LANGUAGE LEARNING STRATEGIES

LANGUAGE LEARNING STRATEGIES

What Every Teacher Should Know

Rebecca L. Oxford

The University of Alabama

NEWBURY HOUSE PUBLISHERS, New York
A division of Harper & Row, Publishers, Inc.
Grand Rapids, Philadelphia, St. Louis, San Francisco
London, Singapore, Sydney, Tokyo

Director: Laurie E. Likoff
Production Coordinator: Cynthia Funkhouser
Cover Design: 20/20 Services, Inc.
Compositor: Crane Typesetting Service, Inc.

NEWBURY HOUSE PUBLISHERS
A division of Harper & Row, Publishers, Inc.

 Language Science
Language Teaching
Language Learning

Language Learning Strategies: What Every Teacher Should Know

Library of Congress Cataloging in Publication Data

Oxford, Rebecca L.
    Language learning strategies : what every teacher should know / by
Rebecca L. Oxford.
        p.   cm.
    ISBN 0-06-632607-9
    1. Language and languages—Study and teaching.   I. Title.
P51.094   1989
418'.0071—dc20   89-13109
                                                                              CIP

63-26078   90 91 92 93 9 8 7 6 5 4 3 2 1

This book is dedicated to my family—David, Merry Lou, George, Tom, Ellie, and Mac—my most loving supporters.

It is also dedicated to the memory of Charles Meister, my favorite and best teacher, by whom I was first challenged to learn.

Foreword

In recent years there has been a shift in focus from the teacher to the learner—from exclusive focus on the improvement of teaching to an increased concern for how learners go about their learning tasks in a second or foreign language. It has become clearer that much of the responsibility for success at language learning rests with individual learners and with their ability to take full advantage of opportunities to learn. This being the case, books which train language learners directly and those which are intended to train teachers to train learners, such as this volume by Rebecca Oxford, are now clearly in vogue.

The appearance of Oxford's book marks a turning point in the treatment of learner strategies in foreign and second language learning. For the first time since learners and their strategies have begun to receive prime attention, there appears on the market a solo-authored volume that combines a solid theoretical basis and an astute mastery of the research literature with an impressive array of practical suggestions to teachers concerning how to train their students to be more successful language learners. The book presents, among other things, a new strategy classification system, suggested means for assessing students' learning strategies, and a model for strategy training accompanied by numerous strategy training exercises. The concept of strategy training is brought to life by a chapter describing a number of actual strategy training projects.

As a further testimonial to the value of the book, the volume underwent field testing and was received quite favorably by teachers, teacher trainees, and language learners. It was found, for example, that incorporating strategy training exercises into regular classroom activities, and treating learning strategies as a means of enhancing progress that students were already making, was more beneficial than having the exercises constitute a separate entity, disconnected from ongoing classroom work. This book was found to heighten an awareness of how to learn in general, not just how to learn languages.

It is most fortunate that the field of foreign and second language learning has a researcher, teacher trainer, and learner trainer as dedicated as Rebecca Oxford, and her book should serve the field well for many years to come.

Andrew D. Cohen
Jerusalem

Preface

A more practiced eye,
A more receptive ear,
A more fluent tongue,
A more involved heart,
A more responsive mind.

These are the characteristics we want to stimulate in students to enable them to become more proficient language learners. This book helps teachers encourage such qualities by means of *language learning strategies*, actions taken by second and foreign language learners to control and improve their own learning. Learning strategies are keys to greater autonomy and more meaningful learning. Although learning strategies are used by students themselves, teachers play an important role in helping students develop and use strategies in more effective ways.

A PERSONAL TALE

Language Learning Strategies: What Every Teacher Should Know is the result of years of struggling with issues of language learning and teaching. In my own school and university experience, most of the foreign language instruction was in the grammar-translation mode, consisting of memorized word lists, recited passages, verbatim translations scribbled in book margins, and no real interaction in the language. It was a painful shock to discover that most of my language teachers did not view communication as a priority, and the few who did care about communication knew little or nothing about how to help their students learn to communicate. Therefore, I spent many years making straight A's in my language courses but secretly feeling like a communicational failure.

Totally discouraged with language instruction as I experienced it, I began to take events into my own hands. Against what seemed to be insurmountable institutional odds, I started assuming some personal responsibility for my own language learning. I invented my own private strategies for learning new languages, techniques including making mental linkages, grouping and comparing words, and using pictures and colors. Eventually it dawned on me that new languages could be learned more readily through foreign travel, living abroad, and correspondence with foreign friends, and with great personal effort I began to use those techniques, too. Little did I know that these and other strategies had been potentially accessible the whole time, but that the instructional establishment had simply not understood the need to encourage learners to use such strategies.

By the time I became a language teacher, audiolingualism had arisen as a challenge to grammar-translation, and they both shared the stage as the primary language instructional methodologies. The language teaching profession was still not ready for much real communication. Nevertheless, I ventured to bring some homemade communicative instructional activities into the classroom. I also shared a few treasured learning strategies with my students, though I had no name for them; language learning strategies had not yet been "discovered."

Much has changed since that time. Communication at last seems to be a priority in many language classrooms. Communicative language instruction and its measurement-focused twin, proficiency-oriented instruction, have taken hold. Language learning strategies, based on the idea of learner self-direction, are beginning to command attention around the world. Now teachers require a practical and simple guidebook to help them in two ways: to understand learning strategies, and to train students in using better strategies in the context of a communicative approach to language learning. Born of my own grappling with language instruction, this book is intended to meet teachers' need for such a guidebook.

WHO CAN BENEFIT FROM THIS BOOK

This book is mainly for teachers of second or foreign languages at secondary, university, and adult levels, but language teachers in elementary schools are sure to find many useful ideas here as well. It will be especially useful for teachers seeking ways to help students become more active, self-directed, and effective learners. This book need not be used only by teachers in traditional academic settings; language trainers in international business settings, government agencies, and military institutions will also find it valuable. *Language Learning Strategies* can be used as a text for experienced teachers enrolled in advanced degree programs or in-service training workshops on learning strategies, communicative language instruction, proficiency-oriented instruction, or active learning of any kind. In addition, the book will be helpful as a course text for individuals who are training to become language teachers.

Because many learning strategies useful for languages are also applicable to other subject areas, teachers outside the language field may find a wealth of practical ideas within these covers. In this book, researchers are likely to uncover new areas of investigation, and language students may obtain useful strategy suggestions.

WHAT THIS BOOK OFFERS

Because the field of language learning strategies is so new, few books currently exist on the topic. This book is unlike other existing resources in that it

- Contains a clear, eight-step model for strategy training and a large number of ready-to-use-or-adapt strategy training exercises covering all four language skills.
- Presents useful surveys for assessing students' learning strategies with clear directions for administration and use, along with student profile sheets.
- Contains a new strategy system covering six main types of strategies in a coherent and consistent way, with visual and verbal cues throughout the book to help readers remember the system.
- Offers a networking chapter with real-life illustrations of learning strategies in action around the world.
- Is based on the latest language learning strategy research, which is interwoven in a practical, useful fashion throughout the text with detailed references in the chapter notes.
- Provides concrete examples of language learning strategies using different languages, such as English, French, German, Spanish, Russian, Italian, and Japanese, and different learning tasks and situations.
- Has been thoroughly field-tested with teachers in a variety of language learning settings.
- Makes extensive use of pictures and diagrams to highlight important material and spark interest.

ACKNOWLEDGMENTS

Thanks go especially to David Crookall of the University of Toulon, France (now at the University of Alabama). For almost two years he shared his rich instructional experience, computer skills, and affection as I wrote this book, thereby aiding me more than I can say. David also kindly provided some of his own student exercises for inclusion in this book.

I am deeply grateful to the five people who led the field test: H. Douglas Brown of San Francisco State University, San Francisco, California; W. Flint Smith and Joseph Wipf of Purdue University, West Lafayette, Indiana; Roberta Z. Lavine of the University of Maryland, College Park, Maryland; and Will Sutter of the Danish Refugee Council and the North Jutland Department of Adult Education, Aalborg, Denmark. Their comments were invaluable to me in making the final revisions, and their conclusions will be helpful to many readers. Flint was particularly adept and generous in helping me make key editorial decisions. Equally important was the support of my esteemed colleague and friend from the School of Education of the Hebrew University of Jerusalem, Andrew D. Cohen, whose constant letters gave me encouragement and excellent ideas.

To my "right arm" during the final draft stages, Haru Yamada, I give my loving gratitude. Mary Ann Zima and Melissa Eliason offered their expert editorial skills and gently assisted the book through labor and birth. Olivia Stockard, independent consultant and long-time friend, checked the sources of many favorite quotations. The editors at Newbury House Publishers, first Leslie Berriman and later Laurie Likoff, Director, facilitated my effort in several ways, most especially by suggesting the field test, the results of which increased the practical usefulness of the book. My dear friend and research colleague, Martha Nyikos of Indiana University, and her talented sister, Katalin Nyikos of Georgetown University, were helpful in modifying a previous version of the Strategy Inventory for Language Learning for use with learners of English. Another close friend and colleague, Madeline Ehrman of the Foreign Service Institute (FSI), has worked with me for almost four years on research studies and has been a catalyst for my thinking about learning styles and strategies.

For their strategy-related suggestions and material contributions, past or present, I am personally indebted to Judith Englert Brooks of the Army Research Institute for the Behavioral and Social Sciences (ARI), Anna Uhl Chamot of InterAmerica Research Associates, Kuan-Yi Rose Chang of the University of West Virginia, Donald Dansereau of Texas Christian University, Sally Hague of Duval County (Florida) Public Schools, Betty Leaver and John Lett of the Defense Language Institute Foreign Language Center, Anne Lomperis of Dade County Public Schools, Maria Matheidesz of the International House in Budapest (Hungary), Barbara McCombs of the Denver Research Institute, Douglas Morgenstern of the Massachusetts Institute of Technology, J. Michael O'Malley of Georgetown University, Joan Rubin of Joan Rubin Associates, Anna Smith of Project GRASP (England), and Anita Wenden of the City University of New York.

Finally, I am thankful to the more than one thousand language teachers who have attended my strategy workshops or have written or called to ask for information about strategies. Your enthusiasm underscores the value of language learning strategies. This book is chiefly directed to you and your teaching colleagues around the world. My challenge to all language teachers is to help students use better learning strategies, so that their eyes will be more practiced, their ears more receptive, their tongues more fluent, their hearts more involved, and their minds more responsive.

Rebecca L. Oxford
Tuscaloosa, Alabama

Contents

List of Tables   xix

List of Figures   xxi

Chapter **1**   Looking at Language Learning Strategies   1

Chapter **2**   Direct Strategies for Dealing with Language   37

Chapter **3**   Applying Direct Strategies to the Four Language Skills   57

Chapter **4**   Indirect Strategies for General Management of Learning   135

Chapter **5**   Applying Indirect Strategies to the Four Language Skills   151

Chapter **6**   Language Learning Strategy Assessment and Training   193

Chapter **7**   **Networking at Home and Abroad**   **213**

Epilogue   **Where to Go from Here**   **235**

Notes   **237**

References   **261**

Appendix **A**   **General Instructions to Administrators of the Strategy Inventory for Language Learning (SILL)**   **277**

Appendix **B**   **Strategy Inventory for Language Learning— Version for English Speakers Learning a New Language**   **283**

Appendix **C**   **Strategy Inventory for Language Learning— Version for Speakers of Other Languages Learning English**   **293**

Appendix **D**   **Sources of Quotations**   **301**

Appendix **E**   **How to Find Activities for Readers**   **305**

Appendix **F**   **How to Find Exercises to Use with Your Students**   **311**

Appendix **G**   **Strategy Applications Listed According
to Each of the Four Language Skills**   **317**

Index   **331**

Credits   **341**

About the Author   **343**

List of Tables

1.1. Features of Language Learning Strategies   9

3.1. Personal Characteristics Grid for Jigsaw Listening   109

5.1. Indirect Strategies as Related to the Four Skills   174

5.2. Weekly Schedule   176

5.3. Questionnaire for Determining Language Learning Goals and Objectives   179

5.4. Opportunity Knocks!   181

5.5. Self-Evaluation Questionnaire   183

5.6. Taking Your Emotional Temperature: A Checklist for Language Learners   188

5.7. Stress Checklist   190

6.1. Interviewer Guide for Reading Strategies   196

6.2. Steps in the Strategy Training Model   204

6.3. Activity on Strategy Assessment Options   210

List of Figures

1.1. Interrelationships Between Direct and Indirect Strategies and Among the Six Strategy Groups   15

1.2. Diagram of the Strategy System: Overview   16

1.3. Diagram of the Strategy System Showing Two Classes, Six Groups, and 19 Sets   17

1.4. Diagram of the Strategy System Showing All the Strategies   18

2.1. Diagram of the Direct Strategies: Overview   38

2.2. Diagram of the Memory Strategies   39

2.3. Diagram of the Cognitive Strategies   44

2.4. Diagram of the Compensation Strategies   48

3.1. Diagram of the Direct Strategies to Be Applied to the Four Language Skills   58

3.2. Diagram of the Memory Strategies to Be Applied to the Four Language Skills   59

3.3. Example of a Semantic Map for "Bullfight" (*La Corrida de Toros*) Using Related Words   63

3.4. Example of a Semantic Map for "Hair" Using Related Words   64

3.5. Example of a Semantic Map for "Hair" Using Pictures and Words   65

3.6. An Illustration of Structured Review (Spiraling)   67

3.7. Diagram of the Cognitive Strategies to Be Applied to the Four Language Skills   69

3.8. Shopping List Note Form   87

3.9. T-Formation Note Form   88

3.10. Standard Outline Structure   89

3.11. Diagram of the Compensation Strategies to Be Applied to the Four Language Skills   91

3.12. English Road Map   107

3.13. German Road Map   108

3.14. Guessing with Pictures   113

3.15. Inventions   116

3.16. Match the Captions with the Pictures for Hobbies   119

3.17. Match the Captions with the "Peanuts" Cartoon   120

3.18. Russian Telegram Form   131

4.1. Diagram of the Indirect Strategies: Overview   136

4.2. Diagram of the Metacognitive Strategies   137

4.3. Diagram of the Affective Strategies   141

4.4. Diagram of the Social Strategies   145

5.1. Diagram of the Indirect Strategies to Be Applied to the Four
      Language Skills   152

5.2. Diagram of the Metacognitive Strategies to Be Applied
      to the Four Language Skills   153

5.3. Diagram of the Affective Strategies to Be Applied to the Four
      Language Skills   163

5.4. Diagram of the Social Strategies to Be Applied to the Four
      Language Skills   169

7.1. The Flower Model   222

Chapter 1

Looking at Language Learning Strategies

It takes better teachers to focus on the learner.
PETER STREVENS

PREVIEW QUESTIONS

1. Why are language learning strategies important?
2. How can this book best be used to understand learning strategies?
3. What terms are useful for understanding the learning strategy concept?
4. What are the most important features of language learning strategies?
5. How can language learning strategies be classified?

WHY LEARNING STRATEGIES ARE IMPORTANT

Learning strategies are steps taken by students to enhance their own learning. Strategies are especially important for language learning because they are tools for active, self-directed involvement, which is essential for developing communicative competence. Appropriate language learning strategies result in improved proficiency and greater self-confidence.

Although researchers have formally discovered and named language learning strategies only recently, such strategies have actually been used for thousands of years. One well-known example is the mnemonic or memory devices used in ancient times to help storytellers remember their lines. Throughout history, the best language students have used strategies, ranging from naturalistic language practice techniques to analytic, rule-based strategies.

Now, for the first time, learning strategies are becoming widely recognized throughout education in general. Under various names, such as learning skills, learning-to-learn skills, thinking skills, and problem-solving skills, learning strategies are the way students learn a wide range of subjects, from native language reading through electronics troubleshooting to new languages. Within the language instruction field, teachers are starting to discuss learning strategies among themselves. Learning strategy workshops are drawing big crowds at language teachers' conventions. Researchers are identifying, classifying, and evaluating language learning strategies, and these efforts are resulting in a steady stream of articles on the topic. Most encouraging of all, increasing numbers of language learners are beginning to recognize the power of their own strategies.

This chapter explains the organization and best use of this book, some important terms, key characteristics of language learning strategies, and a comprehensive classification system for language learning strategies.

ORGANIZATION AND BEST USE OF THIS BOOK

The major purpose of this book is to make learning strategies understandable to teachers of second and foreign languages, so they can enable students to become better learners. Others, too, may find useful ideas here [1]. To use the book most effectively, observe how its chapters are organized and notice their practical emphasis. Each chapter offers preview questions, a summary, activities to help you expand your understanding, and exercises to use with your students. In two "applications" chapters (3 and 5), the activities and exercises are intentionally as long as the chapter narrative, thus underscoring the hands-on nature of the book.

Appendices A through C present a useful strategy assessment survey. Appendix D lists sources of quotations used in this book. To make it easier for you to locate activities and exercises relevant to your own needs, *How to Find Activities for Readers* (Appendix E) and *How to Find Exercises to Use with Your Students* (Appendix F) are included. If you want to find all the strategies connected with a particular language skill, consult *Strategy Applications Listed According to Each of the Four Language Skills* (Appendix G).

The chapter you are now reading presents a general overview of the concept of language learning strategies. Chapter 2 examines three kinds of direct strategies for dealing with a new language, and Chapter 3 applies those strategies to the language skills of listening, reading, speaking, and writing. Chapter 4 explores three kinds of indirect strategies for managing learning, while Chapter 5 shows how these indirect strategies are used in developing all language skills. Chapter 6 describes techniques for assessing language learning strategies and presents a model for training with these strategies. Chapter 7 gives examples of learning strategy use around the world. Finally, the epilogue offers specific ideas about the next steps to take, and the notes provide crucial research data.

Guidelines for General Readers

Most readers of this book might be called general readers, who are interested equally in gaining a broad understanding of language learning strategies and in discovering a variety of applications. If you are one of these readers, you will want to read the chapters in the order in which they are given. By following this sequence, you will find out about language learning strategies in a step-by-step way, going from the overall strategy system to specific strategies, then moving to assessment and training applications and real-life examples.

To get the most from this book, read *actively* by using such strategies as purposeful reading and getting the idea quickly by using the preview questions (see Chapters 2 and 4 for definitions of these two strategies). Many of the reading strategies described in this book are as valuable for reading in one's own native language as they are for reading in a second or foreign language. Pay attention to the examples and illustrations. Do some or all of the readers' activities at the end of the chapters. With creative adaptation, almost all of the activities can be done in a variety of ways— alone, in a pair, or in a group.

Go beyond the readers' activities to the exercises you can use with your students. These are classroom exercises which make language learning strategies come alive for your own learners. Assess your students' learning strategies and give them information about their strategies. Ask them to focus on what they *do* in the process of learning the new language. Conduct learning strategy training with your students, making the training relevant to regular classroom language activities.

Apply the information in this book as much as you can. Reflect on it. Talk with your colleagues about it. Ask for help from others. Come back to the book for further guidance whenever you need it. Any book like this one, filled with ideas and suggestions, can be a valuable resource and a good friend to have around for a long time.

Guidelines for Readers Interested Mainly in Specific Strategy Assessment and Training Techniques

Some readers might have chosen this book primarily to find out about particular strategy assessment and training techniques. If you are such a reader, you might read this chapter to obtain an overview of the strategy system and then move immediately to Chapter 6, where strategy assessment and training are the focus. However, don't forget to return later to Chapters 2 through 5 in order to learn more about specific strategies and their applications, and don't miss the examples of strategies in action around the world as described in Chapter 7. Be sure to try out the activities and exercises. Strategy assessment and training are meaningful only if you understand particular strategies and how they can be used in real instances.

A WORD ABOUT TERMINOLOGY

Like any book, this book uses terms in certain ways, and it is helpful to understand these at the outset. The following are some important terms: *learning and acquisition, process orientation, four language skills, second language and foreign language, communication, communicative competence,* and *learning strategies.*

Learning and Acquisition

According to one well-known contrast, *learning* is conscious knowledge of language rules, does not typically lead to conversational fluency, and is derived from formal instruction. *Acquisition,* on the other hand, occurs unconsciously and spontaneously, does lead to conversational fluency, and arises from naturalistic language use [2]. Some specialists even suggest that learning cannot contribute to acquisition, i.e., that "conscious" gains in knowledge cannot influence "subconscious" development of language.

However, this distinction seems too rigid. It is likely that learning and acquisition are not mutually exclusive but are rather parts of a potentially integrated range of experience. "Our knowledge about what is conscious and what is subconscious is too vague for us to use the [learning-acquisition] distinction reliably," says one expert [3]; moreover, some elements of language use are at first conscious and then become unconscious or automatic through practice. Many language education experts [4] suggest that both aspects—acquisition and learning—are necessary for communicative competence, particularly at higher skill levels. For these reasons, a learning-acquisition continuum is more accurate than a dichotomy in describing how language abilities are developed [5]. In this book the term *learning* is used as a shorthand for the longer phrase *learning and acquisition.* The term *language learner* (or just *learner*) is used here in preference to more awkward terms, such as *language acquirer* or *language learner or acquirer.*

Language learning strategies contribute to all parts of the learning-acquisition continuum. For instance, analytic strategies are directly related to the learning end of the continuum, while strategies involving naturalistic practice facilitate the acquisition of language skills, and guessing and memory strategies are equally useful to both learning and acquisition. For ease of expression, the term *learning strategies* is used in this book to refer to strategies which enhance any part of the learning-acquisition continuum.

Process Orientation

Interest has been shifting from a limited focus on merely *what* students learn or acquire—the *product* or *outcome* of language learning and acquisition—to an expanded focus that also includes *how* students gain language—the *process* by which learning or acquisition occurs. This new emphasis involves looking at a variety of process factors: the development of an interlanguage (the learner's hybrid form of language use that ranges somewhere in between the first or native language and the actual new language being learned), the kinds of errors and mistakes the learner makes and the reasons for them, the learner's social and emotional adaptation to the new language and culture, the amount and kind of activities available to the learner inside and outside of class, and the learner's reactions to specific classroom techniques and methods and to out-of-class experiences with the language. Most relevant to this book, the process orientation also implies a strong concern for the learner's strategies for gaining language skills.

Interestingly, the process orientation (building on general systems theory, in which all phenomena are part of a dynamic system) forces us to consider not just the language learning process itself but also the *input* into this process. The general term *input* might include a variety of student and teacher characteristics, such as intelligence, sex, personality, general learning or teaching style, previous experience, motivation, attitudes, and so on. Input might also include many societal and institutional factors, such as unspoken and often inaccurate generalizations about particular students or about whole groups (e.g., simplistic expectations like "Girls must learn to be good wives and mothers, while boys must go out and conquer the world with their achievements," or overly stereotypical attitudes like "All Asian students are 'grinds' who study all the time"). It is important to identify the input factors in order to understand and interpret more clearly both the process and the outcome of language learning or acquisition.

Four Language Skills

Gaining a new language necessarily involves developing four modalities in varying degrees and combinations: listening, reading, speaking, and writing. Among language teachers, these modalities are known as the *four language skills*, or just the *four skills*. Culture and grammar are sometimes called skills, too, but they are somewhat different from the Big Four; both of these intersect and overlap with listening, reading, speaking, and writing in particular ways. The term *skill* simply means ability, expertness, or proficiency. Skills are gained incrementally during the language development process.

Second Language and Foreign Language

The *target language*, or language being learned, can be either a *second language* or a *foreign language*. Throughout this book the term *target language* is used as a generic phrase to cover the two circumstances, second language learning and foreign language learning. This "second versus foreign" distinction is often baffling to teachers, students, parents, and the general public. Nevertheless, it is important to understand the difference, since these terms appear so often in language instructional texts and sometimes galvanize competing camps of educators.

The difference between learning a second language and learning a foreign language is usually viewed in terms of where the language is learned and what social and communicative functions the language serves there. A *second language* has social and communicative functions within the community where it is learned. For example, in multilingual countries like Belgium or Canada, people need more than one language for social, economic, and professional reasons. Refugees or immigrants usually have to learn a second language in order to survive in their adopted country. In contrast, a *foreign language* does not have immediate social and communicative functions within the community where it is learned; it is employed mostly to communicate elsewhere. For instance, one might learn Russian in the USA, English in France, or German in Australia [6].

This book accepts that the differences between second language contexts and foreign language contexts are real, and that these differences occasionally have implications for language learning strategies. Some learning strategies might be easier to use in second language contexts than in foreign language settings, or vice versa. However, most learning strategies can be applied equally well to both situations. Therefore, in the rest of this book it is usually unnecessary to highlight the distinctions between second language learning strategies and foreign language learning strategies.

Communication, Communicative Competence, and Related Concepts

The word *communication* comes from a Latin word for "commonness," including the prefix *com-* which suggests togetherness, joining, cooperation, and mutuality. Therefore, communication is definable as "a mutual exchange between two or more individuals which enhances cooperation and establishes commonality" [7]. Communication is also seen as dynamic, not static, and as depending on the negotiation of meaning between two or more persons who share some knowledge of the language being used [8].

Communicative competence is, of course, competence or ability to communicate. It concerns both spoken or written language and all four language skills [9]. Some people mistakenly think of communication as occurring only through the medium of speech. In fact, even language learning experts have commonly used the term *communication strategies* to refer only to certain types of speaking strategies, thus unwittingly giving the false impression that the skills of reading, listening, and writing—and the language used via these modalities—are not really equal partners in communication [10].

One very useful model [11] provides a comprehensive, four-part definition of communicative competence:

1. *Grammatical competence* or *accuracy* is the degree to which the language user has mastered the linguistic code, including vocabulary, grammar, pronunciation, spelling, and word formation.
2. *Sociolinguistic competence* is the extent to which utterances can be used or understood appropriately in various social contexts. It includes knowledge of speech acts such as persuading, apologizing, and describing.
3. *Discourse competence* is the ability to combine ideas to achieve cohesion in form and coherence in thought, above the level of the single sentence [12].
4. *Strategic competence* is the ability to use strategies like gestures or "talking around" an unknown word in order to overcome limitations in language knowledge.

Ways in which language learning strategies contribute to the goal of communicative competence are described later in this chapter.

Learning Strategies

To understand learning strategies, let us go back to the basic term, *strategy*. This word comes from the ancient Greek term *strategia* meaning generalship or the art of war. More specifically, strategy involves the optimal management of troops, ships, or aircraft in a planned campaign. A different, but related, word is *tactics*, which are tools to achieve the success of strategies [13]. Many people use these two terms interchangeably. The two expressions share some basic implied characteristics: planning, competition, conscious manipulation, and movement toward a goal. In nonmilitary settings, the strategy concept has been applied to clearly non-adversarial situations, where it has come to mean a plan, step, or conscious action toward achievement of an objective [14].

The strategy concept, without its aggressive and competitive trappings, has become influential in education, where it has taken on a new meaning and has been transformed into *learning strategies* [15]. One commonly used technical definition says that learning strategies are operations employed by the learner to aid the acquisition, storage, retrieval, and use of information [16]. This definition, while helpful, does not fully convey the excitement or richness of learning strategies. It is useful to expand this definition by saying that learning strategies are specific actions taken by the learner to make learning easier, faster, more enjoyable, more self-directed, more effective, and more transferrable to new situations.

Important terms used in this book have just been presented, including some general definitions of the concept of language learning strategies. Now it is time to explain the central features of such strategies.

FEATURES OF LANGUAGE LEARNING STRATEGIES

Key features of language learning strategies are discussed below and summarized in Table 1.1 [17]. To illustrate some of these features, certain strategies or strategy groups are briefly mentioned here. Subsequent chapters offer complete strategy definitions and applications.

Communicative Competence as the Main Goal

All appropriate language learning strategies are oriented toward the broad goal of communicative competence. Development of communicative competence requires realistic interaction among learners using meaningful, contextualized language. Learning strategies help learners participate actively in such authentic communication. Such strategies operate in both general and specific ways to encourage the development of communicative competence.

It is easy to see how language learning strategies stimulate the growth of communicative competence *in general*. For instance, metacognitive ("beyond the cognitive") strategies help learners to regulate their own cognition and to focus, plan, and evaluate their progress as they move toward communicative competence. Affective strategies develop the self-confidence and perseverance needed for learners to involve themselves actively in language learning, a requirement for attaining communicative competence. Social strategies provide increased interaction and more empathetic understanding, two qualities necessary to reach communicative competence.

Table 1.1 FEATURES OF LANGUAGE LEARNING STRATEGIES

Language learning strategies:
1. Contribute to the main goal, communicative competence.
2. Allow learners to become more self-directed.
3. Expand the role of teachers.
4. Are problem-oriented.
5. Are specific actions taken by the learner.
6. Involve many aspects of the learner, not just the cognitive.
7. Support learning both directly and indirectly.
8. Are not always observable.
9. Are often conscious.
10. Can be taught.
11. Are flexible.
12. Are influenced by a variety of factors.

Source: Original.

Certain cognitive strategies, such as analyzing, and particular memory strategies, like the keyword technique, are highly useful for understanding and recalling new information—important functions in the process of becoming competent in using the new language. Compensation strategies aid learners in overcoming knowledge gaps and continuing to communicate authentically; thus, these strategies help communicative competence to blossom.

As the learner's competence grows, strategies can act in specific ways to foster *particular* aspects of that competence: grammatical, sociolinguistic, discourse, and strategic elements. For instance, memory strategies, such as using imagery and structured review, and cognitive strategies, such as reasoning deductively and using contrastive analysis, strengthen *grammatical accuracy*. Social strategies—asking questions, cooperating with native speakers, cooperating with peers, and becoming culturally aware— powerfully aid *sociolinguistic competence*. Strategies related to communication in a natural setting and with social involvement also foster the development of sociolinguistic competence. Many kinds of strategies— compensation strategies, including using contextual clues for guessing, social strategies, such as cooperating and asking questions, and cognitive strategies, like recombination and use of common routines—encourage greater amounts of authentic communication and thus enhance *discourse competence*. Compensation strategies—guessing when the meaning is not known, or using synonyms or gestures to express meaning of an unknown word or expression—are the heart of *strategic competence* [18].

Greater Self-Direction for Learners

Language learning strategies encourage greater overall self-direction for learners [19]. Self-direction is particularly important for language learners, because they will not always have the teacher around to guide them as they use the language outside the classroom. Moreover, self-direction is essential to the active development of ability in a new language.

Owing to conditioning by the culture and the educational system, however, many language students (even adults) are passive and accustomed to being spoon-fed [20]. They like to be told what to do, and they do only what is clearly essential to get a good grade—even if they fail to develop useful skills in the process. Attitudes and behaviors like these make learning more difficult and must be changed, or else any effort to train learners to rely more on themselves and use better strategies is bound to fail [21]. Just teaching new strategies to students will accomplish very little unless students begin to *want* greater responsibility for their own learning.

Learner self-direction is not an "all or nothing" concept; it is often a gradually increasing phenomenon, growing as learners become more comfortable with the idea of their own responsibility. Self-directed students gradually gain greater confidence, involvement, and proficiency.

New Roles for Teachers

Teachers traditionally expect to be viewed as authority figures, identified with roles like parent, instructor, director, manager, judge, leader, evaluator, controller, and even doctor, who must "cure" the ignorance of the students. As Gibson said, "You've got to make [students] toe the line all the time, you cannot assume that they'll come in, sit down and get on with the job." According to Harmer, "The teacher *instructs*. This is where [s]he explains exactly what the students should do" [22]. These familiar roles will stifle communication in any classroom, especially the language classroom, because they force all communication to go to and through the teacher.

The specter of role change may discomfort some teachers who feel that their status is being challenged. Others, however, welcome their new functions as facilitator, helper, guide, consultant, adviser, coordinator, idea person, diagnostician, and co-communicator. New teaching capacities also include identifying students' learning strategies, conducting training on learning strategies, and helping learners become more independent [23]. In this process, teachers do not necessarily forsake all their old managerial and instructional tasks, but these elements become much less dominant. These changes strengthen teachers' roles, making them more varied and more creative. Their status is no longer based on hierarchical authority, but on the quality and importance of their relationship with learners [24]. When students take more responsibility, more learning occurs, and both teachers and learners feel more successful.

Other Features

Other important features of language strategies are problem orientation, action basis, involvement beyond just cognition, ability to support learning directly or indirectly, degree of observability, level of consciousness, teachability, flexibility, and influences on strategy choice.

Problem Orientation Language learning strategies are tools. They are used because there is a problem to solve, a task to accomplish, an objective to meet, or a goal to attain. For example, a learner uses one of the reasoning or guessing strategies to better understand a foreign language reading passage. Memory strategies are used because there is something that must be remembered. Affective strategies are used to help the learner relax or gain greater confidence, so that more profitable learning can take place.

Action Basis Related to the problem orientation of language learning strategies is their action basis. Language learning strategies are specific actions or behaviors accomplished by students to enhance their learning. Examples are taking notes, planning for a language task, self-evaluating, and guessing intelligently. These actions are naturally influenced by the learners' more general characteristics or traits, such as learning style (broad, generalized approach to learning, problem solving, or understanding oneself or the situation), motivation, and aptitude, but they must not be confused with these wider characteristics.

Involvement Beyond Just Cognition Language learning strategies are not restricted to cognitive functions, such as those dealing with mental processing and manipulation of the new language. Strategies also include metacognitive functions like planning, evaluating, and arranging one's own learning; and emotional (affective), social, and other functions as well. Unfortunately, many language learning strategy experts have not paid enough attention to affective and social strategies in the past. It is likely that the emphasis will eventually become more balanced, because language learning is indisputably an emotional and interpersonal process as well as a cognitive and metacognitive affair.

Direct and Indirect Support of Learning Some learning strategies involve direct learning and use of the subject matter, in this case a new language.

These are known as *direct strategies*. Other strategies, including metacognitive, affective, and social strategies, contribute indirectly but powerfully to learning. These are known as *indirect strategies*. Direct and indirect strategies are equally important and serve to support each other in many ways.

Degree of Observability Language learning strategies are not always readily observable to the human eye. Many aspects of cooperating, a strategy in which the learner works with someone else to achieve a learning goal, can be observed, but the act of making mental associations, an important memory strategy, cannot be seen. It is often difficult for teachers to know about their students' learning strategies, because some strategies are hard to observe even with the help of videotape and closed-circuit television. Another problem with observing learning strategies is that many strategies are used (as they should be!) outside of the classroom in informal, naturalistic situations unobservable by the teacher.

Level of Consciousness The ancient Greek definition of strategies, given above, implies consciousness and intentionality. Many modern uses of learning strategies reflect conscious efforts by learners to take control of their learning, and some researchers seem to suggest that learning strategies are always conscious actions [25]. However, after a certain amount of practice and use, learning strategies, like any other skill or behavior, can become automatic. In fact, making *appropriate* learning strategies fully automatic—that is, unconscious—is often a very desirable thing, especially for language learning [26].

Perhaps paradoxically, the strategies some learners use—either appropriate or inappropriate ones—are already employed instinctively, unthinkingly, and uncritically. Strategy assessment and training might be necessary to help these learners become more aware of the strategies they are using and to evaluate the utility of those strategies.

Teachability Some aspects of the learner's makeup, like general learning style or personality traits, are very difficult to change. In contrast, learning strategies are easier to teach and modify. This can be done through strategy training, which is an essential part of language education [27]. Even the best learners can improve their strategy use through such training. Strategy training helps guide learners to become more conscious of strategy use and more adept at employing appropriate strategies.

Strategy training is most effective when students learn why and when specific strategies are important, how to use these strategies, and how to transfer them to new situations. Strategy training must also take into account learners' and teachers' attitudes toward learner self-direction, language learning, and the particular language and culture in question. As a strategy trainer, the language teacher helps each student to gain self-awareness of how he or she learns, as well as to develop the means to maximize all learning experiences, both inside and outside of the language area.

Flexibility Language learning strategies are flexible; that is, they are not always found in predictable sequences or in precise patterns. There is a great deal of individuality in the way learners choose, combine, and sequence strategies. The ways that learners do so is the subject of much current research (see the following discussion of factors influencing learners' choice of strategies).

However, sometimes learners *do* combine strategies in a predictable way. For instance, in reading a passage, learners often preview the material by skimming or scanning, then they read it more closely while using guessing to fill in any gaps, and finally they organize the material by taking notes or summarizing. In addition, some learning strategies contain within themselves an *internal* sequence of steps; for instance, deductive reasoning requires first considering a rule and then applying it to a new situation.

Factors Influencing Strategy Choice Many factors affect the choice of strategies: degree of awareness, stage of learning, task requirements, teacher expectations, age, sex, nationality/ethnicity, general learning style, personality traits, motivation level, and purpose for learning the language [28].

In a nutshell, learners who are more aware and more advanced seem to use better strategies. Task requirements help determine strategy choice; learners would not use the same strategies for writing a composition as for chatting in a cafe. Teacher expectations, expressed through classroom instructional and testing methods, strongly shape learners' strategies; for instance, classroom emphasis on discrete-point grammar-learning will result in development of learning strategies like analysis and reasoning, rather than more global strategies for communication.

Older learners may use somewhat different strategies than younger learners. Recent studies indicate that females may use a much wider, or at least a very different, range of strategies than males for language learning. Nationality or ethnicity influences strategy use; for example, Hispanics seem to use social strategies more than do some other ethnic groups. General learning style, such as field dependence-independence, analytic-global orientation, or the judging-perceiving mode, has a strong effect on the strategies that language learners use.

More highly motivated learners use a significantly greater range of appropriate strategies than do less motivated learners. Motivation is related to language learning purpose, which is another key to strategy use. For instance, individuals who want to learn a new language mainly for interpersonal communication will use different strategies than learners who want to learn a new language merely to fulfill a graduation requirement.

This review of the characteristics of language learning strategies is a useful background to the new strategy classification system, discussed next. Many elements of this system have already been touched upon, and they will be explained in greater detail now.

A NEW SYSTEM OF LANGUAGE LEARNING STRATEGIES

The strategy system [29] presented here differs in several ways from earlier attempts to classify strategies. It is more compehensive and detailed; it is more systematic in linking individual strategies, as well as strategy groups, with each of the four language skills (listening, reading, speaking, and writing); and it uses less technical terminology. Visual and verbal cues are used throughout this book for understanding and remembering the system.

Figure 1.1 presents a general overview of the system of language learning strategies. Strategies are divided into two major classes: direct and indirect. These two classes are subdivided into a total of six groups (memory, cognitive, and compensation under the direct class; metacognitive, affective, and social under the indirect class). This figure indicates that direct strategies and indirect strategies support each other, and that each strategy group is capable of connecting with and assisting every other strategy group. Figure 1.2 shows a different view of the same strategy system.

So far only general strategy definitions have been given. Complete strategy definitions are offered in Chapter 2 (for all the direct strategies) and Chapter 4 (for all the indirect strategies). Chapters 3 and 5 present detailed applications of direct and indirect strategies, respectively.

Mutual Support

What does it mean to say that direct and indirect strategies support each other, or that the six strategy groups (three direct and three indirect) interact with and help each other? To understand this, consider an analogy from the theater.

The first major class, direct strategies for dealing with the new language, is like the Performer in a stage play, working with the language itself in a variety of specific tasks and situations. The direct class is composed of memory strategies for remembering and retrieving new information, cognitive strategies for understanding and producing the language, and compensation strategies for using the language despite knowledge

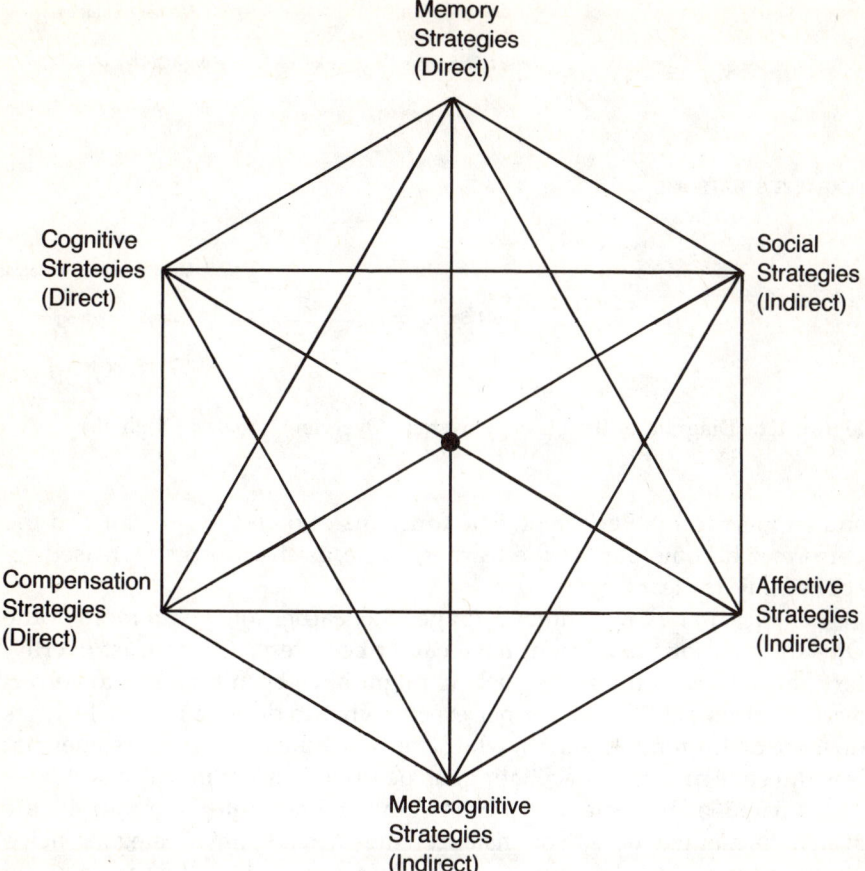

Figure 1.1 Interrelationships Between Direct and Indirect Strategies and Among the Six Strategy Groups. (*Source*: Original.)

gaps. The Performer works closely with the Director for the best possible outcome.

The second major strategy class—indirect strategies for general management of learning—can be likened to the Director of the play. This class is made up of metacognitive strategies for coordinating the learning process, affective strategies for regulating emotions, and social strategies for learning with others. The Director serves a host of functions, like focusing, organizing, guiding, checking, correcting, coaching, encouraging, and cheering the Performer, as well as ensuring that the Performer works cooperatively with other actors in the play. The Director is an *internal* guide

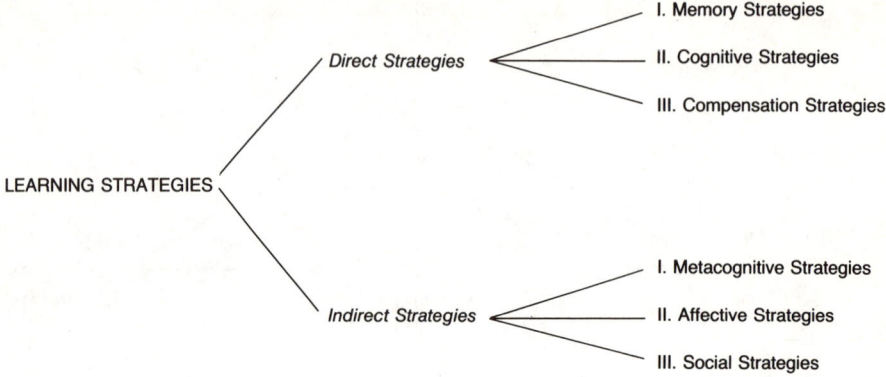

Figure 1.2 Diagram of the Strategy System: Overview. (*Source*: Original.)

and support to the Performer. The functions of both the Director and the Performer become part of the learner, as he or she accepts increased responsibility for learning.

The teacher allows and encourages the learner to take on more of the Director functions that might have earlier been reserved, at least overtly, for the teacher. In the past, teachers might have been the ones to correct learner errors and tell the learner exactly what to do when. Now learners do more of this for themselves, while teachers' functions become somewhat less directive and more facilitating, as described earlier in this chapter.

A large overlap naturally exists among the strategy groups in the system presented here. For instance, the metacognitive category helps students to regulate their own cognition by assessing how they are learning and by planning for future language tasks, but metacognitive self-assessment and planning often require reasoning, which is itself a cognitive strategy! Likewise, the compensation strategy of guessing, clearly used to make up for missing knowledge, also requires reasoning (which explains why some specialists call guessing a cognitive strategy), as well as involving sociocultural sensitivity typically gained through social strategies.

Figure 1.3 indicates how the six strategy groups are subdivided into a total of 19 strategy sets. Figure 1.4 shows the entire learning strategy system, including 62 strategies.

Cautions

It is important to remember that *any* current understanding of language learning strategies is necessarily in its infancy, and *any* existing system of strategies is only a proposal to be tested through practical classroom use

DIRECT STRATEGIES   INDIRECT STRATEGIES

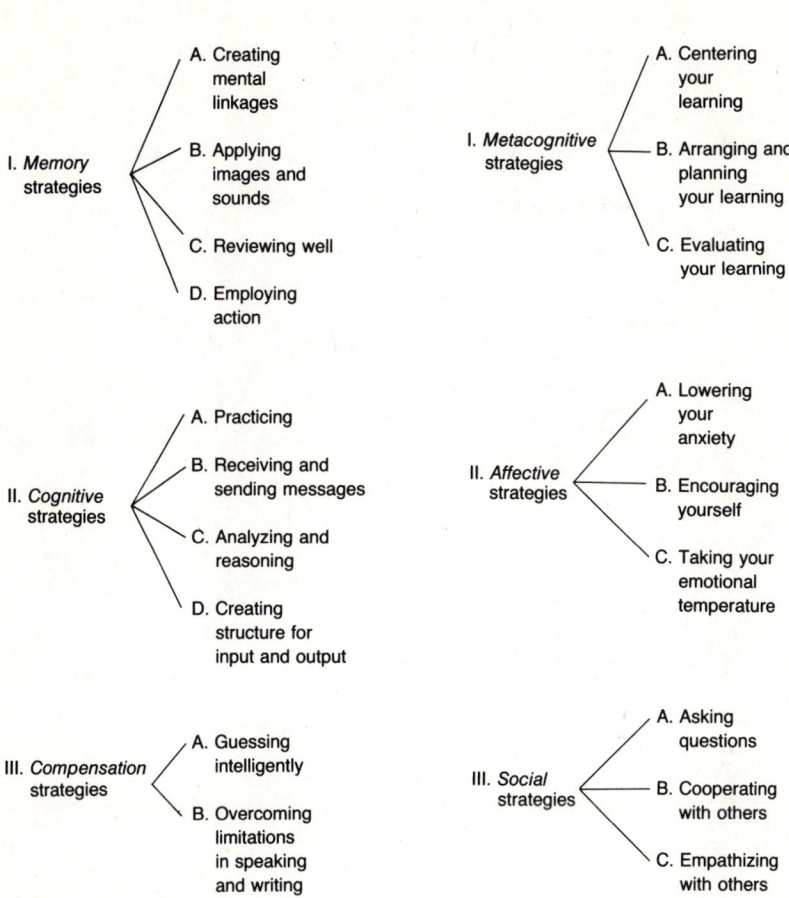

Figure 1.3 Diagram of the Strategy System Showing Two Classes, Six Groups, and 19 Sets. (*Source*: Original.)

and through research. At this stage in the short history of language learning strategy research, there is no complete agreement on exactly what strategies are; how many strategies exist; how they should be defined, demarcated, and categorized; and whether it is—or ever will be—possible to create a real, scientifically validated hierarchy of strategies. Some language learning strategies, such as naturalistic practice, are very broad, containing many possible activities, while others, like the keyword technique, are narrower, but breadth or narrowness cannot be the sole basis of a hierarchical structure for strategies.

Classification conflicts are inevitable. A given strategy, such as using synonyms if the exact word is not known to the learner, is classed by some

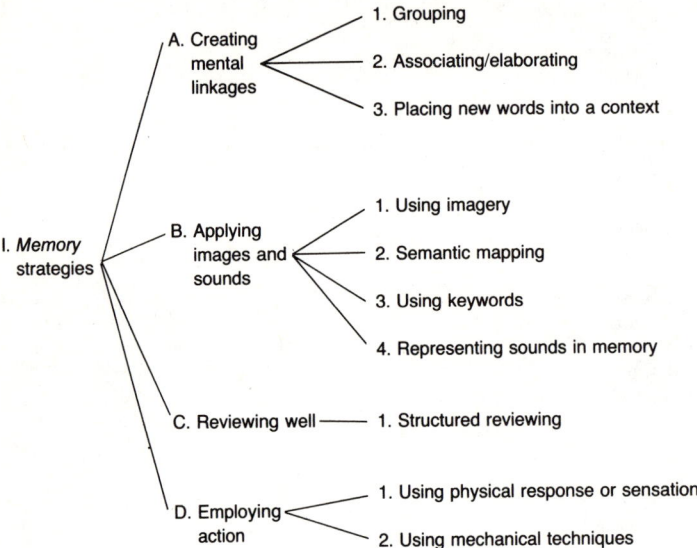

DIRECT STRATEGIES

(Memory, Cognitive, and Compensation Strategies)

A. Creating mental linkages
1. Grouping
2. Associating/elaborating
3. Placing new words into a context

I. *Memory* strategies

B. Applying images and sounds
1. Using imagery
2. Semantic mapping
3. Using keywords
4. Representing sounds in memory

C. Reviewing well
1. Structured reviewing

D. Employing action
1. Using physical response or sensation
2. Using mechanical techniques

Figure 1.4 Diagram of the Strategy System Showing All the Strategies. (*Source:* Original.)

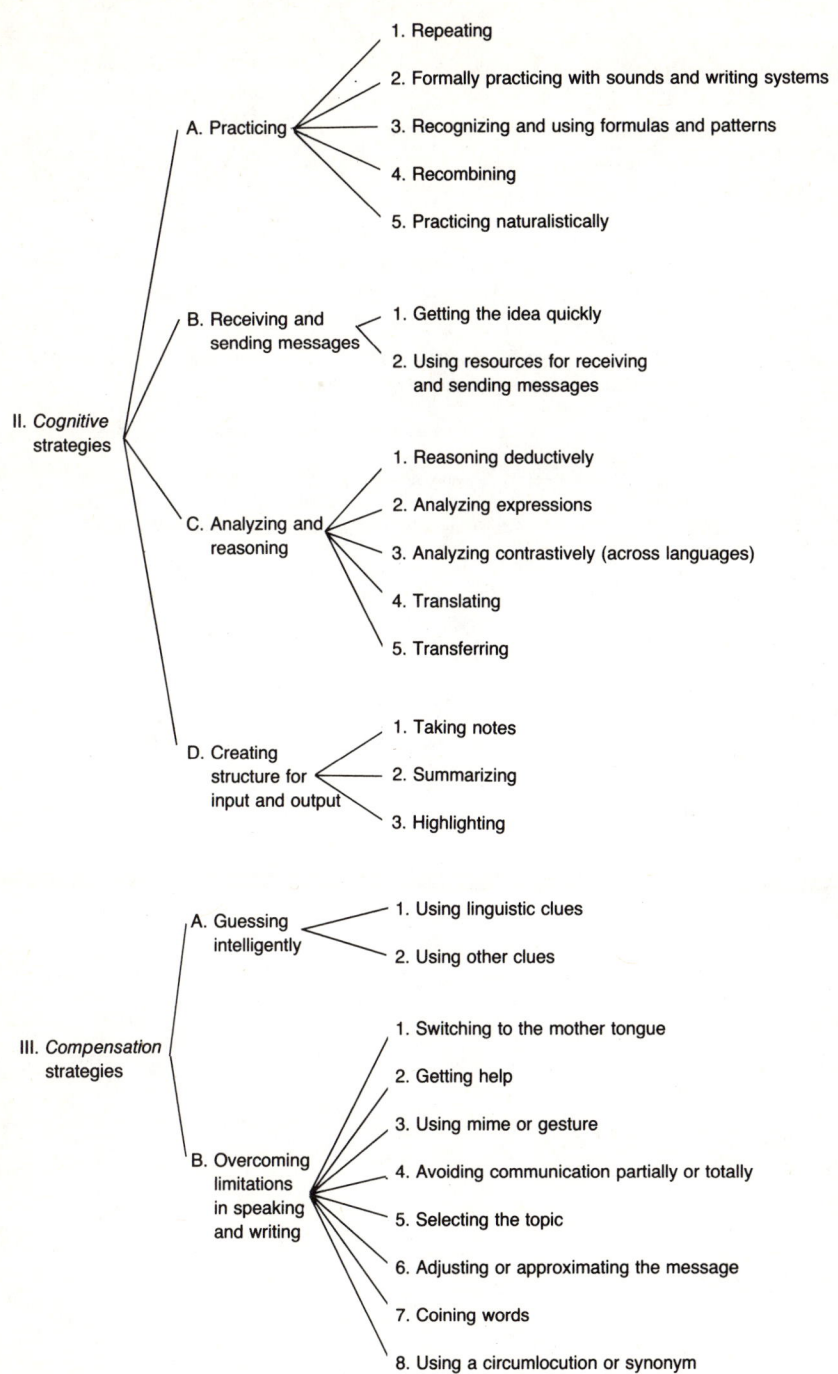

II. *Cognitive* strategies

- A. Practicing
  1. Repeating
  2. Formally practicing with sounds and writing systems
  3. Recognizing and using formulas and patterns
  4. Recombining
  5. Practicing naturalistically

- B. Receiving and sending messages
  1. Getting the idea quickly
  2. Using resources for receiving and sending messages

- C. Analyzing and reasoning
  1. Reasoning deductively
  2. Analyzing expressions
  3. Analyzing contrastively (across languages)
  4. Translating
  5. Transferring

- D. Creating structure for input and output
  1. Taking notes
  2. Summarizing
  3. Highlighting

III. *Compensation* strategies

- A. Guessing intelligently
  1. Using linguistic clues
  2. Using other clues

- B. Overcoming limitations in speaking and writing
  1. Switching to the mother tongue
  2. Getting help
  3. Using mime or gesture
  4. Avoiding communication partially or totally
  5. Selecting the topic
  6. Adjusting or approximating the message
  7. Coining words
  8. Using a circumlocution or synonym

Figure 1.4 *(Continued)*

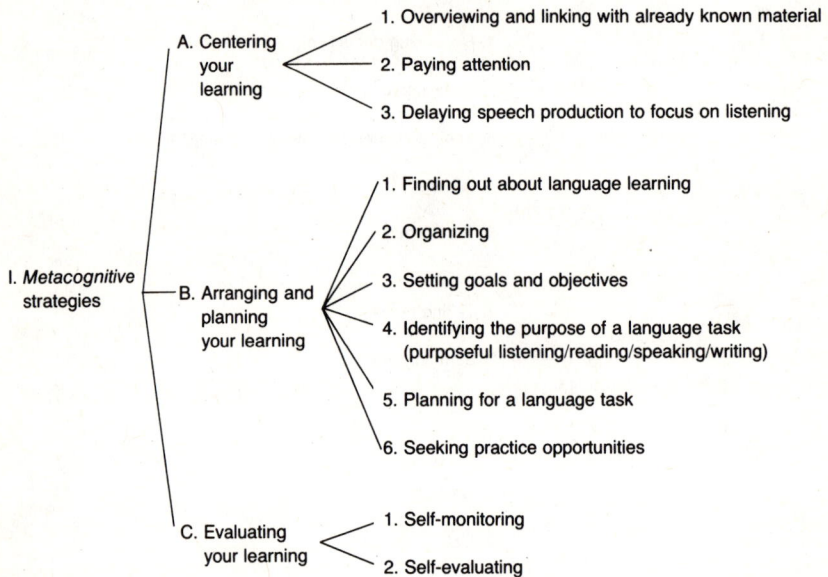

INDIRECT STRATEGIES
(Metacognitive, Affective, and Social Strategies)

A. Centering your learning
1. Overviewing and linking with already known material
2. Paying attention
3. Delaying speech production to focus on listening

I. *Metacognitive* strategies

B. Arranging and planning your learning
1. Finding out about language learning
2. Organizing
3. Setting goals and objectives
4. Identifying the purpose of a language task (purposeful listening/reading/speaking/writing)
5. Planning for a language task
6. Seeking practice opportunities

C. Evaluating your learning
1. Self-monitoring
2. Self-evaluating

Figure 1.4   *(Continued)*

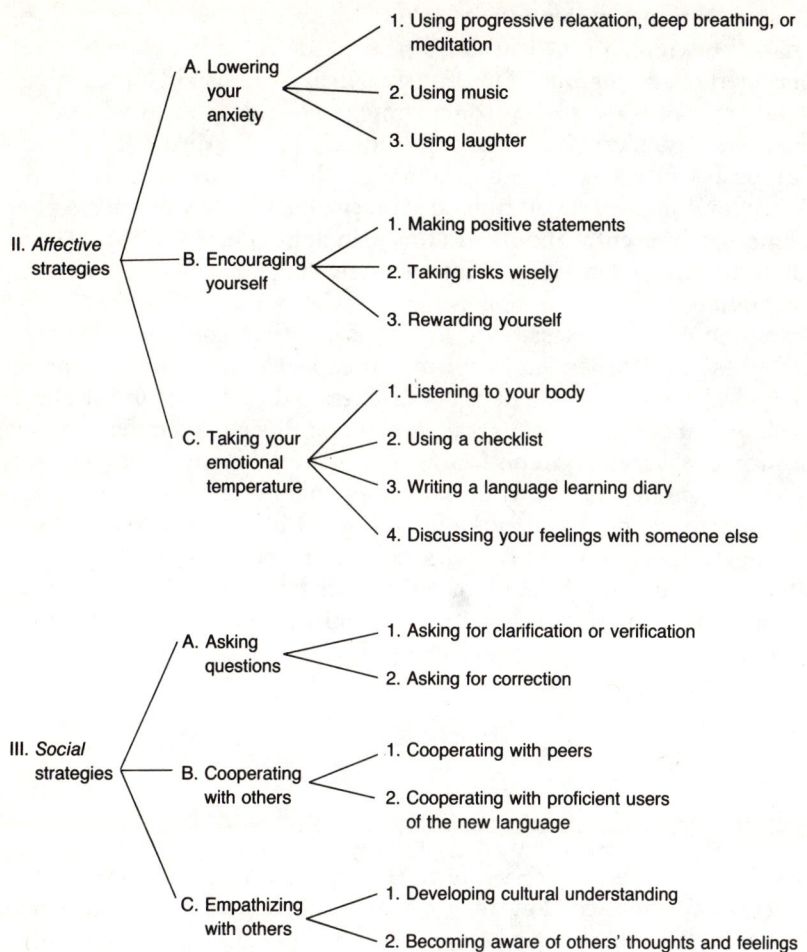

II. *Affective* strategies

A. Lowering your anxiety
1. Using progressive relaxation, deep breathing, or meditation
2. Using music
3. Using laughter

B. Encouraging yourself
1. Making positive statements
2. Taking risks wisely
3. Rewarding yourself

C. Taking your emotional temperature
1. Listening to your body
2. Using a checklist
3. Writing a language learning diary
4. Discussing your feelings with someone else

III. *Social* strategies

A. Asking questions
1. Asking for clarification or verification
2. Asking for correction

B. Cooperating with others
1. Cooperating with peers
2. Cooperating with proficient users of the new language

C. Empathizing with others
1. Developing cultural understanding
2. Becoming aware of others' thoughts and feelings

Figure 1.4 *(Continued)*

experts as a learning strategy (it is included here as such) but is unceremoniously thrown out of the learning strategy arena by other experts, who think it is merely a communication strategy which is not useful for learning. Also, there is confusion among some strategy specialists as to whether a particular strategy, like self-monitoring, should be called direct or indirect; this may be because researchers disagree on the basic definitions of the terms *direct* and *indirect*. Even individual researchers often classify a particular strategy differently at different times, in light of new insights. These difficulties are understandable, given the early stage of investigation concerning language learning strategies [30].

Despite problems in classifying strategies, research continues to prove that strategies help learners take control of their learning and become more proficient, and the experience of many teachers indicates that the strategy system shown above is a very useful way to examine such strategies. This system provides, albeit in imperfect form, a comprehensive structure for understanding strategies. It includes a wide variety of affective and social strategies which are not often enough considered by strategy researchers, teachers, or students. It unites the whole range of compensation strategies, so confusingly separated in other strategy classification schemes. Finally, it organizes well-known metacognitive, cognitive, and memory strategies so that you can access them easily.

SUMMARY

This chapter has explained the importance of language learning strategies and has discussed the best way you can use this book. In this chapter central terms are defined, key features of strategies explained, and the overall strategy classification system presented. Later chapters will provide more details on strategies and show how they are used to make language learning more effective.

ACTIVITIES FOR READERS

Activity 1.1. Brainstorm the Features of Learning Strategies

With others or by yourself, brainstorm all the characteristics of learning strategies that you can think of, listing them on a large sheet. Then organize them into categories, giving examples. How does your list compare with the one in this chapter?

Activity 1.2. Place Strategies on the Learning-Acquisition Continuum

Assume that learning and acquisition form a continuum. Draw this continuum on a flip-chart or backboard as follows:

ALL	MAINLY	BOTH	MAINLY	ALL
LEARNING	LEARNING	EQUALLY	ACQUISITION	ACQUISITION

Take each of the six strategy groups (and the 19 strategy sets into which these groups are divided), as listed in this chapter. Place each one along the continuum in the spot where you think it belongs. Explain your reasoning.

Activity 1.3. Consider Degrees of Learner Responsibility

Henri Holec [31] advocates that language learners take charge of their learning in *all* respects, including determining the objectives, defining the content and progressions, selecting methods and techniques to be used, monitoring the procedures (rhythm, time, place, etc.), and evaluating what has been learned. Teachers can help learners take this responsibility, according to Holec, but the ultimate responsibility lies with the learners themselves.

What is your opinion about Holec's assertion that learners should take charge of their learning in all the respects listed above? Explain any reservations or agreements, and give examples.

Brainstorm specific ways learners might take responsibility for each of the language learning aspects cited by Holec.

Activity 1.4. Discuss Teacher Roles

Read the following list of classroom management behaviors, and then answer the questions.

Behaviors

1. Giving learners plenty of encouragement for their efforts.
2. Establishing a position of dominance over learners.
3. Ignoring disruptive behavior and praising appropriate behavior.
4. Giving pupils responsibility for their learning.
5. Learning the names of pupils quickly.
6. Keeping grading and attendance lists up to date.
7. Being warm, friendly, and open with the learners.

8. Establishing a daily and weekly routine.
9. Threatening with punishment learners who misbehave.
10. Setting learning tasks which are completed in total silence.

Questions

1. Which do you think are the most appropriate classroom management behaviors?
2. Which ones require the imposition of the teacher's power?
3. Which ones involve a lessening of social distance between teacher and students?
4. Which of these behaviors are task-oriented?
5. In what ways do these behaviors influence student motivation?
6. Which behaviors do your own learners expect? Which do their parents expect (if relevant)? Which does the administration expect?
7. How do these behaviors relate to the six groups of learning strategies included in this chapter?

Source Adapted from T. Wright (1987, pp. 52–53).

Activity 1.5. Consider Your Own Strategy Use

Think back to when you were learning a new language. Which of the six groups of strategies—memory, cognitive, compensation, metacognitive, affective, and social—did you use most often? Least often? Indicate any strategy groups you *never* used and discuss whether use of such strategies might have helped you.

Describe how you used language learning strategies, giving examples. Discuss how you used learning strategies in at least one other subject area and provide examples.

EXERCISES TO USE WITH YOUR STUDENTS

Exercise 1.1. Embedded Strategies Game

Purpose

This game helps participants to become acquainted with language learning strategies and can be used with either teachers or students as participants. Participants are asked to determine which language learning strategies (from the list in this chapter) are embedded in, or suggested by, certain language activities. The game is a process of matching a number of language activities with the names of the relevant strategies, and thus acquaints participants with the whole system of strategies.

Materials

Each participant gets a copy of the strategy system from this chapter (Figure 1.4) and a list of language activities (given below).

Time

This game, which takes 1 to 2 hours, can be spread over several class periods. Total time required depends on the number of language activities used.

Instructions

1. *Introduction*   Give out the materials (strategy system in Figure 1.4 and list of language activities below). Explain that participants will be divided into small groups. Each small group will try to identify the language learning strategies embedded in, or suggested by, the series of language activities. Explain that all the language activities refer to the target language. Every language activity can be matched with *one or more language learning strategies*.

It is not necessary to consider the language activities in the order in which they are listed. Explain that participants must choose relevant strategies to match any given language activity on the list; but they must be able to justify or explain their selection of strategies! You might also tell participants they will not have access to complete definitions of the strategies; they will have only the strategy system, which lists the name of each strategy and shows how the strategies are grouped. The names are intentionally descriptive, so most participants will not have any trouble understanding the meaning of the strategies.

If you want to give a quick introduction to the strategy system itself, tell participants that some strategies deal directly with the target language, while other strategies do not deal with the language but instead support language learning indirectly through metacognitive, emotional, and social means. Do not give any more detail on the strategy system now; let the participants teach themselves to understand and use the system as they play the game.

Announce the time limit in advance. It does not really matter how many language activities a small group chooses to cover; the key is the number of relevant, justifiable strategies named. But encourage small groups to try to cover at least 15 language activities to get a general feeling for a variety of strategies.

NOTE: SCORING IS OPTIONAL. If you decide to score the game, explain how scoring works. Scoring: 1 point for each relevant strategy listed for any activity. The winning group is the one with the greatest number of *relevant* strategies matching the listed language activities within the time allowed. If you decide not to use scoring, Step 4 (below) can just be a whole-group explanation of the strategy choices, with each small group contributing its ideas but without counting points.

2. *Practice*   Run through one or two examples with the whole group before breaking up into smaller groups. To do this, read a language activity description (for instance, the description for LISTENING IN—see list below) to the whole group, and get participants to call out any strategies that are suggested by the activity (e.g., practicing naturalistically, paying attention). Ask for a *very brief* (one sentence) explanation or justification for each strategy named. Make sure everyone understands how to play.

3. *Play*   Divide everyone into groups of three to five people. Each small group now works through the list of activities (in any order), writing down on one or more large sheets of paper the strategies they consider relevant and useful for each activity and making sure they can explain or justify their choices.

4. *Explanation of strategy choices and determination of scores*   Reconvene the whole group and ask each small group to post its list visibly at the front of the room. Now ask a spokesperson from each group to discuss the language activities covered by the group, and explain the strategies the group matched with each activity. (Other members of the small group can help the spokesperson, if needed, by adding explanations or justifications.) If the whole group generally agrees that the choice of a given strategy is a good one, the small group gets 1 point.

The easier and more obvious activity-and-strategy matchings can be explained or justified in just a sentence, but participants might want to discuss in a little more detail the more difficult or borderline cases. You need to keep this discussion condensed enough so that all small groups will have an equal chance to present their findings.

Note that the small groups presenting later may have a slight advantage over the small groups that present earlier, in that they have heard what the earlier groups have said. Urge the later-presenting groups not merely to repeat what has been said, but to add something new, if they can, to justify their strategy choices.

If you feel any small group's reasons for choosing a strategy are off course, ask questions to lead the group to understand, rather than just telling them the answer. Remember, there is often not just one solution to dealing with any given language activity; many strategies are often appropriate.

If you have decided to score the game, it is now time to let the small groups count up the number of points they have earned. Decide on a winning group—the one with the greatest number of relevant strategies (regardless of the number of language activities covered).

5. *Discussion*   Be sure to leave at least 15 to 25 minutes for this discussion, which helps participants understand and consolidate what they have learned. Discuss what the participants learned about strategies, using the following questions as a guide. Were certain strategies relevant across

a number of language activities? Why might this be the case? Were there any *combinations of strategies* that recurred across language activities? Which strategies seem to go together? Which strategies seem to operate on their own? Which strategies do the participants tend to use themselves, when, and why? How can this game help participants in dealing with tasks in the foreign or second language?

List of Language Activities for the Embedded Strategies Game

ALL THE NEWS THAT FITS, WE PRINT—Read the newspaper in the target language to practice the language and keep up with events.

AS THE WORLD TURNS—Watch a soap opera every day to practice understanding the target language.

BRAINSTORM—Brainstorm with other language learners some possible topics for writing in the new language.

BREAK-DOWN—Break down into parts any long words and expressions in the new language that you find overwhelming.

CANNED TALK—Learn some common "canned" routines by heart in the new language so you can rattle them off easily when you need them in social conversation.

CHECK-UP—Check yourself to see the kinds of errors you make in the new language and then try figure out why.

CINEMA CITY—Go to a foreign film festival to get more exposure to the new language.

COLORS—Color-code your language notebook so you can find things easily.

CUISINE—Read and follow recipes in the target language.

DATING GAME—To meet a person of the opposite sex, read the computer dating company advertisement in the newspaper—in the new language, of course.

'FRAIDY CAT—Make positive statements to yourself in order to feel more confident and be more willing to take risks.

GETTING IT ALL TOGETHER—When preparing to give a talk in the new language, figure out the requirements, your own capabilities, and what else you will have to do in order to give a good talk.

GOOD OLD SHERLOCK—While reading the new language, constantly look for clues to the meaning.

GOSSIP—While a friend is telling you some juicy gossip in the new language, listen carefully so you can get it right when you tell it to someone else.

GUESS WHAT—While listening to a politician's TV speech in the new language, guess what the politician will say next.

HANDOUTS—Send off for free items advertised in target language magazines and newspapers.

HELP!—When you can't seem to find the word to say in the new language, ask for help from somebody else.

HELP, I NEED YOU—Look for native speakers who can help you practice speaking the new language or who can explain things to you about the new culture.

HOLY, HOLY, HOLY—Read a hymnbook, bible, prayerbook, etc., in the new language. See if there is anything similar to what you know from your own background. When you don't understand something, guess.

HOW AM I DOING?—Ask someone else for feedback on whether you have understood, said, or written something correctly in the new language.

HOW COME?—Try to figure out the reason for doing a certain language activity, so that you can prepare yourself better.

IT'S BEEN A HARD DAY—Schedule a break from language learning when you are tired.

KEEP QUIET—Try to just listen and understand the new language for a while because your speaking skills aren't so hot yet.

LISTENING IN—While the old lady ahead of you on the bus is chastising a young man in your new language, listen to their conversation to find out exactly what she's saying to him.

LOOKING AHEAD—Use preview questions or other ways to look ahead at the new target language reading material, so that you can orient yourself.

MARKERS—In reading the new language, look for markers in the text (headings, subheadings, topic sentences) to give you clues about the meaning.

MIND IMAGES—When learning a list of words in the new language, create a picture in your head of the words and the relationships among them.

MOUTHING—When trying to learn the sounds of the new language, pay attention to how a native speaker shapes his or her mouth when talking; then you do the same while looking at a mirror.

MUSIC TIME—Listen to song lyrics in the target language and try to sing along and learn the words.

NITPICKING—While reading or listening to the target language, look for specific new words, forms, or pieces of information.

PEERS WITHOUT TEARS—Stop competing with your fellow students and learn to work together in learning the new language.

PENPALS—Meet a native speaker visiting from another country and then keep in touch with that person by writing in the new language after the person returns home.

PHYSICAL TRAINING—In class, follow commands of your teacher, such as "Stand up. Go to the blackboard. Pick up the chalk. Write your name."

PICTURES ON THE WALL—Go to the art museum, get a target language brochure about the paintings, read about them, go to see the ones you are most interested in, and write your impressions.

REWARDS—Having done very well on a language test, reward yourself with a special treat.

SCRABBLE—While playing a game of Scrabble in the target language, use a dictionary but no other aids.

SECRETS—Keep a journal of your language learning progress and write down new words and expressions.

SHORT-HAIRED (OR LONG-HAIRED) DICTIONARY—Find a pal who is a native speaker of the target language, and get your pal to explain to you the meanings of new words in the target language.

SNOOP AROUND—Make it a point to look around at signs, billboards, names of streets and buildings, headlines, magazine covers, and all the visual symbols of the new language and culture.

SOUNDS OF THE CITY—Listen to city sounds (announcements, discussions, speeches, mumblings, commercials, arguments), trying to figure out what people are saying in the new language.

SPREAD 'EM OUT—Plan your sessions for reviewing new material in the target language so that the sessions are at first close together and then more widely spread out.

STEERING CLEAR—When the conversation in the new language gets onto topics for which you don't know the vocabulary, change the subject or just don't say anything.

TAKING THE PULSE—Stop to determine whether you are feeling especially nervous before you go into language class.

TALKING TO YOURSELF—Tell yourself that you really *can* learn this language; bad experiences you might have had before don't count anymore.

T-TIME—Take notes on what you hear or read in the new language by drawing a big T on the paper, writing the key idea or title at the top of the T, then listing details in the left column and examples in the right column.

WALKING AROUND TOWN—To take a walk around the foreign city, get a guidebook and map in the new language, mark the best places, wander a bit, stop at a cafe, and meet some interesting people.

WATERY WORLD—Go down to the bay or the river, count the ships, read their names written in the new language, and ask people where the ships come from and where they are going next.

WHAT'S THE BIG IDEA?—Find all sorts of ways to locate the main idea as you are reading a passage in the new language.

WRITER'S CRAMP—To combat your "mental block" against writing a report in the new language, try to calm down and relax by means of music and breathing exercises.

Source Original [32].

Exercise 1.2. Strategy Search Game

Purpose

This game helps participants, either teachers or students, to determine which language learning strategies are embedded in, or suggested by, certain language tasks/situations. These are a little more complicated than the language activities in the preceding Embedded Strategies Game (Exercise 1.1 above). The Strategy Search Game is a process of matching language tasks/situations with the names of relevant language learning strategies. Like the Embedded Strategies Game, this exercise acquaints participants with the whole range of strategies. It can follow the Embedded Strategies Game as a more in-depth look at strategies, or it can be used instead of Embedded Strategies if participants already know something about strategies and their use.

Materials

Each participant gets a copy of the strategy system from this chapter (Figure 1.4) and a list of language tasks/situations (given below).

Time

This game, which lasts 1 to 2½ hours, can be spread over several class periods. Total time required depends on the number of tasks/situations used.

Instructions

Follow the instructions for the Embedded Strategies Game (Exercise 1.1) above. However, in place of "language activity" substitute "language task or situation." A reminder: Again, leave plenty of time at the end for a discussion of what has been learned about language learning strategies!

Alternatives

1. Instead of giving each small group the *complete* list of *all* the tasks/ situations from which to choose, let each small group pick a certain number of task/situation strips randomly from a well-shuffled set, so that no small group has the same task/situation strips as any other small group. Then each group must come up with all the relevant strategies for each of the task/situation strips it has randomly drawn. In Step 4 (explanation of strategy choices and determination of scores), small groups must read or describe each task/situation aloud to the whole group (so that everybody will know what the task or situation is). The explanation or justification operates as usual.

The rest of the game operates the same way as for the Embedded Strategies Game.

2. A small group makes up its own language tasks/situations, in addition to using the ones provided here within the time allowed. Strategies would be matched with the new tasks/situations in the same way as with the ones provided here.

3. Small groups act out their language tasks/situations. This works well with participants who are uninhibited or who know each other fairly well already.

Language Tasks/Situations for Strategy Search Game

(Cut into strips)

PRESENTING A PAPER: You are a Hungarian chemist in an industrial exchange program in the United States. Your task is to prepare a scientific paper to present orally to a group of your American colleagues. Your paper must be about 45 minutes long and must explain your research in some detail. Your oral English skills are not too good, but you know the technical vocabulary for your field and have a pretty fair grasp of English grammar. You are feeling nervous. Which language learning strategies do you need to use?

STRANGER: You are a 35-year-old refugee from Laos who has arrived in the United States. Your four children also escaped and are now with you. Your husband has died, and you are living on welfare funds. You are almost illiterate in your own language, as well as in English. You had a short course in English at the refugee processing camp, but all of your English skills are very poor. You need to learn enough English so that you can go shopping by yourself, deal with the social worker and the welfare office, take care of your family, and become adjusted to a totally new cultural situation. Which language learning strategies do you need to use?

ESPIONAGE: You are a spy. Your job deals with overhearing and understanding target language conversations in person, over the phone, and on tape. Your task is to track a covert group which has been conducting international sabotage and to uncover secrets about this group's activity. You have studied the language (called Unca) spoken by this group, but are not an expert; you need to work on your Unca listening skills—fast! Which language learning strategies do you need to use?

CARTOON: You are an English-speaking high school student learning Italian. You have a good sense of humor and enjoy jokes and cartoons. You decide to buy an Italian cartoon book. It is about 100 pages long, full of cartoons. You want to read the book, understand the cartoons, and explain some of the cartoons to your friends who do not know Italian at all. Which language learning strategies do you need to use?

TRAVEL AGENT: It is September. You are a British college student just starting a year's study in France. You want to go home for the Christmas holidays, and you've been told that you must book your tickets early or else you won't be able to get reservations. You have to take a train from Aix to Paris, another train from Paris to Cherbourg, and a ferry from Cherbourg to Plymouth, across the English Channel. You don't have much money, so you have to find the cheapest fare possible. Furthermore, you have some time constraints; you must return from England in time to see your girlfriend/boyfriend in France before the next semester starts. Your task is to talk to the travel agent, who does not understand English, and convey as much of this information as is relevant. Your French is rather limited, since you have not had much speaking practice yet. Which language learning strategies do you need to use?

ON TOUR: You are an Australian tourist in Greece. You have never been here before, and your study of Greek has been limited to skimming the Berlitz phrasebook. You managed to find your hotel with the help of a taxi driver. You went out for a walk on your own and got lost. Nobody around you seems to speak English. Your task is to find out where you are and get back to your hotel before it gets dark. You have 2 hours to do this. You are getting a little worried! Which language learning strategies do you need to use?

CHURCH: You are a visitor from the United States in Germany. It is Friday, and you want to prepare yourself to go to church on Sunday to worship, participate in the service, and possibly meet some German people afterwards. You had 2 years of German study, but that was a very long time ago. Which language learning strategies do you need to use?

NEWSWORTHY: You are a French student learning English in France. You try to read the *International Herald Tribune* regularly so you can practice English, but you keep getting stuck on unfamiliar words. You use a dictionary to find out the meaning of every word you don't know, but that slows you down too much, and not all the words are in the dictionary, anyway! It is very upsetting to have such difficulty, and you are about to give up. Which language learning strategies do you need to use?

VISITING GRANNY: You are in your 30s. Three months from now you will go to Warsaw to visit your grandmother, whom you have never met. You know from your parents that your grandmother speaks only a few words of English. You speak only a few words of Polish. You need to learn as much Polish as you can in the next 3 months, so you can find out all you can about your grandmother's life, the family history, and your Polish relatives when you get to Poland. Which language learning strategies do you need to use?

CHILD OF THE MIDLANDS: You are a Pakistani child in a medium-size city in the English midlands. You live in a Pakistani enclave. Your parents, brothers and sisters, and friends do not speak English at home or in the neighborhood. But in school there are children from 15 different language and cultural groups, and English is the primary language of communication across these groups. You need to learn English to get along with the other children and to get good grades in school. Which language learning strategies do you need to use?

DOWN IN TEXAS: You are a 13-year-old Mexican student. Your family has just moved to Texas from a small town in Mexico. You are in an English-as-a-second-language program at school with lots of other Mexicans. They call it a "transitional" program, because it is supposed to prepare you for regular classes. You feel annoyed and upset because you don't know much English, but you are highly motivated to learn. You want to be able to go to technical school or college after high school. You especially want to develop your language skills so that you will understand what your teacher says and so that you will be able to move more quickly into regular classes. Which language learning strategies do you need to use?

THE PLAY'S THE THING: You are an American high school student in your third year of French. Your task is to work with a small group to write and participate in a 30-minute play, all in French, about teenagers in France. You don't know much about teenagers in France, and you are terrified about speaking French in the play, but you are relieved that your friends are involved in it with you. Which language learning strategies do you need to use?

LEARNING RUSSIAN: You are a student of Russian in a university. You have not found any Russian natives in your town, except for your own professor. You realize that your speaking and listening skills are shaky, though you are doing OK in reading and writing (for instance, you can pick your way through a journal article or short story in Russian and can write a passable letter). Your task is to find ways to improve your speaking and listening skills so that you feel more confident. Which language learning strategies do you need to use?

FOREIGN POSTING: Your spouse has an offer of a high-level management post in a multinational firm that makes shoelaces in Costa Rica. You don't know Spanish. You studied a little bit of French and German in school many years ago, but that does not seem to help much. You are very interested in other cultures. Your task is to learn enough Spanish to be able to get along socially and to help you take care of daily needs once you get to Costa Rica. Which language learning strategies do you need to use?

TROPICS: You are a new Peace Corps volunteer in the Philippines. You have been studying the local dialect that you will need to speak when you are posted in the north. You have completed about half of the language training so far, but you don't feel much confidence in your skills. You know you will be working with village irrigation programs when you finish your language training, so you will need technical language about irrigation. But you also know that the Filipinos are very friendly and sociable, so you think it will be important to develop social language. Your task is to figure out whether to concentrate your language training on developing technical, job-related language skills and/or social, non-job-related language skills, and then to make the most of language training so that you will be able to get along in a new and unfamiliar situation. Which language learning strategies do you need to use?

NEWSPAPER: You are a foreign language student in your second year of study. With your classmates, you are writing and publishing a newspaper in the target language. Your task is to use written pieces of target language information given to you and then to transform that information into articles—news, features, editorials—and format them into a readable newspaper. Which language learning strategies do you need to use?

READING A CHAPTER: You are a graduate student in nuclear physics. One of the latest and best books on the subject is in Russian and has not yet been translated into your own language. You and your friends have decided to read this book together by having each of you read and summarize a chapter. You are looking at your chapter. You don't understand all of the text word for word, but you can see that it is fairly well organized and that it contains a lot of technical words you already know. Your task is to read and understand your chapter and provide a written summary of it to present to others. Which language learning strategies do you need to use?

TOOTHACHE: You are a student living in another country, whose language you speak only a little. One of your teeth fell out last night. It dropped on the floor, and you cannot find it. You don't like going to the dentist, but you know you have to. You have a dictionary and a phrasebook. You must learn how to ask about finding a dentist and how to get the telephone number and address. Then you must be able to call the dentist's office to explain the problem and set an appointment time. Once in the dentist's office, you need to be able to cooperate with the dentist in having the problem treated, and arrange for payment. Which language learning strategies do you need to use?

ERRANDS: You are a Canadian student who has just come to Austria to learn German. You must run the following errands in town. First you have to go to the market to get some fruit and vegetables, then to the pharmacy for bandages and toothpaste, then to the bakery for bread, and then to the post office for stamps. You don't yet have all the vocabulary you need for these errands, but you have about an hour to practice the language before you need to run the errands. Which language learning strategies do you need to use?

Source Original.

Chapter 2

Direct Strategies for Dealing with Language

Trying to learn to use words, and every attempt is . . . a raid on the inarticulate.

T. S. Eliot

PREVIEW QUESTIONS

1. What are direct strategies?
2. How do they differ from indirect strategies?
3. Why are direct strategies important for language learning?
4. What are the three groups of direct strategies?

INTRODUCTION TO DIRECT STRATEGIES

Language learning strategies that directly involve the target language are called *direct strategies*. All direct strategies require mental processing of the language, but the three groups of direct strategies (memory, cognitive, and compensation) do this processing differently and for different purposes. *Memory strategies*, such as grouping or using imagery, have a highly specific function: helping students store and retrieve new information. *Cognitive strategies*, such as summarizing or reasoning deductively, enable learners to understand and produce new language by many different means. *Compensation strategies*, like guessing or using synonyms, allow learners to use the language despite their often large gaps in knowledge. Figure 2.1 highlights these three groups of direct strategies.

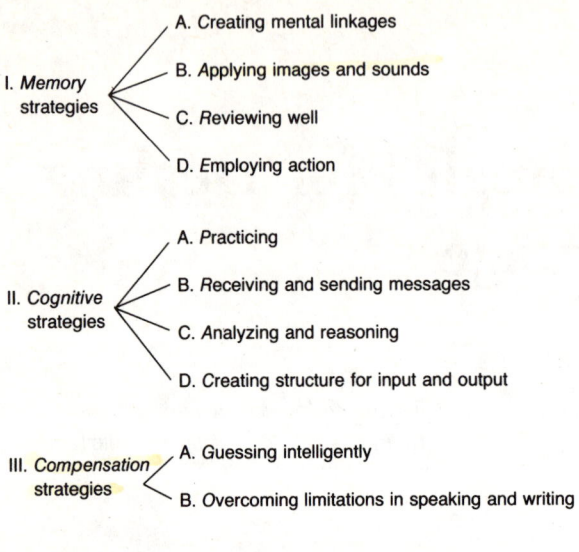

I. *Memory strategies*
- A. Creating mental linkages
- B. Applying images and sounds
- C. Reviewing well
- D. Employing action

II. *Cognitive strategies*
- A. Practicing
- B. Receiving and sending messages
- C. Analyzing and reasoning
- D. Creating structure for input and output

III. *Compensation strategies*
- A. Guessing intelligently
- B. Overcoming limitations in speaking and writing

Memory Aids: CARE, PRAC, GO

Figure 2.1   Diagram of the Direct Strategies: Overview. (*Source*: Original.)

MEMORY STRATEGIES

Memory strategies, sometimes called mnemonics, have been used for thousands of years. For example, orators in ancient times could remember a long speech by linking different parts of the speech with different rooms of a house or temple, and then "taking a walk" from room to room [1]. Before literacy became widespread, people used memory strategies to remember practical information about farming, weather, or when they were born. After literacy became commonplace, people forgot their previous reliance on memory strategies and disparaged those techniques as "gimmicks." Now memory strategies are regaining their prestige as powerful mental tools. The mind can store some 100 trillion bits of information, but only part of that potential can be used unless memory strategies come to the aid of the learner.

Memory strategies fall into four sets: Creating Mental Linkages, *Ap*plying Images and Sounds, *Reviewing Well*, and *Employing Actions* (see Figure 2.2). The first letters of each of these strategy sets spell CARE, an acronym that is itself a memory aid: "Take CARE of your memory and your memory will take CARE of you!" Memory strategies are clearly more effective when the learner simultaneously uses metacognitive strategies, like paying attention, and affective strategies, like reducing anxiety through deep breathing.

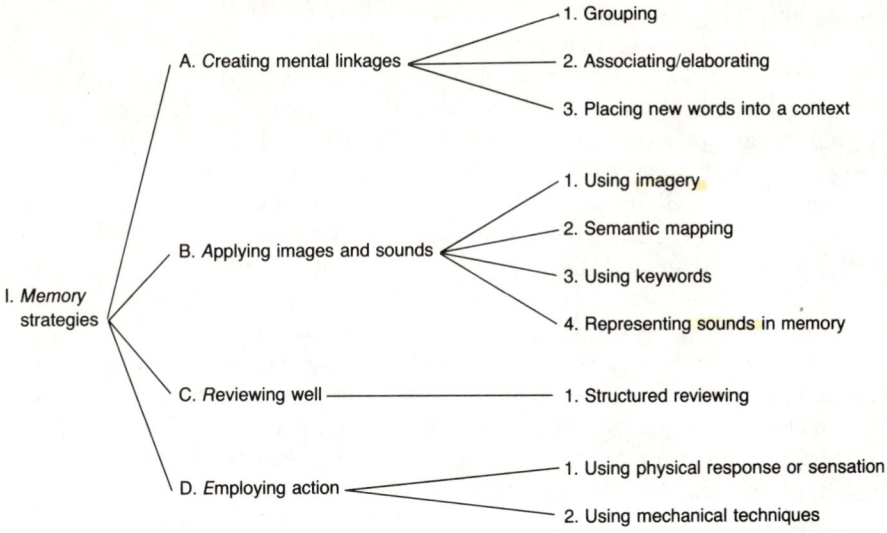

Memory Aid: CARE

"Take CARE of your memory, and
your memory will take CARE of you!"

> *The memory strengthens as you lay burdens upon it,*
> *and becomes trustworthy as you trust it.*

Thomas de Quincy

Figure 2.2   Diagram of the Memory Strategies. (*Source*: Original.)

Memory strategies reflect very simple principles, such as arranging things in order, making associations, and reviewing [2]. These principles all involve *meaning*. For the purpose of learning a new language, the arrangement and associations must be personally meaningful to the learner, and the material to be reviewed must have significance [3].

Though some teachers think vocabulary learning is easy, language learners have a serious problem remembering the large amounts of vocabulary necessary to achieve fluency. "Vocabulary is by far the most sizeable and unmanageable component in the learning of any language, whether a foreign or one's mother tongue" because of "tens of thousands of different meanings," according to Lord [4]. Memory strategies help language learners to cope with this difficulty. They enable learners to store verbal material and then retrieve it when needed for communication. In addition, the memory strategy of structured reviewing helps move information from the "fact level" to the "skill level," where knowledge is more procedural and automatic [5]. When information has reached the skill level, it is more easily retrieved and less easily lost after a period of disuse [6].

Memory strategies often involve pairing different types of material. In language learning, it is possible to give verbal labels to pictures, or to create visual images of words or phrases. Linking the verbal with the visual is very useful to language learning for four reasons. First, the mind's storage capacity for visual information exceeds its capacity for verbal material. Second, the most efficiently packaged chunks of information are transferred to long-term memory through visual images. Third, visual images may be the most potent device to aid recall of verbal material. Fourth, a large proportion of learners have a preference for visual learning [7].

While many language learners benefit from visual imagery, others have aural (sound-oriented), kinesthetic (motion-oriented) or tactile (touch-oriented) learning style preferences and therefore benefit from linking verbal material with sound, motion or touch. Certain memory strategies are designed to do this [8]. In memory strategies, as in other kinds of learning strategies, "different strokes for different folks" should be the cardinal rule.

Although memory strategies can be powerful contributors to language learning, some research shows that language students rarely report using these strategies [9]. It might be that students simply do not use memory strategies very much, especially beyond elementary levels of language learning. However, an alternative explanation might be that they are unaware of how often they actually *do* employ memory strategies. Below are the definitions of each memory strategy, as clustered into appropriate strategy sets.

Creating Mental Linkages

In this set are three strategies that form the cornerstone for the rest of the memory strategies: grouping, associating/elaborating, and using context.

1. Grouping

Classifying or reclassifying language material into meaningful units, either mentally or in writing, to make the material easier to remember by reducing the number of discrete elements. Groups can be based on type of word (e.g., all nouns or verbs), topic (e.g., words about weather), practical function (e.g., terms for things that make a car work), linguistic function (e.g., apology, request, demand), similarity (e.g., warm, hot, tepid, tropical), dissimilarity or opposition (e.g., friendly/unfriendly), the way one feels about something (e.g., like, dislike), and so on. The power of this strategy may be enhanced by labeling the groups, using acronyms to remember the groups, or using different colors to represent different groups.

2. Associating/Elaborating

Relating new language information to concepts already in memory, or relating one piece of information to another, to create associations in memory. These associations can be simple or complex, mundane or strange, but they must be meaningful to the learner. Associations can be between two things, such as bread and butter, or they can be in the form of a multipart "development," such as school–book–paper–tree–country–earth [10]. They can also be part of a network, such as a semantic map (see below).

3. Placing New Words into a Context

Placing a word or phrase in a meaningful sentence, conversation, or story in order to remember it. This strategy involves a form of associating/elaborating, in which the new information is linked with a context. This strategy is not the same as guessing intelligently, a set of compensation strategies (described later) which involve using all possible clues, including the context, to guess the meaning.

Applying Images and Sounds

Four strategies are included here: using imagery, using keywords, semantic mapping, and representing sounds in memory. These all involve remembering by means of visual images or sounds.

1. Using Imagery

Relating new language information to concepts in memory by means of meaningful visual imagery, either in the mind or in an actual drawing. The image can be a picture of an object, a set of locations for remembering a sequence of words or expressions, or a mental representation of the letters of a word. This strategy can be used to remember abstract words by associating such words with a visual symbol or a picture of a concrete object.

2. Semantic Mapping [11]

Making an arrangement of words into a picture, which has a key concept at the center or at the top, and related words and concepts linked with the key concept by means of lines or arrows. This strategy involves meaningful imagery, grouping, and associations; it visually shows how certain groups of words relate to each other.

3. Using Keywords [12]

Remembering a new word by using auditory and visual links. The first step is to identify a familiar word in one's own language that sounds like the new word—this is the "auditory link." The second step is to generate an image of some relationship between the new word and a familiar one—this is the "visual link." Both links must be meaningful to the learner. For example, to learn the new French word *potage* (soup), the English speaker associates it with a pot and then pictures a pot full of *potage*. To use a keyword to remember something abstract, such as a name, associate it with a picture of something concrete that sounds like the new word. For example, Minnesota can be remembered by the image of a *mini soda* [13].

4. Representing Sounds in Memory

Remembering new language information according to its sound. This is a broad strategy that can use any number of techniques, all of which create a meaningful, sound-based association between the new material and already known material. For instance, you can (a) link a target language word with any other word (in any language) that sounds like the target language word, such as Russian *brat* [брат] (brother) and English *brat* (annoying person), (b) use phonetic spelling and/or accent marks, or (c) use rhymes to remember a word.

Reviewing Well

This category contains just one strategy, structured reviewing. Looking at new target language information once is not enough; it must be reviewed in order to be remembered.

1. Structured Reviewing [14]

Reviewing in carefully spaced intervals, at first close together and then more widely spaced apart. This strategy might start, for example, with a review 10 minutes after the initial learning, then 20 minutes later, an hour or two later, a day later, 2 days later, a week later, and so on. This is sometimes called "spiraling," because the learner keeps spiraling back to what has already been learned at the same time that he or she is learning new information. The goal is "overlearning"—that is, being so familiar with the information that it becomes natural and automatic.

Employing Action

The two strategies in this set, using physical response or sensation and using mechanical tricks, both involve some kind of meaningful movement or action. These strategies will appeal to learners who enjoy the kinesthetic or tactile modes of learning.

1. Using Physical Response or Sensation [15]

Physically acting out a new expression (e.g., going to the door), or *meaningfully relating a new expression to a physical feeling or sensation* (e.g., warmth).

2. Using Mechanical Techniques

Using creative but tangible techniques, especially involving moving or changing something which is concrete, in order to remember new target language information. Examples are writing words on cards and moving cards from one stack to another when a word is learned, and putting different types of material in separate sections of a language learning notebook.

COGNITIVE STRATEGIES

Cognitive strategies are essential in learning a new language. Such strategies are a varied lot, ranging from repeating to analyzing expressions to summarizing. With all their variety, cognitive strategies are unified by a common function: manipulation or transformation of the target language by the learner [16]. Cognitive strategies are typically found to be the most popular strategies with language learners [17].

Four sets of cognitive strategies exist, as shown in Figure 2.3: Practicing, Receiving and Sending Messages, Analyzing and Reasoning, and Creating Structure for Input and Output. The first letters of each of these strategy sets combine to form the acronym PRAC, because "Cognitive strategies are PRACtical for language learning."

Strategies for practicing are among the most important cognitive strategies. Language learners do not always realize how essential practice is. During class, potential practice opportunities are often missed because one person recites while the others sit idle. Even when small group activities increase the amount of classroom practice, still more practice is usually needed to reach acceptable proficiency, a goal which requires hundreds or even thousands of hours of practice, depending on the difficulty of the language and other factors [18]. Given these facts, the practicing strategies—including repeating, formally practicing with sounds and writing systems, recognizing and using formulas and patterns, recombining, and practicing naturalistically—take on special value. Research has underscored the importance of naturalistic practice at all levels of language learning [19].

Strategies for receiving and sending messages are necessary tools. One such strategy, known as getting the idea quickly, helps learners locate the main idea through skimming or the key points of interest through scanning. This strategy implies that it is not necessary for learners to focus on every single word. Another strategy in this group, using resources, is useful for

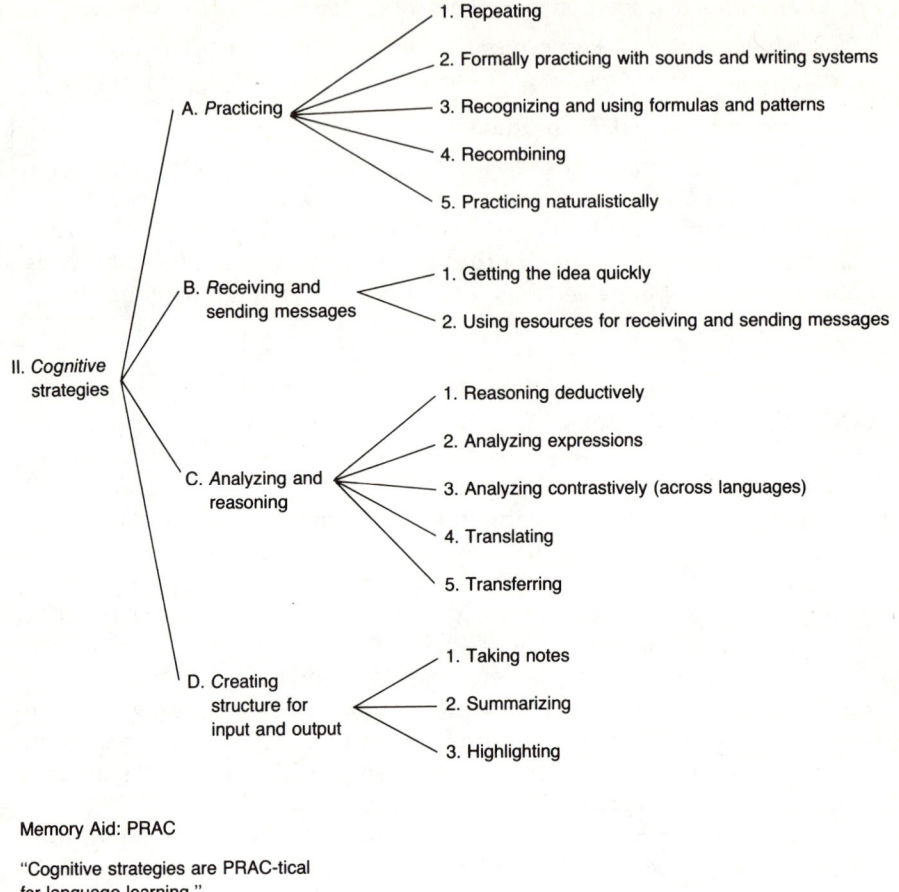

Memory Aid: PRAC

"Cognitive strategies are PRAC-tical
for language learning."

Wild and whirling words!
William Shakespeare

Figure 2.3 Diagram of the Cognitive Strategies. (*Source*: Original.)

both comprehension and production. It helps learners take advantage of a variety of resources, print or nonprint, to understand and produce messages in the new language.

Analyzing and reasoning strategies are commonly used by language learners. Many learners, especially adults [20], tend to "reason out" the new language. They construct a formal model in their minds based on analysis and comparison, create general rules, and revise those rules when new information is available. This process is extremely valuable. However, sometimes students make mistakes by unquestioningly generalizing the rules they've learned or transferring expressions from one language to another, typically from the mother tongue to the new language. Such mistakes characterize the "interlanguage," a hybrid form of language that lies somewhere between the native language and the target language [21]. Inappropriate use of literal translation also contributes to the interlanguage [22]. Interlanguage is a predictable, normal phase of language learning, but some language learners fail to leave that phase because they misuse or overuse some of the analyzing and reasoning strategies.

Language learners often feel besieged by "whirling words" from radio and TV programs, films, lectures, stories, articles, and conversations. To understand better, learners need to structure all this input into manageable chunks by using strategies such as taking notes, summarizing, and highlighting. Such structure-generating strategies are also helpful in preparing to use the language for speaking and writing.

Following are the definitions of important cognitive strategies.

Practicing

Of the five practicing strategies, probably the most significant one is practicing naturalistically.

1. Repeating

Saying or doing something over and over: listening to something several times; rehearsing; imitating a native speaker.

2. Formally Practicing with Sounds and Writing Systems

Practicing sounds (pronunciation, intonation, register, etc.) in a variety of ways, but not yet in naturalistic communicative practice; or *practicing the new writing system* of the target language.

3. Recognizing and Using Formulas and Patterns

Being aware of and/or using routine formulas (single, unanalyzed units), such as "Hello, how are you?"; *and unanalyzed patterns* (which have at least one slot to be filled), such as, "It's time to ———."

4. Recombining

Combining known elements in new ways to produce a longer sequence, as in linking one phrase with another in a whole sentence.

5. Practicing Naturalistically

Practicing the new language in natural, realistic settings, as in participating in a conversation, reading a book or article, listening to a lecture, or writing a letter in the new language.

Receiving and Sending Messages

Two strategies for receiving and sending messages are (a) getting the idea quickly and (b) using resources for receiving and sending messages. The former uses two specific techniques for extracting ideas, while the latter involves using a variety of resources for understanding or producing meaning.

1. Getting the Idea Quickly

Using skimming to determine the main ideas or scanning to find specific details of interest. This strategy helps learners understand rapidly what they hear or read in the new language. *Preview questions often assist.*

2. Using Resources for Receiving and Sending Messages

Using print or nonprint resources to understand incoming messages or produce outgoing messages.

Analyzing and Reasoning

This set of five strategies concerns logical analysis and reasoning as applied to various target language skills. Often learners can use these strategies to understand the meaning of a new expression or to create a new expression.

1. Reasoning Deductively

Using general rules and applying them to new target language situations. This is a top-down strategy leading from general to specific.

2. Analyzing Expressions

Determining the meaning of a new expression by breaking it down into parts; using the meanings of various parts to understand the meaning of the whole expression.

3. Analyzing Contrastively

Comparing elements (sounds, vocabulary, grammar) of the new language with elements of one's own language to determine similarities and differences.

4. Translating

Converting a target language expression into the native language (at various levels, from words and phrases all the way up to whole texts); *or converting the native language into the target language;* using one language as the basis for understanding or producing another.

5. Transferring

Directly applying knowledge of words, concepts, or structures from one language to another in order to understand or produce an expression in the new language.

Creating Structure for Input and Output

The following three strategies are ways to create structure, which is necessary for both comprehension and production in the new language.

1. Taking Notes

Writing down the main idea or specific points. This strategy can involve raw notes, or it can comprise a more systematic form of note-taking such as the shopping-list format, the T-formation, the semantic map, or the standard outline form.

2. Summarizing

Making a summary or abstract of a longer passage.

3. Highlighting

Using a variety of emphasis techniques (such as underlining, starring, or color-coding) to focus on important information in a passage.

COMPENSATION STRATEGIES

Compensation strategies enable learners to use the new language for either comprehension or production despite limitations in knowledge. Compensation strategies are intended to make up for an inadequate repertoire of grammar and, especially, of vocabulary. Ten compensation strategies exist, clustered into two sets: *Guessing Intelligently in Listening and Reading,* and *Overcoming Limitations in Speaking and Writing* (see Figure 2.4). These two sets can be remembered by the acronym GO, since "Language learners can GO far with compensation strategies."

Guessing strategies, sometimes called "inferencing," involve using a wide variety of clues—linguistic and nonlinguistic—to guess the meaning when the learner does not know all the words [23]. Good language learners, when confronted with unknown expressions, make educated guesses. On the other hand, less adept language learners often panic, tune out, or grab the dog-eared dictionary and try to look up every unfamiliar word—harmful responses which impede progress toward proficiency.

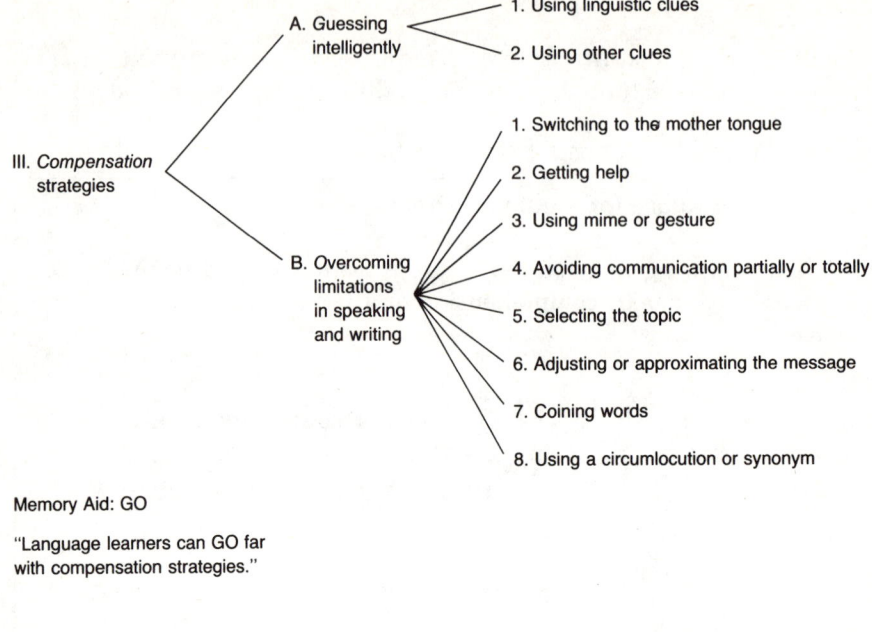

Memory Aid: GO

"Language learners can GO far
with compensation strategies."

Necessity is the mother of invention.
16th-century proverb

Figure 2.4 Diagram of the Compensation Strategies. (*Source*: Original.)

Beginners are not the only ones who employ guessing. Advanced learners and even native speakers use guessing when they haven't heard something well enough, when they don't know a new word, or when the meaning is hidden between the lines. Guessing is actually just a special case of the way people typically process new information—that is, interpreting the data by using the immediate context and their own life experience. "Meaning is in fact created by the receiver in light of the experience which [s]he already possesses," said MacBride [24]. It is this experience which provides the source of many intelligent guesses for both language experts and novices.

Compensation occurs not just in understanding the new language but also in producing it. Compensation strategies allow learners to produce spoken or written expression in the new language without complete knowledge. Researchers have typically paid attention only to compensation strategies for speaking [25]. It is true that certain compensation strategies, like using mime or gestures, are used in speaking. However, other compensation strategies—adjusting or approximating the message, coining words, using a circumlocution or synonym, or selecting the topic—can be used in informal writing as well as in speaking.

Many compensation strategies for production are used to compensate for a lack of appropriate vocabulary, but these strategies can also be used to make up for a lack of grammatical knowledge. For instance, if learners do not know how to express the subjunctive form of a verb, they might use a different form to get the message across.

Just as advanced learners and native speakers occasionally use guessing to help them understand, they sometimes use compensation strategies when experiencing a temporary breakdown in speaking or writing performance. Less proficient language learners need these compensatory production strategies even more, because they run into knowledge roadblocks more often than do individuals who are skilled in the language.

Compensation strategies for production help learners to keep on using the language, thus obtaining more practice. In addition, some of these strategies, such as adjusting or approximating the message, help learners become more fluent in what they already know. Still other compensation strategies, like getting help and coining words, may lead learners to gain new information about what is appropriate or permissible in the target language [26]. Learners skilled in such strategies sometimes communicate better than learners who know many more target language words and structures.

Here are definitions of some key compensation strategies.

Guessing Intelligently in Listening and Reading

The two strategies which contribute to guessing intelligently refer to two different kinds of clues: linguistic and nonlinguistic [27].

1. Using Linguistic Clues

Seeking and using language-based clues in order to guess the meaning of what is heard or read in the target language, in the absence of complete knowledge of vocabulary, grammar, or other target language elements. Language-based clues may come from aspects of the target language that the learner already knows, from the learners' own language, or from another language. For instance, if the learner does not know the expression *association sans but lucratif* ("nonprofit association," in French), previous knowledge of certain words in English (association, lucrative) and French (*sans* = without) would give clues to the meaning of the unknown word, *but* (aim, goal), and of the whole expression.

2. Using Other Clues

Seeking and using clues that are not language-based in order to guess the meaning of what is heard or read in the target language, in the absence of complete knowledge of vocabulary, grammar, or other target language elements. Nonlanguage clues may come from a wide variety of sources: knowledge of context, situation, text structure, personal relationships, topic, or "general world knowledge." For example, if the learner does not know what is meant by the words *vends* or *à vendre* in the French newspaper, noticing that these words are used in the context of classified ads, and that they are followed by a list of items and prices, provides clues suggesting that these terms probably refer to selling.

Overcoming Limitations in Speaking and Writing

Eight strategies are used for overcoming limitations in speaking and writing. Some of these are dedicated solely to speaking, but some can be used for writing, as well.

1. Switching to the Mother Tongue

Using the mother tongue for an expression without translating it, as in *Ich bin eine girl*. This strategy may also include adding word endings from the new language onto words from the mother tongue.

2. Getting Help

Asking someone for help by hesitating or explicitly asking for the person to provide the missing expression in the target language.

3. Using Mime or Gesture

Using physical motion, such as mime or gesture, in place of an expression to indicate the meaning.

4. Avoiding Communication Partially or Totally

Partially or totally avoiding communication when difficulties are anticipated. This strategy may involve avoiding communication in general, avoiding certain topics, avoiding specific expressions, or abandoning communication in mid-utterance.

5. Selecting the Topic

Choosing the topic of conversation in order to direct the communication to one's own interests and make sure the topic is one in which the learner has sufficient vocabulary and grammar to converse.

6. Adjusting or Approximating the Message

Altering the message by omitting some items of information, making ideas simpler or less precise, or saying something slightly different that means almost the same thing, such as saying *pencil* for *pen*.

7. Coining Words

Making up new words to communicate the desired idea, such as *paper-holder* for *notebook*.

8. Using a Circumlocution or Synonym

Getting the meaning across by describing the concept (circumlocution) or using a word that means the same thing (synonym); for example, "what you use to wash dishes with" as a description for *dishrag*.

SUMMARY

This chapter has explained direct strategies, which involve use of the new language, and has described these groups of direct strategies: memory, cognitive, and compensation. Definitions of a variety of specific strategies in each group were also given. In the next chapter, these strategies will be applied to the four language skills.

ACTIVITIES FOR READERS

Activity 2.1. Check Your Attitudes Toward Memory Strategies

Consider your attitudes toward memory strategies. Were you brought up to believe that memory strategies are just gimmicks or tricks that are not used by serious people? Or have you generally believed that memory strategies are valuable tools for improving mental power? Explain how your attitude toward memory strategies has or has not changed through reading this chapter.

List at least eight new ideas about memory strategies you gained from this chapter. Put one star beside each of the ideas which might benefit you personally. Put two stars beside each of those which might help your students as well.

Activity 2.2. Examine Memory Strategies in Different Settings

Brainstorm the ways that memory strategies might be used in two different settings: the language classroom and a naturalistic language setting outside of the classroom (for example, a local cultural event where the language is used). Be as specific as possible.

Activity 2.3. Think About Language Loss

Have you or your students experienced loss of language skills through nonuse? If so, under what circumstances? What kinds of memory strategies might have helped prevent this loss?

Activity 2.4. Consider the Nature of Practicing

Draw a continuum ranging from more realistic to less realistic. Now classify the five practicing strategies on that continuum. List the differences between the more realistic practicing strategies and the less realistic ones. Indicate when each would be useful.

Activity 2.5. Work with Skimming and Scanning

The next time you read the newspaper in your own language, pay attention to how you read. Notice whether you use skimming or scanning to get the idea quickly, or whether you try to comprehend every word. Consider how you can help your students develop and practice their own skimming and scanning skills in the target language.

Activity 2.6. Find Resources

Make a list of the resources that students might use to understand, say, or write something in the new language. Indicate where those resources might be found. Consider how you can help your students know about these resources.

Activity 2.7. List the Pros and Cons of Analyzing/Reasoning

List all the ways that analyzing and reasoning can assist language learning. Now list all the ways that analyzing and reasoning can inhibit progress toward language proficiency. Discuss how teachers can help their students avoid traps such as overgeneralization.

Activity 2.8. Consider the Need for Structure

List ways in which people might use structuring strategies such as note-taking, summarizing, and highlighting in everyday life. Now discuss how these strategies can be used in learning a new language.

Activity 2.9. Notice Students' Compensatory Speaking Strategies

Notice your students' compensation strategies as they speak with each other and with you in the target language. Make a list of these strategies.

Indicate which of the strategies occur most often and least often. Note whether this depends on the student, with some students using certain compensation strategies more than others.

Activity 2.10. Consider Learning and Communication

Do you feel that the saying "Learning takes place *through* communication" is accurate in regard to your students? Explain.

EXERCISES TO USE WITH YOUR STUDENTS

Exercise 2.1. Ask Students to Identify Their Memory Strategies

Purpose

This exercise helps students consider the kinds of memory strategies they use and introduces them to new ones.

Materials

Large sheets of paper for the list.

Time

This exercise, lasting 20 minutes or more, can be done periodically in order to add to the list.

Instructions

Ask your students to identify their own memory strategies. It is not necessary to try to classify those strategies according to the list in this chapter. Just let students come up with their own strategy descriptions and share them with each other. Add to the list as time goes by, on the basis of classroom activities involving vocabulary learning. Encourage students to keep sharing their memory strategies.

Source Original.

Exercise 2.2. Get the Message

Purpose

This exercise helps students practice a variety of strategies for understanding an oral message.

Materials

Film, cartoon, or news program; equipment to play it.

Time

It takes 30 minutes to 1 hour, depending on the length of the material.

Instructions

Get hold of a short suspense film, cartoon, or TV news program in the target language. Play it for your students, asking them in advance to pay attention to the ways they receive the message. Afterwards, have them brainstorm the ways they used skimming, scanning, guessing, or other strategies to understand.

Alternatively, run the show *twice*—the first time without the sound but with the visual input, and the second time with both sound and visual input. After each run, ask your students to explain (a) what they understood and (b) the clues they used to help them understand.

Source Original.

Exercise 2.3. Play Twenty Questions

Purpose

This exercise gives practice in guessing using a familiar game.

Materials

None.

Time

The exercise takes 20 to 45 minutes.

Instructions

Play the game Twenty Questions, first in the native language and then in the target language. To play the game, one person thinks of an expression, such as "hiking in the mountains." Then that person provides clues about the expression to the other participants, so they can guess what the expression is. They can ask only 20 questions, which must be answerable by either "yes" or "no." Permissible extra clues include whether the expression refers to something animal, vegetable, or mineral; the number of words in the expression; and whether the expression contains the definite article (*the*) or the indefinite article (*a, an*), for those languages which have such articles. After one round is over, switch roles so that a different participant thinks of an expression, and the others guess. Use this game as a spring-board to a discussion of the uses of guessing strategies.

Source Traditional parlor game.

Exercise 2.4. Hold a Conversation

Purpose

This exercise enables students to consider the kinds of strategies they use in a conversation and how often they use them.

Materials

Paper for a list.

Time

Lasts 30 to 45 minutes.

Instructions

Ask your students to hold a 5-minute conversation in the new lan-guage, on any topic, with a classmate. Ask them to list the strategies they used either to understand what was said or to produce expressions when they did not know the precise words. Ask them to make a rough estimate of the number of times each strategy was used by each person in the conversation. Now ask them how they felt when they used these strategies (happy to keep on in the conversation, ignorant because unable to think of the right word, pleased to be understood, etc.).

Source Original.

Chapter 3

Applying Direct Strategies to the Four Language Skills

It is better to see once than to hear a hundred times.

RUSSIAN PROVERB

PREVIEW QUESTIONS

1. How can the direct strategies be applied to the four language skills?
2. How are these strategies applied differently to the four skills?
3. Are any direct strategies especially useful to the development of a particular skill?

INTRODUCTION TO APPLYING THE DIRECT STRATEGIES

This chapter discusses how the three groups of direct strategies—memory, cognitive, and compensation strategies (see Figure 3.1)—are used to develop each of the four language skills: listening, reading, speaking, and writing. These direct strategies work best when supported by indirect strategies, which are described in detail in Chapter 4.

Underlying the discussion are two assumptions. First, all four language skills are important and deserve special attention and action [1]. Second, learning strategies help students to develop each of the skills. In this chapter, the language skills related to each strategy are noted, following the section title, like this: Ⓛ (listening), Ⓡ (reading), Ⓢ (speaking), Ⓦ (writing), Ⓐ (all skills).

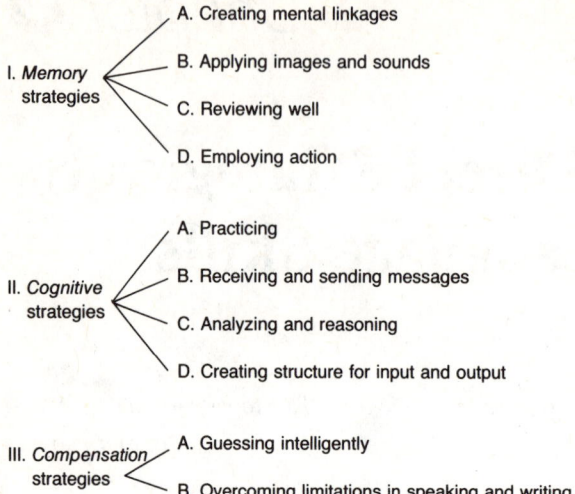

I. *Memory* strategies
- A. Creating mental linkages
- B. Applying images and sounds
- C. Reviewing well
- D. Employing action

II. *Cognitive* strategies
- A. Practicing
- B. Receiving and sending messages
- C. Analyzing and reasoning
- D. Creating structure for input and output

III. *Compensation* strategies
- A. Guessing intelligently
- B. Overcoming limitations in speaking and writing

Figure 3.1   Diagram of the Direct Strategies to Be Applied to the Four Language Skills. (*Source*: Original.)

APPLYING MEMORY STRATEGIES TO THE FOUR LANGUAGE SKILLS

Storage and retrieval of new information are the two key functions of memory strategies. These strategies, as shown in Figure 3.2, help learners *store* in memory the important things they hear or read in the new language, thus enlarging their knowledge base. These strategies also enable learners to *retrieve* information from memory when they need to use it for comprehension or production. Descriptions of memory strategies below focus mostly on the storage function, because that is the initial key to learning, but some general comments are included about the retrieval function as well.

Creating Mental Linkages

Three kinds of strategies are useful for making mental linkages: grouping, associating/elaborating, and placing new words into a context. These are the most basic memory strategies and the foundation of more complex memory strategies.

Grouping Ⓛ Ⓡ Grouping involves classifying or reclassifying what is heard or read into meaningful groups, thus reducing the number of un-related elements. It sometimes involves labeling the groups, as well. Notice

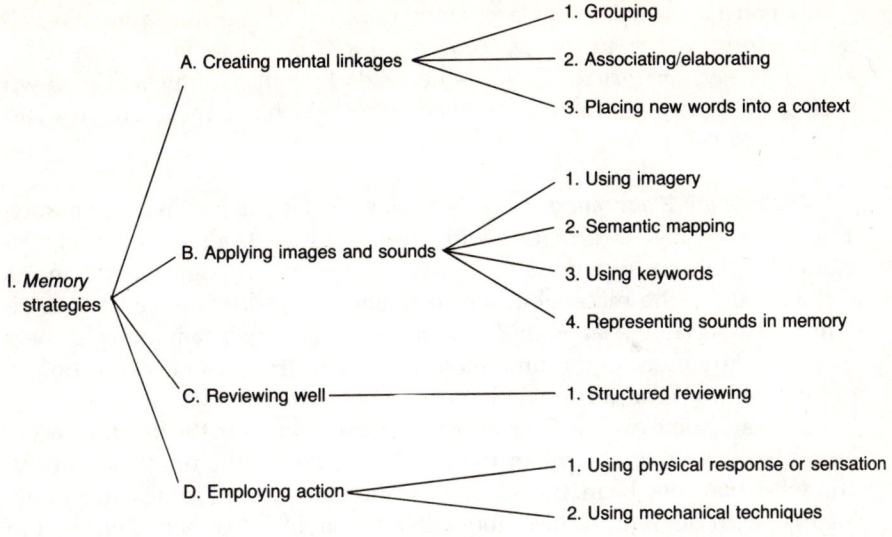

This is the use of memory: For liberation.
T. S. Eliot

Figure 3.2 Diagram of the Memory Strategies to Be Applied to the Four Language Skills. (*Source*: Original.)

that some of the examples below involve other strategies, too, such as paying attention or taking notes.

The following examples show ways to group material that has been heard in the new language [2]. First, Norberto, who is learning English, writes down in his notebook new words when he hears them, and he categorizes them grammatically: for example, *you, he, she, they, someone; hard, easy, kind, soft; quickly, heatedly, markedly, completely.* Then he labels these categories: pronouns, adjectives, and adverbs. Second, Jennie, a student of French, is listening to a talk about computers. She writes down the important words, such as *l'informatique* (computer science), *l'ordinateur* (computer), *le moniteur* (monitor), *l'écran* (screen), *le clavier* (keyboard), *la puce* (chip, literally flea!), *l'unité centrale* (central processing unit), and *les touches* (the keys). Then she groups these words according to whether they are masculine or feminine.

Here are some examples of grouping of written material that has been read. First, Lucien, a French speaker learning English, groups new words that he reads by conceptual similarities (e.g., *hot, warm, fire*), and in reading he actively looks for the opposites, such as *cold, cool, ice.* Second, while Stephanie is reading, she jots down new Russian verbs that she encounters, putting them into various categories, such as motion verbs and nonmotion verbs. Third, Donny makes a column for each of the important French prefixes (e.g., *e-*, *en-/m*, *entre-*, *para-*, *sou-*) and each of the suffixes (e.g., *-able*, *-age*, *-ier*, *-oir*, *-eux*). Then, as he reads French, Donny writes down interesting examples of words he encounters which use these prefixes and suffixes.

Associating/Elaborating Ⓛ Ⓡ This memory strategy involves associating new language information with familiar concepts already in memory. Naturally, these associations are likely to strengthen comprehension, as well as making the material easier to remember. Below are some real instances of associating/elaborating that are personally significant to the learners involved. Any association must have *meaning* to the learner, even though it might not make a geat deal of sense to someone else.

Here are some examples of associating/elaborating in the listening area. First, Mike wants to remember the name of Solange, the university librarian, who has just been introduced in French. He associates the name Solange with something else about her by saying "*So long*, library, I'm leaving!" or "Solange's face is *so long*." Second, Corazon, a learner of English, hears the word *billboard*. She associates it with a previously learned word, *board*, used for displaying; therefore she understands and remembers *billboard* more effectively.

Following are some examples of associating/elaborating in reading. First, Benjamin reads a German story that contains the word *Wissenschaft* (knowledge). He associates this word with the English words *wise* and *shaft* and remembers the German word by thinking of knowledge as a *shaft of wisdom*. Second, Glennys reads the Russian word *soyuz* [союз] (union); to remember this word, she associates it with her friend Susie.

Placing New Words into a Context Ⓐ This strategy involves placing new words or expressions that have been heard or read into a meaningful context, such as a spoken or written sentence, as a way of remembering it. As an example in listening, Michel has heard the names of the Great Lakes in the United States and wants to remember them. To do so, he uses the acronym *HOMES* (standing for Huron, Ontario, Michigan, Erie, and Superior) and puts it in the context of the spoken sentence, "My *HOME'S* on the Great Lakes."

Written selections often present new words in a meaningful context. However, students sometimes encounter written lists of words or phrases they must learn with no supporting or explanatory context. In such cases, it helps for learners to create their own context. For example, Katya, a learner of English, encounters a list of words and expressions related to sewing, such as *hook, eye, seam, zipper, button, snap, thread, needle, baste, hem*, and *stitch*. She writes a little story to put these words into a meaningful context. And Keith, while reading his German language book, finds a list of verbs that are unrelated in meaning, though they have some grammatical similarities (e.g., *ankommen*, to arrive, *aufstehen*, to get up, *ausgehen*, to go out, *fortfahren*, to go on, *einsteigen*, to get in, *wegnehmen*, to take away, *abreisen*, to set out, *zumachen*, to shut). He creates a funny tale that contains all these verbs.

Applying Images and Sounds

The four strategies for applying images and sounds are useful for remembering new expressions that have been heard or read. These strategies include using imagery, semantic mapping, using keywords, and representing sounds in memory. One of these strategies, semantic mapping, is immediately helpful for comprehension, too.

Using Imagery Ⓛ Ⓡ A good way to remember what has been heard or read in the new language is to create a mental image of it. Here are some illustrations. First, Adel, a Spanish bank manager learning English, tries to remember the American phrase *tax shelter*, which he has just heard [3]. He uses a mental image of a small house protecting or sheltering a pile of money inside. Second, Quang remembers a whole set of verbs related to household chores (e.g., *cooking, cleaning, washing, cutting, buying*) by making a mental image of the situation in which he first heard these words during an English class in the refugee camp. Third, Helen has just read the phrase *les mouettes blancs* (French for the white seagulls), and she mentally pictures white seagulls flying in the sky. Fourth, Jeff has read the Russian sentence *Ya hochu pisat' pis'mo* [Я хочу писать письмо] (I want to write a letter), and he pictures these Russian words in his mind.

One kind of imaging has special value in reading. It involves remembering a written item by picturing the place where it is located. For instance, Mariette remembers new English verbs by imagining the place where they are on the page. Jill remembers the expression *Cédez le passage* (yield) by picturing the road sign where she first read it.

The imagery used to remember expressions does not have to be purely mental. Drawings can make mental images (of objects like *house* or *tree*, or descriptive adjectives like *wide* or *tall*) more concrete. Even abstract words like *evil* or *truth* can be turned into symbols on a piece of paper for the purpose of remembering. For many prepositions, such as the equivalent of *above, over, under, among, between, below*, or *into*, learners can draw diagrams with arrows to illustrate meanings. These visual products do not need to be artistic. Just about anyone can draw stick figures, sketches, or diagrams to communicate a concept worth remembering.

Semantic Mapping Ⓛ Ⓡ This strategy involves arranging concepts and relationships on paper to create a semantic map, a diagram in which the key concepts (stated in words) are highlighted and are linked with related concepts via arrows or lines. Such a diagram visually shows how ideas fit together. This strategy incorporates a variety of other memory strategies: grouping, using imagery, and associating/elaborating. This strategy is valuable for improving both memory and comprehension of new expressions. It can be used for prelistening or prereading activities designed to help learners understand and remember vocabulary that will be heard or read. It can also be used as the basis for an entire listening or reading activity by giving the main concept or expression and asking students to listen and fill in the rest. Semantic mapping also provides a good note-taking format. Of course, in an exercise based on semantic mapping, there is no single "right answer," because different students will have different approaches to clustering ideas—unless a particular formula is taught (not a useful practice if the purpose is for learners to make their *own* associational linkages) [4].

Three examples of semantic mapping appear in Figures 3.3, 3.4, and 3.5. In the first illustration (Figure 3.3), *la corrida de toros* (the bullfight) is the key concept, and sets of related vocabulary are listed around this central theme and linked with it by means of lines. The next two figures (3.4 and 3.5) show a different example, in which the concept *hair* is mapped with its related concepts. Figure 3.4 is a simple version, mainly using words connected with lines. Figure 3.5 enhances the meaning of the words by using abundant pictures of objects. On their own, learners can make semantic maps like this to cluster or group related concepts visually, thus making the concepts easier to remember.

Using Keywords (L) (R) This strategy combines sounds and images so that learners can more easily remember what they hear or read in the new language. The strategy has two steps. First, identify a familiar word in one's own language or another language that sounds like the new word. Second, generate a visual image of the new word and the familiar one interacting in some way. Notice that the target language word does not have to sound exactly like the familiar word. (Additional pronunciation practice may be needed via the strategy of formally practicing with sounds and writing systems.)

Here are some examples of keywords for remembering what is heard or read. Brian links the new French word *froid* (cold) with a familiar word, *Freud*, then imagines Freud standing outside in the cold. *Sobor* [собор] is the Russian word for council, so Alice links this new word with *so bored*, picturing a bunch of councillors "so bored" with their meeting. Howard links the new Spanish word *sombrero* (hat with a large brim) with *somber*, and imagines a somber man wearing a sombrero. Fourth, in Italian the word for fly is *mosca*, so Bernie pictures flies invading Moscow. Julianne reads the new Spanish word for waitress, *camarera*, relates it to a *camera*, then imagines a waitress with a camera slung around her neck. Jeremy

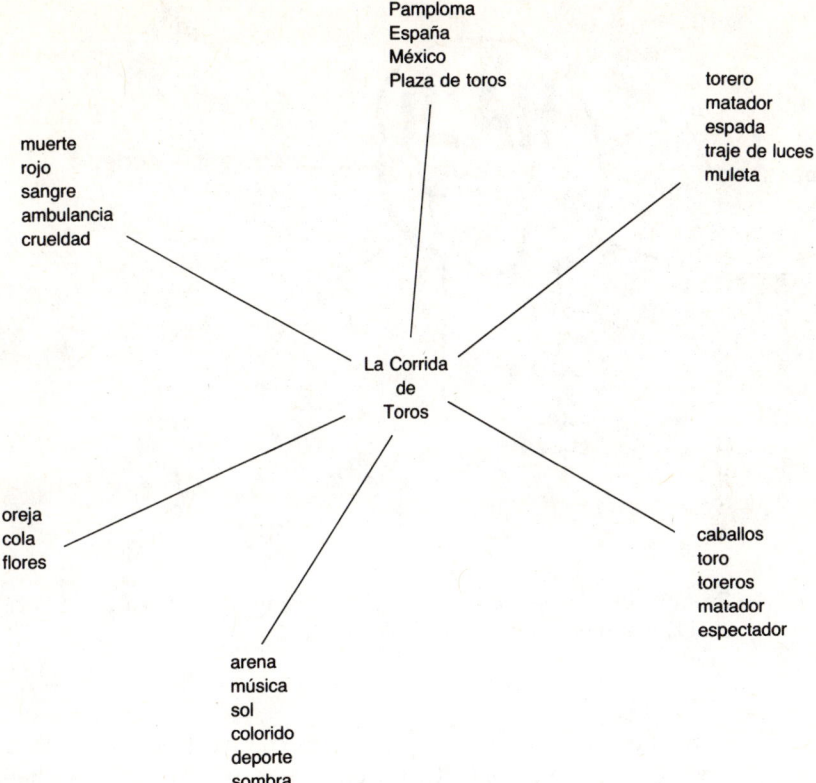

muerte
rojo
sangre
ambulancia
crueldad

Pamploma
España
México
Plaza de toros

torero
matador
espada
traje de luces
muleta

La Corrida
de
Toros

oreja
cola
flores

caballos
toro
toreros
matador
espectador

arena
música
sol
colorido
deporte
sombra

Figure 3.3   Example of a Semantic Map for "Bullfight" (*La Corrida de Toros*) Using Related Words. (*Source*: Hague (1987, p. 222).)

reads a new French word, *grève* (strike), and links it with a familiar English word that sounds similar, *grievance*, picturing a group of strikers taking a list of grievances to their employer. Yolande, a French speaker, reads the English word *pool*. To remember it, she thinks of the French word *poulet* (chicken, also slang for policeman) and imagines a chicken (or a policeman!) with sunglasses sitting by a pool.

Representing Sounds in Memory (L) (R) (S) This strategy helps learners remember what they hear by making auditory rather than visual representations of sounds. This involves linking the new word with familiar words or sounds from any language: the new language, one's own language, or any other.

Rhymes are a well-known example of representing sounds in memory. Most English speakers know the helpful spelling rhyme "*I* before *E* except

Figure 3.4 Example of a Semantic Map for "Hair" Using Related Words. (*Source*: Brown-Azarowicz, Stannard, and Goldin (1986, p. 32).)

after C." Learners can use rhymes, especially in context (see the strategy of placing new words into a context), to remember new vocabulary they have heard. Here are three examples. Rollande uses rhyme to learn the sounds of English words, such as *goat, coat, boat, float, moat, dote,* and she makes up nonsense rhymes using these words. Antonio creates the nonsense rhyme "I hit a parrot with my carrot. The parrot said I am dead!" Rudy associates the new French word *poubelle* (trash can) with a similar-sounding French phrase, *plus belle* (more beautiful), and he puts these into humorous rhyme by saying, *la plus belle poubelle* (the prettiest trash can).

Rhymes are not the only way to represent sounds mentally. Consider these other ways. Kelley links the new Russian word *gazyeta* [газета] with the English word *gazette*, which has a similar sound and meaning. Carlos links the new word *cart* with the familiar Spanish word *carta* because of similar sounds, though the words have different meanings. Gerard, a learner of Russian, encounters the word *moloka* [молока] (milk) in a story. He sounds out the new word in his mind and associates it with an English word that sounds similar (milk) and means the same thing. Kiri is reading an article and finds the new English word *familiar*. It sounds like a word she knows, *family*, so she can remember the new word by the auditory link.

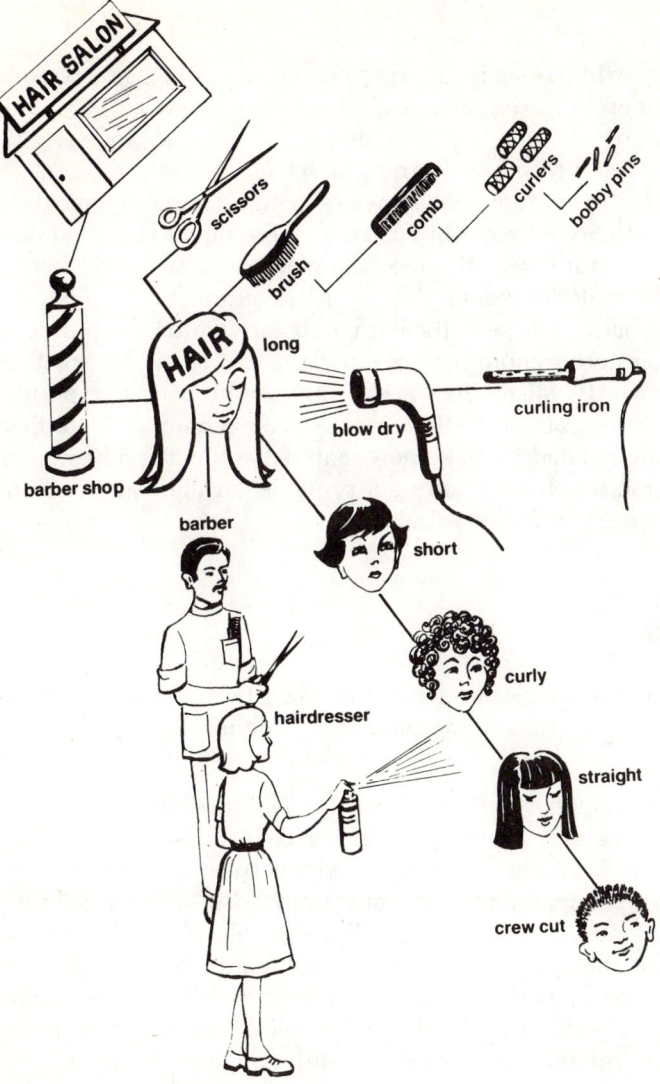

Figure 3.5 Example of a Semantic Map for "Hair" Using Pictures and Words. (*Source*: Brown-Azarowicz, Stannard, and Goldin (1986, p. 33).)

Reviewing Well Ⓐ

The sole strategy in this set is structured reviewing, which is especially useful for remembering new material in the target language. It entails reviewing at different intervals, at first close together and then increasingly far apart. For instance, Misha is learning a set of vocabulary words in English. He practices them immediately, waits 15 minutes before practicing them again, and practices them an hour later, three hours later, the next day, two days later, four days later, the following week, two weeks later, and so on until the material becomes more or less automatic. In this way, he keeps spiraling back to these particular vocabulary words, even though he might be encountering more material in class. Each time he practices these vocabulary words, Misha does it in a meaningful way, like putting them into a context or recombining them to make new sentences. Naturally, the amount of time needed to make new material automatic depends on the kind of material involved. Figure 3.6 provides an illustration of one way to approach structured reviewing.

Employing Action

The two memory strategies under employing action are using physical response or sensation and using mechanical techniques.

Using Physical Response or Sensation Ⓛ Ⓡ This strategy may involve physically acting out a new expression that has been heard. The teaching technique known as Total Physical Response [5] is based on this strategy; students listen to a command and then physically act it out (and later are able to give commands to other people). For example, Akram is told by the teacher, "Take the pencil, go to the pencil sharpener, sharpen the pencil, write your name with it, and then give it to Maria." As Akram carries out these instructions, he finds that physical movement helps engrave the new information in memory. A different use of the strategy involves associating the heard expression with a physical sensation. For instance, Jack trains himself to get a feeling of physical heat whenever he hears a new feminine noun in German, a feeling of cold for masculine noun, and a feeling of moderate temperature for a neuter noun; this helps him to remember the gender of the new nouns he hears.

The strategy of using physical response or sensation can also be applied for remembering written material. Learners can act out what they read, or associate physical sensations with specific words found in reading passages.

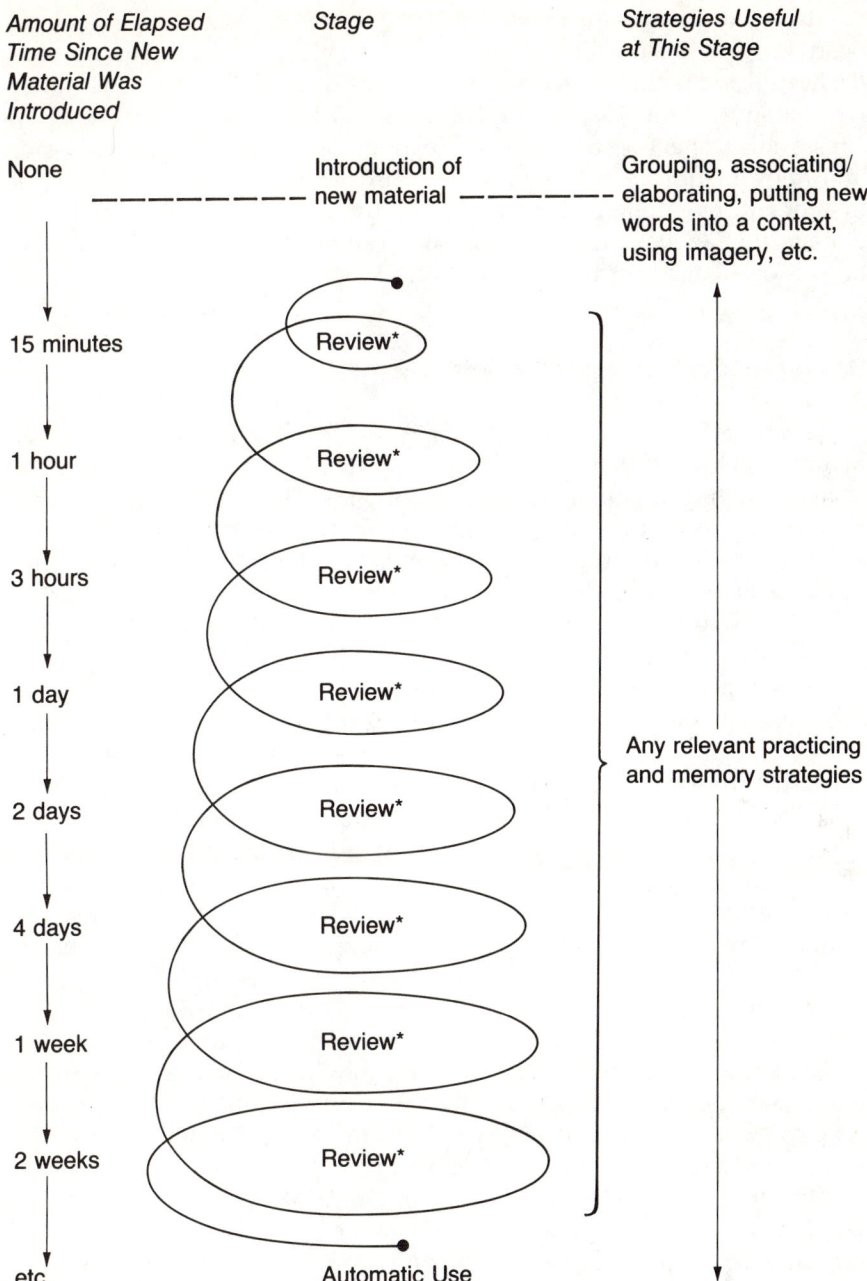

Amount of Elapsed Time Since New Material Was Introduced	Stage	Strategies Useful at This Stage
None	Introduction of new material	Grouping, associating/ elaborating, putting new words into a context, using imagery, etc.
15 minutes	Review*	
1 hour	Review*	
3 hours	Review*	
1 day	Review*	
2 days	Review*	Any relevant practicing and memory strategies
4 days	Review*	
1 week	Review*	
2 weeks	Review*	
etc.	Automatic Use	

Figure 3.6 An Illustration of Structured Review (Spiraling). (*)*Review as needed* in increasingly separated intervals until the stage of automatic use is reached. Goal is to retain the material in long-term memory and to retrieve it easily and automatically when required. (*Source*: Original.)

Using Mechanical Techniques Ⓛ Ⓡ Ⓦ To remember what has been heard or read, mechanical techniques are sometimes helpful. For instance, flashcards, with the new word written on one side and the definition written on the other, are both familiar and useful. To contextualize a new expression and get writing practice, learners can write the new expression in a full sentence on a flashcard. Flashcards can be moved from one pile to another depending on how well the learner knows them. Separate sections of the language learning notebook can be used for words that have been learned and words that have not.

Using Memory Strategies for Retrieval Ⓐ

Learners can use memory strategies to retrieve target language information quickly, so that this information can be employed for communication involving any of the four language skills. The same mechanism that was initially used for getting the information into memory (for instance, a mental association) can be used later on for recalling the information. Just thinking of the learner's original image, sound-and-image combination, action, sensation, association, or grouping can rapidly retrieve the needed information, particularly if the learner has taken the time to review the material in a structured way after the initial encounter.

Here are some examples of retrieving information through memory strategies. Bud, a student of French, initially learned the 17 *être* verbs (i.e., verbs that take *être* instead of *avoir* in the perfect tense) by using the acronym *DR. MRS. VANDERTRAMPP*, another example of the strategy of placing new words into a context. This acronym stands for *devenir, revenir, monter, rester, sortir, venir, aller, naître, descendre, entrer, rentrer, tomber, retourner, arriver, mourir, passer*, and *partir* [6]. Later, whenever Bud has to use one of these verbs in the perfect tense in speaking or writing, he immediately thinks of *DR. MRS. VANDERTRAMPP* and knows the right form.

Mathilde wants to remember the Italian word for drawer (*cassetto*), so she can write a note to her Italian friend explaining that the important papers are in the drawer. Mathilde originally learned the word by using the keyword strategy, which involved making a mental picture of herself keeping *cassettes* in a drawer. In writing the note, Mathilde recalls this picture and remembers the required word, *cassetto*.

Finally, Lih originally used the acronym *BAGS*, a form of placing new words into a context, along with a mental image of bags, to learn which French adjectives come before nouns (pronominal adjectives), unlike the majority of adjectives: *B* for beauty words like *beau, joli; A* for age words, like *jeune, vieux, nouveau; G* for goodness words, like *bon, mauvais, vrai;* and *S* for size words, like *petit, grand, gros, long*. When Lih has to use any adjective in speaking or writing, she just remembers *BAGS* and knows where to put the adjective.

As just discussed, memory strategies are valuable for storing and retrieving new information in the target language. In addition, a variety of cognitive strategies—the second group of direct strategies—can be used for learning a new language.

APPLYING COGNITIVE STRATEGIES TO THE FOUR LANGUAGE SKILLS

Four sets of cognitive strategies (see Figure 3.7) are practicing, receiving and sending messages, analyzing and reasoning, and creating structure for input and output. All these bring benefits to language learners.

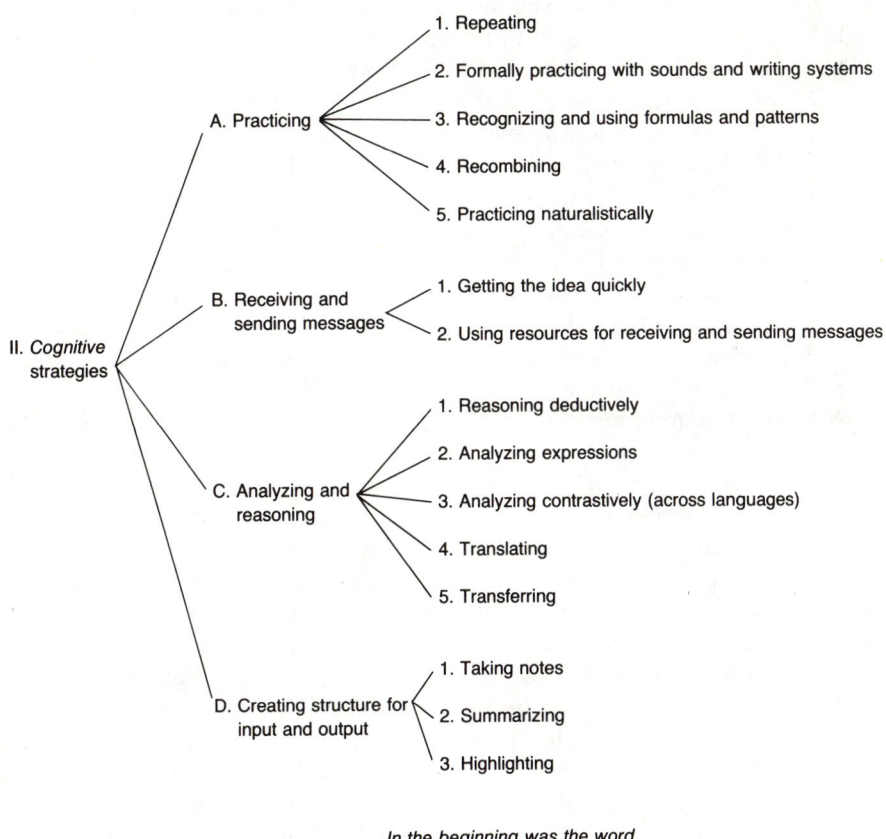

Figure 3.7   Diagram of the Cognitive Strategies to Be Applied to the Four Language Skills. (*Source*: Original.)

Practicing

The first and perhaps most important set of cognitive strategies, practicing, contains five strategies: repeating, formally practicing with sounds and writing systems, recognizing and using formulas and patterns, recombining, and practicing naturalistically.

Repeating (A) Although the strategy of repeating might not at first sound particularly creative, important, or meaningful, it can be used in highly innovative ways, is actually essential for all four language skills, and virtually always includes some degree of meaningful understanding [7].

One use of this strategy is repeatedly listening to native speakers of the new language on a tape or record, with or without silent rehearsal (repeating the words to oneself mentally). Here are some examples. Milton listens to the weather report in French every day while eating breakfast. He is now very familiar with weather-related terms such as *le soleil* (sun), *chaud* (hot), *froid* (cold), and *il fait beau* (the weather is fine). Lyle, who is learning Russian, repeatedly plays a song, *Moskovskiye Vechera* [Московские Вечера] ("Moscow Evenings") and listens to the Russian words, trying to understand them while silently rehearsing them.

The strategy of repeating might mean reading a passage more than once to understand it more completely. A profitable technique is to read a passage several times, each time for different purposes: for example, to get the general drift or the main ideas, to predict, to read for detail, to write down questions, and so on. The learner might also take notes about a reading passage and then review them several times.

Repetition might involve saying or writing the same thing several times. For instance, Lori repeats orally or in writing the item in the *same* way each time, as a way of making it automatic. Yacoub, on the other hand, says or writes a single expression or passage in *different* ways. A well-known language teaching method, Suggestopedia, asks teachers and students to repeat the same oral passage several times, each time saying the passage at a different speed by matching it to the cadence of a different kind of music being played.

Repeating something in different ways can be a means of emphasizing it, as in the "tell 'em" rule often used in speaking and writing: "Tell 'em what you're *going* to tell 'em, then *tell* 'em, and then tell 'em what you *told* 'em." This rule, which works well for certain kinds of oral or written reports in many languages and cultures, means there is an introduction laying out the main points, followed by the body of the text explaining the main points in greater detail, and finally a brief summary of these points phrased somewhat differently. A related but different principle involving repeating is called the "lead paragraph" rule, which is widely used in written and oral journalism. This principle involves putting into the lead paragraph (that is, the first or leading paragraph) all the salient details of who, what, when, where, why, and how—the essence of the entire story in a few hard-hitting introductory sentences. The paragraphs following the lead paragraph flesh out this skeleton, giving more information and background details, usually in order of decreasing importance. Sometimes there is a real conclusion or summary at the end, and sometimes not [8].

Imitation of native users of the language is another repeating technique used for both speaking and writing. Mindless or meaningless imitation is generally not worthwhile [9]. In imitating native speakers, learners can improve their pronunciation and their use of structures, vocabulary, idioms, intonation, gestures, and style. Help your students by providing varied examples of target language speech and writing for them to imitate. Consider the following examples of imitation of native users of the language. Marian, learning German, imitates aloud the intonation patterns and word order used by her German friend Heidi, as in *Wir haben Tennis gespielt* (we have played tennis). Adrienne imitates a word or phrase (along with the appropriate gestures) used by her Italian-speaking friend Giovanni, who takes this as a sign that Adrienne is truly involved and interested in the conversation. Steve, an advanced student of Russian, imitates the writing he finds in *Pravda* [Правда], while Maya, an intermediate Russian student, imitates the composition style she finds in simplified, vocabulary-controlled Russian texts. Elisabeth, a French speaker studying English, imitates the tone and format of business letters written in English.

In writing, still another use of the repeating strategy is revising, that is, going through a written draft in detail (usually more than once) in order to correct or amend it. Nothing ever rolls off the pen or the keyboard perfectly the first time, so revising is almost always necessary. Writers revise in different ways. For instance, some treat writing and revision as distinct phases, while others revise as they write in a continuous, ongoing process. Also, not every detail is always covered in any single revising effort. Sometimes writers concentrate on specific things for one revision (for instance, expressing the main themes clearly) and other things for another revision (e.g., checking punctuation). Help your students learn the best way to revise their writing, and help them avoid becoming bogged down in a premature and fruitless quest for perfection.

Formally Practicing with Sounds and Writing Systems (L) (S) (W) In listening, this strategy is often focused on perception of sounds (pronunciation and intonation) rather than on comprehension of meaning [10]. In listening *perception* exercises (as opposed to listening *comprehension* exercises), it is essential to keep visual and contextual clues to a minimum; therefore, recordings, not live speech, are recommended for listening perception [11].

Here are some instances of formally practicing with sounds. Leni marks the stress in the English sentence "I'm terribly tired; I think I'll go and have a rest" (I'm /terribly /tired; I /think I'll /go and /have a /rest). Haruko, a learner of English, listens to different words containing the letters *ough*, a combination that sounds different in various words: *through, though, tough,* and *trough*. She creates her own phonetic spelling of these words (*throo, thow, tuff,* and *troff*) to understand them better. Parker listens to the French vowel sounds of *eu, e, a,* and so on. He does a listening exercise with a tape, checking off the vowel sounds that he hears.

This strategy can be extended to include not just listening but also speaking. Tapes or records assist this strategy well. Some tape arrangements allow learners to record themselves so they can hear and compare their own voices with a native speaker's voice. Lisha, who is learning French, practices the many sounds of *ille* [12] by taping her speech, comparing it with that of a native speaker, and looking in the mirror so she can see herself when saying these sounds.

This strategy also centers on learning new writing systems necessary for using the target language. Of course, language learners do not always have to learn a new writing system, but many languages have alphabets, syllabaries, or idiographic systems that differ from the learners' own writing system. With a language such as Russian, Arabic, or Hebrew, the alphabet might be different from the learners' own. Some languages, like Thai, do not have alphabets but instead rely on syllabaries—nonalphabetic characters that represent sounds of whole syllables. In contrast, Chinese has thousands of idiographs—pictures representing ideas or objects. Japanese uses Chinese idiographs but also has two distinct syllabaries. Korean is moving from an idiographic system to a syllabary-based system. Formal practice with writing systems can include copying letters, copying words, comparing similar-sounding words in the native and target languages in terms of their written representation, using visual imagery and humor to remember new symbols, and putting symbols into meaningful verbal contexts [13].

Recognizing and Using Formulas and Patterns (A) Recognizing and using routine formulas and patterns in the target language greatly enhance the learner's comprehension and production. *Formulas* are unanalyzed expressions, while *patterns* have at least one slot that can be filled with an alternative word. Teach students such expressions as whole chunks early in their language learning process. These routines will help build self-confidence, increase understanding, and enhance fluency.

Here are some examples of common formulas:

Hello.

Good-bye.

How are you?

The weather's nice, isn't it?

D'accord. (*OK,* as a sign of agreement in French)

Spasibo [Спасибо]. (*thanks* in Russian)

Ça va? and *Ça va.* (*Hello,* literally *How's it going?* and *OK* in French)

Wie geht's dir? or *Wie geht es Ihnen?* (*How are you?* in German)

¿Habla usted inglés? (*Do you speak English?* in Spanish)

A demain. (*until tomorrow* in French)

Bis später. (*until later* in German)

Jaa ne. (*see you later* in Japanese)

A tout à l'heure! (*see you later* in French)

Es geht mir gut. (*I like it* in German)

Spokoinoi nochi [Спокойной ночи]. (*good-night* in Russian)

Chotto matte. (*just a minute* in Japanese)

Perdóneme. (*pardon me* in Spanish)

Tout à fait. (*completely* in French)

Dommage or *Tant pis.* (*too bad* in French)

Some formulas are most often used for the express purpose of managing conversations. Teach learners to recognize these formulas as used by native speakers, and to say these formulas to continue in a conversation or show interest. Conversation management formulas include target language equivalents of expressions like this:

Yes, that's right.

And what happened then?

That's not so bad.

Hey, that's great!

Tell me more.

This is a funny story.

I know what you mean.

That's interesting.

In addition to all the formulas above, many useful patterns exist in every language. Help your students to understand these patterns when they hear or read them, and to say or write them when appropriate. Examples include the following:

I don't know how to . . .

I would like to . . .

U menya [У меня] . . . (*I have* . . . in Russian)

Hajimemashite . . . *to moshimasu.* (*My name is* . . . in Japanese)

Per piacere, dov'è . . . (*Please, where is* . . .? in Italian)

Il y a . . . (*There is* . . . in French)

Qu'est-ce que c'est que . . . (*What is* . . .? in French)

Mieux vaux . . . (*It's best to* . . . in French)

Recombining Ⓢ Ⓦ The strategy of recombining involves constructing a meaningful sentence or longer expression by putting together known elements in new ways. The result might be serious or silly, but it always provides useful practice. For instance, Sam, a learner of German, knows the expression *Ich bin so gut wie Sie* (I am as good as you), *Sie sind gut* (you are good), and *sie ist besser* (she is better). He strings them together in new ways, using connecting words to say: *Sie sind gut, und ich bin so gut wie Sie, aber sie ist besser* (You are good, and I am as good as you, but she is better). Rosine knows the three expressions *weather's fine, I think I'd like* . . ., and *take a walk*. In practicing her spoken English, she creates the following new sentence from these three expressions with some additional words: *The weather's fine today, so I think I'd like to take a walk.*

The recombining strategy can be used in writing as well as in speaking. One way to use it is to string together two or more known expressions into a written story. For example, Ferenc, who is learning English, knows some terms for everyday tasks, such as *going to the store, going to the laundromat, washing clothes, getting some gas,* and *going to the library.* He writes a little story about a man who does all these things in the same afternoon.

But the recombining strategy does not always imply stringing together items in this way; it might involve using known forms, such as *going to the concert*, with different pronouns, such as *he, she, we, they, you.* For instance, Natalya writes, *He's going to the concert, but she's not. We're going to the concert, too. I hope you'll go with us!*

Practicing Naturalistically Ⓐ This strategy, of course, centers on using the language for actual communication. Any of the four skills, or a combination, might be involved. Because you as a teacher often have a great influence on the availability of practice opportunities, the following discussion details certain *instructional or teaching strategies* that you can use to make it easier for your students to exercise the *learning strategy* of practicing naturalistically.

As applied to listening, this learning strategy involves understanding the meaning of the spoken language in as naturalistic a context as possible. Help your students feel they are learning a language they can use, and give them confidence in their ability to succeed in listening tasks. To do this, use live speech for listening comprehension exercises as much as possible. Speech need not be completely authentic for listening exercises; in fact, it is often better to use an approximation to authentic speech, somewhat modified to take into account the learners' proficiency level. Employ semiscripts or notes rather than reading from a fixed script. If unedited authentic listening materials are used, these should be short segments of recorded broadcasts or live or taped interviews with native speakers on familiar topics [14].

Construct listening comprehension exercises around a specific task, in which students are required to do something in response to what they hear. For example, they might be required to express agreement or disagreement, take notes, mark a picture or diagram according to instructions, or answer questions. This requirement gives learners a purpose for listening. Learners should respond throughout the task, not just at the very end. Choose listening tasks that demand some kind of judgment or thinking and that are geared to the learners' level. Listening exercises should not include tasks that require a lot of reading (such as answering multiple-choice questions) or writing (such as extensive or detailed note-taking), unless the intention is to develop several skills jointly. Base the task on easily grasped visual materials (diagrams, pictures, grids, maps) and quick, simple responses (physical movement, checking off responses, or writing one-word answers). Students can also practice listening to directions for a task that they need to do. For instance, describe a picture while they draw it, or ask students to act out a pantomime as you tell them a story, or give directions for a physical action or sequence of actions. Help your students in class to practice using the telephone in role-plays with each other; this makes the telephone less intimidating. Tell students the correct answers immediately after the exercise, so they can check their own performance, then explain in more detail the reasons why certain responses are preferred. This encourages learners to use strategies such as self-monitoring and self-evaluating, which are powerful motivators and enhancers of understanding [15].

Technology offers many opportunities for naturalistic listening practice inside or outside of the classroom. Learners can use tapes and records to practice on their own. Learners can even make their own tapes of recorded material from radio or records. Audiocassette decks are useful for listening practice. International shortwave radio stations offer a huge variety of programs in many languages at various proficiency levels [16].

The addition of a visual image often provides learners with an invaluable context to which they may relate the spoken form. Realia, drawings, and homemade videos are very basic visual tools to enhance listening practice. Films are a wonderful sound-and-image resource. Towns and cities with large foreign populations often show films in other languages. It is also possible to borrow films from public libraries, boards of education, regional educational centers, universities, national film boards, and even aerospace centers. Television provides other sound-and-image possibilities. Local TV does not usually carry much in the way of multilingual programming, but there are some notable exceptions, such as Spanish programs in many parts of the United States, bilingual (English-Japanese) news and movies on Japanese TV, and multilingual TV channels in frontier regions of Europe. For second language learners who are in the midst of the target language community, TV is a great resource for listening practice. TV soap operas provide excellent listening practice and an interesting slant on the culture. Alternatives to film and TV for listening practice are the videocassette and direct broadcasting by satellite (DBS) [17].

Practicing naturalistically also means using the language in an authentic way for reading comprehension. The most common medium for reading material is, of course, print. Print material in just about any target language is easy to come by and comparatively inexpensive. Target language newspapers and magazines are often available at newsstands, or readers can subscribe. In addition, books in other languages are obtainable in libraries and shops or by mail order. Readily available menus, advertisements, brochures, pamphlets, department store catalogues, comic books, university catalogues, travel brochures, and timetables all provide cultural information as well as practice in reading the language. Spend some class time having students write letters to request some of these materials. Also encourage students to collect and share print material in the new language (from any source) as a basis for reading exercises. Help your students practice their reading by giving them active and interesting reading tasks. Use simulations in which learners are required to read the instructions or the main documents (such as scenarios) in the new language. Do jigsaw reading exercises to involve readers in cooperatively sharing and rearranging information that they gain from reading. Find out what your students' main interests are, and provide reading materials and activities that address those interests. Encourage students to read in the new language outside of class. Consider giving them credit for out-of-class reading. Develop and provide a lending library of materials in the new language so that learners can check out books and magazines for home reading. Provide information on where and how they can obtain other reading materials on their own.

In the speaking area, practicing naturalistically involves practice in speaking the language for realistic communication. Speaking with other people in natural settings provides interactive, rapid, personal communication. Being in the country or community where the target language is spoken natively, either as a permanent resident or a temporary visitor, is the best way to find opportunities for practice in speaking. Living in a place where the language is normally spoken is an informal immersion in the language and culture. In such a situation, the learner generally has no choice but to communicate and to understand how the language is used in its wider social context. Subtleties of gestures, facial expressions, and tone of voice become much clearer and more understandable in the cultural setting where the language is spoken natively. However, even without traveling to the country where the language is spoken, it is often possible to converse with native speakers right in the learners' home community. Making friends with native speakers of the target language is possible, usually by seeking them out individually or by finding an association, such as an international friendship club, where there are numerous native speakers. Casual chatting with friends in the target language—either abroad or at home—is a fine way to improve communication skills. For most language learners, making friends with target language speakers is one of the most important reasons for language learning [18]. Help your students find these opportunities for using the language conversationally.

The classroom itself can provide practice that combines listening and speaking and thus approaches natural language use. Role-plays, drama activities, games, simulations, and structured communication exercises offer practice that takes learners' attention away from language learning and directs it toward the communication of meaning. In doing these activities, learners sometimes become so engrossed in communicating that they forget they are trying to use a new language! Such activities can increase learners' confidence in their oral communication skill. Greater confidence leads to better attitudes and increased motivation to continue using the new language. In addition to providing interesting and challenging communication activities, you can also change the classroom environment to facilitate naturalistic practice. Transform the room into a place where communication can occur normally and easily. Move the chairs so they are not in straight rows. Put students into small groups or pairs to converse. Let the classroom come alive with talk. Banish the teacher-centered mode in which all communication occurs between the teacher and one student at a time, with everyone else sitting, waiting, and daydreaming. Encourage learners to express their own personality and needs. Bring in native speakers whenever possible. Invite learners to hold communication sessions on their own without your being present. Occasionally go out of the room for short periods during normal classes, so that learners realize they don't need you to tell them to speak. Give them materials to help them organize themselves while you are gone, if necessary. (Note that the other two language skills, reading and writing, can often be integrated with listening and speaking by means of role-plays, simulations, games, and other activities.)

Practicing naturalistically is very important for developing writing skill [19]. It can involve many different activities, such as creation of separate products by individuals, individual contributions to multipart products, coauthorship of a single piece by multiple writers, or exchanges of written messages between individuals or teams. In all of these activities, real readers are involved. Often students read the writings of their peers. Therefore reading and writing skills can be jointly developed.

The first of the naturalistic writing modes is creation of separate products by individuals. Individual writing efforts might include all sorts of formats: autobiographical sketches, interviews of family or friends, factual reports, stories, poems, diary entries in the target language, and so on. The length can vary from a sentence or paragraph to 20 or more pages, depending on the language proficiency of the learners.

The second naturalistic writing mode is joint writing projects composed of individual contributions. Examples include newspapers, newsletters, literary magazines, sports digests, scrapbooks, or scripts for simulated radio and TV programs, in which each person contributes his or her own different items to a written product. Excellent simulations exist for producing radio scripts, such as RADIO COVINGHAM, and news bulletins and newspapers, like NEWSIM [20]. These provide the experience of writing with a real purpose for a defined audience, as well as working together to create a product. Another suggestion for joint writing practice is to have learners interview each other using a semistructured format, and then turn the interviews into feature articles which are, after revisions, published in a class magazine. Student-created literary magazines containing poetry, stories, pictures, and other items are sometimes very popular.

The third naturalistic writing mode is coauthorship of a single product. Two or more learners can work together to write one piece—a single article, short story, play—as is often done in "real life" outside of the classroom. Because they are equally invested in a single, integrated product, writing partners provide constant encouragement and feedback to each other. A more playful way to use coauthorship is jigsaw writing. Learners are given unrelated target language story fragments, a sentence or two each, and are required to write a story that weaves all the story lines together into a reasonably coherent whole, transitions and all. The results are entertaining and often comical, and the process gives learners practice in finding (or making) interesting linkages.

The last naturalistic writing mode involves exchanges of written messages between individuals or teams. This includes journal exchanges, letter writing, and computer interaction. Dialogue journals are one way of making writing a more interactive process, in which learners exchange messages with their teachers. Language students write anything they want in their dialogue journals and share these journals with the teacher, who responds with comments—not in a threatening, red-ink, corrective mode but in a supportive, nonjudgmental, idea-evoking way. The process continues, back and forth, with both sides learning from each other as students get increasing practice with writing. Dialogue journals are very effective and highly motivating for language learning [21]. Letter writing to pen-friends or for business purposes is another kind of written exchange between individuals, but not just between teachers and students. In correspondence, learners know their writing is meaningful and important to someone else, they get practice using the language for both writing and reading, they learn all sorts of things about new cultures and their own culture as well, and they begin to view writing as part of a rewarding social process.

Exchanges between individual writers or teams of writers are also stimulated by computer interaction. Computers don't have to be used just for drill and practice; they can be a medium of real communication in the target language, including composing and exchanging messages with other students in the classroom or around the world [22]. Language teachers are helping their students at all proficiency levels set up local, regional, national, and international networks for the exchange of student-created messages with other students, who may be either native speakers or learners of the target language. An outstanding example of such an information exchange is the Computer Chronicles Newswire operating from San Diego, California. A month-long, computerized international simulation, ICONS, has teams of students writing messages in various languages and sending them to teams representing other countries around the globe [23]. In addition to student-oriented computer interactions, established computerized information networks not originally designed for educational purposes sometimes encourage useful written exchanges. In any computerized exchange, communication is both meaningful and urgent. Because on-line cost is a factor, it is necessary to write quickly, so learners must also think quickly and appropriately in the new language. In addition, learners use the target language for a practical purpose and cease to focus on the language as a mere object of study. Of course, the computer does not guarantee the instant development of writing skill. However, it does allow collaborative exchanges which dramatically increase students' motivation to write, and it also provides potentially large amounts of interactive writing practice.

It is possible to publish or disseminate material that your students have written for their language class. For instance, the BBC World Service reads aloud original stories on its "Short Story" program, and these are occasionally written by students [24]. Newsletters, specialty publications (such as magazines about refugee resettlement or Hispanic issues), local newspapers, language teaching journals, and other outlets might be willing to publish your students' materials. Hearing their work broadcast or seeing it in print is an incredibly motivating experience for students.

The foregoing discussion has concerned the strategy of practicing naturalistically. A good deal of attention was devoted to this strategy and its instructional manifestations, since this is one of the most essential learning strategies. Now we will turn to some highly specific and useful strategies for receiving and sending messages.

Receiving and Sending Messages

This set consists of two strategies: getting the idea quickly and using resources for receiving and sending messages.

Getting the Idea Quickly Ⓛ Ⓡ This strategy is used for listening and reading. It helps learners home in on exactly what they need or want to understand, and it allows them to disregard the rest or use it as background information only. Two techniques constituting this strategy are skimming and scanning. *Skimming* involves searching for the main ideas the speaker wants to get across, while *scanning* means searching for specific details of interest to the learner.

Preview questions help learners to skim and scan more easily. For beginning learners of the target language, preview questions often provide many clues and require simple "true/false," "yes/no" responses or a choice from a set of answers. With more proficient learners, fewer clues are given by preview questions. Provide preview questions to help learners skim; for instance, "What are the three key ideas in this reading passage?" or "What is the theme of this passage?" Ask skimming questions in the learners' native language or in the new language, depending on the skill level of the learners. Preview questions for scanning, on the other hand, focus readers not so much on the main ideas but rather on specific facts, like "Who is the man in the dark hat? Where does he come from? What does he want from the old woman?" There are advantages and disadvantages to asking scanning questions in the target language. Using the target language gives hints about the vocabulary the readers should look for, but readers might be tempted to search for those expressions and answer without fully understanding.

Charts to complete, lists to write, diagrams to fill out, and other mechanisms also provide clues about what kind of general points or specific details the learners need to pick up in a listening or reading passage. These help learners get the idea quickly and efficiently. In the beginning, these charts, lists, and diagrams may provide a lot of clues about what to listen or read for, and later, as the learners progress, fewer clues might be given. Another useful tip: Skimming and scanning in the classroom setting are often enhanced by another strategy, taking notes.

Two instances of skimming are as follows. Jean-Claude is listening to get the main ideas of the talk on American architecture given at the international social club. Monica is trying to get the gist of a front-page article in the Chinese newspaper. Here are some examples of scanning. Rowena has agreed to listen for certain details in Spanish, such as the names, ages, professions, and general background of three visitors from South America, while Jim will scan for other information, such as how long the visitors will stay, what they want to do on their visit, or whom they want to meet.

Waiting in the Köln train station, Pascual (a learner of German) is worried about his late train, and therefore he listens closely for an announcement of its estimated arrival time and scans the schedule board periodically.

Remember that not all listening or reading involves getting the idea quickly. For instance, the techniques of skimming and scanning might not be too useful for listening to a radio play or for reading poems or stories. Irony, suspense, and humor can sometimes be ruined by too much skimming and scanning. Thus, the efficiency of skimming and scanning, while often useful, is not the only approach to listening or reading.

Using Resources for Receiving and Sending Messages (A) This strategy involves using resources to find out the meaning of what is heard or read in the new language, or to produce messages in the new language. To better understand what is heard or read, printed resources such as dictionaries, word lists, grammar books, and phrase books may be valuable. Encyclopedias, travel guides, magazines, and general books on culture and history can provide useful background information so that learners can better understand the spoken or written language. Printed resources on just about any topic can be found in the target language. Nonprint resources include tapes, TV, videocassettes, radio, museums, and exhibitions, among others. These cannot easily be used during speaking, but they can help learners prepare for speaking activities. Printed resources like thesauruses, target language dictionaries, and bilingual dictionaries are especially helpful for writing.

Here are some examples of using resources to understand a spoken or written message. Rusty, a beginning learner of Spanish, uses a Spanish/English dictionary to look up the definitions of new words he has written down in his language learning notebook. Sandrine, who is more advanced in Spanish, uses an all-Spanish dictionary to look up definitions and variations of new words. Susan, a learner of French, has heard many similar phrases in the new language, but she does not always understand the differences, so she uses reference resources. For instance, she uses a phrase book to look up the meaning of *Fais gaffe!* (be careful). She wants to know how this phrase relates to different-sounding expressions with similar meanings, such as *Attention!* and *Fais attention!*, and to similar-sounding expressions with entirely different meanings, such as *faire une gaffe* (make a mistake). Pablo, who is learning German, uses the German grammar book to look up information on separable prefixes, since he has had a hard time understanding them on the German tape. Marc, a learner of Spanish, is reading a Spanish short story filled with modern slang terms. Most of the time he succeeds in grasping the meaning from the context, but when totally baffled he finds it necessary to use a dictionary of Spanish slang.

Following are some examples of using resources to produce the target language in speaking or writing. Akira uses a dictionary and a grammar book in composing an English-language talk about a favorite hobby, sailing. Ellen looks up a few useful social phrases in her German phrase book before she goes to the cafe to meet her German acquaintances. Louisa uses all the background material she can find—articles, books, and TV news shows—to gather information about the terrorist movement in Spain in preparation for writing a report in Spanish on the subject.

Analyzing and Reasoning

The five strategies in this set help learners to use logical thinking to understand and use the grammar rules and vocabulary of the new language. These strategies are valuable, but they can cause problems if overused.

Reasoning Deductively Ⓐ This strategy involves deriving hypotheses about the meaning of what is heard by means of general rules the learner already knows. Reasoning deductively is a common and very useful type of logical thinking. Here are examples of successful use of this strategy for the four skills. First, Julio, who is learning English, hears his friend say, "Would you like to go to the library with me at five o'clock?" Julio correctly understands that he is being asked a question to which he must respond, because he recognizes that part of the verb comes before the subject (a general rule he has learned). Second, Roberta is reading a Russian story involving a character named Elisavyeta Ivanovna. Roberta has not encountered this name before, but she knows that *-ovna* means "daughter of," so she understands immediately that the person must be Elizabeth, Ivan's daughter. Third, Marcie, who is learning French, knows the general rule that the future tense is not used for things that will happen very soon, and that the *futur proche* (near future) tense or even the present tense would be better. So, when she wants to say in French the equivalent of "I'm leaving soon," Marcie applies the general rule and says *Je vais bientôt partir* or *Je pars bientôt*, not *Je partirai bientôt*. Fourth, in writing, Marianne applies the general rule that an article (definite or indefinite) is ordinarily used in front of a French or German noun.

Sometimes the strategy of reasoning deductively results in overgeneralization errors, as in the following examples. Spanish-speaking Lugo knows that the past tense in English uses *-ed*, so he applies this rule to say *bringed* and *goed*. The perfectly good English questions "What is it?" and "Where are they?" are overapplied by Josef in the sentence *I don't know what is it* and by Marcello in *Find out where are they*. Sometimes an expression is overgeneralized to a situation where its semantic limitations become painfully obvious, as when Gabriele says, "He is pretty." Miko, a Japanese speaker, knows the general rule that the English plural is formed by adding

-s or -es; this works very well with *house/houses*, but not so well with *mouse/ mouses*. Cesar, learning English, overuses the progressive, as in *We are not knowing the rules*. *Who can Angela sees?* is an example produced by Mario, another learner of English, who applies the rule for forming the third-person-singular verb ending when it should not be used.

Analyzing Expressions Ⓛ Ⓡ To understand something spoken in the new language, it is often helpful to break down a new word, phrase, sentence, or even paragraph into its component parts. This strategy is known as analyzing expressions [25]. If the learner is in the midst of a conversation there may not be enough time to analyze the new expression, but it is sometimes possible to jot down the expression (phonetically if need be) and analyze it later. Analysis is a good strategy for learners of Welsh, who encounter very long words—such as the longest place name in the UK, *Llanfairpwllgwyngyllgogerychwyrndrobwllllantysyliogogogoch*. (This means St. Mary's church in a hollow by the white hazel, close to the rapid whirlpool, by the red cave of St. Tysilio.) Just think of trying to grasp this word if you heard it in a casual conversation! Admittedly, Welsh provides some of the most exciting and extreme instances of the need for analyzing expressions, but any language with compound words can benefit from this strategy. Though analyzing expressions is helpful for listening, it is even more useful for reading, because readers have more time to go back and analyze complicated expressions when reading than when listening.

Here are some helpful examples of analyzing expressions. First, Martina is learning English. She does not immediately understand the phrase *premeditated crime*, which she hears in a TV news broadcast. She breaks down this phrase into parts that she does understand: *crime* (bad act), *meditate* (think about), and *pre-* (before). Thus, she figures out the meaning of the whole phrase: an evil act that is planned in advance. Second, Lloyd, a learner of French, hears the French phrase *le génie inépuisable*, in a radio program about the German composer Wagner. He knows that Wagner was a brilliant person, a genius. Using analysis, he divides the unknown word, *inépuisable*, into parts to understand it: *in* (not), *épuis* (from *épuiser*, meaning to exhaust), and *-able* (able). Putting these back together, Lloyd knows that the phrase must mean that Wagner was an inexhaustible genius. Third, Marijane reads a new German word, *Deutschlehrerverband*. She divides it into *Deutsch* + *lehrer* + *verband* (capitalization would differ if these were really being used as separate words, of course) to understand the meaning, *German teachers' association*. Fourth, David understands the meaning of *parapluie* (umbrella) by breaking it into *para* (for) and *pluie* (rain).

Analyzing Contrastively Ⓛ Ⓡ This strategy is a fairly easy one that most learners use naturally. It involves analyzing elements (sounds, words, syntax) of the new language to determine likenesses and differences in comparison with one's own native language. It is very commonly used at the early stages of language learning to understand the meaning of what is heard or read. Here are some examples of analyzing contrastively in listening and reading. Stanley recognizes through contrastive analysis that the German word *Katze* sounds like the English word *cat*. Nora recognizes the similarities between *chair* in English and *chaise* in French. In reading an English passage, Luis immediately understands the word *cream*, which corresponds to the French word *crème* and the Spanish word *crema*. Rita, an English speaker, is fascinated by the similarities in a number of words she finds in reading other languages, such as *sister* (English), *syestra* [сестра] (Russian), *Schwester* (German), and *soeur* (French). She figures out that the English word *sorority* is related to the others. John is interested in the different ways his own name is expressed in other languages: *Jean* (French), *Joan* (Portuguese), *Juan* (Spanish), and *Johann* (German). A beginner in Japanese, Reba finds that many current Japanese words are simply English words with a Japanese phonetic veneer: *orengi* (orange), *remon* (lemon), *chokoreto* (chocolate), *pankeiki* (pancakes), *hamueggu* (ham and eggs), *soseji* (sausage), *sarada* (salad), *sandowitchi* (sandwich), *aisukurimu* (ice cream), *appurupai* (apple pie), *puddingu* (pudding), *jusu* (juice), *supu* (soup), *resutoran* (restaurant), *basu* (bus), *tenisu* (tennis), *takushi* (taxi), and *chekku* (check) for example.

However, remind your students to beware of "false friends," sometimes called by their French name, *faux amis*. These are the target language words that sound or look like words in the learners' own language, but whose meaning is very different. French is full of false friends for English users, as Lillian learns from the following examples. *Actuellement* does not mean *actually*; it means right now. *Assister* has nothing to do with *assisting*; it means to attend. And *attendre* is not the same as attend; it means to wait. Imagine the misunderstandings caused by these words!

Some of the most significant and embarrassing "false friends" to warn your students about are those with sexual overtones. For instance, in some countries *preservatives* are used to keep food fresh, but Brooke discovers to her chagrin that *preservatif* in France means a male contraceptive. Ron learns that the Japanese word *guramaa* is originally borrowed from the English word *glamorous*, but it now implies that the *guramaa* woman has big breasts. Richard, an American visitor to Madrid, tries to apologize for a Spanish error, saying ¡*Estoy embarazada!*—and when he finds out his intended apology means *I'm pregnant*, then he is truly embarrassed.

Translating (A) Translating can be a helpful strategy early in language learning, as long as it is used with care. It allows learners to use their own language as the basis for understanding what they hear or read in the new language. It also helps learners produce the new language in speech or writing. However, word-for-word (verbatim) translation, though a frequent occurrence among beginners, can become a crutch or provide the wrong interpretation of target language material. Furthermore, translating can sometimes slow learners down considerably, forcing them to go back and forth constantly between languages.

The following examples show how translating can be used, and misused, for understanding what is heard or read in the new language. In a conversation when the Russian speaker says, *Ya chitayu zhurnal* [Я читаю журнал], Billie mentally translates this to mean "I'm reading the newspaper," the English equivalent. In this case a straight translation is correct. Herb, a learner of German, hears his German friend say, *Du hast Recht*. He doesn't understand; the sentence cannot be translated directly into English. He discovers later that the friend was saying, "You're right." Lauren finds it impossible to understand in English the literally translated meaning of the French phrase, *il y a . . .* (roughly meaning *there is/are . . .*). Elton reads the words *beau-frère* and *belle-soeur* in French. He tries to understand them through literal translation, but they just come out as "handsome brother" and "beautiful sister"! Later he discovers that they mean brother-in-law and sister-in-law.

Beginning speakers and writers often rely on the strategy of translating to produce messages in the target language. For instance, in Spanish it is correct for Amado to say or write *No comprendo*, but translating this directly into English produces *No understand*, a rather primitive expression in English. And there's no single verbatim translation of *I've got to go* in French; Martha learns to say one of the following, all of which have slightly different connotations: *Il faut que j'y aille, Je dois partir, Il faut que je parte, Il faut que je m'en aille, Je dois aller, On m'attend*, and so on.

Transferring Ⓐ The last of the analyzing and reasoning strategies is transferring, which means directly applying previous knowledge to facilitate new knowledge in the target language. This strategy relates to all four skills. Transferring can involve applying linguistic knowledge from the learner's own language to the new language, linguistic knowledge from one aspect of the new language to another aspect of the new language, or conceptual knowledge from one field to another. Transferring works well as long as the language elements or concepts are directly parallel, but most of the time they are not! It can lead to inaccuracy if learners transfer irrelevant knowledge across languages.

The following are some correct examples of transferring. When Dwight hears the expression *weekend* in French, he correctly knows through transfer that it means the same as in English, and that *bon weekend* means "Have a good weekend." Reading German, Erwin finds that it is easy to understand through transfer from English the German names for most of the months of the year.

Here are some less appropriate instances of transferring. Mildred is reading a French article about a scandal involving a *notaire*. An American notary is a clerk who has certain official rights such as stamping and sealing legal papers. On the basis of incorrect transfer, Mildred thinks that a French *notaire* is the same thing, but she finds out later that a *notaire* is a trained lawyer with a much higher level of education and professional status than a typical American notary. Jana is writing a letter in French. She discovers that transferring the word *possibly* into *possiblement* doesn't work, because the latter does not exist in French; *peut-être* (meaning perhaps) is correct. Transfer errors frequently occur in word order, as illustrated by Fritz, a German speaker learning English, who says, *Donald always fools so much around*, with *around* incorrectly placed at the end of the clause like a German separable prefix [26].

Like translating, transferring has its perils. Learners cannot expect that all the varied hues of meaning will be the same for words and concepts across two languages; sometimes there is just no equivalent from one language to the other. In addition, grammatical differences are sometimes very great.

Creating Structure for Input and Output

This is another set of strategies that aids all four skills. The three strategies in this group—taking notes, summarizing, and highlighting—help learners sort and organize the target language information that comes their way. In addition, these strategies allow students to demonstrate their understanding tangibly and prepare for using the language for speaking and writing.

Taking Notes Ⓛ Ⓡ Ⓦ This is a very important strategy for listening and reading, but learners generally are not taught to use it well, if at all. The focus of taking notes should be on understanding, not writing. Note-taking is often thought of as an advanced tool, to be used at high levels of proficiency—such as when listening to lectures. However, developing note-taking skills can begin at very early stages of learning. Key points can be written in the learners' own language at first. Depending on the purpose, later note-taking can be in the target language, thus involving writing practice. Or you can also allow a mixture of the target language and the learners' own language, with known vocabulary words written in the target language and the rest in the native language.

There are many different ways to take notes, the simplest and most common form being that of raw notes, which are unstructured and un-transformed [27]. For raw notes to become useful, learners need to go back immediately (before they forget what was said) and organize the notes using a different system. A better way is to use the "shopping list" or T-formation as the very first step, omitting the raw notes. The advantage of using one of these formats initially is that they help learners organize what they hear while they are hearing it, thus increasing the original understanding and the ability to integrate new information with old.

If your students ordinarily take notes word for word, as in a dictation exercise, give them practice in listening for and taking notes on only the key points of information. After they are able to note the main points, help them to develop their skill in noting details. Use graphics and visuals wherever possible to highlight the main ideas as your students take notes. Teach your students to use various kinds of note-taking formats and then to choose the ones they like the best.

The shopping list format is extremely simple, but it does impose some sort of order and organization on the spoken material. It involves writing down information in clusters or sets that have some internal consistency or meaning. An example of the shopping list format is shown in Figure 3.8.

The T-formation is shown in Figure 3.9 using the same language material as for the shopping list. This format is similar in intent to the shopping list format, but it allows learners to use the space on the paper in a more effective way. First draw a large T on a piece of paper, taking up the whole sheet. Then write the main theme or title on the top line (the crossbar of the T). On the left side of the vertical line, write the basic categories or topics that have been discussed; on the right side of the vertical line, write details, specific examples, follow-up questions, or comments.

A semantic map is also a useful note-taking format, requiring learners to indicate the main word or idea and to link this with clusters of related words or ideas by means of lines or arrows; see examples of this format under memory strategies earlier in this chapter. Another useful form for notes is the tree diagram, sometimes transformed into a flow chart by means of arrows, diamonds, circles, and so forth. Examples of the tree diagram format are found throughout this book [28]. In addition, the standard outline form (using Roman numerals, letters, etc.) deserves special mention as a note-taking format. This outline structure, shown in Figure 3.10, can be extended to as many levels of detail as learners might ever

Banana Cake Ingredients	lemon juice	baking powder	milk
	walnuts	sugar	butter
	bananas	cream cheese	vanilla
	eggs	confectioner's sugar	
Equipment Needed	large bowl	measuring cup	fork
	greased pan	spoon	

Figure 3.8 Shopping List Note Form. (*Source*: Hamp-Lyons (1983, p. 112).)

Banana Cake

ingredients needed	lemon juice milk sugar bananas vanilla eggs (etc.)
equipment needed	large bowl measuring cup fork greased pan spoon

Figure 3.9   T-Formation Note Form. (*Source*: Hamp-Lyons (1983, p. 118).)

need. Just add more symbols, such as (a), (b), (i), (ii), or (iii), as needed. An alternative numbering system involves decimals (e.g., 1, 1.1). Well-structured reading passages lend themselves to the standard outline form, one version of which is shown in Figure 3.10.

Provide exercises that require your students to take notes on their listening and reading (including the instructions you give them in class). Allow students to take notes either in their own language or the target language at first, but encourage them to move toward taking notes mostly or solely in the target language if possible.

Note-taking techniques can be integrated with regular language activities and materials as a natural element in language learning. A metacognitive strategy closely associated with note-taking is organizing, which includes keeping a notebook for gathering new language information and for tracking progress (see Chapters 4 and 5). Any notes should be kept neatly and organized in some fashion; a loose-leaf notebook is perhaps the best way. For students who are writing substantial pieces in the target language, it is helpful to jot down ideas as soon as they pop into the head. Therefore, the notebook should be kept close at hand at all times.

Summarizing Ⓛ Ⓡ Ⓦ Another strategy that helps learners structure new input and show they understand is summarizing—that is, making a condensed, shorter version of the original passage. Writing a summary can be more challenging (and sometimes more useful) than taking notes, because it often requires greater condensation of thought.

At the early stages of language learning, summarizing can be as simple as just giving a title to what has been heard or read; the title functions as a kind of summary of the story or passage. Another easy way to summarize

I.
   A.
   B.
II.
   A.
   B.
      1.
      2.
         a.
         b.
         c.
III.
   A.
      1.
      2.
         a.
         b.
            (1.)
            (2.)
   B.
IV. (etc.)

Figure 3.10   Standard Outline Structure. (*Source*: Original.)

is to place pictures which depict a series of events in the order in which they occur in the story. This is a very useful exercise, especially for beginners, because it links the verbal with the visual.

As students advance in their knowledge of the language, their summaries can be made in the target language, thus allowing more writing practice. The summaries they construct can also become more complex; for example, learners can write complete sentences or paragraphs (called a "précis" or an "abstract") summarizing what they have heard or read.

Highlighting Ⓛ Ⓡ Ⓦ Learners sometimes benefit by supplementing notes and summaries with another strategy, highlighting. This strategy emphasizes the major points in a dramatic way, through color, underlining, CAPITAL LETTERS, Initial Capitals, **BIG WRITING**, **bold writing**, ★ stars ★, boxes, circles and so on. The sky's the limit in thinking of ways to highlight.

The three structuring strategies are often, but not always, used together. For instance, Monte uses the shopping list note form for his initial class notes, and later the same day he cleans up his notes, underlines the important points, and makes a short written summary. Eli is preparing to give an oral report on irrigation problems in a Central American country. He takes notes on the subject, summarizes the problems involved, and highlights the main issues. Gilberto, learning Russian, uses different colors to highlight different types of information (vocabulary, grammar points, cultural concepts) in his Russian textbook, and he outlines these in his language learning notebook.

A new twist in using these strategies is to have learners take notes on, summarize, or highlight *each other's* speaking or writing when it has reached a fairly well-developed stage. This procedure has two benefits. First, it allows learners to know what it is like to have a real audience trying to get the gist of their message. Second, the notes, summaries, and highlightings will tell learners whether or not they have succeeded in getting their main points across clearly. If you try this procedure in your classes, be sure to review the techniques of taking notes, summarizing, and highlighting so that everyone knows how. Otherwise, the benefits of this activity will be lost.

The cognitive strategies, a large and varied group, have been discussed. Now it is time to examine applications of compensation strategies, the last group of direct strategies.

APPLYING COMPENSATION STRATEGIES TO THE FOUR LANGUAGE SKILLS

The compensation strategies, displayed in Figure 3.11, help learners to overcome knowledge limitations in all four skills. For beginning and intermediate language learners, these strategies may be among the most important. Compensation strategies are also useful for more expert language users, who occasionally do not know an expression, who fail to hear something clearly, or who are faced with a situation in which the meaning is only implicit or intentionally vague.

Guessing Intelligently in Listening and Reading

Guessing is essential for listening and reading. It helps learners let go of the belief that they have to recognize and understand every single word before they can comprehend the overall meaning. Learners can actually understand a lot of language through systematic guessing, without necessarily comprehending all the details. Two compensation strategies relevant to listening and reading involve using linguistic clues and other clues.

Using Linguistic Clues (L)(R) Previously gained knowledge of the target language, the learners' own language, or some other language can provide linguistic clues to the meaning of what is heard or read. Suffixes, prefixes, and word order are useful linguistic clues for guessing meanings. Here are

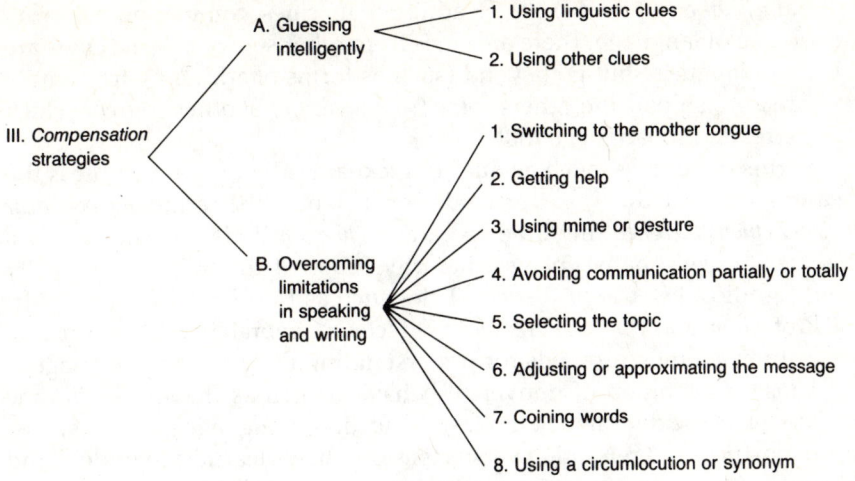

Language grows out of life, out of its needs and experiences. . . . Language and knowledge are indissolubly connected; they are interdependent. Good work in language presupposes and depends on a real knowledge of things.

Annie Sullivan

Figure 3.11 Diagram of the Compensation Strategies to Be Applied to the Four Language Skills. (*Source*: Original.)

some examples of guessing based on partial knowledge of the target language. Andrey recognizes the English words *shovel, grass, mower,* and *lawn,* so he knows that the conversation is about gardening. Wladislaw hears the sentence "*Jim* rejected the offer." The primary stress in this sentence is on Jim, so Wladislaw, alert to the significance of stress patterns in English, figures that Jim is being contrasted with someone else; the meaning would be different if the stress were on "offer" or some other word in the sentence.

Knowledge of the learner's own language provides still more clues for understanding material heard in the new language. For instance, Frank might be able to guess, given his knowledge of English, that *J'arrive!* means *I'm coming!* Sally realizes that every language has polite greetings, so when someone says *Zdravstvuitye* [Здравствуйте] in Russian, she guesses that this is a way of greeting her.

Linguistic clues are the bedrock of many correct guesses about the meaning of written passages [29]. For example, Vivian knows that *le lavabo* (sink) and *la toilette* (toilet) relate to *la salle de bains* (bathroom); so when she encounters *le robinet* (tap, faucet) and *le carrelage* (tiling) in the same advertisement, she figures that these are accessories or parts of the bathroom.

Using Other Clues Ⓛ Ⓡ In addition to clues coming purely from knowledge of language, there are clues from other sources. Some clues are related to language but go beyond (such as forms of address which imply social relationships), and others come from a variety of other sources which are not related to language [30].

Forms of address, such as titles or nicknames, help learners guess the meaning of what they hear or read. For instance, the terms *my pet*, *dear husband*, *mein Liebchen* (my little love), and *chère amie* (dear friend) imply a close relationship between two characters. Use of the formal *vous* or *Ihr* (you) signifies distance or respect. Titles such as *Herr Doktor Professor* (Mr. Dr. Professor) and *P.D.G.* (Président Directeur Général) indicate status. To the learner, all these are aids for understanding the rest of the passage.

Close observation of nonverbal behavior, such as the speaker's tone of voice, facial expression, emphasis, and body language (gestures, distance, posture, and relaxation versus tension), helps learners to understand what is being said. For instance, Broderick, the English-speaking learner of French, does not know the meaning of the word *Salaud!* but is aware of the speaker's angry tone and menacing body language. He uses this nonverbal information to guess that the speaker is saying something insulting or angry.

Knowing what has already been said frequently gives important information for getting the meaning of what is currently being said and for anticipating what will be said. Simone, listening to a dialogue about a policeman questioning a suspect, hears the sentence, "He gave him a real grilling." On the basis of what has been said already in the dialogue, Simone guesses that the word *grilling* in this context has nothing to do with cooking but has something to do with questioning. Molly asks herself questions, such as "What will happen now?" and "What might the author want to say next?" She then answers these questions in light of what has already been said, and checks to see whether her guesses are correct. Given even a hazy understanding of what the writer has said so far in a Brazilian newspaper editorial (maybe aided by background knowledge of the paper's political leanings), Andrew can guess what the writer will say next, even if he doesn't understand all the Portuguese words.

In listening, perceptual clues concerning the situation aid the listener's understanding. These clues can be audible (e.g., background noise) or visual (e.g., the number of people involved, what they appear to be doing). For instance, Miguel, a learner of English, is watching TV. He hears one of the TV characters say to his buddy, "Quick! Let's get out of here!" and at the same time he sees both TV characters start running out the door. Using the situational context, Miguel infers that the phrase means something about leaving. Ismael is listening to the radio. He hears a lot of noise from a crowd and some fast, excited speech, of which he catches a few words; he figures out from these signals that this must be a broadcast of a basketball game. Lisette is watching TV. A woman is reading something from a piece of paper, slowly, deliberately, and with a sense of rhythm, so Lisette immediately understands these clues to indicate that this is a poetry reading.

In listening or reading, an important source of clues to meaning is the text structure—that is, introductions, summaries, conclusions, titles, transitions, and ways of dividing the text. It is possible to obtain many clues by noticing the speaker's or author's structural, organizational use of words, phrases, numbers, and letters that indicate importance or priority; for instance, *first . . ., second . . ., third . . .; the most important idea is . . .;* or *the two main points are. . . .* Structural clues are often given, like *By way of introduction, We will now turn to . . ., So far we have covered . . .,* and *In conclusion . . . .* Proper names may be used over and over to indicate importance. Graphs, pictures, tables, and appendices can help readers get an idea of the meaning.

Descriptions of people in oral or written stories can also give clues about the meaning of the rest of the passage. For instance, if a character is described as sinister or mean, learners will expect the person to behave in a particular way later in the story, and even if they don't know all the words, they can guess the general kinds of things the character might do. Recognizing, even in very general terms, how the people in the listening or reading passage treat each other (kindly, subserviently, cruelly, respectfully) can help readers guess the events and the main message of the story. Identification of the situation described in the passage—a trip by train, a horse race, or a classroom scene—helps provide still more clues.

General background knowledge (including knowledge of the target culture, knowledge of the topic under discussion, and general world knowledge of current affairs, art, politics, and literature) helps language learners to make guesses about what they hear or read. A recent study [31] indicates that associating newly heard information with prior knowledge (see the strategy of associating/elaborating, as described earlier) is a powerful and very frequently used way to guess the meaning of a listening passage. All listeners make mental associations with prior knowledge, but when compared with ineffective listeners, good listeners make many more of these associations, make them more personally meaningful, and intentionally use them for guessing. The same undoubtedly holds true for reading. Here are some examples of using clues from background knowledge to guess meanings. Millicent, who is learning Russian, hears the word *apparatchik* [аппаратчик] used in a discussion of Soviet government. On the basis of her general knowledge of the way governments work, she guesses that the word must refer to the government employee, who is part of the *apparatus* of government. The rest of the discussion confirms her guesses. Knowing about the culture where the language is spoken gives many clues; for instance, in reading Spanish, Hilde might expect to encounter a passage about *la corrida de toros* (the bullfight), but Robert would probably be surprised to encounter such a passage in German.

However, learners do not all have the same kind of knowledge upon which to draw. For instance, an English-as-a-second-language class may be composed of people representing many different languages and nationalities and many kinds of life experiences, some including severe hardship and deprivation. For some learners, such differences are a real handicap to understanding the target language. One solution to this problem is to use a variety of listening and reading materials covering as many different topics as possible. Another solution is to try to anticipate the kinds of materials and topics your students, as a group or individually, will have trouble with and the ones they will find easier. Focus on the easier ones at first, in order to build the students' confidence and give them the sense that they can listen and read (and guess!) in the target language. Move into more difficult topics and formats gradually.

How to Promote Guessing

Build guessing skills systematically by leading students step by step through different stages of guessing. Start with global comprehension. To stimulate guessing, ask students some preview questions before they start reading or listening, or interrupt a story in the middle to ask for predictions about what will happen, or give just the ending and ask for guesses about the beginning. Ask which picture corresponds to what they are hearing or reading. Alternatively, give students a sentence in the new language and ask them to complete it [32]. Whenever you use activities like these, be sure to give students feedback immediately (or soon) about the correctness or appropriateness of their answers. Discuss the source of the guesses, so that students can learn from each other and so you can know whether learners are using all possible sources of clues.

The guessing strategies relate to listening and reading. The next group of compensation strategies is tailored for speaking and writing.

Overcoming Limitations in Speaking and Writing

All the compensation strategies for speaking and writing contribute to learning by allowing learners to stay in conversations or keep writing long enough to get sustained practice. Some of these strategies also provide new knowledge in a more obvious way (e.g., getting help).

Switching to the Mother Tongue (S) This strategy, sometimes technically called "code switching," is used for speaking and involves using the mother tongue for an expression without translating it. Here are some examples of this strategy. Geraldo, a Spanish speaker learning English, uses *balón* for *balloon*, and *tirtil* for *caterpillar*. Trudy, an English-speaking student of French, says, *Je suis dans la wrong maison* (I'm in the wrong house), inserting "wrong" when the French word is unknown. Leslie, an English speaker learning French, states, *Je ne pas go to school*, thus switching back to English in midstream. June, another learner of French, uses the expression *le livre de Paul's* (Paul's book), including the non-French word *Paul's*. And Henri, a French speaker learning English, declares, *I want a couteau*, a knife.

Creatively using this strategy, Norman adds word endings from the target language onto words from the mother tongue, as in *Wir sind Soldieren* (We are soldiers, using the English word *soldier* with the German *-en* tacked on). An English speaker, Nicki, wants to describe a clock over the fireplace, but says instead *Il y a une cloche sur la cheminée* (there's a bell over the fireplace). Of course, these two examples might be misunderstood by native speakers of the new language.

Getting Help Ⓢ This strategy involves asking someone for help in a conversation by hesitating or explicitly asking for the missing expression. This strategy is somewhat similar to the strategy of asking for clarification or verification; the difference is that in getting help, the learner wants the other person to simply *provide* what the learner does not know, not to explain or clarify. For example, Clive, a learner of Spanish, signals a desire for help by saying only the first part of the sentence, as in *El quiere . . .?* (He wants . . .?), and Hector, a native Spanish speaker, finishes the sentence with *qué te vayas* (the whole sentence means, "He wants you to go"). Edna, a learner of French, asks in English, *How do you say "staple" in French?* Terry, another learner of French, says, *Je veux, uh, how do you say it?* (I want . . .). Often this strategy is combined with the next one, using mime or gesture, in order to ask for help.

Using Mime or Gesture Ⓢ In this strategy, the learner uses physical motion, such as mime or gesture, in place of an expression during a conversation to indicate the meaning. Following are some examples. Kirsten does not know the expression for a large wooden desk with drawers, so she makes gestures indicating the size of the desk, the hardness of the wood, and the way the drawers pull out. Not able to say, "I am afraid," Jaime instead mimes the emotion of fear by crouching with his arms crossed over his head. Aviva does not yet know how to say, "Put it over there, please," and instead points to the place, hoping the other person will catch the meaning and put the object down in the right spot. Not knowing how to express approval verbally, Tonio claps loudly to indicate approval, then nods in an exaggerated fashion while saying "yes."

Avoiding Communication Partially or Totally Ⓢ This strategy involves avoiding communication when difficulties are anticipated or encountered.

It includes a total avoidance in certain situations, as when required to use persuasive skills or to compete with others for a turn to speak. It also includes avoiding certain topics for which the learner does not know the words, concepts, or grammatical structures in the new language. This strategy goes against the aim of speaking as much and as often as possible, but it does have an advantage of keeping the learner emotionally protected and possibly more able to speak about other things later in the conversation. The avoidance of a specific expression is illustrated by Constanze, a learner of English, who avoids saying *air pollution* (or any description or synonym for this expression) and says instead, *It's hard to breathe*; this might also be used as an example of the strategy of adjusting or approximating the message. The abandonment of communication midway is exemplified when Miki says, *If I only had a . . .* but then fails to finish the sentence.

Selecting the Topic Ⓢ Ⓦ When using this strategy, the learner chooses the topic of conversation. The reasons for this are obvious. Learners want to make sure that the topic is one in which they are interested and for which they possess the needed vocabulary and structures. For example, Rashid, a learner of English, is interested in football and knows a lot about it, including useful terms, so he often directs conversation to this theme. Marcelle is more comfortable discussing subjects like family, school, and weather and thus frequently attempts to move the conversation toward these topics. Learners using this strategy must be careful not to be overly domineering. They should allow the other person to guide the conversation, too.

Writers in any language sometimes use this strategy, but it is particularly valuable to writers in a language other than their own. Of course, circumstances sometimes force language learners to deal with topics they don't want to write about, but whenever possible learners should select a topic that interests them. The only caveat is that learners, when choosing a topic for writing, need to be aware of their audience's interests, needs, and level of understanding.

Adjusting or Approximating the Message Ⓢ Ⓦ This strategy is used to alter the message by omitting some items of information, make the ideas simpler or less precise, or say something slightly different that has similar meaning [33]. Here are some examples. Omitting details that the learner cannot yet say is illustrated when Vanya, asked about his family, says he has two children but does not indicate that they are now fully grown adults; another learner, Nina, says she has to leave now, but does not indicate that she has an appointment at the dentist's in 20 minutes. Using less precise expressions to substitute for more precise but unknown ones, Carmelita might say *pipe* for *waterpipe*. Using a French word that has a similar meaning to the intended French word, Laura says *bureau* (office) to mean shop, as in *un bureau pour cosmetics et perfume*. Franny, a learner of Spanish, uses "presidente" to mean principal, as in *Señor Smith es el presidente de la escuela* (Mr. Smith is the president of the school).

Writers often resort to this strategy when they simply cannot come up with the right or most desirable expression. For instance, instead of writing the more difficult sentence "I would have liked to have visited Australia, but I could not go because I lacked the necessary funds," Nubia writes "I did not go to Australia, because I did not have money."

Coining Words Ⓢ Ⓦ This simple strategy means making up new words to communicate a concept for which the learner does not have the right vocabulary. For instance, Zoltan might say *airball* to mean *balloon*. A German learner of English, Gottfried, does not know the expression *bedside table* and therefore coins the expression *night table*, a direct translation of the German *Nachttisch*. (Note the use of the strategy of translating in the service of coining words during a conversation.) Lucille, an English-speaking learner of German, does not know how to say *dishwasher* in German and consequently makes up the word *Abwaschmaschine*, a combination of *abwaschen* (to wash up) and *Maschine* (machine). Finally, Omar, a learner of English, is not familar with the word *bucket* and therefore coins *water-holder*.

When there is no time to look up the correct word, or when the dictionary fails them, writers sometimes make up their own words to get the meaning across. For example, Stavros uses the term *tooth doctor* instead of *dentist* when writing a note to indicate where he is going this afternoon.

Using a Circumlocution or Synonym Ⓢ Ⓦ In this strategy the learner uses a circumlocution (a roundabout expression involving several words to describe or explain a single concept) or a synonym (a word having exactly the same meaning as another word in the same language) to convey the intended meaning. Examples of circumlocution are as follows. Renato, a learner of English, does not know *car seatbelt* and therefore says, "I'd better tie myself in." Liz, a learner of French who does not know the word for *stool* (*tabouret*), describes it instead: *une petite chaise de bois, pour reposer les jambes quand on est fatigué, elle n'a pas de dos* (a little wooden chair for resting the legs when one is tired, it doesn't have a back). Osmin, a learner of English, cannot come up with the right word and therefore ambles around the topic: "She is, uh, smoking something. I don't know what's its name. That's, uh, Persian, and we use in Turkey, a lot of." Heinrich does not know how to say *towel* in English, so he says, "a thing you dry your hands on." Domenico uses the close synonym *sofa* or *couch* to mean the specific piece of furniture, *divan*. Frequently learners use high-coverage terms that are very close to (but not quite) synonyms; for instance, *pen* instead of *ballpoint pen*, *fruit* for *strawberry*, or *meat* instead of *ham*.

Synonyms or circumlocutions are sometimes used in informal writing. For instance, Siu cannot think of the word *briefcase*, so he writes, "I lost my leather package that holds papers," a circumlocution that gets the point across.

SUMMARY

The focus of this chapter has been use of direct strategies—memory, cognitive, and compensation strategies—to enhance performance in the four language skills. This chapter has shown how certain direct strategies, like taking notes, work across all four skills, while other direct strategies, like getting the idea quickly, are useful for only a subset of these skills. A huge range of applications of direct strategies has been covered here. However, these strategies, to be used most effectively, require their allies, the indirect strategies, which are detailed in Chapters 4 and 5. Before moving on to those chapters, do some of the following activities and exercises to solidify your understanding and stimulate your students' interest in and comprehension of direct strategies.

ACTIVITIES FOR READERS

Activity 3.1. You Can Quote Me on That!

In the left-hand column below is a list of quotations [34] relating to the four language skills: listening, reading, speaking, and writing. Identify the skill or skills mentioned or implied in the quotation, by writing L, R, S, or W in the middle column next to the quotation. Then in the right-hand column, for *each* quotation list *at least three* direct strategies which would strongly enhance development of *each of the skills* mentioned.

QUOTATION	SKILL(S) (L,R,S,W)	STRATEGIES
The time has come, the Walrus said, to talk of many things. Lewis Carroll		
To read without reflecting is like eating without digesting. Edmund Burke		
There can be no fairer ambition than to excel in talk. Robert Louis Stevenson		
Prick up your ears. Movie title		

QUOTATION	SKILL(S) (L,R,S,W)	STRATEGIES
True ease in writing comes from art, not chance, as those move easiest who have learned to dance. Alexander Pope		
Reading is a psycholinguistic guessing game. June Phillips, quoting Frank Smith		
Lend me your ears. William Shakespeare		
Speak out: What is it thou hast heard, or seen? Lord Tennyson		
Polonius: What are you reading? Hamlet: Words, words, words. William Shakespeare		
Genius is one percent inspiration and ninety-nine percent perspiration. Thomas A. Edison		
I took a course in speed reading, learning to read straight down the middle of the page, and was able to read *War and Peace* in twenty minutes. It's about Russia. Woody Allen		
Dear authors! Suit your topic to your strength, And ponder well your subject And its length. Lord Byron		
A good listener is a good talker with a sore throat. Katherine Whitehorn		
To write simply is as difficult as to be good. Somerset Maugham		

Activity 3.2. Remark on Remembering

This chapter shows how memory strategies are used to *store* new information that is heard or read, and to *recall* or *retrieve* the information later when needed in a situation involving any of the four skills. Give your own examples of these two functions of memory strategies as applied to each of the four language skills.

Activity 3.3. Cogitate About Cognitive Strategies

List all the cognitive strategies that you have observed your students using. Now, next to each strategy, list the language skills (listening, reading, speaking, writing, or some combination) that your students have developed by using the strategy.

Activity 3.4. Accentuate the Positive

Brainstorm all the ways compensation strategies might be useful for listening, reading, speaking, and writing. Give your own examples. How do these strategies help to "accentuate the positive"? What are the reasons why you might place guessing strategies (useful in listening and reading) alongside strategies like circumlocution (useful in speaking and writing)?

Activity 3.5. Stalk the Strategies

Carefully study the exercises below. In the margin or on another sheet, indicate all the strategies that are called for by each of the exercises. Do not be limited by the strategy information in the descriptions of "purpose" at the top of each exercise. List *all* the strategies that *you* think are involved.

EXERCISES TO USE WITH YOUR STUDENTS

Note: The exercises here focus primarily on *direct* strategies—memory, cognitive, and compensation—but in many cases *indirect* strategies—metacognitive, affective, and social—are also necessary to do these tasks. As mentioned earlier, direct and indirect strategies work together for optimal learning.

Exercise 3.1. Memory Practice

Purpose

This exercise helps learners to distribute or space their memory practice with new vocabulary words, using structured review and other memory strategies.

Materials

Large sheet of paper for the list.

Time

Although the exercise takes 30 to 50 minutes, you might also hold short sessions periodically to add to the list later.

Instructions

Ask your students to brainstorm about all the memory strategies they now use, or have used, to learn a language. Make the list as long as possible. Then ask the students to tell which of these were useful and which were not, and have them explain why. Put a star (*) beside those which students describe as effective. Add to the list periodically. (If students cannot think of the memory strategies they use, do a few language learning tasks in class, then ask your students to list all the memory strategies they used for those tasks and to indicate which ones they felt were the most helpful.)

Then explain some of the principles of remembering. For instance, describe in your own words the need for *structured reviewing at increasing intervals*, and give or show them a copy of Figure 3.6. Ask them to learn specific vocabulary for an upcoming lesson by using this strategy. Ask them to report back to the class on the effects.

During a vocabulary learning task in class, give your students practice in making *associations*, using *imagery*, and putting new words into the *context* of a sentence. To do this, ask students to work in small groups and share their associations, images, or contexts (sentences) aloud as they work on learning new expressions.

Source Original.

Exercise 3.2. Grouping and Labeling

Purpose

These tasks help learners see the value of grouping and labeling. Learners get practice with both of these as they learn vocabulary.

Materials

Word lists.

Time

The exercise takes 20 to 30 minutes.

Instructions

Tell your students the following in your own words: Grouping information helps you remember it. Putting a label on the groups you have made can also help you recall it later. Both of these techniques are really organizational functions, which help you sort information and reduce it to smaller, more cohesive units.

Let's show how grouping helps you. First, try to memorize List A after reading through it a few times. (Give learners the list.)

LIST A

cocoa	Indian	bed	soda
post office	hello	soap	what
able	that	registration	personality
rigidity	loop	disk	yellow

Now put the list away and then try to write down as many of the words in the list as you can remember. Then count the number of words you have recalled. (Take a few minutes here to do an informal survey of how many of the 16 words were recalled; get a rough average for the group.) These are your results when you do *not* use any special kind of grouping—that is, when the information in a list is completely unorganized.

Now let's try another experiment. Try to memorize List B. Read through it a few times now. (Give learners the list.)

LIST B
Office Supplies and Equipment

Desk-related:	pens pencils rubber bands paper clips tape stapler desk
Computer-related:	paper ribbon hard disk floppy disk VDT
Telephone-related:	telephone notepad phone book answering machine

Now put the list away and again write down as many of the listed words as you remember. Count the number of words you have written down. (Take time to survey the students again and obtain an average of the number of words. It is likely that students remembered more from List B than they did earlier from List A.) This is how you perform when the information is more organized—that is, grouped and labeled so that it is easier to remember.

We will now try List A again, but this time you'll organize the words and use any labels you want to use. (Give students time, say 3 to 5 minutes, to organize the words from List A into groups of their own making.) Be sure to write down the words as you group them and then put labels on the groups. Put away the list now. Try to write down as many of the words as you remember, and then count the number of words you recall from your "organized List A." (Check how many words have been recalled; it will probably be far more than students remembered the first time they dealt with List A, partly due to grouping and partly due to having a second encounter with the material.)

Though List B was already grouped, you might find it useful to regroup and relabel the words in List B in a way that suits you better personally. Take a few minutes to think of a different grouping system. Jot the words down in their new groups, and give each group a name. Now remember the words. (Do another survey about the words remembered from List B, and see if the average is any better than it was with the original List B.)

Now let's discuss grouping and labeling. How does grouping help you remember? What functions does it serve? What does labeling do for you? Is it better to create labels before or after the groups are formed? Is it better to generate your own groups and labels, or have the groups and labels given to you, or does it make any difference? What role does structured review play, and what role does grouping play? (Let students have time to discuss these questions, possibly in small groups or pairs, reporting to the larger group at the end.)

Source Original.

Exercise 3.3. Make Your Own Groups

Purpose

This exercise gives learners the opportunity to create their own groups of words and consider the best criteria for doing so, as a way of remembering vocabulary.

Materials

Word cards.

Time

This lasts 45 minutes.

Instructions

Give your students 50 to 100 small cards containing vocabulary words in the new language. Let them work in pairs to group the cards and then label their groups. To do this, they should lay the cards out on a table, putting them into as many groups as necessary and then devising labels for each group. Suggest that they transfer this information onto a large sheet and then draw lines between any groups of words that might have some relationship to each other, thus creating a *semantic map*. You might show them an example of a semantic map from this chapter. Students should be able to find relationships, either direct or far-fetched, among many groups!

Then ask the pairs to compare notes with other pairs about their resulting groups, labels, and semantic maps. Ask them to consider what criteria they used for grouping, labeling, and figuring out relations between groups. Ask them to consider which ways of grouping, labeling, and finding relationships helped them remember better.

Alternative

For advanced students, all the discussion could take place in the new language.

Source Original.

Exercise 3.4. Find the Odd Word

Purpose

This activity is an extension of the grouping exercises. It requires learners to find the word that does *not* fit into the groups. This provides more complex grouping practice, helps in discrimination skills, and helps in remembering new words.

Materials

Word lists, instruction sheet.

Time

The exercise takes 15 minutes, more if alternatives are used.

Instructions

Give your students the word lists and instructions below.

Which word does not belong in each of the four lists below? Circle the "odd" word in the cluster and explain why you chose it.

LIST 1	LIST 2
der Regen (rain)	der Friseur (hairdresser)
das Gewitter (thunderstorm)	der Vetter (cousin, masc.)
das Unglück (misfortune)	der Großvater (grandfather)
der Donner (thunder)	die Kusine (cousin, fem.)

LIST 3	LIST 4
das Theater (theater)	breit (broad)
das Gebäude (building)	weit (wide)
die Kirche (church)	eng (narrow)
der Käfig (cage)	weich (soft)

Alternatives

1. Some highly creative students always seem to find relationships among almost any set of words, and they are able to give logical reasons, too! If you are dealing with such students, run the exercise as above. Then run it a second time, this time asking learners to think of reasons why the four words in each group *do* fit together.

2. If learners are more advanced, they can do the exercise, including all discussion, entirely in the target language.

Source Omaggio (1981, p. 27) for basic exercise. Alternatives are original.

Exercise 3.5. Yes/No Game

Purpose

This exercise helps learners to improve their perception and discrimination of sounds in the new language. The exercise involves the strategy of formally practicing with sounds.

Materials

None.

Time

It takes 5 to 10 minutes.

Instructions

Call out two words to the students. Tell them to indicate if the words are the *same* (if so, write YES) or *not the same* (if they are not the same, write NO). Each pair of words will have a number, and YES or NO will be written next to the appropriate number. Give students an example on the board, like this:

WORD PAIR NUMBER	YES (the same) or NO (not the same)?
1. (book/look)	NO
2.	
3.	
4.	
5.	

Alternatives

Call out a series of several words and ask students to indicate which, if any, is not the same as the others. For the set FAR, BAR, FAR, FAR, learners would write down 2 to show that the second word in the series is not like the others.
OR
Give students a page with sets of words listed, two to four at a time. Ask students to circle the words that they hear you read aloud from each set.

Source Original; however, these sound discrimination exercises are fairly standard in any listening comprehension textbook.

Exercise 3.6. Finding Your Way

Purpose

This exercise is a listening comprehension task involving students in marking a route on a map according to spoken directions. It requires a combination of many strategies, such as direct strategies like practicing naturalistically, guessing, and using imagery and indirect strategies like paying attention.

Materials

Map photocopied for each student.

Time

This will take 20 minutes.

Instructions

Get a clear road map of an interesting area (see examples in Figures 3.12 and 3.13). Make copies for all students and yourself. On your own copy, sketch the route you want students to go. Then, without showing your copy to the students, describe in words where to go, adding comments on the scenery and landmarks, discussing the kinds of people you will meet (e.g., the butcher, the minister, the teacher), and mentioning reasons for visiting certain places. These hints will help students as they mark on their map the route you are describing.

Source Original instructions; however, such activities are typically found in good listening comprehension books, such as Ur (1984).

Exercise 3.7. Physical Response

Purpose

This exercise has learners listen carefully for directions about how they should perform physical movement, a useful memory strategy.

Materials

None.

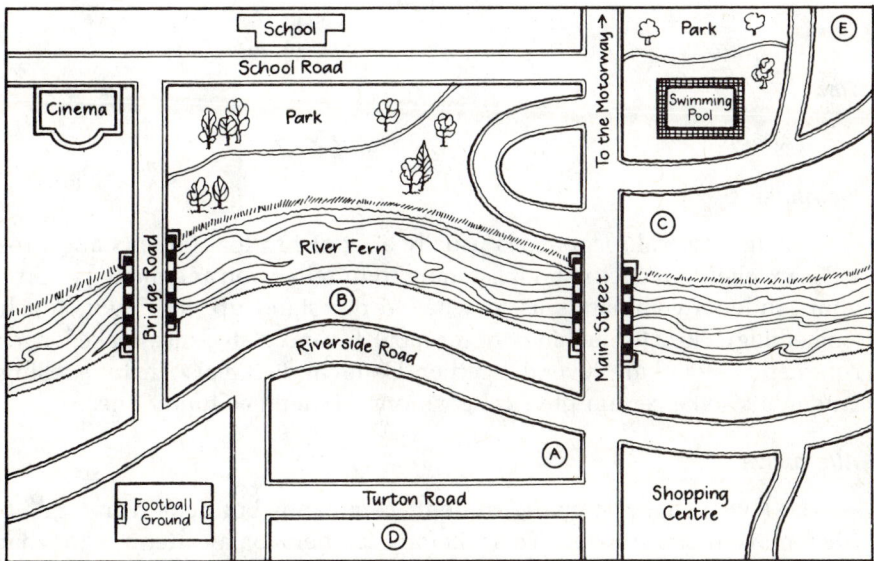

Figure 3.12   English Road Map. (*Source*: Ur (1984, p. 61).)

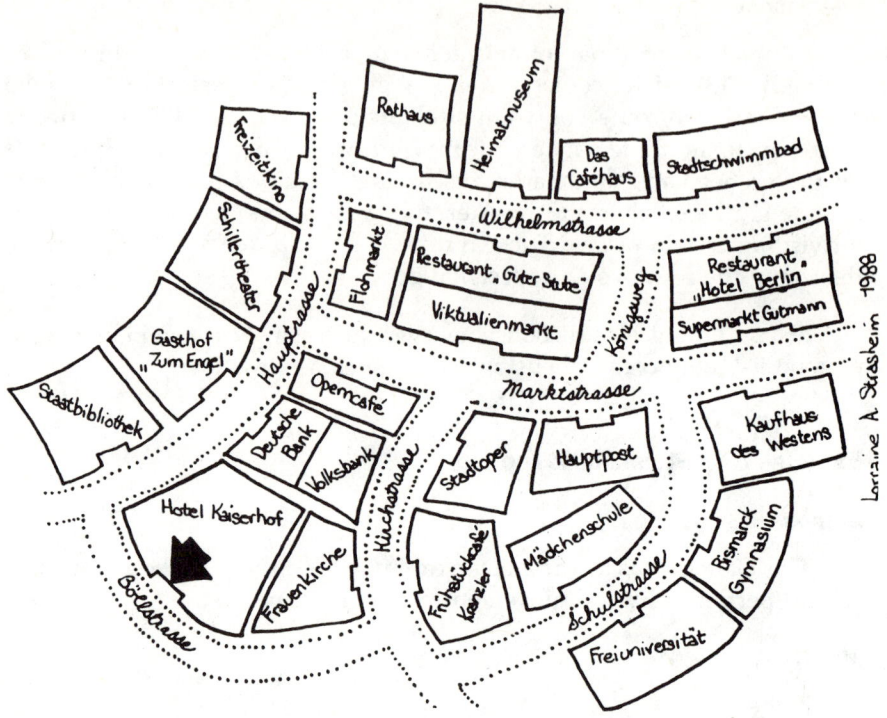

Figure 3.13   German Road Map. (*Source*: Strasheim (1988, p. 3).)

Time

Variable.

Instructions

Using physical response is usually a lot of fun for students and provides excellent practice in both listening comprehension and memory. Give your students commands as to what to do: stand up, sit down, touch (something), close (something); or for more advanced students, make longer commands by linking several together. Commands can also include telling students to take certain physical positions, sometimes funny ones.

Alternative

Ur (1984) suggests giving students commands but demonstrating *different* movements yourself. This will force learners to pay attention to what you are actually saying! You might also try having your students pair up and give each other commands.

Source Original instructions, but these are typical of many Total Physical Response exercises.

Exercise 3.8. Jigsaw Listening

Purpose

This exercise allows students to listen to different extracts from a text and then collate their information in order to get a complete understanding of the situation. It involves direct strategies like practicing naturalistically, guessing, and note-taking, as well as indirect strategies like paying attention and cooperating.

Materials

Tapes containing extracts of a narrative.

Time

Depends on narrative length and proficiency level.

Instructions

Ask your students to fill out a grid (see Table 3.1) by listening to extracts of a narrative on tape, and then pooling information from their extracts. The purpose of the grid is to describe characters in the narrative by name, profession, address, age, and appearance. One-third of the students would have Extract 1, another third Extract 2, and the last third Extract 3.

Table 3.1   PERSONAL CHARACTERISTICS GRID FOR JIGSAW LISTENING

Name				
Profession				
Address				
Age				
Appearance				

Source: Ur (1984), p. 153.

Here are some sample extracts taken from Ur (1984). Note that these are only brief extracts! The real narrative would need to be longer and more detailed.

Extract 1

PAT: Do you know those four people over there by chance?

JON: I know the old man with the beard, Mr. Sutton. He's headmaster of the local school and lives here in Cheston. I think the younger man's also a teacher in the school. I've seen him around, the one that's talking to the doctor.

Extract 2

JASON: Do introduce me to that attractive girl talking to old Mr. Sutton—who is she?

ELSA: No luck, Jason, she's married, that's her husband, the tall man next to her. Name of Smith.

JASON: She looks too young to be married.

ELSA: Rose? She's twenty-two, we were at school together. She works as a secretary in her husband's school—they live quite near here.

Extract 3

GRANDMA: Thelma, do go and ask that nice Dr. Thorndike if she'd come and talk to me for a while.

THELMA: All right, Grandma, which one is she?

GRANDMA: She's that middle-aged, very well dressed lady standing over there talking to Mr. Smith. She lives in London and doesn't come down here very often, so I'd love to have a chat with her.

Note Jigsaw listening tasks such as this one are entertaining and very useful for listening comprehension. However, there are drawbacks: the need for the right number of recordings and machines, and the need to have each group listen to its own extract without being overly distracted by others. See Ur for details and other suggestions for jigsaw listening.

Source Ur (1984, pp. 152–154).

Exercise 3.9. Guessing the Meaning of Reading Passages

Purpose

This exercise helps learners to guess the meaning of a reading passage and explain how they made those guesses.

Materials

Sheet with reading passages.

Time

This takes 30 to 50 minutes, depending on amount of discussion.

Instructions

Explain to your students that they will be practicing their guessing skills in various languages. Give them a sheet containing the following instructions and reading passages (or others of your own selection). Keep the number of passages down to four or five, or whatever you think your students can handle profitably.

Read the following passages and try to guess the general meaning, even if you do not know all the words! You will be answering some questions about these passages at the end.

1. . . . It was really a very nice appetizing bit of pischa they'd laid out on the tray—two or three lomticks of like hot roast beef with mashed kartoffel and vedge, then there was also ice-cream and a nice hot chasha of chai. And there was even a cancer to smoke and a matchbox with one match in it. (Burgess, 1963, p. 99)

2. Dr. Lightfoot, who guffled my aunt's flumps, is a fine surgeon. (Mendelsohn, 1984, p. 70)

3. URSS: LE PLUS ANCIEN DES "REFUSNIKS" VLADIMIR SLEPAK A QUITTÉ MOSCOU POUR ISRAEL. M. Vladimir Slepak, l'un des principaux dissidents juifs soviétiques, est arrivé le dimanche 25 octobre à Vienne, en provenance d'Union Soviétique et à destination d'Israel.

   A leur arrivée dans la capitale autrichienne, le "refusnik" et sa femme Maria ont été accueillis par leur fils Alexandre, qui avait emigré aux Etats-Unis il y a dix ans. Celui-ci a dit espérer que la liberation de ses parents annonçait un tournant dans la politique soviétique à l'égard des juifs.

   En revanche, son père a declaré: "Selon moi, [ma liberation] est un geste en direction de l'Occident parce que les autorités soviétiques ont besoin d'aide et de crédit (. . .) Ce sont des tyrans". (URSS . . ., Le Monde, 1987)

4. Selected Items from Menu from Al-Ikhwa Hotel, Taiz, Y.A.R.: Coloured Soop, Fish with Potatoes & Latic, Fish with Eggs & Potatoes Beas, Rost Meat with Potatoes Beans, Stick Meat with Potatoes & Beas, Kutlet Meat, Small Meat, Dry Meat Shab, Stick with Eggs & Potatoes, Kari Meat & Rice, Kari Hans with Rice, Hans with Potatoes & Beas, Hurts with Eggs & Patatoes Beas, Mukroni with Eggs Meat Bakred, Sandwish Colured, Sweat Boding, Lce and Tea, Lce with Coffee and Milk, Turkey Coffee, Vimto, Franch Lemon, Lec-Cream . . . (Private Eye, 1979, p. 54)

Now answer the following questions, working with another person:

1. Summarize the meaning of each passage in one sentence.
2. How well did you understand the meaning of each of the passages above? Which passages gave you the most trouble, and why?
3. If you did not understand certain words, which ones were they?
4. Did you try to guess the meaning of unknown or unclear words? If so, how often? What are some examples of unknown words you were able to guess? What information did you use to make your guesses?
5. What other information sources might you have used to guess the meanings? List as many sources as you can think of.
6. Did you need to know (or guess) the meanings of all the words in a passage in order to know (or guess) the overall meaning of the *whole* passage? In other words, do you need to get the details in order to get the general idea?

Source Original.

Exercise 3.10. Guessing with Pictures

Purpose

This exercise helps learners practice their guessing strategies using pictures.

Materials

Cartoons without words (as in Figure 3.14).

Time

It will take 10 to 30 minutes, depending on the number of cartoons.

Instructions

Give students cartoons without any words at all, as in Figure 3.14. Ask them to fill in the missing captions with their own words in the target language. Remind them to use all the clues they find in the pictures in order to create appropriate captions.

Source Moran (1984).

Exercise 3.11. Scanning a Reading Passage for Personal Facts

Purpose

This exercise helps learners to scan a reading passage for personal facts.

Figure 3.14 Guessing with Pictures. Use your imagination—and your new language—to fill in the missing captions! (*Source*: Moran (1984).)

Materials

Sheet with reading passages and instructions.

Time

Variable, depending on proficiency level and passage length; you should limit the time for scanning.

Instructions

Tell your students the following in your own words: Below are the names of four characters in the reading passage. (Teacher provides these names from a reading passage the students have not yet read.) For each of the characters listed here, you are to give information from the reading passage about the person's

1. nationality
2. age
3. occupation
4. future plans
5. main traits

(Learners receive the passage and do the task here.)
Here are the correct answers. Check yours against these to see whether you are right. If you made any errors, how might you have been confused by the passage?

Alternatives

Adapt this for use with a listening passage. Or have learners scan a passage for actions, new words, or any other details. See Phillips (1984) for ideas.

Source Adapted from Phillips (1984, p. 291).

Exercise 3.12. Skimming a Reading Passage for the Main Idea

Purpose

This exercise helps learners to skim a reading passage for the main idea.

Materials

Sheet with reading passages, instructions, and headlines.

Time

Variable, depending on proficiency level and length of the passages; you should limit the time for skimming.

Instructions

Tell your students the following in your own words: You will be given a series of short news articles with three possible headlines for each. Read as quickly as you can and choose the most appropriate headline for each article.

(Provide students with articles and possible headlines.) Now that you have finished the task, compare notes with someone else.

Alternatives

An alternative with news or magazine articles has students skim the lead paragraph and decide in which section of the index or table of contents it belongs, such as national news, life-style, sports. Or adapt this for use with a listening passage. Or read a passage and provide a one-word or one-sentence summary of the passage. Or read a passage and provide a one-word summary of each paragraph.

Source Adapted from Phillips (1984, p. 290). For additional skimming exercises, see Phillips (1984).

Exercise 3.13. Inventions

Purpose

This exercise helps readers practice naturalistically, search for meaning, and use information to complete a diagram. This exercise could easily be adapted for any set of chronological facts from any culture or subject area.

Materials

Invention list (below), incomplete diagram (Figure 3.15).

Time

Takes 45 minutes.

Instructions

Give your students the following instructions orally and in writing: The diagram in Figure 3.15 plots the time between the date of conception

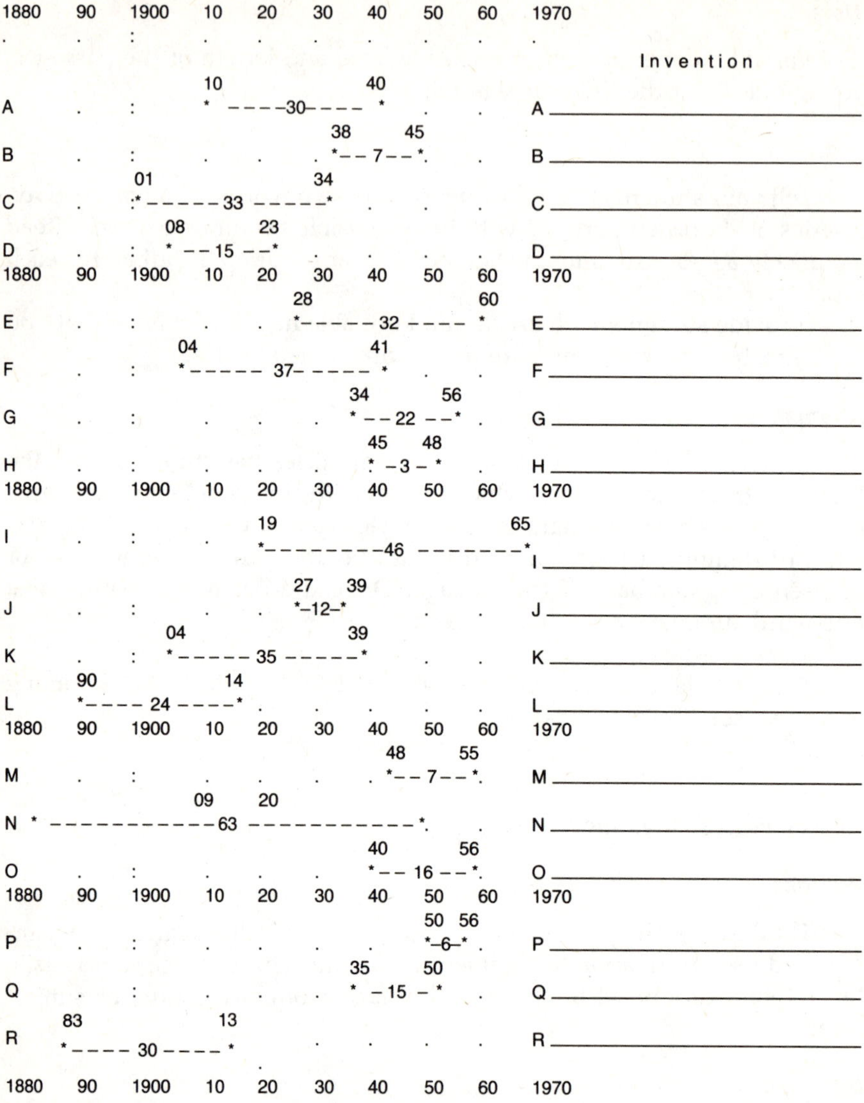

```
1880    90   1900   10    20    30    40    50    60   1970
  .      .    :      .     .     .     .     .     .     .
                                                              Invention
               10                40
A    .    :    * ----30---- *    .          .        A _____
                          38        45
B    .    :         .     . *--7--*.        .        B _____
          01               34
C    .    :* -----33 -----*        .        .        C _____
           08      23
D    .    :  * --15 --*    .        .        .       D _____
1880    90   1900   10    20    30    40    50    60   1970
                          28                     60
E    .    :         .     .*-----32 ---- *           E _____
               04                41
F    .    :    * ----- 37- ---- *    .               F _____
                          34        56
G    .    :         .     . * --22 --* .             G _____
                          45        48
H    .    :         .     . *-3-*    .                H _____
1880    90   1900   10    20    30    40    50    60   1970
               19                          65
I    .    :         .*--------46 -------*            I _____
                     27   39
J    .    :         . *-12-*        .        .        J _____
               04              39
K    .    :    * ----- 35 -----*    .        .        K _____
          90             14
L    *---- 24 ----* .        .        .        .     L _____
1880    90   1900   10    20    30    40    50    60   1970
                                   48        55
M    .    :         .     .     . *--7--*.           M _____
               09    20
N    * ----------- 63 -----------*.        .         N _____
                              40        56
O    .    :         .     .     . *-- 16 --*.        O _____
1880    90   1900   10    20    30    40    50    60   1970
                                   50  56
P    .    :         .     .     .     . *-6-* .      P _____
                              35        50
Q    .    :         .     .     . * -15 - *          Q _____
          83             13
R    *---- 30 ---- * .        .        .        .    R _____
1880    90   1900   10    20    30    40    50    60   1970
```

Figure 3.15 Inventions. (*Source*: Crookall (1984, p. 25).)

and the date of realization for 19 different inventions (A to S). For example, invention A was first thought of in 1910 and did not become a concrete reality until 1940, a time lapse of 30 years; invention M was conceived in 1948 and took 7 years before it was realized in 1955.

Your task is to use the information in the sentences given here to label each invention on the diagram in Figure 3.15. In other words, you have to decide which inventions (mentioned in the sentences) go with which lines in the diagram. The problem is to find out which invention took the least time between its conception date and its realization date.

- The zipper was thought of just one year before the television.
- Both nylon and radar were developed in the same year, but the latter was conceived at the turn of the century, in the same year as the helicopter was thought of.
- The long-playing record took less than half the time, from conception to realization, than the roll-on deodorant.
- Antibiotics took the same time as the zipper to be made, while the heart pacemaker and fluorescent lighting took, respectively, 2 and 3 years longer.
- Instant coffee was thought of in the same year as fluorescent lighting was produced, and the same relationship holds for the transistor and antibiotics.
- The invention which took the most time between its conception and its realization was the television.
- The VTR (video tape recorder) took only half as long as nylon to be made, and one-quarter the time that radio took.
- The Xerox copier and frozen foods each took as much time to produce as the combined time it took for the ballpoint pen and the VTR (video tape recorder), and each took half as long as the zipper.
- The television took 17 years longer to become a reality than did nuclear power.
- The roll-on deodorant took just a little longer to come into being than did the VTR (video tape recorder), and both were conceived and produced more or less concurrently.

Source Adapted from Crookall (1984a, pp. 24–25).

Exercise 3.14. Jigsaw Reading

Purpose

This exercise asks learners to put together two or more pieces of a written text that have been separated, thus requiring that learners guess by using text structure and content clues. Other strategies, such as a range of cognitive strategies, are involved.

Materials

Books, articles, advertisements, or stories cut up (see below).

Time

Variable, depending on the materials used.

Instructions

Jigsaw reading involves cutting up a text and asking the students to put it back together. This exercise can take many forms: (a) matching headlines with the relevant newspaper articles, (b) matching pictures with the stories, advertisements, or articles from which they came, (c) matching cartoons with their captions, (d) matching two parts of an interview, i.e., the interviewer's questions with the interviewee's answers, (e) putting together in the proper sequence all the questions and answers from an interview, (f) matching pictures, captions, and text that have been split and putting them all into the right order, and so on.

You can make up your own variations, and you can make them as simple or complex as you want. Simple matching of one thing with another, e.g., cartoons with their captions, is interesting, fun, and easy. See Figures 3.16 and 3.17 for examples.

More challenging but also exhilarating for students is the matching of various elements (captions, split-up text, pictures) and putting them all *in the right order*. Note that some texts (e.g., advertisements that contain lists of testimonials) do not always have a particular order. However, most texts do have an order based on meaning, and learners can gain a great deal by having to search for the meaning for the purpose of putting the material into the right order.

It is best to have students work in pairs for the more complicated jigsaw reading tasks, but they may work individually for the easier ones. After the task is done, the pair (or individual) compares results with other pairs (or other individuals). For beginning and intermediate learners, the discussion will likely lapse into the mother tongue, but since the focus is on the meaning of the reading passage, this may be all right. For more advanced learners, the discussion should be in the target language if possible.

Note For an excellent combination of jigsaw reading with a writing task (writing a memo), see Withrow (1987), p. 54. For details on the conceptual skills involved in jigsaw reading, and various aspects of this activity, see Crookall and Watson (1985).

Figure 3.16   Match the Captions with the Pictures for Hobbies. To use this with your students, remove the captions and list them in random order on another sheet. Ask students to match the captions with the pictures of various hobbies (*Freizeitbeschäftigungen*). (*Source*: Picture is from *Kinder Monatszeitschrift*, VIII (3), 1986.)

Figure 3.17 Match the Captions with the "Peanuts" Cartoon. To use this with your students, remove the captions and list them in random order on another sheet. Ask students to match the captions with the "Peanuts" cartoon. (*Source*: Picture is from *Kinder Monatszeitschrift*, VIII (6), 1986.)

Source Original description of Jigsaw Reading. *Kinder Monatszeitschrift* VIII (3) (1986) for Figure 3.16 and VIII (6) (1986) for Figure 3.17.

Exercise 3.15. Alibi

Purpose

This exercise is an adaptation of the parlor game Alibi. It aims to get students communicating authentically, putting together information, and guessing meanings in a suspenseful situation.

Materials

None.

Time

This exercise takes 1 hour.

Instructions

In the original Alibi game, two people go out of the room and make up a story about what they did together during a given period, say between 6:00 P.M. and 9:00 P.M. the previous day. The first person comes back in, tells his or her version of the story, and is questioned for detail by the jury—that is, the rest of the people. The second person then comes in, tells his or her version of the story, and is cross-examined. These two people are suspected of committing a crime during the given period, so they must have an "alibi," a reasonable story that proves they are not guilty, and their two versions of the story must be consistent with each other.

This game has been adapted for use in the language classroom, so that the two people are interrogated at the *same time* by different juries (different sets of classmates), so that more time is spent in actual communication in the target language. Some participants have to defend themselves and refute accusations, while others act as their juries. They all become totally involved in the activity and engaged in heated communication in the new language.

It is important that for every variation of the game, each jury must consist of *two to five students*.

Variation 1 (Class Size: 6–12; 2 Suspects and 2 Juries)

Stage A—Story Creation and Interrogations The two suspects, A and B, go out and make up their story. The class is split into two juries, 1 and 2.

When the suspects return, jury 1 interrogates suspect A, and jury 2 questions suspect B. After a while the two suspects change over for a second round of interrogations: Jury 1 now has suspect B, and jury 2 has A.

Stage B—Further Cross-Examination (and Optional Preparation) For this stage, there are at least three possible procedures: (1) The whole class comes together and the two juries can now cross-examine the suspects further to cover anything so far missed. Suspect A is not allowed to intervene if the question is directed at B, and vice versa. The juries must enforce this rule, which itself involves meaningful language use. (2) Alternatively, the suspects go back to their original juries for further cross-examination. (3) Instead of, or following, (1) or (2), the suspects come together again and prepare their final defense, which occurs in Stage C. To do this they will have to find out what discrepancies have emerged during their separate interrogations. At the same time, juries will meet together and discuss their strategies.

Stage C—Final Defense With the whole class together, each jury now presents the contradictions it has found in the suspects' alibi stories. This time the suspects are allowed to interrupt and respond freely. They must explain any discrepancies, refute accusations, make excuses, etc.

Variation 2 (Class Size: 9–18; 3 Suspects and 3 Juries)

Stage A—Story Creation and Interrogations For the first round of interrogations, suspect A goes to jury 1, suspect B to jury 2, C to 3. For the second round, suspects move to the next jury (A to 2, B to 3, C to 1). The decision to have a third round will depend on length of previous rounds, students' level, and complexity of the alibi.

Stage B—Further Cross-Examination (and Optional Preparation) Might be useful, but not really necessary if a third round of interrogations has taken place in Stage A.

Stage C—Final Defense Same as Stage C under Variation 1.

Variation 3 (Class Size: 19–24; 4 Suspects and 4 Juries)

Variation 3 uses the same stages as Variation 2.

Source Adapted from Crookall (1979).

Exercise 3.16. What We Have in Common

Purpose

This exercise allows learners to work in pairs to communicate naturalistically about things of personal significance. Can be used as an ice-breaker.

Materials

None.

Time

Takes 20 minutes.

Instructions

1. Split the class up into groups of about eight. Within these groups, ask people to pair off and find five things they have in common with their partner and five things they don't have in common. Tell them to note these down.

2. Once the questioning in pairs is over, ask the students to report to their group of eight. The reports in the groups go on simultaneously. If the students are elementary level give them structures to help the reporting, for example:

We both like . . .   S/he lives in . . . but I . . .
We are both wearing . . .   I prefer . . . , but s/he prefers . . .

Note In using this exercise as an ice-breaker, don't prescribe structures for the paired questioning. Listening to how they go about this unguided will prove a golden diagnostic opportunity for you.

Source Frank and Rinvolucri (1983, p. 17).

Exercise 3.17. What's My Line?

Purpose

This exercise allows development of guessing and naturalistic practice skills in an entertaining format.

Materials

None.

Time

Takes 20 to 30 minutes, depending on number of rounds.

Instructions

Tell your students the following in your own words: One person will take the role of a "secret person" who has a certain occupation ("line"). The other student(s) will ask questions that can be answered by either yes or no; their task is to find out what the occupation of the person is. The "secret person" can be famous (e.g., Napoleon) or not famous (e.g., a bricklayer).

Alternative

You can make up many variations of this game. One variation is to ask students to select only a famous person as their "secret person." This gets into all sorts of interesting historical and cultural information. If students figure out that the secret person is dead, they can use the past tense; if the secret person is alive, they can use the present tense.

Source Old American TV show, "What's My Line?"

Exercise 3.18. Picture Stories

Purpose

This exercise gives students a chance to create a new story; use memory strategies, particularly imagery, to remember sequences; practice naturalistically; and compensate for missing information.

Materials

Pictures on small cards, about 80 in all (reusable).

Time

Takes 30 minutes.

Instructions

First you create the cards, one picture per card. These can be cut out of magazines, travel brochures, advertisements, mail order catalogues, etc., and should be clear, interesting, colorful, and varied. (You can get your students to bring in picture materials and help you make the cards! It will take much less time and will be fun for them.) On the back of each card, write the vocabulary related to the picture (e.g., "tennis/have a game of tennis/play tennis/racket/court"). Now you are ready to have your students play the game.

Stage 1—Story Construction Split the class into four groups (preferably equal in size). Each group sits at four different tables, A through D. Explain to the students that they will each be dealt a number of cards, say three or four, to use for constructing a story. The first student in each group starts the game by placing one of his or her cards on the table and making up a sentence related to the picture. The second student then chooses a card from his or her set, places it next to the first card, and says a sentence related to that picture and linking the story with what the previous person said. The third person does likewise, continuing the story. Encourage students to create real linkages, no matter how improbable; the result should be a story, not a set of discrete sentences. Also let students know that they are not allowed to write down their story; they need to remember it, using the pictures as cues. Continue the process until the group runs out of cards, or until you stop the proceedings. If a group runs out of cards before the other groups, give them a few more cards and let them continue their story-making. While all this is going on, you go from table to table and give each person a number, 1 to 4; tell the students to remember their numbers because they will need them later.

When a group has about 15 or 20 cards down on the table, take up the unused cards. Explain to the group that it should now go over the story so as to remember it well, since in a moment they will have to tell it to another group. Go around to each group and explain the same thing. Students may be surprised, and they usually respond with a noticeable increase in concentration. (Slower groups may not have a chance to go completely through their story again, but that is all right.)

Stage 2—Telling the Stories Students are told that some will move and that some will stay where they are, but that they shouldn't move until they all know where to go. All students who have the number 1 stay where they are. All the other students (numbers 2, 3, and 4) will move to the next table; that is, students 2, 3, and 4 at table A go to table B; students 2, 3, and 4 at table B go to C; C to D, and D to A. Then they move. The task now of student 1 is to tell the story to the "new" students who have just arrived at the table.

Stage 3—Retelling the Stories Here all students who have number 2 are told that they have to stay where they are (i.e., with the new story they have just been told). Students 1, 3, and 4 at table A move to B, and B to C, etc. They move, and it is now the turn of student 2 to tell the story to the other three who've just sat down. This time the story is being told not by one of its creators but by someone to whom it has just been told. Since no one who made up the story is present, there is now a tendency for students to comment on the story.

Stage 4—Retelling the Stories Same as previous two stages, except that it is now the turn of student 3 to tell the story.

Stage 5—Checking the Original This is the last stage of the game. Students are told that they must listen carefully because they will not move in exactly the same way as they've done before. Student 4 does stay where he or she is, but the others (1, 2, and 3) go back to their original tables, to the tables of the story they made up at the beginning of the game. Once in their places, student 4 has to tell the story and the others see what changes have been made to their original story, noticing in what ways it has been deformed over the various "tellings." Sometimes very little will have changed, while in some cases important details and even whole chunks will have been completely left out, new things put in, and so on. These changes can provoke some interesting discussion and even heated debate.

Alternatives

1. The game as described above is for 16 students. For classes of more or fewer than 16, here are some possible alternatives: 9 students = 3 groups, 3 students/group, 4 stages; 25 students = 5 groups, 5 students/group, 6 stages; 18 students = as for 9 students, but 2 separate games; 10 students = as for 9 students, but 2 of the 9 students work as 1. Other figures are given in Crookall (1983b). You will need more than 80 cards for classes of greater than 16. NOTE THAT IN EVERY CASE, THE NUMBER OF PEOPLE IN A GROUP MUST BE EQUAL TO, OR LARGER THAN, THE NUMBER OF GROUPS.

2. It is possible to follow this with a writing assignment in which students write up the stories.

Source Adapted from Crookall (1983b). More details on this game are found there.

Exercise 3.19. Crystal Ball

Purpose

This exercise allows students to develop prediction/guessing skills, which are often required for understanding a reading passage.

Materials

Reading passage.

Time

Variable, depending on amount of discussion.

Instructions

1. You and the students silently read a specified portion of the selection. In the beginning, this should be no more than a few lines or a short paragraph.

2. With your book closed, invite the students to ask you as many questions as they can about the portion that was read. The students may refer to the text during this phase, and all speaking is done in the new language.

3. When the students have exhausted their questions, they must close their books, and you ask them questions about the same portion of the text.

4. Repeat steps 1, 2, and 3 several times.

5. At a predetermined point, stop the reciprocal questioning routine and ask the students to predict the outcome of the story or selection. Their predictions are written on the board.

6. Then you and the students silently read the remainder of the story.

7. Discuss the outcome of the story with the students, comparing the predictions with the actual ending.

Alternatives

1. Work with only the ending of a story, and make predictions about the beginning; then read the beginning and find out whether the predictions were correct.

2. Adapt this procedure for use with a listening passage.

Source The ReQuest procedure developed by Manzo (1969) as described by Hague (1986a).

Exercise 3.20. Protest

Purpose

To make guesses from context and to write meaningfully and authentically.

Materials

Newspaper article (one copy per student).

Time

Variable, depending on amount of discussion.

Instructions

Tell your students in your own words: Read the newspaper article I will give you. Then, working with a partner, write what you think each person said. Here is a copy of the article:

"Protest Gets Nasty—41 Arrested" by Birney Jarvis

About 200 anti-war demonstrators went wild yesterday, invading stores, knocking down pedestrians, and breaking windows before police moved in to arrest them.

The problem began when a small group of punk rockers, "skin-heads," admitted anarchists, and students ran into one of the department stores at Post and Powell streets at 6 p.m. pushing and shoving customers. Some were knocked down, witnesses said.

Within seconds, several squads of police in riot gear and 30 motorcycle officers and mounted police moved in. A total of 41 people were arrested.

The Police Commander, Ray Canepa, said _____

_____

_____

_____

_____. A store owner on Powell Street said _____

_____

_____

_____

_____. One of the protesters, a high school student at

Concord High, said _____

_____

_____

_____

_____, and one of the customers who was pushed around by

the rioters said _____

_____

_____

_____

_____. The mayor, who came down to the scene

of the riot, said _____

_____

_____

_____

_____.

Now that you have finished this part, discuss the following questions with your partner:

1. How do you feel about demonstrations? Do they help a cause? How?
2. Can a demonstration hurt a cause? How?
3. Do you think the demonstration in the article helped the anti-war cause? Why or why not?

Source Jones and Kimbrough (1987, pp. 60–61).

Exercise 3.21. Interviews

Purpose

This exercise stimulates meaningful spoken and written communication, is personally meaningful to learners, and encourages group solidarity. It involves direct strategies like using resources, practicing naturalistically, taking notes, summarizing, and guessing, along with various indirect strategies.

Materials

Reference books (e.g., dictionaries, grammar books).

Time

Variable, depending on proficiency level and your own intention for how to use this multiphase project.

Instructions

1. List Interview Questions.   Ask your students as a group to call out questions that would be good to use in interviewing each other. Make a list in the new language. Post it on the board or give everyone a copy. Tell the students they do not have to use all these questions, and they can make up additional ones.

2. Conduct Interviews.   Ask the students to find a partner to interview. One student in the pair interviews the other one, finding out interesting details about that person's life. Then they switch roles, with the second person interviewing the first. You should put a realistic time limit on the interviews and inform the students of this in advance. (They can meet at another time on their own if they want to continue.)

3. Write Articles, Get Feedback, and Revise.   Now each student uses the information from the interview to write an article about the interviewee. The writer checks what he or she has written with the interviewee to make sure that the facts are all correct and that the person is willing to have those facts in print! In addition, the partners help each other with style, tone, organization, and language. Then each pair meets with another pair to swap articles and get further feedback on content, style, tone, organization, and language.

4. Publish Articles.   When the articles are as good as they can be on the basis of this feedback, they are posted on the bulletin board, or else put together in a class magazine.

Note   You may have to help students with vocabulary and grammar from time to time, but restrain yourself from "red-inking" all the errors. The point is to get the message across, even if it is not perfect. Provide plenty of printed resources in accessible places so students can help themselves to improve their writing after the interview phase is over.

Source   Original.

Exercise 3.22. Sending a Telegram

Purpose

This exercise gives learners a chance to express themselves in writing in an important and personally meaningful situation, just as in real life. Many cognitive and compensation strategies are required to do this task.

Materials

Telegram forms (see Figure 3.18 for an example in Russian).

Ф. ТГ-1

ПЕРЕДАЧА

го ——— час. ——— мин.

№ связи

Передал.

Служебн. отметки

МИНИСТЕРСТВО СВЯЗИ СССР

ТЕЛЕГРАММА

Из

№

сл. ——— го ——— час. ——— мин.

Плата

руб. коп.

С л о в

Итого

Принял

Категория и отметки особого вида:

Куда, кому

Фамилия отправителя и его адрес (в счет слов не входят, не оплачиваются и по телеграфу не передаются).

Тип «Ставр. правда», 1971 г. №1 13.900.00

куда, кому.

В начале телеграммы перед текстом пишется категория (срочная), особый вид (уведомление телеграфом, вручить лично, ответ и др.),

Figure 3.18 Russian Telegram Form. (*Source:* Culhane (1986, p. 20.)

Time

Variable.

Instructions

Give your students the following instructions, *modified to fit the language and culture:* You will work in pairs. Person 1 is due to go from Leningrad to Moscow by plane. Person 1 discovers that Pulkovo Airport in Leningrad is closed and will not be open for another 4 days. Person 1 will have to send a telegram to Person 2 saying that Person 1 will be coming by train instead of plane, arriving in Moscow at 10:00 a.m. on Wednesday, August 8. Person 2 needs to respond to that telegram with another telegram, telling Person 1 that Person 2 got the message and indicating exactly where Person 2 will meet Person 1 at the Moscow train station (by the magazine racks, at the information desk, etc.).

Source Adapted from Culhane (1986, pp. 115 and 120).

Exercise 3.23. Doctor's Appointment

Purpose

This exercise gives learners practice in planning an upcoming language task and then demonstrating comprehension and production. A range of direct strategies is necessary, such as taking notes, practicing naturalistically, recombining, guessing, and using synonyms—along with indirect strategies of various types.

Materials

(Optional) Teacher-prepared audiotapes and scripts of conversations relevant to the task.

Time

The exercise is divided into three 1-hour segments.

Instructions

Tell students the following in your own words: You need to make a doctor's appointment for yourself over the telephone.

1. Identify the situation. The task, making a doctor's appointment over the telephone, requires that you have to speak with the receptionist, explain the symptoms, and arrange a convenient time. (What are your

symptoms? Define them. If the symptoms are acute, you'll need an immediate appointment! If not, the appointment is not so urgent.)

2. Consider the general functions required by the task. You will probably need greetings, requests, giving biographical information, describing symptoms, getting directions, thanking, and leave-taking.

3. Check your own resources. This means considering whether you are able to do all the functions—that is, whether you have all the vocabulary and forms needed.

4. Decide what else is needed and work on it. For instance, if you cannot yet describe symptoms in the target language, this is what you will need to work on.

5. Now listen to several samples of relevant conversations provided by the teacher on audiotape, and analyze scripts of the conversation by identifying expressions that accomplish the necessary functions (e.g., greetings, requests). Take notes of the key expressions.

6. If audiotapes of the situation are not available, work with others in a small group and discuss possible expressions that would accomplish the necessary functions (e.g., greetings, requests). Possibly ask for help from a native speaker. Take notes of the key expressions.

7. With other people, think of problems or issues that might arise, and expressions that would be necessary to handle them. Take notes.

8. Rehearse the key expressions, putting them together in a reasonable sequence, as for a real telephone conversation.

9. Now that you are ready, role-play the telephone call to the doctor's office, with one person playing the sick person and the other playing the receptionist. It is possible to do this in fours, with two people playing the sick person and coaching each other (helping by adding information that may have been forgotten) and two people playing the receptionist in the same way.

10. Now evaluate the results—what was understood and what was not, and reasons why. Make notes of specific problems: word order, sounds, politeness expressions. Decide why these problems might have occurred and what to do next time.

Alternative

You, rather than a student, might play the doctor's receptionist in the role-play if desired. It might be less tense if learners played both roles, however.

Source Adapted from Stewner-Manzanares, Chamot, O'Malley, Kupper, and Russo (1985, p. 33).

Chapter 4

Indirect Strategies for General Management of Learning

They know enough who know how to learn.

HENRY ADAMS

PREVIEW QUESTIONS

1. What are indirect strategies?
2. How do they differ from direct strategies?
3. Why are indirect strategies important for language learning?
4. What are the three groups of indirect strategies?

INTRODUCTION TO INDIRECT STRATEGIES

This chapter discusses the indirect strategies that underpin the business of language learning. Indirect strategies are divided into metacognitive, affective, and social (see Figure 4.1). Metacognitive strategies allow learners to control their own cognition—that is, to coordinate the learning process by using functions such as centering, arranging, planning, and evaluating. Affective strategies help to regulate emotions, motivations, and attitudes. Social strategies help students learn through interaction with others. All these strategies are called "indirect" because they support and manage language learning without (in many instances) directly involving the target language. The indirect strategies explained here work in tandem with the direct strategies described earlier. Indirect strategies are useful in virtually all language learning situations and are applicable to all four language skills: listening, reading, speaking, and writing.

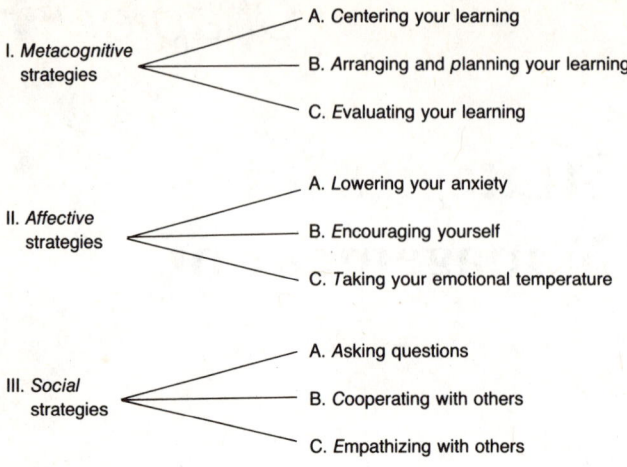

I. *Metacognitive* strategies
- A. Centering your learning
- B. Arranging and planning your learning
- C. Evaluating your learning

II. *Affective* strategies
- A. Lowering your anxiety
- B. Encouraging yourself
- C. Taking your emotional temperature

III. *Social* strategies
- A. Asking questions
- B. Cooperating with others
- C. Empathizing with others

Memory Aids: CAPE, LET, ACE

Figure 4.1   Diagram of the Indirect Strategies: Overview. (*Source*: Original.)

METACOGNITIVE STRATEGIES

"Metacognitive" means beyond, beside, or with the cognitive. Therefore, metacognitive strategies are actions which go beyond purely cognitive devices, and which provide a way for learners to coordinate their own learning process. Metacognitive strategies include three strategy sets: Centering Your Learning, *A*rranging and *P*lanning Your Learning, and *E*valuating Your Learning. Ten strategies form these three groups, the acronym for which is CAPE (see Figure 4.2). Remember these strategy sets by saying, "Metacognitive strategies make language learners more CAPE-able."

Metacognitive strategies are essential for successful language learning. Language learners are often overwhelmed by too much "newness"—unfamiliar vocabulary, confusing rules, different writing systems, seemingly inexplicable social customs, and (in enlightened language classes) nontraditional instructional approaches. With all this novelty, many learners lose their focus, which can only be regained by the conscious use of metacognitive strategies such as paying attention and overviewing/linking with already familiar material.

Other metacognitive strategies, like organizing, setting goals and objectives, considering the purpose, and planning for a language task, help learners to arrange and plan their language learning in an efficient, effective way. The metacognitive strategy of seeking practice opportunities is especially important. Learners who are seriously interested in learning a new

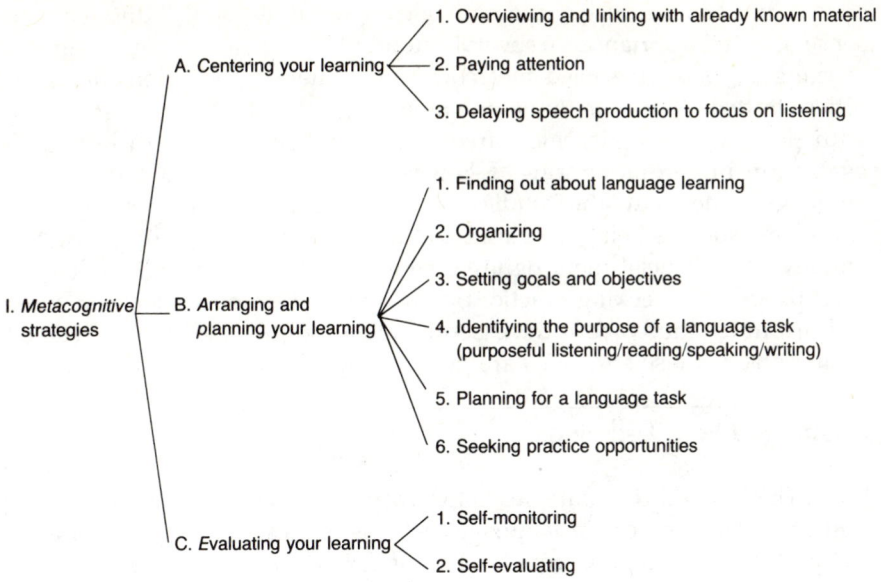

A. Centering your learning
1. Overviewing and linking with already known material
2. Paying attention
3. Delaying speech production to focus on listening

I. *Metacognitive* strategies

B. *Arranging and planning your learning*
1. Finding out about language learning
2. Organizing
3. Setting goals and objectives
4. Identifying the purpose of a language task (purposeful listening/reading/speaking/writing)
5. Planning for a language task
6. Seeking practice opportunities

C. *Evaluating your learning*
1. Self-monitoring
2. Self-evaluating

Memory Aid: CAPE

"Metacognitive strategies make language learners more CAPE-able."

A mighty maze! But not without a plan.
Alexander Pope

Figure 4.2   Diagram of the Metacognitive Strategies. (*Source*: Original.)

language must take responsibility to seek as many practice opportunities as possible, usually outside of the classroom. Even in a second language situation, ripe with opportunities for practice, learners must actively search for, and take advantage of, these possibilities.

Sometimes language learners have problems in realistically monitoring their errors. Students may become traumatized when they make errors, thus failing to realize that they will undoubtedly make them and should therefore try to learn from them. Students may also underrate or overrate their proficiency. Confusion about overall progress is made worse by the academic grading system, which generally rewards discrete-point rule-learning rather than communicative competence. These problems—unrealistic monitoring of errors and inadequate evaluation of progress—can be ameliorated by using the metacognitive strategies of self-monitoring and self-evaluating [1].

Though metacognitive strategies are extremely important, research shows that learners use these strategies sporadically and without much sense of their importance. In several studies of second and foreign language learning [2], students used metacognitive strategies less often than cognitive strategies and were limited in their range of metacognitive strategies, with planning strategies most frequently employed and with little self-evaluation or self-monitoring. Likewise, university and military foreign language students in other studies [3] reported using certain metacognitive strategies, such as being prepared and using time well, but they failed to employ other crucial metacognitive strategies, like accurately evaluating their progress or seeking practice opportunities. Obviously, learners need to learn much more about the essential metacognitive strategies. Detailed definitions of these strategies are given below.

Centering Your Learning

This set of three strategies helps learners to converge their attention and energies on certain language tasks, activities, skills, or materials. Use of these strategies provides a focus for language learning.

1. Overviewing and Linking with Already Known Material

Overviewing comprehensively a key concept, principle, or set of materials in an upcoming language activity and associating it with what is already known. This strategy can be accomplished in many different ways, but it is often helpful to follow three steps: learning why the activity is being done, building the needed vocabulary, and making the associations [4].

2. Paying Attention

Deciding in advance to pay attention in general to a language learning task and to ignore distractors (by *directed attention*), and/or *to pay attention to specific aspects* of the language or to situational details (by *selective attention*).

3. Delaying Speech Production to Focus on Listening

Deciding in advance to delay speech production in the new language either totally or partially, until listening comprehension skills are better developed. Some language theorists encourage a "silent period" of delayed speech as part of the curriculum, but there is debate as to whether all students require this [5].

Arranging and Planning Your Learning

This set contains six strategies, all of which help learners to organize and plan so as to get the most out of language learning. These strategies touch many areas: finding out about language learning, organizing the schedule and the environment, setting goals and objectives, considering task purposes, planning for tasks, and seeking chances to practice the language.

1. Finding Out About Language Learning

Making efforts to find out how language learning works by reading books and talking with other people, and then using this information to help improve one's own language learning.

2. Organizing

Understanding and using conditions related to optimal learning of the new language; organizing one's schedule, physical environment (e.g., space, temperature, sound, lighting), and language learning notebook.

3. Setting Goals and Objectives

Setting aims for language learning, including long-term goals (such as being able to use the language for informal conversation by the end of the year) or short-term objectives (such as finishing reading a short story by Friday).

4. Identifying the Purpose of a Language Task

Deciding the purpose of a particular language task involving listening, reading, speaking, or writing. For example, listening to the radio to get the latest news on the stock exchange, reading a play for enjoyment, speaking to the cashier to buy a train ticket, writing a letter to persuade a friend not to do something rash. (This is sometimes known as *Purposeful Listening/Speaking/Reading/Writing.*)

5. Planning for a Language Task

Planning for the language elements and functions necessary for an anticipated language task or situation. This strategy includes four steps: describing the task or situation, determining its requirements, checking one's own linguistic resources, and determining additional language elements or functions necessary for the task or situation.

6. Seeking Practice Opportunities

Seeking out or creating opportunities to practice the new language in naturalistic situations, such as going to a second/foreign language cinema, attending a party where the language will be spoken, or joining an international social club. Consciously thinking in the new language also provides practice opportunities.

Evaluating Your Learning

In this set are two related strategies, both aiding learners in checking their language performance. One strategy involves noticing and learning from errors, and the other concerns evaluating overall progress.

1. Self-Monitoring

Identifying errors in understanding or producing the new language, determining which ones are important (those that cause serious confusion or offense), tracking the source of important errors, and trying to eliminate such errors.

2. Self-Evaluating

Evaluating one's own progress in the new language, for instance, by checking to see whether one is reading faster and understanding more than 1 month or 6 months ago, or whether one is understanding a greater percentage of each conversation.

AFFECTIVE STRATEGIES

The term *affective* refers to emotions, attitudes, motivations, and values. It is impossible to overstate the importance of the affective factors influencing language learning. Language learners can gain control over these factors through affective strategies. As shown in Figure 4.3, three main sets of affective strategies exist: Lowering Your Anxiety, Encouraging Yourself, and Taking Your Emotional Temperature (10 strategies in all). The acronym LET comes from the first letter of each one of these strategy sets—"affective strategies help language learners LET their hair down!"

"The affective domain is impossible to describe within definable limits," according to H. Douglas Brown [6]. It spreads out like a fine-spun net, encompassing such concepts as self-esteem, attitudes, motivation, anxiety, culture shock, inhibition, risk taking, and tolerance for ambiguity [7]. The affective side of the learner is probably one of the very biggest influences on language learning success or failure. Good language learners are often those who know how to control their emotions and attitudes about learning [8]. Negative feelings can stunt progress, even for the rare learner who fully understands all the technical aspects of how to learn a new language. On the other hand, positive emotions and attitudes can make language learning far more effective and enjoyable. Teachers can exert a tremendous influence over the emotional atmosphere of the classroom in three different ways: by changing the social structure of the classroom to give students more responsibility, by providing increased amounts

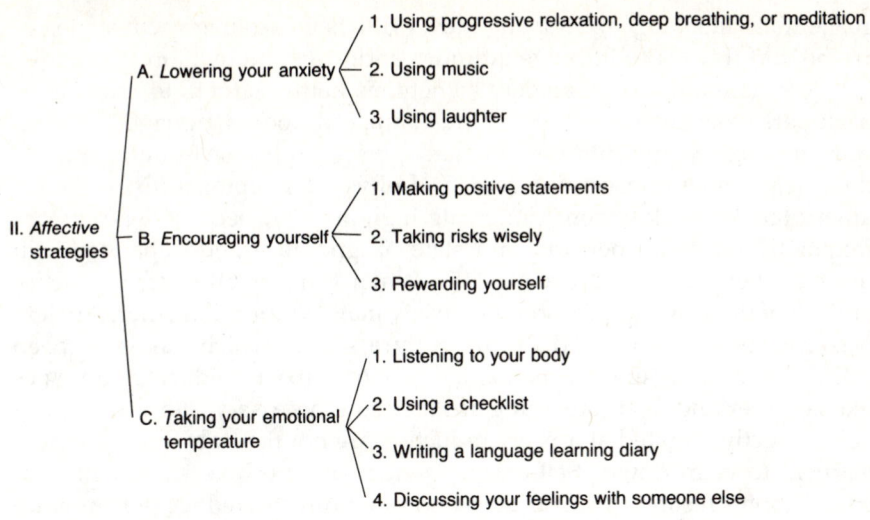

> *The mind is its own place, and in itself can make a Heaven of Hell, a Hell of Heaven.*
> John Milton

Figure 4.3 Diagram of the Affective Strategies. (*Source*: Original.)

of naturalistic communication, and by teaching learners to use affective strategies.

Self-esteem is one of the primary affective elements. It is a self-judgment of worth or value, based on a feeling of efficacy—a sense of interacting effectively with one's own environment [9]. Low self-esteem can be detected through negative self-talk, like "Boy, am I a blockhead! I embarrassed myself again in front of the class." The three affective strategies related to self-encouragement help learners to counter such negativity.

The sense of efficacy that underlies self-esteem is reflected in attitudes (mental dispositions, beliefs, or opinions), which influence the learner's motivation to keep on trying to learn [10]. Attitudes are strong predictors of motivation in any area of life, and especially in language learning [11]. Just as attitudes affect motivation, attitudes and motivation work together to influence language learning performance itself—including both global language proficiency and proficiency in specific language skills, such as listening comprehension, reading comprehension, and oral production [12]. In addition, research findings suggest that the combined attitude/motivation factor strongly influences whether the learner loses or maintains language skills after language training is over [13]. Self-encouragement strategies are powerful ways to improve attitudes and, thus, motivation [14].

A certain amount of anxiety sometimes helps learners to reach their peak performance levels, but too much anxiety blocks language learning. Harmful anxiety presents itself in many guises: worry, self-doubt, frustration, helplessness, insecurity, fear, and physical symptoms. Even the ordinary language classroom can create high anxiety, because learners are frequently forced to perform in a state of ignorance and dependence in front of their peers and teacher [15]. When learners attempt to practice outside of the language classroom, anxiety may mount still further. Anxiety becomes most pronounced during culture shock, which has even been called a form of temporary mental illness [16]. Anxiety-reducing strategies like laughter and deep breathing are therefore necessary. However, strategies directly targeted at anxiety reduction are not the only ones that help learners to calm down. Self-encouragement via positive statements can change one's feelings and attitudes and can indirectly reduce performance anxiety, including the tension which surrounds test taking [17]. In addition, the self-assessment strategies listed under Taking Your Emotional Temperature help learners realize when they are anxious. Listening to bodily signals is an especially helpful strategy for discovering and controlling anxiety.

The language learner who is overly anxious, either in a typical language classroom or in a more serious culture shock situation, is likely to be inhibited and unwilling to take even moderate risks. Successful language learning necessitates overcoming inhibitions and learning to take reasonable risks, as in guessing meanings or speaking up despite the possibility of making a mistake [18]. Inhibited learners are paralyzed by actual or anticipated criticism from other people and from themselves, so they try to ensure that there are as few "chinks in their armor" as possible [19]. Self-encouragement and anxiety-reducing strategies can help learners lower their inhibitions and take appropriate risks [20].

Tolerance of ambiguity—that is, the acceptance of confusing situations—may be related to willingness to take risks (and also reduction of both inhibition and anxiety). Moderate tolerance for ambiguity, like moderate risk taking, is probably the most desirable situation. Learners who are moderately tolerant of ambiguity tend to be open-minded in dealing with confusing facts and events, which are part of learning a new language. In contrast, low ambiguity-tolerant learners, wanting to categorize and compartmentalize too soon, have a hard time dealing with unclear facts and events. One study [21] discovered that tolerance for ambiguity was one of the two factors that predicted success in foreign language learning. Other studies have found that language learners who are tolerant of ambiguity are more successful in certain language tasks [22] and may use somewhat more effective learning strategies than learners who are less tolerant of ambiguity and who need to seek rapid closure [23].

Again, self-encouragement and anxiety-reducing strategies help learners cope with ambiguity in language learning.

Few studies have examined the frequency of use of affective strategies, but those which have done so reveal that these strategies are woefully underused—reported by about 1 in every 20 language learners [24]. This situation is distressing, given the power of affective strategies. These strategies are useful for the vast majority of language learners who have ordinary hang-ups and difficulties. However, these strategies are not intended as a substitute for psychotherapy or a mechanism for solving deep psychological problems, nor can they single-handedly change general traits, such as low global self-esteem [25]. With this in mind, consider the following affective strategies and their definitions.

Lowering Your Anxiety

Three anxiety-reducing strategies are listed here. Each has a physical component and a mental component.

1. Using Progressive Relaxation, Deep Breathing, or Meditation

Using the technique of *alternately tensing and relaxing* all of the major muscle groups in the body, as well as the muscles in the neck and face, in order to relax; or the technique of *breathing deeply* from the diaphragm; or the technique of *meditating by focusing* on a mental image or sound.

2. Using Music

Listening to soothing music, such as a classical concert, as a way to relax.

3. Using Laughter

Using laughter to relax by watching a funny movie, reading a humorous book, listening to jokes, and so on.

Encouraging Yourself

This set of three strategies is often forgotten by language learners, especially those who expect encouragement mainly from other people and do not realize they can provide their own. However, the most potent encouragement—and the *only* available encouragement in many independent language learning situations—may come from inside the learner. Self-encouragement includes saying supportive things, prodding oneself to take risks wisely, and providing rewards.

1. Making Positive Statements

Saying or writing positive statements to oneself in order to feel more confident in learning the new language.

2. Taking Risks Wisely

Pushing oneself to take risks in a language learning situation, even though there is a chance of making a mistake or looking foolish. Risks must be tempered with good judgment.

3. Rewarding Yourself

Giving oneself a valuable reward for a particularly good performance in the new language.

Taking Your Emotional Temperature

The four strategies in this set help learners to assess their feelings, motivations, and attitudes and, in many cases, to relate them to language tasks. Unless learners know how they are feeling and why they are feeling that way, they are less able to control their affective side. The strategies in this set are particularly helpful for discerning negative attitudes and emotions that impede language learning progress.

1. Listening to Your Body

Paying attention to signals given by the body. These signals may be negative, reflecting stress, tension, worry, fear, and anger; or they may be positive, indicating happiness, interest, calmness, and pleasure.

2. Using a Checklist

Using a checklist to discover feelings, attitudes, and motivations concerning language learning in general, as well as concerning specific language tasks.

3. Writing a Language Learning Diary

Writing a diary or journal to keep track of events and feelings in the process of learning a new language.

4. Discussing Your Feelings with Someone Else

Talking with another person (teacher, friend, relative) to discover and express feelings about language learning.

SOCIAL STRATEGIES

Language is a form of social behavior; it is communication, and communication occurs between and among people. Learning a language thus involves other people, and appropriate social strategies are very important in this process. Three sets of social strategies, each set comprising two

specific strategies (see Figure 4.4), are included here: *Asking Questions,
Cooperating with Others,* and *Empathizing with Others.* These can be
remembered by using their acronym, ACE: "ACE language learners use
social strategies!"

One of the most basic social interactions is asking questions, an action
from which learners gain great benefit. Asking questions helps learners
get closer to the intended meaning and thus aids their understanding. It
also helps learners encourage their conversation partners to provide larger
quantities of "input" in the target language and indicates interest and
involvement. Moreover, the conversation partner's response to the learner's question indicates whether the question itself was understood, thus
providing indirect feedback about the learner's production skills. The content of questions is important, of course. One social strategy concerns
asking questions for clarification (when something is not understood) or
verification (when the learner wants to check whether something is correct).
A related social strategy involves asking for correction, which is especially
useful in the classroom. The classroom setting provides much more overt
correction than do natural, informal social settings.

In addition to asking questions, cooperating in general—with peers
and with more proficient users of the target language—is imperative for
language learners. Cooperation implies the absence of competition and the
presence of group spirit. It involves a cooperative task structure or a cooperative reward structure [26], either of which can encourage "positive

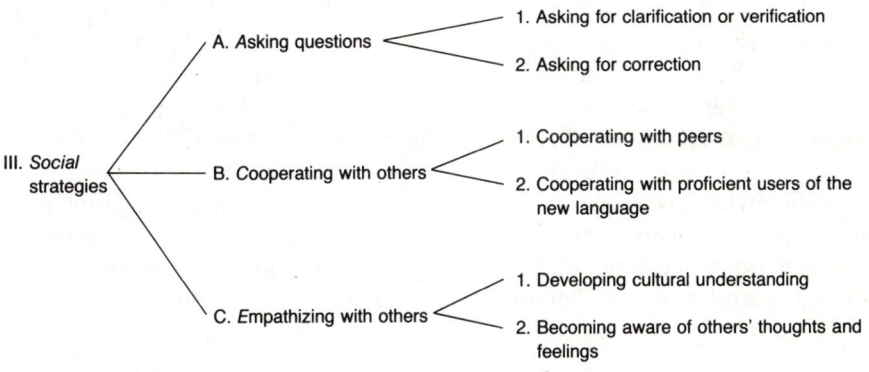

Memory Aid: ACE

"ACE language learners use social strategies!"

*Probably no greater need exists than to learn how to participate effectively. . . . Humans are, and always
have been, social animals.*

James Botkin

Figure 4.4   Diagram of the Social Strategies. (*Source*: Original.)

interdependence" and mutual support [27]. Many studies outside of the language learning field have strongly demonstrated the utility of cooperative learning strategies [28]. Cooperative learning consistently shows the following significant effects: higher self-esteem; increased confidence and enjoyment; greater and more rapid achievement; more respect for the teacher, the school, and the subject; use of higher-level cognitive strategies; decreased prejudice; and increased altruism and mutual concern [29]. In the area of language learning, cooperative strategies have accrued the same benefits, as well as the following additional advantages: better student and teacher satisfaction, stronger language learning motivation, more language practice opportunities, more feedback about language errors, and greater use of different language functions [30].

However, cooperative strategies might not be second nature to all language learners. Research shows that on their own, with no special training or encouragement, language learners do *not* typically report a natural preference for cooperative strategies [31]. Competition is strongly reinforced by the educational establishment, with schools often pitting students against each other in competition for approval, attention, and grades in all subject areas, including language learning [32]. Although competition might sometimes result in a positive desire to improve and do better than other people, more often it results in debilitating anxiety, inadequacy, guilt, hostility, withdrawal, fear of failure, and desire for approval [33]. To promote cooperative language learning strategies, either inside or outside the classroom, it might be necessary to help learners confront—and possibly modify—their culturally defined attitudes toward cooperation and competition.

Empathy is the ability to "put yourself in someone else's shoes" in order to better understand that person's perspective. Empathy is essential to successful communication in *any* language; it is especially necessary, although sometimes difficult to achieve, in learning another language. People differ in their natural ability to feel and demonstrate empathy. However, social strategies can help all learners increase their ability to emphathize by developing cultural understanding and becoming aware of others' thoughts and feelings. Following is a list of social strategies and their definitions.

Asking Questions

This set of strategies involves asking someone, possibly a teacher or native speaker or even a more proficient fellow learner, for clarification, verification, or correction.

1. Asking for Clarification or Verification

Asking the speaker to repeat, paraphrase, explain, slow down, or give examples; asking if a specific utterance is correct or if a rule fits a particular case;

paraphrasing or repeating to get feedback on whether something is correct.

2. Asking for Correction

Asking someone for correction in a conversation. This strategy most often occurs in conversation but may also be applied to writing.

Cooperating with Others

This set of two strategies involves interacting with one or more people to improve language skills. These strategies are the basis of cooperative language learning, which not only increases learners' language performance but also enhances self-worth and social acceptance.

1. Cooperating with Peers

Working with other language learners to improve language skills. This strategy can involve a regular learning partner or a temporary pair or small group. This strategy frequently involves controlling impulses toward competitiveness and rivalry.

2. Cooperating with Proficient Users of the New Language

Working with native speakers or other proficient users of the new language, usually outside of the language classroom. This strategy involves particular attention to the conversational roles each person takes.

Empathizing with Others

Empathy can be developed more easily when language learners use these two strategies.

1. Developing Cultural Understanding

Trying to empathize with another person through learning about the culture, and trying to understand the other person's relation to that culture.

2. Becoming Aware of Others' Thoughts and Feelings

Observing the behaviors of others as a possible expression of their thoughts and feelings; and when appropriate, asking about thoughts and feelings of others.

SUMMARY

This chapter described the significance of three groups of indirect strategies: metacognitive, affective, and social. For each of these groups, specific strategies were identified and defined. Indirect strategies are an essential counterpart to direct strategies, which were described in Chapters 2 and 3.

ACTIVITIES FOR READERS

Activity 4.1. Consider a Difficult Subject

Although you might be a teacher, consider your previous experience as a student. This will help you understand what students face as they cope with a new subject.

1. Write down three examples of times when a new subject seemed overwhelming to you owing to its novelty, complexity, difficulty, or scope.
2. Then choose the single most interesting example and discuss what made that subject so difficult to you.
3. Now list your affective (emotional and attitudinal) responses to that subject and explain what strategies you used to cope with those responses.
4. Consider your metacognitive control over the subject. For instance, describe how you tried to focus your efforts and organize your environment, schedule, and materials. Explain what you did about setting goals and finding practice opportunities. Cite any efforts to evaluate your own progress.

Activity 4.2. Experiment with Metacognitive and Affective Strategies

Metacognitive and affective strategies are useful for any area of learning or work. This week try out at least one metacognitive strategy and one affective strategy you do not ordinarily use. Write down the effects of your experiment and discuss them with other people. What did you do that was most effective? What did you do that was least effective?

Activity 4.3. Ask Questions

Consider your questioning style by trying the following:

1. When you are talking with native speakers of a language that is not your own, observe how often you ask questions for clarification, verification, or correction.
2. Do you tend to use questioning techniques more often with some people than with others? Why or why not?

3. Observe your own behavior in your native language. Do you ask questions for clarification, verification, or correction in your own native language? If so, under what circumstances, and with whom? Do you use questioning in the same way in your native language as in the target language?

Activity 4.4. Judge Your Empathy

How much empathy do you have for others? Do you think you identify well with others or not? How do you feel this influences your ability to learn languages? To get along with other people? Give specific examples to back up your statements. How can the strategies listed under Empathizing with Others help you increase your empathy? How can you help others, especially your students, strengthen their empathy?

Activity 4.5. Weigh Competitiveness and Cooperation

In a small group or by yourself, answer the following questions:

1. Do you agree with the statements in this chapter about the effects of competitiveness and cooperation in language learning? Why or why not?
2. Have you ever felt competitive in a language learning experience? If yes, what were the circumstances? What aspects of the situation, or of yourself, might have encouraged you to feel competitive? Is this a typical learning mode for you?
3. In what ways have you exercised cooperation in language learning? Was this in a classroom setting or in a naturalistic language situation? What differences in types of cooperation exist between these two kinds of environments?

EXERCISES TO USE WITH YOUR STUDENTS

Exercise 4.1. Listen to Self-Talk

Ask your students how often they say positive things to themselves about language learning. Ask them to list all the positive things they say and to explain how these statements make them feel about themselves and about continuing their language learning.

Now request that your students list all the negative things they say to themselves, and ask how these negative statements affect their self-esteem as language learners.

Exercise 4.2. Let Students Consider Cooperation and Competition

Run a cooperative learning activity—one which has either a cooperative task or a cooperative reward or both, and which therefore encourages cooperative learning strategies. Afterwards, discuss with your students how they felt about that activity and about learning cooperatively in general. Ask them how they have reacted to cooperative learning experiences in other classes, and encourage them to give specific examples.

Now ask students about their feelings of competition with their peers, both in the language class and in other classes. Find out whether they are more comfortable with competition than with cooperation. Discuss with your students what they would need to increase their use of cooperative strategies in the language class.

Exercise 4.3. Try Out Indirect Strategies

In order to stimulate greater use of a range of indirect strategies, ask students to do any or all of the following activities listed above for readers of this book: Activities 4.1, 4.2, 4.3, or 4.4. Assess results. You might need to modify some of the directions slightly for use with students. Make sure there is time to discuss the results.

Chapter 5

Applying Indirect Strategies to the Four Language Skills

Order is the shape on which beauty depends.

PEARL BUCK

PREVIEW QUESTIONS

1. How can the indirect strategies be applied to the four language skills?
2. How are these strategies applied differently to the four skills?
3. Are any indirect strategies especially useful to development of a particular skill?

INTRODUCTION TO APPLYING THE INDIRECT STRATEGIES

This chapter shows how learners can apply the indirect strategies—metacognitive, affective, and social—to each of the four language skills. These powerful strategies are shown in Figure 5.1. As in Chapter 3, examples of applications of strategies to the different skills are indicated after the section title, like this: Ⓛ (listening), Ⓡ (reading), Ⓢ (speaking), Ⓦ (writing), Ⓐ (all skills). Although this chapter focuses on applications of indirect strategies, remember that indirect strategies work best when used in combination with direct strategies. By definition, *direct strategies* involve the new language directly, whereas *indirect strategies* provide indirect support for language learning through focusing, planning, evaluating, seeking opportunities, controlling anxiety, increasing cooperation and empathy, and other means.

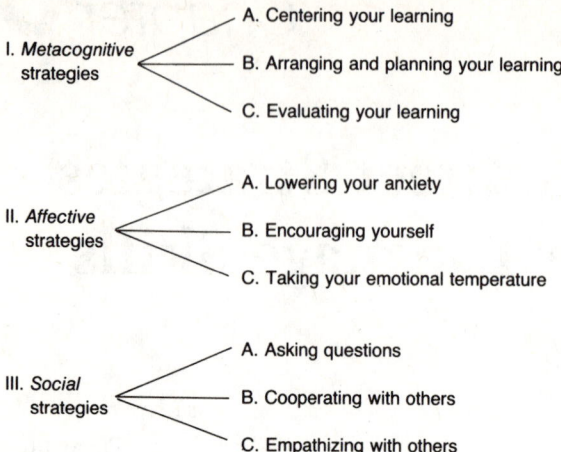

I. *Metacognitive* strategies
- A. Centering your learning
- B. Arranging and planning your learning
- C. Evaluating your learning

II. *Affective* strategies
- A. Lowering your anxiety
- B. Encouraging yourself
- C. Taking your emotional temperature

III. *Social* strategies
- A. Asking questions
- B. Cooperating with others
- C. Empathizing with others

Figure 5.1 Diagram of the Indirect Strategies to Be Applied to the Four Language Skills. (*Source*: Original.)

APPLYING METACOGNITIVE STRATEGIES TO THE FOUR SKILLS

The three sets of metacognitive strategies displayed in Figure 5.2 (Centering Your Learning, Arranging and Planning Your Learning, and Evaluating Your Learning) are useful in developing all the language skills.

Centering Your Learning

Finding a focus or center for learning is important no matter what the language skill. Without appropriate strategies for centering, language learners face merely confusion and noise.

Overviewing and Linking with Already Known Material (A) This strategy involves previewing the basic principles and/or material (including new vocabulary) for an upcoming language activity, and linking these with what the learners already know. Exactly how this strategy is used depends in part on the skill level of the learners. With higher-level students, you can be less directive in helping them learn to use this strategy. Regardless of the students' level, let students express their own linkages between new material and what they already know, rather than pointing out all the associations yourself. Following are examples of the overviewing/linking strategy applied to each of the four language skills. Although the target

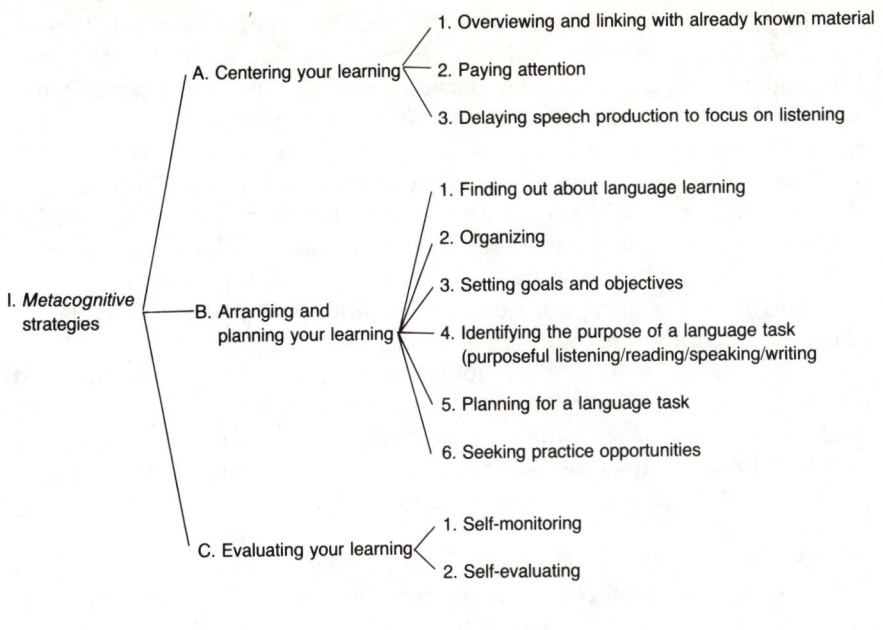

The gods help them that help themselves.

Aesop

Figure 5.2 Diagram of the Metacognitive Strategies to Be Applied to the Four Language Skills. (*Source*: Original.)

language is sometimes shown in these examples, the main focus is on the act of overviewing/linking, not on how the language is used in that act.

Preparing for a listening exercise, Ricky and his classmates preview French vocabulary about irritation and exasperation, like *C'est insupportable, inadmissable, inacceptable, révoltant, dégoûtant, incroyable!, Ça m'énerve*, and so on, because they know their upcoming task will be to check off these phrases as they hear them on the tape. As they preview, Ricky and his friends demonstrate each expression in the context of a sentence, add some other relevant French expressions they already know, and finally compare the French expressions for irritation with those in their own language.

Anh, a refugee learning English, sees that the next story to be read is about workers in a big city. She overviews the material and considers how the troubles of the workers in the story relate to her own struggles to get a good job. Mac overviews the upcoming Russian lesson in the grammar book concerning seasons and times of day. He rapidly sees that the handling of seasons and times is different in Russian and English, as in the contracted Russian expressions *lyetom* [летом] (in the summer), *utrom* [утром] (in the morning), among others.

In preparing for an Italian role-play about a family going to Naples on vacation, Katalin and her small group create role descriptions of each of the family members. Then they discuss their best and worst family vacations and identify ways in which an Italian vacation might be different from their own experiences.

Getting ready to do a writing assignment, Saskia does 10 minutes of "nonstop writing," a kind of written brainstorming in which ideas are not censored [1]. At other times, Saskia brainstorms out loud with a small group or participates in debates to generate ideas for writing [2]. Such activities help her bring out her own existing ideas and start expanding them as preparation for the future writing task.

In any of the skill areas, vocabulary building can be an important part of the overviewing/linking strategy. Students can help each other create and expand lists of relevant vocabulary for an upcoming language task, putting those expressions into context and considering similar (or contrasting) expressions in the native language.

Paying Attention Ⓐ The strategy of paying attention is necessary for all of the language skills. This strategy involves two modes, *directed attention* and *selective attention*. Directed attention (almost equivalent to "concentration") means deciding *generally or globally* to pay attention to the task and avoid irrelevant distractors. In contrast, selective attention involves deciding in advance to notice *particular details*. Encourage directed attention by providing interesting activities and materials, reducing classroom distractions, reminding students to focus, and rewarding them when they do so. Facilitate selective attention by giving learners an incomplete chart to fill out, a table or checklist on which to mark details, or some other activity which requires attention to specifics.

Both of these attention modes, directed and selective, are important for listening. For instance, Murray's mind begins to wander when he is listening to someone talk in the new language, so he consciously directs his attention to the conversation. In a Spanish-language simulation about catching a plane at the airport, Reinhardt quickly learns that he must notice the announcements about times of arrival and departure for his plane. Janos selectively notes expressions as he hears them, using a checklist provided by the teacher.

In reading, Emily decides to pay close attention to the way characters in her German short story bring conversations to a close and how they use polite phrases. In reading a Tolstoy novel in Russian, Chloë focuses on the names and tries to remember who's who—sometimes a tall order! Bertolt decides to focus on ways in which the French past tense forms are used in front-page articles in *Le Monde*.

Full participation in spoken communication demands directing attention to the general context and content. Learners can also pay selective attention to particular elements of the speech act, such as pronunciation, register, style, physical distance from other speakers, grammar, and vocabulary. For instance, Lorraine, a student of Russian, decides to engage herself fully in the conversation with her Russian friends, and in the conversation she intends to pay special attention to using the correct forms of nouns and pronouns after prepositions. In his oral report in German, Alain concentrates on making his spoken argument as logical as possible. Rifka tries to set a melancholy mood as she tells her story in English.

Writing in the new language, like writing in the native language, requires directed attention. For instance, Sangeeta determines she will concentrate wholeheartedly on writing a letter in her new language, Chinese, blocking out noise and interruptions until she is finished. For writing, selective attention may mean deciding in advance which aspects of the writing to focus on at any given time, like structure, content, tone, sentence construction, vocabulary, punctuation, or audience needs. Especially for beginners, it is hard to pay attention to all these elements at once. Here are some examples of selective attention applied to writing. In writing his French paper Karl keeps constantly in mind the informational needs of the reader and tries to structure the paper to address those needs. Marijke decides to focus on phraseology in writing her article in Spanish. Juan, fresh from a small group discussion, wants to make sure his English essay includes all of the key points from the discussion. These three students are focusing attention on specific aspects of their writing.

Delaying Speech Production to Focus on Listening (L) (S) This strategy relates to listening and speaking rather than reading and writing. You do not have to teach or encourage this strategy, because many learners do it automatically by postponing their speaking in the target language for hours, days, weeks, or possibly even months. This phenomenon is often viewed as a way of focusing on listening comprehension before students feel comfortable enough to speak. The speech delay may be total (no target language speech) or partial (for instance, saying only stock phrases but no creative sentences). The delay occurs because listening is more rapidly developed than speaking, and because speaking seems more threatening to many students. Some instructional theorists have stressed the importance of allowing a "silent period" for all learners, and various language teaching methods reflect this emphasis, but research evidence concerning the significance and optimal length of the silent period is mixed [3]. Help build solid listening comprehension skills, and encourage students to speak as soon as they are ready, without any externally imposed delay.

Here are some examples of delaying speech production. Judy lets others speak in her German class, while she repeats silently to herself, because she does not yet feel confident enough to speak. Aleta, a learner of Russian, says routine phrases such as *dobry den'* [добрый день] (good day), and *do svidaynia* [до свидания] (good-bye), but she does not yet say anything more than these standard phrases. Jon, a traveler in Israel, decides he is ready to try pronouncing the names of the items on the menu, but he feels unable to speak the language in normal conversations with Israelis.

Arranging and Planning Your Learning

The six strategies for arranging and planning are helpful in developing all language skills. These concern discovering the nature of language learning, organizing to learn, establishing aims, considering task purposes, planning for tasks, and looking for chances to practice.

Finding Out About Language Learning (A) This strategy means uncovering what is involved in language learning. Learners often do not know much about the mechanics of language learning, although such knowledge would make them more effective learners. Books about language learning are a good source of information [4]. Help your students by allowing them to talk about their language learning problems, ask questions, and share ideas with each other about effective strategies they have tried. Taking class time to talk about the learning process will reap rewards for the students [5]. All four skills are aided by this strategy, especially if time is allotted to talk about special problems in each of the skills.

Organizing (A) This strategy includes a variety of tools, such as creating the best possible physical environment, scheduling well, and keeping a language learning notebook. First, having the right physical environment is important for every language skill. Listening and reading especially require a comfortable, peaceful setting without too much background noise. Help establish a good classroom environment, and encourage your students to create an appropriate setting for learning at home.

Second, assist your students in developing practical weekly schedules for language learning, with plenty of time devoted to outside-of-class practice in the language skills which are most needed. Note that certain skills like reading and writing are, for many students, best developed with unbroken stretches of time. Relaxation time should be built into the schedule, too, because students can become exhausted with too much work, leading to lowered performance.

Finally, a language learning notebook is an excellent organizational aid to learners. The notebook is useful for writing down new target language expressions or structures and the contexts in which they were encountered, class assignments, goals and objectives, strategies which work well, things to remember, and so on. Encourage your students to obtain a language learning notebook and organize it for the best use.

Setting Goals and Objectives (A) Goals and objectives are expressions of students' aims for language learning. Students without aims are like boats without rudders; they do not know where they are going, so they might never get there! Goals and objectives should be noted in the language learning notebook, along with deadlines for accomplishing them and an indication as to whether those deadlines were met. *Goals* are generally considered to be long-range aims referring to the outcome of many months or even years. *Objectives* are short-term aims for hours, days, or weeks. Aid your students in determining goals and objectives in each of the skill areas, realizing that different students will have different aims. In the examples below, some of the aims reflect full-blown communicative competence, while others reflect relatively minimal skill development.

Some possible goals for listening might be to attain an advanced listening proficiency rating, to be an effective listener in occasional conversations with native speakers, to understand the language well enough for foreign travel, or to be able to hold a job that depends on skilled, in-depth listening. Examples of listening objectives might be as follows. Betty will tune in to the Spanish-language news this evening and will try to understand at least half of it. Bill will visit his French-speaking uncle twice this week and work to improve his listening comprehension. Alden plans to listen to a Chinese tape on the way to work daily for the next 3 weeks.

Reading goals might be to become proficient enough to read professional materials in a technical area, to read magazines or newspapers for pleasure, to read short stories with ease, to understand signposts in the foreign country, to reach a superior reading proficiency level, or to pass the reading exam required for graduate school entrance. Reading objectives might look like these. Johann decides to master the Cyrillic alphabet by Friday, so he can proceed with learning simple Russian words. Kathleen wants to learn a set of vocabulary words this afternoon, so it will be easier for her to read the Italian story tonight. Muriel, who is learning French, plans to finish the Camus novel by the end of the month.

Speaking goals might be to develop sufficient speaking skill to survive in a second language environment, to communicate occasionally with acquaintances who speak the target language, to get a job requiring daily spoken communication in the language, to negotiate foreign travel arrangements, and the like. Sample speaking objectives might be as follows. Sonya decides to master the common German greetings before the next class meets. Manning plans to practice the Russian past tense verb endings this week until he can say them perfectly. Alfonso will speak English for half an hour with his teacher and will apply some of the new conversation management techniques he has just learned.

Goals for writing might include developing enough writing skill to maintain correspondence with foreign friends, to succeed in school or university courses conducted entirely in the target language, to write acceptable business letters, to write scientific articles publishable in international journals, or to pass the language course. Writing objectives might be like the following. Marianne wants to finish her essay within the next few days. Helmuth wants to share the first draft of his autobiography with Wilhelm by the following Tuesday. Edward hopes to meet his early and intermediate writing deadlines, so that he can avoid a "crash" writing effort at the end.

Identifying the Purpose of a Language Task (A) This strategy involves determining the task purpose—an act useful for all language skills. (However, *carrying out* that purpose is the subject of various direct strategies, such as analyzing expressions, guessing, and practicing.) The strategy of considering the purpose is an important one, because knowing the purpose for doing something enables learners to channel their energy in the right direction. Help your students understand the purpose by allowing them to discuss the purpose before doing the task itself.

Figuring out the purpose for listening or speaking is made easier by understanding the kind of speech being used—for instance, casual speech, deliberate speech, reading aloud from a written text, and speaking from a memorized script [6]. Here are some examples of considering the purposes of listening and speaking tasks. When he meets his Italian-speaking friends for a casual lunch on Tuesday, Pierre's chief communication purposes are to have fun, find out how his friends are, and tell them what he has been doing. Juana, who has a job interview in English, has more serious purposes in mind. Her listening purpose is to understand key questions, and her speaking purpose is to respond appropriately and convince the interviewer that she is qualified for the job. In listening to a lecture in Polish, Michael has as his main purpose to understand and take notes on the most salient ideas. Going to a German-language suspense film, Leonida and Pasha have the purpose of using the visuals to help them enhance their understanding of the language and the plot. Meredith's purpose is to ask for information about Nice-to-Paris train schedules and about overnight sleeping accommodations, and to understand that information well enough to purchase an appropriate ticket. Classroom listening and speaking exercises need to become more like these authentic communication tasks, so that task purposes are clear and realistic.

Reading activities are also enhanced by having a clear purpose. Teach your students to look for the purpose in light of the situation and the type of material. Various formats suggest different purposes for reading: looking quickly through the piece to get the main idea or gist (skimming), searching rapidly for a particular piece of information (scanning), reading a longer text for pleasure (extensive reading), and reading a shorter text carefully and in detail (intensive reading) [7]. Following are some examples of reading with a purpose. Myra races through the news article to understand the key idea. Caroline pages rapidly through the German telephone book to find the phone number of the cinema. Sandor relishes the English novel as he reads slowly for pleasure. Bridget reads a Spanish editorial carefully and in detail, trying to separate the assumptions and opinions from the facts.

The purpose of a writing task is related to the type of written format and the needs of the potential audience. Language learners will have a great advantage if they know some possible purposes for writing, such as providing factual information, convincing the audience of the validity of a point, persuading someone to act or think in a certain way, entertaining the audience, making the reader feel an emotion deeply, or evoking a certain mood (light, happy, serious, somber, tense, fearful). Here are some examples of writing with a purpose. Writing a letter to her American pen-pal, Danni, Sibella includes a long list of things that Danni might do in Germany when she comes to visit; the purpose is to make a clear, factual list that will enable her friend to choose among alternatives. Walt wants to write a funny story in Spanish to entertain his classmates. Karen's purpose is to write a serious report in Japanese about the influence of Japanese investments in North America. Gert, a German speaker, is making a written list of duties in English for his summer assistant from Britain, who has just arrived in Munich and does not yet know much German.

Planning for a Language Task (A) Regardless of the language skill(s) involved, this strategy always involves identifying the general nature of the task, the specific requirements of the task, the resources available within the learner, and the need for further aids. These four steps can be illustrated for each of the language skills.

Felicia, a student of Russian, wants to listen to the Radio Moscow news. In planning for this task she first identifies the nature of the task— that is, listening to a news program that is likely to be mainly political and economic. Then she figures out the probable elements, like nuclear arms, diplomatic talks, warships, American and Soviet attitudes, economic change. Next she checks her own internal resources and decides she knows most of the political words but not the economic terminology. Therefore, she looks up terms which she might need but does not yet know. Of course, she cannot determine everything in advance, but she can anticipate and prepare for many of the topics and thus become better prepared for the listening activity.

The same steps are used for a reading task. Janette decides to read an article about fashion in the German women's magazine *Burda*. She figures this task will require her to recognize and understand a variety of words related to women's attire, such as clothing items, styles, and colors. She considers whether she has the needed vocabulary, realizes she knows a few fashion-related words, and assumes she can guess many more expressions from the pictures and the text. To help her if she gets completely stumped, Janette decides to keep a dictionary handy.

Here is an example of preparing for a spoken presentation in the target language. In the first step, describing the nature and purpose, Christoph decides to talk in Spanish about Mexican education in the year 2000. The next step is identifying the language elements needed—for instance, the future tense, comparatives, and vocabulary for primary and secondary schools, universities, vocational schools, education ministries, and so on. Christoph then checks whether he has the necessary knowledge and finally works to develop any missing elements.

In using this strategy for a writing task, Livia realizes first that she wants to write a letter to a friend overseas. Next she decides her letter will require a range of specific language functions (like asking questions, describing, and explaining), a number of structures (such as past, present, future, and conditional), and vocabulary that is adequate to talk about personal things to her friend. After considering whether she has the necessary knowledge, she seeks additional resources by asking a native speaker for help with certain colloquial expressions. (In a longer piece of writing, the planning steps would occur repeatedly, with plans made and remade as ideas evolve.)

Seeking Practice Opportunities (A) Language learners must seek out—or create—opportunities to practice any and all of the four language skills. If students want to reach moderate to high proficiency, classroom time cannot usually provide adequate practice opportunities. Therefore, students will need to find additional chances to practice the language and must realize it is *up to them* to search for these occasions. This strategy underscores students' responsibility to generate their own opportunities to practice. Challenge your students to look for such chances whenever and wherever possible. For ideas about practice possibilities, read the discussion of the strategy of practicing naturalistically in Chapter 3.

Here are some examples of seeking practice opportunities. Viva, who is learning Spanish, decides to practice her listening comprehension skills by listening to popular songs on the radio. Sachi actively seeks out new American friends to talk with at the local community club. Bob decides to submit his name and address to the German magazine's pen-pal list so that he can begin a correspondence in German. Eva takes out a subscription to Le Monde as a way of pushing herself to practice reading French every day. Each of these examples involves a conscious decision to look for or create new chances to practice the target language.

Evaluating Your Learning

The two strategies in this set relate to monitoring one's own errors and evaluating one's overall progress. Both are useful in all the skill areas.

Self-Monitoring (A) This strategy does not center as much on using the language as it does on students' conscious decision to monitor—that is, notice and correct—their own errors in any of the language skills. Encourage your students to write down their most significant difficulties in their language learning notebooks and try to eliminate them. In considering a particular *faux pas*, learners can often benefit from trying to determine the reason why it was made. Tracking the cause of the problem, such as overgeneralization from a native language rule, or inappropriate verbatim translation, helps learners understand more about the new language or about their own use of learning strategies [8]. However, error analysis—even this positive kind—must not be too strongly emphasized, or else learners will become overly self-conscious about their performance.

Although monitoring one's own errors is often thought to be used mainly in speaking and writing, it is frequently used for listening and reading as well. One study [9] reported that self-monitoring is extensively used by effective listeners, who check whether they correctly understand the meaning of whole chunks of the message, monitor any confusion they encounter, and correct inaccurate guesses. A similar process occurs in reading. Readers often skim or scan, make guesses about what will come next, and correct any misinterpretations as they move ahead. Here are some specific cases of self-monitoring for listening and reading. Lyla is talking with Uwe in German, and she misinterprets what he says about the age of his nephews. Later she corrects her understanding of their ages as Uwe continues to talk about the nephews' school activities. Briggi is reading a detective novel in English. She guesses whenever she does not fully understand the details of the plot, like who is where at what time, but she subsequently corrects her understanding as she gets more facts.

Self-monitoring is important for speaking, but students should not become obsessed with correcting every speech difficulty, because this would kill communication. Without expecting to be perfect, learners should notice and rectify their important speech problems, such as those which are socially offensive or which cause confusion. Here are some examples of self-monitoring of speech. Phyllis notices that the French school director is offended when she uses just a single-word response instead of saying the more polite expression, *Oui, Madame la Directrice,* so Phyllis quickly corrects herself. Hans, a German learning English, transfers *am Telefon* directly into English, as in the incorrect statement, *I promised it to you at the telephone* [10]. Carlos, a Spanish speaker, makes English speech errors like *I want to explain you the problem.* The difficulties of Hans and Carlos are not serious or offensive at the beginning stage of language learning, so they might not need immediate correction—although more experienced language learners should know and use the correct forms. Encourage your students to keep track of and correct their important speech problems.

For writing, avoid teachers' frequent practices of appropriating the whole error-monitoring function and splashing fountains of red ink over students' compositions. These practices can lead to a sense of defeat for both you and your students [11]. Learners can help each other monitor their writing difficulties without your constant intervention. If the classroom climate is sufficiently nonthreatening, peers can read and comment on each others' written drafts. Mark the most important writing problems, or certain kinds of problems, and then ask students to figure out the correct forms with help from their friends and from reference books. Encourage students to use published checklists to monitor their own errors in spelling, punctuation, vocabulary, organization, content, and tone [12]. Here is an example of self-monitoring in writing. Alberto, an Italian student of English, is writing a letter to Beth, his English-speaking friend, in order to make plans for a trip. Alberto mistakenly uses an Italian *pensare*-type construction when he writes, "We think to come by car." In rereading the letter, he realizes this is an inappropriate construction and changes it to: "We are thinking of coming by car."

Self-Evaluating Ⓐ This strategy involves gauging either general language progress or progress in any of the four skills. Global impressions are often faulty, and the more specific the learner is in self-evaluating, the more accurate the evaluation [13]. Of course, any self-evaluation must take into consideration the difficulty of the situation or the language. Checklists, diaries, or journals can help learners evaluate their progress, at the same time as getting in touch with feelings. For instance, an advanced ESL student wrote in his journal, "My research paper has turned out decently. . . . I definitely failed to make the topic enchanting but I hope I described it satisfactorily and showed my point of view. . . . Life is blossoming again" [14]. See the exercises at the end of this chapter for applications of checklists and diaries for self-evaluation. Following are some ideas about how to evaluate progress in each of the four skills.

Listeners can check with the speaker to determine whether what they understood is really accurate. They can estimate what percentage of a conversation has been understood (for instance, less than half, more than half, almost all). They can assess whether they are at the stage of listening comprehension they expected or wanted to be at this time. Students can consider whether their listening has improved since last week or last month, based on what they understand.

As applied to reading, self-evaluating might consist of learners' assessing their proficiency in a variety of ways. For instance, learners might consider whether their speed or comprehension is acceptable at this point. They might estimate whether their reading skills have improved since the last check. They might consider what proportion of a reading passage they understand, and whether this represents any sign of progress.

In speaking, there are many ways to self-evaluate. Learners may record their own speech on a tape recorder and then listen to the recording to find out how they sound compared with native speakers. During a face-to-face interaction or a telephone conversation, they can make a rough count of the number of times they are asked to repeat something. Learners can also pay attention to the responses of native-speaking listeners when they speak: Do they appear confused or comprehending, upset or calm, alienated or involved? Learners can ask themselves whether, given such signs, their speaking seems to have improved since last month or last year.

Finally, learners can learn to use self-evaluating effectively for writing. They can review samples of their own work, note the style and content of the writing, and assess progress over time. They can compare their writing with the writing of more proficient language users and with that of their peers. Some important criteria are sentence length, complexity of thought, power of arguments, written organization, accuracy, and social appropriateness.

APPLYING AFFECTIVE STRATEGIES TO THE FOUR SKILLS

The three sets of affective strategies are highlighted in Figure 5.3 and explained below as they apply to various language skills.

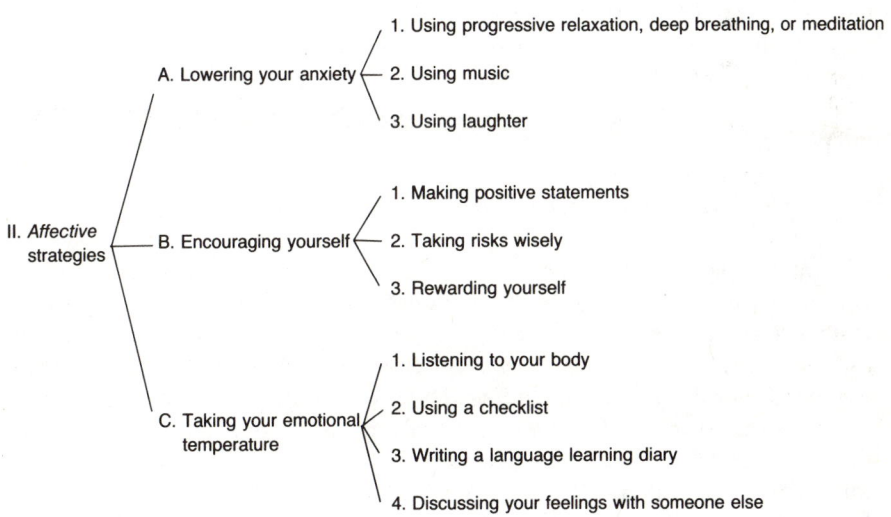

The heart has such an influence over the understanding that it is worthwhile to engage it in our interest.
Lord Chesterfield

Figure 5.3 Diagram of the Affective Strategies to Be Applied to the Four Language Skills. (*Source*: Original.)

Lowering Your Anxiety

In any of the four skills, anxiety can play a strong role, short-circuiting potential learning. Speaking the new language often causes the greatest anxiety of all, but some learners also experience tremendous anxiety when listening, reading, or writing the new language. The following strategies help learners to lower their anxiety, no matter which skill or combination of skills is involved.

Using Progressive Relaxation, Deep Breathing, or Meditation Ⓐ These techniques are all effective anxiety reducers, according to scientific bio-feedback research. Progressive relaxation involves alternately tensing and relaxing all the major muscle groups, one at a time. Deep breathing is often an accompaniment to progressive relaxation. It involves breathing low from the diaphragm, not just from the lungs. The simple act of deep breathing brings greater calmness almost immediately. Meditation means focusing on a mental image or sound to center one's thoughts, and it, too, helps to reduce the anxiety that often dogs language learners. All of these techniques can be used in the classroom or just about anywhere else. Learners do not need to lie down or assume yoga poses to benefit from any of these techniques. A few minutes of relaxation in the classroom or at home using progressive relaxation, deep breathing, or meditation will help learners accomplish their learning tasks more peacefully and more efficiently. Train your students to use these techniques.

Specific examples of this strategy are as follows. Daniela, who is learning German, is frightened by the prospect of the upcoming Goethe Institute examinations, which are known to be tough but fair. She relaxes by using deep breathing techniques before entering the testing room. Libby, a student of Spanish, uses progressive relaxation and meditation for a few minutes before giving a talk in Spanish.

Using Music Ⓐ This strategy is useful before any stressful language task. Five or 10 minutes of soothing music can calm learners and put them in a more positive mood for learning. The language teaching method known as Suggestopedia is based partly on the use of baroque music to alter students' moods and mental states. The powerfully relaxing capabilities of music cannot be denied in the language learning context. As an illustration of using music to relax, Flint listens to his favorite, most upbeat country music before practicing Russian. Sara relaxes with classical music before her German study sessions.

Using Laughter Ⓐ Laughter is the best medicine, as the saying goes. The use of laughter is potentially able to cause important biochemical changes to enhance the immune system, so many hospitals are now using "laughter therapy" to help patients relax [15]. Language learners, too, can benefit from laughter's anxiety-reducing powers. Laughter brings pleasure to the classroom. Laughter is not just the result of teacher-centered joke-telling or Rassias-type dramatics; it can be stimulated by many kinds of classroom activities, such as role-plays, games, and active exercises in which learners are allowed to play as they learn. Laughter is part of a general atmosphere of enjoyment for students of all ages. As an example, Marguerita reads comic books in French for relief, relaxation, and language practice. Ingmar tells jokes and laughs with his friends, so that he can unwind and study more effectively. Grace enjoys doing comical role-plays in class.

Encouraging Yourself

Teaching students some self-encouragement strategies will pay off in all of the skill areas. Language learners often need to find ways to keep their spirits up and persevere as they try to understand or produce the new language.

Making Positive Statements (A) The strategy of making positive statements can improve each of the four language skills. Demonstrate the kinds of positive statements your students can privately make to themselves. Urge them to say those statements regularly, especially before a potentially difficult language activity. Here are some examples:

I understand a lot more of what is said to me now.

I'm a good listener (reader, speaker, writer).

I pay attention well.

I enjoy understanding the new language.

I can get the general meaning without knowing every word.

I'm reading faster than I was a month ago.

People understand me better now.

I had a very successful conversation today.

I can tell my fluency is increasing.

I enjoy writing in the new language.

Writing helps me discover what's on my mind.

I don't have to know everything I'm going to write before I start.

I'm confident and secure about my progress.

I'm taking risks and doing well.

It's OK if I make mistakes.

Everybody makes mistakes; I can learn from mine!

When used before or during a language activity, positive statements are for *self-encouragement*. For example, before presenting a talk in Japanese, Rose says to herself, "I'm sure I can get my point across, even if I make errors." When used after a very good performance, such statements also take on a *self-reward* function (see the strategy of rewarding yourself, described below). For instance, Udo says, "I really did a good job this time!"

Taking Risks Wisely Ⓐ This strategy involves a conscious decision to take reasonable risks regardless of the possibility (or probability) of making mistakes or encountering difficulties. It also suggests the need to carry out this decision in action—that is, employing direct strategies to use the language despite fear of failure. This strategy does not imply wild, unnecessary risks, like guessing at random or saying anything at all regardless of its degree of relevance. Risk taking must therefore be tempered by good judgment. Deciding to be a wise risk taker may require the supportive use of other affective strategies, such as making positive statements or rewarding yourself.

For example, Grigori decides to prod himself to speak in his beginning English class, though he is afraid of sounding like a fool, but he intends to say something sensible and not just blurt out something irrelevant. Mohammad decides to guess at meanings in the article he is reading, even though his guesses might not always be right.

Rewarding Yourself Ⓐ Learners often expect to be rewarded only by external sources, such as praise from the teacher, a good grade on a test, or a certificate of accomplishment. However, learners need more reward than they can get externally. They also need it more regularly and more often. Some of the most potent and useful rewards come from within the learners themselves. Therefore, learners need to discover how to reward themselves for good work in language learning. Naturally, self-reward relates to all four language skills. Rewards differ from one person to another and must be personally meaningful to the individual.

Rewards need not be tangible or visible. They can also come from the very act of doing a good job. Students can learn to relish their own good performance. For instance, they can begin to value more highly a well-crafted composition in the new language, or a conversation in which the learner participates fully and communicates as well as possible. Positive statements, when used after a particularly good performance on the part of the learner, can become a form of self-reward, as seen above.

Here are some examples of more tangible rewards. Hildegarde rewards herself for good work by watching a favorite TV show. Elgard eats a big pizza. Lindsay goes out shopping. Lois calls up a friend for a long chat. Frederick goes to hear a beautiful opera. Ernie takes his family out for a drive by the lake. These are potent rewards for the individuals involved.

Taking Your Emotional Temperature

This set of strategies for affective self-assessment involves getting in touch with feelings, attitudes, and motivations through a variety of means. Language learners need to be in touch with these affective aspects, so that they can begin to exert some control over them. The strategies described here enable learners to notice their emotions, avert negative ones, and make the most of positive ones.

Listening to Your Body Ⓐ One of the simplest but most often ignored strategies for emotional self-assessment is paying attention to what the body says. Performance in all four language skills is affected by the learner's physical state. Negative feelings like tension, anxiety, fear, and outrage tighten the muscles and affect all the organs of the body. Positive feelings like happiness, pleasure, contentment, and excitement can have either a stimulating or a calming effect, but certainly an effect that is discernibly different from the effect of negative feelings. Language learners need to learn to pay attention to these physical sensations frequently. "Tuning in" to the body can be a first step toward greater emotional self-understanding and control. For example, Regina feels her stomach knotting up and her legs going weak just before she has to talk with a native speaker of Thai, so she knows she is nervous and decides to do something about it. Pardee, a learner of German, has a headache, realizes that it is coming from tension about performing in German, and determines that he will relax a bit more every day.

Using a Checklist Ⓐ A checklist helps learners in a more structured way to ask themselves questions about their own emotional state, both in general and in regard to specific language tasks and skills. Learners can use a checklist every day or every few days to assess their feelings and attitudes about language learning. Encourage students to complete check-lists periodically at home, or else give students 10 or 15 minutes of class time on a regular basis to do checklists. Use checklists to stir up class discussions of feelings about language learning. Here are examples of this strategy in action. Liselotte uses a checklist each night to note her changing attitudes about her intensive Chinese course, her teacher, and her own progress in learning Chinese. Alton's teacher asks the members of the class to complete a checklist every Monday morning, then Alton discusses the checklist responses with his language partner. Zaria realizes through using a checklist that she feels more at ease and less scared about learning English than she felt before.

Writing a Language Learning Diary Ⓐ Language learning diaries or jour-nals are narratives describing the learners' feelings, attitudes, and perceptions about the language learning process. They can also include specific information about strategies which learners find effective or ineffective for each of the four language skills. You can either give guidelines for your students' diaries or allow those diaries to be freewheeling [16].

Some learners like to share their diaries or journals with other people. In Vladimir's English class, students use diaries to understand and keep track of their thoughts, attitudes, and language learning strategies, and if they feel comfortable enough, they share their diary entries during group discussion in class once or twice a week. Lorelei, a student of Spanish, gets a new perspective by sharing her language learning diary with her sister, who is not studying Spanish.

Other learners prefer to keep their diaries or journals private. For example, while writing in her diary, Bea admits she is bored in her Polish class and does not like the Polish textbook. This realization, which she does not share with her Polish teacher or classmates, makes Bea decide to inject more energy and variety into the learning situation.

Discussing Your Feelings with Someone Else (A) Language learning is difficult, and learners often need to discuss this process with other people. As noted above, written checklists and diaries can be used as input to oral discussions about feelings and needs related to any of the language skills. Learners can benefit from discussing these topics with peers—and with you! Amazing transformations of classroom activity and atmosphere can occur because of these discussions; anxieties and inhibitions diminish, and learners feel they have more control over their own fate. Discussions of feelings can also take place outside of class with a friend, a parent, a counselor, or a native speaker of the language. Encourage students to express their feelings about the language learning process and discover what they need to be better learners. Examples of discussions with other people inside and outside the language classroom have already been given for Alton, Vladimir, and Lorelei (see above).

APPLYING SOCIAL STRATEGIES TO THE FOUR SKILLS

Sometimes people mistakenly think that social strategies (see Figure 5.4) are used only for listening and speaking, but social strategies are helpful and indeed essential to all four language skills.

Asking Questions

This set of strategies includes both asking for clarification or verification and asking for correction. These two strategies are used differently in the

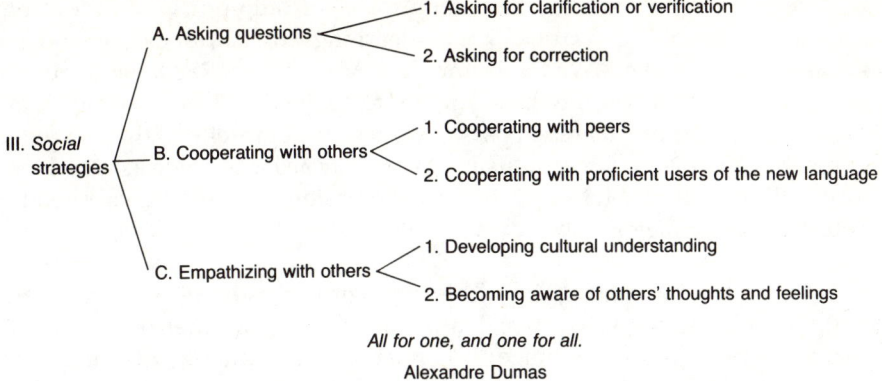

All for one, and one for all.
Alexandre Dumas

Figure 5.4 Diagram of the Social Strategies to Be Applied to the Four Language Skills. (*Source*: Original.)

four skill areas. In listening and reading, asking questions for clarification or verification is used more often than asking for correction. In speaking and writing, asking for correction is more prevalent.

Asking for Clarification or Verification Ⓛ Ⓡ Asking for clarification in listening involves asking the more proficient speaker to slow down, paraphrase, repeat, explain, or otherwise clarify what he or she has said. Asking for verification in listening means checking to make sure that something has been rightly understood. Learners need to learn acceptable ways to ask for clarification or verification, since it is done differently in different cultures and different languages. Help your students learn appropriate conversational questions like the following:

Would you repeat that, please?
Please speak more slowly.
I'm sorry, I don't understand.
Pardon me.
What was that again?
Did you say———?
What does _____ mean?

Learners who are reading in the new language may also use the strategy of asking for clarification or verification. Usually they ask someone more proficient in the target language, although students at the same proficiency level can often provide clarifying or verifying information. In jigsaw listening or reading exercises, or in other activities involving these two skills, this strategy is commonly used.

Here are some instances of asking for clarification or verification for listening and reading. Marina, who is learning English, does not understand when Rae says, "Wadja wanna do?" Marina asks Rae to slow down and repeat, and Rae clarifies by saying more distinctly, "What do you want to do?" Vicki, reading a French passage, does not comprehend the meaning of the phrase *à toute allure*, confusing it with *à tout à l'heure*. She asks Helene for clarification and is told that the first expression means "at great speed" and the second means "see you very soon."

Asking for Correction Ⓢ Ⓦ This strategy is mostly used in speaking and writing, because errors which are most obvious to other people occur in producing the new language. It is related to the strategy of self-monitoring, in which students notice and correct their own difficulties.

In a spoken conversation, learners can ask the other person for correction of important problems—that is, those which cause confusion or offense. However, the other person cannot be expected to correct all errors made by the learner, because this would intimidate the learner, halt the conversation, and turn the conversation partner into a "speech cop."

Language learners should ask for correction of some writing difficulties, but the kind and amount of correction depends on the level of the learner and the purpose of the writing. Heavy-handed correction, especially in the beginning stages of language learning, can have two possible negative effects: students' morale plummets, or students simply ignore the corrections. If advanced learners are expected to create a polished written product, they might ask for a greater amount of correction, or at least a noting of problems which they themselves can correct.

Following are specific examples of asking for correction. Paige is sure that she has made an error when her Spanish friend looks surprised at what she says, so she asks to be corrected. Aurelius wants to improve his writing, so he asks the teacher to mark his most serious difficulties, for which he then tries to find the correct form on his own. Felix asks his Russian teacher for correction of the written phrase representing "date of birth, 16th of April, 1959" (*data rozhdyeniya, 16oye apryelya 1959 goda* [дата рождения, 16ое апреля 1959 года]). The teacher says that no correction is needed.

Cooperating with Others

Because language in all its aspects is a social act, cooperating with other people is essential. This cooperation requires that the learner interact well with both peers and more proficient language users. Some of the actions mentioned here under cooperating are similar to those in Chapter 3 under the cognitive strategy of practicing naturalistically.

Cooperating with Peers (A) This strategy involves a concerted effort to work together with other learners on an activity with a common goal or reward. Games, simulations, and other active exercises challenge students to develop their ability to cooperate with peers while using a variety of language skills.

Here are some examples of cooperating with peers in listening and speaking. Agnes's small group is working on French jigsaw listening activities, which require individual language learners to listen to different pieces of a story and then figure out the whole story by putting the pieces together in the right order. In another kind of listening exercise, Johanna and José listen to the same passage in English, and Johanna summarizes it in English, with José asking questions and prompting. Then, while listening to a different passage, they reverse their roles. Barbro and Stefan, regular language learning partners at the advanced level of English, have daily telephone conversations with each other, thus receiving listening and speaking practice in the company of a friend.

Reading, though usually considered an independent activity, can be a cooperative enterprise as well. For example, Wally works with his small group on a Russian-language jigsaw reading activity. Each group member has part of the story to read, and together they have to figure out the entire story through a process of negotiating, questioning, and cooperating. At first they do this in English. Later, when they are more advanced, they do it in Russian; when this happens, listening and speaking skills enter the reading act. No matter how it is done, jigsaw reading encourages cooperation with peers.

Writers in any language are often viewed as lonely figures, cloistered in some dim and drafty nook, scribbling silently or pounding the keys of their word processor or typewriter. Though such views might have more than just a grain of truth, writing can also be a social, cooperative activity. For instance, Manolo writes a journal and shares it with his English-language classmate, who responds with comments. Beate participates in brainstorming activities to generate ideas for writing. Daniel takes notes on his friend Max's writing and shares comments with him. Charlene writes in Portuguese to a pen-pal in Lisbon. Before sending a letter, Charlene shows it to her language partner, Sue, to obtain feedback.

Cooperating with Proficient Users of the New Language (A) This strategy applies to all four skills. When used for listening and speaking, this strategy involves taking specific steps to enhance communication with a proficient user of the new language. For example, Lynda reminds herself to keep Rudolph, her German-speaking friend, informed of her own listening needs (e.g., slowing down, repeating). She knows she must listen actively, ask questions, and observe natural feedback, like gestures, facial expressions, and body distance.

In reading and writing the target language, students often need to cooperate with proficient language users. This frequently happens when language learners encounter proficient language users on the job, in the classroom, or on a trip. For instance, Sean needs to get help from Jean-Louis in order to understand some highly technical written instructions while on the job. Diana seeks advice from her Danish friends as she writes reports in Danish. Belinda cooperates with Germans, who help her understand the German tour book.

Empathizing with Others

Understanding and producing the new language involves empathy with other people, especially with individuals from the target culture.

Developing Cultural Understanding (A) Background knowledge of the new culture often helps learners understand better what is heard or read in the new language. Such knowledge also helps learners know what is culturally appropriate to say aloud or in writing. Help students sharpen their cultural understanding by injecting short cultural discussions into classroom activities, and by comparing and contrasting behavior in the students' native culture and the target culture. Turn the language classroom into a cultural laboratory. In second language classes, where many nationalities may be represented and where students are learning the language of the immediate community, learners can bring in materials from their own cultural group to share and can discuss how their background differs from that of the culture in their new homeland. In foreign language classes, where learners are learning a language from a distant country and are generally from a homogeneous cultural background, students can bring in cultural artifacts from traveling abroad or from visiting any ethnic enclaves that exist in their own community.

Outside of the classroom, encourage students to find out all they can about the target culture through reading, going to lectures, or watching films in the target language. All these activities develop greater cultural awareness, which is necessary for achieving proficiency in the new language.

Here are some instances of developing cultural understanding. Paco, who is studying in England, listens to the BBC to try to get a flavor of the culture. Clem and his classmates sign up for a trip to Central America so they can learn about the culture in person as they speak the Spanish language. Lucretia looks at department store catalogs from France to understand more about French culture.

Becoming Aware of Others' Thoughts and Feelings (A) Learners can purposefully become aware of fluctuations in the thoughts and feelings of particular people who use the new language. Such awareness brings learners closer to the people they encounter, helps them understand more clearly what is communicated, and suggests what to say and do.

Observing the behavior of others during face-to-face communication often sharpens this awareness. Listening carefully to what is said, and what is left unsaid, enables learners to become more aware of the mindset of other people. For instance, Rosalee carefully listens to the tone and expression of the mother in the Italian "host family," so that she can be more sensitive to the mother's feelings. Ramon observes the physical signals and speech of his teacher, so he can be more aware of the teacher's mood and thoughts. With this knowledge, Rosalee and Ramon both understand better what they themselves should say.

In addition, learners can become aware of the feelings of others as expressed in writing. Students can sense the feelings of people with whom they communicate informally through letters, notes, or memos. Formal writing like novels, stories, and articles can be understood more easily when learners consciously try to "get inside the skin" of the writer to understand the writer's point of view. For informal or formal writing, this awareness might mean reading on two levels: the literal, verbatim level and the covert, between-the-lines level. The literal meaning might be perfectly sensible in many instances, but sometimes meanings are expressed in both explicit and subtle ways, and learners need to read for both types of meanings. For example, Mickey reads the letter from his Asian friend on both levels to determine what is directly expressed and what is implied. This helps Mickey know how to respond in the next letter he writes to his friend. Sandy reads the Tredyakovsky poem in Russian, being aware of both possible levels of meaning.

SUMMARY

This chapter presented information on how the three kinds of indirect strategies—metacognitive, affective, and social—can be applied to the four language skills. These strategies provide a rich and powerful support to any language learning effort. They work in concert with direct strategies, which were presented earlier in Chapters 2 and 3. The following activities and exercises are geared toward applications of indirect strategies.

ACTIVITIES FOR READERS

Activity 5.1. Examine Indirect Strategies in the Four Skills

On a large sheet write five columns and give them the following labels: *strategy* in Column 1, and the four skills, *listening, reading, speaking,* and *writing,* in Columns 2–5, as in Table 5.1. In the strategy column, list all the indirect strategies shown earlier in this chapter in Figures 5.2, 5.3, and 5.4. Now consider how strongly each of these indirect strategies enhances learners' growth in each of the four skills. Put one check in the skill box if a particular strategy supports development of the skill to a moderate level, and two checks in the skill box if a particular strategy strongly facilitates skill development. Leave the box blank if you feel the strategy is totally irrelevant to the skill. (This will rarely be the case!) Discuss your results with someone else. Note differences and similarities.

Table 5.1   INDIRECT STRATEGIES AS RELATED TO THE FOUR SKILLS

Strategy	Four skills			
	Listening	Reading	Speaking	Writing

Source: Original.

Activity 5.2. Consider Your Use of the Indirect Strategies

Think back to when you were a language learner yourself. Which of the indirect strategies did you use often? sometimes? rarely or not at all? Which ones do you wish you had known about and tried? Explain your answers.

Activity 5.3. Ponder the Purposes of Writing and Speaking

In one column on a large sheet of paper, list all the kinds of writing formats you can think of (e.g., reports, stories, letters, memos, personal notes, lists, catalogs, plays). List at least 20. Now, in another column, list the purposes for which the author might be using this format (for instance, convincing, entertaining, challenging the reader). Next, do the same thing for speaking: List a variety of formats, and then note the purposes for using each format. Then put a star (*) by the formats and purposes that might be useful for your students as they learn a new language. Finally, brainstorm ways you could help learners consider the multiple purposes for speaking and writing.

EXERCISES TO USE WITH YOUR STUDENTS

Exercise 5.1. Make a Weekly Schedule

Purpose

This exercise produces a generalized, weekly schedule for language learning. Learners can then add details and make changes week by week.

Materials

Anything necessary to make a schedule (paper, ruler, pen).

Time

Takes 20 minutes for general schedule, 20 minutes a week thereafter.

Instructions

Tell the students the following in your own words: Make a schedule of your typical week, including classes, independent study, time for practicing the language with others, job (paid or unpaid), sleeping, eating, and so on. Block out your major time slots. Pay special attention to the amount of time you have available for language learning. Also note any time conflicts you have that need to be worked out. Leave plenty of time for relaxing and taking breaks, since "time off" increases your efficiency. Keep in mind that shorter, more frequent study sessions are better than longer, less frequent ones.

Also consider the basic principles of structured reviewing. You should review a lesson or piece of information frequently at first, and then less frequently (for example, at first once every 30 minutes, then once an hour, then at gradually greater intervals), coming back to it periodically even after you have moved on to new material.

Table 5.2 WEEKLY SCHEDULE

	Morning	Midday	Afternoon	Evening
Sun.				
Mon.				
Tues.				
Wed.				
Thurs.				
Fri.				
Sat.				

Source: Original.

If you want, you can reproduce this schedule and use it in a more detailed way each week to organize your language learning. Week by week, write down your plans for learning the language. List times you will do language assignments, times you plan to meet with native speakers or your regular language partner, special events in the target language, and so on. Table 5.2 provides a possible model for the schedule.

Source Original.

Exercise 5.2. Create a Language Learning Notebook

Purpose

This exercise helps learners create a notebook that will help them throughout their language learning.

Materials

Notebook, dividers.

Time

It will take 1 hour to consider contents and make divisions. Time needed for using the notebook is up to the learner!

Instructions

Tell your students the following in your own words: If you don't already have one, create a language learning notebook. This will help you organize your language learning. Your notebook can be used for any of the following purposes, or other purposes that you might think of:

To record your goals and objectives for learning the language

To write down assignments given by the instructor

To keep a list of new words or expressions you have learned or want to learn

To write down words you have heard or read that you want to ask someone about or look up in the dictionary

To write down grammar rules you have learned or figured out in some way

To keep notes about conversations you have had in the language

To summarize what you read in the new language

To keep a record of errors you want to work on, and your hunches about why you might have made those errors

To comment on strategies you have used successfully or unsuccessfully

To record the amount of time you spend each week studying or using the target language

Make your notebook as simple or detailed as you want. The structure of your notebook depends on your learning style, your personality, and your purposes for using the notebook. If you want to color-code the sections of the notebook, go ahead. Write in your language learning notebook every day or as often as possible. Use it as a good friend in the language learning process. It is one of the best ways to get organized and to manage your learning.

Source Original.

Exercise 5.3. Set Your Goals and Objectives

Purpose

This exercise helps learners set their goals and objectives.

Materials

Copy of questionnaire below, additional paper.

Time

Setting long-term goals: 15 minutes to 1 hour. Setting short-term objectives: should be done periodically; amount of time varies.

Instructions

Tell your students the following in your own words: Let's work on setting goals and objectives for language learning. Your goals and objectives may differ from those of your friends in the class, but that is not important. What is important is that you become clear about why you are learning the language and what you want to get from language learning. To do this, answer the questions in Table 5.3.

Alternative

Learners can work in pairs on this. Or they can work individually and then compare their goals and objectives with those of others.

Source Original.

Table 5.3 **QUESTIONNAIRE FOR DETERMINING LANGUAGE LEARNING GOALS AND OBJECTIVES**

1. *Setting long-term goals*   First set some long-term goals for yourself. To do this, answer the following questions:

   a. Why are you learning this language? (check one or more)

   _____ For advancement

   _____ For good grades

   _____ For a new or better job

   _____ For travel

   _____ Because the language is required for graduation

   _____ To get to know people from the new culture

   _____ Because it's fun

   _____ Other (list) _____

   b. Which skills are the most important to you? Given the purposes you have identified, decide which skills are the most important and how you need to spend your learning time. Indicate below the importance of each skill area (1 = least important, 5 = most important). Then indicate how proficient you want to become in each of these skills (low, medium, high).

Skill	Importance (list 1 to 5)	Desired proficiency (list Low, Med, High)
Listening	_____	_____
Speaking	_____	_____
Reading	_____	_____
Writing	_____	_____

   c. On the basis of your purposes for learning the language and of your skills priorities, what are your long-term goals for learning the new language for the next months or years? Sample goals: being able to hold a long social conversation in the new language; reaching a certain overall proficiency level; being able to give instructions in the new language without constantly using a dictionary. Goals should be realistic.

   _____

   _____

   _____

   _____

   _____

   Now go back and write down a date for each goal—a time by which you expect to reach the goal. Setting such a date will enable you to check your progress toward meeting your goals.

Table 5.3   Continued

2. *Setting your objectives*   After you have set long-term goals, set yourself some short-term objectives, too. These are aims for the next few hours, days, or weeks. Sample short-term objectives include memorizing a set of vocabulary words; mastering the past tense of regular verbs; reading a specific text or complete a particular assignment. Some of these objectives might take only a few hours, while others might take several weeks. Again, set a deadline for yourself for achieving these objectives so you can check your progress. (Repeat this process as needed.)

_____

_____

_____

_____

_____

3. Now put this questionnaire in your language learning notebook to remind you of your goals and objectives. Review periodically so that you will remember them and gear your learning toward them. Revise them as needed.

Source: Original.

Exercise 5.4. Opportunity Knocks!

Purpose

This exercise helps learners to consider the possibilities that exist for practicing the new language.

Materials

Paper, pen, instruction sheet.

Time

Takes 30 minutes.

Instructions

Provide your students with an instruction sheet with the following details:

On a sheet of paper, mark off two columns, numbering them Column 1 and Column 2, as shown in Table 5.4.

In Column 1, list *all* the opportunities that you can think of for practicing the new language *in any of the four language skills: listening, reading, speaking, and writing.* These can be existing opportunities or opportunities that you might create. (You don't have to be taking advantage of these opportunities now.) Be specific! Example: reading a newspaper in the new language every day. Now count up the number of ideas you have listed in Column 1, and write down this number where Table 5.4 says "Total number of opportunities."

In Column 2, next to each opportunity you have just listed (see Column 1), indicate whether or not you are now taking advantage of that opportunity. If yes, write 1; if no, write 0. For example, if you are already reading a target language newspaper regularly, put a 1; if not, put a 0. Now add up the points in this column, and write down this number where Table 5.4 says "Total points."

In Column 3 multiply the number of ideas (Column 1) by the number of points (Column 2), and write down the result where Table 5.4 says "Grand total."

Finally, evaluate your results using the scale in Table 5.4.

Source Original.

Table 5.4   OPPORTUNITY KNOCKS!

Column 1	Column 2	Column 3
List opportunities	Now taking advantage? Yes = 1, No = 0	Multiply total number of opportunities by total points
a.		
b.		
c.		
d.		
e.		
f.		
g.		
h.		
i.		
j.		
etc.		
Total number of opportunities _____	Total points _____	Grand total _____

Evaluating Your Results
If you have 15 or more points—GREAT!
If you have 11–14 points—WELL DONE!
If you have between 7–10 points—OK!
If you have between 3–6 points—BETTER LUCK NEXT TIME!
If you have 0–2 points—GOSH!?!

Source: Original.

Exercise 5.5. Gauge Your Skill Progress

Purpose

This exercise helps learners to assess their own progress in language learning skill by skill.

Materials

Paper, pen.

Time

Up to the students.

Instructions

Tell your students the following in your own words: As you learn the new language, you need to measure how well you are progressing—not according to what the teacher says but according to your own criteria of what is important for you. Sometimes learners tend to be too hard or too lenient on themselves. This is because they do not know how to evaluate their efforts. Rate yourself on your progress on each skill and then overall, using Table 5.5.

If you rated yourself as a 3 in any of the skill areas or overall, what can you do about it? What strategies might you use to improve your performance? If you want to keep your ratings private, that is OK, but you might get some benefit out of discussing them with another student or with the teacher.

Source Original.

Table 5.5   SELF-EVALUATION QUESTIONNAIRE

Listening
1. What percentage of a typical conversation with a native speaker do you understand (less than half, more than half, all of it)? _____
2. What percentage of a typical listening comprehension exercise in class do you understand (less than half, more than half, all of it)? _____
3. Has your listening comprehension improved since last month, i.e., do you understand more now than you did then? _____
4. Are you generally able to guess the meanings of what you hear? _____

On the basis of these questions, give yourself a rating on *listening* (circle one):

1. Doing just fine, about where I should be
2. Not too bad, nothing to worry about
3. Serious problems

Table 5.5   Continued

Reading

1. How much do you understand of a typical reading passage in a magazine or newspaper in the new language (less than half, more than half, all of it)? _____
2. How much do you understand of a typical classroom reading passage (less than half, more than half, all of it)? _____
3. Has your reading comprehension improved since last month? _____
4. Are you generally able to guess the meanings of what you read? _____

On the basis of these questions, give yourself a rating on *reading* (circle one):

1. Doing just fine, about where I should be
2. Not too bad, nothing to worry about
3. Serious problems

Speaking

1. When you speak to native speakers of the new language, do they seem to understand you most of the time, without your being asked to repeat? ____
2. In class do your classmates generally understand what you say in the new language? _____
3. Has your speaking improved since last month in terms of quality and quantity? _____
4. Do you find ways to express yourself orally even if you don't know all the words? _____

On the basis of these questions, give yourself a rating on *speaking* (circle one):

1. Doing just fine, about where I should be
2. Not too bad, nothing to worry about
3. Serious problems

Writing

1. When you write in the new language outside of class, do people generally understand your meaning? _____
2. When you write in the new language in class, do people generally understand your meaning? _____
3. Has your writing improved since last month in terms of quality and quantity? _____
4. Do you find ways to express yourself in writing even if you don't know all the words? _____

On the basis of these questions, give yourself a rating on *writing* (circle one):

1. Doing just fine, about where I should be
2. Not too bad, nothing to worry about
3. Serious problems

Now, on the basis of these evaluations of each skill, give yourself an *overall rating* for your general language progress so far (circle one):

1. Doing just fine, about where I should be
2. Not too bad, nothing to worry about
3. Serious problems

Source: Original.

Exercise 5.6. Relaxing

Purpose

This exercise helps learners to relax so that they are able to deal more effectively with language learning.

Materials

None.

Time

This might take 10 to 15 minutes each time (can be more or less, depending on the learner).

Instructions

Tell your students the following in your own words: Tension and anxiety get in the way of language learning. You can learn how to relax. This will help you in language learning and in many other aspects of your life. First, tighten up your lower arm muscles as much as you can, and hold this position for 20 or 30 seconds. It probably hurts a little. Now let go and see how much better it feels. Many of us go around most of the time—especially in times when we have to use the new language—all tensed up, when we could relax instead.

Now let's relax all over by using progressive relaxation. Loosen your clothes a bit around the neck and waist. If you can, lie down; if not, sit in a comfortable position. Tense your feet, and then relax them. Now move up to the ankles, and do the same. Move up to the thighs, then the hips, then the lower back, and on up all the way to your shoulders, tensing and relaxing each major group of muscles. Do the same to your neck muscles and your face muscles, where a lot of tension is stored. By now you should feel really comfortable and relaxed. To maintain this feeling, for a few minutes imagine a lovely, relaxing scene, like a beach or a forest. Center your thoughts on this beautiful spot, meditating on it gently as you breathe deeply. This is a scene you can return to as often as you want, to help you relax.

Source Original.

Exercise 5.7. Calm Down Through Meditation and Music

Purpose

This exercise helps learners to focus and become calm, so that language learning does not feel so stressful.

Materials

None.

Time

Takes 10 to 20 minutes a day (can be more or less, depending on the learner).

Instructions

Tell your students the following in your own words: You can meditate for a few minutes at a time, several times a day. You will be surprised at how focused and calm this can make you, and how much readier you will feel to deal with the new language.

All you have to do is to sit comfortably in a quiet place and think of one thing: an object, a word, a syllable, or a pretty place. Your mind will wander at first, but bring it back to the thing you are thinking about. As you meditate, breathe slowly and deeply from your abdomen, not from your chest. That's the basic idea. If it helps you, you might also play some peaceful background music while you meditate. Try this now in class, and repeat it in the morning and the evening at home. Do it any time you feel tension as a way of relaxing your body and centering your mind.

Source Original.

Exercise 5.8. Praise Be!

Purpose

In this exercise, learners praise themselves for good work and encourage themselves to keep on learning.

Materials

Small cards (optional).

Time

The exercise takes 5 to 10 minutes each day.

Instructions

Tell the students the following in your own words: Pay attention to your *specific* accomplishments and successes in learning, and make positive comments (sometimes called "affirmations") to yourself about your work. Such comments might include things like:

I understood almost everything the teacher said today.

I'm reading much faster now in Spanish than I was a month ago.

I was able to understand and write down the telephone number in French when the caller left a message.

I didn't get paralyzed when I made an error today; I just kept right on going.

I took a risk in using that new expression today, and I'm glad I did it.

It was hard for me to talk in English class today, but I tried.

I held a very successful conversation in German today.

I met with my language partner today, and I can tell that my Russian fluency is increasing.

Make statements that are relevant to you and what you have specifically accomplished. These statements help you change negative attitudes about yourself as a language learner, and they can speed up the process of learning by convincing you that you will succeed. Say positive statements to yourself at least three to five times a day, more if possible.

You can also make more *general* statements that will help you feel more confident. These might include:

I am a good language learner.

I am confident and secure in language learning.

I am progressing well in my language learning.

I can learn from my errors and do not have to be afraid of them.

It's OK if I take risks in language learning.

I don't have to understand everything all at once.

I can tolerate a bit of confusion.

My warm personality helps me in language learning.

Make up your own favorite (and most relevant) general statements to encourage yourself. You might write these statements on little cards and look at them in the morning and at night—or more frequently during the day—as a psychological suggestion to yourself. Gradually you might memorize them, and you might not have to look at the cards anymore. Saying general statements to yourself several times a day helps you internalize these concepts and believe them at a deeper level. You'll be surprised at the power these simple statements can have! If you have a language learning partner whom you trust, you might share your positive statements with that person, and vice versa.

Make positive statements several times a day for a week. (If you miss one time, don't give up. Go back to the schedule and keep on encouraging yourself!) After the first week, check on the success of your efforts. Are you feeling more confident? Better able to help yourself and manage your emotions? More committed to learning the language? Write down your evaluative comments in your language learning diary or notebook.

Source Original.

Exercise 5.9. Assess Your Emotions

Purpose

This exercise helps learners use a checklist to assess their emotional state regularly and often, and to link their emotional state with the events of their language learning and other aspects of their lives.

Materials

Checklist.

Time

Takes 5 minutes each day.

Instructions

Tell your students the following in your own words: Use the checklist in Table 5.6 to keep tabs on your feelings. The checklist is simple to use, requires little time, gives you a record for comparison from time to time, is private, and helps you link your feelings with the language tasks and events in which you are involved. If you decide to use this checklist, you should do so at least once a week, but you could use it every single day. This checklist is not a complicated psychological profile that tells deep secrets about you! It is an easy way for you to keep in touch with yourself in a private, personal, and regular way, so that you can better handle the demands of language learning.

Source Original.

Table 5.6   TAKING YOUR EMOTIONAL TEMPERATURE: A CHECKLIST FOR LANGUAGE LEARNERS

Part A

Date: _____   Language studied: _____

Period covered (check one):

_____ Day   _____ Week   _____ Other   (specify): _____

Part B   List language tasks or events in which you have just been involved, for example, giving an oral report, writing a letter, doing drills, holding a conversation. (Give whatever details are useful to you, including, if you want, the other people involved. Don't skip this; it shows you how certain tasks/events trigger particular feelings!)

_____

_____

_____

_____

_____

Part C   Describe how you're feeling now, especially in relation to the learning tasks or events above. (Check the one descriptor per line that *best describes you*. Realize that nothing is either black or white, and that any single descriptor is not necessarily better than its opposite.)

_____ happy   _____ unhappy

_____ proud   _____ ashamed

_____ confident   _____ unconfident

_____ peaceful   _____ anxious

_____ unafraid   _____ afraid

_____ risk-taking   _____ cautious

_____ clear-thinking   _____ confused

_____ friendly   _____ unfriendly

_____ interested   _____ bored

_____ calm   _____ angry

_____ strong   _____ weak

_____ energetic   _____ tired

_____ outgoing   _____ shy

Table 5.6 Continued

_____ accepting	_____ critical
_____ able to tolerate contradictions	_____ unable to tolerate contradictions
_____ want to learn the language	_____ don't want to learn the language
_____ want to know the culture	_____ don't want to know the culture

Source: Original.

Exercise 5.10. Stress Check

Purpose

This exercise helps learners to assess their stress level, which directly influences language learning.

Materials

Checklist.

Time

Variable, depending on students' needs.

Instructions

Provide students with the stress checklist in Table 5.7, and give them oral instructions as well as printed ones.

Here is what you can say to students, in your own words, of course: You might be feeling under a little or a lot of pressure lately. You might not yet know what is causing the problem. If you are feeling stressed, think about what the cause might be. Don't just mask the stress with alcohol, drugs, TV, or something else; think about what's causing you to worry. Are you worried about how you are doing in your studies? About money? About roommate or family problems? About a friend or lover— or the lack of one?

The first thing to do is to identify, if you can, what it is that is bothering you most about the problem or situation. Is there anything you can do about it? What steps might you take to solve the problem or address the main issue? What would your best friend or a respected adviser do about the problem if faced with it?

Try to look for someone to talk to about the problem. Get new ideas about how you might deal with it. If the problem is truly serious, seek professional help from a teacher, counselor, or other person.

It is also useful to consider the worst thing that might happen if the problem does not get resolved. Paint the "worst case scenario" in your mind, and consider what it feels like. Is there any way that you might be able to accept such a situation and learn to live with it? How could you minimize your discomfort under those circumstances?

Can you take your mind off the problem a bit by doing something else that is interesting and positive? Is there anything in your life that feels really good just now? Make a list of the good things that exist, and read the list to yourself a couple of times each day. In this way you might be able to develop some perspective about the difficulties you face.

Source Original.

Table 5.7   STRESS CHECKLIST

Circle each of the signs of stress that you have noticed in yourself lately.		
Anger	Inability to think, concentrate, or make decisions	Tight muscles
Isolation	Depression	Headaches
Exhaustion	Anxiety	Sleeping too much or too little
Pickiness	Fear	Eating too much or too little
Irritability	Worry	Reliance on alcohol or drugs

Source: Original.

Exercise 5.11. Keep a Diary

Purpose

The purpose of a language learning diary is to record feelings about the language learning process.

Materials

Diary.

Time

Variable.

Instructions

Tell your students the following in your own words: Use a diary or journal to express your feelings about learning the new language. Feel free to write whatever you want, but write something every day. The diary describes *how you are learning the language and how you feel about it.* Diary entries do not have to be long and involved. In fact, a few lines or a few paragraphs a day might be enough. When you want to explore a particular problem or a happy event in more detail, you can write more than usual. The diary is for you, and you can use it any way you want: to describe emotions, desires, issues, difficulties, achievements, other people, learning strategies, conversations, how you spent your time. You will probably want to use the diary to evaluate the general progress (or lack of it) that you feel you are making.

Unless the diary is used as a class assignment, you don't have to show it to anyone else. You can decide what you want to write and can be completely honest and open. You won't hurt anyone else by writing down your feelings, even the angry ones, and you will open the door to an important new world inside yourself.

In addition to providing a record of emotions, writing a diary is actually a form of therapy in itself. Diaries are useful for "letting off steam," helping you sort through conflicting feelings, and sometimes coming to new conclusions about how to feel, think, and act. Diaries can help you think through your learning problems and identify your accomplishments.

Source Original.

Chapter *6*

Language Learning Strategy Assessment and Training

We cannot teach another person directly; we can only facilitate his [or her] learning.

CARL ROGERS

PREVIEW QUESTIONS

1. What techniques exist for finding out what language learning strategies students use?
2. When are various techniques appropriate?
3. Which of these techniques might be useful to you?
4. Is it possible to help someone learn how to learn?
5. If so, what methods can be used most effectively?

INTRODUCTION TO STRATEGY ASSESSMENT AND TRAINING

Now that you know how language learning strategies can be applied to the four language skills, you are ready to put strategies into action. The first step involves identifying and diagnosing your students' strategies so that the training program you devise will be effective. The second step is conducting the training.

STRATEGY ASSESSMENT

Some of the most important strategy assessment techniques include observations, interviews, "think-aloud" procedures, note-taking, diaries or journals, and self-report surveys.

Observations

Many language learning strategies take place mentally and cannot be observed by the teacher. For instance, associating/elaborating, using imagery, and guessing intelligently are "invisible" or "mentalistic" strategies in terms of standard observation schemes. However, cooperating with peers, asking for clarification or verification, and overcoming limitations in speaking through gesture or mime are activities that are directly observable and can yield information on how your students currently go about learning languages.

Keeping in mind that any observation scale will miss many of the mentalistic strategies, you can choose a good scale from several that have been published and are readily available [1]. Or you can devise your *own* observation form by making a list of the strategies you think are important and which you wish to observe. On this observation form you can record the strategies in several ways:

- By taking impressionistic or structured notes.
- By checking off the strategies you see in a certain period of time, such as during one class period.
- By combining these two approaches.

Also, consider the level of detail you plan to observe. If you have the time, and perhaps another colleague to help out, you can observe and record detailed information about the context in which strategies are used.

In addition, consider the focus of your observations. You can (perhaps very roughly) observe the strategies typically used by the whole group, you can track the strategies of one small group of students, or you can observe the strategies of one student, including this student's interactions with others. You also need to decide whether you will observe for brief intervals or for a long session, and whether you will repeat your observations. Think about how to select or sample the observation times so they will reflect typical situations.

Videotaping of observation sessions can be valuable. It provides a permanent record of the sessions, so you can replay them for detail. The videotape medium will lose some peripheral information—activity that takes place outside the frame of the picture—but it will also capture details that you might not notice on first viewing.

Observations are just one way to gather strategy data. Other ways include interviews and think-aloud procedures.

Interviews and Think-Aloud Procedures

These techniques can be used together or separately. Totally unstructured interviews, in which there is no particular questioning technique or no data coding form, are difficult to use because they require you to create all your categories for analyzing and interpreting *after* the interview. Slightly more structured techniques are easier to handle.

A Model for Interviewing   The Cohen-Hosenfeld interview model [2] helps you gather data on unobservable mental processes. In this model, the three dimensions of activity, time, and content can be applied to language learning strategies.

Activity: Thinking aloud and self-observation are two ways to observe learning strategies. By *thinking aloud*, the student lets his or her thoughts flow verbally in a stream-of-consciousness fashion without trying to control, direct, or observe them. In *self-observation*, the subject consciously "watches" and analyzes his or her own thoughts to some degree.

Time: Varying amounts of time can elapse between the use of a learning strategy and its verbalization. Think-aloud data must reflect the present time (within a few seconds of the thought). Students "think aloud" as they learn. In contrast, self-observation can take place later, not just when the learning is under way [3].

Content: Thoughts may be focused on a topic, such as a particular language learning task, especially if guided by a researcher [4].

A Guide for Think-Aloud Interviews   The Interviewer Guide developed by Carol Hosenfeld and her colleagues [5] is valuable for assessing reading strategies. Originally, the guide (see Table 6.1) was used for preliminary diagnosis of strategies before training, and then to assess changes in strategy use after training.

To use this guide, ask a student to perform a language task and to think aloud, describing what he or she is doing to accomplish the task. Record the learner's general behavior while the learner says out loud what he or she is doing. In just a few minutes per student, you can check the first 13 strategies. If you have more time, you can assess all 20. The guide is a useful and concise format for think-aloud interviews, except that more space will be needed for comments. You might want to adapt the Interviewer Guide to include the strategies found in this book for any of the four skill areas [6].

Of course, not all interviews actually involve performing a task and simultaneously thinking aloud about the strategies employed. The next technique describes a way to obtain interview information on what students *usually* do, without having them perform the task during the interview.

Interviews Involving Self-Observation   J. Michael O'Malley, Anna Uhl Chamot, and their colleagues developed a useful Student Interview Guide [7] which asks learners to think about what they generally do when faced with familiar language tasks, such as pronunciation, oral grammar exercises, vocabulary learning, following directions, communicating in a social

Table 6.1   INTERVIEWER GUIDE FOR READING STRATEGIES

Student's name _____

General reading behavior (circle 1)

Rarely translates; guesses contextually	Translates; guesses noncontextually
Translates; guesses contextually	Translates; rarely guesses

Circle the strategies mentioned	**Comments**
1. Keeps meaning in mind.	_____
2. Skips unknown words (guesses contextually).	_____
3. Uses context in preceding and succeeding sentences and paragraphs.	_____
4. Identifies grammatical category of words.	_____
5. Evaluates guesses.	_____
6. Reads title (makes inferences).	_____
7. Continues if unsuccessful.	_____
8. Recognizes cognates.	_____
9. Uses knowledge of the world.	_____
10. Analyzes unknown words.	_____
11. Reads as though he or she expects the text to have meaning.	_____
12. Reads to identify meaning rather than words.	_____
13. Takes chances in order to identify meaning.	_____
14. Uses illustrations.	_____
15. Uses side-gloss.	_____
16. Uses glossary as last resort.	_____
17. Looks up words correctly.	_____
18. Skips unnecessary words.	_____
19. Follows through with proposed solutions.	_____
20. Uses a variety of types of context clues.	_____

Source: Adapted from Hosenfeld et al. (1981).

situation, and two levels of listening comprehension in class (getting the main idea and making inferences). Students are not required to perform the language task itself during the interview but are asked to consider how they typically do the task. This technique allows the learners to provide information in their own words about their learning strategies. Such interviews work well in small groups or with individuals, and lend themselves well to taping.

Semi-structured Interviews Semi-structured interviews are very useful for gathering information on your students' strategies. Here is one well-tested example by Anita Wenden. Some days before a semi-structured interview, students are given a list of broad questions outlining the main areas to be covered. They are asked to complete a grid of daily activities, on which they indicate the settings (e.g., TV watching, social conversation) in which they ordinarily find themselves during the week and what learning activities they employ in those settings. Students list only those settings in which they use the target language. During the interview, the learners answer broad questions, using information they have written down on their grid [8].

Think-Aloud Procedures Used Without Interviewing Just as you can interview students without using the think-aloud procedure, you can also use the think-aloud procedure without interviewing (that is, without any prompts or questions by the teacher or researcher). Betty Leaver has had success taping the conversations of a small group of adult Russian learners as they tried to figure out the meaning of taped listening comprehension dialogues. She also recorded the reactions of two children who were asked to figure out the meaning of taped dialogues. Tapes were transcribed and analyzed to determine the approach and strategies used by the students [9].

With this procedure, you must develop a way to categorize or make sense of the data. You can develop the scheme before the think-aloud data are analyzed or afterward, using the think-aloud material you have collected as a basis for defining categories. However, open-ended data collection like this requires skillful interpretation.

Like observations, interviews, and think-aloud procedures, note-taking can provide valuable information on students' strategy use.

Note-Taking

Note-taking is a self-report technique that can be extended to any language task. It is especially valuable when paired with interviewing. Here are three note-taking techniques for strategy assessment. First, a group of students is asked to note down their learning difficulties when performing a language task and to use these notes in an interview. A second use of note-taking involves a daily grid and occurs prior to the semistructured interview, already mentioned. A third technique asks students to take notes on a grid, describing the strategies they employ; then they rate those strategies in terms of frequency of use, enjoyment, usefulness, and efficiency [10]. As you can see, these note-taking schemes impose a bit of useful structure on students as they keep track of their strategy use. Another way for students to focus on how they use strategies is to write in a diary or journal.

Diaries or Journals

Diaries or journals are forms of self-report which allow learners to record their thoughts, feelings, achievements, and problems, as well as their impressions of teachers, fellow students, and native speakers. Diarists become "participant observers" in their own personal, ethnographic research [11]. You have already seen in Chapters 4 and 5 that keeping a diary or journal is a very useful learning strategy in itself, and this strategy can be used to help learners become aware of their whole range of strategies.

Most diaries tend to be subjective and free-form, without constraints on style or content, but some teachers find it helpful to provide guidelines. If you give your students some guidance as to subject matter or style for their diaries, these diaries are likely to be less personal, but the writers might object less to sharing their writing with you. You can ask students to use their diaries to focus specifically on language learning strategies. In some cases, learners need suggestions on how to report their strategy use and may need to take notes so as not to forget which strategies they used. If you are planning to read your students' diaries, you should, of course, tell students in advance, since diaries are frequently considered private.

Though learners are often asked to share their diaries with the teacher, students can also share their diaries among themselves. In addition, some teachers have used diaries as a stimulus to class discussions of strategy use. Some teachers set aside class time once a week to allow students to discuss their diaries.

The final strategy assessment procedure is self-report surveys, discussed next.

Self-Report Surveys

Self-report surveys are instruments used to gather systematic, written data on language learning strategy use. These surveys can vary from less structured to more structured.

Less-Structured Surveys Less-structured self-report surveys, also called subjective surveys, do not provide much organization for students in terms of the responses elicited. Such surveys contain open-ended questions designed to get the learner to describe his or her language learning strategies freely and openly in writing. The advantage is that learners can say what they want, and a lot of interesting information is generated. However, the results may be difficult to summarize across students. One survey first asks learners what kinds of strategies they generally use for certain learning tasks, and then asks them to reflect on their strategies in writing after completing a learning task [12].

More-Structured Surveys More-structured surveys, also called objective surveys, usually ask multiple-choice questions which can be objectively scored and analyzed. Because more-structured surveys use standardized categories for all respondents, such surveys make it easier to summarize results for a group and objectively diagnose problems of individual students. However, these surveys might miss the richness and spontaneity of less-structured formats [13].

The Strategy Inventory for Language Learning (SILL), in Versions 5.1 and 7.0, is a structured survey based on the strategy system used in this book. Earlier versions have been extensively field-tested, demonstrated to be highly valid and reliable, and used for both research and classroom practice. New, shorter versions (see Appendices B and C) are being field-tested and analyzed [14]. In various versions, the SILL has been used in many parts of the world with learners of many different languages, including Chinese, English, French, German, Italian, Japanese, Korean, Russian, Spanish, Thai, and Turkish.

Version 5.1 contains 80 items assessing the frequency of strategy use and takes about 30 minutes to complete. This form is shorter than many previous versions, is easier to self-score, and is keyed to the language learning strategies used throughout this book. Appendix B contains the SILL directions and items, the worksheet for answering and scoring, and the student profile of results. This version is for native English speakers.

SILL Version 7.0, containing 50 items, is geared to students of English as a second or foreign language (see Appendix C) and takes about 30 minutes to complete, depending on the skill level of the students. The language is very simplified, but this version operates similarly to Version 5.1 in most other respects.

The SILL's 5-point scale (for all versions) ranges from "never or almost never" to "always or almost always." The overall average indicates how often the learner tends to use learning strategies in general, while averages for each part of the SILL indicate which strategy groups the learner tends to use most frequently.

How to Choose a Technique
for Checking Your Students' Strategies

All of the techniques described here are valuable for checking your students' use of language learning strategies. How do you know which one(s) you should use? To make a decision, think about why you want to discover your students' strategies: because of personal interest on your part, for use in orienting your teaching practices, for providing feedback to your students on their strategy use, or as a prelude to strategy training? Also, consider the kind of information you want to obtain, the amount of time you and your students have to devote to strategy assessment, the amount of detail you need, and the relative ease or difficulty of administration and analysis. These considerations, and Activity 6.1 below, will help you select the assessment techniques that will suit your needs the best.

How to Use Strategy Assessment Results

One of the soundest reasons to assess your students' learning strategies is so you can provide training on how to improve those strategies. It is always best to provide your students with the results of your assessment. No one likes to be treated like a guinea pig. Besides, they will be curious and eager to know something new about themselves. Interpretive feedback can be woven into the training itself, or it can be presented separately, depending on how you structure your training. You might like to divide your students into small groups by ethnic/national/cultural background to discuss their strategy assessment results. Students from similar backgrounds often find that they use strategies in similar ways. Then provide training so they can learn new strategies.

STRATEGY TRAINING

Once you know how students are currently learning, you can help them to learn more effectively. This section will help you plan and carry out training in language learning strategies.

Training of language learning strategies is called many things: "strategy training," "learner training," "learning-to-learn training," "learner methodology training," and "methodological initiation for learners." This book uses the term *strategy training*, because it is both descriptive and general enough to serve our needs.

The Scope of Strategy Training

The best strategy training not only teaches language learning strategies but also deals with feelings and beliefs about taking on more responsibility and about the role change implied by the use of learning strategies. Unless learners alter some of their old beliefs about learning, they will not be able to take advantage of the strategies they acquire in strategy training [15]. In addition, strategy training can cover more general aspects of language learning, such as the kinds of language functions used inside and outside the classroom, significance of group work and individual efforts in language learning, trade-offs between accuracy and fluency, fear of mistakes, learning versus acquisition, and ways in which language learning differs from learning other subjects [16].

The Need for Strategy Training

Learners need to learn how to learn, and teachers need to learn how to facilitate the process. Although learning is certainly part of the human condition, *conscious* skill in self-directed learning and in strategy use must be sharpened through training [17]. Strategy training is especially necessary in the area of second and foreign languages. Language learning requires active self-direction on the part of learners; they cannot be spoon-fed if they desire and expect to reach an acceptable level of communicative competence.

Many language teachers advocate *explicit* training of language learners in the "how to" of language study. The general goals of such training are to help make language learning more meaningful, to encourage a collaborative spirit between learner and teacher, to learn about options for language learning, and to learn and practice strategies that facilitate self-reliance [18]. Strategy training should not be abstract and theoretical but should be highly practical and useful for students.

No one knows everything about how people learn languages, but there is strong support for sharing, through strategy training, what we *do* know. Research shows us that learners who receive strategy training generally learn better than those who do not, and that certain techniques for such training are more beneficial than others.

How to Prepare Yourself to Conduct Strategy Training

Two issues should be considered as you prepare yourself for conducting strategy training: your knowledge of language learning strategies and your attitudes about role changes.

Expanded Knowledge of Language Learning Strategies The more you know about language learning strategies, the better trainer you will be. There is a great deal you can do to expand your knowledge in this area, beginning with a review of the parts of this book that are of greatest interest to you. Read other books and articles on the topic; see the reference list in this book for abundant suggestions. Attend language learning strategy sessions at professional conferences. Find or create in-service training activities that stress language learning strategies. Get your institution to sponsor such training for language teachers. Find out all you can!

But you do not have to wait until you become an expert on strategies before you can provide effective training for your students. If you follow the guidelines in this chapter and use what you know about learning strategies, you will be able to make a difference in your students' ability to learn languages.

Reconsider Your Attitudes About Roles Think through your assumptions about the roles of students and teachers, because these roles often undergo change when learners start to take more responsibility for their success in the language classroom. Having read thus far, you probably do not need intensive restructuring of your beliefs about learner and teacher roles. You are probably open-minded and may have already experimented with classroom activities allowing you to be more a facilitator than a director. Or perhaps you are interested in experimenting with such activities but do not know exactly where to begin. Talk with other teachers, particularly those who are open to new ideas about roles. Look for games, simulations, and structured exercises in which you and your students can experiment with new teacher and learner roles in class.

Three Types of Strategy Training

Language learning strategies can be taught in at least three different ways: awareness training, one-time strategy training, and long-term strategy training.

Awareness Training Awareness training is also known as consciousness-raising or familiarization training. In this situation, participants become aware of and familiar with the general idea of language learning strategies and the way such strategies can help them accomplish various language tasks. In awareness training, however, participants do not have to use the strategies in actual, on-the-spot language tasks.

Awareness training is very important, because it is often the individual's introduction to the concept of learning strategies. It should be fun and motivating, so that participants will be encouraged to expand their knowledge of strategies at a later time. For this reason, it is best not to use the lecture format for awareness training. Participants can be teachers, students, and anyone else interested in language learning processes; no special background in learning theory or strategies need be assumed. Two examples of exercises for awareness training are found at the end of Chapter 1: the Embedded Strategies Game and the Strategy Search Game.

One-Time Strategy Training One-time strategy training involves learning and practicing one or more strategies with actual language tasks, usually those found in the regular language learning program. This kind of training gives the learner information on the value of the strategy, when it can be used, how to use it, and how to evaluate the success of the strategy. However, one-time training is not connected to a long-term sequence of strategy training. One-time training is appropriate for learners who have a need for particular, identifiable, and very targeted strategies that can be taught in one or just a few session(s). An example is in the teaching of certain memory strategies without integrating them into a more prolonged strategy training approach. In general, one-time training is not as valuable as long-term training.

Long-Term Strategy Training Long-term strategy training, like one-time strategy training, involves learning and practicing strategies with actual language tasks. Again, students learn the significance of particular strategies, when and how to use them, and how to monitor and evaluate their own performance. Like one-time training, long-term training should be tied to the tasks and objectives of the language program. However, long-term training is more prolonged and covers a greater number of strategies. It is likely to be more effective than one-time training.

A Model for Strategy Training

The following eight-step model for strategy training, summarized in Table 6.2, assumes that you have already assessed your students' current learning strategies using one or more of the techniques described earlier.

This model focuses on the teaching of learning strategies themselves, rather than on the broader aspects of language learning. It is especially useful for long-term strategy training, usually closely tied to regular language learning, but can be adapted for one-time training by selecting specific units. Of course, you do not need to use this model if you are concerned only with awareness training at this point. The steps might not always have to be done in this order; some can be performed at the same time, or in a slightly different order [19].

The first five are planning and preparation steps, while the last three

Table 6.2   STEPS IN THE STRATEGY TRAINING MODEL

1. Determine the learners' needs and the time available.
2. Select strategies well.
3. Consider integration of strategy training.
4. Consider motivational issues.
5. Prepare materials and activities.
6. Conduct "completely informed training."
7. Evaluate the strategy training.
8. Revise the strategy training.

Source: Original.

involve conducting, evaluating, and revising the training. As you proceed through the design steps (1–5), try to get feedback from other people if possible. It always helps to get useful comments and suggestions. Better yet, work with a training partner, such as another teacher, throughout the whole sequence.

Step 1: Determine the Learners' Needs and the Time Available The initial step in your training program is to consider the needs of the learners and determine the amount of time you have for the activity. Consider first who the learners are and what they need. Are they children? Adolescents? College students? Graduate students? Adults in continuing education? Refugees or immigrants? Are they advanced language students? Intermediates? Beginners? What is their verbal ability [20]? What are their strengths and weaknesses? What learning strategies have your students been using, according to the strategy assessment results? Which strategies do you think they need to learn? Is there a wide gap between the strategies they have been using and those you think they need to learn? If so, do cultural factors play a role? How do these students view their roles as language learners? Do they take responsibility, or will you need to help them change their attitudes about learning? Have you given the learners a chance to express their desires about strategies they might like to learn? If so, what kinds of strategies were they interested in?

Consider how much time you and your students have available for strategy training, and when you might do it. Are you pressed for time, or can you work strategy training in with no trouble? Can you relate strategy training to the language tasks already under way, so that the strategies become immediately applied and learners can understand and practice them?

Step 2: Select Strategies Well First, select strategies which are related to the needs and characteristics of your learners. Note especially whether there are strong cultural or other biases in favor of (or against) a particular type of strategy, as shown by the strategy assessment you have conducted earlier. If strong biases exist, you might need to choose strategies that do not completely contradict what the learners are already doing, or if you do choose to train strategies which are counter to what learners now prefer, you might need to introduce the new strategies gradually while building on what the learners prefer.

Second, choose more than one kind of strategy to teach (by deciding the kinds of compatible, mutually supporting strategies that are important for your students). Third, choose strategies that are generally useful for most learners and transferable to a variety of language situations and tasks. Fourth, choose some strategies that are very easy to learn, and some strategies that are very valuable but might require a bit more effort. In other words, do not include all easy strategies or all difficult strategies.

Think of this training process as more than just teaching metacognitive and cognitive strategies, the usual fare of strategy training. Other kinds of strategies—memory, compensation, affective, and social—are also very important for strategy training.

The following sequence describes an example of a *broad focus* in strategy training, combining four groups of strategies: affective, compensation, social, and metacognitive. Learners initially try to listen to a target language passage that contains many words they do not know. They discuss their feelings (an affective self-assessment strategy) about trying to understand such a difficult passage. Then they learn and practice guessing strategies (a form of compensation strategy) in pairs or small groups, thus using social strategies. Next, learners evaluate the success of their guessing strategies (via the metacognitive strategies of self-monitoring and self-evaluating), and, finally, they discuss how they feel about themselves and about these strategies (another use of affective self-assessment). This sequence allows the interweaving of many different categories of strategies. It is not necessary to use this many different kinds of strategies in the same training exercise, but it is certainly feasible. This broad focus, including multiple strategy types, trains learners in large segments of the whole strategy classification system, shows students how strategies interact, and may give students a new understanding of the language learning process. However, this broad focus does not allow precise assessment of training effectiveness in reference to any specific strategy.

On the other hand, it is also possible to use a *narrow focus*, centering on the training of just one or two learning strategies rather than an integrated set of many strategies. The narrow focus leads to less overall training time, reduces the possibility of overloading the learner with diverse strategies, and allows more precise assessment of the effectiveness of the strategy training, but it does *not* allow for multiple strategies to interact to maximize learning potential. Note that the narrow focus is not necessarily the same as one-time strategy training, which concerns the amount of time spent. It is possible to do strategy training with a narrow focus over a long period of time, just as broad-focus training can be long-term.

A *combination* approach to training might be as follows: The trainer presents many strategies and strategy groups (*broad focus*), and learners are asked to rate subjectively the use of different strategies or strategy groups. Then, given these ratings, specific strategies are selected for more focused training and assessment (*narrow focus*) [21]. This is an excellent way to approach strategy training. It gives learners the "big picture" at first, then moves into specific strategies which the learners have chosen themselves. The element of learner choice in structuring training is very important, since learning strategies are the epitome of learner choice and self-direction.

Step 3: Consider Integration of Strategy Training In general, as hinted above, it is most helpful to integrate strategy training with the tasks, objectives, and materials used in the regular language training program. Attempts to provide relatively detached, content-independent strategy training have been at best only moderately successful. Learners sometimes rebel against strategy training that is not sufficiently linked with their own language training [22].

When strategy training is closely integrated with language learning, learners better understand how the strategies can be used in a significant, meaningful context [23]. Needless to say, meaningfulness makes it easier to remember the strategies. However, it is also necessary to show learners how to transfer the strategies to new tasks, outside of the immediate ones.

It is also possible to provide detached, nonintegrated strategy training (for instance, a short course on strategies unconnected with current language learning activities), followed by integrated, course-related strategy training. One way to do this is to provide short, well-planned programs of detached training on selected strategies, followed by unobtrusive "prompting" of learning strategies integrated into actual language instruction. The prompts or cues to use certain strategies are gradually faded during regular instruction, so that responsibility for initiation of appropriate learning strategies is eventually transferred from the teacher (or the materials) to the student [24].

Step 4: Consider Motivational Issues Consider the kind of motivation you will build into your training program. Decide whether to give grades or partial course credit for attainment of new strategies, or whether to assume that learners will be motivated to learn strategies purely in order to become more effective learners. Possibly a combination of both motivations will work. Of course, if learners have gone through a strategy assessment phase, their interest in strategies is likely to be heightened, and if you explain how using good strategies can make language learning easier, students will be even more interested in participating in strategy training. Another way to increase motivation is to let learners have some say in selecting the language activities or tasks they will use, or to let them choose the strategies they will learn.

A different type of motivational issue, already hinted at, relates to preexisting cultural (or other) preferences for certain types of strategies. If learners are brought up all their lives to prefer particular learning strategies, like analyzing grammar or memorizing word lists, they may not be highly motivated to drop these preferences and instantly learn a whole new set of strategies. Or they might become confused. You need to be sensitive to learners' original strategy preferences and the motivation that propels these preferences. Being sensitive to this issue does not mean, however, that you should avoid introducing new strategies! It means that you might need to phase in very new strategies gently and gradually, without whisking away students' "security blankets," no matter how dysfunctional you might consider those old strategies to be.

Step 5: Prepare Materials and Activities The materials you are using for language instruction will double well for strategy training materials. In addition, you might develop some handouts on when and how to use the strategies you want to focus on. You might even develop a handbook for learners to use at home and in class, especially if you are planning long-term strategy training. Better yet, get the learners to develop a strategy handbook themselves! They can contribute to it incrementally, as they learn new strategies that prove successful for them. In any case, choose language activities and materials that are likely to be interesting to the learners—or have the students select their own language activities and materials, as mentioned under Step 4.

Step 6: Conduct "Completely Informed Training" As you conduct strategy training, make a special point to inform the learners as completely as possible about why the strategies are important and how they can be used in new situations. Provide practice with strategies in several language tasks, and point out how transfer of strategies is possible from task to task. Give learners the explicit opportunity to evaluate the success of their new strategies, exploring the reasons why these strategies might have helped. Research shows that strategy training which fully informs the learner (by indicating why the strategy is useful, how it can be transferred to different tasks, and how learners can evaluate the success of the strategy) is more successful than training that does not [25].

The following sequence might be useful in presenting a new strategy: First, students try a language task *without* any training in the target strategy, and they comment on the strategies they spontaneously used to do the task. Second, you explain and demonstrate the new strategy. As you do so, build on what the learners said they were doing in the first step and show how they might either improve use of their current strategies or employ an entirely new strategy. Third, learners apply the new strategy to the same language task as before, or a similar one. Depending on the nature of the strategy, it is possible to get pairs of learners to work together to practice the strategy, with one student using the strategy and the other prompting; then they change roles [26].

Of course, completely informed training is undoubtedly the best and most effective training technique. However, in the *very rare* instances when this technique proves impossible, more subtle training techniques might be necessary. For example, when learners are, through cultural influences, adamantly opposed to new learning strategies, you might need to camouflage the new strategies, or introduce them very gradually, paired with strategies the learners already know and prefer [27].

Step 7: Evaluate the Strategy Training Learners' own comments about their strategy use are part of the training itself. These self-assessments provide practice with the strategies of self-monitoring and self-evaluating, and they offer useful data for you. Your own observations, during and after the training and following, are useful for evaluating the success of strategy training. Possible criteria for evaluating training are task improvement, general skill improvement, maintenance of the new strategy over time, transfer of strategy to other relevant tasks, and improvement in learner attitudes [28].

Step 8: Revise the Strategy Training As in any training effort, the evaluation (Step 7) will suggest possible revisions for your materials. This leads right back to Step 1, a reconsideration of the characteristics and needs of the learners in light of the cycle of strategy training that has just occurred. Of course, many of the steps will pass much more quickly after the first cycle. It is not necessary to start from scratch with each step after one cycle has been completed.

Concrete Examples of Strategy Training

A general curricular sequence developed for promoting good reading strategies for language learners, an example of informed training, involves three main procedures: (a) diagnosing the strategies learners already use via a think-aloud procedure, (b) setting the class climate by giving learners a few learning tasks and asking them to explain the strategies they use, and (c) introducing the new strategies and providing plenty of practice [29].

In addition to promoting the use of guessing strategies (a form of compensation strategy), this training sequence also encourages learners to express openly, in a group, their feelings about the effectiveness of the guessing strategies. This kind of evaluative discussion brings in organizational strategies (e.g., self-evaluating), affective strategies (e.g., discussing your feelings with someone else), and social strategies (cooperating with peers, becoming aware of others' thoughts and feelings).

This training sequence illustrates the teaching of strategies for improving target language reading skill, but it can be used for other language skills as well. In addition, any kind of language learning strategies can be taught with this kind of sequence.

Another example of a strategy training sequence, this time focused specifically on English as a second language [30], is similar to the sequence above in informing learners of the value of the strategies and in encouraging the mutually supportive use of different kinds of learning strategies. This sequence suggests encouraging ESL students to practice the new strategies outside of class and asking them to report on their extracurricular use of strategies. It also recommends reminding learners to use the new strategies in other tasks and checking with learners to make sure they are using the new strategies.

In addition to these two strategy training sequences, Chapter 7, on networking, describes many more examples of strategy training modes. The information already presented here and the examples to be presented in the next chapter will help you as you design your own strategy training sequence.

SUMMARY

This chapter has presented tips on assessing your students' strategies and conducting strategy training. The concrete techniques in this chapter will be very valuable in the assessment and training process.

ACTIVITIES FOR READERS

Activity 6.1. Think of Reasons for Assessing Strategy Use

Brainstorm all the reasons you can think of for assessing the kinds of language learning strategies people use. Make a list, then categorize the results.

Activity 6.2. Consider the Strategy Assessment Options

Which types of strategy assessment seem the most relevant to your students? Which could you apply in your own role as teacher? To answer these questions, complete Table 6.3.

Table 6.3   ACTIVITY ON STRATEGY ASSESSMENT OPTIONS

Strategy assessment technique	Purpose	Kind of information gained	Amount of detail (too much, too little, just right?)	Amount of time needed	Ease of adminis- tration and analysis
Observations					
Interviews					
Think-aloud procedures					
Note-taking					
Diaries					
Less- structured surveys					
More- structured surveys					
Combination (specify:					
_____					
_____					
_____)					

Source: Original.

Activity 6.3. Assess Your Own Strategies

Choose a technique of strategy assessment described in this chapter. Assess your own language learning strategies. When you have done this, consider what you may have learned about yourself that you did not know before. What implications does this new information have for you as a teacher?

Activity 6.4. Go Fishing

An ancient proverb says, "Give a man a fish and he eats for a day. Teach him how to fish and he eats for a lifetime" [31]. Explain what this saying means to you in the area of language learning and teaching. Give examples from your own experience, or give examples of the way you *wish* your own experience had been.

Now consider Tyacke and Mendelsohn's (1986, p. 178) response to this proverb: "But just as there are many different kinds of rods, different kinds of bait and different fishing locations, all of which offer a variety of choices and experiences, there are different ways of learning language." What does this rejoinder mean to you? How does it affect what you think of the proverb as applied to strategy training? What are the pros and cons of conducting strategy training, from your perspective?

Activity 6.5. Design a Strategy Training Sequence

This chapter offered tips for conducting strategy training. An eight-step system for planning and conducting strategy training was presented, as well as some concrete examples of strategy training designs. Consider these ideas, as well as the examples of real strategy training projects described in Chapter 7. Keeping these recommendations in mind, *design a strategy training sequence for a specific group of learners.*

If you are currently teaching, choose a class that could benefit from strategy training, and focus on designing a training sequence to meet their needs. Alternatively, think of a class you have taught in the past, or describe a hypothetical group of students who have certain characteristics (which you define).

Be as specific as possible in terms of the language activities and materials involved, as well as the strategies to be taught. Go through the first five planning and preparation steps in the training model presented in this chapter. Get feedback from others on your planning and preparation. Then explain in detail how you would handle the next three steps (conducting, evaluating, and revising the training).

EXERCISES TO USE WITH YOUR STUDENTS

Exercise 6.1. Assess Your Students' Strategies

Assess your students' language learning strategies using *at least two* of the techniques described in this chapter. Provide feedback to your students on their strategy use. Discuss which of the assessment techniques seemed to provide the most accurate information.

Exercise 6.2. Implement Strategy Training

Now that you have designed a strategy training program (Activity 6.5), implement it with your students. To do this, use Steps 6, 7, and 8 of the strategy training model. Make your own observations about the most effective and least effective aspects of the training, and ask for feedback from students, too. Consider ways to improve the strategy training.

Exercise 6.3. Develop a "Successful Strategies" Handbook

Ask your students to start contributing to a "Successful Strategies" handbook. It can contain tips on strategies the students find most useful, examples of strategies applied to specific kinds of tasks or materials, comments made during strategy training, selections from learners' diaries about strategies, or any other strategy-related information. Develop the handbook throughout the language course, with students adding to it and using it as a way to share strategy ideas. A loose-leaf notebook will allow easiest access and expansion.

Exercise 6.4. Discuss Diaries

Hold "diary discussions" once a week, perhaps every Friday, as a means of sharing ideas and impressions among students, based on use of strategies with their usual language learning tasks. If you want, provide short amounts of class time periodically for students to write in their diaries. Use of diaries can thus become part of a regular, ongoing strategy assessment and training effort, integrated with normal language activities.

Chapter 7

Networking at Home and Abroad

Example is better than precept.

LATIN PROVERB

PREVIEW QUESTIONS

1. How have language learning strategies been used in diverse settings and programs around the world?
2. What practical differences exist between explicit and implicit encouragement of strategy use?
3. Where can I find resources concerning language learning strategies?

INTRODUCTION TO NETWORKING

As you put language learning strategies into action, you might want to make connections with other people who are interested in strategies and active learning. You are not alone in your interests; other people can help you, and you can help them. You can develop a support network starting at home and reaching around the world. This chapter presents examples of language learning strategies in action in many countries. These resources will provide you with lots of good ideas, as well as people or institutions to contact for more information. The examples are in two general groups: *explicit encouragement of language learning strategies* and *active but implicit stimulation of language learning strategies*. Language learners involved in these examples include tourists, refugees, immigrants, government workers, businesspeople, military personnel, Peace Corps volunteers, and students of all ages enrolled in primary, secondary, and university language programs. They include children, teens, adults, and senior citizens. These examples suggest a wide range of options for using language learning strategies.

213

EXPLICIT ENCOURAGEMENT OF LANGUAGE LEARNING STRATEGIES

This group includes 11 examples of explicit learning strategy use from the United States, France, the Philippines, England, Denmark, and Israel. Learning strategies are a consistent focus but are handled differently in each of these examples.

The Language Learning Disc: A Videodisk for Training Language Learning Strategies (USA)

Joan Rubin, a founder of the research area of language learning strategies, has produced an exciting instructional tool known as the "Language Learning Disc" [1]. The disk, designed for adults (high school and above), is a two-sided (1-hour) interactive videodisk with five acompanying diskettes providing an average of 8 hours of instruction. This level 3 disk is programmed to run on a Pioneer LDV-1000 player, a Sony PVM 1271Q monitor, and an IBM PC with a Microkey 1000 interface card. With a Microkey 1125 card, other equipment can be substituted. The disk is currently being converted to run on the Sony View system as well.

Intended for use before beginning an introductory-level foreign language course, the disk is designed to help students take charge of their progress by learning how to learn a language. Says Rubin, disk users can expect to

1. Gain insights into their own approach to learning.
2. Learn to choose strategies appropriate to a task and learning purpose.
3. Learn to use these strategies in a classroom, self-study, or job situation.
4. Learn to use strategies specific to reading, listening, and conversation.
5. Be able to define strategies for improving memory for language learning.
6. Learn how to effectively transfer knowledge about language and communication from one language to another.
7. Learn to use resources wisely.
8. Be able to deal more effectively with errors.

Learners can accomplish these purposes using a wide range of topics, including reading an instructional manual to connect a videocassette recorder, watching a spy story, comparing elements of cross-cultural communication, reading a scuba text for new words, or comparing elements used in borrowing money to recognize speech variation. Students can work with 20 languages in this instructional program, thus gaining experience in the process of language learning. The disk includes 13 major dramatic scenarios, 48 locations, and some 60 actors. The four major characters—a military attaché assigned to Korea, a plant manager assigned to Argentina, a Russian translator who will be working on Russian texts and broadcasts, and a Japanese sales manager who will promote Japanese pharmaceuticals in the United States—all provide authentic role models.

Materials are presented in an integrated fashion so that students are exposed to the same strategy in several different lessons. If they don't grasp a strategy in one presentation, they can get it in another. Throughout the material, students can choose the language, the topic, and the level of difficulty. Coaching is provided throughout via inductive inferencing; that is, learners are given clues as to the most appropriate response. As a result of using this instructional material, learners focus on the *process of learning* in order to improve their learning of a foreign language.

The disk uses video in three ways: first, to model natural foreign language communication so that students can observe foreign language speakers using their native language; second, to enable students to participate and get feedback on their choices in a foreign language; and third, to model cognitive approaches to problem solving in foreign language situations. The disk is divided into three main sections: An Introduction; General Language Learning Strategies; and Strategies Related to Reading, Active Listening or Conversation [2]. Field testing of the materials with learners at the Defense Language Institute and at a large international corporation helped to refine the instructions and provide an evaluation of the disk. Responses were very positive.

The disk offers an appealing array of strategies and authentic situations. The technical quality of the presentation and the use of qualified native speakers makes the disk especially valuable. The disk holds promise for a range of language learners in secondary schools, universities, and other institutions. For more information, contact Joan Rubin, P.O. Box 143, Pinole, CA 94564, USA.

CALLA: A Model of Content-Based Language Learning Which Includes Training in Strategies (USA)

The Cognitive Academic Language Learning Approach (CALLA) has been designed by two of the most prolific contributors to the learning strategy area, Anna Uhl Chamot and J. Michael O'Malley. This model [3] embeds training in learning strategies within activities for developing both language skills and content area skills. CALLA provides transitional instruction for upper elementary and secondary students at intermediate and advanced levels of English as a second language. This model also teaches students to use relevant learning strategies to bolster both their language skills and their skills in various content areas. CALLA's purpose is to help learners use English, their new language, to learn through the integration of language and content. The model has three components:

1. The *content component* of the CALLA model represents declarative knowledge, e.g., concepts, facts, and skills for science, mathematics, and social studies, or (in the language area) grammatical, rhetorical, or literary knowledge.
2. The *English language development component* of CALLA aims to teach procedural knowledge that students need to use language as a tool for learning. Students are given practice using language in academic contexts so their language skills become automatic.
3. The *learning strategies instruction component* of the CALLA model suggests ways in which teachers can foster autonomy in their students [4].

Chamot and O'Malley rightly feel that strategies for learning languages and for learning other subjects are often the same, and that learning strategies can give limited English proficient learners a boost as these students prepare to make a transition or move into mainstream classes. The learning strategy instruction component of CALLA therefore shows students how to apply the strategies, suggests a variety of strategies for different tasks, provides examples throughout the curriculum to enhance transfer, and shows how teachers' prompting of strategies can gradually be reduced. Learning strategies are embedded in sample lesson plans in the areas of science, mathematics, and social studies [5]. In addition, the CALLA model includes a generalized lesson plan, divided into five phases: Preparation, Presentation, Practice, Evaluation, and Follow-Up Expansion.

Programs using CALLA are now being implemented in several school districts, and the model is continuing to be refined. The model is valuable for four reasons. First, the linkage between language and content skills using the CALLA model is fruitful. Second, the structured nature of the CALLA lesson plan helps teachers to include the right elements, such as learning strategies, language development, content skills, and ways to assess all three. Third, the model suggests cooperation between language teachers and mainstream content area teachers. While this kind of cooperation is often logistically difficult, it is truly necessary if limited English-proficient learners are to get the best education possible. Fourth, the CALLA model awakens teachers and learners to the possibilities of using learning strategies for both language development and content area skill development.

More information on the model is available from Anna Uhl Chamot, P.O. Box 40937, Washington, DC 20016, USA; or J. Michael O'Malley,

Evaluation Assistance Center-East, Georgetown University, 1916 Wilson Boulevard, Suite 302, Arlington, VA 22201, USA.

The CRAPEL Model of Self-Directed Language Learning (France)

CRAPEL, the Centre de Recherches et d'Applications Pédagogiques en Langues, is part of the Université de Nancy II in France. Since 1974 CRAPEL has been the hub of European research and experimentation on self-directed language learning [6]. CRAPEL provides self-directed language learning opportunities for a variety of learners, such as university students, outside students, and employees in local organizations desiring on-site courses [7]. A variety of course structures is offered, all of which allow some degree of learner autonomy—the ultimate goal.

Learners who choose immediate autonomy are assigned to a "helper," who is a native or competent speaker of English experienced in assisting autonomous learners. The helper consciously avoids the role of tutor or teacher and instead aids the learner in learning how to learn [8]. The helper assists learners at any stage of the learning process, acts as an objective observer, is open to discussion, and gives advice when asked. In addition, the helper provides opportunities for the learner to receive feedback in authentic situations, helps match the learner with peers and with appropriate tasks, offers materials when needed, helps the learner use strategies, keeps detailed notes on the learner, shows sincere caring, and prepares the learner psychologically and environmentally for the task of learning [9].

The learner's role is to take major responsibility for defining needs, goals, priorities; furnishing or selecting materials; organizing learning experiences; determining the pace and time of study; diagnosing his or her own learning difficulties; developing adequate learning techniques; self-monitoring; evaluating progress; and, in general, guiding and planning his or her own learning process. All of these are metacognitive strategies. The learner is also expected to maintain a high level of motivation, which would of course involve affective strategies [10].

The institution must provide a flexible structure allowing for self-direction, rapid availability and reproduction of materials, equipment when needed, contacts with native speakers, and logistical and financial management [11].

The individualized learner–helper design is not the only structure available. In 1977–1978 CRAPEL introduced a group self-tuition structure for senior citizens and others with available free time. In this structure, the group (10 to 15 people) has responsibility for organizing its own learning, after participating in five consecutive half-day sessions on how to do it. Each group defines its objectives, schedules, procedures, and materials.

Helpers take no part in the groups unless called upon, but they and various native speakers are available when needed.

Ongoing research and development occurs constantly at CRAPEL. For more information on CRAPEL and its programs, write Henri Holec, CRA-PEL, Université de Nancy II, Nancy, France.

Training in Language Learning Strategies for Peace Corps Language Instructors and Volunteers (Philippines)

In the tropical heat of the Philippines an experiment was undertaken to improve the language learning strategies of students by (a) providing learning strategy materials and (b) influencing the teaching strategies of instructors. The project was a joint effort designed and led by Anne Lomperis, formerly of the Refugee Service Center (Manila Office) of the Center for Applied Linguistics, Washington, DC, USA, and Bibbet Palo, Language Specialist of the Peace Corps/Philippines. These project leaders saw a need for training both instructors and learners in strategies for communicative language teaching and learning as part of a larger training effort.

The language learners were Peace Corps Volunteers (PCVs) learning a variety of languages spoken in the Philippines in preparation for taking on their 2-year assignments in that country. Their language instructors and coordinators were native speakers from the Philippines, who were expected to provide 180 to 190 hours of language instruction to each of the PCVs. They previously had little or no intensive instruction in communicative language teaching strategies or student self-direction.

To help language instructors, coordinators, and PCVs, the Washington staff developed a language learning strategy handbook known as *Improving Your Language Learning: Strategies for Peace Corps Volunteers* [12]. This handbook is simple, direct, and geared toward the specific needs of the Peace Corps in Southeast Asia. The whole range of language learning strategies is included. Using this handbook and other training materials, the project leaders conducted teacher-training sessions on communicative language instruction. Response to the training was very positive. "The [strategy-related] materials . . . were useful and exciting to all; [the language instructors and coordinators] especially were fascinated by the concepts," said one of the leaders [13].

Language instructors and coordinators wanted more information on how learning strategies could be promoted by specific teaching activities. Inspired by the training, one language coordinator created a booklet of teaching activities matched with selected language learning strategies, to be shared with other instructional personnel. The training process had a "spillover effect" throughout the Southeast Asian region. Learning strategy materials were shared with other Peace Corps language staffers at a regional training session in Chieng Mai, Thailand.

In addition to teacher training, diagnosis of strategies was also an important part of the project. Using a short form of the Strategy Inventory for Language Learning (SILL), included in this volume, the project leaders gathered data about language learning strategies typically used by PCVs. For more information, contact Allene Grognet, Center for Applied Linguistics, 1118 - 22nd Street NW, Washington, DC 20037, USA.

A Eurocentre Experiment in Autonomy (England)

As described by Henri Holec, the Eurocentre language training institute in Bournemouth (UK) caters mainly to students who want to be able to live in the country of the target language, and who are less concerned with professional or vocational language requirements. An experiment in autonomous language learning was conducted at the Eurocentre language training institute [14]. This experiment involved continuous self-assessment of oral communicative skills. Even though teachers maintained their traditional, rather directive roles, it was possible to introduce some elements of learner autonomy by using self-assessment strategies. Self-assessment served two purposes: (a) aiding learners to discover and use assessment criteria, and (b) helping them evaluate their own progress in order to plan future activities.

In this project self-assessment was done by means of five diverse activities, ranging from more structured to less structured. Learners were taught to compare their self-assessments with those of others, although this technique had the danger of implying the existence of a single correct judgment. Furthermore, the assessment tools were mostly of the academic type and might not have been greatly relevant to extracurricular situations [15]. However, this was still an interesting and useful experiment in encouraging one important set of learning strategies in a traditional language learning environment. For further information, contact Bournemouth Eurocentre, Bournemouth, Dorset, England.

GRASP: An In-Service Teacher Training Project
Involving Self-Direction for Teachers and Learners (England)

Project GRASP (Getting Results and Solving Problems) is a multiyear British project jointly funded by the Department of Trade and Industry; the Comino Foundation, a private educational trust; and Dudley Local Education Authority. This project is coordinated by Anna Smith and Peter

Revill of the Dudley L.E.A. in the English Midlands [16]. The project is concerned with the entire teaching-learning process. It focuses on providing in-service training to teachers, with the objective of encouraging active learning, self-direction, and problem solving for both teachers and students. The expectation is that the effort will lead to better results in the education system as a whole. Project leaders feel that the best way to encourage active learning in students is to train teachers in *teaching strategies* which will facilitate appropriate *learning strategies*. Teacher training must involve active learning and self-responsibility on the part of the teachers themselves, if the ultimate goal is to get students to become active learners [17].

The project involves 12 schools: four comprehensive secondary schools and eight primary schools. Eighty teachers are involved in the project at the moment, but this number will probably grow. Project teachers have responsibility for children aged 8 to 14. Five of the 12 schools are multiethnic and multicultural. Therefore, many project teachers—especially at the primary level—have become, of necessity, teachers of English as a second language as part of their instructional duties. The teaching and learning strategies fostered by this project are designed to have repercussions in all curriculum areas, including language.

To date the in-service has taken the following forms: (a) two 2-day residential conferences for project teachers, (b) one 2-day residential conference for school coordinators, (c) in-house in-service training in each of the schools, and (d) 2-day residential training for each school on team-building strategies. In-service conferences and sessions include active learning for teachers in the form of games, simulations, and other experiential exercises. For active learning purposes, traditional lectures are avoided, though they are not seen as inherently "wrong" in all circumstances. Through a variety of active exercises, teachers experientially learn a curriculum development sequence that consists of designing clear objectives, thinking of as many solutions as possible for achieving each objective (divergent thinking), selecting the best solution or solutions, putting the solution(s) into action, and reviewing the success of the solution(s). Teachers are learning how to make their own teaching strategies more open and more responsive to learners' characteristics. They are encouraged to use these new strategies in their classes and share their experiences with each other.

In this project the teachers are learning new roles and beliefs. They are consciously moving from the role of "fount of all knowledge" to "facilitator of learning," and from the belief of "I'm here to tell you the way" to "I'm here to help you." These changes involve some movement of responsibility to the children and a greater concern for learning strategies. For more details, contact Mrs. A. Smith, Project Deputy, GRASP Project, Dudley Teachers' Centre, Laburnum Road, Kingswinford, West Midlands, DY6 8EH, England.

Strategy Training in Primary School Classes
Involving English as a Foreign Language (Denmark)

"The Flower Model" is the evocative name of Leni Dam's approach to primary school language instruction in Denmark [18]. The model assumes learner responsibility from the start and has been used with full classes in the range of 20 to 30 students. The children are in their first year of English and have 4 hours per week of English. In this model, students work out their own needs and interests, arrange their own syllabuses, make decisions, and form contracts with the teacher.

The model of language education is represented as a series of petals on a flower, as shown in Figure 7.1. In the center of the flower is the word NEGOTIATION. The petals include Objectives, Activities, Outcomes, Evaluation, Pupils' Contributions, and Materials. On each of the petals its concept is broken down into components; for example, the concept Pupils' Contributions is divided into emotions, attitudes, values, background, abilities, strategies, needs, interests, knowledge, and skills. There are arrows from the central part, NEGOTIATION, to each of the petals, and each of the petals is linked with all the other petals through a network of arrows. The Teacher's Contributions/Role is shown at the bottom of the flower in a rectangle.

At the beginning of the course learners are asked why they are learning English and what they want to do with the language. This helps learners decide on their own language needs. In the initial period, no text is used, and learning is based on materials the learners bring in themselves: stickers, stamps, children's books, jokes, magazines. Grammar is not taught explicitly, but children work out structure inductively and then make grammar wall-posters with the help of their teacher. Children are given interesting activities from which to choose. The teacher introduces a completed worksheet, and later students learn to do their own worksheets, gradually taking increased responsibility for choosing topics, deciding on what to achieve, specifying objectives, and evaluating progress. Specifying objectives is often very difficult for the students, who need a lot of help from the teacher at first but who gradually learn to do it. Regular self-evaluation is also part of the process. Learners' self-evaluations are generally very positive, both toward their language progress and toward their ability to make decisions about their own learning.

In this ambitious scheme, primary-school language learners are motivated by a variety of materials and activities, a range of possible strategies, and the chance to make decisions for themselves. Dam's own students are typically from working-class backgrounds and are *not* college-bound. That the model could work for such children makes the possibility of transfer to many other settings even greater. For information, write Leni Dam, Paedagogisk Central, Hundige Boulevard 11, 2670 Greve Strand, Denmark.

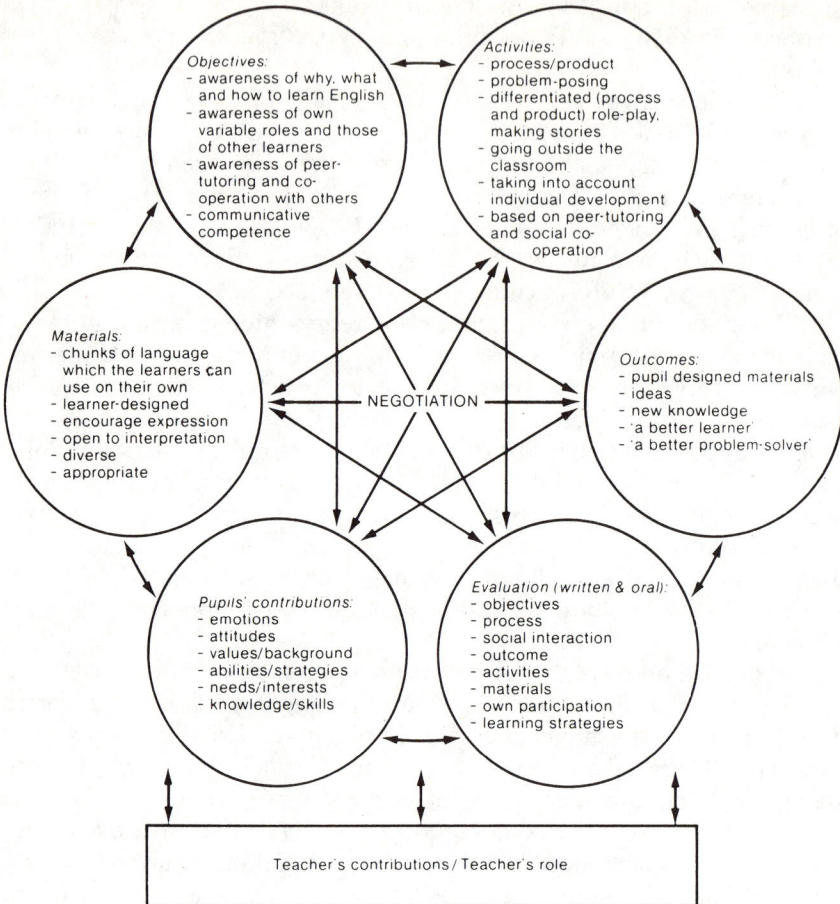

Figure 7.1 The Flower Model. (*Source*: Dam, cited in Dickinson (1987, p. 62).)

Exploring Language Learning in a University Language Institute (USA)

In a project at the intensive American Language Program of Columbia University, Anita Wenden explored a variety of language learning aspects, one of which was learning strategies [19]. She developed materials to be used with two multiethnic groups of very advanced learners of English. Wenden told the students that 2 of the class hours ordinarily devoted to developing conversational fluency would focus on the topic of language learning. According to Wenden, the goal was to sharpen and expand student awareness of various aspects of their language learning experience, including the following:

1. Strategies they utilized.
2. Aspects of language they attended to.
3. Their evaluation of their language proficiency (i.e., performance and competence as the outcome of their learning endeavors).
4. Criteria used for judging the usefulness of various learning contexts and strategies.
5. Their objectives.
6. Themselves as facilitating or inhibiting language learning (e.g., feelings, language aptitude, personality).
7. Their beliefs about how best to learn a language.

Each of these aspects formed the basis of a module, with modules reflecting "informed training" (see Chapter 6). As described by Wenden, materials comprised minilectures and readings about language learning, research findings on learning strategies, and student accounts of their learning. She provided training tasks, such as comprehension exercises, class discussions based on the reading or listening passages, outside language practice, and writing diaries.

As explained by Wenden, one class mutinied against the training program and dropped out, except for a small cadre of learners who met after school; the other class cooperated in a purely mechanical fashion. She traced the problem to the lack of integration of the learner training materials with the language training tasks and objectives. After she revised the materials to integrate them more closely with the language tasks and objectives, students became much more interested, thus underscoring the power of integrated rather than detached strategy training (see Chapter 6). It might also have helped to give the learners a choice about the nature of the training and to make sure that the materials were geared directly to the needs of these very advanced students. A less dedicated individual than Wenden might have given up in frustration, but she wisely persevered—with much more successful results after the revision. For complete details, contact Anita Wenden, 97-37 63rd Road, 15E, Forest Hills North, NY 11374.

"Language Therapy" in a Multiage Setting (Israel)

Andrew Cohen, a well-known researcher and teacher from the Hebrew University of Jerusalem, has become an unofficial "language therapist" for students of many ages at Ulpan Akiva in South Netanya, Israel [20]. Ulpan Akiva was founded 30 years ago by Shulamith Katznelson, who is still the director. Katznelson won the Israeli Knesset Education Prize for her outstanding work in bringing together peoples of different races, religions, ethnic backgrounds, and nations for "more than just language learning," as Cohen puts it. Striving to create peace, the Ulpan serves a variety of students—Jewish immigrants trying to improve their Hebrew, West Bank and Gaza Arabs sent by their employers to study Hebrew, other resident non-Jews such as diplomats, and tourists wanting to learn Hebrew. Ages range from teens to 80s.

Cohen's work at Ulpan Akiva started when he went there 8 years ago to study Arabic. As soon as he arrived as a student, the Ulpan put him to work as a lecturer because of his language instruction background. He has been going there once a month ever since, each time giving two formal, hour-long talks to the current students, usually about 40 to 50 students per talk. One of the sessions is in English and the other in Hebrew (for more advanced students). The talks concern various aspects of strategy use and self-direction. Themes vary—for instance, strategies for paying attention, for vocabulary learning, and for developing speaking, writing, and reading skill. When discussing strategies for speaking and writing, Cohen stresses that the payoff of error correction depends on when and how the correction is offered and how the learner relates to it. The talks are spontaneous and lively, trying to awaken students from their apathy. Cohen's particular challenge is coaching senior citizens learning Hebrew; he calls it "the old dog/new tricks syndrome." No empirical research exists on the effects of the talks, but Cohen receives feedback—sometimes ebullient—from students who try new strategies.

During his monthly visits, Cohen not only gives the two talks described above, but he also leads two informal rap sessions, each an hour long, one in Hebrew and the other in English. The title of the rap sessions is "Everything you ever wanted to know about language learning but were afraid to ask." Says Cohen, "And the students really do ask! In many ways I have become a language therapist at Ulpan Akiva."

Cohen is a rare combination of hard-nosed researcher and empathetic human being, with the knack of applying learning strategy research to practical language learning situations. At the Ulpan he provides awareness training (see Chapter 6), which gives encouragement as well as basic information about a variety of strategies. Because he visits the Ulpan only once a month, he cannot conduct continuous, integrated strategy training from day to day. Instead, he inspires learners to try better strategies on their own through his mixture of new information, humor, and friendly cajoling. For further information, contact Andrew Cohen, School of Education, Hebrew University, 91905 Jerusalem, Israel.

Strategy Training in a Typical University Spanish Class (USA)

Roberta Lavine, coordinator of teaching assistants and professor of Spanish at the University of Maryland, applied the concepts in this book to explore the use of strategies with a class of 22 second-semester Spanish students [21]. She initially used formal presentations about strategies but soon found that students' strategies improved most when strategy training was integrated into regular classroom activities in an informal, natural way rather than remaining abstract and disconnected from ongoing classroom work.

During the strategy training process she used a range of communicative classroom activities, some suggested by this book and some self-created, each time making specific suggestions to her students about the kinds of learning strategies they might employ with these activities. Students responded positively to these efforts and began to examine their strategies for the first time. Lavine successfully changed the classroom climate by introducing affective strategies to reduce anxiety. She also stressed that it was all right to make mistakes or ask friends for help in class—new ideas to most of the students.

Through diaries, classroom discussions, and peer sharing, the students periodically evaluated their old and new learning strategies, identifying the ones that worked best. Students liked sharing their strategies and coaching each other on how to learn more effectively. Of the newly introduced strategies, some of the most useful were metacognitive strategies, especially purposeful listening and planning for language tasks; social strategies, such as cooperating with peers and asking questions; compensation strategies, like guessing meanings and "talking around" an unknown word; and affective strategies, including the use of laughter and deep breathing. Before the training began, the students were unaware that they were already using a fairly extensive range of memory strategies, especially those involving imagery. Strategy training helped them become conscious of their ordinary use of these strategies. During the training they greatly increased their use of association and other memory strategies.

After the training, Lavine stated, "The difference is mindblowing. The great majority of the students show an openness and willingness to try things. Before it was just fear. . . . What my students gained was an awareness of an attitude for life, for learning in general, not just for learning Spanish. The most beneficial, long-lasting effect wasn't learning any particular strategy; it was a general awareness of how to learn, listen, speak, and better themselves. . . . This means willingness to assume responsibility." In regard to learners, here is the most telling comment of all: "Students are now saying, 'I never knew before that you could *use* this language!'"

Strategy training had an effect on Lavine's teaching. "It was really exciting for me. It helped me realize that I had to write on the board more, had to provide more visual clues, had to explain some things in English and not just in the target language. Before this, the frustration level was so high . . . and some students tuned out. Now I am changing my own teaching habits."

Other teachers have expressed keen interest in finding out about the learning strategies, so Lavine has started organizing in-service training sessions for them. She is continuing to work with strategy training and assessment in her own classes and is now analyzing data from studies of learners' diaries. For additional information, contact Roberta Z. Lavine, 4120 Alfalfa Terrace, Olney, MD 20832, USA.

Strategy Training with Adult Refugees (Denmark)

Will Sutter, an Australian-born language teacher and administrator in the Danish Refugee Council and the North Jutland Department of Adult Education in Aalborg, Denmark, conducted strategy training with approximately 100 students of Danish as a second language (DSL) in 12 classes [22]. The classes, which were chosen to include a variety of nationalities, ages, proficiency levels, and amounts of DSL-learning experience, were taught by Sutter and other teachers at the language training school of the Danish Refugee Council. Participating teachers used the strategy training exercises presented in this book for 2 months in any way they desired, with no restrictions on how or how often. According to Sutter, the most effective teachers were those who intentionally incorporated strategy training exercises into regular classroom activities, treated learning strategies as a means of enhancing the progress students were already making, and showed a consistent desire to enable students to take more responsibility for their own learning. Less successful teachers had very different characteristics. They did not try to integrate strategy training with normal classroom activities, they used the exercises in an obviously remedial, last-ditch effort to help demoralized students, or they viewed strategy training as a "vacation" from language teaching.

Three-fourths of the students found the strategy training exercises highly useful. According to Sutter, even more students would have profited from the exercises if strategy training had been made an integral part of the language course from the start. Particular students, notably those culturally accustomed to obeying authority without question, gave up their old strategies without understanding why, just because their teachers presented new strategies. These students could have used special help in learning to assess the value of various strategies.

In describing the most positive aspects of the training, Sutter said, "The students felt it was fun exploring new strategies and discovering their already existing learning processes. Certainly the more entertaining brain-teaser activities were very popular and students caught on quickly. Catching on made the exercises even more appealing. Many of the strategy training exercises (particularly those with communicative undertones) are already embodied in the teaching materials used daily; however, regarding them as strategy exercises had some surprisingly positive effects. I was also pleasantly surprised by how *teachers* became eager to make use of the exercises as their own personal 'think-aloud' tests of their students," said Sutter.

Students especially liked memory strategies, such as grouping and labeling, and enjoyed exercises which had humor or intellectual challenge, like Inventions (see Chapter 3), which they practiced repeatedly in their own free time. Metacognitive strategies were also well accepted. Students' willingness to participate in group learning activities blossomed with their increased awareness of the benefits of social strategies and with their realization that these activities made learning more fun. One class used the affective strategy of diary-keeping as the basis for a weekly discussion.

According to Sutter, language teachers specifically require two things: first, to be helped "out of the pit of 'approach-consciousness'—that is, a focus on particular instructional methods—so that they can pay more attention to learning strategies; and second, to be equipped to use more formalized strategy training practices." Sutter concluded, "It's very important to teach students how to transfer strategies and apply them to new language tasks. It's also important to work on the attitudes of teachers, so that they believe in learning strategies and want to integrate them into the regular language program." More information on Sutter's work with learning strategies (and his research on learning styles) is available by writing to Will Sutter, Terpetvej 160, 9830 Taars, Denmark.

The previous examples have described explicit strategy training in settings around the world. However, strategies can be implicitly encouraged even without overt strategy training, as you will see next.

ACTIVE BUT IMPLICIT SIMULATION OF LANGUAGE LEARNING STRATEGIES

The following examples—two from the United States, one worldwide, and one from Hungary—are outstanding cases of experiential language learning, in which the learners become highly motivated to use a wide range of learning strategies. These examples do not point out to the learners the specific language learning strategies they are using, why those strategies are good, and how they might be transferred to other settings or tasks. These excellent illustrations of active language learning might be even more powerful if strategy training were overtly included.

Language Learning Strategies in High-Technology Simulations (USA)

Language learning strategy use is fostered by imaginative and innovative high-technology simulations developed at the Massachusetts Institute of Technology. The Athena Language Learning Project, directed by Janet Murray at the Massachusetts Institute of Technology and sponsored by the Annenberg/CPB Project, is now producing high-technology prototypes for Spanish, French, German, Russian, Japanese, and English as a second language. Described here are two of these prototypes, both simulations combining a communicative approach to language learning with technological capabilities in an interactive videodisk [23].

NO RECUERDO ("I Don't Remember") is an interactive videodisk project now in development with Douglas Morgenstern as the instructional director. The language learner types in the original input in Spanish; the output consists of various combinations of still photos, film and video segments, audio, text, and graphics. This is a highly contextualized, long-term simulation using real-world data—principally based on explorations of Bogota, Colombia—combined with a fictional story containing elements of romance, intrigue, and science fiction. The learner "communicates" with two protagonists and often sees scenes from their conflicting memories. The result is a system of "multiple realities" with which the learner must deal.

DIRECTION PARIS, instructionally directed by Gilberte Furstenberg, is a sequence of activities based on three half-hour videodisks. One of these is a narrative, *A la rencontre de Philippe*, which focuses on Philippe, who asks the student to help him find an apartment in Paris. The student travels around the city, visiting numerous apartments. In Philippe's current apartment the student uses the telephone and the answering machine and finds clues to other apartments to rent. The student must make quick decisions about which apartments to see and whether to relay information from one character to another. Instead of helping Philippe find an apartment, the student may choose to make a guidebook to Paris by using a second videodisk, a documentary providing an incomplete guidebook; or the student may explore the neighborhood of St. Gervais by using the third videodisk, a documentary called *A la découverte d'un quartier*.

In these high-technology simulations, learners are entertained and motivated by interaction with various characters and exploration of diverse locales. In addition, the nature of the material challenges learners to rely on themselves and especially to call upon their own cognitive, metacognitive, affective, compensation, and memory strategies. If these simulations were adapted for use with small groups, social strategies would also be involved. Thus, the best computer-assisted language learning, especially when enhanced by interactive videodisk capabilities, can be an exciting, strategy-rich means of language learning. For more details on Project

Athena, contact Janet H. Murray, 20B-231, Massachusetts Institute of Technology, Cambridge, MA 02139, USA.

Language Learning Strategies in Low-Technology Simulations for Learning Spanish (USA)

A number of low-technology, classroom-based simulations not requiring computer or videodisk were designed by Douglas Morgenstern [24] for students of Spanish, but they could easily be adapted to other languages and other cultural settings. These simulations have been successfully run at Stanford University, Harvard University Extension (adult classes), and Massachusetts Institute of Technology as a regular part of the curriculum.

One of these simulations is called NEW IDENTITY, which lasts from 1 to 2 hours and can be spread over several classes. Each participant receives a handout sheet to complete as an assignment or else at the beginning of the in-class activity. Each person is to take on a new identity as a Hispanic residing in an unspecified Latin American city. Participants are given a choice of four Hispanic surnames and four places of work (restaurant, clinic, store, or bank). They are asked to form new family groups and workplace groups by a process of negotiation and information exchange.

After this preparatory work, semi-improvised scenes are presented, first by family groups and then by workplace groups. An interesting audience–performer relationship is created, because members of the audience are referred to and can later react when it is their time to perform. Debriefing occurs after scenes are presented. The facilitator gives observations on linguistic and cultural appropriateness of the performers' behavior, and a lively discussion often ensues.

This is just one of the simulations created by Morgenstern. All are different in tone and format, but each simulation encourages use of a wide array of language learning strategies—sometimes even more than do high-technology simulations. Unaided by fancy computers, low-technology simulations like NEW IDENTITY generally promote greater use of social strategies and authentic communication among learners. For more information contact Douglas Morgenstern, Foreign Languages and Literatures, Massachusetts Institute of Technology, Cambridge, MA 02139, USA.

Strategies in a Multilingual, International Simulation Using Telecommunications (Worldwide)

Another simulation, known as ICONS (International COmmunication and Negotiation Simulation), encourages the use of diverse language learning strategies in a worldwide, computer-networked telecommunications effort involving multiple teams and many languages [25]. ICONS was developed by Jonathan Wilkenfeld and Richard Brecht at the University of Maryland, and is based on POLIS, pioneered by Robert Noel at the University of California at Santa Barbara. European coordination of ICONS is traditionally provided by David Crookall in France, and South American coordination by Leopoldo Schapira in Argentina.

ICONS currently involves about 20 university teams and seven languages: English, French, German, Hebrew, Japanese, Russian, and Spanish. Each university team represents a different country in an international political scenario. Some of the teams represent their own countries, e.g., Argentina, Brazil, Chile, Canada, England, France, Israel, Japan, and the United States. Other countries are represented by nonnatives; for example, American teams currently represent the Soviet Union and China. Month-long simulation sessions occur twice a year. Throughout the simulation, an electronic newspaper, *The Diplomat*, inserts new data into the simulation and also plays the role of an ordinary newspaper. A range of international policy issues is explored: superpower relations, European integration, Middle-East conflicts, North–South relations, world economic policies, human rights, the Gulf War, NATO, OECD, and international trade, for example.

Communications between country-teams occur through a variety of computer technologies, which allow the simulation to run in "real time." Local microcomputers are equipped with word processors, telecommunications software, and modems. The microcomputers are linked via international telecommunications data networks—i.e., national packet switching systems connected by satellite—into a central computer (situated at the University of Maryland and equipped with sophisticated and easy-to-use software). While electronic mail is the primary mode, occasional "real-time" teleconferences are held in which participants throughout the world gather at their computer terminals for simultaneous discussions or negotiations on particular issues.

Many metacognitive, cognitive, compensation, and social strategies are implicitly encouraged by ICONS. Two broad types of foreign language skills are involved, translation and reading. In ICONS, a foreign language is no longer an abstract system devoid of meaning or consequence; it becomes a purposeful, authentic, and communicative activity, because the state of the world depends upon a full understanding of foreign language messages. Typically more than 3,000 messages, many over a page in length, are exchanged during a month-long exercise. For more information, contact Jonathan Wilkenfeld, Department of Government and Politics, Lefrak Hall, University of Maryland, College Park, MD 20742, USA.

Learning Strategies Encouraged by Games for Students of English as a Foreign Language (Hungary)

Maria Matheidesz and her colleagues are using a series of games for students of English as a foreign language in Budapest, Hungary. These games call forth the use of learning strategies in many of the same ways as did the simulations described above [26]. In a 2-year project funded by the Soros Foundation, Matheidesz is working with English language teachers at four Hungarian secondary schools. The skilled and enthusiastic project teachers have decided to concentrate on the age range of 15- to 16-year-olds, i.e., Form 2. This project involves just one selected class per teacher (generally 15 to 20 students per class). Thus, four groups/classes of students are included in the project. Project teachers are working together to make games more popular among other teachers, who receive demonstration classes and seminars about language games.

The English teaching-learning situation in Budapest is typical of foreign language teaching and learning in many other places. Class exposure is limited to 3 to 5 hours per week. Access to English-language materials (newspapers, magazines, and films) and native English speakers is severely limited. Although plenty of English pop music is available, it provides only listening practice, not speaking practice. In this relatively impoverished English-language situation, teachers must seek out interesting, communicative classroom activities so their students can develop the English-language skills they desire. The Hungarian government and the school each provide a syllabus or set of instructional guidelines for English-language teachers, but teachers are also allowed to improvise to a certain extent.

Matheidesz is working with the teachers in her project to use a set of low-technology games which she personally developed. Teachers are encouraged to fit the games, which last from 10 to 45 minutes, into their normal classroom activities whenever they can. Some of these games have been commercially published under the name "96," also known as SPEAKING FACES [27]. SPEAKING FACES games deal with packs of 96 cards, each card containing a professional-quality photograph of a face. Many kinds of faces are included: young, old, plain, attractive, sad, happy, tired, animated, multiethnic. The learners' self-generated descriptions of the people represented by these faces form the basis of many SPEAKING FACES games. All communication takes place using English as a foreign language. Not all 96 cards are used for every activity.

The many games available through SPEAKING FACES demonstrate six principles. First, faces of people are endlessly interesting, providing many clues about emotions, occupations, ages, education levels, experiences, and family relationships. Second, imagery is a powerful motivator as well as a useful learning strategy. Third, students can communicate using the same set of materials over and over in different ways—without ever getting bored or frustrated. Fourth, any teacher, just like Matheidesz, can think creatively and come up with interesting materials for communicative language learning. Fifth, low technology can work as well as high technology in encouraging students to learn. Sixth, good materials foster the use of an extensive array of language learning strategies [28].

Informal observations show that learners become very involved in the games. Students communicate with each other more naturally and use a wider variety of cognitive, metacognitive, affective, compensation, and social strategies in the games than in traditional classroom activities. Formal questionnaires so far indicate that students and teachers feel very positive about the games. Later on, Matheidesz will videotape each group to analyze in more detail the language learning strategies used during game playing [29]. Contact Maria Matheidesz, Budapest XII, Borbala 3, 1121 Hungary, for more information.

SUMMARY

This chapter has presented examples of language learning strategies in action around the world. The first group of examples includes explicit training or discussion of strategies. The second group of examples demonstrates how active learning techniques implicitly stimulate the use of language learning strategies.

It would be good to bring together the two modes—that is, to wed the explicit strategy focus with the focus on general active learning principles and techniques. This aim could be accomplished in two ways. First, make sure that active learning techniques and a degree of participant choice are the basis of all training—of learners and teachers alike—which focuses on language learning strategies. Second, add to active language learning experiences an explicit element of strategy training.

ACTIVITIES FOR READERS

Activity 7.1. Assess the Relevance of Examples for Your Own Setting

Review the examples given here. On the basis of the descriptions in this chapter, which examples provide the most useful ideas for your own setting? Why? How could you use the ideas presented in these examples? Be as specific as possible.

Activity 7.2. Follow Up on Your Three Favorite Examples

Write or call the contact people listed for at least three of the examples. Ask for information. When you receive the information, determine what is useful to you and how you can apply it.

Activity 7.3. Take a Closer Look at Explicit Training Examples

Answer the following questions, either alone or with others. Use brainstorming techniques where appropriate.

1. How were the needs of the learners taken into consideration by the 11 examples of explicit strategy encouragement?
2. Which of these examples used active, experiential learning principles?
3. Which seemed to most clearly embody self-direction and autonomy for learners in the way the activities or materials were structured?
4. Which were examples of informed training, in which the value and significance of the strategies were made clear?
5. In which of the examples did you find complete integration between strategy training and language instruction? a moderate level of integration? no integration?

Activity 7.4. Take a Closer Look at Implicit Strategy Encouragement

Answer the following questions, either alone or with others. Use brainstorming techniques when appropriate.

1. Look at each of the four examples of implicit strategy encouragement. In what way could strategy use be made more explicit in each of these examples? What would be the effect?
2. What do all these examples have in common? List as many characteristics as you can think of.
3. What makes these examples so exciting and effective in a language learning situation?
4. What other examples of active, experiential language learning do you know about? Have you used some of these? How successful were they, and why? How did they implicitly or explicitly involve language learning strategies?

EXERCISES TO USE WITH YOUR STUDENTS

Exercise 7.1. Experiment!

After contacting some of the resource people mentioned in this chapter, try out their programs, activities, games, or simulations with your students.

Exercise 7.2. Find Out Which Strategies Are Used

In conducting the experiment in Exercise 7.1, observe the strategies of your students, or better yet, do think-aloud interviews to find out what strategies your students are using. Ask your students if they are learning any differently as a result of the new activities, and allow them to discuss this among themselves.

Epilogue

Where to Go from Here

The best is yet to be.
ROBERT BROWNING

You have been on a journey with this book. Your travels began as you examined language learning strategies in general terms in the first chapter. Next you discovered direct strategies—memory, cognitive, and compensation—and applied them to the four language skills. Then you explored indirect strategies—metacognitive, affective, and social—and learned how they could enhance all the language skills. Traveling on, you considered techniques for assessing and teaching language learning strategies. Finally, you found a number of resources for strategic networking, some relatively close to home and some in distant countries. In the course of these travels, you encountered a wealth of practical activities to do yourself and exercises to use with your students.

Now you have reached the epilogue, a milestone in your travels. However, your journey does not end here; in a real sense it has just begun. Do not put this book on the shelf and say, "That's nice, but I'm too busy to do anything with language learning strategies." Use what you have learned here to help your students become better language learners, able to use their new language communicatively both now and when you are no longer there to help them. Language skills and self-reliance *can* and *must* develop together. You can assist this process by helping your students use appropriate strategies.

If you have not already begun to work with learning strategies, quickly review the first five chapters to make sure you understand the principles and applications. Then assess your students' strategies and begin to conduct strategy training using the eight-step model (see Chapter 6), as well as the student exercises found throughout this book. If you need help, start creating a support network for yourself by calling or writing some of the experienced individuals mentioned in the book, especially those in Chapter 7. Find other sources of ideas using the reference list. Your understanding of strategies will grow by leaps and bounds once you begin putting strategies into practice.

Maybe you have been fostering good language learning strategies in your students for a long time. Even if you are already a promoter of strategies or a veteran strategy expert, you might use this book as a springboard to deeper explorations of strategies in all four language skill areas. Adapt this book's exercises, activities, and training and assessment procedures to your own needs, and expand your existing network of strategy colleagues.

Of course, this book is not the final word on language learning strategies. Much more remains to be discovered about how people learn languages and exactly how conscious use of learning strategies aids the process. Although some technical mysteries still exist, research and practice both indicate that strategies can increase learners' language proficiency, self-confidence, and motivation. Continue your explorations, and help your students tap the power of language learning strategies.

Notes

CHAPTER 1

1. This book has a very practical slant and is directed mainly toward teachers of second or foreign languages. Other very different but helpful kinds of resources might include edited books, each containing a variety of viewpoints (e.g., O'Neil, 1978; Weinstein, Goetz, & Alexander, 1988; Wenden & Rubin, 1987), books presenting hints for language learners (e.g., Rubin & Thompson, 1982), books on self-directed language learning (e.g., Holec, 1980, 1981; Dickinson, 1987), books on communication strategies (e.g., Faerch & Kasper, 1983b), and books addressing both learners and teachers simultaneously (e.g., Cohen, in press). For research findings, see notes below.

2. Krashen (1982).

3. Littlewood (1984).

4. These include Campbell and Wales (1970), Canale and Swain (1980), Hymes (1972), and Omaggio (1986).

5. See, e.g., H. D. Brown (1984).

6. Littlewood (1984) explains in greater depth the differences between foreign and second language learning.

7. Lobuts and Pennewill (1989, p. 177).

8. See Savignon (1983).

9. Other concepts related to communicative competence are *proficiency* and *achievement*. Proficiency is the degree of skill measured without reference to a particular curriculum, and achievement is the degree of skill measured with reference to a particular curriculum. Proficiency and achievement each have two parts: *competence*, i.e., what the learner knows, and *performance*, which reflects competence and is observable/measurable (Savignon, 1972). Chomsky (1965) proposed yet another distinction between competence and performance. Canale (1983) stated that the distinction between competence and performance is not well understood, and he circumvented the issue by avoiding the term *performance* (i.e., using the term *actual communication* instead of, for example, *communicative performance*). For further information on issues related to perfor-

mance or competence, see Bachman (forthcoming), Clark (1972), Munby (1978), Omaggio (1986), Rivera (1984), and Wesche (1983).

10. For instance, see Faerch and Kasper (1983a).

11. This well-known model is by Canale and Swain (1980), further developed by Canale (1983).

12. The concepts of coherence and cohesion were originally described by Widdowson (1978).

13. A specific example of this is the statement "Tactics is the art of using troops in battle; strategy is the art of using battles to win wars" (Von Clausewitz, cited in James, 1984, p. 15).

14. The *adversarial, competitive* aspect of strategy use has prevailed for centuries. The concept of strategy has spread outside the bounds of physical warfare into a variety of other conflict or threat situations, such as business, politics, games, and even conversations—all of which have been viewed by some as battles of will or wits. However, recent examples exist of the *nonadversarial, cooperative* use of strategies to reach a goal or complete an action. For instance, strategies are used by depressed people to escape from their mental prisons (Rowe, 1983), by spiders to spin webs (Koestler, 1964), by gamers to cooperate rather than to compete with each other (Colman, 1982; Hart & Simon, 1988; Oppenheimer & Winer, 1988), by speakers to communicate (Faerch & Kasper, 1983b; Littlewood, 1984), and by language learners to operate a computer simulation (Diadori, 1987). Riley (1985) explicitly calls for linguists to formally recognize the collaborative aspect of strategies.

15. Alternative terms which have been used (appropriately or not) for learning strategies include *tactics, techniques, potentially conscious plans, consciously employed operations, learning skills, functional skills, cognitive abilities, processing strategies, problem-solving procedures,* and *basic skills* (Wenden, 1987). Learning strategies have also been called *thinking skills, thinking frames, reasoning skills, basic reasoning skills,* and *learning-to-learn skills.* Most, but not all, of these terms focus on the rational, cognitive aspects of learning strategies, ignoring—at our own peril and that of our students—the emotional and social aspects.

16. See Rigney (1978) and Dansereau (1985).

17. These features are distilled from many sources. See the lists of features of language learning strategies in Chamot (1987), Wenden (1987), Oxford (1985a, 1986f), Oxford, Lavine, and Crookall (1989), and other sources in the reference list.

18. See Oxford, Lavine, and Crookall (1989) for more details on the communicative approach and language learning strategies.

19. Two terms, *learner self-direction* and *learner autonomy,* are often applied in relation to language learning strategies. These terms have been used in various ways. For instance, Dickinson (1987) used *self-direction* to refer to the learner's attitude of responsibility, and he used *autonomy* to refer to the learning mode, situation,

or techniques associated with the responsible attitude. Holec (1980, 1981) used the same two terms in reverse, with *self-direction* referring to the learning mode, situation, or techniques and *autonomy* referring to the learner's attitude.

20. See Knowles (1976).

21. See Wenden (1987).

22. These two quotations are by Gibson (1973, p. 72) and Harmer (1983, p. 203). Other interesting comments on teachers' roles are found in T. Wright's (1987) chapter, "Teaching Tasks and Strategies."

23. See Wenden (1985a) for more details on teachers' expanded role.

24. See Holec (1981).

25. For instance, Chamot (1987) says, "Learning strategies are intentional on the part of the learner."

26. A very different example of unconscious use of learning strategies occurs when the lesson itself encourages the learner to use certain strategies. For example, lesson-controlled preview questions, comprehension questions, and metaphor-based explanation techniques all encourage learners to use certain strategies, although learners might not be aware of doing so. Learning in this way can be very efficient. However, if learners become *aware* of the strategies they are using in these instances and how such strategies work, they will find it easier to transfer them to new situations or other kinds of materials.

27. This book rejects the unnecessary distinction between training and education, in which trainers sometimes view educators as impractical, grandiose, and insufficiently grounded, and educators occasionally see trainers as superficial, mechanistic, and representative of stimulus-response behaviorism.

28. See Oxford (1989) for a complete review of these factors.

29. Leaning toward caution, this book avoids the term *taxonomy*, which implies a clear set of hierarchical relationships. None of the strategy classification systems currently available should be called a taxonomy, despite earlier usage of the term (see Oxford, 1985a, 1986f). The strategy classification system in this book owes a great deal to the excellent work of Chamot, O'Malley, Dansereau, and Rubin, but the present author takes responsibility for the categories and definitions used here.

30. For the most detailed discussion of problems in defining and classifying language learning strategies, see Oxford, Cohen, and Sutter (in press). See also O'Malley, Chamot, Stewner-Manzanares, Küpper, and Russo (1985).

31. Holec (1981, p. 3).

32. The Embedded Strategies Game is original. However, in another context Bob Burbridge of the UN Language School also thought of the idea of giving funny names to language learning strategies. He cleverly devised such strategy names as Samuel Pepys, Mona Lisa, Fortunetelling, Freebies, and Dental Work. Figure those out!

CHAPTER 2

1. This is called the "loci" or "places" technique. For a wonderful explanation of oral memory strategies, see Ong (1987).

2. The precise physical workings of memory are much more complex and less well understood than these simple memory principles. Memory is still the "black hole in the center of neurobiology" (Begley, Springen, Katz, Hager, & Jones, 1986a, p. 48). See human neurobiology texts for information on brain processes, including memory; see also Begley et al., 1986a, 1986b, for a simplified discussion of memory-related brain structures and of electrochemical and biochemical changes caused by memory formation. The traditional belief is that the left hemisphere of the brain is for storage of speech and language, while the right is for spatial, pictorial, and other nonverbal stimuli. However, new evidence (Goleman, 1986; Van Lancker, 1987) suggests that this distinction may not be totally accurate. Researchers have made progress in understanding the physical aspects of short-term and long-term memory, such as protein synthesis and modification (Leaver, 1984). Short-term and long-term memory appear to be differently constructed systems. Moreover, there are different kinds of long-term memory (Baddeley, 1986; Tulving, 1985) and even different kinds of short-term memory. Howard (1983) provides a succinct and interesting discussion of network theories of long-term memory, including episodic and semantic memory.

3. Thompson (1987) raises questions about whether memory strategies lead the learner *away* from meaning. However, the correct use of memory strategies to learn languages necessarily involves meaning. After all, that is what semantic memory is all about!

4. Lord, quoted in Hague (1987, p. 221).

5. Cognitive psychologists such as Anderson (1976, 1983, 1985) have identified two major kinds of knowledge: *declarative knowledge* (facts, definitions, rules, images, and sequences) and *procedural knowledge* (skills, such as applying and using rules). Both knowledge types are helpful in language learning, especially for adolescents and adults. Declarative and procedural knowledge are stored differently in memory. Anderson assumes that declarative knowledge is stored as nodes, associated by links of various types, while procedural knowledge is stored via "production systems" (if-then systems involving conditions and actions) in three stages, ranging from conscious to automatic. For details on how this theory relates to language learning, see O'Malley, Chamot, and Walker (1987). A simplified explanation of the assumptions and tenets of Anderson's theory is found in Howard (1983).

6. Forgetting the language is a serious problem after formal language training is over, when the learner no longer has the support of a teacher, or of classmates and structured lessons. A new research field called "language skill attrition" or "language loss" has been identified to investigate this problem (see Lambert & Freed, 1982; Oxford, 1982a, 1982b; Weltens, 1986).

7. For details on visual imagery as used for memory, see Nyikos (1987), Miller (1956), Shephard (1967), Bower (1970), Higbee (1979), and Goleman (1986).

8. For information on language learning style preferences relating to sensory modalities, see Reid (1987) and Rossi-Le (1988).

9. The frequency of use of memory strategies is under debate. Some research (e.g., Nyikos & Oxford, 1987; Reiss, 1985) has found that university students report using memory strategies infrequently. On the other hand, other studies using different research methods (for example, Cohen & Aphek, 1981; Nyikos, personal communication, February 8, 1987) revealed that memory strategies were indeed widely used, and that these strategies made vocabulary learning easier and more effective over the long term. The utility of memory strategies for vocabulary learning was reconfirmed by McDonough and McNerney (reported in Tyacke & Mendelsohn, 1986). Successful students in a foreign language writing study used memory strategies (Amber, as reported by Tyacke & Mendelsohn, 1986). However, use of memory strategies can sometimes make initial learning slower, although more effective (Cohen & Aphek, 1981).

10. A. Wright (1987, p. 53).

11. Semantic mapping is not just a good memory strategy, but it is also useful as a prelistening or prereading strategy for aiding comprehension. It can also be the basis of an entire reading or listening lesson (see Hague, 1987). Semantic mapping is discussed at length by Hague (1987) and Oxford (1988). This technique has been used for many years under a variety of labels. This technique was employed by Novak and Gowin (1984) under the name of Conceptual Mapping as the basis of an entire "learning how to learn" system. This technique is also known as a Semantic Network (Halff, 1986), used as a basis for artificial intelligence by computer; a Concept Tree (Brown-Azarowicz, Stannard, & Goldin, 1986), used for memorizing foreign language vocabulary; and Note Mapping (A. Wright, 1987), used for taking notes on reading. All of these usages can be related to psychological concepts about how knowledge is stored as a network, as discussed in Note 5 above. For details, see Oxford (1988). In a different vein, some sociolinguistic experts might have questions about whether semantic mapping might isolate or decontextualize a concept or set of words; these experts might prefer to talk in terms of "frames," "schemes," and "scripts" (Haru Yamada, personal communication, June 11, 1988). The counterargument is that semantic mapping is actually a way of contextualizing a word or concept in an expanding network of related words or concepts, and that such a strategy helps learners make important linkages that carry over into more richly contextualized communication situations.

12. Unlike many memory techniques for foreign and second languages, the keyword has benefited from a good deal of research, all of which shows that it is remarkably successful for vocabulary learning (see the research summaries in Oxford, 1985b, 1986f). One caution with the keyword is that some of the auditory links may not be perfect. That is, the new word in the target language may not sound exactly like the familiar word in one's own language. The

keyword strategy, under the name of Link Word, has been used as the foundation of a whole language learning system, the Link Word Language System, which includes not only vocabulary but grammar points as well (Gruneberg, 1987a, 1987b). This system currently has instructional books available in Spanish, Italian, French, and German. For more information, write Corgi Books, Transworld Publishers, 61–63 Uxbridge Road, Ealing, London W5 5SA, England (also published in Australia and New Zealand by Transworld). The Link System of Lorayne and Lucas (1974) involves keywords (a combination of sound and image) in a sequential and interactive chain—a task not usually necessary for language learning. A different memory strategy, called the pegword (or the memory hook), is also used to remember a string of words in a certain order; see Lorayne and Lucas (1974) and A. Wright (1987) for information on the pegword strategy.

13. From Lorayne and Lucas (1974).

14. Memory for verbal information in one's own language is influenced by time factors, such as primacy, recency, duration, spacing, pacing, and crowding of stimuli; things that are stored together tend to be recovered together (Stevick, 1976). This suggests that scheduling is very important, and the memory strategy of structured reviewing is therefore crucial. Structured reviewing, which encourages spaced review intervals, is related to other strategies: (a) the cognitive strategy of repeating and (b) the metacognitive strategy of organizing. Repeating is a broad strategy that involves both imitating native speakers and repeating target language material. Organizing involves, among other things, scheduling one's learning but does not suggest any particular intervals for reviewing.

15. Asher's (1966a, 1966b) language instructional practice called Total Physical Response involves this memory strategy.

16. Cognitive strategies are often defined as including memory strategies and guessing strategies. Memory strategies are given their own niche in this book because of their specialized function, helping learners store and retrieve new information. Guessing strategies are placed among compensation strategies, because they compensate for missing knowledge in listening and reading.

17. O'Malley et al. (1985a, 1985b) and Chamot, O'Malley, Küpper, and Impink-Hernandez (1987) found that high school ESL students and university foreign language students used considerably more cognitive strategies than metacognitive strategies; however, Chamot et al. (1987) discovered that the use of metacognitive strategies increased somewhat as learners progressed to higher levels of language learning. Russo and Stewner-Manzanares (1985) found that U.S. Army soldiers studying ESL reported using cognitive strategies with simpler tasks and metacognitive strategies with more complex tasks. Many other studies have examined the use of cognitive strategies, among other types of strategies. See, for example, Grandage (in Tyacke & Mendelsohn, 1986), Nyikos and Oxford (1987), Papalia and Zampogna (1977), and Reiss (1985).

18. See Oxford and Rhodes (1988) for estimates of the amount of time to reach proficiency in various languages.

19. The importance of practice—especially naturalistic practice involving communication—has been demonstrated repeatedly; see, for instance, Rubin (1975), Bialystok (1981), and Ramirez (1986).

20. Read Leaver (forthcoming) for interesting data on the use of analytic and reasoning strategies and commentary on whether or not this use is related to age.

21. See Selinker (1972, 1981), the originator of the term *interlanguage*.

22. For example, see Hosenfeld (1977).

23. Amazingly enough, guessing strategies—which compensate for a limited language repertoire in listening and reading—have never before been linked in any way with compensation strategies for speaking or writing, despite the obvious similarity in compensatory function. Guessing strategies are used for listening comprehension (Grandage in Tyacke & Mendelsohn, 1986; Henner-Stanchina, 1986), reading comprehension (Papalia & Zampogna, 1977; Ramirez, 1986), and vocabulary learning (McDonough & McNerney in Tyacke & Mendelsohn, 1986). Note that Ellis (1986) uses the term "compensatory strategies" (coined independently from the term "compensation strategies" as used here) to refer only to production-oriented strategies which compensate for missing knowledge—a far narrower scope than that of "compensation strategies" as described in this book.

24. MacBride (1980, p. 28).

25. Researchers have used the term *communication strategies* in a very restricted sense, referring to strategies which compensate for missing knowledge only during conversational speech production. Tarone's (1977, 1980, 1983) list of communication strategies includes paraphrasing (approximating, word coinage, and circumlocution), borrowing (literal translation, language switch, appeal for assistance, and mime), and avoidance (topic avoidance and message abandonment). As Tarone uses it, the term *communication strategies* refers only to the speaking situation, and this usage might seem to imply that communication does not occur when the learner is engaged in the other three skills, listening, reading, and writing—certainly an erroneous implication. Another difficulty with the term *communication strategies* is that some researchers feel these strategies cannot simultaneously be learning strategies, on the assumption that the purpose is communication, not learning (Chamot, personal communication, July 4, 1987). The argument that communication strategies cannot also be learning strategies is inaccurate. It is often impossible to determine whether the learner intends to use a given strategy to communicate or to learn; often the motivations are mixed, and besides, learning often results even if communication is the main goal (Tarone, 1983; Rubin, 1987a). Simply put, "Learning takes place *through* communication" (Faerch & Kasper, 1983a, p. xvii). "Communication, learning, and instruction interact and influence each other" (Candlin, 1983, p. x). To paraphrase Howatt, learners can either "learn to use the language" or "use the language to learn it" (Howatt, 1984). To avoid the false split between communication strategies and learning strategies, as well as the overly narrow (one-skill) interpretation of communication embodied in most uses of the term *communication strategies*, this book refers instead to *compensation strategies*.

26. Littlewood (1984) explains the uses of these kinds of strategies for learning, not just communicating.

27. Mendelsohn (1984) distinguishes among linguistic, paralinguistic, and extra-linguistic clues for guessing. Somewhat similarly, Bialystok (1978) lists three sources of information for guessing: explicit linguistic knowledge, implicit linguistic knowledge, and general knowledge of the world.

CHAPTER 3

1. People do use all four skills, though in different amounts or to varying degrees. Adults spend 40 to 50% of their communication time listening, 25 to 30% speaking, 11 to 16% reading, and 9% writing, according to Rivers (1981). However, the need for concerted effort to develop each of the four skills might be a novel idea to some people. For instance, Krashen and colleagues (1984, pp. 263 and 273) have suggested that the development of the two production skills, speaking and writing, does not require any special effort, on the assumption that these skills cannot be taught but will "emerge" simply through sufficient exposure to listening and speaking. Conversely, other people have neglected listening on the grounds that it is a passive skill or merely a means of teaching speaking (see Morley, 1984; Mendelsohn, 1984; Brown, 1984, for criticisms of such a viewpoint). However, *there is no evidence to support the concept that any one of the language skills will simply "emerge" solely through practicing other skills, or that one skill is just a means of teaching another skill. The neglect of any of the four skills is likely to restrict the degree of proficiency a student can attain.* Each skill deserves attentive instruction and practice, and many exercises exist for instruction and practice in all four skills.

2. The examples in this chapter come from the following sources. Original (created by the author): Norberto, Jennie, Lucien, Stephanie, Mike, Corazon, Benjamin, Glennys, Katya, Keith, Adel, Quang, Helen, Jeff, Mariette, Jill, Brian, Alice, Howard, Jeremy, Yolande, Rollande, Rudy, Kelley, Gerard, Kiri, Misha, Akram, Jack, Milton, Lyle, Lori, Yacoub, Marian and Heidi, Adrienne and Giovanni, Steve, Maya, Elisabeth, Haruko, Parker, Lisha, Sam, Rosine, Ferenc, Natalya, Jean-Claude, Monica, Rowena and Jim, Pascual, Rusty, Sandrine, Susan, Pablo, Marc, Akira, Ellen, Louisa, Julio, Roberta, Marcie, Marianne, Lugo, Marcello, Martina, Lloyd, Marijane, Stanley, Nora, Luis, Rita, John, Reba, Lillian, Billie, Herb, Lauren, Elton, Amado, Martha, Dwight, Erwin, Mildred, Jana, Monte, Eli, Gilberto, Frank, Sally, Vivian, Broderick, Molly, Andrew, Miguel, Millicent, Hilde, Robert, Norman, Terry, Kirsten, Jaime, Marcelle, Vanya, Nina, Nubia, Stavros, Domenico, and Siu. Grucz and McKee (1986) provided the following examples: Donny, Bud, and Lih. The Antonio example is from A. Wright (1987). Stewner-Manzanares, Chamot, Kupper, and Russo (1984) offered the examples of Carlos and Rashid. Leni's example is from Ur (1984), while Michel's is from Lorayne and Lucas (1974). Gruneberg (1987c) provided examples of Bernie, Julianne, and Mathilde. Examples of Josef, Gabriele, Leslie, June, Henri, Clive and Hector, Edna, Constanze, and Heinrich are from Tarone, Cohen, and Dumas (1983). Littlewood (1984) offered the

examples of Miki, Cesar, Mario, Fritz (adapted), Trudy, Aviva, Laura, Gottfried, Lucille, Omar, and Renato. Andrey, Wladislaw, Simone, Ismael, and Lisette are from Mendelsohn (1984). Tarone (1983) contributed the examples Geraldo, Tonio, Carmelita, Franny, Zoltan, and Osmin. Examples of Nicki and Liz are from Bialystok (1983). My colleagues also contributed examples from their own personal experience or that of their friends. The example of David is from David Crookall. Haru Yamada offered the examples of Brooke and Ron, and Richard's example is from MaryAnn Zima. Roger Rexroth contributed the example of cross-dialect transfer in note 26.

3. This is called a *tax haven* in British English.

4. See Howard (1983) for formal structures proposed by network theories of long-term memory to describe how people make associations and remember information. These structures are maps or networks, related in a very loose way to the semantic maps spontaneously generated by language learners. See also Hague (1987) and Oxford (1988).

5. See Asher (1966a, 1966b).

6. Such a complicated acronym must work rapidly when the learner needs to retrieve the target language information. Therefore, the learner must know the acronym very well, to the point of automaticity. It is necessary to expend some initial energy learning the particular memory device, in this case an acronym. This process might seem to slow learners down, but the longer-term retention caused by using such devices often makes the initial effort worthwhile. See Cohen and Aphek (1981) for a discussion of speed and effectiveness of memory strategies.

7. Repeating words (orally or in writing) that are *not* understood prevents students from accessing background knowledge or setting the new words in an understandable context.

8. Of course the "tell 'em" and "lead paragraph" rules do not fit well into the discourse styles of some languages, which require less direct, more oblique modes of expression.

9. See Brown (1987, p. 30).

10. Ur (1984) provides a number of exercises for formally practicing with sounds. See also Wong (1987).

11. Listening *comprehension* exercises, as opposed to listening *perception* exercises, benefit from having live speech.

12. It is usually pronounced *ee*, as in *famille* and *gentille*, but it is sometimes pronounced *eel*, as in *ville* and *Lille*, or pronounced *iye*, as in *paille*.

13. See Leaver (1984) and Brown-Azarowicz et al. (1986), for detailed suggestions about how to practice new writing systems.

14. Authentic speech contains many ungrammatical, reduced, and incomplete forms, as well as hesitations, false starts, repetitions, fillers, and pauses (up to 30–50% of the conversation!). Moreover, the topic often shifts rapidly. Learners

need to become used to these features as they occur in the target language. Geddes and White (1978) distinguish between two kinds of "authentic speech": (a) unmodified authentic discourse produced for nonteaching purposes, and (b) simulated authentic discourse produced for teaching purposes but having many features that are likely to occur in genuine communication. Omaggio (1986), like many others, calls the second kind of authentic speech "teacher talk" or "caretaker talk," which is typically slower and simpler than the first kind of authentic speech but still contains redundancies, hesitations, backtracking, and so on. The second kind of authentic speech is often better for classroom activities, especially in the early stages of language learning.

15. Language learners need as much realistic listening comprehension practice as possible. However, many classroom listening comprehension exercises do not reflect real-world listening, in which we listen with a purpose; are often required to respond; can usually see the speaker; have the benefit of environmental cues; deal with rapid, short, redundant chunks of speech; and are interested in what is being said (Ur, 1984; Mendelsohn, 1984; Meyer, 1984). Because many listening exercises lack these characteristics, they are boring, childish, and meaningless. Many language teaching specialists—such as Ur (1984), Omaggio (1986), Geddes and White (1978), Mendelsohn (1984), Morley (1984), and Meyer (1984)—have shown how listening exercises can be planned to be more effective. See especially Ur (1984) for a wide variety of useful and relevant listening comprehension exercises.

16. Radio stations often broadcast in foreign languages; the BBC, for instance, broadcasts in some 35 languages. Listening to target language songs on the radio often provides an interesting, nonthreatening way to catch accents and intonations. Listening to radio gives the flavor of the language as spoken at its normal speed and with all its subtle cues to meaning. Some radio stations also broadcast lessons for learners (foreign and native) who want to improve their language skills; for instance, Radio Moscow carries Russian lessons, and the BBC broadcasts the excellent and well-known "English by Radio" series (see Norbrook, 1984). For further information on shortwave broadcasting, see Crookall (1983c, 1984b), or purchase a recent, detailed description of international shortwave broadcasting known as *Passport to World Band Radio* (available from the BBC World Shop, Bush House, London, England). You can use these radio resources in class, and you can give your students sheets describing the radio resources they can use at home.

17. Problems exist with the videocassette, such as finding sources of prerecorded tapes or of material to record oneself. Prerecorded tapes in other languages are not typically found in video shops and clubs, but there are services which specialize in foreign language films (for instance, Facets Video Rental-by-Mail, Facets Cinemathèque, 1517 West Fullerton Avenue, Chicago, IL 60614, USA; Films Incorporated, 1213 Willmette Avenue, Willmette, IL 60091, USA). It is possible to ask one's friends who live abroad to record programs from their TV sets, but this raises technical problems with compatibility of standards. There are three main video/TV standards in the world: NSTC is used in the United States, SECAM in France, and PAL in the UK, in most of Europe, and

in many other countries. Overcoming compatibility problems may involve use of multistandard equipment (for information contact Cartridge King, 825 West End Avenue, New York, NY 10025, USA) or copying and conversion services. One further source of listening material is DBS. For example, in Europe many programs in different languages from neighboring countries can be accessed via DBS using a dish antenna. In the United States dish antennae can pick up programs by DBS from the Soviet Union and other countries, and many of these are being transformed (for example, by the Defense Language Institute in Monterey, California) by means of computers into a means for interactive listening practice. Legal and practical constraints must, of course, be considered. See also Krashen et al. (1984, p. 273) for further information on listening materials using sound only or sound plus image.

18. Aston (1987) provides an excellent discussion of the "comity" (friendship) aspects of learning a new language.

19. See the following writing texts, which might be of use in your foreign or second language classroom: Hamp-Lyons and Heasley (1987), McKee (1981), Hartfiel, Hughey, Wormuth, and Jacobs (1985), Cramer (1985), Blanchard and Root (1984), Raimes (1983), Oshima and Hogue (1985, 1988), Clark (1985). Houpt (1984) provides specific ideas about using conversation as a prewriting stimulus to composition in the new language. Also watch the language teaching journals for reviews of good books on writing.

20. See Jones (1985) for RADIO COVINGHAM; see Crookall (1985) for NEWSIM.

21. For more information on dialogue journals, see Staton (1980, 1987), and Staton, Shuy, and Kreeft (1982). A different kind of written student–teacher exchange is called the "working journal" (Spack & Sadow, 1983). Like dialogue journals, working journals are ungraded, uncorrected, and nonthreatening. However, working journals differ from dialogue journals in two ways. First, the topic of working journals is somewhat less free-ranging and is specifically focused on the learners' description of, and feelings about, the writing process (but it is easy to see how this topic could be extended to the language learning process more generally). This slant is intended to give students a flavor of writing for an audience on a focused topic. Second, the teacher regularly writes journals to the entire class on the same subject and includes in those journals selected student journal entries. Working journals, like dialogue journals, have produced excellent results with language learners at various proficiency levels.

22. Cummins (1986) describes microcomputer communication networks for social and cultural exchange.

23. See Cummins (1986) for details on the Newswire, and Crookall and Wilkenfeld (1985) for information on ICONS.

24. For information on sending students' short stories to the BBC World Service, see Crookall (1986).

25. Sentence diagramming is a familiar form of analyzing expressions. This technique, which has lost much of its appeal in recent years, can help many learners

understand sentence structure. The danger with such techniques is that teachers sometimes focus on them to the exclusion of face-to-face communicative activities.

26. Transferring inappropriately can even occur across different dialects of the same language. For instance, in the United States, it is entirely possible to talk about the lovely embroidered *napkins* on the table, but you should not do so in Australia, where the correct term is *serviettes* and where the term *napkins* has a very restricted usage and is not typically mentioned in polite conversation.

27. The term *raw notes* is used in a different way from that used by Hamp-Lyons (1983), who says that the shopping list and the T-list (i.e., T-formation) can both be used at the raw note stage. I feel that the shopping list and the T-list are one step up from raw notes, which are often chaotic and completely unorganized.

28. See Hamp-Lyons (1983) for another example of the tree diagram for taking notes.

29. Clarke and Nation (1980) have shown how to use linguistic clues to guess meanings in a reading passage.

30. Many of these clues come from what sociolinguists might call frames or scripts.

31. O'Malley, reported in Chamot (1987).

32. Mendelsohn (1984) suggested these examples: (a) On the one hand he was right, but on the other hand . . . (students complete); (b) The dying king called for a priest to . . . (students complete); (c) The man dropped his shopping bag and everything spilled out. He went up to a young girl watching and . . . (students complete).

33. The definition of adjusting or abandoning is from Littlewood (1984).

34. References for the quotations in Activity 3.1 are found in Appendix D.

CHAPTER 4

1. See Rubin (1975), Amber in Tyacke and Mendelsohn (1986), and Oskarsson (1984). For information on self-awareness of language learners, see Wenden (1986b). For comments on self-monitoring in writing, see Bialystok (1981).

2. See, for instance, O'Malley et al., (1985a); Chamot et al., (1987).

3. Nyikos and Oxford (1987), Oxford (1986d), and Oxford and Nyikos (1989). McGroarty (1987) found that even when language learners were surrounded by practice opportunities in the community, they did not necessarily take advantage of those chances to practice.

4. This learning strategy is related to the instructional strategy called *advance organizers*. Advance organizers have been in existence as a formal instructional strategy since the early 1900s, but they were more recently popularized by

Ausubel (1963), who defined them in the specific sense of *overviews* used for simultaneously (a) previewing concepts in detailed written material, (b) reviewing concepts already in the learner's mind, and (c) linking both sets of concepts. See Barnes and Clawson (1975) for an excellent review of research on this instructional strategy.

5. Many language theorists (e.g., Dulay, Burt, & Krashen, 1982) have espoused the "silent period" as a necessary precursor to oral production, and some have called for it to be part of the curriculum. During this period, learners are said to comprehend the language but are unable to speak it. The period might last for only a few hours for adults but could take from 1 to 6 months for children (Krashen & Terrell, 1983). However, in an article reviewing numerous studies of the silent period, Gibbons (1985) disputed the nature of the silent period, stating that (a) this period probably begins as a period of *silent incomprehension* rather than *silent comprehension*; (b) if prolonged, the silent period may represent psychological withdrawal rather than language acquisition; and (c) consequently, initial silence in the target language is not necessarily desirable.

6. Brown (1987, p. 99).

7. The classification of certain learner variables—for example, anxiety, risk taking, inhibition, tolerance for ambiguity, empathy, and culture shock—as either cognitive, affective, or social is often a matter of judgment or taste. Each of these learner variables contains cognitive, affective, and social elements in differing degrees. Three specific classifications might be questioned by some readers. *Tolerance for ambiguity* could have been classified as an aspect of overall cognitive style (Brown, 1987; Shipman & Shipman, 1985) or sociocultural adjustment (Ruben, 1987), but it is included here as an affective factor because it often manifests itself in emotional reactions. *Culture shock*, while sometimes listed as a sociocultural aspect of language learning (e.g., by Brown, 1987), is reflected so strongly and often so negatively in the emotions of the learner that it must be discussed among the affective factors. In addition, *empathy* is sometimes included as an affective trait (Brown, 1987), but because empathy is so socially loaded (Ruben, 1987), it is included here as a social variable. These classifications are not as important as an understanding of the basic concepts.

8. Naiman, Fröhlich, and Todesco (1975). See also Wenden (1986b), who describes how learners analyze their own feelings and attitudes.

9. See White (1959). Global self-esteem emerges about mental age 8 and is based on one's self-perceived success or competence in various broad areas—such as academic competence, athletic competence, social competence, social acceptance, physical appearance, and behavior/conduct—combined with one's judgments of how important these areas are (McCombs, 1987). Global self-esteem can be altered by helping students succeed better in these broad areas, or alternatively by helping students discount the importance of the areas where they are unsuccessful but which they think are extremely important (Harter, 1986). Learners with high self-esteem maintain positive evaluations of themselves through perceiving the world in a rosy, not necessarily accurate way (Tesser & Campbell, 1982, in McCombs, 1987). High self-esteem students often

exaggerate their competence or adequacy, whereas low self-esteem students frequently judge themselves harshly (Harter, 1985). Amber (in Tyacke & Mendelsohn, 1986) found that unsuccessful language learners had lower self-esteem than successful language learners.

10. Over the last 30 years, language learning motivation has been viewed in terms of two primary orientations: instrumental and integrative (see Gardner, 1985). Some studies (e.g., Gardner & Lambert, 1972; Spolsky, 1969) indicate that integrative motivation is a more significant influence on language proficiency than is instrumental motivation, but other studies (e.g., Lukmani, 1972) show that instrumental motivation sometimes results in better language learning than does integrative motivation. Many factors influence the relative importance of these two motivational orientations on language proficiency: the environment where the language is being learned, perceived target community support, and learner attitudes toward the target community. Moreover, there may not be as great a difference between instrumental and integrative motivation as once thought, since they correlate with each other statistically; and other motivations besides instrumental and integrative may also operate in learning a new language.

11. See Gardner (1985).

12. Results on global language proficiency come from research by Clément, Major, Gardner, and Smythe (1977), Clément, Gardner, and Smythe (1980), Gardner and Lambert (1959), Gardner and Smythe (1975a, 1975b) and Gardner (1985). Results on specific components of language proficiency come from Tucker, Hamayan, and Genesee (1976) and Genesee (1978).

13. Gardner, Lalonde, Moorcroft, and Evers (1985).

14. For an effective and comprehensive training system for improving learner motivation, see especially McCombs and Dobrovolny (1982), and read McCombs (1987, 1988) for background information. Various components of McCombs's training system include all three sets of affective strategies listed in this chapter (under different names), combined with metacognitive strategies such as goal setting and social strategies such as cooperation.

15. See Littlewood's (1984) description of typical language classrooms and their effects.

16. "Culture shock . . . is . . . a form of anxiety that results from the loss of commonly perceived and understood signs and symbols of social intercourse" (Adler, 1987, p. 25). While not all language learning involves the identity crisis of culture shock, language learners living in the target culture frequently experience it (see Blair, 1983). Culture-shocked learners may experience regression, panic, anger, self-pity, indecision, sadness, alienation, "reduced personality," and physical illness. However, if handled effectively, culture shock can become a cross-cultural learning experience involving increased cultural awareness, increased self-awareness, and reintegration of personality (Adler, 1987).

17. Adler & Vogel (1986).

18. Beebe (1983).

19. Stevick (1976).

20. Alcohol and tranquilizers might help lower inhibitions (see experiments described in Brown, 1987), but few language teachers would recommend these to their students! Some recent teaching practices, such as Community Language Learning, the Silent Way, and Suggestopedia, all focus on lowering inhibitions.

21. Naiman, Fröhlich, Stern, and Todesco (1978).

22. Chapelle (1983).

23. Ehrman and Oxford (1989) and Oxford and Ehrman (1989).

24. See, for instance, Chamot et al. (1987).

25. Another affective element influencing language learning is extraversion-introversion, i.e., the degree to which the person is energized by other people or by the inner world of ideas. For information on this dimension, see Brown (1987), Ehrman and Oxford (1989), and Oxford and Ehrman (1989).

26. Jacob and Mattson (1987) and Slavin (1983).

27. Kagan (1986) and Kohn (1987).

28. Kohn (1987) and Dansereau (1983, 1988).

29. In addition, research on cooperative learning outside of the language area indicates the following. Such learning succeeds best when students are not just grouped into small units, such as pairs or triads, but are also trained in the kinds of strategies to use in their small groups. When students in a cooperative group are *similar in learning style*, they do better. However, students of *different ability levels* help each other more than students whose ability levels are the same. Cooperative groups do not benefit from competing against other groups. Cooperation does not always mean agreement. Finally, the optimal size for a cooperative group appears to be two or three, except for complex tasks that demand up to six. See References for citations on this topic.

30. See, for example, Sharan et al. (1985), Bejarano (1987), Gunderson and Johnson (1980), Bassano and Christison (1988), Wong Fillmore (1985), Gaies (1985), and Seliger (1983). Cooperation is at the heart of many current language instruction practices, such as Community Language Learning, derived from Counseling-Learning. This model encourages students to value each other and cooperate in developing a supportive learning community.

31. Reid (1987) and O'Malley et al. (1985a). However, this might differ by sex, since females show a more cooperative social orientation than do males (Maccoby & Jacklin, 1974; Gilligan, 1982; Bardwick, 1971). See Oxford, Nyikos, and Ehrman (1988) for sex differences in language learning strategies.

32. Kohn (1987).

33. See Bailey's (1983) review of diary studies for information on competitiveness

in language learning. See also Lobuts and Pennewill (1989) for an analysis of destructive competition.

CHAPTER 5

1. Prewriting exercises like nonstop writing (McKee, 1981) help learners overview the content of the next writing task and link it with what they already know. In nonstop writing, students write for 10 minutes without censoring their ideas or expression in any way. If they can't think of a word, they can write, "I can't think of it," and just proceed. This can be done in one's native language or, better yet, in the target language, then shared in a small group to get feedback and expansion of the thoughts.

2. See Houpt (1984) for ideas about prewriting debates and discussions.

3. See Gibbons (1985).

4. Two relatively recent, easy-to-read, helpful books are *How to Be a More Successful Language Learner* (Rubin & Thompson, 1982) and *Yes! You Can Learn a Foreign Language* (Brown-Azarowicz et al., 1986). Wenden (1986a) lists some other helpful resources, some a bit dated and some more recent: Cornelius (1955), Crawford and Leitzell (1980), Hall (1973), Kraft and Kraft (1966), Moulton (1966), Nida (1957), Pei (1966), Pimsleur (1980), and Politzer (1965). See Wenden (1986a) for still other books of guidance for language learners. Ambitious students able to deal with technical details might value Wenden and Rubin (1987), Stern (1983), Rivers (1981), and Omaggio (1986), even though these books are geared more toward researchers and teachers than toward students.

5. Crookall (1983a) provides excellent ideas for such discussions.

6. For information on the nature and purpose of various speech forms, see Byrnes (1984). For details on the importance of spontaneous free speech, as in friendly conversations, read Aston (1987). A fascinating discussion of differences between orality and literacy is given by Ong (1987).

7. See Grellet (1981) for details.

8. See Omaggio (1981) for information on how to use error analysis to determine the source of errors.

9. O'Malley (reported in Chamot, 1987).

10. The examples of Hans and Alberto are from Littlewood (1984). All the other examples in this chapter which bear the names of learners (e.g., Ricky, Anh) are original.

11. See discussion in Semke (1984).

12. See, for example, the useful diagnostic profile for writing provided by Hartfiel et al. (1985).

13. Oskarsson (1984).

14. Quoted in Spack and Sadow (1983, p. 586).

15. Information on laughter therapy is found in Long (1987).

16. See various applications of diaries in Rubin (1981) and Bailey (1983).

CHAPTER 6

1. A number of strategy observation scales have been published and are readily available. One useful scale is the Observation Schedule of Language Learners (Rubin, 1981). The Class Observation Guide (O'Malley et al., 1985b, pp. 563–564) includes information on the source of a given language learning strategy, the activity in which it is used, the setting, the materials involved, and the approach of the teacher and the students during strategy use.

2. See Cohen and Hosenfeld (1981) for complete details.

3. Self-observation that takes place immediately is called *introspection*. Self-observation that occurs later is called *retrospection*, and it introduces the forgetting factor.

4. Recent revisions of this model (Cohen, 1987b) include three categories: self-report (the frequently used mode in which learners tell what they *usually* do or think, not what they are doing in a particular learning event); self-observation (introspection and retrospection); and self-revelation (thinking aloud and talking aloud, the latter occurring when thoughts are already in verbal form in the learner's mind).

5. See Hosenfeld, Arnold, Kirchofer, Laciura, and Wilson (1981). A few minor criticisms can be mentioned concerning the content of the Interviewer Guide, such as the confusing sequence of strategies, but in general the guide is useful for gathering information on strategies which cannot be observed.

6. A more intensive think-aloud procedure was developed by Chamot and her colleagues (1987) for a longitudinal study of learning strategies. In this study, learners of Russian and Spanish described the strategies they used while working on various language tasks. Students received training and practice in thinking aloud, as well as a warm-up and other preparation before being assessed. Data collection in this study took about 1 to1½ hours per student, much longer than Hosenfeld's procedure for think-aloud interviews described earlier in Chapter 6. During the actual think-aloud assessment, interviewers asked questions like "What are you thinking?" or "How did you figure that out?" Other questions were tied to specific tasks, e.g., "Are you listening word by word, or to groups of words, or to whole sentences?" for the listening tasks. When certain non-verbal behaviors occurred, such as staring, long silences, or looking back over the word, interviewers asked about those behaviors. Painstaking analysis, recently completed, determined how the effective learners and the ineffective learners differed in the strategies they reported. This excellent adaptation of the think-aloud procedure produced interesting information for the entire lan-

guage field. For most teachers, this use of the procedure is too complex for classroom use, but researchers of language learning strategies will find it valuable.

7. For a copy of this guide, see O'Malley et al. (1985b).

8. See Wenden (1986a, 1986b) for more details.

9. See Leaver (forthcoming) for complete information on the procedure used.

10. The three techniques are described, respectively, in Cohen, Glasman, Rosenbaum-Cohen, Ferrara, and Fine (1979), Wenden (1986a, 1986b) and Allwright (1980).

11. See Long (1979) for the participant-observer concept of diaries. For diary studies focusing on psychological and social themes, see, for example, Jones (1977) and Schumann and Schumann (1977). Bailey's article (1983) discusses competitiveness and anxiety as expressed in language learning strategies. Bailey and Ochsner (1983) suggested ways to shape diaries to make them suitable as research documents. Rubin (1981) provides information on guided and unguided diary-keeping. Spack and Sadow (1983) discuss "working journals," which students use to describe their efforts to develop language skills and their feelings about the process. "Dialogue journals" (see Staton, 1980, 1983, 1987; Staton et al., 1982) are useful for describing thoughts and feelings of any kind. For working journals and dialogue journals, the teacher responds in writing.

12. Martha Nyikos of Indiana University developed this technique. An example is shown in her survey called "Assuming Responsibility for Learning: Study Strategy Worksheet" (Nyikos, n.d).

13. Some examples of relevant self-report surveys include the following: **Strategy Questionnaire:** An unnamed but published strategy questionnaire was used by Politzer (1983). This 51-item survey includes strategies explicitly categorized into three scales: general behaviors, classroom behaviors, and interaction with others outside of class. This survey uses a 5-point Likert-type scale ranging from 0 to 4. **Behavior Questionnaire:** This published survey was used in the Politzer and McGroarty study (1985). It contains 66 items, divided into three scales: classroom behavior, learning behavior during individual study, and interacting with others outside the classroom. Learners are to respond either yes or no to each item. Politzer and McGroarty described the survey in their article (p. 107): "The behaviors included in the three parts of the questionnaire do not correspond to any unified psychological construct. They represent a collection of ideas put together from intuition and existing suggestions," i.e., suggestions from the work of Rubin (1981) and Naiman et al. (1978). The authors stated that internal consistency of each of the three scales was low, but it improved to a moderate level (.51, .61, .63) when problematic items were removed. **Language Learning Strategy Student Questionnaire:** This is another example of an objective survey. The 56-item survey was developed by McGroarty (1987) and was based on work by Politzer and McGroarty. This survey uses a 7-point Likert-type scale ranging from 0 (not applicable) to 6 (always) in reference to the frequency of use of the various learning strategies.

Again, the items are divided into three distinct scales: strategies used in the classroom, interacting with others outside the class, and individual study. **Learning Strategies Inventory:**   This is a 48-item questionnaire describing various things a student might do when learning a foreign language. It is divided into five sections: listening to the language in class, speaking the language in class, listening and speaking outside the class, writing the language, and reading the language. The items relate to different ways of applying a total of 16 strategies. The survey asks students to respond (on a 4-point scale) that the statement is almost always true of them, usually true, sometimes true, or almost never true. This survey was used in the series of three studies conducted by Chamot and her colleagues (Chamot et al., 1987).

14. The SILL was originally developed for the Language Skill Change Project, which periodically assesses the amount of change found in language skills after the learner's foreign language training has been completed. This longitudinal study is jointly sponsored by the Defense Language Institute Foreign Language Center, Monterey, California, and the Army Research Institute for the Behavioral and Social Sciences, Alexandria, Virginia. Versions of the SILL have been used with groups of foreign language learners in high schools and universities around the world, as well as at the Defense Language Institute, the Foreign Service Institute, and the Peace Corps/Philippines. Adults learning English as a second language and English as a foreign language in several countries have also used the SILL. It is now being translated into several languages, such as Chinese, Japanese, and Spanish. Items in various forms of the SILL were based on the author's strategy system, and additional items were adapted from early surveys and strategy lists by O'Malley, Chamot, and Rubin. Version 5.1 in Appendix B has 80 items, and Version 7.0 in Appendix C has 50 items. Reliability and validity data are now being assessed for these two versions.

   A slightly earlier, 121-item version of the SILL has been most extensively studied from a psychometric viewpoint. Internal consistency reliability of the 121-item form using Cronbach's alpha is .96 for a 1,200-person university sample (Nyikos & Oxford, 1987; Oxford & Nyikos, 1987; Oxford, Nyikos, & Crookall, 1987) and .95 for a 483-person military sample (Oxford, 1986a, 1986b, 1986c). Reliability of 9 of 10 factors (obtained from a factor analysis) found in the military sample is moderate to high, ranging from .60 to .86, while the 10th factor is lower (.31) (Oxford, 1986a, 1986b, 1986c). Content validity is .95, based on classificatory agreement between two independent raters, who "blindly" matched each of the SILL items with the strategies in the comprehensive list shown elsewhere (Oxford, 1986a, 1986b, 1986c). Concurrent validity of the 121-item form is found in strong, statistically significant relationships between SILL results and self-ratings of target language proficiency and motivation in the 1,200-person university sample (Nyikos & Oxford, 1987; Oxford & Nyikos 1987; Oxford et al., 1987). Learners who were more proficient and more motivated consistently reported on the SILL that they used a wider range of strategies, and used them more frequently, than did learners who were less proficient and less motivated. Another piece of evidence for concurrent validity comes from a Foreign Service Institute study (Ehrman & Oxford, 1989; Oxford & Ehrman, 1989). In that study of approximately 80 adults, the more highly skilled linguists reported more intense and wide-ranging strategy use than less-skilled linguists. Interestingly, females have consistently reported greater strategy use than males on the SILL. Social desirability response bias—the tendency to falsify responses in order to make a good impression (give responses that are thought to be desirable)—was empirically monitored with three samples: 23 clinical trial subjects in the Washington, DC, area in 1985, 483 field test subjects at DLI in 1985, and the 1,200 university students in 1986. Both statistical and ethnographic data were checked. No evidence of social desirability response bias appeared for the three samples.

15. See Wenden (1987).

16. Crookall (1983a) provides details on training that covers these topics.

17. Holec (1981), Riley (1982), Crookall (1983a), and Prowse (1983) eloquently explain the need for strategy training.

18. See Crookall (1983a), Oxford (1986f), and Rodgers (1978) for aims of such training.

19. The author has never seen any detailed, comprehensive, step-by-step guidelines on how to structure language learning strategy training. However, a number of sources provide good ideas about various pieces or aspects of strategy training. See, for example, Wenden's (1986a) criteria for strategy training; and research on strategy training by Brown, Campione, and Day (1980a, 1980b), Dansereau (1985), Derry and Murphy (1986), Stewner-Manzanares et al. (1985), and Weinstein and Underwood (1985).

20. Strategy training is often most successful with those who are in the middle range of verbal ability, rather than at the very top or the very bottom, according to Dansereau (1985). But *all* learners can benefit from strategy training, no matter what their ability level.

21. Dansereau (1985) describes the broad, narrow, and combination approaches.

22. However, Wenden (1986a) notes that in some instances, strategy training which is relatively unintegrated with language training may actually be preferable. For example, some adult learners who have very limited time and need to work autonomously might prefer a separate strategy training course, not closely integrated with language training. By and large, however, greater integration with language training is usually more effective.

23. Dansereau (1985) recommends using integrated strategy training (he calls it content-dependent), starting with more general strategies and moving to more specific ones. Integration of learning strategies with standard subject matter is the approach successfully used in the Chicago Mastery Learning Reading Program with Learning Strategies, or CMLR/LS (Jones, 1983; Jones, Aniran, & Katias, 1985). Another approach that successfully integrates strategy training with content training is found in the Cognitive Academic Language Learning Approach, or CALLA (Chamot & O'Malley, 1986, 1987), which is described in Chapter 7.

24. This compromise is suggested by Derry and Murphy (1986), based on Rigney (1980).

25. Informed training is much more useful than uninformed training. Four levels of information are possible in strategy training. Level A consists of *encouragement of strategy use in general without special training*. In Level A, stimulating activities promote an unfocused, unselected, wide range of strategies without providing any kind of special training or information about these strategies. Because of the interesting activities, learners are stimulated to use whatever strategies suit their fancy. The problem at Level A is that learners, although encouraged in general, might not focus on the most appropriate strategies. They will not know how to assess the value of particular strategies or how and when to transfer strategies to new tasks. Level B is called *blind training*. At this level the tasks or materials themselves call for the use of *particular* strategies, which are often unconsciously used by the learner and are thus called "hidden strategies." No information is given about the significance of those strategies. "Blind training leaves the trainees in the dark about the importance of the activities (strategies) they are being induced to use" (Wenden, 1986a, p. 316). Blind training results in improved performance in the immediate task, but learners generally do not continue to use the strategy, nor do they transfer the strategy to other relevant situations (Brown et al., 1980a, 1980b; Brown, Bransford, Ferrara, & Campione, 1983; Rigney, 1978). Bright students are exceptions to this rule; they sometimes, without any help, figure out the strategy and how to use it in other settings. Examples of blind training are preview questions, advance organizers, inserted questions, comprehension questions at the end, explanation techniques based on metaphor or analogy, and material already blocked into categories for the learner. Of course, the moment these examples are openly discussed with the learner in terms of their function and value, they are no longer "hidden strategies," and there has been a move to the next level. Level C is *informed training*. At this level some, but not complete, information is given about the significance of the strategies being trained. Informed training tells the learner that a particular strategy can be helpful and explains why. In informed training the learner is both induced to use a particular strategy and given some information concerning the significance of that strategy (Brown et al., 1980a, 1980b). For example, learners might be taught to rehearse and be given feedback about their improved performance, or they might be taught to rehearse a task in multiple contexts so they can see the utility of the strategy. Informed training results in (a) improved performance on the task, (b) maintenance of the strategy across time, and (c) some degree of transfer of the strategy to other similar tasks (Brown et al., 1980a, 1980b). Thus, informed strategy training is more effective than blind strategy training. Level D consists of *completely informed training (strategy-plus-control training* or *self-control training)*. At this level, complete information is given about the strategy and how to use, control, and transfer it. This is an even more explicit mode of strategy training. In this mode, the learner "is not only instructed in the use of strategy, but is also explicitly instructed in how to employ, monitor, check and evaluate that strategy" (Brown et al. 1980a, p. 5). Most learners perform best with completely informed training (Brown et al., 1980a).

26. Some of these ideas came from Dansereau (1985).

27. Thanks to Will Sutter for his suggestions regarding initial camouflaging of strategies which are new and very different from what particular learners prefer.

28. See Wenden (1986a) for suggestions concerning these evaluation criteria. More technical evaluation of strategy training, involving statistical analysis, is discussed in Dansereau (1985) and Weinstein and Underwood (1985).

29. Hosenfeld et al. (1981) developed this sequence.

30. This sequence was developed by Stewner-Manzanares et al. (1985).

31. Quoted from Wenden (1985b, p. 1).

CHAPTER 7

1. See, for example, Rubin (1985; 1987b, p. 275); also read more detailed reports by Rubin (1986, 1989). The description in this chapter comes directly from these sources and from Joan Rubin (personal communication, February 24, 1988).

2. Current price at the time of this writing is $995 for a 1-hour disk, five diskettes, and an instruction manual. Price subject to change; check with Dr. Rubin.

3. See Chamot and O'Malley (1986, 1987) and O'Malley and Chamot (1989).

4. These principles appear to be largely based on John Anderson's theory of declarative and procedural knowledge (1976), Jim Cummins's view of contextualized language and task complexity (1982, 1983), and Bernard Mohan's concepts of content-based language learning (1986).

5. See Chamot and O'Malley (1986).

6. This description is summarized from explanations given by Henner-Stanchina (1976), Henner-Stanchina and Holec (1977), Holec (1981), and Dickinson (1987, pp. 44–46). For more information, see reports by Abé, Henner-Stanchina, and Smith (1975), Moulden (1978, 1980), and Wenden (1986a).

7. Dickinson (1987).

8. Dickinson (1987).

9. Henner-Stanchina (1976).

10. Henner-Stanchina and Holec (1977).

11. Henner-Stanchina (1976).

12. This handbook, based on earlier strategy work by Shleppegrell and Oxford, is by Grala, Oxford, and Schleppegrell (1987). A later version designed for the whole Peace Corps organization, not just for the Peace Corps/Philippines, is by Schleppegrell and Oxford (1988).

13. Anne Lomperis (personal communication, September 3, 1987).

14. See Holec (1981).

15. These cautions are from Holec (1981).

16. This information is based on an interview conducted with Mrs. Smith at a recent international conference of the Society for the Advancement of Games and Simulations in Education and Training (SAGSET), Cardiff, Wales.

17. As Keeler (1982, p. 259) stated, "In their training courses teachers must be given the opportunity to experience the methodology and to put it into practice themselves. Training courses should be 'do'-courses."

18. Described by Dickinson (1987).

19. Wenden describes the project (1986a, pp. 130–131).

20. Summarized from Andrew Cohen (personal communication, December 13, 1987).

21. Information obtained from Roberta Lavine (personal communication, May 6, 1988).

22. Details provided by Will Sutter (personal communication, May 15, 1988).

23. See Morgenstern (1987) and Murray, Morgenstern, and Furstenberg (1989).

24. See Morgenstern (1987).

25. Information on ICONS comes from a variety of sources: personal observation of ICONS sessions at the University of Toulon, France; a national ICONS training workshop at the University of Maryland, USA; discussions with developers and coordinators of ICONS; and various publications about ICONS (especially Crookall & Wilkenfeld, 1985, 1987; Noel, Crookall, Wilkenfeld, & Schapira, 1987; Crookall, Oxford, Saunders, & Lavine, 1989).

26. The information here comes from my own observations, a personal interview with Matheidesz at an international conference (Society for the Advancement of Games and Simulations in Education and Training, Cardiff, Wales), written communications, and published articles and games (Matheidesz, 1987a, 1987b, 1988a, 1988b).

27. Matheidesz (1987a).

28. In addition to games using the 96 faces, Matheidesz is also training the teachers to use a board game involving "gift giving" to stimulate classroom communication in English and to train learners in certain sociolinguistic skills, such as taking turns. Another game, RUNNING ERRANDS (Matheidesz, 1987b), is also included in the project.

29. Matheidesz has also worked with language teachers and programmers to produce a series of computer-assisted language games, all available in English and some available in Spanish, German, and Russian. These computer games, like the other games, encourage a large range of strategies. In addition to these efforts, Matheidesz has completed the Teletext English Language Scheme, a full year's program which is now on Hungarian TV each day.

References

Abé, D., Henner-Stanchina, C., & Smith, P. (1975). New approaches to autonomy: Two experiments in self-directed learning. *Mélanges Pedagogiques.*

Adler, B., & Vogel, M. (1986). True or false? Test anxiety is potent and common. *Washington Post,* May 29, p. B-5.

Adler, R. S. (1987). Culture shock and the cross-cultural learning experience. In L. F. Luce & E. C. Smith (Eds.), *Towards internationalism: Readings in cross-cultural communication* (2nd ed., pp. 24–35). New York: Newbury House.

Allwright, R. L. (1980). *What do we want teaching materials for?* Paper presented at the annual meeting of TESOL.

Anderson, J. R. (1976). *Language, memory, and thought.* Hillsdale, NJ: Erlbaum.

Anderson, J. R. (1983). *The architecture of cognition.* Cambridge, MA: Harvard University Press.

Anderson, J. R. (1985). *Cognitive psychology and its implications* (2nd ed.). New York: W. H. Freeman.

Asher, J. J. (1966a). The learning strategy of the total physical response: A review. *Modern Language Journal, 50,* 3–17.

Asher, J. J. (1966b). The strategy of the total physical response: An application to learning Russian. *International Review of Applied Linguistics, 3,* 291–300.

Aston, G. (1987). Casual chat and the teaching of language as comity. *Lingua e Nuova Didattica (LEND),* 16(1), 26–41.

Ausubel, D. A. (1963). *The psychology of meaningful verbal learning: An introduction to school learning.* New York: Grune & Stratton.

Bachman, L. F. (in press). *Fundamental considerations in language testing.* Reading, MA: Addison-Wesley.

Baddeley, A. (1986). *Your memory: A user's guide.* Harmondsworth: Penguin.

Bailey, K. N. (1983). Competitiveness and anxiety in adult second language learning: Looking at and through the diary studies. In H. W. Seliger & M. H. Long (Eds.), *Classroom-oriented research in second language acquisition* (pp. 67–103). Rowley, MA: Newbury House.

Bailey, K. N., & Ochsner, R. (1983). A methodological review of the diary studies: Windmill tilting or social science. In K. N. Bailey, M. H. Long, & S. Peck (Eds.), *Second language acquisition studies* (pp. 188–198). Rowley, MA: Newbury House.

Bardwick, J. (1971). *Psychology of women: A study of biocultural conflicts.* New York: Harper & Row.

Barnes, D. R., & Clawson, E. U. (1975). Do advance organizers facilitate learning? Recommendations for further research based on analysis of 32 studies. *Review of Educational Research,* 45(4), 637–659.

Bassano, S., & Christison, M. A. (1988). Cooperative learning in the ESL classroom. *TESOL Newsletter, 22*(2), 1, 8–9.

Beebe, L. M. (1983). Risk-taking and the language learner. In H. W. Seliger & M. H. Long (Eds.), *Classroom-oriented research in second language acquisition* (pp. 39–66). Rowley, MA: Newbury House.

Begley, S., Springen, K., Katz, S., Hager, M., & Jones, E. (1986a). Memory: Science achieves important new insights into the mother of the Muses. *Newsweek,* September 29, pp. 48–54.

Begley, S., Springen, K., Katz, S., Hager, M., & Jones, E. (1986b). The maze of memory. *Newsweek on Health,* Winter, pp. 16–20.

Bejarano, Y. (1987). A cooperative small-group methodology in the language classroom. *TESOL Quarterly, 21*(3), 483–504.

Bialystok, E. (1978). A theoretical model of second language learning. *Language Learning, 28,* 69–83.

Bialystok, E. (1981). The role of conscious strategies in second language proficiency. *Modern Language Journal, 65,* 24–35.

Bialystok, E. (1983). Some factors in the selection and implementation of communication strategies. In C. Faerch & G. Kasper (Eds.), *Strategies in interlanguage communication* (pp. 100–118). London: Longman.

Blair, K. (1983). *Cubal analysis: A post sexist model of the psyche.* Weston, CT: Magic Circle Press.

Blanchard, K., & Root, C. (1984). *Ready to write.* New York: Longman.

Bower, G. W. (1970). Analysis of a mnemonic device. *American Scientist, 50,* 495–510.

Brown, A. L., Bransford, J. D., Ferrara, R., & Campione, J. C. (1983). Learning, remembering, and understanding. In J. N. Flavell & E. M. Markham (Eds.), *Carmichael's manual of child psychology* (Vol. 1). New York: Wiley.

Brown, A. L., Campione, J. C., & Day, J. D. (1980a). Learning to learn: On training students to learn from texts. *Educational Researcher, 10,* 14–21.

Brown, A. L., Campione, J. C., & Day, J. D. (1980b). *Learning to learn: On training students to learn from texts.* Manuscript, Center for the Study of Reading, University of Illinois.

Brown, H. D. (1984). The consensus: Another view. *Foreign Language Annals, 17*(4), 277–280.

Brown, H. D. (1987). *Principles of language learning and teaching* (2nd ed.). Englewood Cliffs, NJ: Prentice-Hall.

Brown-Azarowicz, M., Stannard, C., & Goldin, M. (1986). *Yes! You can learn a foreign language.* Lincolnwood, IL: Passport Books.

Burgess, A. (1963). *A clockwork orange.* New York: Mouton.

Byrnes, H. (1984). The role of listening comprehension: A theoretical base. *Foreign Language Annals, 17*(4), 317–329.

Campbell, R., & Wales, R. (1970). The study of language acquisition. In J. Lyons (Ed.), *New horizons in linguistics.* Harmondsworth: Penguin.

Canale, M. (1983). From communicative competence to communicative language pedagogy. In J. Richards & R. Schmidt (Eds.), *Language and communication.* London: Longman.

Canale, M., & Swain, M. (1980). Theoretical bases of communicative approaches to second language teaching and testing. *Applied Linguistics, 1,* 1–47.

Candlin, C. (1983). Preface. In C. Faerch & G. Kasper (Eds.), *Strategies in interlanguage communication* (pp. ix–xiv). London: Longman.

Carver, D. (1984). Plans, learner strategies, and self-direction in language learning. *System, 12*(2), 123–131.

Chamot, A. U. (1987). The power of learning strategies. *Ohio Bilingual-Multicultural Update*, March, 4, 6–11.

Chamot, A. U., & O'Malley, J. M. (1986). *Cognitive Academic Language Learning Approach: An ESL content-based curriculum.* Rosslyn, VA: National Clearinghouse for Bilingual Education, and InterAmerica Research Associates.

Chamot, A. U., & O'Malley, J. M. (1987). The Cognitive Academic Language Learning Approach: A bridge to the mainstream. *TESOL Quarterly, 21*(2), 227–249.

Chamot, A. U., O'Malley, J. M., Kupper, L., & Impink-Hernandez, M. V. (1987). *A study of learning strategies in foreign language instruction: First year report.* Washington, DC: InterAmerica Research Associates.

Chapelle, C. A. (1983). *The relationship between ambiguity tolerance and success in acquiring English as a second language in adult learners.* Unpublished doctoral dissertation, University of Illinois.

Chomsky, N. (1965). *Aspects of theory of syntax.* Cambridge, MA: M.I.T. Press.

Clark, B. L. (1985). *Talking about writing: A guide for tutor and teacher conferences.* Ann Arbor: University of Michigan Press.

Clark, J. L. D. (1972). *Foreign language testing: Theory and practice.* Philadelphia: Center for Curriculum Development.

Clarke, D. F., & Nation, J. S. R. (1980). Guessing the meaning of words from context: Strategy and techniques. *System, 8*(3), 211–220.

Clément, R., Gardner, R. C., & Smythe, P. C. (1980). Social and individual factors in second language acquisition. *Canadian Journal of Behavioural Science, 12*, 293–302.

Clément, R., Major, L., Gardner, R. C., & Smythe, P. C. (1977). Attitudes and motivation in second language acquisition: An investigation of Ontario francophones. *Working Papers on Bilingualism, 12*, 1–20.

Cohen, A. D. (1987a). Recent uses of mentalistic data in reading strategy research. *D.E.L.T.A., 3*(1), 57–84. (Depto. de Línguistica, Pontifícia Universidade Católica de São Paulo).

Cohen, A. D. (1987b). Studying learner strategies: How we get the information. In A. Wenden & J. Rubin (Eds.), *Learner strategies in language learning* (pp. 31–40). Englewood Cliffs, NJ: Prentice-Hall.

Cohen, A. D. (in press). *Second language learning: Insights for learners, teachers, and researchers.* New York: Newbury House/Harper & Row.

Cohen, A. D., & Aphek, E. (1981). Easifying second language learning. *Studies in Second Language Acquisition, 3*(2), 221–236.

Cohen, A. D., Glasman, H., Rosenbaum-Cohen, P. R., Ferrara, J., & Fine, J. (1979). Reading English for specialized purposes: Discourse analysis and the use of student informants. *TESOL Quarterly, 13*(4), 551–564.

Cohen, A. D., & Hosenfeld, C. (1981). Some uses of mentalistic data in second language research. *Language Learning, 31*(2), 285–313.

Colman, A. (1982). *Game theory and experimental games: The study of strategic interaction.* Oxford: Pergamon.

Cornelius, E. J., Jr. (1955). *How to learn a foreign language*. New York: Thomas Crowell.

Cramer, N. A. (1985). *The writing process: 20 projects for group work*. Rowley, MA: Newbury House.

Crawford, C., & Leitzell, E. M. (1980). *Learning a new language*. Los Angeles: University of Southern California.

Crookall, D. (1979). Variations on the theme of "Alibi." *Modern English Teacher, 7*(1), 12–13. Reprinted in S. Holden (Ed.), (1983), *Second selections from Modern English Teacher*. Harlow: Longman.

Crookall, D. (1983a). Learner training: A neglected strategy—Parts 1 and 2. *Modern English Teacher, 11*(1), 31–33; *11*(2), 41–42.

Crookall, D. (1983b). Picture stories. *Modern English Teacher, 10*(4), 16–19.

Crookall, D. (1983c). Voices out of the air: World Communications Year, international broadcasting and foreign language learning. *System, 11*(3), 295–302.

Crookall, D. (1984a). Comparing facts and figures. *Practical English Teaching, 4*(3), 24–25.

Crookall, D. (1984b). Rigs and posts: Radio reception technology for FLL. *System, 12*(2), 151–167.

Crookall, D. (1985). Media gaming and NEWSIM: A computer-assisted, "real news" simulation. *System, 13*(3), 259–268.

Crookall, D. (1986). Writing short stories for the BBC World Service. *System, 14*(3), 295–300.

Crookall, D., Oxford, R., Saunders, D., & Lavine, R. (1989). Our multicultural global village: Foreign languages, simulations and network gaming. In D.Crookall & D. Saunders (Eds.), *Communication and simulation: From two fields to one theme*. (pp. 91–106) Clevedon, Avon: Multilingual Matters.

Crookall, D. & Watson, D. R. (1985). Some applied and theoretical perspectives on a jigsaw reading exercise. *ITL Review of Applied Linguistics, 69*, 43–79.

Crookall, D., & Wilkenfeld, J. (1985). ICONS: Communications technologies and international relations. *System, 13*(3), 253–258.

Crookall, D., & Wilkenfeld, J. (1987). Information technology in the service of worldwide multi-institutional simulation. In J. Moonen & T. Plomp (Eds.), *Developments in educational software and courseware* (pp. 157–162). Oxford: Pergamon.

Culhane, T. (1986). *Russian language and people*. London: BBC Books.

Cummins, J. (1982, February). Tests, achievement, and bilingual students. *Focus*, No. 9. Wheaton, MD: National Clearinghouse for Bilingual Education.

Cummins, J. (1983). Conceptual and linguistic foundations of language assessment. In S. S. Seidner (Ed.), *Issues of language assessment: Language assessment and curriculum planning* (Vol. 2, pp. 7–16). Wheaton, MD: National Clearinghouse for Bilingual Education.

Cummins, J. (1986). Cultures in contact: Using classroom microcomputers for cultural interchange and reinforcement. *TESL Canada Journal, 3*(2), 13–31.

Dansereau, D. F. (1983). *Cooperative learning: Impact on acquisition of knowledge and skills* (Technical Report No. 586). Alexandria, VA: Army Research Institute for the Behavioral and Social Sciences.

Dansereau, D. F. (1985). Learning strategy research. In J. W. Segal, S. F. Chipman, & R. Glaser (Eds.), *Thinking and learning skills: Relating learning to basic research* (pp. 209–240). Hillsdale, NJ: Erlbaum.

Dansereau, D. F. (1988). Cooperative learning strategies. In C. E. Weinstein, E. T. Goetz, & P. A. Alexander (Eds.), *Learning and study strategies: Issues in assessment, instruction, and evaluation.* New York: Academic Press.

Derry, S. J., & Murphy, D. A. (1986). Designing systems that train learning ability: From theory to practice. *Review of Educational Research, 56*(1), 1–39.

Diadori, R. (1987). Simulation strategy and communicative approach in CALL. In D. Crookall, C. S. Greenblat, A. Coote, J. H. G. Klabbers, & D. R. Watson (Eds.), *Simulation-gaming in the late 1980s* (pp. 111–115). Oxford: Pergamon.

Dickinson, L. (1987). *Self-instruction in language learning.* Cambridge: Cambridge University Press.

Dulay, H. C., Burt, M. K., & Krashen, S. (1982). *Language two.* New York: Oxford University Press.

Ehrman, M., & Oxford, R. (1989). Effects of sex differences, career choice, and psychological type on adult language learning strategies. *Modern Language Journal, 73*(1), 1–13.

Ellis, R. (1986). *Understanding second language acquisition.* Oxford: Oxford University Press.

Faerch, C., & Kasper, S. (1983a). On identifying communication strategies in interlanguage production. In C. Faerch & G. Kasper (Eds.), *Strategies in interlanguage communication* (pp. 210–238). London: Longman.

Faerch, C., & Kasper, S. (1983b). Plans and strategies in foreign language communication. In C. Faerch & G. Kasper (Eds.), *Strategies in interlanguage communication* (pp. 20–60). London: Longman.

Frank, C., & Rinvolucri, M. (1983). *Grammar in action: Awareness activities for language learning.* Oxford: Pergamon.

Gaies, S. J. (1985). *Peer involvement in language learning.* New York: Harcourt Brace Jovanovich.

Gardner, R. C. (1985). *Social psychology and second language learning: The role of attitudes and motivation.* London, Ontario: Edward Arnold.

Gardner, R. C., & Lambert, W. E. (1959). Motivational variables in second language acquisition. *Canadian Journal of Psychology, 13,* 266–272.

Gardner, R. C., & Lambert, W. E. (1972). *Attitudes and motivation in second language learning.* Rowley, MA: Newbury House.

Gardner, R. C., Lalonde, R. H., Moorcroft, R., & Evers, F. T. (1985). *Second language attrition: The role of motivation and use* (Research Bulletin 638). London, Ontario: University of Western Ontario.

Gardner, R. C., & Smythe, R. C. (1975a). *Second language acquisition: A social psychological approach* (Research Bulletin No. 322). London, Ontario: Department of Psychology, University of Western Ontario.

Gardner, R. C., & Smythe, R. C. (1975b). Motivation and second language acquisition. *Canadian Modern Language Review, 31,* 218–238.

Geddes, M., & White, R. (1978). The use of semi-scripted simulated authentic speech in listening comprehension. *Audiovisual Language Journal, 16*(3), 137–145.

Genesee, F. (1978). Second language learning and language attitudes. *Working Papers on Bilingualism, 16,* 19–42.

Gibbons, J. (1985). The silent period: An examination. *Language Learning, 26,* 267–280.

Gibson, J. (1973). Teachers talking. Quoted in S. Delamont, *Interaction in the classroom* (2nd ed.). London: Methuen.

Gilligan, C. (1982). *In a different voice: Psychological theory and women's development.* Cambridge, MA: Harvard University Press.

Goleman, D. (1986). Mental images: New research helps clarify their role. *New York Times,* August 12, C1, C6.

Grala, M., Oxford, R., & Schleppegrell, M. (1987). *Improving your language learning: Strategies for Peace Corps volunteers.* Washington, DC: Center for Applied Linguistics.

Grellet, F. (1981). *Developing reading skills.* Cambridge: Cambridge University Press.

Grucz, M. M., & McKee, E. (1986). Mnemonic devices: Pegs on which to hang your students' memory. *AATF National Bulletin, 11*(3), 8–11.

Gruneberg, M. M. (1987a). *The Link Word language system: French.* London: Corgi.

Gruneberg, M. M. (1987b). *The Link Word language system: German.* London: Corgi.

Gruneberg, M. M. (1987c). *The Link Word language system: Italian.* London: Corgi.

Gruneberg, M. M. (1987d). *The Link Word language system: Spanish.* London: Corgi.

Gunderson, B., & Johnson, D. (1980). Building positive attitudes by using cooperative learning groups. *Foreign Language Annals, 13*(1), 39–43.

Hague, S. A. (1986a). Bridging the gap between learning to read and reading to learn: A remedy that works. *Northeast Conference Newsletter, 19,* 46–47.

Hague, S. A. (1986b). Learning to read and reading to learn: Bridging the gap in second language acquisition. *Hispania, 69*(2), 400–402.

Hague, S. A. (1987). Vocabulary instruction: What L2 can learn from L1. *Foreign Language Annals, 20*(3), 217–225.

Halff, H. M. (1986). Instructional applications of artificial intelligence. *Educational Leadership,* March, 24–31.

Hall, R., Jr. (1973). *New ways to learn a foreign language.* Ithaca, NY: Spoken Language Services.

Hamp-Lyons, L. (1983). Review of *Survey of materials for teaching advanced listening and note-taking. TESOL Quarterly, 17*(1), 109–121.

Hamp-Lyons, L., & Heasley, B. (1987). *Study writing: A course in written English for academic and professional purposes.* Cambridge: Cambridge University Press.

Harmer, J. (1983). *The practice of English language teaching.* Harlow: Longman.

Hart, J., & Simon, N. (1988). Iterative Prisoner's Dilemma: A program for instructional and experimental use. In D. Crookall (Ed.), *Simulation/gaming and the new technolgies.* Special issue of *Simulation/Games for Learning, 18*(1).

Harter, S. (1986). Feeling good about yourself isn't enough. *Today, 8*(2), 2–3.

Hartfiel, V. F., Hughey, J. B., Wormuth, D. R., & Jacobs, H. (1985). *Learning ESL composition.* Rowley, MA: Newbury House.

Henner-Stanchina, C. (1976). Two years of autonomy: Practise and outlook. *Mélanges Pedagogiques.*

Henner-Stanchina, C. (1986). *Teaching strategies for listening comprehension.* Paper presented at the Fourth Annual Conference on Learning Strategies, LaGuardia (NY) Community College.

Henner-Stanchina, C., & Holec, H. (1977). Evaluation of an autonomous learning scheme. *Mélanges Pedagogiques.*

Higbee, K. L. (1979). Recent research on visual mnemonics: Historical roots and educational fruits. *Review of Educational Research, 49*(4), 611–629.

Holec, H. (1980). Learner training: Meeting the needs of self-directed learning. In H. B. Altman & C. V. James (Eds.), *Foreign language teaching: Meeting individual needs*. Oxford: Pergamon.

Holec, H. (1981). *Autonomy and foreign language learning*. Oxford: Pergamon.

Hosenfeld, C. (1977). *A learning-teaching view of second-language instruction: The learning strategies of second language learners with reading-grammar tasks*. Unpublished doctoral dissertation, Ohio State University.

Hosenfeld, C., Arnold, V., Kirchofer, J., Laciura, J., & Wilson, L. (1981). Second language reading: A curricular sequence for teaching reading strategies. *Foreign Language Annals, 14*(5), 415–422.

Houpt, S. (1984). Inspiring creative writing through conversation. *Foreign Language Annals, 3*(17), 185–189.

Howard, D. V. (1983). *Cognitive psychology: Memory, language, and thought*. New York: Macmillan.

Howatt, A. P. R. (1984). *A history of English language teaching*. Oxford: Oxford University Press.

Hymes, D. (1972). On communicative competence. In J. B. Pride & D. Hymes (Eds.), *Sociolinguistics*. Harmondsworth: Penguin.

Jacob, E., & Mattson, B. (1987). *Using cooperative learning with language minority students: A report from the field*. Washington, DC: Center for Language Education and Research, Center for Applied Linguistics.

James, B. G. (1984). *Business wargames*. Harmondsworth: Penguin.

Jones, B. F., Aniran, M., & Katias, M. (1985). Teaching cognitive strategies and text structures within language arts programs. In J. W. Segal, S. F. Chipman, & R. Glaser (Eds.), *Thinking and learning skills* (Vol. 1, pp. 259–297). Hillsdale, NJ: Erlbaum.

Jones, K. (1985). *Graded Simulations 1: SURVIVAL, FRONT PAGE, RADIO COVINGHAM*. Oxford: Basil Blackwell.

Jones, L. (1983). *Eight simulations: For upper-intermediate and more advanced students of English*. Cambridge: Cambridge University Press.

Jones, L., & Kimbrough, V. (1987). *Great ideas: Listening and speaking activities for students of American English*. Cambridge: Cambridge University Press.

Jones, R. A. (1977). *Psychological, social and personal factors in second language acquisition*. Unpublished master's thesis, English Department (ESL Section), University of California at Los Angeles.

Kagan, S. (1986). Cooperative learning and sociocultural factors in schooling. In *Beyond language: Social and cultural factors in schooling language minority students* (pp. 231–290). Bilingual Education Office, California State Department of Education.

Keeler, S. (1982). Practising what we preach: Teaching teachers about self-directed learning through the integrated use of self-access environments in the teacher training course. *System, 10*(3), 258–268.

Kinder Monatszeitschrift. (1986). *VIII*(3).

Kinder Monatszeitschrift. (1986). *VIII*(6).

Knowles, M. (1975). *Self-directed learning: A guide for learners and teachers*. Chicago: Association Press.

Koestler, A. (1964). *The art of creation*. London: Hutchinson.

Kohn, A. (1987). It's hard to get out of a pair—Profile: David and Roger Johnson. *Psychology Today*, October, pp. 53–57.

Kraft, C. H., & Kraft, M. E. (1966). *Where do I go from here? A handbook for continuing language study in the field.* United States Peace Corps.

Krashen, S. D. (1982). *Principles and practice in second language acquisition.* Oxford: Pergamon.

Krashen, S. D., & Terrell, T. D. (1983). *The natural approach to language acquisition in the classroom.* Oxford/San Francisco: Pergamon/Alemany.

Krashen, S. D., Terrell, T. D., Ehrman, M. E., & Herzog, M. (1984). A theoretical basis for teaching the receptive skills. *Foreign Language Annals, 4*(17), 261–275.

Lambert, R. D., & Freed, B. F. (Eds.). (1982). *The loss of language skills.* Rowley, MA: Newbury House.

Leaver, B. L. (1984). Twenty minutes to mastery of the Cyrillic alphabet. *Foreign Language Annals, 17*(1), 215–220.

Leaver, B. L. (forthcoming). *The acquisition/learning dichotomy: Another look.* Submitted for publication.

Littlewood, W. (1984). *Foreign and second language learning: Language acquisition research and its implications for the classroom.* Cambridge: Cambridge University Press.

Lobuts, J. F., & Pennewill, C. L. (1989). Individual and organizational communication and destructive competition. In D. Crookall & D. Saunders (Eds.), *Communication and simulation: From two fields to one theme* (pp. 177–187). Clevedon, Avon, UK: Multilingual Matters.

Long, M. (1979). *Inside the "black box": Methodological issues in research on teaching.* Paper presented at the annual meeting of TESOL, Boston, MA.

Long, P. (1987). Laugh and be well? *Psychology Today*, 28–29.

Lorayne, H., & Lucas, J. (1974). *The memory book.* New York: Ballantine.

Lukmani, Y. (1972). Motivation to learn and language proficiency. *Language Learning, 22*(2), 261–273.

MacBride, S., et al. (1980). *Many voices, one world.* London: Kogan Page, UNESCO.

Maccoby, E. E., & Jacklin, C. (1974). *The psychology of sex differences.* Stanford, CA: Stanford University Press.

Manzo, A. (1969). The ReQuest procedure. *Journal of Reading, 13,* 123–126.

Matheidesz, M. (1987a). *96 (SPEAKING FACES).* Budapest: Babilon.

Matheidesz, M. (1987b). Running errands: A communication board game. *Simulation/Games for Learning, 17*(3), 120–126.

Matheidesz, M. (1988a). Games for language learning. In D. Saunders, A. Coote, & D. Crookall, (Eds.), *Learning from experience through games and simulation.* Loughborough, Leics, UK: Society for the Advancement of Games and Simulations in Education and Training.

Matheidesz, M. (1988b). Self-access language practice through CALL games. In D. Crookall, (Ed.), *Simulation/gaming and the new technologies.* Special issue of *Simulation/Games for Learning, 18*(1).

McCombs, B. L. (1987). *The role of affective variables in autonomous learning.* Paper presented at the annual meeting of AERA, Washington, DC.

McCombs, B. L. (1988). Motivational skills training: Combining metacognitive, cognitive, and affective learning strategies. In C. E. Weinstein, E. T. Goetz, & P. A. Alexander (Eds.), *Learning and study strategies: Issues in assessment, instruction, and evaluation.* New York: Academic Press.

McCombs, B. L., & Dobrovolny, J. L. (1982). *Student motivational skill training package: Evaluation for air force technical training* (Technical Report No. AFHRL-TR-82-31). Air Force Human Resources Laboratory, Air Force Systems Command, Brooks Air Force Base, Texas; Logistics and Technical Training Division, Technical Training Branch, Lowry Air Force Base, Colorado.

McGroarty, M. (1987). *Patterns of persistent second language learners: Elementary Spanish.* Paper presented at the annual meeting of TESOL, Miami, Florida.

McKee, E. (1981). Teaching writing in the second language composition/conversation class at the college level. *Foreign Language Annals, 14*(4–5), 273–278.

Mendelsohn, D. J. (1984). There ARE strategies for listening. *TEAL Occasional Papers, 8,* 63–76.

Meyer, R. (1984). "Listen my children, and you shall hear . . ." *Foreign Language Annals, 17*(4), 343–344.

Miller, G. A. (1956). The magical number seven, plus or minus two: Some limits on our capacity for processing information. *Psychological Review, 63,* 81–90.

Mohan, B. A. (1986). *Language and content.* Reading, MA: Addison-Wesley.

Moran, P. R. (1984). *Lexicarry: An illustrated vocabulary-builder for second languages.* Brattleboro: ProLingua.

Morgenstern, D. (1987). Artifice vs. real-world data. In D. Crookall, C. S. Greenblat, A. Coote, J. H. G. Klabbers, & D. R. Watson (Eds.), *Simulation-gaming in the later 1980s* (pp. 101–109). Oxford: Pergamon.

Morley, J. (1984). *Listening and language learning in English as a second language: Developing a self-study activities for listening comprehension.* Orlando: Harcourt Brace Jovanovich/Center for Applied Linguistics.

Moulden, H. (1978). Extending self-directed learning of English in an engineering college: Experiment year one. *Mélanges Pedagogiques,* 81–102.

Moulden, H. (1980). Extending self-directed learning of English in an engineering college. Experiment two. *Mélanges Pedagogigues,* 83–116.

Moulton, W. G. (1966). *A linguistic guide to language learning.* New York: Modern Language Association to America.

Munby, J. (1978). *Communicative syllabus design.* Cambridge: Cambridge University Press.

Murray, J. M., Morgenstern, D., & Furstenberg, G. (1989). In W. F. Smith (Ed.), *Modern technology in foreign language education* (pp. 97–118). Lincolnwood, IL: National Textbook Company.

Naiman, N., Fröhlich, M., & Todesco, A. (1975). The good second language learner. *TESL Talk, 6*(1), 58–75.

Naiman, N., Fröhlich, M., Stern, H. H., & Todesco, A. (1978). *The good language learner.* Research in Education Series, 7. Toronto: Ontario Institute for Studies in Education.

Nida, E. (1957). *Learning a foreign language: A handbook prepared especially for missionaries.* Friendship Press for the National Council of Churches in the USA.

Noel, R. C., Crookall, D., Wilkenfeld, J., & Schapira, L. (1987). Network gaming: A vehicle for international communication. In D. Crookall, C. S. Greenblat, A. Coote, J. H. G. Klabbers, & D. R. Watson (Eds.), *Simulation-gaming in the late 1980s* (pp. 5–21). Oxford: Pergamon Press.

Norbrook, H. (1984). Extensive listening: How can radio aid comprehension? (Parts 1 and 2). *Modern English Teacher, 12.*

Novak, D., & Gowin, D. B. (1984). *Learning how to learn*. Cambridge: Cambridge University Press.

Nyikos, M. (1987). *The effect of color and imagery as mnemonic strategies on learning and retention of lexical items in German*. Unpublished doctoral dissertation, Purdue University.

Nyikos, M. (n.d.). *Assuming responsibility for learning: Study strategy worksheet*. West Lafayette, IN: Purdue University.

Nyikos, M., & Oxford, R. (1987). *Strategies for foreign language learning and second language acquisition*. Paper presented at the Conference on Second Language Acquisition and Foreign Language Learning, University of Illinois, Champaign-Urbana.

Omaggio, A. C. (1981). *Helping learners succeed: Activities for the foreign language classroom*. Washington, DC: Center for Applied Linguistics.

Omaggio, A. C. (1986). *Teaching language in context: Proficiency-oriented instruction*. Boston: Heinle & Heinle.

O'Malley, J. M., & Chamot, A. U. (1989). *Learning strategies in second language acquisition*. Cambridge: Cambridge University Press.

O'Malley, J. M., Chamot, A. U., Stewner-Manzanares, G., Küpper, L., & Russo, R. (1985a). Learning strategies used by beginning and intermediate ESL students. *Language Learning, 35*(1), 21–46.

O'Malley, J. M., Chamot, A. U., Stewner-Manzanares, G., Russo, R., & Küpper, L. (1985b). Learning strategy applications with students of English as a second language. *TESOL Quarterly, 19*(3), 557–584.

O'Malley, J. M., Chamot, A. U., & Walker, C. (1987). Some applications of cognitive theory in second language acquisition. *Studies in Second Language Acquisition, 9*(3).

O'Neil, H. F., Jr. (Ed.). (1978). *Learning strategies*. New York: Academic Press.

Ong, W. J. (1987). *Orality and literacy: The technologizing of the word*. London: Methuen.

Oppenheimer, J., & Winer, M. (1988). Using and creating a simulation authoring system: Cooperation and conflict. In D. Crookall (Ed.), *Computerized simulation in the social sciences: Issues and practices*, Special Issue of *Social Science Computer Review, 6*(1).

Oshima, A., & Hogue, A., (1983). *Writing academic English*. Reading, MA: Addison-Wesley.

Oshima, A., & Hogue, A. (1988). *Introduction to academic writing*. Reading, MA: Addison-Wesley.

Oskarsson, M. (1984). *Self-assessment of foreign language skills: A survey of research and development work*. Strasbourg, France: Council of Europe, Council for Cultural Cooperation.

Oxford, R. (1982a). Research on language loss: A review with implications for foreign language teaching. *Modern Language Journal, 66*(2), 168–169.

Oxford, R. (1982b). Technical issues in designing and conducting research on language skill attrition. In R. Lambert & B. F. Freed (Eds.), *The loss of language skills*. Rowley, MA: Newbury House, pp. 119–137.

Oxford, R. (1985a). *A new taxonomy of second language learning strategies*. Washington, DC: ERIC Clearinghouse on Languages and Linguistics.

Oxford, R. (1985b). Second language learning strategies: What the research has to say. *ERIC/CLL News Bulletin, 9,* 3–5.

Oxford, R. (1986a). *Development and psychometric testing of the Strategy Inventory for Language Learning (SILL)* (ARI Technical Report 728). Alexandria, VA: Training Research Laboratory, US Army Research Institute for Behavioral and Social Sciences.

Oxford, R. (1986b). *Development of a new survey and taxonomy for second language learning.* Paper presented at the Fourth Annual Conference on Learning Strategies, LaGuardia (NY) Community College.

Oxford, R. (1986c). *Development of the Strategy Inventory for Language Learning.* Paper presented at the Language Testing Research Colloquium, Monterey, CA.

Oxford, R. (1986d). Research on the successful language learner. *Minibib.* Washington, DC: ERIC Clearinghouse on Languages and Linguistics.

Oxford, R. (1986e). *Researching and assessing strategies for learning a second language.* Paper presented at the annual meeting of AERA, San Francisco.

Oxford, R. (1986f). *Second language learning strategies: Current research and implications for practice.* Los Angeles: Center for Language Education and Research, University of California at Los Angeles.

Oxford, R. (1988). *Problems and solutions in foreign/second language vocabulary learning: The potential role of semantic mapping.* Reston, VA: Advanced Technology.

Oxford, R. (1989). Use of language learning strategies: A synthesis of studies with implications for strategy training. *System, 17*(2).

Oxford, R., Cohen, A., & Sutter, W. (in press). Language learning strategies: Evolution of a concept.

Oxford, R., & Crookall, D. (1988). Learning strategies. In J. Berko-Gleason (Ed.), *You CAN take it with you: Helping students maintain second language skills* (pp. 23–49). Englewood Cliffs, NJ: Prentice-Hall.

Oxford, R., & Ehrman, M. (1989). Psychological type and adult language learning strategies: A pilot study. *Journal of Psychological Type, 16,* 22–32.

Oxford, R., Lavine, R., & Crookall, D. (1989). Language learning strategies, the communicative approach, and their classroom implications. *Foreign Language Annals, 22*(1), 29–39.

Oxford, R., & Nyikos, M. (1987). *Second language learning strategies: New research findings.* Paper presented at the Symposium on Second Language Learning Styles and Strategies, Center for Applied Linguistics, Washington, DC.

Oxford, R., & Nyikos, M. (1989). Variables affecting choice of language learning strategies by university students. *Modern Language Journal, 73*(2).

Oxford, R., Nyikos, M., & Crookall, D. (1987). *Learning strategies of university foreign language students: A large-scale study.* Paper presented at the annual meeting of TESOL, Miami, FL.

Oxford, R., Nyikos, M., & Ehrman, M. (1988). Vive la différence? Reflections on sex differences in use of language learning strategies. *Foreign Language Annals, 21*(4), 321–329.

Oxford, R., & Rhodes, N. C. (1988). U.S. foreign language instruction: Assessing needs and creating an action plan. *ERIC/CLL News Bulletin, 11*(2), 1, 6–7.

Papalia, A., & Zampogna, J. (1977). Strategies used by foreign language students in deriving meaning from a written text and in learning vocabulary. *Language Association Bulletin,* 7–8.

Pei, N. (1966). *How to learn languages and what languages to learn*. New York: Harper & Row.

Phillips, J. K. (1984). Practical implications of recent research in reading. *Foreign Language Annals*, 17(4), 285–296.

Pimsleur, P. (1980). *How to learn a foreign language*. Boston: Heinle & Heinle.

Politzer, R. L. (1965). *Foreign language learning: A linguistic introduction*. Englewood Cliffs, NJ: Prentice-Hall.

Politzer, R. L. (1983). An exploratory study of self-reported language learning behaviors and their relation to achievement. *Studies in Second Language Acquisition*, 6(1), 54–65.

Politzer, R. L., & McGroarty, M. (1985). *An exploratory study of learning behaviors and their relation to gains in linguistic and communicative competence*. Unpublished manuscript, Stanford University.

Private Eye. (1979). *Bumper book of boobs*. London: Private Eye/Deutsch.

Prowse, R. (1983). Talking about learning. *TESOL-France News*, 3(2), 18–19.

Raimes, A. (1983). *Techniques in teaching writing*. Oxford: Oxford University Press.

Ramirez, A. G. (1986). Language learning strategies used by adolescents studying French in New York schools. *Foreign Language Annals*, 19(2), 131–141.

Reid, J. M. (1987). The learning style preferences of ESL students. *TESOL Quarterly*, 21, 87–111.

Reiss, M-A. (1985). The good language learner: Another look. *Canadian Language Review/La Revue Canadienne des Langues Vivantes*, 41(3), 511–523.

Rigney, J. W. (1978). Learning strategies: A theoretical perspective. In H. F. O'Neil, Jr. (Ed.), *Learning strategies* (pp. 165–205). New York: Academic Press.

Rigney, J. W. (1980). Cognitive learning strategies and dualities in information processing. In R. E. Snow, R. Federico, & W. E. Montague (Eds.), *Aptitude, learning and instruction* (Vol. 1, pp. 315–343). Hillsdale, NJ: Erlbaum.

Riley, P. (1982). Topics in communicative methodology: Including a preliminary and selective bibliography on the communicative approach. *Mélanges Pedagogiques*, 93–132.

Riley, P. (1985). "Strategy": Conflict or collaboration. *Mélanges Pedagogiques*, 91–116.

Rivera, C. (Ed.). (1984). *Language proficiency and academic achievement*. Clevedon, UK: Multilingual Matters.

Rivers, W. N. (1981). *Teaching foreign language skills* (2nd ed.). Chicago: University of Chicago Press.

Rodgers, T. S. (1978). Towards a model of learner variation in autonomous foreign language learning. *Studies in Second Language Acquisition*, 2(1), 73–97.

Rossi-Le, L. (1988). *The perceptual learning differences and the relationship to language learning strategies in adult students for English as a second language*. Unpublished dissertation proposal, Drake University.

Rowe, D. (1983). *Depression: The way out of the prison*. London: Routledge & Kegan Paul.

Ruben, B. D. (1987). Guidelines for cross-cultural communication effectiveness. In L. F. Luce & E. C. Smith (Eds.), *Towards internationalism: Readings in cross-cultural communication* (2nd ed., pp. 36–48). New York: Newbury House.

Rubin, J. (1975). What the "good language learner" can teach us. *TESOL Quarterly*, 9(1), 41–51.

Rubin, J. (1981). Study of cognitive processes in second language learning. *Applied Linguistics, 11*(2), 118–131.

Rubin, J. (1985). *The Language Learning Disc.* Descriptive pamphlet, Joan Rubin Associates, Berkeley, CA.

Rubin, J. (1986). *The Language Learning Disc.* Paper presented at SALT conference.

Rubin, J. (1987a). Learner strategies: Theoretical assumptions, research, history, and typology. In A. Wenden & J. Rubin (Eds.), *Learner strategies in language learning* (pp. 15–30). Englewood Cliffs, NJ: Prentice-Hall.

Rubin, J. (1987b). Videodisc teaches language learning skills. FL News, *Foreign Language Annals, 20*(3), 275.

Rubin, J. (1989). The Language Learning Disc. In W. F. Smith (Ed.), *Modern technology in foreign language education* (pp. 269–275). Lincolnwood, IL: National Textbook.

Rubin, J., & Thompson, I. (1982). *How to be a more successful language learner.* Boston: Heinle & Heinle.

Russo, R. P., & Stewner-Manzanares, G. (1985). *The training and use of learning strategies for English as a second language in a military context.* Rosslyn, VA: InterAmerica Research Associates.

Savignon, S. J. (1972). *Communicative competence: An experiment in foreign language teaching.* Philadelphia: Center for Curriculum Development.

Savignon, S. J. (1983). *Communicative competence: Theory and practice.* Reading, MA: Addison-Wesley.

Schleppegrell, M., & Oxford, R. (1988). *Language learning strategies for Peace Corps volunteers.* Washington, DC: Center for Applied Linguistics.

Schumann, F. E., and Schumann, J. N. (1977). Diary of a language learner: An introspective study of second language learning. In H. D. Brown, C. A. Yorio, & R. Crymes (Eds.), *On TESOL '77: Teaching and learning ESL.* Washington, DC: TESOL.

Seliger, H. W. (1983). Learner interaction in the classroom and its effect on language acquisition. In H. W. Seliger & M. H. Long (Eds.), *Classroom-oriented research in second language acquisition.* Rowley, MA: Newbury House.

Selinker, L. (1972). Interlanguage. *International Review of Applied Linguistics, 10*(3), 201–231.

Selinker, L. (1981). Updating the interlanguage hypothesis. *Studies in Language Acquisition, 3*(2), 201–228.

Semke, H. D. (1984). Effects of the red pen. *Foreign Language Annals, 17*(3), 195–202.

Sharan, S., Kussell, R., Hertz-Lazarowitz, R., Bejarano, Y., Raviv, S., & Sharan, Y. (1985). Cooperative learning effects on ethnic relations and achievement on Israeli junior-high-school classrooms. In R. Slavin, S. Sharan, S. Kagan, R. Hertz-Lazarowitz, C. Webb, & R. Schmuck (Eds.), *Learning to cooperate, cooperating to learn* (pp. 313–343). New York: Plenum.

Shephard, R. N. (1967). Recognition memory for words, sentences, and pictures. *Journal of Verbal Learning and Verbal Behavior, 6*, 156–163.

Shipman, S., & Shipman, V. C. (1985). Cognitive styles: Some conceptual, methodological, and applied issues. *Review of Research in Education* (Vol. 12, pp. 229–291). Washington, DC: American Educational Research Association.

Slavin, R. (1983). *Cooperative learning.* New York: Longman.

Spack, R., & Sadow, C. (1983). Student-teacher working journals in ESL freshman composition. *TESOL Quarterly, 17*(4), 575–594.

Spolsky, B. (1969). Attitudinal aspects of learning. *Language Learning, 19,* 271–283.

Staton, J. (1980). Writing and counseling: Using a dialogue journal. *Language Arts, 57*(5), 514–518.

Staton, J. (1983). Dialogue journals: A new tool for teaching communication. *ERIC/CLL News Bulletin, 6,* 1–2, 6.

Staton, J. (1987). New research on dialogue journals. *Dialogue, IV*(1), 1–24.

Staton, J., Shuy, R., & Kreeft, J. (1982). *Analysis of dialogue journal writing as a communicative event* (Vol. 1) (Final report to the National Institute of Education). Washington, DC: Center for Applied Linguistics.

Stern, H. W. (1983). *Fundamental concepts in language teaching.* Oxford: Oxford University Press.

Stevick, E. W. (1976). *Memory, meaning, and method: Some psychological perspectives on language learning.* Rowley, MA: Newbury House.

Stewner-Manzanares, G., Chamot, A. U., Küpper, L., & Russo, R. P. (1984). *A teacher's guide for using learning strategies in English as a second language instruction.* Rosslyn, VA: InterAmerica Research Associates.

Stewner-Manzanares, G., Chamot, A. U., O'Malley, J. M., Küpper, L., & Russo, R. P. (1985). *Learning strategies in English as a second language instruction: A teacher's guide.* Rosslyn, VA: InterAmerica Research Associates.

Strasheim, L. A. (1988). *Getting around in a German-speaking city: Testing the Indiana level one listening competence.* Indianapolis: Center for School Improvement and Performance.

Tarone, E. (1977). Conscious communication strategies in interlanguage: A progress report. In H. D. Brown, C. A. Yorio, & R. Crymes (Eds.), *On TESOL '77: Teaching and learning ESL* (pp. 194–203). Washington, DC: TESOL.

Tarone, E. (1980). Communication strategies, foreigner talk, and repair in interlanguage. *Language Learning, 30*(2), 417–31.

Tarone, E. (1983). Some thoughts on the notion of "communication strategy." In C. Faerch & G. Kasper (Eds.), *Strategies in interlanguage communication* (pp. 61–74). London: Longman.

Tarone, E., Cohen, A. D., & Dumas, G. (1983). A closer look at some interlanguage terminology: A framework for communication strategies. In C. Faerch & G. Kasper (Eds.) *Strategies in interlanguage communication.* London: Longman.

Tesser, A., & Campbell, J. (1982). *Self-evaluation maintenance processes and individual differences in self-esteem.* Paper presented at the annual meeting of the American Psychological Association, Washington, DC.

Thompson, J. (1987). Memory in language learning. In A. Wenden & J. Rubin (Eds.), *Learner strategies in language learning* (pp. 43–56). Englewood Cliffs, NJ: Prentice-Hall.

Tucker, G. R., Hamayan, E., & Genesee, F. H. (1976). Affective, cognitive, and social factors in second language acquisition. *Canadian Modern Language Review/La Revue Canadienne des Langues Vivantes, 32,* 214–226.

Tulving, E. (1985). How many memory systems are there? *American Psychologist, 40*(4), 385–398.

Tyacke, M., & Mendelsohn, D. (1986). Student needs: Cognitive as well as communicative. *TESOL Canada Journal,* Special Issue 1, 171–183.

Ur, P. (1984). *Teaching listening comprehension*. Cambridge: Cambridge University Press.

URSS: Le plus ancien des "refuseniks" Vladimir Slepak a quitté Moscou pour Israel. *Le Monde*, Octobre 27, 1987, p. 48.

Van Lancker, D. (1987). Old familiar voices. *Psychology Today, 21*(11), 12–13.

Weinstein, C. E., Goetz, E. T., & Alexander, P. A. (Eds.) (1988). *Learning and study strategies: Issues in assessment, instruction, and evaluation.* New York: Academic Press.

Weinstein, C. E., & Underwood, V. L. (1985). Learning strategies: The how of learning. In J. Segal, S. Chipman, & R. Glaser (Eds.), *Relating instruction to basic research* (pp. 241–259). Hillsdale, NJ: Erlbaum.

Weltens, B. (1986). The attrition of foreign-language skills: A literature review. *Applied Linguistics, 8*(1), 22–36.

Wenden, A. L. (1985a). Facilitating learning competence: Perspectives on an expanded role for second-language teachers. *Canadian Modern Language Review/ La Revue Canadienne des Langues Vivantes, 41*(16), 981–990.

Wenden, A. L. (1985b). Learner strategies. *TESOL Newsletter, 19*(5), 1–7.

Wenden, A. L. (1986a). Helping language learners think about learning. *ELT Journal, 40*(1), 3–12.

Wenden, A. L. (1986b). What do second-language learners know about their language learning? A second look at retrospective accounts. *Applied Linguistics, 7*(2), 186–205.

Wenden, A. L. (1987). Conceptual background and utility. In A. Wenden & J. Rubin (Eds.), *Learner strategies in language learning* (pp. 3–13). Englewood Cliffs, NJ: Prentice-Hall.

Wenden, A. L., & Rubin, J. (Eds.). (1987). *Learner strategies in language learning*. Englewood Cliffs, NJ: Prentice-Hall.

Wesche, M. B. (1983). Communicative testing in a second language. *Modern Language Journal, 67*(1), 43–55.

White, R. H. (1959). Motivation reconsidered. *Psychology Review, 66*(5), 297–333.

Widdowson, H. G. (1978). *Teaching language as communication*. Oxford: Oxford University Press.

Withrow, J. (1987). *Effective writing: Writing skills for intermediate students of American English*. Cambridge: Cambridge University Press.

Wong, R. (1987). *Teaching pronunciation: Focus on English rhythm and intonation*. Englewood Cliffs, NJ: Prentice-Hall.

Wong Fillmore, L. W. (1985). Second language learning in children: A proposed model. *Issues in English language development*. Rosslyn, VA: National Clearinghouse on Bilingual Education.

Wright, A. (1987). *How to improve your mind*. Cambridge: Cambridge University Press.

Wright, T. (1987). *Roles of teachers and learners*. Oxford: Oxford University Press.

General Instructions to Administrators of the Strategy Inventory for Language Learning (SILL)

Important—Please Read Carefully

List and Explanation of Student Materials

1. Each student will receive:
   a. Directions and Items.
   b. Worksheet for Scoring and Administering the SILL (1 sheet). For the convenience of the students, do not staple the Worksheet directly to the Directions and Items; keep it as a separate page. However, give the Worksheet to students at the same time as Directions and Items.
   c. Profile of Results on the SILL. *The Profile should not be given to students until they have completed the Worksheet! This is very important.* If students receive the Profile at the same time as they receive Directions, Items, and Worksheet, bias can be introduced into the results. Students might be tempted to respond in what they think is a "socially desirable" way, given the descriptions on the Profile. To avoid this situation, simply distribute the Profile sheets when it appears that most students have completed their Worksheets.
   d. Background Questionnaire (Optional). See below.
2. Be sure to read carefully all the student materials listed above, so that you will be familiar with them and be able to answer any questions students might have.

Time Requirements

1. Allow approximately 30 minutes for students to complete the SILL (longer for beginning ESL or EFL students), plus about 15–20 minutes for them to

fill out the Worksheet and the Profile. Times will vary with the students' age, maturity, and familiarity with completing questionnaires.

2. If your class periods are an hour long, you might want to use one period for students to complete the Worksheet and the Profile, and part or all of another class period for a discussion of the Profiles and of language learning strategies in general.

Advance Preparation

1. It is helpful to give students a little advance notice, perhaps 1 to 3 days ahead, that they will be taking the SILL on a certain day. Explain (in your own words) that the SILL is designed to help students understand better how they learn a new language and that the information helps them become better learners.
2. In addition, you might stimulate interest by asking students to be thinking about and noticing the things they do to learn a new language; this is not required but might be useful.
3. Make the needed copies of student materials.
4. Gather a few extra pens or pencils.
5. (Optional) Gather a few hand calculators to speed up the scoring when students use their Worksheets. However, the calculations are fairly simple; most students can easily do them without calculators, as previous administrations of the SILL have demonstrated.

The Confidentiality/Anonymity Question

1. In most SILL research in the past, we have asked students to complete the SILL using their own names, i.e., not anonymously. This method is simple and allows you to use the results to help individual students improve their strategies. Assure students that the *results for each student will not be publicly posted or shared with other students, will not be compared with the results of any other individual student, will not be used for grading or for any negative purpose, and will be used only to help them become better learners*; then you are likely to have no problems.
2. However, if you feel that your students might require anonymity in order to be candid, you can assign each student a code number to be used in place of the name. They will need to use the *same code number consistently on the Worksheet and the Profile* (and on the optional Background Questionnaire, if used).

What to Do When Administering the SILL

1. Just before handing out the SILL Directions, Items, and Worksheet, make sure that everyone has a pen or pencil. Then provide the following general overview aloud, preferably in your own words:

The Strategy Inventory for Language Learning (SILL) is designed to assess how you go about learning a language. Most students who have taken the SILL have found it interesting and fun. Each item represents a particular kind of language learning behavior. The results will help you know more about yourself as a language learner, and it will help me [or, "your teacher"] to help you learn more effectively.

So that you will get your SILL results quickly, you will score your own SILL and complete your own Profile. Taking the SILL will probably raise a number of interesting issues for you about language learning. We will have plenty of time to discuss these issues after you have completed the SILL.

Respond to the items in terms of what you typically do to learn the language you are now studying [or if not studying a language now, what you did to learn the language you most recently studied]. Remember there are no right or wrong answers. Your SILL results will be kept in complete confidence and will not affect your grade or anyone's opinion about you.

2. Now distribute the Directions, Items, and Worksheet.
3. Tell students to write their own name (or a code number) at the top of the Worksheet. See confidentiality/anonymity discussion above. Remind students to use the same name or number on the Profile, which they will receive later (and on the Background Questionnaire, if used).
4. Ask students to read the Directions sheet silently and then raise their hands if they have any questions about the Directions. ESL students might need some help with understanding, depending on their level of proficiency.
5. As students take the SILL, they write down their answers on the Worksheet. Then they calculate their averages on the same Worksheet following the detailed directions given there. You may allow use of hand calculators to speed up the arithmetic, although they are in no way essential (as noted earlier).
6. When it appears that most students have finished the Worksheet, it is time to distribute the Profile. (Do not distribute the Profile earlier; see above.) The Profile is self-explanatory in terms of how it should be completed. Students should complete the Profile as soon as they have finished the Worksheet.
7. (Optional) Have students graph their results if desired. Many students like to see their results in a graphic form, in which comparisons of frequencies of strategy types are easy to understand.
8. (Optional) If you do not have time to discuss the Profiles in the same class period when the SILL is administered, it might be advantageous to take up the Profiles, along with all the rest of the SILL materials, so that nothing gets lost.

Discussing the Results

1. Make sure each student has his or her own completed Profile. This is essential.
2. Remind students that there are no right or wrong answers.
3. Discuss in general the meaning of each of the categories of language learning behaviors (strategies). Rather than going through the categories one by one

in a boring way, it is best if you *ask students to suggest their favorite categories and describe which strategies they like to use in those categories.* Encourage students to ask questions about categories or specific strategies they do not fully understand.

4. Explain that the higher a student's *average for a given SILL category,* the more frequently the student uses that particular category of language learning strategies. The higher a student's *overall SILL average across all categories,* the more frequently the student uses language learning strategies in general.

5. To get a good discussion going, you might want to raise three or four of the following questions. (Or make up your own!)
   a. *Which language strategies do you think people use the most and why?*
   b. *Which kinds of strategies do you think are the most effective in general for most people?*
   c. *Which kinds of language learning strategies might help you personally become a better language learner?*
   d. *Are there some new language learning strategies in the SILL which you have not considered before and which you might like to try in the next few weeks or months?*
   e. *How do you think your own motivation for language learning might be related to the kinds of language learning strategies you choose?*
   f. *Which kinds of language learning strategies do you think are useful for different kinds of people (e.g., younger, older; in school, out of school; in a new country, in their own country; people who learn best by hearing, by sight, or by touch/ movement; people who like to analyze vs. people who like to get an overall impression; impulsive vs. reflective people)?*
   g. *Is it possible that males and females have contrasting patterns of using language learning strategies? What might those patterns be?*
   h. *How might people from various nationalities or cultural backgrounds use different kinds of language learning strategies?*
   i. *In what ways would people who have different reasons for language learning (e.g., travel, job, academic advancement, pleasure) use contrasting strategies for learning a new language?*
   j. *How might different languages affect the choice of learning strategies?*
   During the discussion, do not overwhelm students with research findings; in the discussion, students should be encouraged to provide most of the input and come to their own conclusions as much as possible. *Use research information as background for yourself—or bring it up from time to time as part of the discussion only if students are interested.*

6. Remind students that *people learn languages differently, and no single formula is right for everybody.* BUT: *There may be some strategies that are generally useful in most circumstances,* such as actively seeking practice opportunities, practicing the language in authentic situations, using all possible clues to guess meanings, asking questions, paying attention. It is best to let the students themselves identify any generally useful strategies as part of the discussion.

7. Do not compare one student's results with another student's results in front of the whole group. If students want to compare results with each other on their own or if they volunteer their findings, that's OK, as long as they

refrain from judging their results on the basis of those of others. (You might want to divide students into small groups to compare their results. These groups might be based on ethnicity or cultural background.)

8. (Optional) You might want to collect the Profiles temporarily so as to figure out class averages for each of the categories and for the overall SILL. This can be helpful information for planning any strategy training. If you share the class averages with the students, *be careful how you handle this information*. Some students might feel that if they do not fit the class averages they are doing something wrong, and this might not be the case at all!

9. (Optional but very useful) You might use the discussion of SILL results as a bridge to actual strategy training. It's usually best to integrate strategy training with regular language learning activities. Design strategy training based on what you know from the SILL about the learning strategies the students are already using (or not using).

(Optional) Using the Background Questionnaire

1. The Background Questionnaire (see below) is included as an optional feature. It has been used in SILL research studies to provide additional inforation on student characteristics. This information helps teachers and students better understand the SILL results in context.

2. You might revise the Background Questionnaire or invent one of your own. If you already know the answers to some of the questions—i.e., if age or mother tongue are the same for all your students—then delete such questions as irrelevant. The wording might need to be simplified for ESL students.

3. The Background Questionnaire takes about 10 minutes and can be administered just before the SILL or at another time. It is preferable not to administer it just after the SILL.

BACKGROUND QUESTIONNAIRE

1. Name _____ 2. Date _____

3. Age _____ 4. Sex _____ 5. Mother tongue _____

6. Language(s) you speak at home _____

7. Language you are now learning (or have most recently learned) List one language only

   _____

8. How long have you been studying the language listed in #7?

   _____

9. How do you rate your overall proficiency in the language listed in #7 as compared with the proficiency of *other students in your class*? (Circle one)

   Excellent   Good   Fair   Poor

10. How do you rate your overall proficiency in the language listed in #7 as compared with the proficiency of *native speakers of the language*? (Circle one)

    Excellent   Good   Fair   Poor

11. How important is it for you to become proficient in the language listed in #7? (Circle one)

    Very important   Important   Not so important

12. Why do you want to learn the language listed in #7? (Check all that apply)

    _____ interested in the language

    _____ interested in the culture

    _____ have friends who speak the language

    _____ required to take a language course to graduate

    _____ need it for my future career

    _____ need it for travel

    _____ other (list): _____

    _____

13. Do you enjoy language learning? (Circle one)   Yes   No
14. What other languages have you studied?

    _____

15. What has been your favorite experience in language learning?

    _____

    _____

    _____

Strategy Inventory for Language Learning (SILL)

Version for English Speakers Learning a New Language

Strategy Inventory for Language Learning (SILL)

Version 5.1
(c) R. Oxford, 1989

Directions

The STRATEGY INVENTORY FOR LANGUAGE LEARNING (SILL) is designed to gather information about how you, as a student of a foreign or second language, go about learning that language. On the following pages, you will find statements related to learning a new language. Please read each statement. On the separate answer sheet, mark the response (1, 2, 3, 4, or 5) that tells how true the statement is in terms of <u>what you actually do when you are learning the new language</u>.

1. Never or almost never true of me
2. Generally not true of me
3. Somewhat true of me
4. Generally true of me
5. Always or almost always true of me

<u>Never or almost never true of me</u> means that the statement is very rarely true of you ; that is, you do the behavior which is described in the statement only in very rare instances.

<u>Generally not true of me</u> means that the statement is usually not true of you; that is, you do the behavior which is described in the statement less than half the time, but more than in very rare instances.

<u>Somewhat true of me</u> means that the statement is true of you about half the time; that is, sometimes you do the behavior which is described in the statement, and sometimes you don't, and these instances tend to occur with about equal frequency.

<u>Generally true of me</u> means that the statement is usually true of you; that is, you do the behavior which is described in the statement more than half the time.

<u>Almost or never true of me</u> means that the statement is true of you in almost all circumstances; that is, you almost always do the behavior which is described in the statement.

Use the separate Worksheet for recording your answers and for scoring. Answer in terms of how well the statement describes you, not in terms of what you think you should do, or what other people do. Answer in reference to the language you are now learning (or the language you most recently learned). There are no right or wrong responses to these statements. Work carefully but quickly. You will score the SILL yourself using the attached Worksheet. On the Worksheet, write your name, the date, and the language learned.

(Version 5.1, © R. L. Oxford, 1989)

EXAMPLE

1.   Never or almost never true of me
2.   Generally not true of me
3.   Somewhat true of me
4.   Generally true of me
5.   Always or almost always true of me

Read the item, and choose a response (1 through 5 as above), and write it in the space after the item.

I actively seek out opportunities to talk with native speakers of the new language. _____

You have just completed the example item. Answer the rest of the items on the Worksheet.

Strategy Inventory for Language Learning

Version 5.1

(c) R. Oxford, 1989

1.   Never or almost never true of me

2.   Generally not true of me

3.   Somewhat true of me

4.   Generally true of me

5.   Always or almost always true of me

(Write answers on Worksheet)

Part A

When learning a new word . . .

1.   I create associations between new material and what I already know.

2.   I put the new word in a sentence so I can remember it.

3.   I place the new word in a group with other words that are similar in some way (for example, words related to clothing, or feminine nouns).

4.   I associate the sound of the new word with the sound of a familiar word.

5.   I use rhyming to remember it.

6.   I remember the word by making a clear mental image of it or by drawing a picture.

7.   I visualize the spelling of the new word in my mind.

8.   I use a combination of sounds and images to remember the new word.

9.   I list all the other words I know that are related to the new word and draw lines to show relationships.

10.   I remember where the new word is located on the page, or where I first saw or heard it.

11.   I use flashcards with the new word on one side and the definition or other information on the other.

12.   I physically act out the new word.

When learning new material . . .

13.   I review often.

14.   I schedule my reviewing so that the review sessions are initially close together in time and gradually become more widely spread apart.

15.   I go back to refresh my memory of things I learned much earlier.

1.   Never or almost never true of me

2.   Generally not true of me

3.   Somewhat true of me

4.   Generally true of me

5.   Always or almost always true of me

(Write answers on Worksheet)

Part B

16.   I say or write new expressions repeatedly to practice them.

17.   I imitate the way native speakers talk.

18.   I read a story or dialogue several times until I can understand it.

19.   I revise what I write in the new language to improve my writing.

20.   I practice the sounds or alphabet of the new language.

21.   I use idioms or other routines in the new language.

22.   I use familiar words in different combinations to make new sentences.

23.   I initiate conversations in the new language.

24.   I watch TV shows or movies or listen to the radio in the new language.

25.   I try to think in the new language.

26.   I attend and participate in out-of-class events where the new language is spoken.

27.   I read for pleasure in the new language.

28.   I write personal notes, messages, letters, or reports in the new language.

29.   I skim the reading passage first to get the main idea, then I go back and read it more carefully.

30.   I seek specific details in what I hear or read.

31.   I use reference materials such as glossaries or dictionaries to help me use the new language.

32.   I take notes in class in the new language.

33.   I make summaries of new language material.

34.   I apply general rules to new situations when using the language.

35.   I find the meaning of a word by dividing the word into parts which I understand.

36.   I look for similarities and contrasts between the new language and my own.

37.   I try to understand what I have heard or read without translating it word-for-word into my own language.

38.   I am cautious about transferring words or concepts directly from my language to the new language.

39.   I look for patterns in the new language.

1.   Never or almost never true of me

2.   Generally not true of me

3.   Somewhat true of me

4.   Generally true of me

5.   Always or almost always true of me

(Write answers on Worksheet)

40.   I develop my own understanding of how the language works, even if sometimes I have to revise my understanding based on new information.

Part C

41.   When I do not understand all the words I read or hear, I guess the general meaning by using any clue I can find, for example, clues from the context or situation.

42.   I read without looking up every unfamiliar word.

43.   In a conversation I anticipate what the other person is going to say based on what has been said so far.

44.   If I am speaking and cannot think of the right expression, I use gestures or switch back to my own language momentarily.

45.   I ask the other person to tell me the right word if I cannot think of it in a conversation.

46.   When I cannot think of the correct expression to say or write, I find a different way to express the idea; for example, I use a synonym or describe the idea.

47.   I make up new words if I do not know the right ones.

48.   I direct the conversation to a topic for which I know the words.

Part D

49.   I preview the language lesson to get a general idea of what it is about, how it is organized, and how it relates to what I already know.

50.   When someone is speaking the new language, I try to concentrate on what the person is saying and put unrelated topics out of my mind.

51.   I decide in advance to pay special attention to specific language aspects; for example, I focus the way native speakers pronounce certain sounds.

52.   I try to find out all I can about how to be a better language learner by reading books or articles, or by talking with others about how to learn.

53.   I arrange my schedule to study and practice the new language consistently, not just when there is the pressure of a test.

54.   I arrange my physical environment to promote learning; for instance, I find a quiet, comfortable place to review.

55.   I organize my language notebook to record important language information.

56.   I plan my goals for language learning, for instance, how proficient I want to become or how I might want to use the language in the long run.

1.   Never or almost never true of me

2.   Generally not true of me

3.   Somewhat true of me

4.   Generally true of me

5.   Always or almost always true of me

(Write answers on Worksheet)

57.   I plan what I am going to accomplish in language learning each day or each week.

58.   I prepare for an upcoming language task (such as giving a talk in the new language) by by considering the nature of the task, what I have to know, and my current language skills.

59.   I clearly identify the purpose of the language activity; for instance, in a listening task I might need to listen for the general idea or for specific facts.

60.   I take responsibility for finding opportunities to practice the new language.

61.   I actively look for people with whom I can speak the new language.

62.   I try to notice my language errors and find out the reasons for them.

63.   I learn from my mistakes in using the new language.

64.   I evaluate the general progress I have made in learning the language.

Part E

65.   I try to relax whenever I feel anxious about using the new language.

66.   I make encouraging statements to myself so that I will continue to try hard and do my best in language learning.

67.   I actively encourage myself to take wise risks in language learning, such as guessing meanings or trying to speak, even though I might make some mistakes.

68.   I give myself a tangible reward when I have done something well in my language learning.

69.   I pay attention to physical signs of stress that might affect my language learning.

70.   I keep a private diary or journal where I write my feelings about language learning.

71.   I talk to someone I trust about my attitudes and feelings concerning the language learning process.

Part F

72.   If I do not understand, I ask the speaker to slow down, repeat, or clarify what was said.

73.   I ask other people to verify that I have understood or said something correctly.

74.   I ask other people to correct my pronunciation.

75.   I work with other language learners to practice, review, or share information.

76.   I have a regular language learning partner.

1.   Never or almost never true of me

2.   Generally not true of me

3.   Somewhat true of me

4.   Generally true of me

5.   Always or almost always true of me

(Write answers on Worksheet)

77.   When I am talking with a native speaker, I try to let him or her know when I need help.

78.   In conversation with others in the new language, I ask questions in order to be as involved as possible and to show I am interested.

79.   I try to learn about the culture of the place where the new language is spoken.

80.   I pay close attention to the thoughts and feelings of other people with whom I interact in the new language.

Your Name _____   Date _____

Language Learned Now or Most Recently _____

Worksheet for Answering and Scoring

the Strategy Inventory for Language Learning (SILL)

Version 5.1 (c) R. Oxford, 1989

1.   Write your response to each item (that is, write 1, 2, 3, 4, or 5) in each of the blanks, which are numbered to correspond to each item on the SILL.

2.   Total each column and put the result on the line marked "SUM".

3.   Divide by the number under "SUM" to provide an average for each column. Round this average off to the nearest tenth, as in 3.4. Because the only possible response for a SILL item is 1, 2, 3, 4, or 5, your average across items for each part of the SILL should be between 1.0 and 5.0. You can make sure your fiiguring is correct by checking whether your average for each part is within the range of 1.0 to 5.0.

4.   Calculate your overall average. To do this, add up all the SUMS for the different parts of the SILL. This will give you the total raw score. Divide by 80, the number of items on the SILL. This will give you the overall average, which should be within the range of 1.0 and 5.0.

5.   When you have completed this Worksheet, your teacher will give you the Profile of results on the Strategy Inventory for Language Learning (SILL). Transfer your averages (for each part and for the whole SILL) from the Worksheet to the Profile in order to obtain an interpretation of your SILL results.

SILL Worksheet (continued)

Version 5.1
(c) R. Oxford, 1989

Part A	Part B	Part C	Part D	Part E	Part F	Whole SILL
1. ____	16. ____	41. ____	49. ____	65. ____	72. ____	SUM Part A ____
2. ____	17. ____	42. ____	50. ____	66. ____	73. ____	SUM Part B ____
3. ____	18. ____	43. ____	51. ____	67. ____	74. ____	SUM Part C ____
4. ____	19. ____	44. ____	52. ____	68. ____	75. ____	SUM Part D ____
5. ____	20. ____	45. ____	53. ____	69. ____	76. ____	SUM Part E ____
6. ____	21. ____	46. ____	54. ____	70. ____	77. ____	SUM Part F ____
7. ____	22. ____	47. ____	55. ____	71. ____	78. ____	
8. ____	23. ____	48. ____	56. ____		79. ____	
9. ____	24. ____		57. ____		80. ____	
10. ____	25. ____		58. ____			
11. ____	26. ____		59. ____			
12. ____	27. ____		60. ____			
13. ____	28. ____		61. ____			
14. ____	29. ____		62. ____			
15. ____	30. ____		63. ____			
	31. ____		64. ____			
	32. ____					
	33. ____					
	34. ____					
	35. ____					
	36. ____					
	37. ____					
	38. ____					
	39. ____					
	40. ____					

SUM ____	SUM ____	SUM ____	SUM ____	SUM ____	SUM ____	SUM ____
$\div 15 =$ ____	$\div 25 =$ ____	$\div 8 =$ ____	$\div 16 =$ ____	$\div 7 =$ ____	$\div 9 =$ ____	$\div 80 =$ ____ (OVERALL AVERAGE)

Your Name _____   Date _____

Language Learned Now or Most Recently _____

Profile of Results on the Strategy Inventory for Language Learning (SILL)

Version 5.1

(c) R. Oxford, 1989

You will be given this Profile after you have completed the Worksheet for Answering and Scoring the Strategy Inventory for Language Learning (SILL). This Profile will summarize your results on SILL and show the kinds of strategies you use in learning a new language. Please note that there are no right or wrong answers and no "best" average scores for each part, since people learn languages differently.

To complete this Profile, transfer your averages for each part of the SILL, and for the whole SILL, from the Worksheet.

Part	What Strategies Are Covered	Your Average on This Part
A.	Remembering More Effectively: Grouping; making associations; placing new words into a context to remember them; using imagery, sounds, sound-and-image combinations, actions, etc. in order to remember new expressions; reviewing in a structured way; going back to review earlier material.	_____
B.	Using Your Mental Processes: Repeating; practicing with sounds and writing systems; using formulas and patterns; recombining familiar items in new ways; practicing the new language in a variety of authentic situations involving the four skills (listening, reading, speaking, and writing); skimming and scanning to get the idea quickly; using reference resources; taking notes; summarizing; reasoning deductively (applying general rules); analyzing expressions; analyzing contrastively via comparisons with another language; being cautious about word-for-word translating and direct transfers from another language; looking for language patterns; adjusting your understanding according to new information.	_____
C.	Compensating for Missing Knowledge: Using all possible clues to guess the meaning of what is heard or read in the new language; trying to understand the overall meaning and not necessarily every single word; finding ways to get the message across in speaking or writing despite limited knowledge of the new language; for instance, using gestures, switching to your own language momentarily, using a synonym or description, coining new words.	_____
D.	Organizing and Evaluating Your Learning: Overviewing and linking with material you already know; deciding in general to pay attention; deciding to pay attention to specific details; finding out how language learning works; arranging to learn (schedule, environment, notebook); setting goals and objectives; identifying the purpose of a language task; planning for a language task; finding practice opportunities; noticing and learning from your errors; evaluating your progress.	_____
E.	Managing Your Emotions: Lowering your anxiety; encouraging yourself through positive statements; taking risks wisely; rewarding yourself; noting physical stress; keeping a language learning diary; talking with someone about your feelings/attitudes.	_____
F.	Learning with Others: Asking questions for clarification or verification; asking for correction; cooperating with peers; cooperating with proficient users of the new language; developing cultural awareness; becoming aware of others' thoughts and feelings.	_____

YOUR OVERALL AVERAGE   _____

Version 5.1

(c) R. Oxford, 1989

Key to Understanding Your Averages

High	Always or almost always used	4.5 to 5.0
	Generally used	3.5 to 4.4
Medium	Sometimes used	2.5 to 3.4
Low	Generally not used	1.5 to 2.4
	Never or almost never used	1.0 to 1.4

Graph Your Averages Here

If you want, you can make a graph of your SILL averages. What does this graph tell you? Are you very high or very low on any part?

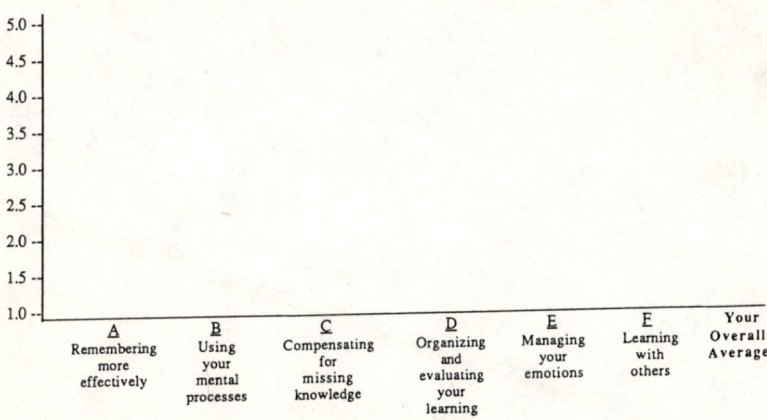

What These Averages Mean to You

The overall average indicates how frequently you use language learning strategies in general. The averages for each part of the SILL show which groups of strategies you tend to use the most in learning a new language. You might find that the averages for each part of the SILL are more useful than your overall average.

Optimal use of language learning strategies depends on your age, personality, stage of language learning, purpose for learning the language, previous experience, and other factors. Nevertheless, there may be some language learning strategies that you are not yet using which might be beneficial to you. Ask your teacher for more information on language learning strategies.

Strategy Inventory for Language Learning (SILL)

Version for Speakers of Other Languages Learning English

Strategy Inventory for Language Learning (SILL)

Version 7.0 (ESL/EFL)
(c) R. Oxford, 1989

Directions

This form of the STRATEGY INVENTORY FOR LANGUAGE LEARNING (SILL) is for students of English as a second or foreign language. You will find statements about learning English. Please read each statement. On the separate Worksheet, write the response (1, 2, 3, 4, or 5) that tells HOW TRUE OF YOU THE STATEMENT IS.

1. Never or almost never true of me
2. Usually not true of me
3. Somewhat true of me
4. Usually true of me
5. Always or almost always true of me

NEVER OR ALMOST NEVER TRUE OF ME means that the statement is very rarely true of you.

USUALLY NOT TRUE OF ME means that the statement is true less than half the time.

SOMEWHAT TRUE OF ME means that the statement is true of you about half the time.

USUALLY TRUE OF ME means that the statement is true more than half the time.

ALWAYS OR ALMOST ALWAYS TRUE OF ME means that the statement is true of you almost always.

Answer in terms of how well the statement describes you. Do not answer how you think you should be, or what other people do. There are no right or wrong answers to these statements. Put your answers on the separate Worksheet. Please make no marks on the items. Work as quickly as you can without being careless. This usually takes about 20-30 minutes to complete. If you have any questions, let the teacher know immediately.

(Version 7.0 [EFL/ESL] © R. L. Oxford, 1989)

EXAMPLE

1.   Never or almost never true of me
2.   Usually not true of me
3.   Somewhat true of me
4.   Usually true of me
5.   Always or almost always true of me

Read the item, and choose a response (1 through 5 as above), and write it in the space after the item.

I actively seek out opportunities to talk with native speakers of English. _____

You have just completed the example item. Answer the rest of the items on the Worksheet.

Strategy Inventory for Language Learning

Version 7.0 (ESL/EFL)

(c) R. Oxford, 1989

1.   Never or almost never true of me

2.   Usually not true of me

3.   Somewhat true of me

4.   Usually true of me

5.   Always or almost always true of me

(Write answers on Worksheet)

Part A

1.   I think of relationships between what I already know and new things I learn in English.

2.   I use new English words in a sentence so I can remember them.

3.   I connect the sound of a new English word and an image or picture of the word to help me remember the word.

4.   I remember a new English word by making a mental picture of a situation in which the word might be used.

5.   I use rhymes to remember new English words.

6.   I use flashcards to remember new English words.

7.   I physically act out new English words.

8.   I review English lessons often.

9.   I remember new English words or phrases by remembering their location on the page, on the board, or on a street sign.

Part B

10.   I say or write new English words several times.

11.   I try to talk like native English speakers.

12.   I practice the sounds of English.

13.   I use the English words I know in different ways.

14.   I start conversations in English.

15.   I watch English language TV shows spoken in English or go to movies spoken in English.

16.   I read for pleasure in English.

17.   I write notes, messages, letters, or reports in English.

18.   I first skim an English passage (read over the passage quickly) then go back and read carefully.

1.   Never or almost never true of me

2.   Usually not true of me

3.   Somewhat true of me

4.   Usually true of me

5.   Always or almost always true of me

(Write answers on Worksheet)

19.   I look for words in my own language that are similar to new words in English.

20.   I try to find patterns in English.

21.   I find the meaning of an English word by dividing it into parts that I understand.

22.   I try not to translate word-for-word.

23.   I make summaries of information that I hear or read in English.

Part C

24.   To understand unfamiliar English words, I make guesses.

25.   When I can't think of a word during a conversation in English, I use gestures.

26.   I make up new words if I do not know the right ones in English.

27.   I read English without looking up every new word.

28.   I try to guess what the other person will say next in English.

29.   If I can't think of an English word, I use a word or phrase that means the same thing.

Part D

30.   I try to find as many ways as I can to use my English.

31.   I notice my English mistakes and use that information to help me do better.

32.   I pay attention when someone is speaking English.

33.   I try to find out how to be a better learner of English.

34.   I plan my schedule so I will have enough time to study English.

35.   I look for people I can talk to in English.

36.   I look for opportunities to read as much as possible in English.

37.   I have clear goals for improving my English skills.

38.   I think about my progress in learning English.

1.   Never or almost never true of me

2.   Usually not true of me

3.   Somewhat true of me

4.   Usually true of me

5.   Always or almost always true of me

(Write answers on Worksheet)

Part E

39.   I try to relax whenever I feel afraid of using English.

40.   I encourage myself to speak English even when I am afraid of making a mistake.

41.   I give myself a reward or treat when I do well in English.

42.   I notice if I am tense or nervous when I am studying or using English.

43.   I write down my feelings in a language learning diary.

44.   I talk to someone else about how I feel when I am learning English.

Part F

45.   If I do not understand something in English, I ask the other person to slow down or say it again.

46.   I ask English speakers to correct me when I talk.

47.   I practice English with other students.

48.   I ask for help from English speakers.

49.   I ask questions in English.

50.   I try to learn about the culture of English speakers.

Your Name _____   Date _____

Worksheet for Answering and Scoring

the Strategy Inventory for Language Learning (SILL)

Version 7.0 (ESL/EFL)

(c) R. Oxford, 1989

1. The blanks (_____) are numbered for each item on the SILL.

2. Write your response to each item (that is, write 1, 2, 3, 4, or 5) in each of the blanks.

3. Add up each column. Put the result on the line marked SUM.

4. Divide by the number under SUM to get the average for each column. Round this average off to the nearest tenth, as in 3.4.

5. Figure out your overall average. To do this, add up all the SUMS for the different parts of the SILL. Then divide by 50.

6. When you have finished, your teacher will give you the Profile of Results. Copy your averages (for each part and for the whole SILL) from the Worksheet to the Profile.

SILL Worksheet (continued)

Version 7.0 (ESL/EFL)

(c) R. Oxford, 1989

Part A	Part B	Part C	Part D	Part E	Part F	Whole SILL
1. _____	10. _____	24. _____	30. _____	39. _____	45. _____	SUM Part A _____
2. _____	11. _____	25. _____	31. _____	40. _____	46. _____	SUM Part B _____
3. _____	12. _____	26. _____	32. _____	41. _____	47. _____	SUM Part C _____
4. _____	13. _____	27. _____	33. _____	42. _____	48. _____	SUM Part D _____
5. _____	14. _____	28. _____	34. _____	43. _____	49. _____	SUM Part E _____
6. _____	15. _____	29. _____	35. _____	44. _____	50. _____	SUM Part F _____
7. _____	16. _____		36. _____			
8. _____	17. _____		37. _____			
9. _____	18. _____		38. _____			
	19. _____					
	20. _____					
	21. _____					
	22. _____					
	23. _____					

SUM _____	SUM _____	SUM _____	SUM _____	SUM _____	SUM _____	SUM _____
÷ 9 = _____	÷ 14 = _____	÷ 6 = _____	÷ 9 = _____	÷ 6 = _____	÷ 6 = _____	÷ 50 = _____ (OVERALL AVERAGE)

Your Name _____   Date _____

Profile of Results on the Strategy Inventory for Language Learning (SILL)

Version 7.0

(c) R. Oxford, 1989

You will receive this Profile after you have completed the Worksheet. This Profile will show your SILL results. These results will tell you the kinds of strategies you use in learning English. There are no right or wrong answers.

To complete this profile, transfer your averages for each part of the SILL, and your overall average for the whole SILL. These averages are found on the Worksheet.

Part	What Strategies Are Covered	Your Average on This Part
A.	Remembering more effectively	_____
B.	Using all your mental processes	_____
C.	Compensating for missing knowledge	_____
D.	Organizing and evaluating your learning	_____
E.	Managing your emotions	_____
F.	Learning with others	_____
YOUR OVERALL AVERAGE		_____

SILL Profile of Results (continued)

Version 7.0

(c) R. Oxford, 1989

Key to Understanding Your Averages

High	Always or almost always used	4.5 to 5.0
	Usually used	3.5.to 4.4
Medium	Sometimes used	2.5 to 3.4
Low	Generally not used	1.5 to 2.4
	Never or almost never used	1.0 to 1.4

Graph Your Averages Here

If you want, you can make a graph of your SILL averages. What does this graph tell you? Are you very high or very low on any part?

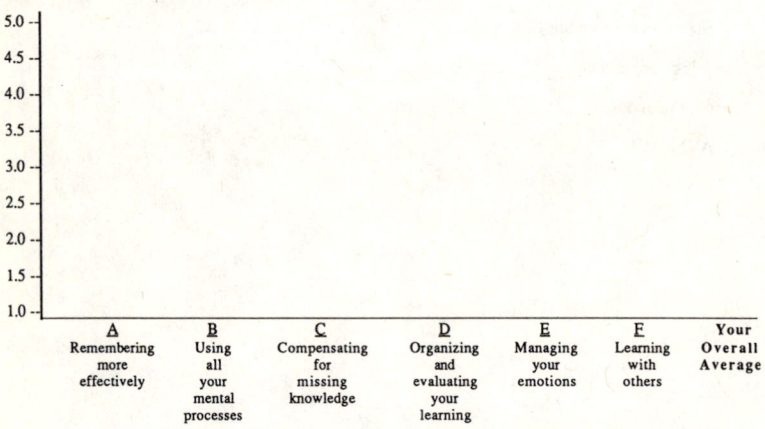

| A Remembering more effectively | B Using all your mental processes | C Compensating for missing knowledge | D Organizing and evaluating your learning | E Managing your emotions | F Learning with others | Your Overall Average |

What These Averages Mean to You

The overall average tells how often you use strategies for learning English. Each part of the SILL represents a group of learning strategies. The averages for each part of the SILL show which groups of strategies you use the most for learning English.

The best use of strategies depends on your age, personality, and purpose for learning. If you have a very low average on one or more parts of the SILL, there may be some new strategies in these groups that you might want to use. Ask your teacher about these.

Sources of Quotations

Preface

John L. Taylor's speech at SIMULTEC '87, Geneva, Switzerland, September 1987, suggested three lines of this verse; I added the other two (a more receptive ear, a more fluent tongue).

Chapter 1

Strevens, P. (1982). In P. S. Green, Review of H. B. Altman and C. W. James (Eds.). (1980), *Foreign language teaching: Meeting individual needs* (Oxford: Pergamon). *System* 10(3), 291.

Chapter 2

Eliot, T. S. (1970). East Coker, *Four quartets* (pp. 30–31). London: Faber & Faber.
DeQuincey, T. (1955). *Confessions of an English opium-eater*, Pt. I. In D. C. Brownling, (Ed.), *Everyman's dictionary of quotations and proverbs* (p. 93). London: Readers' Union, J. M. Dent.
Shakespeare, W. (1987). *Hamlet*, I, v, 137. In S. Wells & G. Taylor, (Eds.), *The complete Oxford Shakespeare, Vol. III: The tragedies*. London: Guild Publishing.
16th-century proverb, in Brownling, p. 487; also Bloomsbury, p. 280.

Chapter 3

Russian proverb, *Newsweek*, June 6, 1988, p. 17.
Eliot, T. S. (1970). Little Gidding, *Four quartets* (pp. 55). London: Faber & Faber.
John 1:1. (1987). *Holy Bible: New International Version*. London: Hodder & Stoughton.
Sullivan, A. Speech, July 1894. In Bloomsbury, p. 339.

Activity 3.1 in Chapter 3

Carroll, L. *Through the Looking-Glass* (chap. 4). In Bloomsbury, p. 93.

Burke, E. (1984). *Letters*. In N. Ewart, *The writer and the reader: A book of literary quotations* (p. 17). Poole, Dorset, England: Blandford.

Stevenson, R. L. (1882). *Talk and talkers*. In R. T. Tripp (Ed.). (1979), *The international thesaurus of quotations* (p. 608). Harmondsworth, Middlesex, England: Penguin.

Prick up your ears. Movie title. From J. Lahr (1987), *Prick up your ears: A biography of Joe Orton*. Harmondsworth, Middlesex, England: Penguin.

Pope, A. *Essay on criticism*. In Brownling, p. 242.

Phillips, J. (1986, September 17). Foreign language reading: Process, practice, and proficiency. Talk at the Foreign Service Institute, Arlington, VA.

Shakespeare, W. *Julius Caesar*, III, ii, 74. In Wells & Taylor.

Tennyson, A., Lord. (1967). Morte d'Arthur. In G. B. Harrison, *A book of English poetry* (p. 371). Harmondsworth, Middlesex, England: Penguin.

Shakespeare, W. *Hamlet*, II, ii, 193–194. In Wells & Taylor.

Edison, T. A. Newspaper interview. In Brownling, p. 108.

Allen, W. (1987). Quoted in A. Wright, *How to improve your mind* (p. x). Cambridge: Cambridge University Press.

Byron, G. G., Lord. *Hints from Horace*. In Ewart, p. 32.

Whitehorn, K. Attrib. In Bloomsbury, p. 375.

Maugham, S. (1978). In W. A. Auden & L. Kronenberger, *The Faber book of aphorisms* (p. 277). London: Faber & Faber.

Chapter 4

Adams, H. (1907). *The education of Henry Adams*, p. 21. In Tripp, p. 347.

Pope, A. *An essay on man*, Epistle i, 1. In Brownling, p. 245.

Milton, J. (1951). *Paradise Lost*, Book I. In A. M. Witherspoon, (Ed.). *The college survey of English literature* (shorter ed., rev., p. 387). New York: Harcourt Brace & World.

Botkin, J. W., et al. (1979). *No limits to learning*. Oxford: Pergamon. In R. M. Smith (1985), *Learning how to learn: Applied theory for adults* (p. 106). Milton Keynes: Open University Press.

Chapter 5

Buck, P. S. (1967). *To my daughters with love*. In Tripp, p. 449.

Aesop, "Hercules and the waggoner," *Fables*. In Bloomsbury, p. 3.

Lord Chesterfield (1979). In Tripp, p. 177.

Dumas, A. (1952). *The three musketeers* (trans. Lord Sudley). Harmondsworth, Middlesex, England: Penguin.

Chapter 6

Rogers, C. R. (1969). *Freedom to learn: A view of what education might become.* Columbus, OH: C. E. Merrill.

Epilogue

Browning, R. (1967). Rabbi Ben Ezra. In Harrison, p. 380.

Appendix E

How to Find Activities for Readers

Each chapter contains activities for you, the reader, to do by yourself or with others. This table provides information which will help you find the readers' activities most relevant for your needs and circumstances. Note that the activities are numbered according to the chapter. For instance, activities in Chapter 1 are numbered 1.1, 1.2, and so on.

NUMBER	NAME	PURPOSE	PAGES
1.1	Brainstorm the Features of Learning Strategies	Obtain an overview of key features.	22
1.2	Place Strategies on the Learning-Acquisition Continuum	Discover how the six strategy groups relate to learning and acquisition.	23
1.3	Consider Degrees of Learner Responsibility	Check your own values on how much responsibility learners should have.	23
1.4	Discuss Teacher Roles	Assess the possible roles teachers might take; again, a values activity.	23–24
1.5	Consider Your Own Strategy Use	Describe your own past use of strategies for learning.	24
2.1	Check Your Attitudes Toward Memory Strategies	Assess your beliefs about mnemonics.	51

NUMBER	NAME	PURPOSE	PAGES
2.2	Examine Memory Strategies in Different Settings	Discover how memory strategies can be used in learning and acquisition.	51
2.3	Think About Language Loss	Consider how memory strategies might have prevented language loss.	51
2.4	Consider the Nature of Practicing	Compare more realistic vs. less realistic practicing.	52
2.5	Work with Skimming and Scanning	Assess your own use of two important reading strategies, skimming and scanning.	52
2.6	Find Resources	List possible student resources.	52
2.7	List the Pros and Cons of Analyzing/ Reasoning	Assess ways that analyzing/reasoning can aid or hinder proficiency.	52
2.8	Consider the Need for Structure	List typical uses of structuring strategies in daily life and in language learning.	52
2.9	Notice Students' Compensatory Speaking Strategies	List students' use of compensation strategies in speech and prioritize by frequency.	52–53
2.10	Consider Learning and Communication	Explain your feelings about how learning might take place through communication.	53

NUMBER	NAME	PURPOSE	PAGES
3.1	You Can Quote Me on That!	List skills and strategies related to a series of quotations; an entertaining way to understand direct strategies.	98–99
3.2	Remark on Remembering	Give examples of functions of memory strategies related to four language skills.	100
3.3	Cogitate About Cognitive Strategies	List observed cognitive strategies and identify skills.	100
3.4	Accentuate the Positive	Brainstorm the utility of compensation strategies.	100
3.5	Stalk the Strategies	Study the students' exercises and indicate the strategies involved.	100
4.1	Consider a Difficult Subject	Consider your own metacognitive and affective control over a difficult subject.	148
4.2	Experiment with Metacognitive and Affective Strategies	Try out new strategies for yourself and see the results.	148
4.3	Ask Questions	Consider your own questioning style.	148–149
4.4	Judge Your Empathy	Assess your degree of empathy and how it affects your language ability.	149
4.5	Weigh Competitiveness and Cooperation	Study your own tendencies toward competitiveness and cooperation.	149

NUMBER	NAME	PURPOSE	PAGES
5.1	Examine Indirect Strategies in the Four Skills	List indirect strategies and determine how they relate to the four language skills.	174, including Table 5.1
5.2	Consider Your Use of the Indirect Strategies	Rate your use of these strategies when you were a language student.	174
5.3	Ponder the Purposes of Writing and Speaking	List writing and speaking formats and determine the purposes.	175
6.1	Think of Reasons for Assessing Strategy Use	Brainstorm reasons for strategy assessment.	209–210
6.2	Consider the Strategy Assessment Options	Complete a table about strategy assessment possibilities.	210, including Table 6.3
6.3	Assess Your Own Strategies	Use an assessment technique from the chapter to check your own strategy use.	210
6.4	Go Fishing	Consider two contrasting positions on strategy training.	211
6.5	Design a Strategy Training Sequence	Use the chapter to design a strategy training sequence for your students.	211
7.1	Assess the Relevance of Examples for Your Own Setting	Consider the real-life strategy use examples in the chapter and their utility to you.	232
7.2	Follow Up on Your Three Favorite Examples	Contact three strategy experts.	232

NUMBER	NAME	PURPOSE	PAGES
7.3	Take a Closer Look at Explicit Training Examples	Answer questions about explicit strategy training techniques.	233
7.4	Take a Closer Look at Implicit Strategy Encouragement	Answer questions about implicit strategy encouragement without explicit training.	233

How to Find Exercises to Use with Your Students

Each chapter contains exercises for you to use with your students. The number and type of exercises are geared to the content of each chapter. Some chapters, notably the ones which focus on applications of strategies (such as Chapters 3 and 5), contain a great number of exercises; other chapters intentionally have fewer exercises.

This table provides information which will help you find the exercises most relevant for your students' needs and circumstances. Note that the exercises are numbered according to the chapter. For instance, exercises in Chapter 1 are numbered 1.1, 1.2, and so on.

NUMBER	NAME	PURPOSE	PAGES
1.1	Embedded Strategies Game	Become acquainted with language learning strategies and see how they are embedded in certain activities.	24–30
1.2	Strategy Search Game	Determine how strategies relate to a set of sometimes complex language learning or acquisition tasks/ situations.	30–35
2.1	Ask Students to Identify Their Memory Strategies	Consider kinds of memory strategies used and keep a running list.	53
2.2	Get the Message	Practice a variety of strategies for understanding an oral message using film, cartoon, or program.	53–54

311

NUMBER	NAME	PURPOSE	PAGES
2.3	Play Twenty Questions	Practice guessing using a familiar game.	54–55
2.4	Hold a Conversation	Consider kinds of strategies used in a conversation.	55
3.1	Memory Practice	Distribute or space memory practice using several memory strategies.	101
3.2	Grouping and Labeling	Discover the value of grouping and labeling while learning vocabulary.	101–103
3.3	Make Your Own Groups	Create new word groups and determine criteria for these groups.	103–104
3.4	Find the Odd Word	Extend grouping exercises by finding the word that does not fit.	104–105
3.5	Yes/No Game	Improve sound perception and discrimination.	105–106
3.6	Finding Your Way	Mark a map route according to spoken directions using combined strategies.	106–107, Fig. 3.12 on 107, Fig. 3.13 on 108
3.7	Physical Response	Listen and physically move.	107–109
3.8	Jigsaw Listening	Listen to different extracts and then, with other people, collate them to understand the whole situation.	109–110, Table 3.1 on 109
3.9	Guessing the Meaning of a Reading Passage	Guess meaning and explain how the guesses were made.	110–112

NUMBER	NAME	PURPOSE	PAGES
3.10	Guessing with Pictures	Guess meaning via pictures.	112, Fig. 3.14 on 113
3.11	Scanning a Reading Passage for Personal Facts	Scan for particular information.	112, 114
3.12	Skimming a Reading Passage for the Main Idea	Skim a passage to locate the central theme.	114–115
3.13	Inventions	Practice naturalistically and use information to complete a diagram.	115–117, Fig. 3.15 on 116
3.14	Jigsaw Reading	Put together pieces of a written text using guessing strategies and other strategies.	117–121, Fig. 3.16 on 119, Fig. 3.17 on 120
3.15	Alibi	Use strategies in a suspenseful, communicative situation.	121–122
3.16	What We Have in Common	Communicate about personally important information using strategies.	123
3.17	What's My Line?	Guess and practice naturalistically in an entertaining format.	123–124
3.18	Picture Stories	Create stories using pictures and a variety of memory strategies and compensation strategies.	124–126
3.19	Crystal Ball	Develop prediction/ guessing skills using reading.	126–127
3.20	Protest	Make guesses from context and write meaningfully about an incident.	127–129

NUMBER	NAME	PURPOSE	PAGES
3.21	Interviews	Use a range of strategies in classroom interviews and in a subsequent write-up.	129–130
3.22	Sending a Telegram	Use cognitive and compensation strategies in a meaningful situation.	130–132, Fig. 3.18 on 131
3.23	Doctor Appointment	Use metacognitive, comprehension, and other strategies to plan for and carry out a multiskill task.	132–133
4.1	Listen to Self-Talk	List positive and negative statements students make about themselves as language learners.	149
4.2	Let Students Consider Cooperation and Competition	Use a cooperative learning activity as a springboard to student discussion of cooperation and competition.	150
4.3	Try Out Indirect Strategies	Experiment with a range of indirect strategies and assess results.	150
5.1	Make a Weekly Schedule	Produce a general schedule useful for each week.	175–177, including Table 5.2 on 176
5.2	Create a Language Learning Notebook	Create a notebook that contains sections for different aspects of language learning.	177–178
5.3	Set Your Goals and Objectives	Establish aims for language learning.	178–180, including Table 5.3 on 179–180

NUMBER	NAME	PURPOSE	PAGES
5.4	Opportunity Knocks!	Consider possibilities for practicing the new language.	180–181, including Table 5.4 on 181
5.5	Gauge Your Skill Progress	Assess progress in language learning skill by skill.	182–183, including Table 5.5 on 182–183
5.6	Relaxing	Use relaxation strategies in order to deal with language learning.	183–184
5.7	Calm Down Through Meditation and Music	Use these two strategies to relax for better language learning.	185
5.8	Praise Be!	Praise yourself for good work using affirmations.	185–187
5.9	Assess Your Emotions	Use an emotional checklist for language learning.	187–189, including Table 5.6 on 188–189
5.10	Stress Check	Use a stress checklist, consider causes of stress, and try to reduce unnecessary stress.	189–190, including Table 5.7 on 190
5.11	Keep a Diary	Record feelings about language learning.	190–191
6.1	Assess Your Students' Strategies	Assess students' strategies using at least two techniques.	211–212
6.3	Implement Strategy Training	Implement a strategy training sequence or program.	212
6.4	Develop a "Successful Strategies" Handbook	Develop a student handbook of the most successful strategies.	212
6.5	Discuss Diaries	Hold regular diary discussions about language learning.	212

NUMBER	NAME	PURPOSE	PAGES
7.1	Experiment!	Try out with your students the programs, activities, games, etc., provided by experts you have contacted.	233
7.2	Find Out Which Strategies Are Used	Assess strategies used in the new activities.	234

Appendix **G**

Strategy Applications Listed According to Each of the Four Language Skills

This table helps you locate definitions and explanations of strategies useful for each of the four skills. The activities and exercises in this book give a wide variety of strategy applications for you to explore after you have read the definitions and explanations indexed below. You may also discover additional strategies that help develop proficiency in the four language skills.

STRATEGIES USEFUL FOR LISTENING

STRATEGY GROUP	STRATEGY SET	STRATEGY	PAGE
Memory	Creating mental linkages	Grouping	40, 58–60
Memory	Creating mental linkages	Associating/ elaborating	41, 60
Memory	Creating mental linkages	Placing new words into a context	41, 60–61, 68
Memory	Applying images and sounds	Using imagery	41, 61
Memory	Applying images and sounds	Semantic mapping	41, 61–62, Fig. 3.3 on 63, Fig. 3.4 on 64, Fig. 3.5 on 65
Memory	Applying images and sounds	Using keywords	41–42, 62–63, 68
Memory	Applying images and sounds	Representing sounds in memory	42, 63–64

317

STRATEGY GROUP	STRATEGY SET	STRATEGY	PAGE
Memory	Reviewing well	Structured reviewing	42, 66, Fig. 3.6 on 67
Memory	Employing action	Using physical response or sensation	43, 66
Memory	Employing action	Using mechanical techniques	43, 68
Cognitive	Practicing	Repeating	45, 70–71
Cognitive	Practicing	Formally practicing with sounds and writing systems	45, 71–72
Cognitive	Practicing	Recognizing and using formulas and patterns	45, 72–74
Cognitive	Praticing	Practicing naturalistically	45, 74–79
Cognitive	Receiving and sending messages	Getting the idea quickly	46, 80–81
Cognitive	Receiving and sending messages	Using resources for receiving and sending messages	46, 81–82
Cognitive	Analyzing and reasoning	Reasoning deductively	46, 82–83
Cognitive	Analyzing and reasoning	Analyzing expressions	46, 83
Cognitive	Analyzing and reasoning	Analyzing contrastively (across languages)	46, 83–84
Cognitive	Analyzing and reasoning	Translating	46, 84–85
Cognitive	Analyzing and reasoning	Transferring	47, 85–86
Cognitive	Creating structure for input and output	Taking notes	47, 86–88, Fig. 3.9 on 88, Fig. 3.10 on 89
Cognitive	Creating structure for input and output	Summarizing	47, 88–89

STRATEGY GROUP	STRATEGY SET	STRATEGY	PAGE
Cognitive	Creating structure for input and output	Highlighting	47, 89–90
Compensation	Guessing intelligently	Using linguistic clues	49, 90–91
Compensation	Guessing intelligently	Using other clues	49, 92–94
Metacognitive	Centering your learning	Overviewing and linking with already known material	138, 152–154
Metacognitive	Centering your learning	Paying attention	138, 154–155
Metacognitive	Centering your learning	Delaying speech production to focus on listening	138, 155–156
Metacognitive	Arranging and planning your learning	Finding out about language learning	139, 156
Metacognitive	Arranging and planning your learning	Organizing	139, 156
Metacognitive	Arranging and planning your learning	Setting goals and objectives	139, 157–158
Metacognitive	Arranging and planning your learning	Identifying the purpose of a language task	139, 158–159
Metacognitive	Arranging and planning your learning	Planning for a language task	139, 159–160
Metacognitive	Arranging and planning your learning	Seeking practice opportunities	139, 160
Metacognitive	Evaluating your learning	Self-monitoring	140, 161–162
Metacognitive	Evaluating your learning	Self-evaluating	140, 162–163
Affective	Lowering your anxiety	Using progressive relaxation, deep breathing, or meditation	143, 164

STRATEGY GROUP	STRATEGY SET	STRATEGY	PAGE
Affective	Lowering your anxiety	Using music	143, 164
Affective	Lowering your anxiety	Using laughter	143, 164–165
Affective	Encouraging yourself	Making positive statements	143, 165–166
Affective	Encouraging yourself	Taking risks wisely	144, 166
Affective	Encouraging yourself	Rewarding yourself	144, 166
Affective	Taking your emotional temperature	Listening to your body	144, 167
Affective	Taking your emotional temperature	Using a checklist	144, 167
Affective	Taking your emotional temperature	Writing a language learning diary	144, 167–168
Affective	Taking your emotional temperature	Discussing your feelings with someone else	144, 168
Social	Asking questions	Asking for clarification and verification	146–147, 169–170
Social	Cooperating with others	Cooperating with peers	147, 171
Social	Cooperating with others	Cooperating with proficient users of the new language	147, 171–172
Social	Empathizing with others	Developing cultural understanding	147, 172–173
Social	Empathizing with others	Becoming aware of others' thoughts and feelings	147, 173

STRATEGIES USEFUL FOR READING

STRATEGY GROUP	STRATEGY SET	STRATEGY	PAGE
Memory	Creating mental linkages	Grouping	40, 58–60
Memory	Creating mental linkages	Associating/ elaborating	41, 60
Memory	Creating mental linkages	Placing new words into a context	41, 60–61
Memory	Applying images and sounds	Using imagery	41, 61
Memory	Applying images and sounds	Semantic mapping	41, 61, 62, Fig. 3.3 on 63, Fig. 3.4 on 64, Fig. 3.5 on 65
Memory	Applying images and sounds	Using keywords	41–42, 62–63
Memory	Applying images and sounds	Representing sounds in memory	42, 63–64
Memory	Reviewing well	Structured reviewing	42, 66, Fig. 3.6 on 67
Memory	Employing action	Using physical response or sensation	43, 66
Memory	Employing action	Using mechanical techniques	43, 68
Cognitive	Practicing	Repeating	45, 70–71
Cognitive	Practicing	Recognizing and using formulas and patterns	45, 72–74
Cognitive	Practicing	Practicing naturalistically	45, 74–79
Cognitive	Receiving and sending messages	Getting the idea quickly	46, 80–81
Cognitive	Receiving and sending messages	Using resources for receiving and sending messages	46, 81–82
Cognitive	Analyzing and reasoning	Reasoning deductively	46, 82–83

STRATEGY GROUP	STRATEGY SET	STRATEGY	PAGE
Cognitive	Analyzing and reasoning	Analyzing expressions	46, 83
Cognitive	Analyzing and reasoning	Analyzing contrastively (across languages)	46, 83–84
Cognitive	Analyzing and reasoning	Translating	47, 84–85
Cognitive	Analyzing and reasoning	Transferring	47, 85–86
Cognitive	Creating structure for input and output	Taking notes	47, 86–88, Fig. 3.9 on 88, Fig. 3.10 on 89
Cognitive	Creating structure for input and output	Summarizing	47, 88–89
Cognitive	Creating structure for input and output	Highlighting	47, 89–90
Compensation	Guessing intelligently	Using linguistic clues	49, 90–91
Compensation	Guessing intelligently	Using other clues	49, 92–94
Metacognitive	Centering your learning	Overviewing and linking with already known material	138, 152–154
Metacognitive	Centering your learning	Paying attention	138, 154–155
Metacognitive	Arranging and planning your learning	Finding out about language learning	139, 156
Metacognitive	Arranging and planning your learning	Organizing	139, 156
Metacognitive	Arranging and planning your learning	Setting goals and objectives	139, 157–158
Metacognitive	Arranging and planning your learning	Identifying the purpose of a language task	139, 158–159

STRATEGY GROUP	STRATEGY SET	STRATEGY	PAGE
Metacognitive	Arranging and planning your learning	Planning for a language task	139, 159–160
Metacognitive	Arranging and planning your learning	Seeking practice opportunities	139, 160
Metacognitive	Evaluating your learning	Self-monitoring	140, 161–162
Metacognitive	Evaluating your learning	Self-evaluating	140, 162–163
Affective	Lowering your anxiety	Using progressive relaxation, deep breathing, or meditation	143, 164
Affective	Lowering your anxiety	Using music	143, 164
Affective	Lowering your anxiety	Using laughter	143, 164–165
Affective	Encouraging yourself	Making positive statements	143, 165–166
Affective	Encouraging yourself	Taking risks wisely	144, 166
Affective	Encouraging yourself	Rewarding yourself	144, 166
Affective	Taking your emotional temperature	Listening to your body	144, 167
Affective	Taking your emotional temperature	Using a checklist	144, 167
Affective	Taking your emotional temperature	Writing a language learning diary	144, 167–168
Affective	Taking your emotional temperature	Discussing your feelings with someone else	144, 168
Social	Asking questions	Asking for clarification and verification	146–147, 169–170
Social	Cooperating with others	Cooperating with peers	147, 171

STRATEGY GROUP	STRATEGY SET	STRATEGY	PAGE
Social	Cooperating with others	Cooperating with proficient users of the new language	147, 171–172
Social	Empathizing with others	Developing cultural understanding	147, 172–173
Social	Empathizing with others	Becoming aware of others' thoughts and feelings	147, 173

STRATEGIES USEFUL FOR SPEAKING

STRATEGY GROUP	STRATEGY SET	STRATEGY	PAGE
Memory	Creating mental linkages	Placing new words into a context	41, 60–61, 68
Memory	Applying images and sounds	Representing sounds in memory	42, 63–64
Memory	Reviewing well	Structured reviewing	42, 66, Fig. 3.6 on 67
Cognitive	Practicing	Repeating	45, 70–71
Cognitive	Practicing	Formally practicing with sounds and writing systems	45, 71–72
Cognitive	Practicing	Recognizing and using formulas and patterns	45, 72–74
Cognitive	Practicing	Recombining	45, 74
Cognitive	Practicing	Practicing naturalistically	45, 74–79
Cognitive	Receiving and sending messages	Using resources for receiving and sending messages	46, 81–82
Cognitive	Analyzing and reasoning	Reasoning deductively	46, 82–83

STRATEGY GROUP	STRATEGY SET	STRATEGY	PAGE
Cognitive	Analyzing and reasoning	Translating	46, 84–85
Cognitive	Analyzing and reasoning	Transferring	47, 85–86
Compensation	Overcoming limitations in speaking and writing	Switching to the mother tongue	50, 94–95
Compensation	Overcoming limitations in speaking and writing	Getting help	50, 95
Compensation	Overcoming limitations in speaking and writing	Using mime or gesture	50, 95
Compensation	Overcoming limitations in speaking and writing	Avoiding communication partially or totally	50, 95–96
Compensation	Overcoming limitations in speaking and writing	Selecting the topic	50, 96
Compensation	Overcoming limitations in speaking and writing	Adjusting or approximating the message	50, 96–97
Compensation	Overcoming limitations in speaking and writing	Coining words	50, 97
Compensation	Overcoming limitations in speaking and writing	Using a circumlocution or synonym	51, 97
Metacognitive	Centering your learning	Overviewing and linking with already known material	138, 152–154
Metacognitive	Centering your learning	Paying attention	138, 154–155

STRATEGY GROUP	STRATEGY SET	STRATEGY	PAGE
Metacognitive	Centering your learning	Delaying speech production to focus on listening	138, 155–156
Metacognitive	Arranging and planning your learning	Finding out about language learning	139, 156
Metacognitive	Arranging and planning your learning	Organizing	139, 156
Metacognitive	Arranging and planning your learning	Setting goals and objectives	139, 157–158
Metacognitive	Arranging and planning your learning	Identifying the purpose of a language task	139, 158–159
Metacognitive	Arranging and planning your learning	Planning for a language task	139, 159–160
Metacognitive	Arranging and planning your learning	Seeking practive opportunities	139, 160
Metacognitive	Evaluating your learning	Self-monitoring	140, 161–162
Metacognitive	Evaluating your learning	Self-evaluating	140, 162–163
Affective	Lowering your anxiety	Using progressive relaxation, deep breathing, or meditation	143, 164
Affective	Lowering your anxiety	Using music	143, 164
Affective	Lowering your anxiety	Using laughter	143, 164–165
Affective	Encouraging yourself	Making positive statements	143, 165–166
Affective	Encouraging yourself	Taking risks wisely	144, 166
Affective	Encouraging yourself	Rewarding yourself	144, 166
Affective	Taking your emotional temperature	Listening to your body	144, 167

STRATEGY GROUP	STRATEGY SET	STRATEGY	PAGE
Affective	Taking your emotional temperature	Using a checklist	144, 167
Affective	Taking your emotional temperature	Writing a language learning diary	144, 167–168
Affective	Taking your emotional temperature	Discussing your feelings with someone else	144, 168
Social	Asking questions	Asking for correction	147, 170
Social	Cooperating with others	Cooperating with peers	147, 171
Social	Cooperating with others	Cooperating with proficient users of the new language	147, 171–172
Social	Empathizing with others	Developing cultural understanding	147, 172–173
Social	Empathizing with others	Becoming aware of others' thoughts and feelings	147, 173

STRATEGIES USEFUL FOR WRITING

STRATEGY GROUP	STRATEGY SET	STRATEGY	PAGE
Memory	Creating mental linkages	Placing new words into a context	41, 60–61, 68
Memory	Applying images and sounds	Using keywords	41–42, 68*
Memory	Reviewing well	Structured reviewing	42, 66, Fig. 3.6 on 67
Memory	Employing action	Using mechanical techniques	43, 68

*NOTE: This strategy is mainly for getting information that has been heard or read into the memory. However, p. 68 demonstrates how it can be employed to retrieve the information to use in writing. It can likewise be employed for retrieval in a speaking situation.

STRATEGY GROUP	STRATEGY SET	STRATEGY	PAGE
Cognitive	Practicing	Repeating	45, 70–71
Cognitive	Practicing	Formally practicing with sounds and writing systems	45, 71–72
Cognitive	Practicing	Recognizing and using formulas and patterns	45, 72–74
Cognitive	Practicing	Recombining	45, 74
Cognitive	Practicing	Practicing naturalistically	45, 74–79
Cognitive	Receiving and sending messages	Using resources for receiving and sending messages	46, 81–82
Cognitive	Analyzing and reasoning	Reasoning deductively	46, 82–83
Cognitive	Analyzing and reasoning	Translating	46, 84–85
Cognitive	Analyzing and reasoning	Transferring	47, 85–86
Cognitive	Creating structure for input and output	Taking notes	47, 86–88, Fig. 3.9 on 88, Fig. 3.10 on 89
Cognitive	Creating structure for input and output	Summarizing	47, 88–89
Cognitive	Creating structure for input and output	Highlighting	47, 89–90
Compensation	Overcoming limitations in speaking and writing	Selecting the topic	50, 96
Compensation	Overcoming limitations in speaking and writing	Adjusting or approximating the message	50, 96–97
Compensation	Overcoming limitations in speaking and writing	Coining words	50, 97

STRATEGY GROUP	STRATEGY SET	STRATEGY	PAGE
Compensation	Overcoming limitations in speaking and writing	Using a circumlocution or synonym	51, 97
Metacognitive	Centering your learning	Overviewing and linking with already known material	138, 152–154
Metacognitive	Centering your learning	Paying attention	138, 154–155
Metacognitive	Arranging and planning your learning	Finding out about language learning	139, 156
Metacognitive	Arranging and planning your learning	Organizing	139, 156
Metacognitive	Arranging and planning your learning	Setting goals and objectives	139, 157–158
Metacognitive	Arranging and planning your learning	Identifying the purpose of a language task	139, 158–159
Metacognitive	Arranging and planning your learning	Planning for a language task	139, 159–160
Metacognitive	Arraning and planning your learning	Seeking practice opportunities	139, 160
Metacognitive	Evaluating your learning	Self-monitoring	140, 161–162
Metacognitive	Evaluating your learning	Self-evaluating	140, 162–163
Affective	Lowering your anxiety	Using progressive relaxation, deep breathing, or meditation	143, 164
Affective	Lowering your anxiety	Using music	143, 164
Affective	Lowering your anxiety	Using laughter	143, 164–165
Affective	Encouraging yourself	Making positive statements	143, 165–166

STRATEGY GROUP	STRATEGY SET	STRATEGY	PAGE
Affective	Encouraging yourself	Taking risks wisely	144, 166
Affective	Encouraging yourself	Rewarding yourself	144, 166
Affective	Taking your emotional temperature	Listening to your body	144, 167
Affective	Taking your emotional temperature	Using a checklist	144, 167
Affective	Taking your emotional temperature	Writing a language learning diary	144, 167–168
Affective	Taking your emotional temperature	Discussing your feelings with someone else	144, 168
Social	Asking questions	Asking for correction	147, 170
Social	Cooperating with others	Cooperating with peers	147, 171
Social	Cooperating with others	Cooperating with proficient users of the new language	147, 171–172
Social	Empathizing with others	Developing cultural understanding	147, 172–173
Social	Empathizing with others	Becoming aware of others' thoughts and feelings	147, 173

Index

This index is divided into two parts. The first of these is the Subject Index, which covers the main topics in the book, as well as many important details. Specific games are noted here in capital letters (e.g., TWENTY QUESTIONS, INVENTIONS). In the interest of conserving space, the Subject Index does not list separately every strategy that is mentioned in the book. In the Subject Index only the main *strategy groups* (memory, cognitive, compensation, metacognitive, affective, and social) and the two *strategy classes* (direct and indirect) are shown. When a particular strategy, such as guessing, is brought up in the text, it is clustered with other related strategies under the broad classifications of group (in this case, compensation strategies) and class (in this instance, direct). See Appendix G for a complete cross-indexing of separate strategies (e.g., translating, writing a language learning diary) applied to each of the four language skills.

The second part of this index is the Index of Authors, Researchers, and Teachers. It lists many people whose ideas have helped strengthen the language learning field and who have been cited in this book.

Subject Index

Achievement and proficiency, distinction between, 237

Acronym use, 60, 68, 245

Acquisition and learning, distinction between and continuum of, 4–5, 23

Advance organizers, 248–249

Affective aspects of language learning, 140–144, 148, 249–251

Affective strategies (*See* Language learning strategy groups, affective.)

ALIBI, 121–122

Ambiguity, tolerance for, 140, 142, 249

Annenberg/CPB Project, 228

Anxiety, 140, 142, 146, 249, 254

Army, U.S., 117

Army Research Institute for the Behavioral and Social Sciences, 255

Artificial intelligence, 241

Attitudes and beliefs, 12, 51, 77, 140, 202 (*See also* Language learning strategy groups, affective.)

Authentic speech (language, discourse), 71, 75, 245–246

Automaticity (unconscious use of strategies), consciousness, awareness, 12, 13, 201, 238, 239, 245 (*See also* Consciously employed operations; Potentially conscious plans.)

Autonomy, 10, 122, 219, 238–239

BBC, 79, 172, 246, 247

Behavior Questionnaire, 254

Bournemouth Eurocentre, 219

Cartridge King, 247

Center for Applied Linguistics, 218

Chicago Mastery Reading Program with Learning Strategies, 256

Cimino Foundation, 219

Class Observation Guide, 253

Cognitive Academic Language Learning Approach (CALLA), 215–217, 256

Cognitive strategies (*See* Language learning strategy groups, cognitive.)

Columbia University, 222

Communication, 4, 6–7, 53 (*Communication is the heart of social strategies, compensation strategies, and many cognitive strategies; see these as listed under* Language learning strategy groups.)

Communication strategies, distinction between language learning strategies and, 243

Community Language Learning, 251

Compensation strategies (*See* Language learning strategy groups, compensation.)

Compensatory strategies and compensation strategies, distinction between terms as used by Ellis and Oxford, 243

Competence and performance, distinction between, 237–238

Competition, competitiveness, 145–146, 149–150, 238, 242, 251–252

Computers, 79, 229–230, 247, 259

Computer Chronicles Newswire, 79

Computer networking, 79 (*See also* Computer Chronicles Newswire; ICONS.)

Concept Tree, 241

Consciously employed operations, 238

Context, contextualizing, 241 (*Almost all compensation strategies and many cognitive and memory strategies employ context; see* Language learning strategy groups. *See also* Decontextualizing.)

Cooperation, 145–146, 149–150, 238, 251 (*Also, many exercises in Chapter 3 involve cooperation.*)

Counseling Learning, 251

CRAPEL, 217–218
Culture, 12, 81, 91–92, 101–133
    (*Communicative instructional activities that
    involve the language can highlight the
    culture as well; see, e.g., the Chapter 3
    exercises that are included here. See also
    Culture shock.*)
Culture shock, 140, 142, 249, 250 (*See also*
    Culture.)

Danish Refugee Council, 226
Decontextualizing, 241 (*See also* Context,
    contextualizing.)
Defense Language Institute Foreign
    Language Center, 247, 255, 256
Department of Trade and Industry (U.K.),
    219
Dialogue journal, 247, 254
Direct broadcasting by satellite (DBS), 76,
    247
DIRECTION PARIS, 228
Discourse coherence and cohesion, 238
Discourse styles, 245 (*See also* Authentic
    speech (language, discourse).)

EMBEDDED STRATEGIES GAME, 24–30
Empathy, 172–173, 249
Error analysis, 161–162, 252
Extroversion vs. introversion, 251

Facets Cinematheque, 246
Facets Video Rental-by-Mail, 246
"False friends," 84
Films (movies), 54, 75
Films Incorporated, 246
Foreign Service Institute, 255
Forgetting (*See* Language loss/attrition.)
Frames, 241, 248
    thinking, 238

Games (*See* Simulation/gaming.)
Georgetown University, 217
Grammar learning, 49, 68, 70–74, 82–85,
    101–133, 242 (*Grammar can be woven into
    all communicative exercises, such as those
    in Chapter 3, as included here.*)

Harvard University, 229
Hemisphericity, brain, 240
"Hidden strategies," 257

ICONS, 79, 229–230, 247, 259
Imitating native speakers, 71, 242

Inhibition, 140, 142, 249, 250, 251
Interactive videodisc, 214–215, 228–229
Introversion vs. extroversion, 251
INVENTIONS, 115–117

Jigsaw listening, 109–110, 171
Jigsaw reading, 76, 117–121, 171
Jigsaw writing, 78

Knowledge
    declarative, 39–40, 240
    explicit linguistic, 244
    general world, 50, 93–94, 244
    implicit linguistic, 244
    missing (*See* Language learning strategy
        groups, compensation.)
    procedural, 39–40, 249

Language Learning Disc, 214–215
Language learning strategies
    in action, case studies of, 213–234
    distinction between communication
        strategies and, 243
    factors influencing choice of, 13
    key features (characteristics) of, 8–14, 22
    problems in the classification of, 16, 22,
        239
    theater, analogy for, 14–16
Language learning strategy classes
    direct, 2, 11–12, 14, 15, 22, 37, 55–133
    indirect, 2, 11–12, 14, 15, 22, 135–191
    mutual support between direct and
        indirect, 14–16, 57, 135
Language learning strategy groups
    affective, 14, 15, 24, 136, 140–141, 149–
        150, 152, 162–168, 182–191, 209, 212,
        214–232, 250, 253
    cognitive, 14, 15, 24, 37, 38, 43–47, 52,
        53–54, 58, 69–90, 100, 105, 106, 109,
        112, 114–126, 127–133, 138, 158, 214–
        232, 241, 242, 243, 245, 247–248
    compensation, 2, 14, 15, 24, 37, 38, 43,
        47–54, 58, 90–97, 100, 106, 109, 110–
        113, 117–133, 209, 214–232, 242, 243,
        244, 248
    memory, 14, 24, 37, 38–43, 51, 53, 58–69,
        87, 93, 100, 101–107, 124–126, 214–232,
        240–242
    metacognitive, 14, 15, 24, 106, 109, 136–
        140, 148, 152–163, 175, 177–183, 209,
        214–232, 242, 250
    social, 14, 15, 24, 109, 136, 144–149, 152,
        168–173, 209, 214–232, 250

Language learning strategy assessment procedures, 2, 3–4, 193–200, 209–211
diaries, 198 (*See also* Language learning strategy groups, affective.)
interviews, 194–197
introspection, 253
note-taking, 197–198 (*See also* Language learning strategy groups, cognitive.)
objective surveys, 199, 254–256
observations, 194
retrospection, 253
self-observation, 195–196, 253
self-report, 253
self-report surveys, 199, 254–256
self-revelation, 253
subjective surveys, 199, 254
thinking aloud, 195, 197, 253
Language Learning Strategy Student Questionnaire, 254
Language learning strategy training, 2, 3–4, 200–209, 211, 212, 214–227, 250, 256, 257–258
Language learning strategy training, eight-step model for, 203–209
Language learning strategy training, focus of, 205–206, 256
Language learning strategy training, types of
awareness training, 202–203
blind training, 257
camouflaged, 208, 257–258
completely informed, 207–208, 257
explicit vs. implicit encouragement of strategy use, 214–233
informed, 223, 257
integrated vs. unintegrated, 206, 256
long-term training, 203
one-time training, 203
strategy-plus-control (self-control), 257
Language learning strategy training
teacher's preparation for conducting, 201–202
Language loss/attrition, 51, 240, 255
Language Skill Change Project, 255
Laughter therapy, 164–165, 253
Learner, roles and responsibilities of, 10, 23
Learning (general), 53
Learning and acquisition, distinction between and continuum of, 4–5, 23
Learning strategies, "hidden," 257
Learning Strategies Inventory, 254
Learning strategy, evolution of the concept of, 8

Left brain, 240
Link System, 242
Link Word Language System, 242
Listening, language learning strategy applications in (*See Appendix G.*)
Literacy, 38, 252 (*See also all the reading and writing applications noted in Appendix G.*)
Literacy and orality, 252

Massachusetts Institute of Technology, 228–229
Meaning, 48, 60, 70, 96, 240 (*Also, almost all strategies involve using material whose meaning is known or knowable by the learner. For illustrations of meaningful language use in strategies and in strategy exercises, see especially Chapters 2–5.*)
Memory
biochemical and electrochemical aspects of, 240
episodic, 240
long-term, 240, 245
network theories of, 240, 245
principles of, 39
semantic, 240
short-term, 240
strategies (*See* Language learning strategy groups, memory.)
Metacognitive strategies (*See* Language learning strategy groups, metacognitive.)
Motivation, 13, 77, 141–142, 206–207, 250 (*See also* Language learning strategy groups, affective; Affective aspects of language learning.)

NEW IDENTITY, 229
NEWSIM, 78, 247
Nonstop writing, 154, 252
NO RECUERDO, 228
North Jutland Department of Adult Education, 226

Observation Schedule of Language Learners, 253
Orality and literacy, 252
Outline, standard, 87–89

Peace Corps, 34, 213, 218–219, 255, 258
Pegword, 242
Performance and competence, distinction between, 237–238
PICTURE STORIES, 124–126

Potentially conscious plans, 238
Practice, importance of, 243
Proficiency, 242
  time needed to reach, 43
Proficiency and achievement, distinction
    between, 237
Project GRASP, 219–220

Radio, 45, 75–76, 78, 81, 246, 247
RADIO COVINGHAM, 78, 247
Raw notes, 86, 248
Reading
  intensive vs. extensive, 158
  language learning strategy applications in
    (*See Appendix G.*)
Records, 75
Reduced personality, 250
ReQuest Procedure, 127
Right brain, 240
Risk-taking, 140, 142, 249
Role-plays (*See* Simulation/gaming.)
RUNNING ERRANDS, 259

Schemes, 241
Scripts, 241, 248
Self-direction (*See* Autonomy.)
Self-esteem, 140–141, 249–250
Sentence diagramming, 247
Shopping list note form, 86–87, 248
Silent period, 155–156, 249
Silent Way, 251
SILL (*See* Strategy Inventory for Language
    Learning.)
Simulation/gaming, 24–35, 54–55, 77, 115–
    117, 121–122, 123–126, 154, 165, 228,
    232, 239, 259
Skill emergence when practicing *other* skills,
    faulty concept of, 244
Skills, 39, 240
  basic, 238
  basic reasoning, 238
  functional, 238
  (four) language, 4, 5–6, 39–40, 244 (*See
    also learning strategy applications to the
    four language skills, Chapters 3 and 5;
    Appendix G.*)
  learning, 2, 238
  learning-to-learn, 2, 238
  problem-solving, 2
  thinking, 2, 238
Social desirability response bias, 256
Social strategies (*See* Language learning
    strategy groups, social.)

Society for the Advancement of Games and
    Simulations in Education and Training
    (SAGSET), 259
Sociocultural factors, 249
Soros Foundation, 231
Speaking, language learning strategy
    applications in (*See Appendix G.*)
SPEAKING FACES (also called "96"), 231
Speech forms, 252
Stanford University, 229
Strategies, processing, 238
Strategy, evolution of the concept of, 7–8
    (*See also* Learning strategy, evolution of
    the concept of.)
Strategy assessment (*See* Language learning
    strategy assessment, procedures.)
Strategy Inventory for Language Learning
    (SILL), 99, 255–256 (*See also Appendices
    A, B, and C.*)
Strategy Questionnaire, 254
STRATEGY SEARCH GAME, 30–35
Strategy training (*See* Language learning
    strategy training.)
Suggestopedia, 251

Tactics, 7, 238
Teacher, roles and responsibilities of, 10–
    11, 23–24, 239
Techniques, 238
Telephone, 75, 163
Teletext English Language Scheme, 259
Television, 45, 54, 76, 81, 91–92, 124, 246,
    259
T-Formation note form, 86–88, 248
Total Physical Response technique, 39, 66,
    109, 242
Tree diagram, 248
TWENTY QUESTIONS, 54–55

Ulpan Akiva, 223–224
Université de Nancy II, 217–218
Université de Toulon, 259
University of Maryland, 225, 229–230, 259

Videocassette, 246
Vocabulary learning, 39, 49, 58–68, 101–
    133, 154, 241–243 (*All communicative
    activities involve some vocabulary learning.
    See the exercises in Chapter 3, as included
    here.*)

Working journal, 247, 254
Writing, language learning strategy
    applications in (*See Appendix G.*)

Index of Authors, Researchers, and Teachers Mentioned in This Book

Abé, D., 258
Adler, B., 250
Adler, R. S., 250
Alexander, P. A., 237
Allwright, R. L., 254
Amber, P., 241, 248, 250
Anderson, J. R., 240, 258
Aniran, M., 256
Aphek, E., 241, 245
Arnold, V., 253
Asher, J. J., 242, 245
Aston, G., 247, 252
Ausubel, D. A., 249

Bachman, L. F., 238
Baddeley, A., 240
Bailey, K. N., 251–254
Bardwick, J., 251
Barnes, D. R., 249
Bassano, S., 251
Beebe, L. M., 251
Begley, S., 240
Bejarano, Y., 251
Bialystok, E., 243, 244, 245, 248
Blanchard, K., 247
Brecht, R., 230
Brooks, J. E., xii
Brown-Azarowicz, M., 64, 65, 241, 245, 252
Burgess, A., 111
Blair, K., 250
Bower, G. W., 241
Bransford, J. D., 257
Brown, A. L., 256, 257

Brown, H. D., xii, 237, 244, 245, 249, 251
Burbridge, B., 239
Burt, M. K., 249
Byrnes, H., 252

Campbell, J., 237, 249
Campbell, R., 237
Canale, M., 237, 238
Candlin, C., 243
Chamot, A. U., xii, 21, 133, 195–196, 215–217, 238, 239, 240, 242, 243, 244, 248, 251, 252, 253, 255, 256, 258
Chang, K-Y. R., xii
Chapelle, C., 251
Chomsky, N., 237
Christison, M. A., 251
Colman, A., 238
Cornelius, E. J., Jr., 252
Cramer, N. A., 247
Crawford, C., 252
Clark, B. L., 247
Clark, J. L. D., 238
Clarke, D. F., 248
Clawson, E. U., 249
Clément, R., 250
Cohen, A. D., vii–viii, xii, 195, 223–224, 237, 239, 241, 244, 245, 253, 254, 259
Coleman, A., 238
Crookall, D., 116, 117, 118,

122, 126, 230, 238, 245, 246, 247, 252, 255, 256, 259
Culhane, T., 131, 132
Cummins, J., 247, 258

Dam, L., 221–222
Dansereau, D., xii, 21, 238, 239, 251, 256, 258
Day, J. D., 256
Derry, S. J., 256
Diadori, R., 238
Dickinson, L., 222, 237, 238, 258, 259
Dobrovolny, J. L., 250
Dulay, H. C., 249
Dumas, D., 244

Ehrman, M. E., xii, 251, 255
Eliason, M., xii
Ellis, R., 243
Evers, F. T., 250

Faerch, C., 237, 238, 243
Ferrara, J., 254
Ferrara, R., 257
Fine, J., 254
Frank, C., 123
Freed, B. F., 240
Fröhlich, M., 249, 251
Furstenberg, G., 259

Gaies, S. J., 251
Gardner, R. C., 250

Geddes, M., 245, 246
Genesee, F., 250
Gibbons, J., 249, 252
Gibson, J., 239
Gilligan, C., 251
Glasman, H., 254
Goetz, E. T., 237
Goldin, M., 64, 65, 241
Goleman, D., 240, 241
Gowin, D. B., 241
Grala, M., 258
Grandage, K., 242, 243
Grellet, F., 252
Grognet, A., 219
Grucz, M. M., 244
Gruneberg, M. M., 242, 244
Gunderson, B., 251

Hager, M., 240
Hague, S. A., xii, 63, 127, 240, 241
Halff, H. M., 241
Hall, R., Jr., 252
Hamayan, E., 250
Hamp-Lyons, L., 247, 248
Harmer, J., 239
Hart, J., 238
Harter, S., 249, 250
Hartfiel, V. F., 247, 252
Heasley, B., 247
Henner-Stanchina, C., 243, 258
Higbee, K. L., 241
Hogue, A., 247
Holec, H., 23, 219, 237, 239, 256, 258
Hosenfeld, C., 195, 196, 243, 253, 258
Houpt, S., 247, 252
Howard, D. V., 240, 245
Howatt, A. P. R., 243
Hughey, J. B., 247
Hymes, D., 237

Impink-Hernandez, M., 242

Jacklin, C., 251
Jacob, E., 251
Jacobs, H., 247
James, B. G., 238

Johnson, D., 251
Jones, B. F., 256
Jones, E., 240
Jones, K., 247
Jones, L., 129
Jones, R. A., 254

Kagan, S., 251
Kasper, G., 237, 238, 243
Katias, M., 256
Katz, S., 240
Katznelson, S., 224
Keeler, S., 259
Kimbrough, V., 129
Kirchofer, J., 253
Knowles, M., 239
Koestler, A., 238
Kohn, A., 251
Kraft, C. J., 252
Kraft, M. E., 252
Krashen, S. D., 237, 244, 247, 249
Kreeft, J. (now Peyton), 247
Kupper, L., 133, 239, 242, 244

Lacuria, J., 253
Lalonde, R. H., 250
Lambert, R. D., 240
Lambert, W. E., 250
Lavine, R. Z., xii, 225–226, 238, 259
Leaver, B. L., xii, 197, 240, 243, 245, 254
Leitzell, E. M., 252
Lett, J., xii
Littlewood, W., 237, 238, 244, 248, 250, 252
Lobbuts, J. F., 237, 252
Lomperis, A., xii, 218–219, 258
Long, M., 254
Long, P., 253
Lorayne, H., 242, 244
Lord (cited in Hague, S. A.), 39, 240
Lucas, J., 242, 244
Lukmani, Y., 250

MacBride, S., 48, 243
Maccoby, E. E., 251
Major, L., 250

Manzo, A., 127
Matheidesz, M., xii, 230–232, 259
Mattson, B., 251
McCombs, B. L., xii, 249, 250
McDonough, M., 241, 243
McGroarty, M., 248, 255
McKee, E., 244, 247, 252
McNerney, V., 241, 243
Mendelsohn, D. J., 111, 211, 241, 242, 243, 244, 245, 246, 248, 250
Meyer, R., 245
Miller, G. A., 241
Mohan, B. A., 258
Moorcroft, R., 250
Moran, P. R., 112–113
Morgenstern, D., xii, 228–229, 259
Morley, J., 244, 246
Moulden, H., 258
Moulton, W. G., 252
Munby, J., 238
Murphy, D. A., 256
Murray, J., 228–229, 259

Naiman, N., 249, 251, 254
Nation, J. S. R., 248
Nida, E., 252
Noel, R. C., 230, 259
Norbrook, H., 246
Novak, D., 241
Nyikos, K., xii
Nyikos, M., 241, 242, 248, 251, 254, 255

Omaggio, A. (now Hadley), 105, 237, 238, 246, 252
O'Malley, J. M., xii, 21, 133, 195–196, 215–217, 239, 240, 242, 248, 251, 252, 253, 254, 255, 256, 258
O'Neil, H. F., Jr., 237
Ong, W., 240, 252
Oppenheimer, J., 238
Oshima, A., 247
Oskarsson, M., 252
Oxford, R. L., 238, 239, 240, 241, 242, 248, 251, 255, 256, 258

Palo, B., 218–219
Papalia, A., 242, 243
Pei, N., 252
Pennewill, C. L., 237, 252
Phillips, J. K., 114, 115
Pimsleur, P., 252
Politzer, R. L., 252, 254
Prowse, R., 256

Raimes, A., 247
Ramirez, A. G., 243
Reid, J. M., 241, 251
Reiss, M-A., 241, 242
Revill, P., 219–220
Rexroth, R., 245
Rhodes, N. C., 242
Rigney, J. W., 238, 256, 257
Riley, P., 238, 256
Rinvolucri, M., 123
Rivera, C., 238
Rivers, W. N., 244, 252
Rodgers, T. S., 256
Root, C., 247
Rosenbaum-Cohen, P. R.,
    254
Rossi-Le, L., 241
Rowe, D., 238
Ruben, B. D., 249
Rubin, J., xii, 21, 214–215,
    237, 239, 243, 248, 252,
    254, 255, 258
Russo, R. P., 133, 239, 242,
    244

Sadow, C., 247, 253, 254
Saunders, D., 259
Savignon, S. J., 237
Schapira, L., 230, 259
Schleppegrell, M., 258
Schumann, F. E., 254

Schumann, J. N., 254
Seliger, H. W., 251
Selinker, L., 243
Semke, H. D., 252
Sharan, S., 251
Shephard, R. N., 241
Shipman, S., 249
Shipman, V. C., 249
Shuy, R., 247
Simon, N., 238
Slavin, R., 251
Smith, A., xii, 219–220, 259
Smith, F., xii
Smith, P., 258
Smythe, R. C., 250
Spack, R., 247, 253, 254
Spolsky, B., 250
Springen, K., 240
Stannard, C., 64, 65, 241
Staton, J., 247, 254
Stern, H. W., 251, 253
Stevick, E. W., 242, 251
Stewner-Manzanares, G.,
    133, 239, 242, 244, 256,
    258
Strasheim, L., 108
Sutter, W., xii, 226–227,
    239, 257, 259
Swain, M., 237

Tarone, E., 21, 243, 244,
    245
Terrell, T., 249
Tesser, A., 249
Thompson, I., 237, 240, 252
Todesco, A., 249, 251
Tucker, G. R., 250
Tulving, E., 240
Tyacke, M., 211, 241, 242,
    243, 248, 250

Underwood, V. L., 256,
    258
Ur, P., 107, 108, 109, 110,
    244, 245, 246

VanLancker, D., 240
Vogel, M., 250
Von Clausewicz, C., 238

Wales, R., 237
Walker, C., 240
Watson, D. R., 118
Weiner, M., 238
Weinstein, C. E., 21, 237,
    256, 258
Weltens, B., 240
Wenden, A. L., xii, 197,
    222–233, 237, 238, 239,
    248, 249, 252, 254, 256,
    257, 258, 259
Wesche, M. B., 238
White, R., 245, 246
White, R. H., 249
Widdowson, H. G., 238
Wilkenfeld, J., 230, 247,
    259
Wilson, L., 253
Wipf, J., xii
Withrow, J., 118
Wong, R., 245
Wong Fillmore, L. W., 251
Wormuth, D. R., 247
Wright, A., 241–242, 244
Wright, T., 24, 239

Yamada, H., xii, 241, 245

Zampogna, J., 242, 243
Zima, M. A. (*now*
    Aquilino), xii, 245

Credits

Activity 1.4: Adaptation from *Roles of Teachers and Learners*, 1987, pp. 52–53, Tony Wright; Oxford University Press, Walton Street, Oxford OX2 6DP, England. **Exercise 3.4:** From *Helping Learners Succeed: Activities for the Foreign Language Classroom*, 1981, p. 27, Alice Omaggio; Center for Applied Linguistics, 118 22nd St. NW, Washington, DC 20008 USA. **Exercise 3.8:** Adapation from *Teaching Listening Comprehension*, 1984, pp. 152–154, Penny Ur; Cambridge University Press, 32 East 57th Street, New York, NY 10022 USA. © Cambridge University Press 1984. Reprinted with the permission of Cambridge University Press. **Exercises 3.11, 3.12:** From "Practical Implications of Recent Research in Reading," *Foreign Language Annals*, 17 (4), 1984, pp. 290–291, June K. Phillips; c/o ACTFL, 6 Executive Blvd., Upper Level, Yonkers, NY 10701 USA. **Exercise 3.13:** From "Comparing Facts and Figures," *Practical English Teaching*, 1984, p. 25, David Crookall; Scholastic Inc., P.O. Box 644, Lyndhurst, NY 07071-0655 USA; Mary Glasgow Publications, Avenue House, 131–133 Holland Park Ave., London W11 4UT, England. **Exercise 3.16:** From *Grammar in Action*, 1983, p. 17, Christine Frank and Mario Rinvolucri; Simon & Schuster, 66 Wood Lane End, Hemel Hempstead, Hertfordshire HP2 4RG. England (for Pergamon Press). **Exercise 3.19:** From "Bridging the Gap Between Learning to Read and Reading to Learn," *Northeast Conference Newsletter*, 20, 1986, pp. 46–47, Sally Hague; Original ReQuest procedure designed by A. Manzo; Northeast Conference on the Teaching of Foreign Languages, P.O. Box 623, Middlebury, VT 05753-0623 USA. **Exercise 3.20:** From *Great Ideas: Listening and Speaking Activities for Students of American English*, 1987, pp. 60–61, L. Jones and V. Kimbrough; Cambridge University Press, 32 East 57th Street, New York, NY 10022 USA. © 1984 Cambridge University Press. Reprinted with the permission of Cambridge University Press. **Exercise 3.22:** *Russian Language and People*, 1986, p. 120, Terry Culhane; BBC Publications, 35 Marlebone High St., London W1M 4AA, England; EMC Publishing, 300 York Ave., St. Paul, MN 55010 USA. **Exercise 3.23:** From *Learning Strategies in ESL Instruction: A Teacher's Guide*, 1985, p. 33, Gloria Stewner-Manzanares, Anna Uhl Chamot, Lisa Kupper, and Rocco Russo; InterAmerica Research Associates, Inc., 7926 Jones Branch Drive, Suite 1100, McLean, VA 22102.

Table 3.1: From: *Teaching Listening Comprehension*, 1984, p. 153, Penny Ur; Cambridge University Press, 32 East 57th Street, New York, NY 10022 USA. © 1984 Cambridge University Press. Reprinted with the permission of Cambridge University Press. **Figure 3.3:** From "Vocabulary Instruction: What L2 Can Learn

From L1," *Foreign Language Annals*, 20 (3), 1987, p. 222, Sally Hague; c/o ACTFL, 6 Executive Blvd., Upper Level, Yonkers, NY 10701 USA.   **Figures 3.4, 3.5:** From: *Yes! You Can Learn a Foreign Language*, 1986, pp. 32–33, M. Brown-Azarowicz, C. Stannard, & M. Goldin; NTC Publishing Group, 4255 Touhy Ave., Lincolnwood, IL 60646-1975 USA.   **Figures 3.8, 3.9:** From "Review Article: Survey of Materials for Teaching Advanced Listening and Note-taking," by Liz Hamp-Lyons, 1983, *TESOL Quarterly 17* (1) pp. 112, 118. Copyright 1982 by Teachers of English to Speakers of Other Languages. Reprinted by permission. c/o TESOL, 1118-22nd St. NW, Washington, DC 20037 USA.   **Figure 3.12:** From *Teaching Listening Comprehension*, 1984, p. 61, Penny Ur; Cambridge University Press, 32 East 57th Street, New York, NY 10022 USA. © Cambridge University Press 1984. Reprinted with the permission of Cambridge University Press.   **Figure 3.13:** From "Getting Around in a German-Speaking City: Testing the Indiana Level One Competence," 1988, Lorraine A. Strasheim, Coord. for School Foreign Language Programs, Office of School Programs, Ed. 253, Indiana University, Bloomington, IN 47405, USA.   **Figure 3.14:** From *Lexicarry: An Illustrated Vocabulary-Builder for Second Languages*, 1984, rev. 1989, Patrick R. Moran; Pro Lingua Associates, 15 Elm St., Brattleboro, VT 05301 USA.   **Figure 3.15:** Adaptation from "Comparing Facts and Figures," *Practical English Teaching*, 1984, p. 25, David Crookall; Scholastic Inc., P.O. Box 644, Lyndhurst, NY 07071-0655 USA; Mary Glasgow Publications, Avenue House, 131–133 Holland Park Ave., London W11 4UT, England.   **Figures 3.16, 3.17:** From *Kinder Monatszeitschrift* VIII (3), 1986 and VIII (6) 1986, c/o European Language Institute, P.O. Box 6, 62019 Recanati, Italy.   **Figure 3.18:** From *Russian Language and People*, 1986, p. 120, Terry Culhane; BBC Publications, 35 Marlebone High St., London W1M 4AA, England; EMC Publishing, 300 York Ave., St. Paul, MN 55010 USA.   **Table 6.1:** Adaptation from "Second Language Reading; A Curricular Sequence for Teaching Reading Strategies," *Foreign Language Annals*, 14 (5), 1981, pp. 415–422, C. Hosenfeld, V. Arnold, J. Kirchofer, J. Laciura, and L. Wilson; c/o ACTFL, 6 Executive Blvd., Upper Level, Yonkers, NY 10701 USA.   **Figure 7.1:** From *Self-Instruction in Language Learning*, 1987, p. 62, Leslie Dickinson (author); Leni Dam (model designer); Cambridge University Press, 32 East 57th Street, New York, NY, 10022 USA. © Leslie Dickinson 1987. Reprinted with the permission of Cambridge University Press.

About the Author

Rebecca L. Oxford is currently Associate Professor of language instructional methodology and Russian at the University of Alabama. She is experienced in foreign languages, English as a second language, and bilingual education. She has taught at both secondary and university levels, has directed an intensive English program for international students at the Pennsylvania State University, and has led teacher training workshops throughout the United States and in Europe and Southeast Asia. She has written widely on language learning styles and strategies for professional journals such as *Modern Language Journal*, *Foreign Language Annals*, and *The Journal of Psychological Type* and has written chapters on these topics for a number of books. With David Crookall she co-edited *Language Learning Through Simulation/Gaming*, which will be published by Newbury House. She holds two degrees in Russian (Vanderbilt University and Yale University) and two in educational psychology (Boston University and the University of North Carolina).

*This book is lovingly dedicated to my wife, Donna Jones,
to my son, Sam Jones, to my daughter, Beth Jones,
and to my parents, Herbert and Dorothy Jones*

CONTENTS

Preface   xi

PART I   THE THEORISTS   1

CHAPTER ONE   1
Edwin Sutherland

CHAPTER TWO   6
Robert Merton

CHAPTER THREE   10
James Q. Wilson

PART II   LAW ENFORCEMENT   15

CHAPTER FOUR   15
Allan Pinkerton

CHAPTER FIVE   21
Thomas Byrnes

CHAPTER SIX   26
Charles Bonaparte

CHAPTER SEVEN   31
Wyatt Earp

CHAPTER EIGHT   35
John Clum

CHAPTER NINE   41
William Burns

CHAPTER TEN   47
Theodore Roosevelt

CHAPTER ELEVEN   52
Lola G. Baldwin

CHAPTER TWELVE   57
August Vollmer

CHAPTER THIRTEEN   61
Samuel Battle

CHAPTER FOURTEEN   64
J. Edgar Hoover

CHAPTER FIFTEEN   70
Harry Anslinger

CHAPTER SIXTEEN   75
O. W. Wilson

CHAPTER SEVENTEEN   81
Eliot Ness

CHAPTER EIGHTEEN   88
Daryl Gates

CHAPTER NINETEEN   93
Herman Goldstein

CHAPTER TWENTY   99
Frank Serpico

CHAPTER TWENTY-ONE   105
Joseph Wambaugh

CHAPTER TWENTY-TWO   111
Buford Pusser

CHAPTER TWENTY-THREE   118
Lee Brown

CHAPTER TWENTY-FOUR   122
Penny Harrington

CHAPTER TWENTY-FIVE   127
Greg MacAleese

PART III   LAW AND THE COURTS   132

CHAPTER TWENTY-SIX   132
Clarence Darrow

CHAPTER TWENTY-SEVEN   137
Roger Nash Baldwin

CHAPTER TWENTY-EIGHT   142
Earl Warren

CHAPTER TWENTY-NINE   146
William Kunstler

CHAPTER THIRTY   154
F. Lee Bailey

CHAPTER THIRTY-ONE   159
G. Robert Blakey

PART IV   CORRECTIONS   165

CHAPTER THIRTY-TWO   165
Thomas Eddy

CHAPTER THIRTY-THREE   170
John Haviland

CHAPTER THIRTY-FOUR   175
John Augustus

CHAPTER THIRTY-FIVE   181
Dorothea Dix

CHAPTER THIRTY-SIX   187
Rutherford B. Hayes

CHAPTER THIRTY-SEVEN   193
Zebulon Brockway

CHAPTER THIRTY-EIGHT   198
Thomas Osborne

CHAPTER THIRTY-NINE   204
Miriam Van Waters

CHAPTER FORTY   210
Joseph Ragen

CHAPTER FORTY-ONE   215
Clinton Duffy

CHAPTER FORTY-TWO   221
George Beto

PART V   JUVENILE JUSTICE   228

CHAPTER FORTY-THREE   228
Jane Addams

CHAPTER FORTY-FOUR   233
Benjamin Lindsey

Epilogue   239

PREFACE

■ ■ ■ ■ ■

The idea for this project came from a book I read in 1981 while I was an undergraduate at the University of Georgia. It contained short biographies of the 100 greatest baseball players of all time. Ever since I started studying crime in earnest, I have wondered why a similar book has not been written about people in criminal justice.

As I read the book on great baseball players, I found myself disagreeing with the author about who had been included and who had been omitted. How, I thought, could you possibly include Mr. X, and how could you possibly exclude Mr. Y? Readers of *Criminal Justice Pioneers in U.S. History* may wonder why I chose to include some of these people, and they will be astounded as to why I left others out. Everyone I spoke with about this project, including some of the subjects themselves, had a suggestion about whom to include. This book is not intended as a definitive list of criminal justice "hall of famers," it is simply my partial list of some of the people who have strongly influenced the operation of America's criminal justice system and public perceptions about crime and criminal justice. I discuss the criteria for inclusion later in this Preface.

The criminal justice system was not created, nor does it currently exist in a political, social, religious, or economic vacuum. It is important to acknowledge the influence of impersonal forces when studying the history of criminal justice. What is also important and sorely neglected are the individual personalities who have helped shape the modern criminal justice system. It allows students of crime to see how human personalities with all their frailties impact the criminal justice system.

An age-old debate among those with an interest in history is whether people make history or history makes people. Two prominent criminal justice figures illustrate this debate. Did Chief Justice Earl Warren create the due process revolution or would any person in his position during the 1950s and 1960s have done as he did given the changing social mood of the country during that time? Did Earl Warren change with the times? Or did his beliefs remain the same throughout his life, and did he actually *change the times* himself? There is no doubt that J. Edgar Hoover's own distinctive personality helped shape the Federal Bureau of Investigation's colorful history, but Hoover's beliefs and prejudices, in many ways, simply reflected those of a majority of Americans throughout the 1930s, World War II, and the Cold War. Would another FBI director have been as prominent a historical figure as Hoover?

The people examined in this book are not saints to be idolized or demons to be vilified. No person is perfectly good, and no one is perfectly evil. Everyone profiled in this book had flaws and strengths. Simply because someone makes a significant contribution to the history of criminal justice does not mean that they should be upheld as role models or as villains to be shunned.

OVERVIEW OF EACH BIOGRAPHY

Each biography is arranged roughly as follows:

  I. Introduction
    a. Summary introduction
    b. Primary accomplishment and notable contribution

  II. Background
    a. Birth date and location
    b. Schooling

  III. Career
    a. Early career
    b. Primary employment
    c. Contributions, controversies

  IV. Summary conclusion
    a. How has criminal justice benefited or been influenced by his or her life and career?
    b. Death (when applicable)

  V. Suggestions for further reading

The book is divided into five parts. Part I, The Theorists, includes biographies of three prominent criminoloical theorists: (1) Edwin Sutherland, (2) Robert Merton, and (3) James Q. Wilson. The study of crime begins with its causes. The study of human behavior, be it on an individual or a group level, is an enormously complex task. The study of criminal behavior is equally complex and hotly debated. Much of the debate about the causes of crime is so esoteric that only the most dedicated criminologists can relate. The study of crime's causes has been hijacked by pure academics that care little for how their study affects public policy. Not so with the three people discussed here. Their work went beyond abstract discussions in college classrooms. They have impacted everyday life both within and beyond criminal justice.

The list of prominent criminological theorists is much longer but these three are among the most prominent in their impact on public policy. I cannot unequivocally state that these are the most important American criminologists ever, but I chose them for inclusion because I think they have affected, perhaps more than most of their colleagues, the way America thinks about crime's causes and our subsequent reactions to crime.

Part II, Law Enforcement, focuses on pioneers in law enforcement: (4) Allan Pinkerton, (5) Thomas Byrnes, (6) Charles Bonaparte, (7) Wyatt Earp, (8) John Clum, (9) William Burns, (10) Theodore Roosevelt, (11) Lola G. Baldwin, (12) August Vollmer, (13) Samuel Battle, (14) J. Edgar Hoover, (15) Harry Anslinger, (16) O. W. Wilson, (17) Eliot Ness, (18) Daryl Gates, (19) Herman Goldstein, (20) Frank Serpico, (21) Joseph Wambaugh, (22) Buford Pusser, (23) Lee Brown, (24) Penny Harrington, and (25) Greg MacAleese.

Many of the pioneers discussed here had few, if any, blueprints to follow when carving out their law enforcement careers. The blueprints that did exist—for example, nondemocratic European models of policing—were not ones that most Americans wanted to follow. Some of the people discussed here performed admirably, and some embody the more unsavory aspects of the history of American policing. Some were pioneers within their gender or ethnic group, bold pioneers in a field historically dominated by Caucasian men.

Police in a democracy represent an inherent contradiction. They restrain citizens who are supposed to enjoy total freedom. The mission of policing a democratic society is complicated and demands a special personality to do it well.

Municipal policing in America did not exist until the 1830s, sixty years after the nation's founding. State law enforcement did not come about until decades later, and the federal government did not get involved in law enforcement until after the Civil War, and then only in counterfeiting cases.

The legacies of all of these people are mixed, leaving some positive legacies and some negative. Irrespective of their individual imperfections, we can learn from their lives and careers to better understand modern policing.

In Part III, Law and the Courts, the reader will find legal pioneers that directly impacted criminal justice, but will find omitted those who may have impacted the other areas of the law. Those included are: (26) Clarence Darrow, (27) Roger Nash Baldwin, (28) Earl Warren, (29) William Kunstler, (30) F. Lee Bailey, and (31) G. Robert Blakey. Of the main components of the criminal justice system, America's legal system is the only one that was directly transplanted from England during America's colonial period. Some of the people who helped shape the American legal system are not included here—that topic goes beyond the subject of this book. A history of the law and the courts takes one in myriad directions aside from crime and criminal justice. In this section, I include legal pioneers that have in my view been intertwined with the criminal justice aspects of the law.

Part IV, Corrections, focuses on institutional and community-based corrections. Corrections has four primary components: probation, jails, prisons, and parole. The history of jails and prisons is greatly intertwined, and the genesis of American parole is wrapped up with the prison and the indeterminate sentence. If the subjects of this section share one thing, it is that they were ultimately frustrated and disillusioned with America's correctional system, even after many years of fervently working to reform it and experiencing some success, reinforcing the maxim, the more things change, the more they stay the same. The subjects of Part IV are (32) Thomas Eddy, (33) John Haviland, (34) John Augustus, (35) Dorothea Dix, (36) Rutherford B. Hayes, (37) Zebulon Brockway, (38) Thomas Osborne, (39) Miriam Van Waters, (40) Joseph Ragen, (41) Clinton Duffy, and (42) George Beto.

Part V, Juvenile Justice, includes (43) Jane Addams and (44) Benjamin Lindsey. Perhaps to an even greater degree than the other subjects of this book, pioneers in the juvenile justice system are products of the Progressive Era (1890–1920), when America sought to improve the quality of life for those on the lower rungs of the social ladder.

CRITERIA FOR INCLUSION

The people discussed in this book pioneered in different ways, some in more ways than one. One prerequisite for inclusion in this book centers on nationality. Everyone discussed in this book is or was American, either born or naturalized, to include people of other nationalities would have made the scope of the book too broad.

In deciding whom to include, I considered several factors. Two of the main factors were purely logistical. First, I could not expand the list too much or the book would have resembled an encyclopedia rather than what it was intended to be. Second, there were a number of people whom I would have liked to include but did not due to lack of available information. I did not include famous outlaws or those whose crimes, alleged crimes, or victimization have made an impact on the criminal justice system, such as Rodney King, O. J. Simpson, and Caryl Chessman. There are plenty of books about famous outlaws.

In the Minority

Caucasian men have dominated criminal justice professions historically, but some people broke gender and racial barriers. Were it not for the efforts of people such as these, criminal justice professions would still be stocked exclusively with white males, and many of the people reading this book would have no chance for a career in criminal justice. Individuals who fall into this category are Penny Harrington, Lola Baldwin, Samuel Battle, and Lee Brown.

Practical Pioneers

We regard others as pioneers because of the contributions they may have made to the mechanical workings of the criminal justice system. Joseph Ragen and Clinton Duffy thought differently from each other in many respects and were world-renowned wardens in Illinois and California, respectively. George Beto administered a well-known Texas prison system during the turbulent 1960s. Thomas Osborne pioneered inmate self-governance at Sing Sing.

Cultural Icons

The mark of a true superstar in any field is becoming a household name not only to those in the field, but to those who know little about that field as well. Those who know little or nothing about baseball still know Babe Ruth. The same is true for Michael Jordan and basketball, Carl Sagan and astronomy, and Elvis Presley and rock music. For some of the people discussed in this book, their legacy has transcended the world of criminal justice, and they have become cultural and social icons, in some respects becoming much bigger in death than they were in life. The legacy surrounding these people often shields the truth about what they may have really been like. Myth can easily become reality when one does not attempt to truly discover the lives of these people. Among the figures in this book that fit this profile are J. Edgar Hoover, Wyatt Earp, Buford Pusser, and Eliot Ness.

Humanitarians

Those who make it their ambition to help others use many methods and institutions to accomplish their mission. Some use religious institutions; others use businesses or educational institutions. Because criminal justice is supposed to help people through one means or another, some of the people we treat as pioneers were humanitarians who used the criminal justice system to accomplish the goal of aiding and improving the lives of other people. Among those who fall into this category are Dorethea Dix, Jane Addams, and John Augustus.

Trendsetters

A *trend* is defined as a tendency, a general direction, or a dominant movement. Some social and legal trends are forged by collective groups of people at a given time, while others are launched by individuals. Many of the policies and laws observed and enforced today are the culmination of efforts made by some of the people covered in this book. Earl Warren led the due process revolution that changed the course of procedural due process. Harry Anslinger was America's first drug war general.

The Thinkers

Aristotle once said, "In general it is a sign of the man who knows, he can teach, and therefore we think art more truly knowledge than experience is; for artists can teach and men of mere experience cannot." Many aspects of modern criminal justice are the brainchild of those who taught or acknowledged the importance of learning from great minds. Just as all disciplines have their great thinkers, criminal justice has its geniuses whose work has helped define the field.

To divorce the great thinkers and writers from those who actually work in the streets, prisons, and courthouses of America would ignore the contributions of many important people. Edwin Sutherland pioneered views on white-collar crime. Robert Merton's research provided the ideological framework for federal efforts to combat crime in the 1960s. August Vollmer improved policing by initiating higher education for police officers. O. W. Wilson literally wrote the book on police administration. Herman Goldstein, one of the best blends of academe and policing, is linked with problem-oriented policing.

The Dark Side

Some individuals will be remembered for their negative contributions to the administration of justice. Brutality, bigotry, and corruption are as much a part of criminal justice history as are justice and mercy. I did not ignore the mistakes, shortcomings, and human frailties of these people. I leave it to the reader to decide where each person's place in history should be.

CONCLUSION

One of the most interesting and inspirational tidbits I discovered while writing this book was that the path to prominence is neither easy nor direct. In his musical tribute to his son, titled "Beautiful Boy," John Lennon wrote, "Life is what happens to you while you're busy making other plans." Many of these people did not embark on a career in criminal justice and they seemed to have little chance of success in the field either as children or even as young adults. George Beto was nicknamed the "accidental penologist," but he is not the only one who could wear such a label. I hope that the readers of this book who are planning a career in criminal justice will be inspired by these biographies, and I am confident that novice and experienced practitioners and academicians will have a better appreciation of America's criminal justice system after reading this book.

ACKNOWLEDGMENTS

I would like to thank the following people for their contributions: Harriet Zuckerman, James Q. Wilson, Herman Goldstein, Frank Serpico, the office of former Houston Mayor Lee Brown, Penny Harrington, Greg MacAleese, G. Robert Blakey, and Dan Beto.

CHAPTER 1

■ ■ ■ ■ ■

EDWIN SUTHERLAND
(1883–1950)

No academician has made a greater impact on the study of criminology than Edwin Sutherland. Perhaps more than anyone else, he can lay claim to making sociology the dominant discipline in the study of crime causation, even though Sutherland was not a pure sociologist. Prior to Sutherland, studying and identifying the roots of criminal behavior laid in the domain of law, biology, medicine, and psychology. Criminal behavior, the thinking went, was predetermined rather than learned. The term *differential association,* a basic staple of criminology, originates with Sutherland.

Few academicians have made a more lasting impact on criminal justice policy than Sutherland; his influence extends beyond colleges and universities. The term *white collar crime,* now a part of everyday criminal justice vocabulary, reflects the culmination of twenty-five years of diligent research by Sutherland.

Edwin Hardin Sutherland was born on August 13, 1883, in Gibbon, Nebraska, one of five children born to Lizzie Pickett Sutherland and George Sutherland, a Baptist minister and history professor at Ottawa College. The Sutherlands moved to Grand Island, Nebraska, in 1893 where George Sutherland assumed the presidency of Nebraska Baptist Seminary. The school's name was soon changed to Grand Island College. The road to prominence in criminology was not a likely one for Sutherland, but his career in academe seemed almost predestined, even though he encountered a few stumbling blocks along the way.

Unlike many academic stars, Sutherland, the most renowned criminologist of the twentieth century, took a path to academic prominence outside the halls of Ivy League universities. Instead, Sutherland made his mark while living and working in America's heartland. He attended Grand Island College, played football there, and graduated with an A.B. degree in 1904. After being rejected for a Rhodes scholarship, Sutherland took a job a Sioux Falls College teaching Greek and Latin.

Although his interests in graduate education were geared toward history and religion at the time, Sutherland, while teaching at Sioux Falls, took his first sociology class, a correspondence course. He left to study at the University of Chicago in 1906 and developed an interest in crime while there. The University of Chicago was renowned for its divinity school, which attracted Sutherland, but it also housed the country's premier sociology department. In 1909 Sutherland returned to Grand Island and taught sociology and psychology, only to return to the University of Chicago in 1911 to focus on studying sociology. Rather than focus exclusively on sociology, Sutherland obtained a Ph.D. degree in sociology and political economy in 1913; the latter discipline would prove useful in his subsequent inquiries into white collar crime.

Sutherland's first position after getting his Ph.D. was with William Jewel College in Liberty, Missouri, where he stayed from 1913–1919, authoring (only) one article while there. Sutherland married Myrtle Crews in 1918; the marriage produced one daughter. Once Sutherland made his move to Big Ten schools, he began to make his mark on criminology through his writings, which was a fortunate decision for Sutherland and those who studied under him. Sutherland was a dry monotone class presenter, but he excelled in small seminars and groups and in one-on-one interaction with graduate students. Plus, he proved an outstanding researcher and writer, and working at large universities offered him research and writing opportunities he never got at small religious colleges.

Sutherland started working at the University of Illinois in 1919. While there, he authored the first of his three true classics in the field of criminology. *Criminology* was released in 1924. Prior to Sutherland's book, the literature on crime causation was dominated by psychology and medicine. With *Criminology*'s publication, Sutherland began the process of capturing the study of crime causation for the field of sociology.

Sutherland suggested that crime was not solely the result of internal factors. This flew in the face of those who advocated sterilization and other medical procedures—an idea in vogue both in the United States and Europe at the time—to address the problem of born criminals or inherited criminality. Sutherland held that individual personal traits are important, but what is more important is how those traits relate to the culture in which a person lives. The culture includes groups large and small, ranging from the culture of an entire nation to that of a particular city, to that of a local neighborhood, and most importantly, the cultures of a person's peer and family groups. In short, Sutherland believed that criminal behavior, like many other behaviors, was not inherited but was learned, and decisions to commit crime are based on rational decisions, rather than being the product of a diseased mind.

Sutherland revised *Criminology* three times, in 1934, 1939, and in 1947. (One of his students, Donald Cressey, revised *Criminology* several times after Sutherland's death.) In his 1939 edition, Sutherland laid out his general theory of criminal behavior and called it "differential association," a theory that is still one of the basic staples of criminology textbooks today. Sutherland's differential association theory originally contained seven propositions, with two more added to the 1947 edition of *Criminology:*

1. Criminal behavior is learned.
2. Criminal behavior is learned in interaction with other persons in a process of communication.
3. The principle part of the learning of criminal behavior occurs within intimate personal groups.

4. When criminal behavior is learned, the learning includes techniques of committing the crime, some complicated and some simple, and the specific direction of motives and attitudes.

5. The specific direction of motives and drives is learned from definitions of the legal codes as favorable or unfavorable.

6. A person becomes delinquent because of an excess of definitions favorable to violation of the law over definitions unfavorable to violation of the law.

7. Differential associations may vary in frequency, duration, priority, and intensity.

8. The process of learning criminal behavior by association with criminal and anticriminal patterns involves all of the mechanisms that are involved in any other learning.

9. Criminal behavior is an expression of needs and values, but it is not explained by those general needs and values since noncriminal behavior is an expression of the same needs and values.

Sutherland was active in other research pursuits during the same time frame. He also changed jobs frequently. Sutherland worked at the University of Minnesota from 1926–1929, then as a researcher with the Bureau of Social Hygiene in New York City from 1929–1930, and as a faculty member with the University of Chicago from 1930–1935. Sutherland took a position with Indiana University in 1935 and remained there for the rest of his career.

One of Sutherland's strengths was that he was not an adherent to any particular method of research. He saw both qualitative and quantitative methods for what they are, means to an end rather than ends in themselves. He made great use of the qualitative method in his research for *The Professional Thief,* which was published in 1937. *The Professional Thief* was the result of detailed questionnaires and more than 80 hours of personal interviews between Sutherland and Chic Conwell, a thief who had been in the business of stealing for more than twenty years, most of his entire adolescent and adult life. The book's table of contents attributes authorship of the book to Chic Conwell, with Sutherland providing annotation.

The Professional Thief paved the way for Sutherland's differential association theory, which would be disseminated two years later. Sutherland opens the book by stating that the professional thief devotes his entire time and energy to larceny, that all thefts are carefully planned, and that the thief has technical skills necessary to perform his job, just as any other professional. Thievery is its own profession, with a code of ethics (a rather questionable conclusion), a professional subculture, and so on. Sutherland provided a glimpse into the mind of a person that thought of himself as a professional criminal, an unusual research venture for its time, and more importantly, one of several groundbreaking qualitative studies conducted through the University of Chicago's sociology department.

In terms of public policy impact, perhaps the most significant work of Sutherland's career was *White Collar Crime,* which was released in 1949. This book introduced the term *white collar crime* into the English vocabulary, but Sutherland had been using it in writings and speeches ten years before the publication of the book. Actually he had been working and refining the concept for more than twenty-five years prior to the book's publication.

The stock market crash in October 1929 signaled the beginning of the Great Depression, a time when millions of Americans were stricken by bankruptcy, unemployment, poverty, and even starvation in many instances. As the number of poor people skyrocketed during the 1930s, so did the study of crime. The Uniform Crime Report, the first attempt to systematically measure crime in the United States, debuted in the 1930s.

Prior to the 1930s, practically all crime studies had focused on crimes committed by the lower class and the poor. What had been neglected were the misdeeds of the upper class. The stock market crash and its aftermath brought into focus a number of unsavory shenanigans committed by big business during the 1920s. In 1932, a public utility tycoon from Chicago named Samuel Insull was charged with mail fraud and embezzlement. Insull's 1934 trial resulted in acquittal. The public outrage over Insull's behavior and his acquittal prompted Congress and President Franklin Roosevelt to authorize creation of the Securities and Exchange Commission, still the primary agency charged with investigating and prosecuting financial crime. Sutherland, also outraged over Insull's acquittal, began studying white collar crime.

Although Sutherland had broken formal ties with his Baptist church roots years earlier, his religious background was still very much in evidence in his attitudes about white collar crime. According to Sutherland, the legal statutes alone should not determine whether something is, in the moral sense, a crime. There must be a higher concept than the law to judge the morality of human actions. He believed that crime was spread among all of the economic classes and not confined to the poor. Plus, Sutherland was a great supporter and believer in American capitalism. Corrupt businessmen, thought Sutherland, were the archenemies of American capitalism.

Sutherland put his background in political economy to work with his white collar crime studies. He researched crimes committed by seventy large business firms during the late 1920s and early 1930s. He found almost 1,000 convictions spread among the seventy firms. The offenses included embezzlement, misappropriation of funds, violation of antitrust laws, patent infringement, and other unfair trade practices. He defined white collar crime as "a violation of criminal law by a person of the upper socioeconomic class in the course of his occupational activity."

Sutherland's first public revelation of his white collar crime concept came in a 1939 speech, titled "The White Collar Criminal," before the American Sociological Society (ASS). He published two journal articles on the subject, one in the *American Sociological Review* in 1940 and the other in *The Annals of the American Academy of Political and Social Science* in 1941, prior to the publication of *White Collar Crime* in 1949. Under pressure from publishers and Indiana University administrators, Sutherland deleted most of the names and identifying information before the book was published. A subsequent edition, released in 1983, was uncut and included the names Sutherland was coerced into deleting.

If numbers alone determined success, Sutherland would not stand out in the field of sociology. If actual impact on criminological thought is important, Sutherland is without peers among academics. His work did not go unnoticed by criminal justice professionals, including FBI director J. Edgar Hoover, who had the Bureau keep secret files on Sutherland, carefully monitoring his writings and public appearances. No one knows just how much Sutherland had stored in his mind that was never published. Many of his writings were simply passed out to a class for discussion and critique and were never published. Sutherland authored four books, three of which stand as classic works in the field of criminology and criminal justice, even today, over fifty years after the last of these three books was published.

From his arrival at Indiana University in 1935, Sutherland chaired the sociology department, the first person to hold that title. Failing health led to his resignation as chair in 1949, but he remained on the faculty. Sutherland died of a stroke on October 11, 1950, while walking to work in Bloomington, Indiana. He was sixty-seven years old.

SOURCES AND SUGGESTED READINGS

Chic Conwell and Edwin Hardin Sutherland, *The Professional Thief* (Chicago: University of Chicago Press, 1937).

Lawrence M. Friedman, *Crime and Punishment in American History* (New York: Basic Books, 1992).

John F. Galliher, "Edwin Hardin Sutherland," *American National Biography Online*, February 2000. www.anb.org, August 19, 2002.

Mike Forrest Keen, *Stalking the Sociological Imagination: J. Edgar Hoover's FBI Surveillance of American Sociology* (Westport, CT: Greenwood, 1999).

Randy Martin, Robert J. Mutchnick, and W. Timothy Austin, *Criminological Thought: Pioneers Past and Present* (New York: Macmillan, 1990).

Edwin H. Sutherland, *Principles of Criminology* (4th ed.) (Philadelphia: J.B. Lippincott, 1947).

———. *White Collar Crime: The Uncut Version* (New Haven, CT: Yale University Press, 1983).

George B. Vold and T. J. Bernard, *Theoretical Criminology* (3rd ed.) (New York: Oxford University Press, 1986).

DISCUSSION QUESTIONS

1. In what ways has Edwin Sutherland impacted criminal justice policy?
2. What does Sutherland's career say to criminal justice students about the importance of understanding other academic disciplines?

CHAPTER 2

ROBERT MERTON
(1910–2003)

Some people believe that a professor's duty is to make the world a better place through their teaching, research, and public service. Others believe that if they cannot make the world better, perhaps they can at least explain in understandable terms how the world works. This is true in both the physical and the social sciences. Although some professors do this job well and some do not, no professor did a better job of explaining crime than Robert Merton. With the possible exception of Edwin Sutherland, no criminologist has had a greater impact on crime-related policy or the way that the public perceives the causes of crime than Merton. Like Sutherland, Merton also bears the distinction of introducing scientific terms into everyday vocabulary and making an impact on everyday life and language, even outside the realm of criminology.

Robert King Merton, the son of Jewish immigrants from Eastern Europe, was born Meyer Schkolnick on July 4 (or 5), 1910, in the slums of South Philadelphia, Pennsylvania. His father scraped out a living by working at a number of jobs, including carpentry, truck driving, and selling dairy products. Meyer Schkolnick developed a love of books early in life, but he was also streetwise. Merton once stated that growing up in Philadelphia provided him "with every sort of capital—social capital, cultural capital, human capital, and above all, what we may call public capital." The young Meyer Schkolnick also developed a fondness for magic—and an aptitude for slight of hand—and began performing shows in public around age twelve. He decided to take the stage name Robert Merlin, in deference to the mythical medieval magician, but was persuaded that the name Merlin was a cliche. He had his name legally changed to Robert Merton within a few years.

Merton graduated from South Philadelphia High School for Boys in 1927 and entered Temple College on a scholarship. His initial interest was philosophy but he soon became enamored with the fledgling field of sociology. He graduated in 1931 and entered Harvard University to pursue a graduate degree in sociology. Merton was part of the first cohort of graduate students to enter Harvard's sociology department. He graduated with his Ph.D. in 1936. In 1934, while he was at Harvard, Merton met and married Suzanne Carhart, a social worker. The couple had three children.

Merton stayed at Harvard as an instructor after graduation. He soon realized that he would not be able to attain a position as a professor; in fact no new positions were created during Merton's time there because of the impact of the Great Depression. Merton had always been fascinated with New Orleans, and when he realized

Harvard was a dead end, he decided he wanted to live somewhere besides the Northeast. When a position at Tulane University was offered to him in 1939, he accepted. Within two years, Merton had achieved the rank of full professor and department chair. In 1941, Merton left Tulane for Columbia University for an Assistant Professor position, where he would spend the rest of his career. While at Columbia, Merton would make the contributions to crime, American culture, and sociology that made him famous.

The Great Depression profoundly affected Merton's intellectual development and worldview. Like other sociologists of his time, Merton observed "the collapsing and deregulation of social traditions and the effect that it had on both individuals and the institutions of society." He was strongly influenced by President Franklin Roosevelt's attempt to rebuild societal structures through his New Deal programs.

One of the lessons that many modern professors can learn from Merton is his insistence on reading the original works of great authors and thinkers, instead of merely reading from modern text writers that discuss the great thinkers. His reasons for doing so mirror those who advocate the study of history. Merton believed that students should study the classics because:

1. It avoids reinventing the wheel;
2. It aids in the clear formulation of ideas;
3. It ensures that ideas will stand up to previously issued challenges;
4. It provides a model for theory development; and
5. The reader gleans something different each time a classic work is read.

Merton's 1965 book *On the Shoulders of Giants* expands on that idea and on the complex connections between accumulated past knowledge and new contributions. The title of his book was taken from Isaac Newton, who once said, "If I have seen farther, it is by standing on the shoulders of giants." The book explores the history of the phrase, so often attributed to Newton, and traces it back to Bernard of Chartes, a twelfth-century French philosopher. By standing on a giant's shoulders, we get a better view of the future, that is, the past provides the basis for new contributions to knowledge but is not their only source.

Merton was the cofounder of the "focus group," an achievement that will solidify his place in American history. Now a staple of commercial marketing and political campaigns, Merton came across the concept somewhat by accident. At the request of Paul Lazarsfeld, a colleague, Merton went to a radio studio where Lazarsfeld wanted his assistance in observing a small audience's reactions to a radio program. Merton and Lazarsfeld became fascinated with what was occurring, and brainstormed on ways to improve the process. Together Merton and Lazarsfeld founded the Bureau of Applied Social Research at Columbia. There the focus group idea was refined and used in a more sophisticated fashion; later the focus group was so frequently used and abused that it repulsed Merton, who wished he had gotten a royalty from the concept.

Merton also played a part in one of the most significant decisions ever handed down by the United States Supreme Court. In 1954, under the leadership of newly confirmed Chief Justice Earl Warren, the Court ruled unconstitutional the "separate but equal" doctrine that had perpetuated racial segregation for several decades; the ruling was handed down in *Brown v. Board of Education of Topeka.* In his writings, Merton had written about the benefits of racially integrated communities and Kenneth Clark, one of the attorneys preparing a brief for the Supreme Court, worked with Merton on the arguments presented to the Court.

Merton made great contributions to sociology and other facets of American society. He is also regarded as one of the premier criminological theorists of the twentieth century. The four concepts that defined Merton's contributions to criminological thought are ones that are basic to all students of criminology today. They are (1) *anomie,* (2) *strain,* (3) *self-fulfilling prophecy,* and (4) *role model.*

Anomie was a term Merton borrowed from the French sociologist Emile Durkheim. It refers to a state of normlessness, usually caused by a sudden social upheaval. An individual cannot cope with the new rules or the lack of rules, which leads to strain or a sense that nothing matters.

Strain, which Merton devised while he was in his twenties, has been the most dominant criminological theory of the past sixty years. It has guided policy decisions for decades, especially during the 1960s, as it meshed with the ideology of the Kennedy and Johnson presidential administrations. More specifically, it spun off opportunity theory, which laid the theoretical groundwork for the Mobilization for Youth program of the 1960s. Merton's theory suggests that most or all individuals in American society strive for the common goal of material success. Stumbling blocks such as poverty, racism, or class bias stand in the way of some people attaining those goals, and those individuals choose one of five mindsets to guide their behavior. These options are (1) conformity, meaning that they accept both the goals and the legitimate (i.e., legal) means of achieving those goals; (2) they may innovate, meaning that they accept the goals but reject the legal means of achieving them; (3) ritualism, in which they do not accept the goals but go through the motions of achieving them; and (4) they may retreat, rejecting both the goals and the means of achieving success; (5) they may rebel, meaning that the individual goes outside the social structure in order to change it.

Another important contribution to the study of criminology from Merton is his idea of the self-fulfilling prophecy, a phrase that has made its way into the everyday American vocabulary. The self-fulfilling prophecy provides an example of Merton's idea to blend creativity with simplicity in a way that makes people wonder why they had never thought of it themselves. The term first surfaced in 1948, in an *Antioch Review* article penned by Merton. The *self-fulfilling prophecy* is a false definition of a situation, that is, it is a prediction that is false, not true, but then becomes the basis for "a new behavior which makes the originally false conception come true." In other words, it is the belief that bad or good will happen. The self-fulfilling prophecy has found applications in all spheres of life, including criminology. It laid the groundwork for labeling theory, in which a person, usually a child, is labeled delinquent from an early age, treated as a delinquent, and the child actively fulfills the role imposed by that label.

The term *role model* is used in everyday language throughout the English-speaking world. It too owes its existence to Merton. One answer to delinquency is the presence of individuals that can make a positive difference in the life of a child; by the same token, negative role models can lead a child down the path to delinquency.

Merton retired from Columbia in 1979, assuming the title of university professor emeritus, but he stayed active, usually arising at 4:30 each morning. He married again, to a sociologist named Harriet Zuckerman. In 1994, Merton received a National Medal of Science from President Bill Clinton, becoming the first sociologist to receive such an honor. Merton was cited for "founding the sociology of science and pioneering contributions to the study of social life, especially the self-fulfilling prophecy and the unintended consequences of social action." One magazine interviewer described Merton as possessing "a surprising catholicity of interests and a talent for good conversation, alarmingly well informed about everything from baseball to Kant and ready to tell anybody about it."

During his last years, Merton, while battling six forms of cancer, published a book on the topic of serendipitous scientific discovery, long an interest area of his. On February 20, 2003, he was informed that the book would be published. Merton, nicknamed Mr. Sociology, died three days later on February 23 in New York City at the age of ninety-two. When Merton died, the mainstream media, including ABC, the Cable News Network, the *New York Times,* and all the major British and Italian newspapers, carried his obituary; such was his recognition outside the boundaries of his academic discipline. His son Robert, a Nobel laureate for his work as an economist, said of his father, "If there were a Nobel Prize in sociology, there would be no question he would have gotten it" (Kaufman, 2003).

SOURCES AND SUGGESTED READINGS

Michael T. Kaufman, "Robert K. Merton, Versatile Sociologist and Father of the Focus Group, Dies at 92." *New York Times,* February 24, 2003.

Randy Martin, Robert J. Mutchnick, and W. Timothy Austin, *Criminological Thought: Pioneers Past and Present* (New York: Macmillan, 1990).

Piotr Sztompka, *Robert K. Merton, An Intellectual Profile* (New York: St. Martin's Press, 1986).

George B. Vold and Thomas J. Bernard, *Theoretical Criminology* (3rd ed.) (New York: Oxford University Press, 1986).

DISCUSSION QUESTIONS

1. What has been Merton's impact on the field of criminology? What has been his impact on issues outside the criminology arena?
2. In what ways might it be beneficial for criminal justice students to emulate Robert Merton?

CHAPTER 3

JAMES Q. WILSON
(1931–   )

An unfortunate aspect of academic life is the tendency of professors and researchers to cluster in the academy with their colleagues, to the exclusion of those in the outside world. Since the 1960s one scholar that has risen above such academic isolationism is James Q. Wilson, one of the most prolific and influential public policy scholars of the past four decades. Wilson has had considerable impact on several areas of public policy and social thought, and his most significant impact has been in the area of theories of crime causation and approaches to policing. Criminal justice historian Samuel Walker wrote that Wilson set the tone for criminal justice policy for several decades with his statement that "wicked people need to be separated from the rest of us." Although Wilson rejects the idea that one person, including him, can produce that sort of impact by himself, Wilson's impact on crime and public policy has been significant.

James Quinn (his maternal grandfather's name) Wilson was born in Denver, Colorado, on May 27, 1931, and grew up in Long Beach, California, the state where, as Wilson says, America was headed in the 1930s and 1940s. He received an A.B. degree in political science from the University of the Redlands in 1952. Soon after graduating he entered the Navy and rose to the rank of Lieutenant Junior Grade. After being discharged in 1955, Wilson entered graduate school at the University of Chicago and graduated with a Ph.D. in political science in 1959. Wilson married Roberta, his childhood sweetheart from California.

Looking back at Wilson's early life, his successful career as an academician was predictable. However, like many academic pioneers in criminal justice, he had to make his own way in a new academic discipline that did not enjoy the benefit of decades of precedent as guidance. His first job after obtaining his Ph.D. was as instructor in the University of Chicago's Political Science Department. While he was in graduate school at Chicago, he never took a course in criminology or criminal justice and he showed no interest in the field that would garner him fame in later years. With few exceptions, universities in the 1950s did not even recognize the study of criminal justice as an academic endeavor.

One fortuitous factor that steered Wilson toward criminal justice was attending the University of Chicago. Although Wilson devoted little if any attention to the study of criminal justice while attending Chicago, he was at one of the few universities that had already established a national reputation for the study of crime causation, but that reputation had been established by sociologists, not by political scientists. However, University of Chicago political scientists, due in part to being located in one of America's largest cities, devoted considerable efforts to the study of urban politics. Wilson's first two books, *Negro Politics,* published in 1960 (when Wilson was only twenty-nine years old), and *The Amateur Democrat,* published in 1961, reflected this interest. Wilson moved from Chicago to Harvard University in 1961 as a lecturer in government, and was promoted to the rank of associate professor in 1963.

Wilson claims that he became a criminologist by accident. He wanted to study cities and African American politics, not crime, but history would intervene to change the direction of Wilson's academic career. In the early 1960s, the academic community exhibited an increasing curiosity about how America's criminal justice system functioned. Additionally, a historically significant event would steer Wilson to the study of crime. The 1964 Presidential election pitted incumbent democrat Lyndon Johnson against an abrasive republican challenger from Arizona, Senator Barry Goldwater. Goldwater's campaign featured blunt, acid rhetoric, accusing Johnson and the Democrats of being soft on defense, communism, and crime.

Johnson won the 1964 election in a landslide, but Goldwater's accusation of being soft on crime stung Johnson, and he resolved to address crime and criminal justice in the United States. He established a blue ribbon commission to conduct a multiyear, comprehensive study of the state of crime and criminal justice in the United States. Johnson's commission, which included experts from all areas of America touched by crime, also formed a scientific advisory committee, one member of which was Harvard University's James Vorenberg. Vorenberg, a friend and colleague of Wilson's, advised Wilson to assume an active role in the work of the presidential commission. Wilson replied that he was unqualified and knew nothing about crime. Vorenberg told Wilson not to worry, neither did anyone else; so Wilson started reading up on crime.

Wilson was later appointed to serve on the Science Advisory Committee of President Johnson's Commission on Law Enforcement and the Administration of Justice from 1966–1967. Wilson's star rose within the Johnson administration. He chaired the White House Task Force on Crime in 1967 and cochaired Vice President Hubert Humphrey's Task Force on Order and Justice in 1968. In a 1968 publication titled *Varieties of Police Behavior,* Wilson differentiated three styles of police behavior:

1. The watchman, with an order maintenance function, who uses the law as a means of maintaining order rather than regulating conduct.
2. The legalistic officer, who sets a single standard for the community and enforces the law even if public order is not breached; and
3. The service officer, or the officer who responds as the community desires but is less likely to make an arrest.

While at Harvard, Wilson met Daniel Patrick Moynihan, an astute, outspoken political liberal and renowned author with an immense measure of political and intellectual talent, and a man who had political ambitions and connections to match his talent. Moynihan would go on to serve as United States ambassador to the

United Nations and as a United States senator. Although Moynihan, a liberal demo-crat, and Wilson, who would eventually join the Republican Party, were often on opposite ends of the political spectrum, they remained fast friends and colleagues from the time they met until Moynihan's death. When asked how such a friendship can endure so many political differences, Wilson says that such is the stuff that makes America great and unique.

During Richard Nixon's presidency (1969–1974), Moynihan told Nixon that he simply had to meet James Wilson, because Wilson was the "smartest man in America." Nixon asked Wilson to head the National Advisory Commission on Drug Abuse Prevention, which he did from 1972–1973. Wilson concluded that the Commission was doing nothing that had a positive impact. He suggested to Nixon that the Commission be abolished. Nixon agreed, but he asked that Wilson appear before Congress and advocate the creation of the Drug Enforcement Administra-tion. Wilson and Nixon's efforts were successful and the DEA was created in 1973.

Wilson's writings on crime began receiving more prominent notice during the 1970s. President Gerald Ford, who succeeded Nixon in 1974, was so impressed with Wilson's *Thinking About Crime* that he invited him to the White House to discuss his views in December of 1974. Ford subscribed to Wilson's analysis of core crime issues, namely that most crime is committed by repeat offenders, that the certainty of imprisonment deters crime, and that crime victims deserved more attention than they were getting from the criminal justice system. Ford also agreed with Wilson's belief that local governments could combat crime more effectively than the federal government, and that correctional rehabilitation efforts were much like social welfare policies that not only failed to deliver, but had actually made bad situations worse. Says Wilson, "Our goal is not to enlarge the welfare system but to change it. All about us lies the wreckage of the therapeutic state."

More important than his specific proposals on crime control was his basic moral stance in *Thinking About Crime*—that wicked people exist and that they had to be set apart from innocent people. Moral terms such as *wicked* had been absent from academic discussions about crime for several decades, decades in which soci-etal conditions were viewed as the prime factor in crime causation. While Wilson continued writing about crime and serving on the Harvard faculty, he served Presi-dent Reagan as an adviser on foreign intelligence, overlooking international activi-ties of the Central Intelligence Agency, which had fallen into disrepute with many Americans by the 1970s.

One of the most significant writings of Wilson's career was an article he co-authored with George Kelling for *The Atlantic* in 1982. In that article he and Kelling laid out a prescription for addressing crime in neighborhoods called the "fixing broken windows" approach, which has become a staple of criminal justice study and police work around the country over the past twenty years. The basic premise of broken windows crime prevention is that public order is as important a goal for the police as catching criminals. A subordinate but unverifiable argument is that crime flourishes in neighborhoods that have fallen into disrepair, where panhandling and drug dealing occur in the open, where dilapidated houses serve as meeting places for criminals, and where it appears that neither the police nor the neighborhood residents care about the quality of life in the neighborhood, and that little crimes lead to bigger crimes. The solution is to clean up the neighborhoods, tear down abandoned buildings, harass petty street criminals, and try to improve the overall quality of life in neighborhoods, all of which involve aggressive policing.

No proposal from an academic has made as great an impact on criminal justice policy as the broken windows idea. Police departments large and small around the country have implemented the broken windows approach. Some credit the broken windows approach with the precipitous decline in crime in New York City during the 1990s.

During a telephone interview with Wilson, I informed him that his broken windows idea was being applied outside the context of policing. In fact, a book on housekeeping advocated the broken windows idea in house cleaning. Keep a house clean by performing small maintenance chores regularly, and those who live in the house will take greater pride in keeping the house clean rather than using it as a dumping ground. Wilson laughed at the idea at first, but then stated that he actually applies the broken windows idea to his neighborhood. His house is the only one on his street, and trucks frequently come by, their drivers often depositing their trash on the street. Even though most of the street is not part of his property, Wilson cleans the trash from the street regularly, realizing that a dirty street will simply invite more dirt and trash. According to Wilson, "Arresting a single drunk or a single vagrant who has harmed no identifiable person seems unjust, and in a sense it is. But failing to do anything about a score of drunks or a hundred vagrants may destroy an entire community."

Wilson has been the target of criticism, especially from the political left. He has never shied away from mentioning race as a factor in crime, noting that African Americans are involved in violent crime in higher numbers than other ethnic groups, and he does not attribute factors outside the person as the prime cause of crime. Wilson has been accused of being too conservative, and has even been accused of promoting "scientific racism," or using scientific methods to suggest that African Americans are more prone to commit crime than other racial groups. Charges like this anger Wilson, who states that it is a fact that African Americans are involved in a disproportionate amount of violent crime, that no one explanation can be offered for this involvement, and that social scientists should be seriously engaged in discovering why this phenomenon occurs.

Wilson believes that his unpopularity with the political left also stems from his steadfast and unchanging belief in punishment. According to Wilson, mainstream Americans believe that moral concepts such as punishment have a place in the criminal justice system, but social leftists that dominate colleges and universities do not share that belief.

Wilson is a strong believer in the traditional two-parent family, sex within the context of marriage, and the value of religious influence on young people. He sees the dissolution of the traditional American family as a prime factor in crime causation, and he sees modern culture as a prime factor in that dissolution. Wilson claims that Americans are materially better off than their parents but spiritually worse off. In a 2002 lecture televised on C-Span, Wilson delivered an address on his book *The Marriage Problem*. A female audience member asked at what point in history marriage became the norm for human relationships. He simply replied, "With Eve."

Despite his advocacy of traditional Judeo-Christian principles and behaviors, Wilson is not devoutly religious. He simply sees traditional conservative values as the bulwark of a civilized society. He also argues that the impact of religious beliefs is scientifically testable, and that it is correlated with avoiding crime.

Wilson retired from Harvard in 1987 and moved to California. He served as professor of management and public policy at the University of California at Los Angeles until his retirement. He currently serves as professor emeritus of management at UCLA, and he is active with the American Enterprise Institute for Public Policy, a conservative thinktank. Wilson continues to write and deliver lectures, never wavering from the beliefs about crime, social mores, and ethics that he has espoused since the 1960s. Of all Wilson's writings and quotes, perhaps one more than any other captures both his wry wit and his philosophy about dealing with crime: "There are no more liberals; they have all been mugged."

SOURCES AND SUGGESTED READINGS

American Enterprise Institute Website, www.aei.org, November 28, 2001.

Brainy Media, www.brainymedia.com, November 28, 2001.

George L. Kelling, Catherine M. Coles, and James Q. Wilson, *Fixing Broken Windows: Restoring Order and Reducing Crime in Our Communities* (New York: Touchstone Books, 1998).

Newshour Website, www.newshour.org, November 28, 2001.

James Q. Wilson, November 20, 2001, telephone interview.

James Q. Wilson, *The Marriage Problem: How Our Culture Has Weakened Families* (New York: Harper Collins, 2002).

James Q. Wilson, curriculum vitae.

James Q. Wilson, *Thinking About Crime*, Revised Edition (New York: Basic Books, 1983).

James Q. Wilson, *Varieties of Police Behavior* (Cambridge, MA: Harvard University Press, 1968).

James Q. Wilson, *The Amateur Democrat* (Chicago, IL: University of Chicago Press, 1966).

James Q. Wilson, *Negro Politics: The Search for Leadership* (New York: Free Press, 1960).

James Q. Wilson and G. L. Kelling, 1982. "Broken Windows." *The Atlantic Monthly* 249 (3): 29–38.

James Q. Wilson and Richard Hernstein, *Crime and Human Nature* (New York: Simon and Schuster, 1985).

DISCUSSION QUESTIONS

1. How has James Wilson impacted policing over the past three decades?
2. Do you think that James Wilson has driven changes in criminal justice policy, or have his ideas merely reflected the evolving sentiments of the general public?

CHAPTER 4

ALLAN PINKERTON
(1819–1884)

Private entrepreneurs were much more central to the development of American law enforcement than is often thought. Early innovations in security and sophisticated criminal investigation came primarily from the private sector, and many of those innovations are traceable to the work of Allan Pinkerton, a Scottish immigrant who was a first-class detective, an enormously successful businessman, and America's first private eye.

Allan Pinkerton was born on July 21 (or August 25), 1819, in Glasgow, Scotland, the fourth son of William and Isabella McQueen Pinkerton. Pinkerton was raised in the Gorbals area of Glasgow, one of the poorest, most vice-ridden, and polluted communities in Scotland. Although the Pinkertons were not poor, especially compared to many others in the Gorbals area, their life was far from luxuriant. William Pinkerton worked as a handloom weaver during much of Allan's childhood, but in 1819 he began working in the Glasgow city gaol (jail). Pinkerton had some formal education, but his father's death in 1830 made further education impossible. Like most boys in his community, Pinkerton learned a trade—in his case, coopering (barrel making)—by apprenticing.

Allan Pinkerton's subsequent interest in investigation and security did not stem from any wish to follow in his father's footsteps. In fact, his life as a young adult seemed more a portent of life as a jail inmate than as a detective. Pinkerton immersed himself into a radical political organization called the Chartists. The Chartists, who had confederates and sympathizers throughout Scotland, Wales, England, and Ireland, espoused ideas contrary to the sentiments of many mainstream political officials in nineteenth-century Great Britain, including temperance (abstinence from alcohol), women's suffrage, the abolition of slavery throughout the British Empire, and the right of workers to organize and bargain collectively.

Pinkerton's life as a young man is shrouded in myth and mystery, some of it attributable to Pinkerton himself. In later years, he embellished some of his early exploits. For instance, he claimed that his marriage was conducted secretly. Actually, church records document his marriage to fifteen-year-old Joan Carfrae in 1842. The Pinkertons had four daughters and three sons.

The story behind Pinkerton's decision to leave for North America is murky as well. Pinkerton claimed that he and his wife had to be smuggled aboard a ship for Canada because he was on the run from government authorities because of his Chartist activities. Though his concerns over criminal prosecution may have been legitimate, the likely reason for leaving Great Britain was economic; the chances of making a good living were better in North America. The Pinkertons were not smuggled aboard a ship; they went as registered passengers aboard a commercial vessel bound for Montreal. Pinkerton paid his way by working as the ship's cooper. The Pinkertons arrived in Montreal in May 1842, where he worked as a cooper. Believing that his job prospects would be better in the United States, the Pinkertons moved to Warsaw, Illinois, and later settled in Dundee, a predominantly Scottish immigrant town northwest of Chicago.

Pinkerton's first brush with detective work came by accident. While searching for wood on a small Fox River island, Pinkerton stumbled on a counterfeiting operation. Pinkerton, the local sheriff, and several other Dundee residents raided the island, which was subsequently tabbed Bogus Island to commemorate the counterfeiting bust, and arrested the counterfeiters. His first brush with detective work whetted his appetite for more.

Pinkerton had a reputation as an honest, hardworking craftsman, but his business and personal reputation encountered misfortune severe enough to force his relocation to Chicago. The problem was not financial or political, but religious. Throughout his life, Pinkerton, the son of atheists, never claimed to be devoutly religious, and he attended church more for the sake of social convention than for spiritual enlightenment. Pinkerton's lack of zeal for worship resulted in local townspeople believing he was an atheist. His church placed him on trial for atheism, with the threat of expulsion from the church looming. Pinkerton acquitted himself well, but many townspeople began avoiding him and his family. His business suffered, and when the offer to work as a deputy sheriff in Cook County (Chicago) came along in 1847, Pinkerton jumped at the chance to leave Dundee.

Pinkerton's career as a deputy was unremarkable, but his reputation as a tough, smart, and honest officer grew throughout Chicago. Pinkerton's good name in Chicago political circles led to his appointment as the first detective in the history of the Chicago Police Department in 1849. Political differences led to his dismissal from the police department in 1850, but he quickly assumed a position as a mail agent with the United States Post Office, his primary job being the investigation of commercial theft. While working as a mail agent, Pinkerton also conducted private investigations as a sideline.

In 1856 Pinkerton established a detective agency with Edward Rucker, with Rucker functioning as a silent partner. Pinkerton established principles from which the agency never deviated, at least during his lifetime. The principles were mostly a list of do's and don'ts that reflected Pinkerton's overall philosophy of detective work: (1) Agents could not represent a criminal defendant in court; (2) they could not shadow jurors, public officials, or union representatives; and (3) they could not get involved in divorces or marital disputes.

Pinkerton's successful foray into private detective work was attributable to several factors:

1. His unswerving devotion to hard work and his absolute insistence that those under him work just as hard. Pinkerton, a prime example of the *type A* personality long before the term entered the English vocabulary, typically worked eighteen to twenty hours each day, often getting by on less than four hours sleep per night.

2. Pinkerton was smart and good at what he did. He was an astute businessman (though his tendency to micromanage would hurt him as his agency grew), and he was one of the most effective and most innovative detectives of his day. Pinkerton was excellent at old-fashioned detective techniques such as using informants and using force (often more than would be tolerated today) to exact information. He was also good at networking and establishing good relations with police agencies around the country, unlike many law enforcers of his day.

3. His eagerness to use emerging technology to better his detective work. A prime example was his use of daguerreotyping, a nineteenth-century forerunner of modern photography. Unlike most of his Neanderthal counterparts in municipal police agencies that considered such technology useless, Pinkerton used the daguerreotype to maintain his own gallery of known criminals he encountered. He would circulate posters of wanted men or suspects to his agents and other police agencies, often meeting with great success.

4. The fact that federal law enforcement, for the most part, did not exist. Throughout most of the nineteenth century, there were no federal law enforcement agencies. The FBI, now the closest thing the United States has to a national police force, would not come into existence until the twentieth century. On the relatively rare occasion when the federal government needed law enforcement services, it would usually contract with a local agency or with a private entity. Pinkerton was a frequent recipient of these contracts. As the United States expanded geographically and as Americans became more mobile during the nineteenth century, crime expanded and criminals became more mobile as well. Fleeing to another state after committing a crime was a common means of beating the law because local law enforcement officials had no authority in states beside their own. As a private entrepreneur, Pinkerton was not limited by jurisdiction. He was one of the few people empowered to pursue criminals across state lines.

5. The expansion of the railroad industry. One of the primary forces in the increased mobility of the American population during the nineteenth century was the railroad. With the railroad, Americans no longer had to rely on horses for transportation. With railroads being used to transport passengers and cargo, theft and robbery became an increasing menace to the burgeoning railroad industry. Since local law enforcement was of no use to interstate industries like the railroad, and since there were no federal agencies to employ, railroad management turned to private organizations to ensure security. The Pinkerton agency offered the best protection.

Pinkerton secured contracts with most of the railroad companies of his day. During the course of securing these contracts, he often met with company officials that would be of great benefit to him in other arenas. Two examples were George McClellan and Abraham Lincoln. Pinkerton met McClellan while the latter served as vice president of the Illinois Central railroad company. Though both men were of Scottish extraction, they were different in almost every other respect. McClellan was handsome, charismatic, and well educated (United States Military Academy); Pinkerton was dour, humorless, and of less than noble extraction. Yet the two men developed a strong friendship that would serve them well for the remainder of their lives.

At the time Pinkerton met Abraham Lincoln, Lincoln was a rising star in Illinois republican circles. Lincoln had served terms in the United States Congress and in the Illinois legislature, and he was enjoying a prosperous career as an attorney. One of Lincoln's clients was the Illinois Central railroad, for which he negotiated a security arrangement with the Pinkerton Detective Agency. Pinkerton had much in common with Lincoln; both came from humble origins and had little formal education but were very intelligent; neither man was physically attractive; neither was devoutly religious; and both had critics that viewed them as crude and ill-mannered.

Despite their similarities, Pinkerton's relationship with Lincoln would always be strictly professional. Pinkerton would always be more loyal to George McClellan, the man who would go on to command union forces during the Civil War, only to be fired by Lincoln, and then go on to run for president in an unsuccessful attempt to unseat Lincoln. Nevertheless, Pinkerton's close relationship with both men would serve him and the country well during the 1860s.

In late 1860 and early 1861, on the heels of Lincoln's election to the presidency, several southern states seceded from the United States. Although Lincoln was resolved to preserve the Union at any cost, many Americans, including Pinkerton, were willing to let the South go. Pinkerton, like many Americans, changed his mind when Confederate forces fired on Union forces at Fort Sumter, South Carolina, on April 12, 1861. One of the primary issues that divided north and south was slavery. Just as he vehemently opposed slavery as a Chartist in Great Britain, Pinkerton abhorred American slavery as well. On one occasion Pinkerton observed a slave auction in Louisville, and thought it utterly vile and revolting.

Lincoln probably would have not lived to assume the presidency if not for Pinkerton. In February 1861, as Lincoln was leaving Springfield, Illinois, for Washington, DC, to be inaugurated, Pinkerton learned of a plot to assassinate Lincoln in Baltimore. Since much of Maryland, especially Baltimore, sympathized with the South, the threat did not surprise Pinkerton. Pinkerton took immediate steps to protect Lincoln. Before Lincoln's train left Harrisburg, Pennsylvania, for Baltimore, Pinkerton instructed his agents to cut all telegraph lines between Pennsylvania and Baltimore, lest the conspirators be alerted to Lincoln's whereabouts. Pinkerton agents were posted on the train with Lincoln and along the route as well. Rather than spending the night in Baltimore as planned, the train secretly passed through Baltimore after a brief stop and proceeded to Washington.

When Lincoln decided to wage war on the south, he persuaded George McClellan to resign his position with the railroad and assume the rank of major general in the Union army. When the issue of intelligence gathering and spying arose, both McClellan and Lincoln, especially McClellan, had no doubt about whom to contact. Pinkerton gladly offered his services. Throughout the course of the American Civil War (1861–1865), Pinkerton and his operatives conducted intelligence-gathering operations throughout the South and the North. In the North, and in Union states with large numbers of southern sympathizers, Pinkerton and his operatives would search out and arrest southern spies. One was Rose Greenhow, the notorious "wild rose of the confederacy," who, while living in the nation's capital, obtained vital intelligence from some of the most notable names in the federal government. In the south, Pinkerton and his men, often wearing disguises and/ or using aliases, would discover and monitor troop movements of Confederate forces, relaying to General McClellan estimates of troop numbers and locations. Throughout his tenure as commander, McClellan would often clash with Lincoln for what Lincoln viewed as timidity on McClellan's part. Some historians attribute this timidity to Pinkerton and his operatives, claiming that Pinkerton's agents exaggerated Confederate troop strength on several occasions, causing McClellan to be overly conservative.

Although Pinkerton was proud of the work his agency performed during the Civil War, his lasting regret was that he did not secure the duty of protecting the president on a full-time basis. Instead, the president relied on Washington, DC, police officers to provide protection. The Secret Service would not begin protecting the president full-time until the twentieth century. Although Pinkerton had his differences with Lincoln, especially over Lincoln's treatment of George McClellan, he admired and liked Lincoln, and he was fiercely loyal to his adopted country and the presidency. Pinkerton maintained that had he been in charge of protecting Lincoln, instead of John Parker, a feckless Washington police officer, he would have thwarted Lincoln's 1865 assassination, just as he had done in 1861.

After the Civil War, Pinkerton and his agents resumed doing what they did best, providing security for railroads and conducting fraud investigations. Railroad banditry continued to flourish as America expanded westward and as economic hard times befell the United States in the 1870s. Throughout his career, Pinkerton had enjoyed enormous public popularity, but an event in 1871 brought Pinkerton's name into disrepute. One of the most notorious train robbers of that era was Jesse Woodson James. Along with his brother Frank and a handful of other career criminals, he terrorized the Midwest from 1866–1882. Although James and his gang were nothing more than sociopathic thugs, the public turned the gang into folk heroes, an image that persists to this day.

In 1871, a Pinkerton agent named John Whicher infiltrated the James gang. His true identity was discovered and the James gang murdered and mutilated the young detective. A short time later, another Pinkerton detective was killed in a shootout with John and Jim Younger, two members of the James gang. Outraged, Pinkerton set out to avenge the agents' deaths and bring the James/Younger gang to justice. On January 26, 1875, several Pinkerton agents descended on the home of James's mother where the gang was believed to be holed up. An incendiary device exploded, killing the James brothers' mother and half brother, while the James gang escaped. Public sympathy rested with the James gang rather than the Pinkertons.

Another incident that damaged Pinkerton's reputation involved the Molly Maguires, a group of militant Irish labor activists in Pennsylvania. The Molly Maguires were actually nothing more than extortionists and terrorists using the causes of social justice for the rights of coal miners as a cover for their crimes. Their crimes included theft, extortion, and murder, and the primary targets were Welsh, German, and English miners who would not bend to their demands. In 1877, after vigorous undercover detective work by the Pinkertons, nineteen Molly Maguires were hung. Pinkerton was forever painted as an enemy of organized labor because of his actions against the Molly Maguires, a bitter irony for a man that had fled Great Britain because of his involvement in organized labor.

In 1868, Pinkerton suffered a stroke that left him partially paralyzed on his right side for the rest of his life. Despite this impediment, Pinkerton was able to carry on his work for several years and author several books. He wrote eighteen during his lifetime. He died on July 1, 1884, three weeks after falling and biting his tongue, which led to gangrene and general septicemia.

After his death, the Pinkerton Detective Agency continued to thrive under the leadership of his son William, although some of William's decisions likely would have disappointed his father. The Pinkertons were associated more and more as hired muscle for big businessmen trying to suppress organized labor; that image still persists. Also, Allan Pinkerton had always taken great pride in the fact that he employed female detectives; it would be five decades before most municipal police departments would even hire women as matrons. After his death, all female detectives were dismissed from the agency. What did not change were the trademark and motto that Pinkerton adopted for his agency when it was created. The Pinkerton Agency still uses the trademark human eye as its logo, with the motto that the Pinkertons are "the eye that never sleeps."

SOURCES AND SUGGESTED READINGS

Carl R. Green and William R. Sanford, *Allan Pinkerton* (Springfield, NJ: Enslow Publishers, 1995).

Judith Pinkerton Josephson, *Allan Pinkerton: The Original Private Eye* (Minneapolis: Lerner Publications, 1996).

James A. Mackay, *Allan Pinkerton: The First Private Eye* (New York: Wiley, 1997).

———. *Allan Pinkerton: The Eye Who Never Slept* (Edinburgh: Mainstream, 1996).

Frank Morn, "Pinkerton, Allan," *American National Biography Online,* February 2000, http://www.anb.org, August 19, 2002.

DISCUSSION QUESTIONS

1. If Pinkerton was alive today, what do you think the Pinkerton agency would be like?
2. What factors external to criminal justice aided the rise of Pinkerton's career?

CHAPTER 5

■ ■ ■ ■ ■ ▬▬▬▬▬

THOMAS BYRNES
(1842–1910)

Convenience stores often offer free coffee to police officers in exchange for the presence of a uniformed officer. One criticism of this practice is that convenience stores are essentially paying for police protection, which is supposed to be available to all of the public. Paying publicly employed police officers to essentially act as private security guards is not new. No police officer exemplified this more than Thomas Byrnes, who controlled police activities in Manhattan's financial district during one of New York's most tumultuous periods. However, Byrnes was more than just a glorified rent-a-cop; his life and career make for an interesting story, one from which many lessons can be learned by modern police officers.

Thomas Byrnes was born in Ireland in 1842 and immigrated to New York City as a child. Possessing little formal education, Byrnes trained for a career as a gas fitter. The outbreak of the American Civil War in 1861 changed the course of Byrnes's life and career. Byrnes fought at the first battle of Bull Run while still a teenager. He joined the New York City police force in 1863, and like many Irish immigrants to American cities, Byrnes realized quickly that he had found his niche. Byrnes rose through the ranks rapidly, achieving the rank of roundsman in 1868, then captain in 1870, one year before his thirtieth birthday.

Crime has always been a problem in urban areas, and it was especially acute in New York City during the 1870s. One estimate is that there were 30,000 professional thieves and 2,000 gambling dens in the city. New York City, especially Manhattan, was also the primary center of wealth in the United States. Just as it is today, it was America's epicenter of banking and finance. Byrnes headed the fifteenth precinct where the Manhattan Savings institute was located. Once, $3 million was stolen from the institute. Captain Byrnes apprehended most of the culprits and recovered most of the money. This high-profile bust led to Byrnes's appointment as commander of the detective bureau in 1880.

Although detective work is part and parcel to even small law enforcement agencies today, little detective work was done by municipal police agencies during the 1880s. Order maintenance was the primary task of police agencies; most criminal investigation was done by private agencies. Byrnes virtually built the detective bureau on his own. He had forty detective sergeants and fourteen patrol officers under his supervision.

Byrnes made it his mission to protect the wealthy and powerful in New York's financial district, and he fulfilled his mission very well. He and his men made more than 3,300 arrests in his career. Byrnes boasted, perhaps justifiably, that his precinct was better than Scotland Yard and the Paris police services when it came to apprehending thieves. Byrnes, a robust, broad shouldered man with a powerful neck and piercing eyes, did not possess much formal education, but he was not a rube. Byrnes always dressed immaculately and could often be seen with a cigar in his mouth. He was a smart detective in his own right, and, more importantly, he was a dedicated student of detective work when there were very few publicly employed detectives. Byrnes had a great flair for the dramatic and was skillful at manipulating public opinion. He also equated crime with anarchy, a popular rallying cry in the late nineteenth century.

What motivated Byrnes? Was he a dedicated public servant or was he lining his own pockets by selecting the citizens he deemed most worthy of protection? In March 1880 he laid down a "Dead Line" at Wall Street, proclaiming that anyone who entered the financial district without a proper pass would be arrested and taken away. Although he was bright, Byrnes was not a Sherlock Holmes– or Agatha Christie–type detective who relied solely on inductive reasoning and intellect to solve cases. One of his greatest skills was his ability to cultivate informants and underworld contacts. He covertly informed many of the major underworld figures in the financial district that he would not try to bother them in their pursuits as long as they operated outside of his precinct. It was fine with Byrnes if they victimized the poor and middle class, but he viewed the wealthy scions in Manhattan's financial district as his personal clients.

Byrnes's typical method was that he would listen to the victim and then assure them that their property would be returned within a certain time frame. More often than not he would keep his promise. Byrnes was skilled at training his subordinates, not so much in police work but in the techniques used by criminals, especially thieves and pickpockets. He detested thievery but admired a professional thief's skills just as many thieves grudgingly admired his ability to catch them. But his admiration had limits, as evidenced in his statement, "There is no honor among thieves." At a time when photography was in its genesis and few photographic records were kept by police agencies, Byrnes made a careful study and kept meticulous records of offender photographs, physical descriptions, the types of crimes they usually committed, and their modus operandi. Byrnes's record keeping culminated in the publication of his "rogue's gallery" (now a common phrase) of hundreds of criminals he met. His *1886 Professional Criminals of America,* though primitive, politically incorrect, and unsophisticated by today's standards, was viewed as a virtual encyclopedia of information about property offenders. Here are a few descriptions of the "rogues":

1. Langdon W. Moore, alias Charley Adams, "eyes, have an expression peculiarly their own. When off his guard he is quite nervous."
2. Daniel Watson, alias Dutch Dan, "A cross-looking man. Has a sort of suspicious look about him when he meets a stranger."

3. Charles McLaughlin, alias McLain, "He has quite a respectable appearance and is a good talker."
4. Gustave Kindt, "dresses like a well-to-do mechanic"
5. James White, alias Pop White, "looks like a well-to-do farmer"
6. Robert Hovan, alias Robert Munroe, "inclined to be feminine in his actions"
7. Frank Lowenthal, "Jew, born in United States, dark complexion, Jewish appearance"
8. Rudolph Lewis, "large ears"
9. Walter Price, "quite a clerical-looking old fellow"
10. Joseph Bond, "looks somewhat like a Jew"
11. Thomas McCormack, "looks like a Spaniard, is a good wine drinker"
12. Of a certain female thief, Byrnes said she had a "Roman" nose, "generally wears a long cloak when stealing, very fleshy, coarse woman, talks with somewhat of an Irish brogue"
13. Charles Mason, alias Boston Charley, "Pickpocket, banco (the old English game of eight dice cloth), a very active man for his size"

Byrnes also provided descriptions of the theft profession:

> Of professional pickpockets there are many types. Odd are the notions that some people entertain of the personal appearance of criminals of this class. Some believe them to be a forbidding and suspicious-looking lot of cut-throats, but on the contrary they are very like ordinary individuals, and, unless their faces are known, their appearance or dress would never excite curiosity.
>
> A man of education, refined habits, and possibly a minimum of courage, would not be likely to adopt the criminal walks requiring brute force and nerve. Such a one would be far more likely to become a forger or counterfeiter than a highway robber.
>
> The best safeguard against the bank-sneak thief is to be able to recognize him at sight, and be sure of his real character.
>
> Some of the most prominent forgers are chemists, and by the aid of a secret mixture of acids, they are able to erase figures in ink from the face of notes without destroying or damaging the paper.
>
> Women make the most patient and dangerous pickpockets.

Many of the people that Byrnes helped did not know or care how he solved cases; they only knew he delivered on his promises. Byrnes led the public to believe that he solved cases by using vast amounts of knowledge he acquired through his rogue's gallery and the careful study of criminals. Although this was true to a great degree, Byrnes did not tell the public about one of his most successful methods of solving cases—the third degree. Byrnes's use of the third degree became well known in law enforcement circles around the country. He came across in public as an intellectual, when in fact he often used primitive and brutal methods for solving crimes. Late in his career, Byrnes expressed regret for using physical torture. He admitted using force very frequently; there was little concern over police brutality during the nineteenth century. Byrnes claimed that psychological methods were more effective. One method was bringing in a wax dummy, telling a suspect that the dummy was a corpse and that a similar fate could await anyone who did not cooperate.

What the public also did not see were the rewards Byrnes garnered for his work. Byrnes was very cognizant of who buttered his bread. He did not focus on violent crimes because they offered no reward; likewise for poor victims of property crime. He did not focus on prostitution or other forms of vice. He would leave pickpockets alone as long as they did not victimize his favored patrons and if they agreed to act as his informants. Rich victims in the financial district paid handsome rewards. Once, when Wall Street tycoon and robber baron Jay Gould had his life threatened, Byrnes found the culprit. In return he received stock tips and real estate from Gould. Wall Street bankers and financiers made Byrnes a very wealthy man. By the middle 1890s, Byrnes had accumulated a fortune in cash, stocks, and property of over $350,000, which would translate to approximately $5.7 million today. He claimed he had made all of his money as a result of sound financial advice from some of his wealthy patrons, a claim that had some truth.

Byrnes was named chief of New York City detectives in 1888, and police superintendent in 1892. To appease a few vocal moral reformers, he ordered all saloons to close on Sunday, but the order was mainly for show and did not last. He was as powerful as any man in New York City, but he was not popular with all New Yorkers. *Harper's Weekly* called him a ruthless autocrat. Byrnes was not popular with Reverend Charles Parkhurst, who had mounted a one-man crusade against vice crime and corrupt police officers in New York City. At Parkhurst's urging, the New York State legislature appointed a special commission to investigate the New York City Police Department. The commission, chaired by state senator Clarence Lexow, found the department rife with graft and corruption, blaming Byrnes for much of the problem. The commission stated that detectives refused to act on a case unless rewards were promised beforehand and that detectives had a cozy relationship with pawnbrokers. The commission found that pawnbrokers would often knowingly receive stolen merchandise, then return the merchandise to detectives in a way that benefited both the pawnbroker and the detective, and then the pawnbroker would give the name of the thief to the detective. In 1895, when Theodore Roosevelt assumed his duties as head of the New York City Police Commission, he made getting rid of Byrnes one of his top priorities.

Byrnes did not put up much of a fight against Roosevelt. The police hierarchy did not press Byrnes on the source of his wealth for fear of embarrassing New York City's financial elite. Byrnes had most of his assets placed in his wife's name. He chose to retire quietly in 1895 and live off his considerable wealth and his annual pension of $3,000. He became general manager of the burglary-insurance department of the United States Casualty Company. Byrnes lived in Red Bank, New Jersey, sailed in yacht clubs, and criticized those who came after him in the New York Police Department who claimed conditions had improved. Thomas Byrnes died from stomach cancer on May 7, 1910.

Policing, especially detective work was still in its developmental stages when Byrnes worked in New York City. It is easy to judge Byrnes as a corrupt and brutal tyrant when using twenty-first-century standards of judgment. The truth about Byrnes is a little more complicated. Most of the rules and codes of ethics that govern modern police officers were not in existence in Byrnes's time, nor was the egalitarian idea that all citizens are worthy of equal attention from publicly employed police officers. Perhaps instead of simply judging Byrnes as a hero or villain, it is more useful to see him as a product of his times and to learn from his career about the pitfalls of police officers treating the wealthy more favorably than the rest of the community.

SOURCES AND SUGGESTED READINGS

Thomas Byrnes, *1886 Professional Criminals of America: Thomas Byrnes Police Inspector and Chief of Detectives 1880–1895* (New York: Lyons Press, 2000).

Thomas F. Byrnes, *Rascals and Rogues of Long Ago* (Scotia, New York: Americana Review, 1974, original publication date 1886).

James F. Richardson, *The New York Police: Colonial Times to 1900* (New York: Oxford University Press, 1970).

DISCUSSION QUESTIONS

1. Would you characterize Thomas Byrnes as corrupt, or just a product of policing as it existed during his lifetime?
2. What lessons should modern police officers learn from Thomas Byrnes's tendency to favor wealthy victims and act as their private police officer?

CHAPTER 6

■ ■ ■ ■ ■ ━━━━━━━━━━━━━━━

CHARLES BONAPARTE
(1851–1921)

The Federal Bureau of Investigation did not begin with J. Edgar Hoover. Although Hoover's impact on the FBI was huge, its genesis and early history is linked largely to the work of Charles Bonaparte, the United States attorney general who presided over its founding. The founding of the Bureau is replete with the controversy, political intrigue, and cloak-and-dagger dealings that have followed the Bureau throughout its history.

Charles Joseph Bonaparte was born in Baltimore, Maryland, on June 9, 1851, the second of two sons born to Jerome Napoleon Bonaparte and Susan Williams Bonaparte. Charles Bonaparte's ancestry was an irony not lost on political officials who opposed creating the Bureau of Investigation (which was later renamed the Federal Bureau of Investigation). His father was the son of Jerome Bonaparte, the brother of the French emperor Napoleon Bonaparte, making Charles the grand-nephew of the infamous French conqueror. Charles's connection to the French emperor ended there. Charles's grandmother was a Massachusetts heiress that married Napoleon's brother Jerome in 1803. Furious over his brother's choice of a bride, Napoleon denounced the marriage. Jerome was recalled to France by his emperor brother and never saw his American family again, a family that included Charles's father.

Despite his ancestry, which included Corsican, Italian, and French blood-lines, Charles Bonaparte was an ardent American patriot. He felt little connection to his ancestral roots, even though his father, Jerome, supported the family by managing the Bonaparte family fortune. His mother, Susan Williams Bonaparte, was a puritan New Englander who sided with the Union during the Civil War; this was an uncomfortable position in Maryland, a Union state with many Confederate sympathizers. His mother's Christian beliefs exerted a lasting and profound effect on Bonaparte that would follow him his entire adult life.

Charles Bonaparte grew up in Maryland and moved to Massachusetts to attend Harvard, where he obtained an A.B. degree in 1871; he graduated from Harvard Law School in 1874 with an L.L.B. degree. Bonaparte returned to Maryland in 1874 and was admitted to the Maryland bar to begin private practice in Baltimore. On September 1, 1875, Bonaparte married Ellen Channing Day, the daughter of a wealthy Connecticut lawyer and publisher.

Bonaparte has been described as a patrician reformer, a title that suits him well. He thought that the duty of the well to do was not simply to accumulate and hoard riches, but to be good public servants because the poor did not have the time or ability to do public service work. Bonaparte was an excellent lawyer, just as he had been an excellent law student, claiming once that studying never tired him, but his real passion was public service. More specifically, he saw civil service reform as a moral imperative, in a time, shortly after the Civil War, when the role of the federal government in everyday life was expanding. Bonaparte disliked the spoils system in which government jobs were handed out based purely on political patronage. The worst offender in Bonaparte's view was President Ulysses Grant, who presided over one of the most corrupt administrations in American history, largely because of Grant's habit of appointing corrupt political cronies to civil service positions. Civil service reform would not come easy, as was evidenced by the 1881 assassination of President James Garfield at the hands of a disgruntled (and deranged) federal job seeker. Bonaparte once stated, "Civil service reform is the application of morality and common sense to the choice and tenure of public servants."

Soon after establishing his law practice, Bonaparte began speaking publicly on the issue of civil service reform. In 1881, he helped found the Civil Service Reform League of Maryland and the National Civil Service Reform League. He was a cofounder, in 1885, of the Baltimore Reform League. In 1895 Bonaparte was appointed supervisor of elections in Baltimore, which laid the groundwork for higher political appointments. He gradually drifted toward Republican Party ideals and his stature within the party increased through the 1880s and 1890s. Bonaparte was relentless in his criticism of corrupt political bosses in Baltimore, other cities, and the federal government. He once criticized President Grover Cleveland, stating, "Civil service offices no more belong to him than does the foundation of the White House; and he has as little right, either in law or morals, to place one at the disposal of a complaisant Congressman, as to reward the latter for his vote with a piano or painting for which the Treasury has paid."

Bonaparte's entry into national politics came when Theodore Roosevelt assumed the presidency in 1901, after the assassination of President William McKinley. Bonaparte met Roosevelt in the 1880s at Harvard, and the two became fast friends as a result of their continuing passion for civil service reform. The two men had much in common; both came from affluent families; both considered themselves highly principled and patriotic. Roosevelt, who viewed Bonaparte as just the sort of "fighting lawyer" that would serve him well, appointed him to the Board of Indian Commissioners in 1902, and, in 1903, he appointed Bonaparte as special counsel in the prosecution of two men charged with postal fraud. After the 1904 election, when Roosevelt was elected to the presidency in his own right, he appointed Bonaparte secretary of the Navy. In December 1906, Roosevelt nominated Bonaparte to the position of attorney general; the Senate confirmed him on December 17. One of Roosevelt's primary agendas was battling trusts and monopolies, and the job of enforcing antitrust laws fell primarily on his good friend and soulmate Bonaparte.

At the turn of the twentieth century, most Americans opposed the idea of a national police force. The thought of a national police force conjured images of a secret police, an idea abhorrent to America's founders during the 1780s and an idea still held in disrepute by many Americans.

Bonaparte first requested congressional authorization to establish the Bureau in 1907. He was denied congressional approval on more than one occasion. During congressional hearings with Bonaparte, several congressmen compared a national police force in America to secret police in other countries. A New York congressman stated "that it would be a great blow to freedom and to free institutions if there should arise in this country any such great central secret-service bureau as there is in Russia." At least one press report, in a not so subtle jab at Bonaparte's ancestry, compared a national police force to the work of Fouche, the police minister under Emperor Napoleon, who intimidated and spied on French citizens and imperial subjects.

Congress pronounced in loud, clear terms its opposition to a national police force like the one Attorney General Bonaparte and President Roosevelt requested. Congress passed a law on May 27, 1908, that prohibited the growing practice of the Justice Department borrowing Secret Service agents from the Treasury Department, which was a roundabout way of achieving Bonaparte's objective.

At the turn of the twentieth century, Congress took a much longer recess than it does today. On May 30, 1908, Congress went into recess, returning home to campaign and attend to local political affairs. This was in the days before the media saturation that is so prevalent in Washington, DC, today. There were no television or radio reporters, and there were fewer print media outlets then than there are today. The paucity of media coverage meant that moves could be made in secret by the executive branch while Congress was in recess. On July 1, 1908, while Congress was in recess, Bonaparte secretly established the Bureau on his own, with the approval of President Roosevelt and without the knowledge of Congress.

Why was the Bureau of Investigation created? The answer depends on who is asked. Advocates of the Bureau, such as President Roosevelt and Attorney General Bonaparte, claimed such an agency was needed because the federal government was assuming more importance in the everyday lives of Americans than in previous years, and the Bureau was just another extension of that inevitable progress. Another related argument was that America was becoming much larger geographically and much more mobile. Interstate crime, never considered a serious threat during America's first 125 years of existence, had become a threat due to the rapid ascension of the railroad and the automobile. Local law enforcement could not go after interstate crooks, and the federal government should not have to rely on private agencies such as the Pinkerton and Burns detective agencies to do its detective work. In fact, two of the first statutes the Bureau was called on to enforce were the Dyer Act, which prohibited interstate trafficking of stolen automobiles, and the Mann Act, which prohibited the interstate trafficking of females for immoral purposes.

Roosevelt and Bonaparte's critics saw a different motive. Unscrupulous executive and legislative officials would use the Bureau to spy on and harass political opponents. Their arguments were buttressed by the clandestine manner in which

Bonaparte had created the Bureau. Their worst fears were realized when, soon after the Bureau was created, agents were caught going through the mail of Senator Benjamin Tillman, one of the Bureau's outspoken critics.

When Congress returned from its recess, many members from both houses were outraged at Bonaparte's and Roosevelt's chicanery. Congress authorized an investigation of the Bureau and of the detectives that Bonaparte had hired to conduct the Bureau's business. The responses from Bonaparte and Roosevelt further inflamed congressional resentment toward the new Bureau of Investigation. Using somewhat circular logic, Bonaparte rationalized his actions; in fact he went so far as to blame Congress for the secrecy, claiming it had forced his hand by not giving him the approval he had openly sought, and also that his hand was forced because Congress had prohibited the borrowing of Treasury agents. Roosevelt even accused Congress of siding with criminals by passing that law. Bonaparte tried to assuage Congress by saying that the Bureau was very small and that he had only hired a few agents. Testifying before an angry Congress after the creation of the Bureau, Bonaparte agreed that any police agency is capable of committing serious abuses, and that the temptation to use such an agency for political purposes would be strong, but he assured Congress that the agency would never be used for such purposes. Bonaparte said that the way to prevent such abuses was for the Attorney General to be completely aware of everything the Bureau was doing.

Another concern was the dubious character of the agents that the Bureau was likely to employ. Congress correctly assumed that Bonaparte would choose his agents from the ranks of private detective agencies. Private detectives had an unsavory reputation in 1908, and no agents could match current FBI agents in terms of education. Bonaparte freely admitted that private detectives were not always the most trustworthy people, but he rationalized employing such unsavory types by saying, "It takes a thief to catch a thief." Bonaparte cared little for Congress's concerns, believing that crime control in the increasingly mobile United States was of greater concern than the hypothetical worries about invasion of privacy and government-sponsored spying.

Congress was still upset with Roosevelt and Bonaparte in late 1908 and early 1909, but there was little it could do. Bonaparte had appointed Stanley Finch as the Bureau's first director, and Roosevelt had chosen not to run for reelection, opting instead to support his handpicked successor, William Taft. After assuming the presidency, Taft and Attorney General George Wickersham kept Finch as director.

The opposition to a federal police force was not based on political philosophy alone. It was based on practical factors as well. Early twentieth-century law enforcement was best left to county and municipal governments, so the thinking went. Local governments better understood the needs of a community than did the federal government. In addition, practically all criminal laws at the turn of the twentieth century were enacted at the state and local levels. What laws would they enforce? The Secret Service had been established after the Civil War to combat counterfeiting, and it eventually assumed the task of protecting the president. The United States Postal Service had its law enforcers. What would a federal law enforcement agency do? The answer, said the critics, was that a federal police force would serve as an army of political spies.

It is ironic that Bonaparte, a fervent advocate of civil service reform throughout his entire adult life, had become associated with the very sort of back door dealing he claimed to despise. It is also ironic that most of the first Bureau agents were the sort of political hacks and incompetents that Bonaparte said should not be a part of the federal government. The Bureau of Investigation was beset by scandal until the 1920s when Hoover assumed control and ran the Bureau with an iron fist.

Bonaparte returned to private life and his law practice in March 1909 when President Roosevelt left office. Until his death on June 28, 1921, at the age of seventy, Bonaparte continued to advocate for civil service reform, despite the scandalous clouds over the Bureau of Investigation. He always preached the dictum that the quality of personnel is more important than the systems and rules that rule them. His philosophy toward government service can be summed in a speech he made in Montreal in 1910:

> The one thing indispensable, the one thing without which good government of any kind or degree is impossible, is good *men*. If your places of public trust are filled by ignorant, incompetent, self-seeking or unscrupulous men, you may multiply checks and balances, you may devise all sorts of ingenious and complicated safeguards, but, whatever its scientific merits in theory, your machine of government will in practice work ill.

SOURCES AND SUGGESTED READINGS

Civil Service Auxiliary of Maryland, *Charles Joseph Bonaparte, 1851–1921: An Appreciation* (Baltimore: Author, 1921).

Joseph Bucklin Bishop, *Charles Joseph Bonaparte: His Life and Public Services* (New York: Charles Scribner's Sons, 1922).

Alan Axelrod, Charles Phillips with Kurt Kemper, *Cops, Crooks and Criminologists: An International Biographical Dictionary of Law Enforcement* (New York: Facts on File, 1996).

Lewis L. Gould, "Bonaparte, Charles Joseph," *American National Biography Online,* February 2000, http://www.anb.org, August 19, 2002.

Max Lowenthal, *The Federal Bureau of Investigation* (New York: Sloane, 1950).

DISCUSSION QUESTIONS

1. Did Charles Bonaparte do the right thing in his clandestine creation of the Bureau of Investigation, or should he have conceded to congressional will and not created it?
2. Given the history of the Federal Bureau of Investigation, do you think that Bonaparte's decision to create the Bureau should be judged positively or negatively?

CHAPTER 7

WYATT EARP
(1848–1929)

Folklorists and filmmakers, not academicians, have told the story of law enforcement and justice administration in the early American West. As a result, the lines between myth and reality have blurred over the years. The most notable law enforcement figure from the American West, and one who embodies the blurred lines of myth and reality better than anyone is Wyatt Earp, a small-town frontier marshal who helped shape popular perceptions of western law enforcement and his own place in American history.

Wyatt Berry Stapp Earp was born in Monmouth, Illinois, the fourth of six sons. All of Wyatt Earp's brothers were involved in law enforcement at various points in their lives. Virgil and Morgan Earp have also been granted a prominent place in western folklore. Part of the enigma of the Earp brothers, as with many other early western criminal justice figures, lies in the fact that their reputations as accused lawbreakers stand side by side with their reputations as law enforcement officers.

Wyatt Earp's law enforcement career began in 1870 when he was appointed constable in Lamar, Missouri. He was elected to the post later that year, barely defeating his half brother Newton. As was the pattern throughout his childhood and adult life, Earp's stay in Lamar was short-lived. Shortly after the death of his first wife and a street brawl that pitted Earp and three of his brothers against Wyatt's brothers-in-law, he moved to the Oklahoma territory, where he was charged with stealing horses. Earp was never convicted.

Earp's next significant law enforcement job was as a deputy marshal in Wichita, Kansas, from 1874 to 1876. In Wichita, Earp established a reputation as a tough, stoic law enforcer, though it is believed he never killed anyone while in Wichita. After leaving Wichita, Earp became marshal in Dodge City, Kansas. Earp's reputation grew during his brief stay in Dodge City, thanks in part to the presence of his assistant and lifelong friend, William "Bat" Masterson, already a living legend for his military exploits. It was also during his Dodge City stay that Earp first met the now legendary dentist-turned-gunfighter John Henry "Doc" Holliday, whose name would eventually be linked with Earp and the most famous gunfight in American history.

Earp left Kansas for Texas, but his stay there was brief as well. At the urging of his brother Morgan, Earp left for the Southwest hoping to strike it rich in the mining business. He settled in Tombstone, Arizona, in 1879. The Earp brothers dabbled in mining, saloon keeping, and several other jobs for several months.

Eventually, Tombstone law enforcement was dominated by two rival factions—the Earp brothers, who were the town marshals, and Sheriff Johnny Behan. Behan was Wyatt Earp's competitor for political popularity and for the affections of Josephine Marcus, the woman who would eventually become Wyatt Earp's life-long companion.

In the booming frontier town of Tombstone, many activities that were not openly tolerated in large eastern towns, such as prostitution and gambling, were carried out in full view, and with the protection of law enforcers, including the Earp brothers. The wife of James Earp, another of Wyatt's brothers, was a so-called career madam, often relying on the protection of her husband's brothers. Tombstone's close proximity to the Mexican border and its attraction to get-rich-quick artists made it fertile ground for another organized criminal activity that drew the attention of law enforcement—cattle rustling. Cattle rustlers drew the attention of law enforcement in two ways. Some law officers combated rustlers; others protected them.

One group of rustlers caught the attention of the Earp brothers on several occasions. This group was allied with Sheriff Johnny Behan, the Earps' personal and political rival. The group of rustlers included two sets of brothers, Isaac and Billy Clanton, and Frank and Tom McClary, and a fifth cowboy named William Claiborne. After a series of hostile exchanges, accusations, arrests, and threats, the rivalry between the Clanton-led rustlers and the Earp brothers came to a head on October 26, 1881. The Earps, joined by Doc Holliday, who had arrived in Tombstone some months earlier, went to the OK Corral in Tombstone to settle their score with the rustlers.

The gunfight at the OK Corral lasted around thirty seconds. Contrary to subsequent Hollywood imagery, the battle took place in an area of about eleven by six feet, a space barely large enough to contain all of the combatants. By the time it was finished, the McClary brothers and Billy Clanton were dead. Virgil and Morgan Earp were wounded, as was Doc Holliday. Over two dozen Hollywood movies and dozens more documentaries have depicted the gunfight. Many such films have left the impression that the gunfight was a triumphant finale of good over evil. The truth is murkier. The Earps, especially Wyatt, were not paragons of law enforcement virtue. Some of the cowboys were actually unarmed during the fight; one unarmed cowboy was holding Doc Holliday's shotgun by the barrel when Holliday shot him. Many townspeople sided with the Clantons and McClarys in the battle. Some townspeople accused the Earps and Holliday of instigating the fight and mercilessly slaughtering the rustlers.

The gunfight was not the final chapter in the Earp-Clanton feud. In December 1881, Virgil Earp was shot in the leg and maimed for life. Several months later, Morgan Earp was killed in revenge. A vendetta was triggered. At least two men, and maybe more who were allied with the Clantons and Sheriff Behan were murdered, supposedly by Wyatt Earp, his youngest brother Warren, and Doc Holliday.

Earp and Holliday left Arizona for Colorado to escape the legal consequences of their actions. Sheriff Behan unsuccessfully attempted to have them extradited to face charges relating to the OK Corral gunfight and the ensuing vendetta.

The gunfight at the OK Corral, widely reported in newspapers around the country, made Wyatt Earp a living legend. It also buttressed American images of life and law enforcement on the western frontier. While eastern law enforcement became synonymous with the nightstick, Wyatt Earp had helped create western law enforcement's stereotypical association with the holster and the gun belt.

For the remaining forty-seven years of his life, Earp lived in numerous locales, mainly in California. He dabbled in several businesses and gambling activities, gained some material benefit from notoriety, and in general lived a life of boom and bust with Josephine Marcus. Earp's encounters with law enforcement did not end, except that in most cases, he was on the receiving end of criminal charges. In June 1900 he was arrested in Nome, Alaska, and charged with interfering with an arrest. He was arrested several times for fighting. Usually, the charges were either dismissed or adjudicated by a small fine.

Earp performed one of his most significant post-Tombstone acts in San Francisco. On December 3, 1896, he refereed a heavyweight boxing championship bout between Bob Fitzsimmons and Tom Sharkey. Earp had extensive experience refereeing fights, and his fame brought enormous attention to the already highly anticipated bout. During the eighth round, Earp awarded the match to Sharkey, claiming that Fitzsimmons had delivered a low blow. Many were outraged at Earp's decision. An investigation was conducted, and Earp was never charged with a crime, though his reputation was severely tarnished.

One reason Earp's legend as hero has eclipsed his reputation as a criminal is that, unlike many other western law enforcement pioneers, he lived long enough to tell his side of his colorful life with filmmakers who settled in southern California shortly after the turn of the century. Earp worked as technical consultant and adviser on many early Hollywood westerns. He played a large role in creating the Hollywood image of law enforcement in the American West, and he was able to secure his place as a hero in Hollywood accounts of the OK Corral gunfight, which contradicted many earlier newspaper accounts of his role in the battle. During his later years, Earp became well acquainted with many Hollywood actors and filmmakers, including John Ford, William S. Hart, Tom Mix, and John Wayne, a stagehand at the time. Wayne later stated that he modeled his cowboy movie image on Wyatt Earp.

By the time of his death on January 13, 1929, Wyatt Earp had succeeded in making himself a living legend, due in part to Stuart Lake's 1927 biography about Earp. Earp was not educated, nor was he a visionary; he had no sophisticated notions of how law enforcement should operate in a democracy, but his imprint on the American image of policing has been greater than anyone who lived in the American West at the turn of the twentieth century.

SOURCES

Allen Barra, "Who Was Wyatt Earp?" *American Heritage* 49 (6): 76–85, 1998.
S. N. Lake, *Wyatt Earp: Frontier Marshall* (New York: Simon & Schuster, 1994 [1927]).
Casey Tefertiller, *Wyatt Earp: The Life Behind the Legend* (New York: Wiley, 1997).

DISCUSSION QUESTIONS

1. Of all nineteenth-century western law enforcers, why is Wyatt Earp so famous?
2. How has Wyatt Earp impacted America's views of nineteenth-century American law enforcement?

CHAPTER 8

JOHN CLUM
(1851–1932)

Native Americans had little if any say in how the American criminal justice system was shaped. As with other racial minorities, including Chinese on the West Coast, Hispanics in the Southwest, and African Americans across the country, throughout most of American history, Native Americans bore much of the criminal justice system's wrath without sharing its benefits. There were bright spots in this sordid and complicated history. John Clum, who acquired the Apache title "Nantan-betunnykahyeh," or "white chief of the Apaches," was one of the few white men who, in trying to administer criminal justice with a Native population, treated them as equals and encouraged them to police themselves, rather than treating them as savages or as unruly children.

John Philip Clum was born on September 1, 1851, in Claverack, New York, one of nine children born to William Henry Clum and Elizabeth Van Duesen Clum. Like many people who lived in New York's Hudson River Valley in the nineteenth century, the Clums were of Dutch ancestry. The Clums were a farming family, and like many other farmers they lived on or near land that had once belonged to Native Americans, an irony given John Clum's eventual legacy as a friend to Native Americans in the American Southwest.

John Clum was educated at the Hudson River Institute at Claverack and worked on the family farm. He earned enough money and studied well enough to gain admission to Rutgers College in New Jersey in 1870. A fine athlete, Clum excelled at football, which was then in its infancy as an intercollegiate sport. A lack of funds precluded him from staying around long enough to graduate. After working briefly on the family farm, Clum answered an advertisement to work with a newly established federal meteorological service to be administered by the War Department. Clum went to Washington, DC, passed an examination, and was appointed as an observer-sergeant in the United States Signal Corps. In 1871, he left for Santa Fe, New Mexico, to begin his duties, a New Yorker looking and feeling like the quintessential fish out of water.

Clum took the first atmospheric readings on that part of the American continent in 1871. Being a meteorologist was not a full-time job, so Clum started a private school, the first English-speaking school in Santa Fe. His first exposure to New Mexico's Indian population came in the summer of 1872, when he made a one-hundred-mile horseback trip to the Ute Indian Reservation. The Utes lived peacefully, even though they were relegated to second-class citizenship throughout the New Mexico territory. Conversely, many of New Mexico's and Arizona's Apaches had a relationship with white Americans and Mexicans that was anything but harmonious. The enmity had taken centuries to build up, and the animosity was strong by the time Clum arrived from New York.

Although he was still in his early twenties, Clum rose to prominence in territorial New Mexico's government circles. When the territorial governor traveled to Washington on business during the summer of 1872, Clum assumed the duties of governor, even residing in the official mansion. In November 1873, Clum was offered the position of Indian agent for the San Carlos Reservation in the Arizona territory, the heart of Apache country. Law enforcement prowess had nothing to do with Clum's appointment; he had no law enforcement experience. The reason for Clum's appointment involved a confluence of his ancestry, religion, educational background, and pure happenstance. At that time, several mainline Christian denominations made it their mission to evangelize many Native American groups. The Dutch Reformed Church, in which Clum had grown up, had taken the Apaches under its wing. When Washington Indian Bureau officials were looking for someone to serve as Indian agent for the Apaches, they went to Rutgers College to recruit. Some of the students and faculty at Rutgers knew that Clum was already in the Southwest and that he had a Dutch Reformed background; Bureau officials thought Clum a natural choice for the position. Clum received his official appointment from President Ulysses Grant in February 1874.

Clum never had tolerance for militant Apaches throughout his lifetime; he also had little regard for many of the military officers that warred with Apaches. He was appalled at what would now be perceived as a policy of genocide that the American government had toward the Apaches. Clum's biography (Clum 1936) contains an excerpt from a letter written by an Army General in Apache territory:

> It is useless to negotiate with Apaches. They will observe no treaties, agreements, or truces. There is no alternative but vigorous war, until they are completely exterminated. (p. 123)

What struck Clum was the government's contradictory policy toward the Apaches. On one hand, the Department of Interior appointed people such as himself to work with and aid the Apaches; on the other hand, the Department of War (now Department of Defense) sought their extermination. While not an intellectual visionary, Clum was a frank, intelligent, no-nonsense young man, simply resolved to see that the Apaches got fair and honest treatment.

Although all Indian agents faced challenges, perhaps none were more daunting than the ones facing Clum. Caucasians advised him to go back to New Mexico to save his scalp. Even many other Indians had long enmity with some of the Apaches. Clum's first encounter with the Apaches would bring him one of his closest friends and partners in his efforts to establish an Apache police force. Clum observed twenty Apache prisoners of war at New Camp Grant, shackled and making Adobe bricks. One prisoner in particular caught his attention. When Clum discovered that the prisoner was not being jailed on specific charges, only that the major in charge did not like him, Clum worked to secure his release. The freed prisoner was Eskiminzin, an Arivaipa chief who would become Clum's closest friend and partner for years to come.

Clum would spend much of his time at San Carlos in conflict with battle-scarred Army officials, many of whom took a much more hostile view of the Apaches than did Clum. Believing that the Apaches would be much more peaceful if they engaged in self-governance instead of living under the total subjugation of Caucasians and Mexicans, Clum took steps to establish Apache-run criminal justice institutions. With no law enforcement experience of his own, Clum appointed an Apache police force at a time when American policing among Caucasians was still new, the first large-scale municipal police force having existed for about four decades. Clum's police force numbered more than fifty officers at its peak. Clum also established a court for trying Apache offenders; the trial court was composed of four or five Apache judges with Clum serving as chief justice.

Clum's Apache criminal justice system served as a template for similar systems around the country for the next several decades. If the concept of a police force and an interconnected criminal justice system was novel to Caucasians, it was even stranger to the Apaches, but they accepted the idea primarily because they saw it as a step away from the oppressive thumb of the federal government and the U.S. Army, even if it was established and administered by Clum, a Caucasian. Unlike many other Caucasians, Clum was honest and pleasant, communicated with the Apache men as equals, was courteous to Apache women, and played with Apache children.

One of Clum's first orders was the disarmament of San Carlos's population. Federal law forbade the sale of liquor to Indians, but Clum knew that fellow Apaches were among the worst offenders. Efforts to keep Apaches disarmed and sober were met with resistance, but, given that the criminal justice system in their charge was composed mostly of fellow Indians, and the concomitant view that they had a stake and role in the proceedings, the effort went much smoother than had previous efforts. Much of Clum's work was focused on relatively mundane criminal matters. He also oversaw food rations and other civil administration affairs. While many activities were routine, some challenged Clum's non-Aboriginal mindset. One was polygamy, which was illegal under federal and state laws, but common among Apaches. Domestic violence also presented a challenge to Clum. Apache men felt perfectly within their rights to administer physical punishment to a wife that had "gotten out of line."

There was one Apache with whom Clum never made peace, and who he never respected, without regard to the eventual accolades he received from other federal government officials. That Apache was Geronimo, whose mixed legacy exemplifies the conflicting feelings between Native Americans and Caucasians even to this day. While many Apaches and some Caucasians view Geronimo as a great warrior, Clum, who hated Geronimo, saw him as a cowardly cutthroat who harmed Indians and Caucasians more than anyone else in the American Southwest and

Mexico. In Clum's eyes, Geronimo was not a great or heroic warrior, but a liar and a murderer.

The first face-to-face encounter between Clum and Geronimo was dramatic. Together with their armed entourages, the two met at a prearranged spot in the New Mexico mountains. Clum, much younger and less physically imposing than the older, war-savvy Geronimo, was blunt and direct with the veteran warrior. Clum told Geronimo:

> You and your followers have been killing white men and stealing their cattle. You have violated the peace treaty made between (Apache Chief) Cochise and General (O. O.) Howard. But you spoke with a split tongue; you did not tell the truth. So now we have come to take you back with us. We have come a long way—four hundred miles. (1936, pp. 217, 218)

Geronimo responded:

> Nantan-betunnykahyeh, you talk very brave, but we are not going to San Carlos with you, and unless you are very careful, your bodies will stay here at Ojo Caliente to make food for coyotes. (Clum, 1936, p. 218)

Fortunately, the situation did not escalate (beyond one Apache woman having to be subdued by Apache police) before Clum took Geronimo's rifle. But before his capture Geronimo looked at Clum with a look of intense hatred—a look Clum claimed never to have seen prior or subsequently to that meeting. The non-violent capture of Geronimo won Clum the admiration of many friendly Apaches and the grudging respect of hostile Apaches.

Clum resigned his position as Indian agent in June 1877, due to a dispute over pay and inadequate resources. Clum thought that Geronimo should have been hung as a murderer in August 1877, shortly after his capture and Clum's resignation. Instead, Geronimo, whose name had become a political football to some, was released and resumed his campaign of warfare (in the eyes of his admirers) or murder and brigandage (in the eyes of his critics), for several more bloody years, before coming to an end in 1886 with Geronimo's recapture. Geronimo lived long enough to become a folk hero, even in the eyes of some whites. Clum was disgusted when Geronimo, who was again released shortly after capture, was treated as a visiting dignitary to Washington on the day of President Theodore Roosevelt's inauguration on March 4, 1905. Later, Geronimo became the object of tourist fascination, regaling Caucasians with his tales of western life, just as famous whites like John Clum did.

Clum's Apache police force morphed into the territorial militia and later Arizona's first National Guard unit. Still in his twenties when he resigned as Indian agent, Clum had plenty of living in front of him. He spent the next few years in Arizona, dabbling in business ventures. He ran a Tucson newspaper for a brief period before selling it and moving to Tombstone, Arizona, in 1880 (to capitalize on recently discovered silver mines), where he started a newspaper called the *Tombstone Epitaph*. On October 26, 1881, Clum, watching from his window, was one of only two eyewitnesses to the most famous gunfight in American history, the "Gunfight at the OK Corral" that pitted Wyatt Earp, his brothers, and Doc Holliday against a group of cattle rustlers led by Ike Clanton. Word of the infamous gunfight, now a part of American folk and film lore, was first reported by Clum in the *Epitaph* and then spread to news outlets across the country. Tombstone citizens were divided over who was the villain in the OK Corral gunfight. Some, including the local sheriff, sided with the rustlers. Clum, who also served as Tombstone's Mayor, sided with the Earps and Holliday.

Clum eventually left Tombstone to serve as assistant editor of the *San Francisco Examiner*. He resumed a law enforcement career in 1898 when he was appointed to the position of postal inspector for the Alaska territory, which had experienced a population boom as a result of the Klondike Gold Rush. The position involved much more than law enforcement; Clum was responsible for establishing post offices throughout Alaska, a vast undertaking that involved over 8,000 miles of travel during a five-month period. Clum stayed in Alaska until 1909.

Clum spent the next few years traveling and promoting Western tourism for the Santa Fe and Southern Pacific railroads. He eventually settled in San Dimas, California, operating a citrus ranch, working in local government and teaching Sunday school to little children, where he would also recall tales of the old west. Clum moved to Los Angeles in 1928, where he died four years later at the age of eighty. His first wife had died in Tombstone on December 18, 1880, but his second wife survived him. He was also survived by a daughter and by a son, Woodworth Clum, who wrote his father's biography based mostly on notes left by Clum himself.

John Clum did not cure the tortured relationship between Native and Caucasian Americans. What Clum did was take an important first step in providing some measure of autonomy and self-governance to the Apaches of Arizona. Some historians claim that if more government officials had taken Clum's compassionate approach to dealing with Native Americans, history may have been different. Clum does have one plain legacy; he started a large police force in an area of the United States that had not known one before.

SOURCES AND SUGGESTED READINGS

Woodworth Clum, *Apache Agent: The Story of John P. Clum* (Lincoln: University of Nebraska Press, 1936).

Martha Glauther, "San Dimas Remembered: John P. Clum, Indian Agent," www.sandimasnews.com/history, April 24, 2002.

National Postal Museum Website, "John Philip Clum," www.si.edu/postal/gold/clum.html, April 22, 2002.

Rutgers University, John P. Clum bio page, Rutgers University, http://info.rutgers.edu/University/alumni, April 20, 2002.

DISCUSSION QUESTIONS

1. Did the fact that John Clum was born and raised in the Northeast, rather than the West, affect his outlook toward Native Americans in the Southwest?
2. What lessons can be learned from John Clum's life about relations between Native Americans and the American government?

CHAPTER 9

WILLIAM BURNS
(1858–1932)

William Burns, one of the most famous private detectives of the late nineteenth and early twentieth centuries, is the closest thing to a real-life American Sherlock Holmes. At a time when government agencies lacked both the expertise and the jurisdictional authority to conduct complex criminal investigations, William Burns filled that gap. The *New York Times* called him the "only detective of genius whom the United States has ever produced."

William Jerome Burns was born in October 1858 in Baltimore, Maryland, the son of Michael and Bridgett Treahy Burns, both Irish immigrants. Shortly after William's birth, the Burns family moved to Zanesville, Ohio, where Michael Burns worked as a tailor. The Burns moved again, this time to Columbus, Ohio. William Burns attended parochial schools, where he excelled at drama and debate; both skills would serve him well in his career as a detective. He worked part time at his father's tailor shop, but his passion was acting, something he wanted to do professionally; he settled for participating in local amateur productions.

In 1870, Michael Burns was elected Columbus police commissioner on the Reform ticket. William Burns developed a fascination with detective work, something that few police officers of the 1870s cared for. He would hang around the police station, talking with police officers and the accused criminals they brought in. He loved hearing of criminal exploits and getting inside the minds of criminals, especially professional thieves.

In 1870, even though William was only seventeen, his father entrusted him to interview victims to solve an especially vexing burglary problem that was sweeping Columbus. William noticed that all of the victims had been burglarized while they were out of town and they had advertised the trip in advance in the society page of the newspaper. He concluded that a Columbus man was the culprit, and his work helped solve the case.

Torn between his desire to be an actor, his father's desire that he become a lawyer, and his newfound fascination with detective work, Burns continued working for his father, sometimes as a tailor, while dabbling in detective work, both for the Columbus police department and on his own. He met Anna-Maria Ressler during this period and the two were married in July 1881.

The year 1885 brought Burns his first crack at a high-profile criminal case. In October, allegations of election fraud surfaced in a countywide election. The police cared little about the allegations. Like most municipal police agencies during the nineteenth century, the Columbus police were more preoccupied with order maintenance and violent crimes than with election fraud. The local prosecutor, knowing there would be little interest shown by the local police, hired William Burns to investigate the allegations. Burns's flare for drama served him well. He relished the cloak and dagger of secret detective work, finding it preferable to the daily grind of local law enforcement. He began hanging around the penitentiary, mostly to speak with the guards. He found out that an inmate named John Francis, a professional safecracker and forger who was incarcerated for another crime, had bragged about the crime. Francis also claimed that he was in cahoots with the prison doctor, the brother of the defeated incumbent candidate. The case was solved and Burns's reputation as a detective grew, even though part-time detective work was not held in high regard.

Burns left his tailoring job in 1888 and went to work full time as a freelance detective, performing many jobs for the Furlong Detective Agency of St. Louis. By that time, Anna-Maria Burns had given birth to two sons, George and Charles. A daughter, Florence, was born in 1888; another son, William, was born in 1890, the same year that Charles Burns passed away. William Burns's professional career left little time for a home life. He traveled constantly, mostly chasing criminals throughout the Midwest, leaving the job of child rearing to his wife.

The desire for steady pay led Burns to accept a part-time position with the Secret Service on December 5, 1891, a position that paid $3 a day. Burns, accustomed to dealing with the seediest type of criminal, now spent most of his time tracking down counterfeiters, the primary task of the Secret Service since its inception earlier in the nineteenth century.

Creative, energetic, and dramatic, Burns stood in marked contrast to most Secret Service agents of the day. Once, he received word that Charlie Ulrich, a professional criminal that he had conversed with during his teenage years while hanging around the Columbus police station, was participating in a sophisticated counterfeiting ring in Cincinnati.

Burns uprooted his family and moved to Cincinnati for the sole purpose of conducting surveillance on Ulrich. He rented an apartment near Ulrich's residence, and he had his entire family live under assumed names to divert any suspicion that he was spying on Ulrich. In a move that typified his devotion to his work and his negligence toward his family life, Burns once followed Ulrich to a train station, got on a train to tail Ulrich, and went to New York City where he stayed for five months. There he arrested Ulrich and the engraver.

In 1896, Burns was promoted to a full-time position with the Secret Service, a job that paid $6 per day. His reputation grew, helped in part by his dismantling a counterfeiting ring in New York City at the behest of the government of Costa Rica.

Even though he was paid by the Secret Service, Burns hired himself out for other work. Sometimes the Secret Service would investigate crimes other than counterfeiting, especially when it was suspected that local law enforcement could not be trusted. In September 1897, five inmates at the Versailles, Indiana, jail were lynched in public. The inmates had been accused of burglary and rape, and local police had supposedly done nothing to stop the lynching. The governor of Indiana requested the Secret Service's assistance.

Knowing he would receive no cooperation by just showing up and asking questions, and also knowing that doing so would probably endanger his own life, Burns got a job with New York Life Insurance as a salesman under the name William Burton. He knew that there was a need for an insurance salesman in the town, and he took the time to study and learn the insurance business to make his cover convincing. Burns discovered the identities of those in the lynch mob, but the case went nowhere when the Indiana attorney general decided that a conviction would be impossible after being told that the mob consisted of several prominent citizens.

On May 1, 1903, President Theodore Roosevelt assigned Burns to a new position in the Department of the Interior. Roosevelt, the nation's first conservationist president, was concerned about the amount of public land in the West that was being acquired through fraud. Again, Burns assumed a false identity, this time as a law school professor conducting research on the mechanics of land use statutes. Burns discovered that the General Land Office, which was charged with overseeing public land, was riddled with corruption at all levels. Private commercial interests, with the tacit approval of the General Land Office, were illegally exploiting public land for their own use. Among the people prosecuted as a result of Burns's investigation (which was aided by his son George who was working in Tucson, Arizona) were the head of the U.S. Forestry Division, numerous local government officials in Oregon, and most notably, John Mitchell, a United States senator. Mitchell was convicted and sentenced to prison, but he died while he was free on appeal bond.

Burns's conquests continued, and unlike most law enforcers who concentrated on crime in the streets, Burns enjoyed focusing on crime in the suites; the bigger the prize, the greater the challenge, the greater the drama, and the greater the glory. He conducted an investigation of corruption in San Francisco city government, an investigation paid for by local business interests, one being newspaper magnate William Randolph Hearst (who would later turn on Burns). Corruption in San Francisco was tied to the railroad, trolley car, and restaurant businesses, the proprietors of which had to pay as much as $5,000 to local officials to operate, and some of which were under the control of corrupt government officials.

The investigation netted Mayor Eugene Schmitz, who was indicted for extortion, and Abe Ruef, the man who controlled San Francisco politics. Ruef pleaded guilty and was sentenced to prison. Schmitz opted for a jury trial, one that witnessed the shooting of one of the prosecutors (who survived) at the hands of a small-time crook. The would-be assassin was placed in the city jail, but the police chief would not allow Burns to interview him. The would-be assassin was soon found shot to death in his cell, and the police chief was found dead two weeks later. Mayor Schmitz was convicted, but the conviction was overturned, yet not in time to save his political career.

Burns broke with the Secret Service in 1909 and joined forces with William Sheridan to form the Burns and Sheridan Detective Agency. Like the Pinkerton agency, they vowed never to get involved in divorces. Unlike the Pinkertons, who by that time had become fierce opponents of organized labor, Burns and Sheridan vowed never to be used as strikebreakers. Sheridan sold his interest in the business to Burns in March 1910, and the agency assumed Burns's name alone.

That same year, Burns began work on the biggest case of his career. Early on the morning of October 1, a dynamite explosion rocked the headquarters of the *Los Angeles Times,* a stridently antilabor (and anti-Burns) newspaper. The blast resulted in twenty-one deaths. Los Angeles mayor George Alexander immediately contacted Burns. Burns was already investigating the bombing of a railroad office in Peoria, Illinois, which had occurred in September. Burns suspected a connection, and he immediately turned his attention to militant labor advocates, even though he feared being labeled as antilabor, which had happened to the Pinkerton agency.

Burns investigated the bombings, but the pace was slow, especially in the view of Angelinos that craved immediate vengeance for the killings. The Los Angeles County prosecutor grew frustrated with Burns and had his funding eliminated, but Burns, by now a wealthy man in his own right, funded the investigation with $14,000 of his own money. After months of meticulous investigation, Burns arrested three labor militants, Ortie McManigal, along with brothers James and John McNamara, on April 11, 1911. John McNamara was on the board of directors of the American Federation of Labor (AFL), and all three men were active in the Ironworkers union. The three men told Burns that they would blow up the whole country if it meant them getting their rights.

Burns reveled in the publicity, but organized labor fought back, claiming that the three were being framed. Samuel Gompers, the most prominent labor leader of the era, led the attack against Burns. The AFL hired Clarence Darrow to represent the trio. Burns was theatrical by nature, but his flare for courtroom theater did not match Darrow's, who in his courtroom battles was often long on style and emotional appeal, especially when he had a weak case. Darrow and organized labor bosses even succeeded in getting Burns indicted for kidnapping in Indiana for his "illegal" extradition of the defendants.

Darrow depicted Burns as part of a capitalist conspiracy controlled by the steel industry. Contrary to Burns's wishes, the case became a cause celebre for organized labor. Fortunately for Burns, his case was solid, and Darrow made some serious errors in his defense attempt. Darrow was accused (and eventually indicted, tried, and acquitted) of hiring detectives to bribe members of the jury. Burns was also vindicated by the abrupt decision of the defendants to plead guilty to the bombing, a move that sorely embarrassed labor leader Gompers and Clarence Darrow. Burns collected a $200,000 reward for cracking the case, and his name became a household word. The *New York Times* called him a detective genius; reporters from all over the world sought him out. He began writing accounts of his detective stories, which sold well, even though Burns was a much better speaker than he was a writer.

His career flourished in the 1910s. Unlike the secretive Pinkertons, Burns exploited his own popularity. He loved showing off for the press; he wrote books about himself, and even endorsed a theater production about his exploits. He was photographed with and publicly lauded by Arthur Conan Doyle, the British physician who penned the Sherlock Holmes mysteries.

Burns continued his involvement in high-profile cases, such as the murder of Mary Phagan in Georgia, a crime that resulted in the lynching of Phagan's employer, a Jew named Leo Frank who was eventually killed by a lynch mob. Burns was nearly killed himself in 1914 while investigating the case. The mob accused Burns of being the pawn of northern Jewish business interests when Burns pointed an accusing finger at a janitor that he believed had actually killed Mary Phagan.

He revisited some of the same labor militants who had been involved, but never caught, in the *Los Angeles Times* bombing case. This time, two labor militants accidentally blew themselves up in New York City while attempting to plant a bomb in the financial district. Burns chased two conspirators from the Los Angeles case to Seattle, where they were caught and returned to New York for prosecution.

Burns made the worst mistake of his professional life in 1921 when he accepted President Warren Harding's offer to head the Bureau of Investigation (BI), the forerunner of the FBI. Although Burns was a genius at detective work and running a business, he was no match for the political vultures and corrupt hacks that comprised the BI. Burns was placed in charge of an agency that was mired in corruption, and to make things worse, he had become part of a presidential administration that still bears the title of the most corrupt in American history.

Burns had lost his ability to detect wrongdoing, as evidenced by a huge scandal that took place right under his nose. The Teapot Dome scandal was the finishing blow to Burns's undistinguished tenure as BI chief. Numerous Harding administration officials, including the Secretary of the Interior, were caught granting or selling leases on public land in exchange for kickbacks and bribes. Although Burns was not guilty of a crime, he became a scapegoat for the Teapot Dome scandal, since the crimes took place under his watch and involved some BI agents. He resigned from the Bureau in 1924, a year after President Harding's death.

After his debacle as BI director, Burns still dabbled in detective work, even conducting some criminal investigations related to the Teapot Dome scandal. Health problems began to take their toll on Burns, who had moved to Sarasota, Florida, with his wife. After several years of living a relatively quiet life, Burns died on April 16, 1932, of heart failure; he was seventy-three. The Burns detective agency is still in operation today, but the Burns family divested itself of any involvement in the agency in the years following William Burns's death.

SOURCES AND SUGGESTED READINGS

Gene Caesar, *Incredible Detective: The Biography of William J. Burns* (Englewood Cliffs, NJ: Prentice-Hall, 1968).

William R. Hunt, *Front-Page Detective: William J. Burns and the Detective Profession, 1880–1930* (Bowling Green, OH: Bowling Green State University Popular Press, 1990).

DISCUSSION QUESTIONS

1. How did William Burns's dramatic talent help his career as a private detective?
2. What do you think was the most significant case in Burns's career?

CHAPTER 10

THEODORE ROOSEVELT
(1858–1919)

Theodore Roosevelt is one of American history's true giants. When historians evaluate presidents, Roosevelt consistently ranks as one of the top ten, in the company of Abraham Lincoln, George Washington, Andrew Jackson, and Franklin Roosevelt, his distant cousin. He is remembered as an avid outdoorsman and America's first conservation president. Roosevelt is remembered as a hero in the Spanish-American War as leader of the Rough Riders who led the famous charge up Cuba's San Juan Hill, an act that vaulted him to the office of vice president of the United States. He is generally regarded as the first president to fully recognize America's emergence as a world power and player in international affairs.

Roosevelt's list of historically noteworthy accomplishments extends far beyond the scope and range of this writing. What is not as well remembered about Roosevelt is that he also served as president of the police commission for the largest police department in the United States. In fact, he is one of only two American presidents to have served in an official civilian law enforcement capacity. (The other is Grover Cleveland, who served as a county sheriff in Buffalo, New York.) Even though his tenure as New York City police commissioner was brief, his impact on urban policing and his fervent advocacy for civil service reform make him a significant figure in the history of American criminal justice.

Theodore Roosevelt was born in New York City on October 27, 1858, the second of four children born to Martha Bulloch Roosevelt and Theodore Roosevelt, a wealthy glass importer, merchant, banker, and ardent republican. His childhood education came primarily from private tutoring. As a child of privilege growing up in New York, Roosevelt wanted for nothing, except good health. He had all the amenities a child could want, but he was sickly, very asthmatic, and nearsighted. His later childhood and teen years were spent trying to overcome his physical limitations, and his efforts eventually brought him robust health.

Roosevelt spent his entire life overcompensating for his poor health as a child through athletics and outdoor activities. Roosevelt's overt machismo as an adult was also the result of his father's conduct during the Civil War, which began when the younger Roosevelt was two years old. During the Civil War, it was common for wealthy northerners to avoid serving in the military by paying someone, usually someone poor, to take their place. The elder Theodore Roosevelt did that, and the shame of his father's action never left young Theodore, who spent his adult life eagerly seeking military confrontation, both in the role of civilian politician and as a soldier.

By the time he entered Harvard at age seventeen, Roosevelt was a superb athlete—his best sport was boxing—and an avid hunter and equestrian. He was an excellent student at Harvard, graduating 21st in a class of 177 in 1880. After graduating from Harvard, Roosevelt returned to New York City to attend Columbia Law School, an experience that proved short-lived. He also married shortly after graduating from Harvard, which, tragically, proved short-lived as well. Roosevelt married Alice Lee on his birthday in 1880. Alice Roosevelt died on February 14, 1884, as a result of complications in childbirth. His mother Martha died the same day. Roosevelt's infant daughter Alice survived. Roosevelt married again in 1886, this time to Edith Carow, who would bear five children, two daughters and three sons.

Roosevelt, as the son of a well-connected and wealthy New York republican, viewed politics, not law, as his key to success. In 1881, at the age of twenty-three, Roosevelt was elected to the New York state assembly. Although his legislative record was mediocre, Roosevelt's flair for the dramatic, his outspoken and brash nature, and his colorful personality and oratory served him well, both with Republican Party leaders and the news media. Roosevelt's ability to manipulate the news media would follow him for the rest of his life.

To a much greater degree than is the case today, most civil service jobs, both at local and national levels, were handed out as political favors. Merit exams, the bureaucratic mindset, and formal hiring procedures were practically unknown. Whenever a new mayor, governor, or president would take office, civil service jobs would be given to repay political favors. The spoils system, as this was called, bred incompetence and corruption in civil service work, including police work. Incompetents took most police jobs in New York City and other cities. The primary qualification for becoming a police officer in most American cities was having a friendly relationship with a prominent politician.

In 1889, President Benjamin Harrison appointed Roosevelt to the United States Civil Service Commission. The job paid poorly and offered little prestige or public recognition, but it placed him in positions to which he aspired, in Washington with access to the seat of political power, and in civil service reform, something in which he fervently believed.

Throughout the nineteenth century, a political machine referred to as Tammany Hall dominated New York City politics. Machine politicians controlled most civil service appointments, including police officers. Myriad efforts were launched against Tammany Hall; those seeking change in separate but related areas often joined efforts against Tammany Hall. Reform efforts in New York politics were part of a larger progressive era across the United States. Progressives advocated (1) the introduction of order, rationality, and professionalism in public service and (2) ethics and morality in public service. Roosevelt stated that there are two types of gospel, the gospel of morality and the gospel of efficiency.

One key advocate of political and moral reform in New York City was Reverend Charles Parkhurst, the pastor of the Madison Avenue Presbyterian Church and president of the Society for the Prevention of Crime. Parkhurst openly criticized the New York City police force for not taking a tougher stance against vice crimes. Many police officers were co-opted by wealthy criminals who could bribe them. Others, like Detective Thomas Byrnes, would only investigate crimes in which the victim could offer some sort of reward. Parkman also denounced Chinese opium dens, drag queens parading in public, and male and female prostitution. Parkman thought that ridding the police department of corrupt officers was one key in reducing such activity.

On January 30, 1894, New York Senator Clarence Lexow, no doubt influenced by the complaints of Parkman and others, called for a thorough investigation of the New York Police Department. Actually Lexow was under the control of Tammany Hall, who thought that conducting an investigation on their terms would whitewash the machine. The move backfired on Tammany, both because of the findings of widespread corruption and brutality, and because of Tammany's attempts to influence the Lexow Commission's conclusions. In addition to the expected findings of petty bribes, kickbacks, and brutality directed toward citizens, the commission also found that officers blatantly paid for promotions, $300 for choice patrol assignments, and up to $15,000 for promotions to captain.

The Lexow Commission findings were made public on September 6, 1894, in Madison Square Garden. The result, an anti-Tammany candidate named William Strong won the mayor's seat that year. Theodore Roosevelt was working on his third volume of a book series called *The Winning of the West,* and still serving on the United States Civil Service Commission when Strong was elected, but he had grown frustrated with the job. He campaigned behind the scenes for the police commissioner's job. He worked with Mayor Strong and the Reverend Parkhurst to get some of the police commissioners who stood in his way removed from their positions.

Roosevelt was appointed to head the police commission in May 1895. As with everything else he had done and would do, Roosevelt took on the job with abandon. The job as head of the police commission did not carry any more power than any other position on the commission, but it held more of the spotlight, in which Roosevelt gloried. One of his first tasks was to rid the department of Chief Thomas Byrnes, who after rising through the ranks as detective was very wealthy and powerful. Roosevelt set out to make Byrnes miserable by exposing his wealth, which Byrnes sheepishly claimed he had gotten from good investments. Byrnes left without putting up a fight. Roosevelt also ridded the department of one its most notoriously corrupt and brutal officers, Alexander "Clubber" Williams, who once stated, "There is more law at the end of a policeman's night stick than in any ruling of the U.S. Supreme Court" (Brands, 1997, p. 276).

What made Roosevelt famous was his habit of patrolling the streets of New York, a very risky proposition in the late nineteenth century. He was not trolling for criminals, but for lazy or crooked police officers. Roosevelt set out for the first time on June 7, 1895. On his first night, he discovered two police officers sleeping in public, one of whom was the subject of a search by a waiter trying to bring him some free food; he found another officer having sex with a prostitute, and others engaged in conversation and paying no attention to their duties. He found one officer patrolling out of his district, and asked him what he was doing, to which the officer, not knowing to whom he was speaking, replied, "Why, I'm standing of course." Roosevelt ordered all of the stunned officers to his office the next morning. He reprimanded the officers, and the word was out that Roosevelt was apt to surprise any officer at any time. Once Roosevelt caught an officer drinking beer in a bar. The officer ran from Roosevelt, who gave chase and caught the officer. The officer suffered a heart attack while in Roosevelt's grasp. His nocturnal patrols made Roosevelt the object of both praise and ridicule from the New York press. His caricature featured prominent teeth and the famous eyeglasses that would remain his caricature for the rest of his life.

Roosevelt also succeeded in cleaning New York sidewalks of crates, which had become a nuisance to pedestrians. His method was simple; force officers to enforce already existing laws prohibiting placing crates on the sidewalk. Citizens of that era cared little for improvement in criminal investigation but were more concerned with quality of living issues and what the police could do to address those issues. Like the NYPD of one-hundred years later under the leadership of William Bratton and Mayor Rudolph Giuliani, Roosevelt knew that improving the quality of life for New Yorkers meant making the streets clean and safe.

Another creative move on Roosevelt's part was putting officers on bicycles. A relatively new method of transportation, bicycles experienced a tremendous growth in popularity in the United States in the early 1890s. Roosevelt had ridden a bike himself on his family home on Oyster Bay. Unfortunately, criminals, especially thieves, had capitalized on the bike craze, realizing that bikes were much faster than police officers or citizens on foot, and there were no automobiles in that day. Consequently Roosevelt ordered bike patrols on an experimental basis. The bike squad was expanded, and within one year the squad had made more than 1,000 arrests.

Bold and colorful though his police work was, Roosevelt did not stay long. He grew tired of the long hours and time away from his family. He wanted to resume his writing career, and some of his friends warned him he was becoming overly preoccupied with police work. Roosevelt also realized that corruption and bureaucratic inertia in New York City government were objects immovable even for him. Above all, Roosevelt wanted new challenges on a bigger stage. Knowing that greater things were in store for him, Roosevelt left the New York Police Commission in April 1897.

Roosevelt's career after serving the New York Police Department has literally carved his place in history; his face sits atop Mount Rushmore beside those of George Washington, Thomas Jefferson, and Abraham Lincoln. During his tenure as assistant secretary of the Navy under President McKinley, he strongly encouraged McKinley to wage war with Spain, Roosevelt recognizing America's emergence as a true world power as the twentieth century dawned. He resigned as assistant Navy secretary to head his own regiment to fight in Cuba, despite his relatively advanced age (late thirties), and became a war hero. In 1901, he accepted the republican nomination for vice president of the United States, running with incumbent William McKinley.

Tragedy would intervene to make Roosevelt one of the most important figures in American history. President McKinley was shot on September 6, 1901, in Buffalo, New York. He died on September 14, making the forty-two-year-old Roosevelt the youngest man ever to become president of the United States. His accomplishments as president were legion as well. He asserted American military might as few presidents before him had. He used the threat of force to build the Panama Canal; he won the Nobel Peace Prize for mediating an end to the Russo-Japanese War. He fought monopolies and trusts with a passion. He continued his efforts to institute civil service reform.

After leaving the presidency, Roosevelt retired from the public spotlight, but not for long. Disappointed in the performance of his handpicked successor, William Taft, he launched his own presidential candidacy in 1912, running as an independent. While giving a speech in Milwaukee on October 14, Roosevelt was shot but finished his speech and recovered. After the 1912 election, which Taft and Roosevelt lost to Woodrow Wilson, Roosevelt bitterly criticized Wilson for, among other things, his timidity in keeping the United States out of World War I. The United States eventually entered World War I, which cost Roosevelt the life of his son Quentin. Although Roosevelt publicly claimed that his son had died for a just and noble cause, the loss devastated him, and Roosevelt never recovered from his death. Often overheard by his butler quietly murmuring to himself, "Poor Quinikins; poor, poor Quinikins" (his son's childhood nickname), Roosevelt lived in despondency until his own death from heart failure on January 6, 1919, at the age of sixty. His brother Archie cabled other family members with the simple message, "The old lion is dead."

SOURCES AND SUGGESTED READINGS

Jay Stuart Berman, *Police Administration and Progressive Reform: Theodore Roosevelt as Police Commissioner of New York* (New York: Greenwood Press, 1987).

H. W. Brands, *TR: The Last Romantic* (New York: Basic Books, 1997).

H. Paul Jeffers, *Commissioner Roosevelt: The Story of Theodore Roosevelt and the New York City Police, 1895–1897* (New York: Wiley, 1994).

DISCUSSION QUESTIONS

1. What was Theodore Roosevelt's most important contribution to policing and civil service work?

2. What part did Roosevelt's work as a police commissioner play in his political career?

CHAPTER 11

■ ■ ■ ■ ■ ━━━━━━━━━━

LOLA G. BALDWIN
(1860–1957)

The question of who served as America's first fully sworn police officer is a matter of dispute. Some claim that is was Alice Wells, and others maintain that is was Portland's Lola Baldwin. Irrespective of who deserves the title, Baldwin paved the way for women who work in municipal policing. Although she was a maverick for her time, she was very different from many modern feminists, both in terms of personal mores and her functions as a police officer. Baldwin's work and life reflected the mood of American feminists during the Progressive Era of the early twentieth century, most notably the social hygiene strain of thought that dominated some efforts to improve life in large cities.

Lola Greene was born in 1860 in Elmira, New York; the Greene family moved to Rochester when Lola was a child. The sudden death of her father in 1877, while Lola was still in high school, altered the course of her professional and personal life. As the oldest of three daughters, Lola assumed childcare duties. She was forced to drop out of high school to support herself and her two sisters. Lola secured a teaching license in New York; her first teaching job, at the age of twenty, was in Monroe County, New York. She moved to Lincoln, Nebraska, in 1880 and taught high school. There she met and married LeGrand M. Baldwin, a Vermont native and dry-goods merchant. Instead of teaching, Lola Baldwin worked as a clerk for the Nebraska Public Lands Commissioner. While living in Nebraska, the Baldwins had two sons, Myron and Pierre. The Baldwins left Lincoln in 1893. LeGrand Baldwin plied his dry-goods trade in several cities, all located on the East Coast. Baldwin landed a position with a Massachusetts-based company in 1904. The company transferred him to Portland, Oregon.

It was clear even from her early life that Lola had no intention of being a housewife. Baldwin was feisty, vocal, and opinionated. She described herself as possessing an "Irish temperament," and one who loved a good fight. She stood only five feet three inches and wore steel-rimmed glasses, the visual stereotype of a Victorian-era matron.

Lola Baldwin was a product of the Progressive Era of 1890–1920. A hallmark of the Progressive Era was the social hygiene movement, which maintained that life in America's big cities could be improved by addressing moral issues that were related to public health. Prostitution, seduction at the hands of unscrupulous men, alcohol use, and other forms of vice bred disease and other health maladies, both physical and moral. Wrapped up in this school of thought was the idea that teenaged girls needed protection from the evils of big city life that bred such ills.

Social hygienists saw it as their duty to protect young women from these misfortunes.

Upon moving to Portland, Baldwin immersed herself into social hygiene activities. With the support of several charitable organizations, most notably the YWCA Traveler's Aid, she sought homeless and delinquent girls, trying to shepherd them either into group homes or other protective environments and sometimes taking young women into her home. She would locate families for some runaways, and she also tried to rescue and protect young female immigrants from dishonest immigration brokers.

A prime catalyst for promulgating the social hygiene mentality and Lola Baldwin's career was Portland World's Fair. Americans had been migrating westward for several decades prior to the turn of the twentieth century, and Portland, like other large western cities, had become a magnet for runaways and get-rich quick schemers and scam artists. Portland government officials anticipated that the World's Fair would exacerbate such problems. Baldwin had already played an important role in the establishment of a juvenile court in Portland; the number of juvenile courts had gradually increased since the pioneering efforts of Ben Lindsey in Colorado and Jane Addams in Illinois several years prior. Baldwin, already a vocal force in Portland's government, was appointed by a local judge as an unpaid probation officer and as vice prevention agent. Her task was the protection of Portland's young women from those who would try to lure them into prostitution, sexual assault, or other unsavory behaviors.

Portland officials thought that the need for Baldwin's work would be eliminated after the World's Fair, and so the position was designed to be temporary. However, because of her good work, Baldwin was kept in her position. She worked well with Portland police officers, judicial officials, and local government leaders. She handled hundreds of cases referred by police officers over a three-year period. Unlike many other women reformers of that era, she thought it best that girls be helped by women, as opposed to merely advocating that men in positions of authority pay more attention to the plight of young women with crime-related problems.

As her term as an unpaid probation officer was nearing an end, Baldwin petitioned local government officials to make her position a paid one, and that she be a fully sworn police officer with the Portland Police Department. The primary task of this female police officer would be to aid young women and address the root causes of female delinquency. Baldwin pointed out that the city of Portland had spent more money on dog pounds than on the type of work she wanted to do. Her lobbying paid off, and on April 1, 1908, at the age of forty-eight, Baldwin was sworn in as an officer with the Portland Police Department. Although she was a fully sworn officer, she did not work alongside other officers on a daily basis. Her office was not located in police department headquarters, but in the local YWCA.

Baldwin had no desire to do the same type of police work as most of her male colleagues. She did not show her badge or wear a uniform. Perhaps that was the reason she got along very well with most of her male police colleagues. She was not viewed as a woman trying to do a man's job, and therefore she was not viewed as a threat by the overwhelmingly male police department. Baldwin specialized in dealing with wayward girls, but she pursued what she believed to be the causes of delinquency as vigorously as she did the protection of those who came to her attention.

Baldwin's main priority was preventing the sexual exploitation of women and girls. Like many people of her era, she believed that men committed crime by choice, but that women lacked the capacity to make such decisions on their own, and that most if not all women who were in trouble with the law, especially women under sixteen, were led astray by men. Based on her experience and morals, she identified several causes and venues for promulgating sexual exploitation. Some venues were fairly obvious, such as houses of prostitution that functioned as an open secret throughout Portland at the turn of the century. She waged war against brothels, focusing special wrath on those that employed underage girls. She vigorously pursued cross-dressers. Cross-dressing, considered indicative of homosexuality, was a morals offense in Portland at the time, and offenders were charged with disorderly conduct.

Another venue was the dance hall. Baldwin viewed dance halls as a prime area for luring girls into sexually compromising situations. She did not seek their outright ban, but she succeeded in having many of them licensed and regulated. The situation became especially dicey when Portland residents noted that Baldwin and her colleagues only targeted dance halls populated by the lower classes, while the dance halls frequented by upper-class residents were left alone.

In 1909, with a new group of politicians sweeping into Portland, came the threat of abolishing the women's division of the Portland Police Department, a division that by then included several additional women officers. Baldwin gathered support from the YWCA, the mayor, the local Woman's Club, and the Social Hygiene Society to have an amendment to the city charter placed on the June election ballot. The amendment called for the permanent establishment of a women's police division in Portland; it passed, and the Women's Protective Division became a permanent part of the Portland Police Department. Her ability to lobby successfully for resources was uncanny, especially given the fact that most government leaders of the day paid little attention to the demands of women. At a time when many of America's police departments owned automobiles (the automobile being a recent invention) and very few women knew how to drive, Baldwin convinced the city of Portland to purchase a new 1914 Ford Model T for the exclusive use of the Women's Protective Division.

Baldwin went even further in addressing the roots of female delinquency. She sought out pornography at every turn. Once, she confiscated some objectionable viewing material from a young boy on a train, tracked down the seller and had him prosecuted in a neighboring county.

One of Baldwin's most public moral battles was with Sophie Tucker, a blond, buxom, early-twentieth-century dance hall and nightclub performer whose sexually suggestive shows delighted male audiences, much to the consternation of an increasingly powerful and prudish female population in Portland. After viewing

Tucker's performance in November 1910, Baldwin swore out a warrant for Tucker, charging her with public indecency. Baldwin biographer Gloria Myers quotes Baldwin as saying of Tucker: "Many are wondering why we have so much trouble with the young people. What can you expect when such performances as this one have only one effect on the public mind—that of debauchery and indecency" (Myers 1995, p. 58). Tucker, feeling the glare of Baldwin and the city of Portland, glared right back, threatening Baldwin and the city with legal action. After a series of nasty public exchanges, the case against Tucker was dismissed.

Movie theaters, a new phenomenon during the 1910s, also received Baldwin's scrutiny. It was not the movies to which Baldwin objected. Instead, as with dance halls, she fretted that they were places where girls would go to meet men. Baldwin also enforced laws prohibiting interracial sexual relations, especially when it involved black men (a very small portion of Portland's population) and white women, feeling little need to enforce such laws when the situation was reversed or when it involved other ethnic groups. Although Baldwin was progressive and a maverick in many respects, her beliefs about race reflected that of a majority of American Caucasians just after the turn of the century. Baldwin worked during the same time that lynching of blacks was at its zenith (although she would have abhorred such a practice), and at the same time as the release of the film *Birth of the Nation,* an enormously popular motion picture that depicted the Ku Klux Klan as the heroes of the post–Civil War south.

Her views on race relations notwithstanding, Baldwin became known throughout the United States for her work with transient girls and other female offenders. Her reputation came into play around 1917, when America prepared to enter World War I. New York police czar Raymond Fosdick was appointed by President Woodrow Wilson to head a nationwide "moral martial law" around military facilities. Baldwin was appointed to head efforts to keep military facilities free from prostitutes and other women who might lead servicemen astray. With this assignment, Baldwin sought to protect decent men from unsavory women, a reversal from her past efforts. Baldwin was placed in charge of four states: Washington, Oregon, California, and Arizona. The new job necessitated a move to San Francisco, where she remained for the duration of World War I.

Rather than simply hauling prostitutes and other "wayward girls" off to jail, only to see them back on the streets (or near military facilities) plying their trade, she established four houses that took in prostitutes. She and her colleagues were empowered by wartime emergency laws to hold these female offenders for indeterminate lengths of time. The houses, located in San Diego, Tacoma, Portland, and Los Angeles, targeted prostitutes with venereal disease. Officials in other cities followed Baldwin's lead, and thirteen similar facilities were established around the country.

Baldwin's job with the federal government ended in December 1920, two years after the end of World War I. She returned to her position in Portland and to a warm reception from the citizenry. However, the police department, under the direction of a different police chief, had downsized the women's division that

Baldwin had fought so hard to build. She traveled the country and to other countries, espousing the benefits of women performing police work. Baldwin still advocated that women officers work exclusively with women and girls rather than performing all of the jobs performed by male officers. Neither Baldwin nor any other officer in the women's protective division ever wore a uniform. Baldwin's legacy lived on in this respect for decades to come. No female police officer in Portland wore a uniform until the 1970s.

Baldwin retired from the Portland Police Department on May 1, 1922. She remained active with the parole board and with her sons and husband in the commercial bakery business. She was appalled by the changes in American culture and its effect on social hygiene in its cities. She did not like some of the behaviors (e.g., smoking, provocative clothing) of newly liberated women, all of whom were empowered by receiving the right to vote a few years prior. She watched with dismay what she viewed as the dissolution of the American family. Her Victorian-era morality still intact, she continued to lecture on venereal disease prevention, and she remained active in many of the organizations that she had been involved with during her tenure with the Portland Police Department. As Gloria Myers (1995) writes, Baldwin continued balancing the customary male and female roles, which was a difficult job for professional women during the Progressive Era. Baldwin died on June 22, 1957. at the age of ninety-seven.

Gloria Myers called Baldwin Portland's "municipal mother." She viewed the city of Portland and other West Coast cities as an extension of her own household. She thought she was a mother charged with protecting her children, and anyone, especially a female, was her child, subject to her rules, her mores, and her uncompromising dictates. Although many of her moral beliefs seem at best quaint, and at worst, very objectionable, the fact that she was a major influence on American policing is undeniable. Her stubbornness and myopic view of morality, often a detriment, was also her greatest asset. One of her admirers, Elizabeth Moorad, said of Baldwin: "She couldn't be bought; she couldn't be influenced, and she couldn't be intimidated" (Myers, 1995, p. 162).

SOURCES AND SUGGESTED READINGS

Gloria E. Myers, *A Municipal Mother: Portland's Lola Greene Baldwin, America's First Police-woman* (Corvallis, OR: Oregon State University Press, 1995).

Dorothy Schulz, *From Social Worker to Crime Fighter: Women in the United States* (Westport, CT: Praeger Press, 1995).

DISCUSSION QUESTIONS

1. How does police work performed by contemporary women differ from that done by Lola Baldwin?
2. If Lola Baldwin were alive today, what type of role would she be playing in policing?

CHAPTER 12

■ ■ ■ ■ ■ ▬▬▬▬▬▬▬▬▬▬▬▬▬▬▬

AUGUST VOLLMER
(1876–1955)

August Vollmer was the most important pioneer in municipal policing in the United States. Although his persona does not loom as large in American culture as J. Edgar Hoover, no man did as much as Vollmer to bring American policing into the twentieth century. Vollmer is owed a debt not only by modern police officers for his work, but by everyone that has studied criminal justice in an academic setting. It was Vollmer who first blended the worlds of academe and police work.

August Vollmer was born on March 7, 1876, in New Orleans, the son of German immigrants. His father, John, and his mother, Philipinne, ran a grocery business. John Vollmer died in 1884. Two years after John Vollmer's death in 1884, the Vollmers moved to Germany to live with Philipinne Vollmer's parents for two years. When August was twelve, the family returned to New Orleans, but moved to San Francisco while Vollmer was still a teenager. Raised in a lower-class household, Vollmer was forced to work odd jobs while still attending public schools. In 1891, the Vollmer family moved to Berkeley, California, the city where Vollmer would eventually make a name for himself.

In 1895, at the age of nineteen, Vollmer started a coal and feed business with a man named Ted Patterson. His successful business venture was interrupted by the outbreak of the Spanish-American War in 1898. Vollmer sold his half of the business and enlisted in the Army. He spent the war in the Pacific theater, participating in the capture of Manila from the Spanish. The fighting left Vollmer with a punctured eardrum. He returned to California in August 1899.

Upon his return, Vollmer worked a number of odd jobs before landing a position as a mail carrier, a job he held for four years. In January 1905, a friend who worked with the *Berkeley Daily Gazette* encouraged Vollmer to run for town marshal, thinking that Vollmer's military experience would serve him well in attacking the drug dens and gambling parlors that had become a problem in Berkeley. Although he was reluctant at first, Vollmer ran after receiving further encouragement from the local Republican Party, the mayor, and the local fire chief. The twenty-nine-year-old Vollmer defeated the incumbent by a three-to-one margin.

Vollmer's law enforcement career began on April 15, 1905. His first action was requesting that the city council increase the size of his force from three to twelve and that officers be given uniforms. With each deputy carrying a revolver and a short-handled sixteen-pound sledgehammer, Vollmer began raiding Chinese opium dens, only to be frustrated when the arrestees were immediately bailed out by the Caucasian families for whom they cooked and cleaned. Vollmer realized early on that the support for cleaning up Berkeley would not be unanimous. He also realized that temptation would come his way. He was offered money and real estate in exchange for not raiding lotteries and other gambling operations. Once Vollmer repaid the man who offered him a bribe by immediately raiding his gambling operation.

Vollmer's knack for innovation is seen early in his career. He purchased bicycles for his deputies, which provoked laughter from the San Francisco newspapers but attention from news outlets around the country, as Vollmer was among the first to implement bike patrol. Since bicycles were three times faster than foot patrol, Vollmer viewed it as not as a way to get in touch with the community (as with community policing today) but as a way to catch criminals more efficiently.

In 1905, Vollmer visited Los Angeles and went on patrol with a private detective named Jim Foster. Foster, in the employ of private citizens in Los Angeles, would patrol on bicycle in the hope of preventing burglaries. Foster placed call boxes on telephone poles that were wired to his residence. He would dismount from his bicycle and phone his wife, who would tell him of any reported crimes. Foster later attached a red light to each phone that would light on all phones if it were pressed on any one of them. Although it seems primitive by today's standards, it was innovative for its time.

Eager to implement a similar system across Berkeley, Vollmer persuaded the city council to place a $25,000 bond referendum on the next election ballot that would carry the cost of such a program. After the referendum was approved, Vollmer contracted with Gamewell Signal and Alarm Company to install the system.

In April 1906 an earthquake devastated San Francisco, bringing 50,000 refugees into Berkeley. About half that number remained in Berkeley after the earthquake's immediate aftermath, and the size of Vollmer's marshal force doubled.

The 1907 death of a milkman that was deemed a suicide but which Vollmer believed was a murder convinced him that police officers needed to know more than just how to catch and fight criminals. In an unusual move for a police officer, Vollmer began studying criminal psychology, using it immediately to catch a psychologically maladjusted arsonist. After being reelected by a huge margin, Vollmer devised the idea of having a police school to train officers, realizing that there was very little written about police work and criminal investigation. Vollmer's police school, which was at first met with resistance by line officers who had to attend classes during their spare time, included four teachers. Resistance from line officers never mattered much to Vollmer; he had little faith in the rank and file, assuming that most people were basically lazy and needed strong leadership. Vollmer taught first aid, police methods, public health and sanitation, photography, and basic law. Walter Peterson, an Oakland police captain, taught detective work. Most significantly, Vollmer blended the world of academe and policing for the first time in American history by using William Herms from the University of California Parasitology Department to lecture on sanitation. He had A. M. Kidd from the University of California Law School teach courtroom evidence. Even though he was not a college graduate, Vollmer was the first law enforcement official in the United States to formally integrate police work with academic inquiry.

Vollmer was appointed chief of the Berkeley Police Department on August 13, 1909. He gladly accepted the move, motivated in large part by not having to conduct any more political campaigns. Vollmer's personal life changed soon after becoming police chief. He married Lydia Sturdevant in 1911. The marriage ended in divorce in 1920.

Soon after becoming chief, Vollmer put his officers on motorcycles. In 1913, he gained nationwide publicity by placing his officers in automobiles, though he was not the first to do that. In 1916, Vollmer convinced the city to lure Dr. Albert Schneider away from the University of California Medical School to become a full-time criminologist for the police department, another innovative move. Vollmer demanded that his men accept no gifts, do no special favors, put no juveniles in jail, and use no excessive force or torture, all four of which were common elements of police work in the 1910s. Violators were fired instantly.

One of the most innovative moves of his career was his decision to hire police officers with some college education. Vollmer purchased an advertisement in the *Daily Californian,* the University of California student newspaper. The ad read:

> College men wanted for police force. Interesting experience. Learn a new profession. Serve on the Berkeley police force while you go to college. Contact August Vollmer, Chief of Police.

Psychiatry, a new medical endeavor, was frowned upon by much of the general public and the medical profession in the 1910s. Vollmer, however, saw the need for psychiatric assistance in conducting hires. He employed Dr. Don Ball of the University of California to screen applicants and give intelligence tests to insure that the applicant had high intelligence, sound nerves, "good physique and reliable character."

Some newspapers lampooned the hiring of college graduates by featuring cartoons of boys in caps and gowns wearing pistols, but the move was widely popular. One of Vollmer's first college cops was O. W. Wilson, a man who would be mentored by Vollmer and succeed him as one of the greatest innovators in police work of the twentieth century. Another college recruit, John Larson, helped him develop a method of fingerprinting; he also developed a lie detector in 1921. Vollmer kept a modus operandi file as well. He developed the first police radio car in 1921. That same year he was unanimously elected to serve as president of the International Association of Chiefs of Police (IACP). At the IACP meeting in 1922, Vollmer called for the creation of a national bureau of criminal records and statistics. His efforts culminated in a congressional bill changing the name of the Bureau of Investigation to the Federal Bureau of Investigation, which was charged with maintaining criminal records and statistics.

In 1923, Vollmer agreed to serve a one-year term as police chief in Los Angeles. He brought some of his methods to Los Angeles, hiring UCLA professors to conduct some of the work done by UC professors in Berkeley. He tried to ferret out corrupt police officers through undercover stings. He used the Army Alpha test of intelligence as a tool in making promotion and assignment decisions. He oversaw the construction of a new jail in Los Angeles. Along with bringing professors into the police department, Vollmer, who never attended college, conducted guest lectures on police work at the University of Southern California.

Vollmer was not pleased with his stay in Los Angeles, thinking he had not been able to do enough and believing that corruption and cronyism were well engrained in the Los Angeles Police Department. He returned to Berkeley in 1924, the same year that he married Millicent Pat Fell. He began sharing his police innovations with police chiefs around the world, including chiefs in Detroit, Chicago, and Havana. In 1929 he accepted President Herbert Hoover's offer to serve on the Wickersham Commission, which was formed to conduct the first national study of criminal justice administration in American history. He accepted a part-time teaching position at the University of Chicago and later at the University of California at Berkeley.

Vollmer resigned from the Berkeley Police Department on June 30, 1932, after serving twenty-six years as chief. He became an international consultant, traveling throughout Asia and Europe advising police departments while retaining his teaching position at the University of California. His life slowed down in the 1940s, especially after the death of his wife, Pat, though he continued to write and consult on occasion. In failing health, suffering from depression and deteriorating eyesight, Vollmer committed suicide on November 4, 1955, at the age of seventy-nine.

In an address before the IACP in 1919, Vollmer said that making arrests was not enough in preventing crime. He believed that police officers should "go up the stream a little" by working with families and schools. At the same time, Vollmer's two real hallmarks as a police chief were that policing should be a bureaucratic rather than a political position and that higher education and police work go hand in hand. August Vollmer did more to bring police studies into the educational arena than any person in the first half of the twentieth century.

SOURCES AND SUGGESTED READINGS

Alfred E. Parker, *Crime Fighter, August Vollmer* (New York: Macmillian, 1961).
Samuel Walker, *Popular Justice: A History of American Criminal Justice* (New York: Oxford University Press, 1980).

DISCUSSION QUESTIONS

1. How did August Vollmer forge a link between police work and the academic environment?
2. What lessons can be learned from Vollmer in terms of police management and crime prevention?

CHAPTER 13
■ ■ ■ ■ ■
SAMUEL BATTLE
(1883–1966)

I can take no pride in showcasing racial or ethnic diversity with this book. In fact, a book of this nature in many ways is a showcase of shame on American history and its criminal justice system. Caucasian men have dominated American criminal justice. Racial minorities were not allowed a voice in shaping the criminal justice system. Examples of blacks being employed in the criminal justice system, let alone in great numbers or in leadership positions, are rare. However, a number of individuals have had a tremendous impact by working through the system, former lawyer and Supreme Court Justice Thurgood Marshall among them. A number of African Americans, such as Martin Luther King, Jr., have effected change in the administration of criminal justice by working outside the system. There are many biographies of minority criminal justice pioneers that should be written, but only those within specific locales or small towns might know many of them. One story that should be told is that of Samuel Battle, the first African American police officer in New York City, and a man whose career and impact went far beyond breaking that one barrier.

Samuel Battle, the son of former slaves, was born on 1883 in New Bern, North Carolina. He attended segregated schools in North Carolina. Like many other African Americans of his era, Battle moved north to seek a better life than he could find in the Jim Crow south. He moved to New Haven, Connecticut, to attend a manual training school as a young man. Eventually Battle took a job in New York City as a train porter at Grand Central Station. While he was still working twelve-hour shifts, Battle took the radical and what some may have viewed as insane step of studying for the civil service exam to become a police officer.

Battle passed the exam in 1910, but city officials, uneasy with the prospect of hiring a black officer, delayed his appointment under the pretext of claiming that Battle had a heart condition that might affect his suitability for police work. Nevertheless, Battle was hired as a police officer for the city of New York in June 1911. His first assignment was to New York's West 68th Street station.

American history is filled with sad stories of poor treatment of pioneering minorities. For example, Jackie Robinson, by joining the Brooklyn Dodgers in 1947, became the first African American major league baseball player of the twentieth century and was subjected to incredible torrents of verbal abuse from teammates, opposing players, and fans. Upon his arrival to the New York City Police Department, Battle was greeted mostly with stony silence. Unwelcome by the vast majority of his peers, Battle was subjected to the silent treatment by other police officers that refused to even acknowledge his existence, let alone accept him as a colleague. By one account, two years went by before any of the white officers spoke to him, but Battle did not publicly admit that he was receiving bad treatment from his peers.

Although he was never accepted by many of his colleagues, Battle's perseverance, polite demeanor (an impolite demeanor would have been the death knell for Battle's career), and courage to withstand the hostility of those around him began to pay dividends. New York City police officials, recognizing that African Americans were populating the city's Harlem area in growing numbers, sought an opportunity to use Battle's skin color to their advantage. Thinking that black residents in Harlem would have a better rapport with a black officer than with white officers, they assigned Battle to the West 135th Street station in Harlem.

Battle's transfer to Harlem was well received by the area's black residents. It worked well for Battle too, so well that he was encouraged to apply for a promotion to sergeant in 1919. The year 1919 was one of the worst in American history in terms of urban riots, some of which were race-related. The most infamous was in Chicago, which resulted in the loss of dozens of lives, but a riot broke out that year in Harlem as well. Fitting an all-too-familiar pattern through America's twentieth century, Harlem's Straw Hat riot, as it was called, erupted over the shooting of a young black man by a white police officer. Another white officer, when cornered and in danger of being murdered by a rioting black mob, was saved by Battle. In return, the New York Police Department, which had been holding up Battle's admission to sergeant's school because he lacked the requisite approval from his colleagues, promptly admitted him to sergeant's school, with the blessings of Battle's colleagues.

Battle made high marks on the sergeant's exam but had to wait seven years for his promotion. In 1926, Battle, already the first African American police officer in New York Police Department history, became its first African American sergeant. Battle became the Department's first African American lieutenant in 1935. He continued to advance, becoming a parole commissioner in 1941; his primary task was working with delinquent black youths in Harlem. Part of the reason for this move was Battle's history of reaching out to the Harlem community and his crime prevention measures. In addition to the common sense crime prevention practices he used on his patrol beat, he raised money to buy Thanksgiving dinners and trips to movie theaters for poor Harlem residents.

In 1943, while America was in the throws of World War II, it experienced another outbreak of urban riots, one of which occurred in Harlem, again the result of the shooting of a black man by a white police officer. At the request of New York Mayor Fiorello LaGuardia, Battle took charge of the city's response to the Harlem riots. One of his first orders was that all white civilians including Mayor LaGuardia vacate Harlem's streets. Then he ordered officers placed in strategic rooftop locations and on mounted patrol. Battle personally patrolled the Harlem area, making sure he was visible to the Harlem residents who knew and trusted him.

After the 1943 riots, Battle resumed his work as parole commissioner. Not only did he monitor his charges' whereabouts, he devised methods he saw as conducive to rehabilitation of inner-city youths. He organized and administered summer camps, sports leagues, and other community activities. Battle solicited the involvement of black and white police officers, in hopes of bringing Harlem residents and the police closer together.

Battle kept his position as parole commissioner until his retirement in 1951. He continued working with Harlem's youth in crime prevention and other community activities. In 1964, the New York City Police Department held a special ceremony with the eighty-one-year-old Battle as special guest. The department paid tribute to him, calling him "the father of all Negroes in the Police Department." Battle died on August 7, 1966, at the age of eighty-three, leaving behind his wife, Florence, a son, a daughter, and a legacy as one of America's bravest criminal justice pioneers.

SOURCES AND SUGGESTED READINGS

James I. Alexander, *Blue Coats: Black Skin* (New York: Exposition Press, 1978).
Alan Axelrod and Charles Phillips with Kurt Kemper, *Cops, Crooks and Criminologists* (New York: Facts on File, 1996).

DISCUSSION QUESTIONS

1. If you were faced with the same obstacles as Samuel Battle, could you persevere as he did?
2. In what ways did Samuel Battle go beyond conventional police work to fight and prevent crime? What can be learned from his efforts?

CHAPTER 14

■ ■ ■ ■ ■

J. EDGAR HOOVER
(1895–1972)

Some subjects of this book lived lives that made so great an impact that not even an entire book, let alone one short chapter, can capture that impact. J. Edgar Hoover, the man who directed the Federal Bureau of Investigation from 1924 to 1972, is one such person. His presence still looms larger than life, not only within the FBI, but also over American law enforcement, politics, and culture. Few Americans are neutral on the subject of J. Edgar Hoover. Few Americans have been as admired and simultaneously detested as Hoover. No one was as lionized in life and as vilified after death as Hoover either. Since his death, history has not been kind to him. Much has been written and said about J. Edgar Hoover, some of it true and some of it myth. His personal strengths, accomplishments, and positive contributions to law enforcement, often overlooked by modern historians, are exceeded only by his personal quirks, his fascinating frailties, and his glaring shortcomings.

Some subjects of this book gained fame or infamy by accident. Not so with Hoover, who seemed almost destined from birth to become what he was, a spectacularly successful Washington bureaucrat. John Edgar Hoover was born on January 1, 1895, in Washington, DC, not far from the Capitol building that his great-granduncle helped construct. Of all of the subjects of this book, Hoover was probably the least traveled. He knew or cared little about other places or other cultures. He was very much a product of the small town provincial and bureaucratic atmosphere that was Washington at the turn of the twentieth century. He was the youngest of four children born to Dickerson and Annie Scheitlin Hoover. Dickerson Hoover, who worked for the U.S. Coast and Geodetic Survey, was not a strong influence on him; in fact Dickerson Hoover's institutionalization for mental health problems was a family embarrassment. J. Edgar Hoover's strongest influence was his mother, with whom he lived until her death in 1938.

A devoutly religious child, Hoover at one point aspired to be a Presbyterian minister. Hoover was short and slight of build, and stuttered as a child. Hoover overcame his stuttering by speaking in a rapid-fire, staccato fashion, and he sharpened his speaking skills through participation in high school debate teams. He remained short of stature his entire life, something of which he was very conscious. He avoided social gatherings where tall people were present, and while many FBI field agents were tall, few tall agents worked in FBI headquarters in physical proximity to the diminutive Hoover. Hoover always kept a dais under his desk that he could stand on when anyone entered his office.

Hoover was the valedictorian of his high school graduating class in 1913. Rather than accepting a scholarship from the University of Virginia, Hoover chose to live at home and attend night school at George Washington University. During the day Hoover worked at the Library of Congress, which was located four blocks from his home. It was there that Hoover learned two things that would serve him well throughout his career. One, he honed his ability to research and keep meticulous records, which would lead to his trademark as FBI director, the keeping of thousands of secret files on public figures. Second, Hoover, the son and grandson of Washington bureaucrats and a fledgling bureaucrat in his own right, discovered something about Washington; even the most powerful politicians come and go; bureaucrats, not politicians, are the real power brokers.

Hoover received a bachelor of law degree in 1916, his master of law degree a year later, and passed the District of Columbia bar exam that same year. On July 26, 1917, Hoover took a job as a clerk with the United States Department of Justice (DOJ). The job exempted Hoover from the draft; America had entered World War I three months earlier.

Throughout his life, Hoover viewed people and issues in strict absolute terms; someone or something was either good or evil, with no in-between. What he perceived as un-American was bad, and anyone that did not conform to his idea of a patriotic American was not only wrong, but also evil. Hoover, already a skilled, humorless, patriotic, no-nonsense bureaucrat while still in his early twenties, rose rapidly through Justice Department ranks, heading the DOJ's Alien Enemy Bureau by 1917.

In 1919, Hoover was placed in charge of the DOJ's Radical Division. The first public display of using the criminal law to advance his idea of patriotism came with his role in the deportation of Emma Goldman, Alexander Berkman, and more than 200 other political radicals in 1919, an outgrowth of the Palmer Raids, which he coordinated for Attorney General A. Mitchell Palmer. Hoover took an active part in the prosecution of these radicals, who had been suspected of, among other things, sabotaging America's war effort. He also succeeded in using the news media to proclaim his actions, something he grew increasingly adept at doing as the years progressed. When the raids began to fall into public disfavor, Hoover just as effectively distanced himself.

Hoover was appointed as assistant director of the Bureau of Investigation in 1921, fourteen years before it would be renamed the FBI. During the early 1920s the Bureau was filled with corrupt, feckless agents with shady backgrounds and little in the way of qualifications. Presidents, cabinet officials, and powerful congressional figures had used it almost exclusively as a political football. The Teapot Dome scandal, in which numerous Interior Department officials accepted bribes and kickbacks in exchange for leasing oil rights on government property, led to

President Calvin Coolidge's call for the Bureau and the entire Justice Department to be cleaned up.

Upon the departure of William Burns in 1924, Attorney General Harlan Fisk Stone offered the job of Bureau director to Hoover. Hoover accepted but with conditions. Hoover demanded that the Bureau be divorced from politics and not a "catch-all for political hacks," that appointments and promotions be based on merit, and that Hoover be answerable to the attorney general and the president, not to any member of Congress or other cabinet officials. Stone gladly agreed, effectively giving the twenty-nine-year-old Hoover a blank check to establish the department in his own image and render him virtually unaccountable. Hoover assumed his duties as director on May 10, 1924; he would serve for more than forty-eight years.

As crime increasingly became a national concern, Hoover was determined to make the Bureau the nation's and the world's premier law enforcement agency. To a great extent he did just that. He imposed qualifications for his agents far and above those required by even the most progressive police agencies. Bureau agents were required to have backgrounds in either law or accounting. Bureau agents would be called on to investigate complex financial crimes. Hoover did not want agents working for him who would lose cases in court because of ignorance of the law. Procedural guarantees such as the exclusionary rule, which would not apply to the states until the 1960s, already were required at the federal level.

Hoover took advantage of every available investigation tool he could find. The FBI boasted the world's most highly trained agents and one of the world's top training programs and regimens. Agents were required to be dressed neatly in coat and tie at all times. Utter patriotism and loyalty to the Bureau (and to Hoover personally) were FBI agent trademarks. Hoover, the consummate Washington insider, knew how to get things done and how to get what he needed and wanted, both for himself and his agency. He succeeded in getting a fingerprint identification unit, which was accessed by law enforcement agencies from around the country; he developed a crime laboratory unmatched by any that had ever existed. Not long after Hoover assumed directorship, the FBI became the envy of law enforcers around the world. The FBI represented the unquestioned elite in American law enforcement.

Prior to the 1930s, the United States had no empirical measure of how much crime occurred or how many crimes were reported to police. Hoover oversaw administration of the Uniform Crime Report (UCR), which was started in 1933. Crude and imperfect, especially in its founding stage, the UCR consisted of crimes reported to police agencies, or at least the local agencies that chose to participate by sending their reports to the Bureau. It was the United States' first systematic method for gathering and analyzing crime statistics, and it is still in use today.

Although Hoover was effective at improving the qualifications of his agents and the facilities and technologies at their disposal, his real strength was in selling his agency and himself to the public. Despite the fact that he possessed a dour and colorless personality, Hoover became the object of public fascination and downright adoration. Hoover developed a following like no other American law enforcer before or since his time, even though he made very few actual arrests, all of which, though genuine, were carefully staged and planned in order to bolster Hoover's image as a top-notch cop. He effectively portrayed crime as a public menace, and he offered his own guidance in crime prevention to whoever would listen.

One of Hoover's greatest strengths was his ability to personalize America's crime problem, to put a face on crime, to be able to create in the public mindset the idea that there were good guys and bad guys. Take the bad guys off the street, courtesy of the FBI, and feel a sense of closure and relief. Hoover created this image by creating America's first public enemies list. The public enemies list would consist of America's most-wanted criminals, with their names and faces plastered on federal office buildings around the country. The 1930s in particular was the decade of g-men (FBI agents) hunting down notorious bank robbers and murderers. Hoover simultaneously helped to create reputations for some of his prey, which to some degree hurt the public image of the criminals, but which also inadvertently helped create folk hero images as well. Names such as Lester Gillis, a.k.a. Baby Face Nelson, Alvin "Creepy" Karpis, Charles "Pretty Boy" Floyd, George "Machine Gun" Kelly, "Ma" Barker, and "Handsome" John Dillinger became household words. By tracking down and either capturing or killing such criminals, most of whom were active in the Midwest, Hoover was able to effectively portray the FBI as the agency that "always got its man" (or woman).

Dillinger's case provides some insight into the way Hoover thought. After months of fruitless searches, embarrassing escapes, and shootouts, including one notorious jail escape courtesy of a wooden gun (after Dillinger posed for a photo with the local sheriff, with his arm draped across the local prosecutor's shoulder), Hoover made it his passion to get Dillinger, in part because he was a genuine threat to public safety, but mostly because he had embarrassed Hoover and the Bureau. Bureau agents killed Dillinger in 1934 outside a Chicago theater.

The long-awaited killing of Dillinger, which should have made Hoover ecstatic, instead sent him into a jealous frenzy. The reason, one of his agents, Melvin Purvis, who directly supervised the Dillinger killing, was hailed as a hero. Hoover could not stand for any law enforcer, particularly one of his own agents, to grab the limelight, and any police officer or chief that did could count Hoover as an enemy. His enemy list included Cleveland public safety director Eliot Ness and Wichita police chief O. W. Wilson. The public adulation heaped on Purvis would spell the end of his career with the Bureau.

World War II brought new challenges to Hoover and the FBI. Investigating espionage and industrial sabotage became the top priorities. The FBI investigated numerous such cases, including the case of the bungling German saboteurs that landed ashore in Florida and New York via German submarine, but were easily caught and prosecuted; some were executed.

A sad footnote to America's World War II victory was the forced relocation and internment of Japanese-Americans on the Pacific Coast. Many Americans, including prominent names associated with twentieth-century liberalism, such as Earl Warren (who served as Attorney General of California) and President Franklin Roosevelt, ordered the internment of the Japanese Americans. What is not mentioned by most of Hoover's critics is that Hoover opposed the forced relocation, believing that most Japanese Americans posed no threat to American security and that those who did could be effectively monitored, as was being done on the East Coast and in the Midwest with people of German ancestry.

After World War II, American anger and suspicion was directed at a new enemy, Communism, which had also been viewed as a threat immediately after the end of World War I. This brought Hoover into contact with two people, both of who enjoyed a symbiotic relationship with Hoover, one for only a short time and one for many years to come. Joseph McCarthy, a United States senator from Wisconsin, succeeded in whipping America into a paranoid frenzy over Communism. Richard Nixon, a young California congressman, joined the fray. Hoover and the FBI, with the aid of Nixon, succeeded in prosecuting a high-level State Department official named Alger Hiss on charges of perjury, related to supplying intelligence information to the Soviet Union. With prodding from McCarthy, President Harry Truman, who disliked both Hoover and McCarthy, grudgingly allowed the FBI to conduct background checks on all prospective and current federal employees. Hoover, who had already accumulated hundreds of secret files, delighted in his new duty. He had a virtual blank check to investigate practically anyone.

McCarthy quickly fell from grace, but Hoover and Nixon thrived in the Cold War era. The FBI even successfully led the prosecution of the only Americans of the twentieth century to be executed for espionage during peacetime. Julius and Ethel Rosenberg were convicted and executed in 1953 for selling nuclear secrets to the Soviet Union.

The 1960s, the age of civil rights and anti-Vietnam war protests, brought out even more paranoia in Hoover. Critics and even some agents (quietly) charged that Hoover, who had directed the FBI for more than forty years and who was now in his seventies, was losing touch with reality. The list of people he tracked and secretly (and illegally) investigated grew astronomically. It included Martin Luther King, Jr. (whom Hoover referred to as a degenerate), Malcolm X, Elvis Presley, Edwin Sutherland, John Lennon, the Kennedy family, and literally hundreds of other academics, entertainers, political figures, and public figures, most on the political left.

During his tenure with the FBI, Hoover had working relationships with presidents from across all parts of the political spectrum. Some liked him (Richard Nixon); some disliked him but could not get rid of him because of the feared political fallout (Harry Truman) or they were afraid he would release damaging information about their personal or political lives (John Kennedy and Franklin Roosevelt). Eleanor Roosevelt, the wife of Franklin Roosevelt and a person that Hoover detested, called the FBI an American gestapo. Neither Dwight Eisenhower nor Lyndon Johnson particularly liked Hoover, but they knew he was useful. When asked by an aide why he kept Hoover around, President Johnson replied, "I'd rather have him inside the tent pissing out than outside the tent pissing in" (Dallek, 1998, p. 126).

J. Edgar Hoover died on May 2, 1972, at the age of seventy-seven. Hoover never married and was never known to have dated a woman seriously. Many believe that Hoover had a long-term homosexual relationship with Clyde Tolson, the man who served several decades as assistant director to the FBI and one of the few people with whom Hoover was ever seen in a casual setting, such as lounging around the home or visiting the race tracks, something which any other FBI agent would have been forbidden to do.

Evaluating J. Edgar Hoover's place in American history is not easy. He was in many ways a true giant in the field of law enforcement. The FBI, even with its many faults, still stands as one of the world's elite law enforcement agencies, thanks in large measure to Hoover, for whom FBI headquarters are named. However, as large he was in many ways, he was equally small in other respects. He was petty, small-minded, paranoiac, and bigoted. The question is whether Hoover merely reflected the attitude of most Americans of his era, or whether he was one of the people responsible for shaping mainstream America's attitudes toward crime, civil rights, and left-wing politics. He was smart enough to take on battles he could win, such as nabbing gangsters and spies, but he was also smart enough to avoid battles he knew he could not win, such as prohibition and organized crime. However one chooses to view Hoover, one cannot say his impact on American law enforcement is anything less than profound.

SOURCES AND SUGGESTED READINGS

Robert Dallek, *Flawed Giant: Lyndon Johnson and His Times, 1961–1973* (New York: Oxford University Press, 1998).

Curt Gentry, *J. Edgar Hoover: The Man and His Secrets* (New York: Norton, 1991).

Mike Forrest Keen, *Stalking the Sociological Imagination: J. Edgar Hoover's FBI Surveillance of American Sociology* (Westport, CT: Greenwood Press, 1999).

Max Lowenthal, *The Federal Bureau of Investigation* (New York: William Sloan, 1950).

Richard Gid Powers, *Secrecy and Power: The Life of J. Edgar Hoover* (New York: Free Press, 1987).

DISCUSSION QUESTIONS

1. Was J. Edgar Hoover a case in point of one man being granted too much power? Why or why not?
2. In what respects did J. Edgar Hoover create American perceptions that matched his own, and in what respects did he simply mirror popular perceptions of his time?

CHAPTER 15

■ ■ ■ ■ ■ ▬▬▬▬▬▬▬▬▬▬▬▬▬▬▬▬

HARRY ANSLINGER
(1892–1975)

Harry Anslinger directed the Federal Bureau of Narcotics (FBN) from 1930–1962, a record of longevity in high-level federal law enforcement exceeded only by J. Edgar Hoover. He was the first federal law enforcer to successfully make social and criminal pariahs of narcotics users, and one of the first to paint drugs as a threat to America's existence as a nation. One of the most skillful bureaucrats of the twentieth century, Anslinger's administrative prowess directly affected all Americans during his tenure as FBN director and is still felt today. Anslinger's life and career offer insight into America's strange relationship with narcotics during the twentieth century. His draconian attitude toward drug use and his successful misinformation campaigns about the effects of drugs reflected the uninformed sentiments of the American public and set the pace for American drug policy for his lifetime and beyond.

Harry Jacob Anslinger was born on May 20, 1892, in Altoona, Pennsylvania, the eighth of nine children born to Robert and Christina Anslinger, both of whom immigrated to Ellis Island from Switzerland in 1881. Originally trained as a barber in Switzerland, Robert Anslinger moved to Houtzdale, Pennsylvania, then to nearby Altoona where he worked for the Pennsylvania Railroad. Harry Anslinger attended public schools in Altoona, but, at age fourteen, the immediate attraction of earning money led to his attending school part-time while working for the Pennsylvania Railroad. Anslinger never officially graduated from high school, but he enrolled at Altoona Business College in 1909 and at Pennsylvania State College in 1913, where he earned an associate's degree in engineering and business management while working for the railroad on weekends. He also worked as a piano player for silent movie theaters, hoping to become a concert pianist.

Anslinger's railroad job served as a formative experience for him. While working there, he developed a love of investigations and sleuthing by working as company detective, once discovering that a woman that had been "accidentally" run over by a railroad car had actually been murdered by her husband. He developed a strong hatred for narcotics, witnessing the destructive aspects of morphine addiction on both adults and children in Altoona's lower and middle classes. While working alongside many Italian immigrants, Anslinger also discovered firsthand the existence and ruthlessness of the Italian *Mano Nero* (Black Hand), or mafia, which terrorized fellow Italians who refused to accede to their shakedown attempts. In later years, Anslinger, unlike FBI director J. Edgar Hoover, would claim that the Italian mafia posed a great threat to the well-being of American society and that the mafia was one of the prime actors in the spread of drug use.

Anslinger's entry into the federal government came with America's entry into World War I in 1917. As the son of Swiss immigrants, Anslinger spoke fluent German, a useful skill paired with his attraction to unobtrusive observation. Anslinger was assigned to the Netherlands to work with friendly elements of the German government in a clandestine effort to elicit cooperation with the United States. After the war, Anslinger maintained his employment with the federal government, a relationship that would not be severed until his retirement almost fifty years later. Anslinger began working for the State Department's diplomatic corps in 1918, first assigned to the Netherlands, then in 1921 to Hamburg, Germany, a hotbed of international drug trafficking.

While in Germany, Anslinger married Martha Dennison, the mother of a twelve-year-old son from a previous marriage. To his dismay, Anslinger was assigned to work in La Guaria, Venezuela, in 1923, far away from the European languages and culture he had grown to love and from the educational opportunities his stepson needed. In 1926, at the height of American Prohibition, Anslinger was transferred to the Bahamas, a major transit point for bootleggers and a British colony that was a thorn in the side of American Prohibition agents. Anslinger believed in Prohibition, thinking that corruption within the Treasury's Prohibition Bureau and lax criminal penalties were the reasons for its failure, rather than agreeing with many who saw Prohibition as a fundamentally flawed experiment. As a result of his interaction with Treasury officials, Anslinger, though an employee of the State Department, began advocating stiff penalties for both corrupt Treasury agents and Prohibition violators.

Narcotics enforcement had become an issue of increasing concern since 1914 when the Harrison Act was enacted. The Harrison Act required those dealing in certain drugs to register and pay a tax. Since the Harrison Act was related to tax collection, enforcement was placed in the hands of the Treasury Department, just as had most attempts to enforce Prohibition laws. In fact, the same bureau within the Treasury Department enforced both Prohibition and narcotics laws. Thinking that the two problems merited the full attention of individual bureaus, Congress established the Federal Bureau of Narcotics in June 1930. President Herbert Hoover signed the bill into law, just as America was starting to experience the pangs of the Great Depression.

President Hoover appointed Levi Nutt to head the FBN, but a scandal involving Nutt's son and New York's infamous gambler Arnold Rothstein stained his nomination. Treasury Secretary Andrew Mellon, a relative of Anslinger's wife, appointed Anslinger acting commissioner. Anslinger received a permanent appointment on September 23, 1930, at the age of thirty-eight.

Anslinger set about combating international drug trafficking rings, especially those trafficking in marijuana. The 1930s was the first decade in American history in which marijuana became an issue of national concern. If modern medical researchers and policy makers are unsure about the full effects of marijuana use today, they were completely ignorant of its effects in the 1930s. Marijuana use was largely confined to Hispanics in the Southwest, its native region, and it gradually made its way into the American jazz subculture, where jazz notables like Duke Ellington and Louis Armstrong praised its use. New Orleans, America's jazz capital, was the center of much of the phobia over marijuana use. As long as it was confined to these two subcultures, marijuana was not a matter of national concern. Marijuana became an issue of widespread concern when its use spread to America's white middle class.

Some public officials in the 1930s, Anslinger among them, believed that marijuana, in addition to causing severe hallucinations, was correlated with violent crimes like rape, suicide, and murder. Among the popular magazine articles about marijuana were ones titled "Youth Gone Loco" and "Danger." Anslinger, using his FBN directorship as a bully pulpit, cowrote an article for *American Magazine* called "Marijuana: Assassin of Youth." The article mirrored Anslinger's frequent testimonials before Congress on the subject of marijuana. Not only did they reflect his views on marijuana as a health hazard and link to violent crime, they reflected the racism associated with concerns over marijuana:

> I am of the opinion that those addicted to the use of this drug are far more dangerous than those addicted to the other forms of narcotics in that it makes the user of it very brazen and fearless.
>
> In New Jersey in 1936, a particularly brutal murder occurred, in which case one young man killed another, literally smashing his face and head to a pulp. One of the defenses was that the defendant's intellect was so prostrated from his smoking marihuana cigarettes that he did not know what he was doing.
>
> Colored students at the University of Minnesota partying with female students smoking and getting their sympathy with stories of racial prosecution. Result pregnancy.
>
> West Virginia—Negro raped a girl eight years of age. Two Negroes took a girl fourteen years old and kept her for two days in a hut under the influence of marihuana. Upon recovery she was found to be "suffering from" syphilis.

Anslinger's public war against marijuana and his skillful manipulation of Congress, whose members were as ignorant about marijuana's effects as his, culminated in his greatest coup. In 1937, Congress passed the Marijuana Tax Act, despite scant reliable scientific research on marijuana. The act imposed taxes on marijuana dealers, effectively banning the drug under federal law through strict regulation. Marijuana was not banned outright because some of its uses, such as using hempseed in pigeon feed, were deemed legitimate.

During World War II, Anslinger launched aggressive efforts to investigate and disrupt drug use on military bases. He claimed that narcotics were as great a threat to American security as were foreign armies. He believed that Japan was trying to weaken America by trafficking in opium.

Both during and after the war, Anslinger used actors and other celebrities to promote his agenda. In 1943, San Francisco bureau agents arrested Gene Krupa, a well-known big band leader, on charges of sharing marijuana with a seventeen-year-old boy. Krupa was sentenced to ninety days for marijuana possession and one to two years for corrupting a minor. Krupa's arrest was reported in *Time*, a major publicity coup for Anslinger. An even bigger publicity coup was the 1948 arrest of actor Robert Mitchum. Mitchum was charged with smoking marijuana with a group of other young people. Mitchum's arrest generated enormous public alarm about the moral state of Hollywood, as the movie industry was also fighting charges that it was under Communist control. Mitchum was convicted on February 9, 1949, and sentenced to two years probation; the case was eventually dismissed. Mitchum's career soared anyway and so did Anslinger's.

Throughout his career, Anslinger tied drugs to whatever crisis America confronted. During the 1950s, when the United States was in the throws of the Cold War with the Soviet Union and China, Anslinger portrayed drug importation as a Communist plot perpetrated by the Soviets and especially by the Chinese, just as he had done with the Japanese (China's adversary) during World War II. He saw drugs as more of a social evil than a public health matter, and he thought that those who used and sold them had malicious intentions. Anslinger never had a sympathetic attitude toward drug users, much to the dismay of America's medical establishment, and he believed in preventing the spread of drug use by severely punishing drug dealers, having little faith in medical or therapeutic treatment.

As the 1960s dawned, so did new ways of thinking about many aspects of American life. Many teenaged baby boomers loudly questioned or rebelled against many institutions, including the political establishment and law enforcement. A changing attitude about narcotics was occurring as well, with drug use becoming an increasingly common part of the college experience. Drug use became associated with rock-and-roll music, which had exploded in the 1950s and became even more popular in the 1960s. In 1962 the United States Supreme Court, led by Chief Justice Earl Warren, added its voice to this changing attitude by striking down a California law that criminalized drug addiction and instead calling addiction a disease.

Americans elected John F. Kennedy to the presidency in 1960. Kennedy, in contrast to Dwight Eisenhower, his staid, grandfatherly predecessor, was young, handsome, Ivy League educated, aloof, and intellectual—in many ways the antithesis of a dry career Washington bureaucrat like Anslinger. Kennedy nominated his younger brother Robert to serve as attorney general. Many expected that one of the Kennedy brothers' first acts would be to replace Anslinger with someone new, but the Kennedy brothers surprised them by keeping Anslinger.

Anslinger had worked under four presidents prior to Kennedy, having the greatest respect for Harry Truman. Anslinger biographer John McWilliams states that Anslinger also had great respect for both John and Robert Kennedy; whether the Kennedys had mutual feelings toward Anslinger is not known. So it is not known if Anslinger was forced into retirement on his seventieth birthday in 1962, sixteen months after Kennedy's inauguration, or whether he retired because he had reached the mandatory federal retirement age of 70. It is also possible that the death of Anslinger's wife in 1961 played a role in his decision.

After his retirement, Anslinger continued his fight against narcotics, never wavering in his belief that drugs were an evil and that drug users were criminals rather than sick addicts. In public speeches he continued to advocate stiff penalties for drug use while eschewing treatment. Anslinger lived a relatively quiet existence in Hollidaysburg, Pennsylvania. In 1968, under the leadership of President Lyndon Johnson and Attorney General Ramsey Clark, the Federal Bureau of Narcotics was merged with the Bureau of Drug Abuse Control to form the Bureau of Narcotics and Dangerous Drugs.

Anslinger began experiencing serious health problems in 1973, including an enlarged prostate, serious angina, and total blindness. Ironically, Anslinger, who had battled narcotic use throughout his life, used morphine to relieve the pain of angina. He died of heart failure on November 14, 1975, at the age of eighty-three.

After Anslinger's death, the United States Senate, led by Senator Edward Kennedy, the brother of the former president, held hearings into Central Intelligence Agency (CIA) activities during the 1950s and 1960s. The senators discovered that Anslinger's FBN, in cooperation with the CIA, participated in several bizarre and malign drug experiments during the Cold War. Anslinger personally approved of experiments to find a truth serum consisting of marijuana, peyote, and sodium amytal. Sometimes the experimental subjects were foreign prisoners, sometimes they were CIA researchers, and others were unsuspecting citizens. In one instance, drug-addicted prostitutes in New York City were given a fix in exchange for luring Johns to hotel rooms where the unsuspecting men were given LSD for the purpose of examining the drug's effects.

The debate over how to address drug use in America remains unsettled. Was Anslinger right in seeing drug users as criminals who needed to be punished rather than helped? Or was his mentality horribly misguided, as alleged by the medical establishment throughout his career? Even though Anslinger did not single-handedly shape the American criminal justice system's attitude toward narcotics—many countries have much more punitive policies toward drug use than the United States—his role as America's first true drug warrior has cemented his place in American criminal justice history.

SOURCES AND SUGGESTED READINGS

Rufus King, "Harry Jacob Anslinger," *American National Biography Online,* www.anb.org, March 21, 2003.

John C. McWilliams, *The Protectors: Harry J. Anslinger and the Federal Bureau of Narcotics, 1930–1962* (Newark: University of Delaware Press, 1990).

DISCUSSION QUESTIONS

1. Did Harry Anslinger create America's attitude toward narcotics, or did he merely mirror existing sentiments?
2. How might America's policies toward marijuana be different were it not for Harry Anslinger?

CHAPTER 16

O. W. WILSON
(1900–1972)

If August Vollmer deserves the title of America's premier police pioneer of the twentieth century, O. W. Wilson is entitled to the title of chief protégé of that pioneer. Vollmer's and Wilson's lives and careers were inextricably linked, with Wilson owing his career to Vollmer but still carving his own distinctive niche in the history of American policing. Several labels are appropriate for O. W. Wilson, including academic pioneer, police scholar, police reformer, and consummate police professional.

Orlando Winfield Wilson was born in 1900 in Veblen, South Dakota. His father, Ole Vraalson, was a Norwegian immigrant who changed his last name to Wilson because he thought it would be easier for business purposes. Both he and his wife, Olava, were schoolteachers, while Ole also worked the family farm. Ole also served as county treasurer and state legislator. The Wilsons moved to Saskatchewan in 1905, then to Anderson, California, in 1911, then to Orland, California, in 1913, and finally to Pacific Beach near San Diego. O. W. Wilson graduated from San Diego High School in 1918, and motivated by his interest in a gold mine his father had purchased years earlier, he left San Diego to attend the University of California at Berkeley to pursue a degree in mining engineering.

Shortly after World War I ended in 1918, the United States experienced a severe recession. Ole Wilson fell victim to the bad times and was unable to provide for his son's college expenses. O. W. Wilson needed a job to put himself through college, and he noticed an advertisement in the student newspaper placed by the city of Berkeley, more specifically by August Vollmer, the city's police chief. Vollmer was recruiting college students to work as municipal police officers, something unheard of in American policing at that time. Desperate for funds, Wilson applied for one of Vollmer's "college cop" positions, thinking of it merely as a college meal ticket.

The standards set by Vollmer for police work were much higher than Wilson expected. Wilson scored higher than any of the other applicants on the Army Alpha Test and performed well on the physical examination and the psychological examination. The last step was a personal interview with Chief August Vollmer. Vollmer hired him and informed Wilson that he would have to furnish his own personal vehicle and .38 caliber Smith & Wesson revolver. He started working for the Berkeley Police Department in 1921 at a salary of $140 per month, plus $30 monthly car allowance.

Most police departments in the 1920s were riddled with inefficiency, corruption, political meddling, and uneducated, feckless officers. Not so in Berkeley; Wilson and his young colleagues worked and learned under the most progressive police chief in the country. Wilson learned to work with polygraphs; he learned about using call boxes on streets to contact police, which although crude by today's standards, were innovative for their day. Vollmer's record keeping was ahead of its time as well; Wilson learned to keep a modus operandi file that catalogued robbery and burglary techniques.

Some veteran officers resented the presence of Vollmer's college cops. Wilson managed to overcome this resistance by working hard, not flaunting his education, maintaining a serious, mature demeanor, and doing good police work. Early in his tenure, Wilson captured a notorious escaped prison inmate named Kid Benet by himself, and his reputation as an effective officer was solidified.

Like most Berkeley police officers, Wilson spent much of his time responding to calls from the University of California campus, where he did not make many friends, mostly because of his fraternity house inspections, where he would cite members for city health code violations and for minor thefts in which they had participated. His serious demeanor and the fact that he was the same age as the people being policed did not help him win friends either.

It was at Berkeley that Wilson made contact with people who would play important parts in his personal life and his career. In addition to August Vollmer, one such person was Earl Warren, who as an assistant prosecutor in the Alameda County district attorney's office, worked closely with Wilson. Warren and Wilson became fast friends in the 1920s, mostly because of their shared philosophy in strict law and order and vigorous prosecution of criminal defendants. Forty years later, when Warren, as chief justice of the United States, would lead the due process revolution so despised by many police officers, Wilson called him "treacherous" for turning his back on law enforcement.

While at Berkeley, Wilson met Vernis Haddon, a university student, when he stopped her for speeding in 1921. Haddon was one of the few people Wilson would turn loose for an infraction. Six weeks after they met, Wilson and Haddon eloped and were married in Sacramento, a rare act of impulsivity that he probably regretted in later years.

While working as an officer, Wilson's studies suffered, and he even flunked out of Berkeley for one semester. He returned and changed his major to economics, thinking a career in business would be his future; he graduated in 1925. Chief Vollmer had other plans for Wilson. Realizing that Wilson would prove an invaluable asset to the professionalization of law enforcement, Vollmer strongly recommended that Wilson accept the job of police chief in Fullerton, California.

Wilson accepted the Fullerton police chief job in 1925. The Fullerton experience would prove disappointing. The liberal atmosphere of Berkeley that permitted Vollmer to innovate and experiment was not present at Fullerton. Some citizens were puzzled and alarmed at his call for birth control as a crime prevention measure. Wilson was criticized for being overzealous when he strictly enforced a dog leash law. He was also criticized for curtailing the use of motorcycle patrol, which he saw as inefficient, but which locals liked because the motorcycles made impressive funeral processions. Although he was lauded for many of his efforts, Fullerton civic leaders tired of hearing complaints from citizens about Wilson. He resigned on December 1, 1925, and moved to Los Angeles to work as an investigator for the Pacific Finance Corporation while his wife embarked on an acting career.

In March 1928, again relying on Vollmer's recommendation, Wilson accepted the position of chief of police in Wichita, Kansas, where he would make his historic mark on American law enforcement. Wichita was ripe for reform and posed an enormous challenge for Wilson. It was in many ways still tied to the frontier law enforcement mentality of Wyatt Earp, who had worked in Wichita law enforcement half a century prior. Corruption and inefficiency were the hallmarks of Wichita policing, but during his eleven-year tenure Wilson would turn it into one of the most progressive police departments in the nation. Just as Vollmer did in Berkeley, Wilson would also forge a relationship between law enforcement and academe that would handsomely benefit both entities. Wilson and Wichita State University would create a program that is still heralded as one of the top academic police programs in the United States.

Wilson hit the ground running, refusing to enact reforms slowly. In his first year as chief, he fired more than 20 percent of the force, including anyone even suspected of being corrupt. He required weekly written quizzes in the squad room. Wilson began in-service training, adding both a small library and a gymnasium for that purpose. He established a six-week training program for police cadets, the first of its kind in the United States. When he discovered that the best criminology and police science texts were written in French and German, he had them translated into English. Wilson implemented a sophisticated (for its day) record and report system. Each officer was provided a work sheet on which they were required to log all of their shift activities. He established a modus operandi file. One of his most innovative ideas was in the area of patrol. After careful study, Wilson concluded that two-officer patrol cars were wasteful, that it was not a good way to allocate resources, and that officers spent too much time lollygagging when they were paired together. He implemented one-officer patrols.

Not wishing to repeat the mistakes he made in Fullerton, Wilson not only lectured the community on the work of the police, but he engaged them by seeking their input. He did not do so with his subordinates, because, like his mentor, August Vollmer, one of Wilson's greatest weaknesses as an administrator was that he tended to distrust his rank and file, paying little attention to their concerns or input.

Taking a cue from Vollmer's experience with the University of California, Wilson established a good working relationship with the Municipal University of Wichita, later renamed Wichita State University. He enlisted sociologists to work with his officers in assisting wayward youth. He never hesitated to contact university professors when starting a new project when he thought they might be useful. Wilson, a college graduate himself, never doubted the value of a college education for a police officer. The question was what the police officer should study. Should the police officer specialize in police courses, or would the officer be better off with a degree in the liberal arts? Wilson was not even sure that so-called police science merited university study on its own.

In preparing an academic curriculum for police officers, Wilson began by listing the tasks performed by a police officer. First, he eliminated from university study tasks best taught at a police academy and subjects that would not be worth the time of a university professor. He then decided that political science would be the best vehicle for offering a police studies program, and that seven courses should be taught: (1) criminal law, (2) personal identification, (3) police patrol practices, (4) criminal evidence, (5) traffic control, (6) criminal investigation, and (7) police administration. The curriculum was implemented in 1936.

Wilson's star shone from Wichita throughout the 1930s, in large measure due to his own brilliance and because of support from Wichita city officials. He received praise and support from law enforcement officials from across the United States and other countries. Not surprisingly, Wilson eventually became the enemy of FBI director J. Edgar Hoover, for reasons unknown to Wilson. In all likelihood, Hoover's negative attitude toward Wilson stemmed from the same reason he had negative attitudes toward other prominent law enforcers; he simply could not stand being upstaged.

During the 1930s, Wilson also had the luxury of selecting the best candidates for police work. The Great Depression left many people out of work and desperate, which made the steady pay that police jobs offered highly attractive. Wilson's training was so effective that many of his officers relocated to other jurisdictions to assume jobs as managers and chiefs. Wilson's department acquired the nickname the "West Point of Law Enforcement" because of the number of highly qualified police leaders that passed through its ranks.

As the 1930s came to a close, the situation in Wichita changed. Wilson was no longer able to have his pick of police candidates as Kansans began returning to work. City officials grew increasingly uncooperative. After eleven years, Wilson had finally begun to wear out his welcome in Wichita. He resigned in May 1939 to work as a consultant with the Chicago Police Department, but he still had three monumental tasks before him. Soon after he arrived in Chicago, August Vollmer enticed Wilson to accept a tenured professorship at the University of California at Berkeley. He began his professorship in July of 1939.

The United States entered World War II in 1941. Separated from his wife (he and his wife divorced in 1943) and in his forties, Wilson enlisted in the army and was given a commission with the rank of lieutenant colonel. When it became clear that the tide was turning toward American victory over Germany and Italy, the United States organized a School of Military Government in Charlottesville, Virginia. Its charge was to rebuild civilian police services in postwar Germany in accordance with a democratic system of government. After the war ended in 1945, Wilson went to Germany to work on this task. One of the most controversial aspects of the rebuilding program was installing former Nazi Party members in positions of police responsibility. Nevertheless, Wilson and those around saw it as the only practical move, agreeing with General George Patton's assessment that many Nazis were party members in the same sense that Americans were either Democrats or Republicans. Wilson received the Bronze Star for writing a public safety manual and helping establish a civilian police force in West Germany.

Wilson returned to Berkeley after his work in West Germany. He continued to write and teach with great success. He authored *Police Administration,* the seminal work in that area even today, but his work in municipal government was not done. In 1960, at the age of sixty, Wilson accepted the job of police chief for Chicago. He took over a department with a reputation as the most corrupt in the nation. Though he did not totally rid Chicago policing of corruption, his tenure was marked with great successes, in marked contrast to that of his successor.

The 1960s was the most turbulent decade of the twentieth century. It was marked by riots and protests for many causes, civil rights and antiwar protests topping the list. Police officers around the country found themselves the unwitting front line soldiers in many of these protests. Unlike many other police officials who chose a strictly defensive and hostile posture toward most protesters, Wilson did just the opposite, hoping that Chicago would avoid the black eye given to police departments in Birmingham and other cities for their actions against demonstrators and protesters. In 1966, Martin Luther King, Jr., decided to stage a protest march in Chicago. Wilson was told of King's plans, and invited King to Chicago to meet with him well in advance of the protest. Rather than vowing to fight King as many other police officials had done before, Wilson treated King as an honored guest. He worked patiently with King, giving him a tour of Chicago police facilities, making arrangements for King's and the other marchers' protection, and doing his best to insure that the King-led protest would go off smoothly and without violence. Wilson's treatment of King should have served as a model for handling similar events in the turbulent 1960s, but, unfortunately, few police chiefs, including his successor in Chicago, paid heed.

Wilson resigned in 1967 and returned to California, this time settling in Poway and living with Ruth Wilson, who he had married in 1950. He reworked *Police Administration* but stayed out of the public eye. His children from both marriages were grown and Wilson wanted to live quietly in retirement near his siblings. O. W. Wilson died of a stroke on October 18, 1972, at the age of seventy-two.

Modern police officers and those interested in the academic pursuit of police studies owe a greater debt to O. W. Wilson and August Vollmer than to any other Americans. If Vollmer was the Socrates of modern policing, Wilson was his Plato. After Vollmer, Wilson ranks as the most significant figure in American municipal policing.

SOURCES AND SUGGESTED READINGS

William J. Bopp, *O. W. Wilson and the Search for a Police Profession* (Port Washington, NY: Kennikat Press, 1977).

O. W. Wilson, *Police Administration* (3rd ed.) (New York: McGraw-Hill, 1972).

DISCUSSION QUESTIONS

1. If you were a police manager and had a subordinate who was dating a person they met through a traffic stop, and that subordinate read the story of how O. W. Wilson met his wife, what would you say to the subordinate?
2. What was the most significant act of O. W. Wilson's career?

CHAPTER 17

■ ■ ■ ■ ■ ━━━━━━

ELIOT NESS
(1903–1957)

He has been portrayed as the man that single-handedly brought down the most notorious American gangster of the twentieth century and as a fearless, almost flawless, soldier in the battle against big city corruption during Prohibition. He was the inspiration for Chester Gould's "Dick Tracy" comic strip and his name has been placed in the annals of film and television history through *The Untouchables*. The story of Eliot Ness is a story of two lives, one, a young, handsome, idealistic, crime fighting crusader, the second, a middle-aged playboy and problem drinker whose lifestyle brought an early death.

Eliot Ness was born on April 19, 1903, in Chicago, the second of four children born to Norwegian immigrants Peter and Emma Ness. He was named after George Eliot, the British novelist whose real name was Mary Ann Evans. Peter Ness was a baker; Emma Ness worked as a housewife at the family's South Side Chicago home in the predominantly Scandinavian enclave of Kensington. Eliot Ness was an excellent student, graduating near the top of his high school class and earning good enough marks to gain admission to the University of Chicago, where he graduated in 1925 with degrees in business administration and political science.

Ness's first job after graduation was with the Retail Credit Company, where he conducted investigations on people applying for insurance coverage. America was in the middle of Prohibition, which had been in effect since the ratification of the Eighteenth Amendment and the accompanying Volstead Act of 1920. Prohibition, dubbed "the great experiment" by its proponents, was a failure from its inception. A large number of Americans wanted to consume alcohol, and although making alcohol sale and consumption illegal curtailed consumption, Prohibition demonstrated that the citizenry does not abide by laws with which it does not agree.

Prohibition spawned a plethora of bootlegging enterprises throughout the United States, none greater than in the city of Chicago, and none bigger or more violence-ridden than the one controlled by Al Capone, a hulking, thuggish, Brooklyn-based gangster who still bears the distinction as the most notorious criminal entrepreneur of the twentieth century. Prohibition also led to the creation of law enforcement agencies to enforce temperance laws. One was the Prohibition Bureau, organized by the Department of Justice. The Bureau of Investigation (later renamed the FBI), also housed in the Department of Justice and under the direction of J. Edgar Hoover, wanted as little to do with Prohibition as possible, realizing it was a battle that could not be won. One Prohibition Bureau agent was Alexander Jamie, Ness's brother-in-law. Ness worked with Jamie occasionally, going with him on raids and learning the business of prohibition enforcement. Ness also enrolled in criminology courses at the University of Chicago.

Ness used his connections with Jamie to land a position with the Department of the Treasury, the agency that assumed the bulk of Prohibition enforcement duties. Ness began working with the Treasury Department in 1926, after undergoing a background check conducted by Hoover's Bureau, which had assumed such responsibility for Treasury and Justice Department officers. The agent who investigated Ness characterized him as "reliable in every aspect, a clean young man, morally a fine fellow." This rosy assessment would serve in marked contrast to assessments in later years by J. Edgar Hoover, who became jealous of Ness's fame.

Unlike most other Prohibition agents and many Chicago police officers, Ness was honest, hard working, not beholden to Chicago's bootleggers, and virtually incorruptible. Although he was ambivalent about the wisdom of Prohibition, he believed in the rule of law and thought it was the law enforcers' job to enforce it, regardless of personal opinions. Public sympathy and the sympathies of local police lied with the bootleggers, especially Al Capone, who always maintained that he was just giving the public what it wanted. Treasury agents could not trust the local police, much of the citizenry, the news media, nor each other. Very often, Ness and other agents would arrive at a speakeasy (an illegal bar), a booze warehouse, or a still and find it abandoned or empty, the bootleggers having been tipped off in advance of the impending raid.

It is difficult to say when the tide of public opinion began to turn against the bootleggers, including Al Capone, but turn it did, even as opposition and exasperation toward Prohibition escalated. The event that may have signaled the beginning of the end for Al Capone and other area bootleggers and gangsters occurred on February 14, 1929. Several men, some wearing police uniforms, cold-bloodedly murdered seven bootleggers, and the Chicago media covered the event extensively. No arrests were made, but all eyes turned to Al Capone, who probably ordered the killings. The St. Valentine's Day Massacre was the type of anti-gangster publicity that law enforcement needed. Even President Herbert Hoover got involved. He was determined to wrest control of the city from Capone and his tommy-gun-toting gangsters.

Treasury agents also got a boost from Chicago's business, civic, and political leaders, who realized that Chicago's lawless reputation was damaging its chances of attracting investors and manufacturers. One group of businessmen, dubbed the "secret six" by the local media because of their insistence on remaining anonymous (lest gangsters target them for retribution), was charged by the Chicago Association of Commerce with addressing the city's crime problem. President Herbert Hoover appointed Ness' brother-in-law Alexander Jamie as chief investigator for the secret six. Because of Ness's honest reputation, Jamie appointed Ness to head a squad to pursue Capone's bootlegging operation, despite the concerns of Ness's superiors who thought him too anxious to make a name for himself.

Ness selected a squad of men that he thought trustworthy, not given to drink, and proficient either at investigation, evasive driving, or wiretapping. Over the years, approximately fifteen men worked with Ness, either openly or secretly, with eleven men (not three as portrayed in *The Untouchables*) plus Ness forming the core of the group. The group tenaciously pursued Capone's bootlegging operation, raiding his warehouses, his breweries, and his speakeasies. Although Ness and his men did not put Capone out of business, they irritated him, and forced Capone and other bootleggers to operate clandestinely rather than parading their illegal goods down the streets of Chicago in broad daylight. In 1931, Ness infuriated Capone by phoning him and telling him to look out his window. A convoy of cars that had been confiscated from Capone, containing Ness and his agents brandishing pistols and rifles, rode by Capone's office, taunting the egomaniacal gangster, an unthinkable act in 1931 Chicago. Attempts to bribe Ness and his men were unsuccessful, and threats did not deter them. Their unwillingness to be co-opted or intimidated led Ness's squad to be labeled the "Untouchables" by the local media.

Ness skillfully manipulated the media, making a name for himself and hurting the gangsters' image. He was gracious to reporters, and would often inform them of an impending raid so they could film or view it firsthand, even though this sometimes foiled the raid, either because reporters would alert the gangsters in advance, or would accidentally arrive at the scene before Ness, thus letting the gangsters know that a raid was coming.

Capone made a severe tactical error in 1929. A number of nationally prominent bootleggers wanted to eliminate Capone for the bad publicity generated by the St. Valentine's Day Massacre. In an attempt to lay low, Capone arranged to have himself arrested in Philadelphia on a concealed weapons charge, assuming that he would spend a few weeks in the local jail. To his surprise, the judge imposed a one-year sentence, which Capone served in relative luxury at Eastern State Penitentiary. Unfortunately for Capone, his brother Ralph, left to run the bootlegging business, was inept, which made the Capone organization ripe pickings for Ness and the other officials pursuing him.

A 1927 Supreme Court ruling, coupled with the dogged determination of Ness and Internal Revenue Agents investigating Capone's financial dealings, spelled the end of the notorious gangster's empire. In *U.S. v. Sullivan,* the U.S. Supreme Court held that illegally obtained income was subject to taxation, and that those who failed to file or pay taxes on such income were criminally culpable. Internal Revenue Service officers used the holding to attack Capone while Ness and his agents continued their attack on Capone.

In 1931, after two years of investigations, raids, arrests, indictments, rigged-jury allegations, guilty pleas, plea negotiations, and a jury trial, Capone was found guilty of income tax evasion and failure to file an income tax return. He was sentenced to eleven years in prison and fined $80,000. In their only face-to-face encounter, Ness personally escorted Capone from the courthouse to waiting federal marshals at the Dearborn Street Station on February 27, 1932. Although Ness thought the encounter significant, Capone paid Ness little attention.

Prohibition ended in 1933 with the ratification of the Twenty-First Amendment, and Ness, now made famous by his clash with Capone, was ready for new ventures. He wanted to join the FBI, but J. Edgar Hoover, never one to share the spotlight with any of his subordinates, entertained no thought of hiring Ness.

Ness was offered the position of director of public safety in Cleveland. The job involved oversight of both the local police and fire departments. Rampant corruption within the Cleveland Police ranks had made the department an embarrassment. City leaders, in particular newly elected mayor Harold Burton, were aware of Ness's reputation for honesty, and saw him as an answer to departmental corruption and a poster boy for reform with Cleveland city government, even though he had no experience in municipal law enforcement or fire protection.

Ness started his duties on December 11, 1935, at the age of thirty-two. His impact was immediate. Ness aggressively pursued corrupt officers within Cleveland's ranks, to the hearty approval of city leaders. The soft-spoken, amiable Ness charmed the local media. Many veteran officers were resentful of the young, boyish-looking Ness, often referring to him as a "boy scout" or a "college cop." The fact that he had gained fame as a prohibition agent also generated resentment, as many of the veteran officers had been co-opted by bootleggers during Prohibition.

Ness thought that weeding out corruption in the Cleveland Police Department was key in reducing crime. Unlike most other police chiefs past and present who are reluctant to acknowledge corruption within their agency, Ness reveled in taking down corrupt police officers and making it public. Ness targeted high-ranking officers, namely captains, lieutenants, inspectors, and the like rather than low-ranking officers. Dozens of high-ranking officers were either indicted, fired, or both, most guilty of accepting kickbacks and bribes or running protection rackets for bootleggers and gamblers.

Ness viewed poor training and low qualifications as causal factors in police corruption. He implemented several reform measures considered radical in the 1930s. According to FBI files, Ness wanted to bring "g-man" methods to Cleveland law enforcement. He thought that traditional reactive policing was inadequate in addressing Cleveland's major crime problems. Instead, Ness focused on the financial roots of major crime organizations.

Soon after becoming public safety director, Ness was quoted in a college classroom speech in which he offered his perspective on gambling. It was consistent with his perspective on alcohol. As with alcohol, Ness disliked gambling because he believed it fed crime syndicates. The FBI obtained some of Ness's speech by reading about it in the Cleveland *Plain Dealer*. Ness titled his speech, "Choke Crime by Its Purse." Ness did not attack gambling on a moral basis. Ness said, "It is debatable, for instance, whether gambling is morally wrong, but from the policing standpoint you have an entirely different picture. I am inclined to be liberal in my views of amusements and I do not want to intrude my opinions on others, but as a safety director I must recognize every thing which contributes to a lawless situation. By that I mean major crime."

Even though Ness was officially disengaged from federal law enforcement, he still tried to maintain friendly ties with federal agencies. FBI Director Hoover, ever curious about anyone and everyone that might assume a position of political or social prominence, ordered that agents report any information about Ness, be it personal or professional. In January 1936, an FBI agent was sent to meet with Ness and report back to Hoover. The agent wrote that he believed that Ness was a good man, but that his department was poorly organized, judged by the number of petty interruptions they got while meeting.

The agent also carried some information to Hoover that he had obtained from a Cleveland *Plain Dealer* interview with Ness. In the January 11, 1936, article, Ness laid out a prescription for "curing police evils." Many of his suggestions are standard to police work today and they reflect considerable foresight and sophistication on Ness's part:

1. Immediate establishment of a police training school (he used the FBI Academy as a model)
2. Much more rigid requirements for admittance to civil service examinations given to candidates for appointment as patrolmen (he implemented an exam that weeded out more than half of the applicants)
3. Searching character investigations and the fingerprinting of men in line for appointment to the force
4. Different requirements for admission to and promotion in various branches of the police service
5. Testing of a candidate's temperamental, as well as mental and physical, fitness to become a policeman
6. Weeding out of cadet patrolmen who have not demonstrated proficiency in police work during a two-year probationary period
7. Adoption of measures to improve the morale of the present police force

Ness was America's golden boy of municipal policing. He was admired nationwide and viewed as the poster child for honest, efficient law enforcement. With all of that in his favor, what caused his eventual downfall in Cleveland? The answer is threefold. First was his role in creating the Cleveland Industrial Safety Council in 1939, just after World War II started in Europe. The Cleveland Industrial Safety Council assessed a twenty-five-cent per employee fee on all industrial and manufacturing businesses in Cleveland. The money was given to the council, which Ness chaired, so that undercover agents could be hired to monitor subversive activities in the plants, such as sabotage and espionage. Ness collaborated with the Navy's intelligence division and the Pinkerton Detective Agency in establishing and operating the council. The council had been established in accord with the directive of President Franklin Roosevelt, who had asked local law enforcement to report subversive activities in manufacturing plants to the FBI.

When the activities of the council became public, Cleveland's labor unions were outraged, arguing that the real purpose of the covert surveillance was to subvert organized labor. J. Edgar Hoover denounced the "morally repugnant" council, primarily on the grounds that he distrusted private co-optation of public law enforcement. Hoover, feeling that Ness had usurped his local law enforcement role, believed that such activities should be left to the FBI.

A second reason for Ness's demise was the inability of the Cleveland police to arrest the "mad butcher," a serial killer that terrorized Cleveland's Kingsbury Run area and claimed more than twenty victims over a period of several years during the 1930s. The butcher preyed on Cleveland's homeless population, the ranks of which soared during the Great Depression. Ness was confounded by the inability of police to catch the killer, and he thought such investigations beneath him. Ness enjoyed pursuing rational, profit-driven celebrity criminals instead of irrational sociopathic killers. The mad butcher was never caught.

A third event brought an end to Ness's Cleveland career. After his wife Edna left him in 1938, Ness's personal life took a downward spiral that would continue the rest of his life. Ness became a womanizer and a fixture at Cleveland nightspots. He became one of Cleveland's most well known playboys, to the bemusement of those that had praised him for his fight against alcohol several years earlier. Ness remarried in October 1939, this time to Evaline McAndrews, a Cleveland socialite, but he continued his playboy lifestyle.

On March 5, 1942, after a night of drinking, Ness and his wife had an auto accident in which the driver of the other car was injured. Ness reportedly left the scene and did not report the accident. Ness was never charged with a crime, but when his behavior was discovered, Ness's days as director were numbered. He resigned on April 30, 1942.

Ness moved to Washington, DC, to become director of social protection service of the Federal Security Administration, a position he had already assumed while still serving as Cleveland's public safety director. The service's primary function was to patrol military facilities to investigate and prevent vice crimes, especially organized prostitution. The service was also active in venereal disease prevention efforts, sponsoring films and lectures designed to educate military personnel on the subject. Ness's poor relations with J. Edgar Hoover and the FBI haunted him in this position. Once when an agent recommended to assistant FBI director Clyde Tolson that the FBI partner with Ness, Tolson wrote, "This is Elliot Ness' (sic) outfit. I am opposed to any cooperation."

As World War II came to an end, so did Ness's job. Ness participated in several business ventures, enjoying a great degree of success for a while, and even gaining recognition for his efforts in *Fortune* magazine. In 1944 Ness became board chair of Diebold Safe Company. Despite Ness's many opportunities to succeed in business, his primary devotion was to his playboy lifestyle, which not only affected his personal life but his health as well. He got involved in an import-export business, but bad management on Ness's part eventually doomed the company. He divorced his second wife in 1944 and remarried in 1946, this time to Elisabeth Andersen Seaver. In 1947, Ness unexpectedly ran for mayor of Cleveland and was defeated by an almost two-to-one margin.

As his financial and personal lives continued their downward spiral, Ness, in need of funds and thinking that his battle against Al Capone would be of interest to the general public, collaborated with Oscar Fraley on a book called *The Untouchables*. The book was spun into a television screenplay, and as the projects were being developed, Ness and his family (which included one adopted son, Robert) realized that the Ness portrayed in books and television would be far different than the real-life Ness. The fictional Ness was a swaggering, macho gunslinger, whereas the real-life Ness was soft spoken and mischievous and seldom carried a gun. Nevertheless, the deal offered a much needed $1,000 advance, so Ness went along with the ruse. Although few people remember Ness for his role in other law enforcement jobs, his association with *The Untouchables* made him a television icon.

Ness did not live to see his name mythologized by Robert Stack (who portrayed him in the Emmy-award-winning *Untouchables* television series) or Kevin Costner (who portrayed him in a 1987 movie of the same name) or Tony Amandes (who portrayed him in a 1993 syndicated television series). Kevin Costner's movie portrayal in *The Untouchables* notwithstanding, Eliot Ness did not confront Al Capone in the lobby of a hotel; he did not have a daughter; he seldom carried a weapon (discharging it only once, at a door lock); and he did not push Capone associate Frank Nitti off a courthouse roof to his death. On May 16, 1957, Ness died of a heart attack in Coudersport, Pennsylvania, at the age of fifty-four. He left an estate worth $675.

SOURCES AND SUGGESTED READINGS

Freedom of Information Website, http://Poia.fbi.gov, August 23, 2002.

Stacey Hamilton, "Ness, Eliot," *American National Biography Online,* June 2000, http://www.anb.org, August 19, 2002.

Paul Heimel, *Eliot Ness: The Real Story* (2nd ed.) (Nashville: Cumberland House, 2000).

Eliot Ness with Oscar Fraley, *The Untouchables* (New York: Messner, 1957).

DISCUSSION QUESTIONS

1. What lessons can be learned about Eliot Ness's personal lifestyle while he worked in Cleveland?
2. In what ways was the real Eliot Ness different from the one portrayed in television and film?

CHAPTER 18

■ ■ ■ ■ ■ ━━━━━━━━━ ▬▬▬▬

DARYL GATES
(1926–   )

March 4, 1991, was a night that changed America. It was on that night that a private citizen, using a store-bought video camera, taped police officers pummeling Rodney King, a small-time criminal who had led the officers on a high-speed chase and failed to obey their instructions after exiting the car. A total of fifty-six blows were delivered to King's head and body. The videotape became the lead story of television newscasts around the world. Some thought it represented all that was wrong with race relations in the United States, especially with respect to police officers and African Americans. Its impact went far beyond the boundaries of law enforcement; it even served as the opening for Spike Lee's movie biography of Malcolm X. All eyes turned to Daryl Gates, the controversial chief of the Los Angeles Police Department. The Rodney King beating was the beginning of the end for one of America's most simultaneously admired and despised police chiefs.

In April 1991, Los Angeles mayor and dedicated Gates foe Tom Bradley appointed a special commission headed by international attorney (and future secretary of state) Warren Christopher to investigate the Los Angeles Police Department (LAPD). The Christopher Commission released its report on July 9, 1991, and it placed blame for the LAPD's problems squarely on Gates. Among other criticisms, the commission stated:

> There is a significant number of officers in the LAPD who repetitively use excessive force against the public and persistently ignore the written guidelines of the department regarding force. The failure to control these officers is a management issue that is at the heart of the problem. The LAPD's failure to analyze and act evidences a significant breakdown in the management and leadership of the Department. The Department not only failed to deal with the problem group of officers but it often rewarded them with positive evaluations and promotions.

Gates stepped down in April 1992, ending a forty-three-year career in law enforcement, all spent with the LAPD. What was it about Daryl Gates that evoked such strong feelings? How could a man be so reviled and also be called a hero by several American presidents? The day of the Rodney King beating, Gates was in Washington, DC, attending a presidential forum on crime prevention at the invitation of the attorney general of the United States. A year later he retired in disgrace.

There was little in Daryl Gates's background to indicate he would one day become a police officer, let alone one of the most well-known American police officers of the twentieth century. Daryl F. Gates was born on August 30, 1926, in

Glendale, California. The second of three children, Gates and his family enjoyed a comfortable middle-class life, much like that of many Californians in the bustling 1920s. Gates's father, Paul, worked in the plumbing business and his mother, Arvilla, was a housewife.

The Great Depression hit the Gates family hard. In 1930, the Gates family moved to a poor area of Glendale; money became scarce, and the family lived in abject poverty throughout the 1930s. Economic deprivation took a psychological toll on the Gates family, especially on Paul Gates. During most of Daryl Gates's childhood, Paul Gates drank heavily and was often involved in bootlegging, which brought on numerous, unwelcome visits from police officers.

Police officers actions toward his family did little to ingratiate Daryl Gates to the law enforcement profession. Gates developed an antipolice attitude that stayed with him until he became a police officer himself. The young Gates thought police officers were arrogant, ignorant, insensitive bullies. "No way," Gates constantly told himself and others, "do I ever want to be a dumb cop." His attitude was reinforced by an arrest outside a Los Angeles theater in 1942, in which he and a friend scuffled with police officers. Charges were dropped when the sixteen-year-old Gates, under coercion, apologized to the officer with whom he fought.

After graduating from high school, Gates joined the navy and served in the Pacific theater during the closing days of World War II. After the war, Gates, using money from the GI Bill, started attending college. He enrolled at the University of Southern California but was unsure of what to study, quickly souring on education because he wanted to "punch all of the guys" who annoyed him and date all of the girls he found attractive. In 1949, he and his wife, Wanda Hawkins Gates, who was pregnant with their first child, were in need of a quick, steady paycheck. When he discovered that the LAPD would help fund his college education (Gates eventually obtained a degree in public administration), he was sold, but he had no intention of making a career from policing, thinking that he wanted to go to law school, an irony given the animosity he acquired toward lawyers in subsequent years.

Yet make a career from policing is just what he did. Gates, nicknamed "The Bear" for his muscular physique, took to police work well. After working the normal duties expected of most other rookie police officers, Gates got a transfer that he dreaded, but one that wound up being the most important of his career. In 1950, he was assigned to drive for William Parker, the new chief of the LAPD. Gates saw the assignment not as police work but as a job for a lackey, and he feared Parker because of his reputation. The taciturn Parker, it turned out, was one of the most instrumental figures in Gates's career.

Gates came to admire Parker's blunt, honest, personal manner. Another aspect of Parker's personality that Gates admired was his willingness to stand firm and not compromise when he thought he was right. These are traits that would both serve and disserve Gates in later years. While few ever accused Gates of being wishy-washy, his detractors accused him of being intractable and inflexible. Gates also learned from Parker that a police chief should never turn down an opportunity to communicate with the public, be it via the mass media or through public speaking engagements. However laudable this habit might be, it worked for and against Gates, given his proclivity to, by his own admission, put his foot in his mouth. Soon after becoming chief, he told a group of Latino activists that a certain Latino officer had missed a chance at promotion because he was lazy, a comment that was interpreted as bigoted by the local media. Years later, Gates, suspecting that African Americans were more susceptible to death or serious injury from a chokehold, said, "We may be finding that in some blacks when it is applied the veins or arteries do not open as fast as they do in normal people."

After his job as Parker's assistant was completed, Gates continued advancing through the ranks of the LAPD. He worked in several areas, one of his more notable assignments being with the department's intelligence division, where his primary duty was gathering information on the Los Angeles mafia. Gates spent the 1960s with the LAPD, a decade in which Gates and the department were involved in some of the most high-profile police investigations of the twentieth century, including: (1) the 1962 death of actress Marilyn Monroe; (2) the 1968 assassination of Senator Robert Kennedy; (3) the 1965 Watts riots that resulted in thirty-four deaths, and (4) the 1969 murders of seven people at the hands of Charles Manson and his followers. Amidst the turmoil that gripped the LAPD during the tumultuous 1960s was a shot in the arm from a highly popular television show. *Dragnet,* which portrayed police officers as nearly flawless and incorruptible and had been popular in previous runs as a television show in the 1950s and as a radio drama before then, was based on cases lifted from the LAPD with the department's approval.

One of the most notable accomplishments of Gates's career occurred while he was an inspector. The Watts (a predominantly African American area of Los Angeles) riots, which had been precipitated by rumors of excessive force used against a black suspect by police, occurred in the area supervised by Gates. Despite what he acknowledged was a terrible police response to the riots, Gates gained the label "riot expert" as a result of the riots. He lectured and attended seminars on riot response across the country. Since American cities were beset by riots throughout the 1960s, riot response experts like Gates were in high demand for consultation.

As he studied and analyzed riot responses, both those of the LAPD during the Watts riots and others, Gates became increasingly convinced that most police departments, including the LAPD, were ill-equipped and poorly trained in the techniques needed to deal with siege-like conditions such as riots and hostage taking. At the request of Attorney General Ramsey Clark, Gates wrote a riot control manual for the President's Commission on Civil Disorders, one still studied by law enforcers today.

With that in mind, Gates took lessons not from civilian law enforcement, but from the United States Marines Corps, which was embroiled in the Vietnam War. Counterinsurgency and guerilla warfare tactics were of special interest to Gates. The result was an idea Gates called SWAT. Gates's initial idea was to have SWAT stand for Special Weapons Attack Team. After being told that the terminology was too militaristic for civilian law enforcement, Gates changed the acronym to stand for Special Weapons and Tactics. Although SWAT was not warmly received at first, it is a staple of most law enforcement agencies today, even the smallest ones.

In 1978, the LAPD began the search for a new chief. The selection of LAPD chief is designed to be nonpolitical. A police commission, appointed by the mayor, makes the selection and candidates are ranked based on a number of factors, two of which are a written exam (graded by experts outside city government) and years of experience with the department. Despite the wish of Mayor Tom Bradley (a former LAPD officer himself) to change the mentality within the department by hiring someone other than Gates, Gates emerged as the number one candidate and assumed his duties as chief on March 28, 1978.

During his tenure as chief of the Los Angeles Police Department (1979–1992), Daryl Gates was warmly toasted by American presidents, lauded by many of his colleagues throughout the United States and around the world, and roasted and berated by many high-profile politicians and civil rights leaders. He developed programs and law enforcement innovations that are common to many police departments today.

Although he is remembered for a militaristic approach to law enforcement, such a simple label for Gates would be inappropriate. He developed SWAT and believed in a strict no-nonsense approach to police work and crime control, but Gates should also be remembered for DARE (Drug Abuse Resistance Education). Drug problems hit Gates in a personal way, his son Scott having experienced severe drug problems of his own. Convinced that arrests alone were not a sufficient law enforcement response, Gates approached the Los Angeles School Board in 1983 with the idea of sending police officers into classrooms to speak with children about the dangers of drug abuse. DARE began with ten officers and, as was the case with SWAT, was greeted with cold shoulders from local political officials. Although the effectiveness of DARE has been questioned in several empirical studies, Gates's brainchild, like SWAT, is a basic component of law enforcement agencies around the country today.

However, when listening to his equally numerous critics, it seems that Gates represents all that is wrong with American policing. However one chooses to view him, both his admirers and critics admit that his demise is owed to a short reel of videotape from a home movie camera, featuring four police officers and Rodney King.

The beating of King outraged many Americans. What surprised and angered many others was the acquittal of the officers tried for the beating. The acquittals sparked rioting, first in the South Central area of Los Angeles, and then in cities across the United States and Canada. Dozens of deaths were the result. Once again, Gates was the target of criticism, this time for not anticipating the riots that the acquittals sparked and for an inadequate response to the riots.

In interviews with the Associated Press in 2001 and with the Cable News Network in 2002 commemorating the ten-year anniversary of the 1992 Los Angeles riots, Gates was defiant in his defense of his management of the LAPD and highly critical of his successors. He ridiculed the idea of bringing Washington values to the LAPD by allowing the federal government to have oversight of the agency. In what appeared to be a strange public pitch to reclaim his old position, Gates stated that since his departure from the LAPD officer morale had taken a precipitous drop and that restoring him to the office of chief provided the answer to the LAPD's problems. Gates guaranteed that he would restore morale and credibility to the department within six months. Gates expressed no sympathy for Rodney King. "Here's a guy, a parolee, driving down the freeway between 90 and over 100 in a Hyundai which shouldn't go that fast," Gates told Associated Press reporter Erica Werner. "He would not stop for the police or the CHP (California Highway Patrol), challenged the police when he finally did stop, under the influence of beer, which is a violation of his parole, and he got whacked. Los Angeles made him a hero, gave him $3 million and had a riot that almost tore the city apart. And for what?" (Werner, 2001).

After leaving the LAPD Gates delved into a number of ventures, including talk radio. His first marriage ended in divorce, and soon after his divorce he married a second time, to Sima Lalich. In addition to his son, Scott, Gates has two daughters.

SOURCES AND SUGGESTED READINGS

Daryl F. Gates and Diane K. Shah, *Chief: My Life in the LAPD* (New York: Bantam Books, 1993).
Human Rights Watch web site, http://www.hrw.org, March 27, 2003.
Erica Werner, "Ex Chief Still Defiant," ABC News, www.abcnews.go.com, March 3, 2001.

DISCUSSION QUESTIONS

1. Since his resignation as chief, the media as well as the political and social left have spoken very unfavorably of Daryl Gates. Given his career, how will he be remembered fifty years from now?
2. Did Gates bear too much or not enough responsibility for the Rodney King beating and events stemming from it?

CHAPTER 19

■ ■ ■ ■ ■ ▬▬▬▬▬

HERMAN GOLDSTEIN
(1931–   )

Herman Goldstein is the third in the line of twentieth century American police patriarchs, behind August Vollmer and O. W. Wilson. Goldstein is the patriarch of problem-oriented policing, which subsequently spawned community-oriented policing, the hottest trend in late twentieth-century law enforcement. Marie Rosen provided the best description of Herman Goldstein when she wrote, "Goldstein is a fascinating study in contrasts: a police expert who never wore a uniform; a law professor who was never a lawyer; a giant in his field who prefers to mingle with those in the trenches" (Dodenhoff, 1987, p. 10). Goldstein, a gentle, self-effacing scholar, ranks as one of twentieth-century policing's greatest minds, in part because of his willingness to admit that many ideas, even his own, can run their course.

Goldstein's rise to prominence is the quintessential American dream come true. He was born on December 8, 1931, in New London, Connecticut, the youngest of three children. Goldstein's parents, Max and Bella, were poor though not poverty stricken Jewish immigrants. His father immigrated from Poland, his mother from Lithuania. Both of Goldstein's parents came to America to escape the rising persecution of Jews that swept across Europe throughout the first four decades of the twentieth century. Several members of Bella Goldstein's family died in the holocaust.

Goldstein grew up in a lower-middle-class home in Connecticut and attended public schools. Although Goldstein was cognizant of anti-Semitism as a youth, and he knew that some doors to success were closed to him because of his ethnicity, being Jewish in Connecticut did not present the barriers to success that it did for his extended family in Europe. The plight of his extended family in Europe did not directly affect Goldstein, but the abuses of governmental power throughout Europe left an indelible mark on him. Goldstein is acutely aware that a great number of unspeakable atrocities perpetrated against the citizens of Europe came not only at the hands of an invading German military but through the actions of local police officials and soldiers acting as police officials. As a result, Goldstein has worked to insure that government, especially the police, remains attentive and responsive to the needs of its citizens. Police officers, as representatives of the government in the streets, should act as partners with the public, not cruel oppressors as was the case throughout Europe during the 1930s. According to Goldstein, government officials should be ever cognizant of (1) their ability to oppress its citizens, (2) the anomalousness of police officers in a free society, and (3) the need for government to be ever-ready to place constraints on its own authority.

After graduating from high school, Goldstein enrolled at the University of Connecticut. He earned a bachelor of arts degree in 1953 and then enrolled in the University of Pennsylvania's Wharton School. Goldstein earned a master's in governmental administration in 1955. At the time Goldstein embarked on his career, very few government officials focused on systematic methods of improving police services. Criminal justice as an academic discipline was practically nonexistent. Goldstein did not take courses in criminal justice as a student. When he took his first job as administrative assistant to the city manager in Portland, Maine, his primary interest was in municipal government and public administration, not policing.

Goldstein became a police expert by accident. One of the first problems he noticed was that the study of police management was practically nonexistent. The field was ripe for a young scholar/government administrator to carve out an area of expertise, and Goldstein proceeded to do just that. It was during this time that Goldstein first met O. W. Wilson. Wilson's *Police Administration,* which Goldstein read, had been released five years earlier. Goldstein was called on to assist Wilson in his study of police management in Portland. The Portland collaboration was the beginning of a lifelong friendship and partnership between the two men.

Goldstein's work in Portland did not go unnoticed. From 1956–1957, he worked as a research associate for the American Bar Association's Survey of the Administration of Criminal Justice, focusing his efforts on municipal and state police functions in Michigan and Wisconsin. The ABA study was the first body of empirical data on the daily work of street-level police officers. This marked Goldstein's transition from working strictly for local government to bridging the gap between local governments and research agencies. For the rest of his career, Goldstein would have feet in both the academic/research arena and the everyday operations of government and criminal justice. Goldstein has realized that two things are true about criminal justice research: (1) research findings are useless unless they are shared with criminal justice policy makers and practitioners and (2) researchers can learn much from criminal justice professionals in the field.

From 1957–1958, Goldstein worked as assistant director of the Governmental Research Institute in Hartford, Connecticut. From 1958–1960 he worked as a staff member with the Public Administration Service, a nonprofit organization that provided consulting services to local and state governments. Goldstein made one of the most important moves of his career in 1960 when he moved to Chicago to take a position as executive assistant to the superintendent of police, O. W. Wilson. Goldstein would stay in this position until 1964.

Despite the fact that Goldstein had no experience as a police officer, Wilson was confident that the twenty-eight-year-old "boy wonder genius" would make a great impact on policing in Chicago and around the country as well. Wilson and Goldstein enjoyed some success in Chicago, but they were not successful in creating the mental revolution required to effect significant and long-lasting change in the historically corrupt Chicago Police Department.

Goldstein learned about policing by getting on the street with line officers. While many police managers viewed line level police officers almost as natural enemies, Goldstein discovered that rank and file police officers have much to offer, calling them an area of untapped expertise. One of Goldstein's greatest talents has always been his ability to listen, and his ability to persuade people to change their way of thinking in a gentle, nonthreatening manner. Both traits came in handy when he was observing police officers and explaining his findings.

Goldstein wrote one of the most significant articles on policing in the 1960s while he worked for Wilson in Chicago. Goldstein discovered something that most police officers on the street already knew and that few police managers would admit. He found that policing is more than just running from one call to another. He found that officer discretion is a vital part of police work, and in 1963 he published his views on the importance of individual discretion in *The Public Administration Review*. His article, "Police Discretion: The Ideal Versus the Real" was one of the most important contributions to police literature of the 1960s.

Goldstein's reputation flourished while he was in Chicago. He worked as a police consultant and expert for the Ford Foundation. In addition to his landmark article on discretion, he published an article in *Pubic Management* titled "Guidelines for Effective Use of Police Manpower." His tireless efforts in the street, behind the desk, as a writer, and as a consultant prompted a deputy chief to say, "I hope this guy gets married so he won't be around so much."

Goldstein got married in May 1964 and had three children, but that did not slow him down. He left Chicago in 1964, making the final job change of his career when he took a position as assistant professor at the University of Wisconsin Law School in Madison. On paper, Goldstein seemed an odd choice for law school professor. Goldstein does not have a law degree, never attended law school, and does not have a doctoral degree. He was hired because the school needed someone who knew police operations, not law books. Goldstein attributes his long tenure at the University of Wisconsin to the school's long tradition of studying law in action.

By the time he became a professor, Goldstein had earned a reputation as one of the best police minds in the country. The University of Wisconsin provided fertile ground for the furthering of his career. It has always had a reputation as one of the most politically and socially liberal universities in the United States. Socialist ideals found a home on the Madison campus to a greater extent than most other college campuses in the 1960s. It would seem that academic inquiry into policing, which epitomized the political establishment so despised by many at the University of Wisconsin, would not flourish in such a liberal environment. On the contrary, says Goldstein. The University of Wisconsin, even with its liberal tradition, has always prided itself on practical innovation, be it in policing, political science, or agriculture.

So while police studies were not welcome in some liberal environments, except those that merely engaged in police bashing, Goldstein's career as a police scholar thrived at Wisconsin. He developed a policy-making process aimed at systematically controlling police discretion. Goldstein was promoted to associate professor in 1967 and to the rank of professor in 1968 at the age of thirty-six, a notable accomplishment at one of the nation's most prestigious law schools. Although some officials at Wisconsin had issues with his lack of a law or doctoral degree, the university president, fortunately for Goldstein, was more concerned with accomplishments than educational credentials.

During the 1960s and early 1970s, Goldstein worked on the three most significant criminal justice task forces of the era. He gained inroads into the elite of policing circles in part thanks to O. W. Wilson. The presidential election of 1964 was the first in which crime was a major issue. In keeping with the fervor of the 1964 campaign, Wilson consulted with Goldstein, wanting to know what universities were doing in response to the public concern over crime. Goldstein served on President Johnson's Commission on Law Enforcement and the Administration of Justice from 1964–1967, the task force that practically invented the modern study of criminal justice in higher education. It made *criminal justice system* an everyday term and called for a better-educated criminal justice practitioner as well.

Goldstein worked for the National Advisory Commission on Civil Disorders, commonly referred to as the Kerner Commission, from 1967–1968. The Kerner Commission was a blue-ribbon panel of experts assembled to study urban riots, which had been erupting with increasing regularity in the 1960s. Goldstein also served on New York City's Knapp Commission from 1971–1973, which had investigated corruption in the New York City Police Department and featured Frank Serpico as the star witness. The late 1970s would witness the publication of two more seminal police works by Goldstein. *Policing a Free Society,* released in 1977, is the work that Goldstein points to as his most significant. He discusses the difficulties and complications inherent with police work in a democratic society.

In 1979, Goldstein published an article in the journal *Crime and Delinquency* titled "Improving Policing: A Problem-Oriented Approach." The article signaled the beginning of an entirely new direction in police philosophy. Goldstein believes that giving police a longer leash is a key to problem solving in policing, rather than focusing on how quickly an officer disposes of a case, which Goldstein labeled a disastrous mentality. Goldstein believes that police managers too often sacrifice effectiveness for the sake of efficiency. Problem-oriented policing involves police officers handling cases as a group to discover underlying causes of crime, or at least the underlying reasons for frequent calls for service. According to Goldstein, street officers have an innate sense of what will work and what the problems are on their beats.

The development of problem-oriented policing was the result of an evolution on Goldstein's part, dating back to his 1963 article on police discretion. The idea of police officers as problem solvers evolved from the realization that police officers employ a great amount of discretion in the course of doing their work, and that beat officers have a good idea of how to solve the problems on their beat, if only they are provided the opportunity. Goldstein's embrace of the problem model of policing also signaled his movement away from the professional model of policing that was touted for years by his mentor, O. W. Wilson. Although Goldstein and Wilson remained close friends until Wilson's death, they disagreed over the best approach to policing. In Goldstein's opinion, efficiency and professionalism, the hallmarks of Wilson's approach, are good but are not enough.

One Philadelphia story told by Goldstein demonstrates the basic premise of how problem-oriented policing works. A Philadelphia police officer noticed that he answered several calls for service to one particular neighborhood bar. He was never told the source of the complaint; he was only told that the bar was generating too much noise and that they should quiet down. Finally, the officer decided to get to the bottom of the matter; he discovered that other officers had also been called to the bar repeatedly. He also discovered that all of the complaints came from one person, a woman whose residence adjoined the bar. When he visited the bar owners, they told him that they would be happy to find some solution to the problem. The officer visited the complainant, and she told the officer that the music from the bar came right into her wall. That was the sole basis for her complaints. The officer went back to the bar and noticed that the bar's stereo speakers were placed directly beside the wall that adjoined the woman's wall. The proposed solution was to ask the bar owners to move the speakers to another part of the bar. They complied and the problem was solved, and no more police time and manpower was expended answering complaints at the bar. Giving one officer a longer leash and allowing the officer to get to the root of the problem, instead of just answering the call and doing the minimal amount of work, resolved the problem. In 1990, Goldstein released *Problem-Oriented Policing,* which captured his thoughts about police officers working as problem solvers. Problem-oriented policing and its "cousin," community policing, have some similarities. They developed along parallel lines for two decades, with some elements of problem-oriented policing being incorporated in what became a larger, more umbrella-like concept of community policing. But the two ideas have differences. The main difference is that community policing means involving the community, while problem-oriented policing places its major emphasis on a general reconceptualization of what police do. The problem approach focuses on a wide set of problems, and encourages an analytical approach to solving problems. In a perfect world, police would only need to be reactive, but there will always be problems to solve, so police officers should be proactive. Says Goldstein, "We are constantly in a state of reform because we are constantly trying to catch up."

Goldstein is dismayed by what has happened with his concept in recent years. He believes that the problem-oriented label has become so popular that it has been trivialized, that the label is superficial, and that many who claim to employ his concept lack an understanding about what the concept is all about. Simplistic labels like problem-oriented and community policing are overused. According to Goldstein, the professional model can be just as useful as the problem-oriented approach. Neither should be adopted blindly; what is paramount are the needs of the agency and the community. In fact, Goldstein believes that the question of whether the police can handle crime is the wrong one; the more important question is whether society can handle it.

Goldstein retired from the University of Wisconsin in 1994, but he remained as professor emeritus. He remains active, still believing that researchers can learn more from line-level officers than from administrators. Goldstein stands in awe of the complexity of policing and of the role that police should play in a free democratic society. Goldstein remains cautiously optimistic about the future of policing, saying, "We've suffered greatly in this field from an expectation that you introduce something this month and you reap the harvest the next month. You have to plant seeds and hope that they develop over a period of time" (Goldstein, 2001). When asked what he thinks his legacy will be, Goldstein is unsure. He hopes that police work will advance to the point that in thirty years his work will be viewed as primitive. He does have a wish about what should be placed on his tombstone, "A free society is what is most important" (Goldstein, 2001).

SOURCES AND SUGGESTED READINGS

Peter Dodenhoff, "LEN's 1986 Man of the Year," *Law Enforcement News,* 13 (241): 10–12, 1987.
Herman Goldstein, curriculum vitae, December 1, 2001.
Herman Goldstein, *Policing a Free Society* (New York: Harper and Row, 1988).
Herman Goldstein, *Problem-Oriented Policing* (New York: McGraw Hill, 1990).
Herman Goldstein, telephone interview, November 17, 2001.

DISCUSSION QUESTIONS

1. What role did Herman Goldstein's heritage play in his view of the role of police in American society?
2. How has Goldstein integrated the worlds of law enforcement and academic inquiry?

CHAPTER 20

■ ■ ■ ■ ■ ▬▬▬▬▬▬▬

FRANK SERPICO
(1936–   )

$\mathbf{A}$s a child, as a youth, and as a young man, all Frank Serpico wanted to be was a police officer. He thought that being a police officer, especially in his boyhood home of New York City, was the greatest thing he could do. As a young man who joined the New York Police Department, he wanted nothing more than to earn a detective gold shield. Serpico realized his childhood dream of becoming a New York police officer, and he eventually earned his gold shield, but only after his idealism about the nobility of police work had been shattered beyond repair. Serpico's storied battle against corruption in the New York City Police Department throughout the 1960s has made him a true living legend, and he still fascinates the American public. His frustration with bureaucratic inertia and timid government leadership resonates with anyone who has ever faced similar problems in an organization, except that Serpico's story is much more profound. It is also disgusting. It cost Serpico his career as a police officer, and it nearly cost him his life.

Francesco Vincent Serpico was born on April 14, 1936, in New York City, the youngest of four children. His father, Vincenzo, was an Italian immigrant. His mother, Maria Giovanna, was born in Ohio. As a child growing up in lower-middle-class Brooklyn, Serpico idealized police work. His favorite radio program was *Gangbusters*. He viewed the police officer as the ultimate good guy, a dedicated public servant that protected the weak from the bully. Serpico also viewed the world in black-and-white terms, just as he did as a police officer and just as he does today; what is right is right and what is wrong is wrong.

Although Serpico saw the best of police work as a Brooklyn youth, he also encountered situations that negatively affected his perception of policing, and which made him vow to be different when his time to be a police officer would finally come. Once, a New York police officer came into his father's shop, received a shoe shine from young Serpico, and left without paying. He observed officers helping themselves to free fruit from markets. Things would be different when he became a police officer, so he thought.

Serpico graduated from high school in 1954 and enlisted in the Army. Already fluent in Italian, Serpico also learned to speak French, Spanish, and Japanese. After his discharge from the Army, Serpico returned to New York. He worked as a private investigator and later for the New York Youth Authority, both in preparation for his ultimate goal of becoming a police officer.

Serpico's dream was realized when he joined the New York City Police Department in 1959. He quickly realized that straight, hard, honest police work was not always rewarded, especially when it created work for others or if a little petty corruption did not accompany it. Once, while still an academy cadet, he was assigned to guard a synagogue that had been the frequent target of vandals. He arrested two suspects that were wanted for a string of taxi cab robberies, and this arrest should have gotten him the mayor's trophy for the best arrest among academy cadets. Instead the trophy went to an inspector's son for a minor arrest.

After donning the uniform as a full-fledged police officer, Serpico encountered the oddities of bureaucratic thinking that were a part of the NYPD. He thought that hard work and frequent arrests would earn rewards. Instead, his supervisor became annoyed with the arrests Serpico made because it interfered with his studying for his promotion exam. Unlike other officers, Serpico would not take the rest of the day off after making an arrest. He became known as a "rate-buster," making other officers look bad because he worked more hours and made more arrests than them. He was reprimanded for making an arrest during his off hours in another precinct. He discovered that many officers participated in cooping, or sleeping on duty. What surprised Serpico about cooping was that officers did it en masse, finding an empty building and napping as a group, without fear of being reported.

Serpico acquired distaste for the acceptance of gratuities. Although he had always known of police officers helping themselves to free or discounted services, he never liked it but went along at first. Once he entered a restaurant and was told by the owner to try a certain entree (at a discount). Serpico insisted on ordering something else instead and was given an inferior cut of meat. He realized then that, contrary to the perception of the officers that accepted such favors, they came with strings and restaurateurs actually had little respect for officers that accepted their favors and only used them to get rid of excess inventory. Serpico decided he had had enough. When on one occasion he laid down the full amount of the restaurant tab and walked out, a restaurant employee chased Serpico down the street and offered to give part of his money back. Serpico politely refused. From then onward, Serpico received much better treatment at the restaurant.

In 1966, Serpico transferred to the plainclothes division after he heard that it was the best route to becoming a detective. It was as a plainclothes officer that he fully realized the depths of corruption within the NYPD. Rather than finding that acts of corruption were isolated incidents confined to a few officers (i.e., the classic bad apple theory), Serpico found that corruption was everywhere. He would request a transfer to another precinct in the hopes of getting away from corrupt officers, only to find corruption at the new precinct, with plainclothes officers usually the worst offenders. The corruption took numerous forms. Some officers would shake down suspects or accept bribes; some engaged in protection rackets, protecting gambling or drug operations by accepting regular payoffs. Far from operating discreetly, officers openly informed Serpico of how the rackets worked. Each precinct had a "pad" kept by one officer, which provided a detailed accounting of how the rackets worked, how much each officer was paid, and so on. Other officers insisted that Serpico participate in the payoffs, to which he would simply reply that he did not take money. His failure to participate resulted in his being ostracized by his colleagues and arousing their suspicion.

Part of Serpico's problem with his colleagues stemmed from his unorthodox appearance and lifestyle. During the 1960s and early 1970s, the height of the hippie era, many police officers detested anyone that wore long hair, a beard, or hippie clothing such as bell-bottom pants and sandals. Serpico did all of those things, thinking it necessary to blend in with the community, especially when conducting undercover work and because he felt a closer identity with much of New York's counterculture element than with most of his fellow police officers. While most police officers lived in working class neighborhoods, spent off hours with other cops, and disdained intellectual and cultural pursuits, Serpico did just the opposite. He lived in New York City's Greenwich Village area, long associated with a bohemian lifestyle. In the 1960s it was the hangout for avant garde poets, artists, and hippies. When Serpico went to parties he would not tell anyone he was a police officer unless asked. He went to the theater, literary gatherings, and the ballet, and he loved to associate with New York's intellectual circle, finding police shop talk boring after a full day's work.

Every time Serpico informed his superiors of corruption, he was told that the matter was being addressed and that someone would contact him. After talking with his superiors proved fruitless, he arranged to meet with a member of Mayor John Lindsay's staff, courtesy of a politically connected police colleague named David Dirk. Mayor Lindsay would not heed Serpico's call for a thorough top-to-bottom investigation of corruption in the NYPD because he anticipated a disorderly summer of riots and did not want to alienate the police management of the rank and file officers. Word eventually leaked out that Serpico could not be trusted to keep corrupt activities within the department (because he was not corrupt), and he began to fear for his career and his personal safety. Once, on arrival to a new precinct, he was met by a fellow officer who pulled a knife on him and told Serpico, "We know how to handle guys like you," at which time Serpico disarmed the officer, nearly breaking the officer's wrist and pointing his gun in the officer's face.

His frustration grew to a point where he did the unthinkable; Serpico decided to air the NYPD's dirty laundry to the world. He arranged for a meeting with a *New York Times* reporter, and on April 25, 1970, Serpico's account of corruption within the NYPD exploded with the front-page headline "Graft Paid to Police Here Said to Run into Millions." The story was picked up by other New York papers and was disseminated to media outlets across the country. Several officers were prosecuted for various crimes, usually with Serpico serving as chief witness against them, but Serpico was not satisfied. They only go after the small fish, he thought, while letting the systematic and high-level corruption continue to exist.

On February 3, 1971, Serpico, by then working narcotics, went with other officers to make a bust in the Williamsburgh section of Brooklyn, based on a tip from an informant. When they arrived at the apartment to make the bust, Serpico, who spoke fluent Spanish, was sent to the door to gain access from the Hispanic drug dealers inside the apartment. Serpico knocked and said in Spanish, "I need something. Joe sent me." The door opened slightly and Serpico tried to push the door in. Instead, he found himself wedged between the door and the hallway, with a .22 caliber pistol pointed eighteen inches away from his face. He yelled for help from the two officers behind him, but none came. Serpico was shot in the face from almost point-blank range. He managed to return fire, wounding the drug dealer, before collapsing into the hallway.

The actions of his two partners are in dispute. They claim they tried to assist Serpico, but they never called for a back up and left him there to bleed to death. Instead of receiving attention and reassurance from the two police officers, Serpico recalls lying in the hallway, his head being cradled by an elderly Hispanic man that lived in the building and heard the shot from his apartment. Police records indicate that a call was made by a civilian, but no 10–13 (officer down) call was ever made.

Serpico was rushed to Brooklyn Jewish Hospital, where he spent the next six weeks fighting for his life. At the hospital he was given the last rites of the Roman Catholic Church. He was under constant guard by NYPD officers and he received frequent mail from them, but most of the attention he received was not warm. He once overheard an officer guarding his door tell the officer that came to relieve him, "Don't talk to him. He's no good." Serpico received a sympathy card that read, "WITH SINCERE SYMPATHY, THAT YOU DIDN'T GET YOUR BRAINS BLOWN OUT, YOU RAT BASTARD. HAPPY RELAPSE." He went home and spent the next several months recovering from his wound. In May he was awarded the gold detective shield that he had sought since becoming a police officer twelve years earlier. By then he did not care; in fact he literally told the NYPD representative that informed him of the honor to shove it. He would never return to work as a police officer again.

Between the time of the *New York Times* headline and the time Serpico was shot, Mayor John Lindsay appointed a special independent commission to investigate corruption within the NYPD, to be chaired by Whitman Knapp, a Wall Street lawyer. Knapp fought several obstacles in the course of trying to set up the commission's work, most of it from the rank and file of the NYPD. Before he was shot, Serpico had already begun working with the Knapp Commission. After months of secret deliberations, Knapp scheduled public hearings for October 1971. Serpico, assisted by former Attorney General Ramsey Clark, was the star witness before the Knapp Commission. He uttered simple yet profound words, some of which are presented below, which have become indelibly linked with his efforts to fight police corruption and which summarize the fears and frustration of anyone else who chooses to do the same:

> Because of my attempts to report corruption, I was made to feel that I had burdened them with an unwanted task. The problem is that the atmosphere does not yet exist in which an honest police officer can act without fear of ridicule or reprisal from fellow officers. We create an atmosphere in which the honest officer fears the dishonest officer, and not the other way around. (Maas, 1973)

Wanting to escape New York, Serpico spent the next several years living in various locations, both in Europe and the United States. He has never been married, though he has had some long-term live-in relationships and has one son. Peter Maas chronicled his story in a 1973 best seller titled *Serpico*. A movie based on the book with Al Pacino in the title role was released a short time later.

Today, Serpico works occasionally as a guest speaker for police academies and law enforcement organizations, but he has never been invited to speak to the NYPD. He surfaces in public occasionally, often as a critic of corruption in law enforcement and government. Serpico granted a telephone interview with the author in the spring of 2002, during which time he revealed his thoughts on law enforcement today, his life, and his reflections on his experiences with the NYPD. Serpico is very talkative (the interview lasted for more than one hundred minutes), very opinionated, very friendly and cordial, and is unlike anyone with whom I have ever spoken.

Serpico lives in upstate New York at an undisclosed location. He has a telephone and a computer but no television. He is an occasional contributor to *The Village Voice,* a left-leaning New York newspaper, and other publications. In 1997 he was the subject of the A&E Network's *Biography* series. He harbors no bitterness toward the NYPD. He recently confronted and challenged former NYPD chief Patrick Murphy's integrity in a public forum where Murphy was promoting his own autobiography. In his autobiography, Murphy presented an account of Serpico's shooting that differed from the one presented by Peter Maas. I asked his opinion of the movie *Serpcio* and what he thought of Al Pacino's portrayal of him. He was pleased with the overall tenor and message of the movie and with Pacino's portrayal, as was Hollywood; Pacino received an Oscar nomination for his portrayal of Serpico. But in a comment that made me laugh silently, because it perfectly exemplifies both the irascible personality and unbending honesty of Frank Serpico, he stated that during the making of the movie, for which he served as consultant, he quickly wore out his welcome on the set, because he would have a visible reaction whenever something was portrayed in a manner that was the least bit fictional, such as the scene in which Pacino does not shoot the man that shot him.

I asked Serpico if he thought conditions regarding police corruption had changed since the early 1970s. He replied by telling the following story. Recently, Serpico was a guest speaker at an awards banquet honoring outstanding American police officers. In addition to being the guest speaker, Serpico handed the recipients their awards and shook their hands as they received them. After his speech, when the officers were called forward to receive their awards, several of them leaned over and whispered the same words in his ear. In an action that typified his ability to dominate an interviewer, Serpico repeatedly requested that I try and guess the words they whispered. When I finally gave up, he said he would whisper it to me. I found myself leaning forward in my chair, despite the fact that I was on the telephone with him instead of talking to him from across the desk. He whispered the words "I have to talk to you," to which Serpico replied, "I know." Serpico was saying that nothing has changed in American police work. Good police officers still fear dishonest officers and feckless managers. Many individual officers still work hard at their jobs and do their best to perform as true public servants, but policing is still rife with corruption, callous indifference to the plight of the economically disadvantaged, and selfish ambition of the political officials that administer police departments.

Serpico is an advocate of reform within all levels of government and especially in police work. He is very critical of the negative attention directed at American Muslims in light of September 11, 2001, remembering the extraordinary kindness given to him by a Muslim physician during his hospital stay. He describes himself as very spiritual, but very irreligious, seeing religion as yet another corrupted institution in American society. He is a vegetarian, believing that people must connect on a respectful level with all animals, both human and nonhuman.

Frank Serpico represents what many believe is the ideal in policing. Dogged honesty, a passion for police work, an earnest belief that good policing can improve the quality of life in a community, and a desire to help others, characterize this ideal. Unfortunately, the name Frank Serpico also presents an unfortunate reminder that such idealist aspirations often run afoul of some of the bitter realities of police work and public service in general. Serpico's worldview is summarized in a 1996 afterword that he penned for a new release of Maas's biography. He wrote of a conversation with his father Vincenzo, in which he was told, "Be careful son, there are a lot of bad people out there." To which Frank replied, "I know Pa, but there are a lot of good people, too." Vincenzo said, "Yes, but you don't have to worry about them."

SOURCES AND SUGGESTED READINGS

Peter Maas, *Serpico* (New York: Harper Collins, 1973).
Frank Serpico, telephone interview, May 1, 2002.

DISCUSSION QUESTIONS

1. Had you been in Frank Serpico's position, could you have done what he did? Why or why not?
2. What lessons can be learned from Serpico's life about the difficulty of doing what one thinks is right?

CHAPTER 21

■ ■ ■ ■ ■ ▬▬▬▬▬▬▬▬▬▬▬▬▬▬▬▬

JOSEPH WAMBAUGH
(1937–   )

No one has done more to merge the fields of literature and police work than Joseph Wambaugh, referred to by at least one literary critic as the "poet laureate of police." He is the most successful police-officer-turned-novelist in American history. Numerous detective and crime novelists like Mickey Spillane and Arthur Conan Coyle have glamorized crime detection and investigation, but none has ever shown the gritty, darkly comic, human side of day-to-day police work with greater power than Joseph Wambaugh. Wambaugh no doubt served as the inspiration for Ron Glass's character in the popular 1970s situation comedy *Barney Miller,* in which Glass plays a detective moonlighting as a best-selling author. Some of Wambaugh's books, like *Echoes in the Darkness* and *The Blooding,* depict his own narrative of notable crimes. Others are novels in which Wambaugh provides insight into the mind of a police officer on the beat.

In his most successful and gripping works, Wambaugh presents a view of police officers unlike that which had often been depicted in television and movies. Wambaugh's police officers exhibit the signs of stress in police work; they have the same human frailties and flaws as the population they serve, a population that is not always admiring or appreciative of the work police officers do. But it is presented from the point of view of a person who has done police work and understands what officers experience. Many of his novels are required reading in college criminal justice courses.

Throughout the 1950s and 1960s, the image presented to the American public of Los Angeles police officers came from *Dragnet,* a radio and (later) television series that portrayed the LAPD as a force of idealistic, incorruptible, dedicated, almost saintly group of men (and practically no women). Wambaugh's portrayal of Southern California police officers was quite different from that of *Dragnet.* Police officers in Wambaugh's books experienced cynicism, emotional distress, and marital and other personal problems; they lied in court and used excessive force when they deemed necessary. They expected and demanded free meals and other gifts and gratuities. Wambaugh's police officer was, to say the least, far from saintly. However, Wambaugh cannot be accused of being a stereotypical left-wing police basher. Although his characters are flawed, they are presented in a sympathetic manner. In spite of the officers' imperfections, they still are portrayed as the good guys, fallible heroes with whom the reader identifies and sympathizes.

Joseph Aloysius Wambaugh, Jr., was born in East Pittsburgh, Pennsylvania, on January 22, 1937, the only child in a working-class Roman Catholic family that included his mother, Anne Malloy Wambaugh, a housewife, and his father, Joseph Wambaugh, Sr., a police officer and steelworker. When Wambugh was fourteen, his family moved to Ontario, California, where his father worked as a washing machine repairman.

Wambaugh was a poor student, but he managed to graduate from high school in 1954. Wambaugh loved to read, calling it his escape. A favorite was Jack London's *Call of the Wild,* which he read twelve times. Wambaugh enlisted in the Marines after graduation, where he remained until 1957. While in the Marines, Wambaugh married his high school sweetheart, Dee Allsup.

After leaving the Marines, Wambaugh took a job at a steel mill and began attending night classes at Chaffey College in Alta Loma, California. He graduated with an associate's degree in 1958 and enrolled at California State College in Los Angeles. Wambaugh's childhood fascination with reading carried over to his collegiate career. Hoping to have a career as a teacher, he majored in English and graduated with his bachelor's degree in 1960.

Instead of becoming a teacher, Wambaugh began working with the Los Angeles Police Department in 1960 while still a student at California State. He took the path of law enforcement over education primarily because the police job came available first but also in response to a subconscious desire to follow in his father's footsteps. Although Wambaugh would perform well as a police officer—he began as a patrol officer and eventually rose to the rank of detective sergeant—writing was always Wambaugh's passion, even long before he was actually published, and police work served as a springboard for his literary career. Says Wambaugh, "I was born to be a writer and trained to be a cop. One can learn to be a cop. I don't think one can learn to be a writer. At least a good writer" (Gregory, 1996).

Wambaugh's career with the LAPD was far from dull. He worked the crime-ridden Hollenbeck Division in East Los Angeles, a predominantly Chicano and Hispanic area of the city. He was close at hand in Watts—a predominantly African-American area of Los Angeles—when its infamous riots erupted in August 1965. Wambaugh's observations of the Watts riots would be depicted in his first novel. According to Wambaugh, then a twenty-eight-year-old five-year police veteran, "People were dropping dead all over the place. I have no idea who was shooting. I had no idea what to do about it. All we did was sort of back up and protect our ass" (Dunn, 2000).

Wambaugh kept notes of his police experiences. While on the force, Wambaugh returned to California State, this time to earn a master's degree in English, which he obtained in 1968. Wambaugh's first attempt at publishing was with a short story. He wrote several in the late 1960s and publishers rejected all of them. Wambaugh's break came when he submitted a short story to *The Atlantic.* Editors of the prestigious monthly magazine, rather than reject it outright, sent it to Edward Weeks, a former *Atlantic* editor who had recently become a consultant with *The Atlantic*'s book publication division. Weeks suggested Wambaugh develop the story into a novel. Wambaugh followed the advice, and *The New Centurions* was published in 1971.

The New Centurions examines the first five years of three fictional Los Angeles police officers. The officers begin as idealistic public servants, but their attitudes change and harden; they become cynical, suspicious, and willing to break rules, even to the point of falsifying arrest reports. The gritty, gut-wrenching story of the three officers met with enormous critical and commercial success. *The New Centurions* has sold more than 2 million copies.

Like several of his subsequent books, *The New Centurions* was made into a movie. *The New Centurions* featured fine actors, including Stacy Keach and George C. Scott, but Wambaugh, who has never hesitated to express criticism in honest, blunt terms, called the screenplay and the film a "comic book" version of his novel. Wambaugh's caustic criticism of the film was only the beginning of his battles with filmmakers eager to capitalize on the popularity of his books.

Wambaugh's second book was another novel titled *The Blue Knight*. The novel chronicles the days of soon-to-retire Officer Bumper Morgan. Wambaugh covers Morgan's every thought and action in cynical, humorous, gritty detail. Officer Morgan is portrayed favorably, but with serious shortcomings. Morgan overlooks "minor" illegalities and works with corrupt informants. Morgan's cynical attitude toward defendants, attorneys, and judges culminates in the fictional officer getting caught committing perjury on the witness stand.

The Blue Knight spawned several film projects. First came a 1973 NBC miniseries starring William Holden as Morgan, an effort that received favorable comments from Wambaugh, but only after he fought successfully for a second script to be written. In 1975, CBS made a weekly series based on *The Blue Knight* starring George Kennedy. Wambaugh lambasted the initial episodes of the show as just another shoot 'em up cop show, and he was successful in obtaining control over the show's content.

Wambaugh was hired as a consultant for an NBC weekly series called *Police Story,* which ran from 1973–1977. Wambaugh had a running battle with *Police Story* executives and with other filmmakers over the stereotyping of police officers. Contrary to the perception presented by most filmmakers, Wambaugh claims that police work contains some physical risk, but that these risks are far outweighed by emotional dangers.

Wambaugh's third book may rank as his best in nonfiction. Wambaugh took a six-month leave of absence and invested much of his own money in researching *The Onion Field*. He patterned the book on Truman Capote's *In Cold Blood*. Released in 1973, *The Onion Field* chronicles the lives of four men, two police officers and two murderers. It is an account of the 1963 murder of police officer Ian Campbell, who, along with his partner, Karl Hettinger, was kidnapped and taken to an onion field near Bakersfield, California. The kidnappers, two career criminals named Gregory Powell and Jimmy Smith, cold bloodedly shot and murdered Ian Campbell. The book provides powerful insight into the thinking of Jimmy Smith (who consented to the project); it presents a stinging indictment of the justice system that turned the trials of the two killers into a farce. Most significantly, it follows the tragic life of Karl Hettinger (who also consented to the project), who is so racked with guilt over his inability to prevent Campbell's murder that he suffers a psychological meltdown.

The Onion Field brought Wambaugh the Edgar Allan Poe Award in 1974, and a special award for nonfiction from the Mystery Writers of America. *The Onion Field* also spawned what is to date the best movie, in the author's expert opinion, based on a Wambaugh book. Released in 1979 and starring James Woods and Ted Danson, the movie enjoyed critical acclaim and commercial success.

Wambaugh left the LAPD in 1973 to devote greater energy to his writing, and because his celebrity status interfered with his ability to do police work. His first work published after his departure from the LAPD, *The Choirboys,* was one of his best novels. Wambaugh's publisher initially frowned on the project. The book was too dark, too cynical, too depressing—one that the public would not like. Wambaugh, true to form, stubbornly insisted that the book be published as he wrote it, not with a happy ending rewrite as suggested by the publishers. Wambaugh said, "You can paper your walls with it; I am not rewriting it and I'm not giving you another one" (Dunn, 2000).

Fortunately, Wambaugh prevailed. *The Choirboys* was Wambaugh's biggest seller. It examines the tumultuous personal and professional lives of ten fictitious Southern California police officers that meet regularly in MacArthur Park for "choir practice," which consists of drunken debauchery and the chance to release the frustrations that accompany police work. In preparation for *The Choirboys,* Wambaugh reread Joseph Heller's *Catch-22* and Kurt Vonnegut's *Slaughterhouse-Five.* Wambaugh said, "I'd like to do in a police novel what they did in war novels. I want to make people laugh, but I want them to be embarrassed for laughing at what they're laughing at. I want to really try gallows humor . . . dark, dark, dark satire" (Penfield, 1996). *The Choirboys* blends dark humor and personal tragedy in spectacular fashion. One portion depicts a police officer working an auto accident in which one of the accident victims was decapitated. A group of onlookers stop to ask the officer if anyone had been hurt in the accident. The officer presents the severed head of the accident victim, smiles, and tells the onlookers that "this guy" did not come through so well.

The Choirboys was made into a motion picture that included an outstanding cast of actors including James Woods, Charles Durning, and Lewis Gossett, Jr. But not even that group could save *The Choirboys* from being labeled a "star studded flop." In a *Tonight Show* interview with Johnny Carson, Wambaugh blasted the movie, calling it "filthy," and vented his rage at filmmakers for turning his poignant and tragic novel into a film farce with an upbeat ending. Wambaugh sued Lorimar Productions for "mutilating" *The Choirboys* and was awarded $1,000,000 and had his name removed from the script.

The Black Marble, released in 1978, was Wambaugh's first book that was not well received by the critics. As a movie it enjoyed a much better reception, garnering the Edgar Allan Poe Award for best motion picture. Another significant nonfiction work was *The Blooding,* which took Wambaugh to England. In *The Blooding,* Wambaugh relates the true story of English serial killer Colin Pitchfork. The book is billed as the story of the first criminal case solved by DNA profiling, which is somewhat misleading. In truth, the killer pays someone to provide his DNA sample to police in order to avoid detection, and when caught, the killer confesses to the killings before his DNA matches that found on the victims.

Wambaugh abandoned nonfiction because he was tired of being sued. In Wambaugh's words, the prevailing mentality in the 1980s was, "Hey, let's sue Wambaugh, what have we got to lose?" He explains, "I have to be ready to defend in court everything I write when I do nonfiction because we live in a nation of lawyers, and the second someone sees their name in one of my nonfiction books and realizes that I'm a deep-pockets writer, off they go to some ambulance chaser, and I'm sued and I have to defend" (Gregory, 1996). He was sued for *Echoes in the Darkness,* a 1987 book-turned-miniseries, which tells the story of a schoolteacher's murder in Pennsylvania at the hands of two other teachers.

Lawsuits notwithstanding, Wambaugh expresses a greater love for fiction than nonfiction. Says Wambaugh, "The nonfiction books are my stepchildren. And the fiction books, the novels, are my blood children. They have my DNA" (Gregory, 1996). Nonfiction is just as challenging however, primarily because one must interact with real people that have been involved in traumatic situations. Says Wambaugh, "Now even though there's not as much imaginative work, it's very, very hard because I've got to interview people. A lot of times they're crime victims; they're people who've been terribly, terribly hurt and wounded, and I've got to portray them in a book. And sometimes I need to portray them warts and all, when they've already suffered a lot."

Wambaugh has a love-hate relationship with writing and with the criminal justice system, and his cynical wit comes through in his interviews just as it does in his writings. He calls police patrol working in "the big sewer." Wambaugh claims that he enjoys researching his books, but he has called writing as much fun as a "hemorrhoidectomy." According to Wambaugh, he writes not because he enjoys it, but to get rid of "the thing that's roiling inside." Writing requires a different persona than policing, says Wambaugh. While the police officer must be distant, the writer must be intimate.

Wambaugh is the stereotypical eccentric writer, saying, "I tend to withdraw from society of various kinds. I don't have a sense of community. I walk into this room and there's my community on those shelves. I probably take too many drinks every day. I work seven days a week doing a novel or a nonfiction book. There are no days off until the first draft is finished. I'm absolutely disciplined. All of these writing clichés apply to me." In a 1996 documentary titled *We, the Writer,* Wambaugh claimed that he knew how to use computers, which terrify him. He bought one, then sent it back when he realized it would not write the stories for him. He does not use agents, saying that he used one for one book but could not figure what the agent did to earn 10 percent that Wambaugh could not do himself.

Wambaugh spends most of his time in Southern California. Recently he blasted the media for exaggerating the impact of LAPD's Rampart scandal, in which several officers were fired and prosecuted for a host of illegal activities. He blasted the justice system for the acquittal of O. J. Simpson (the jury ignored the evidence), reiterating his belief that courts need professional jurors, and he speaks out for humane prison conditions (so long as those guys are there and not in the community). He and his wife, Dee, have had three children, one of whom is deceased. Finally, Wambaugh offers this advice, "Don't join a political party, and get a dog for affection."

Other books by Joseph Wambaugh include *Fugitive Nights* (1992), *The Golden Orange* (1990), *The Secrets of Harry Bright* (1985), *The Delta Star* (1983), and *The Glitter Dome* (1981).

SOURCES

Adam Dunn, "Joseph Wambaugh Sounds Off," www.CNN.com, October 13, 2000.

Michael Steven Gregory, *We, the Writer: A Nonfiction Portrait of Writers and the Creative Writing Process* (Author, 1996).

Anne McDermott, "Police Author Wambaugh Weighs in on LAPD Scandal," www.CNN.com, March 10, 2000.

Wilder Penfield, "Laughing Maters," *Toronto Sun,* June 16, 1996.

Wilson Biographies (H. W. Wilson Company, 1980).

DISCUSSION QUESTIONS

1. How has Joseph Wambaugh increased the public's knowledge of American policing?
2. In what ways does the career of Joseph Wambaugh highlight the importance of criminal justice professionals having a worthy appreciation of fictional literature?

CHAPTER 22

■ ■ ■ ■ ■ ━━━━━━━━━

BUFORD PUSSER
(1937–1974)

The early 1970s was a very turbulent period in American history. Many Americans believed that law and order had broken down, that criminals had been given too much freedom, and that recent Supreme Court rulings had handcuffed police officers. Feeling powerless over their inability to improve such problems, Americans turned to the entertainment media as a release. Americans got a chance to see the good guys win and the bad guys lose, often in violent fashion. A real-life tough guy cop that enjoyed celebrity status was Buford Pusser, the six-foot six-inch, 250-pound, *Walking Tall* sheriff of rural McNairy County, Tennessee. Through poetry, song, print, and film, the legend of former Sheriff Buford Pusser became larger than life from the minute the story was told, much larger than Pusser himself, or almost anyone else, could have dreamed of becoming in real life. Despite the fact that much of what has been said and written about Pusser is at best embellishment, and in many respects, downright mythical, Pusser symbolizes the anticrime backlash of that era, and he represents America's ability to use the entertainment media to create superheroes from real-life law enforcers.

Buford Hayse Pusser was born on December 12, 1937, in Finger, Tennessee. His parents, Carl and Helen Pusser, struggled to survive as Depression-era farmers while caring for Buford and their two other children. In addition to his farm work, Carl Pusser worked part-time as a barber and later in a sawmill. The Pussers moved to Adamsville, Tennessee, when Buford was fourteen. Pusser dropped out of school during his junior year at McNairy County's Adamsville High School and went to Oklahoma to work on an oil pipeline. The venture to Oklahoma was short-lived, and Pusser returned to Adamsville High School within two months.

During Pusser's youth, life in McNairy County grew increasingly dangerous and unwholesome, in part because of developments outside its territory. Phenix City, Alabama, a small town that adjoins Columbus and Fort Benning, Georgia, had long been a haven for underworld crime and vice. During Pusser's childhood, Phenix City underwent a modest transformation. Local officials in Phenix City made efforts to rid the town of bootleggers, prostitutes, and vice crime. Much of the vice activity and the accompanying criminal element migrated northwest to McNairy County, Tennessee, and to McNairy's bordering county, Alcorn County (Corinth), Mississippi. Both counties became hotbeds of bootlegging, prostitution, and gambling.

Pusser saw life in his community at its most unsavory when he was sixteen. He also got a chance to see police corruption at its most vile. Pusser went to a gambling house called the White Iris Club and observed its owner, Louise Hathcock, beat a sailor to death with a hammer. The sailor claimed he had been cheated. As Hathcock was murdering the sailor, a deputy sheriff smiled and did nothing.

Pusser graduated from high school in 1956. He turned down an athletic scholarship from Florida State University and joined the Marines that August. He received a medical discharge after only four months because of an asthma condition. Pusser returned to Adamsville, where his father Carl had become police chief.

In early 1957, while recovering from injuries received in an automobile accident, Buford crossed the Mississippi line to Corinth and went to the Plantation Club, which was owned by W. O. Hathcock, Louise Hathcock's brother-in-law. Pusser claimed he had been cheated in a dice game. He was beaten severely enough to require 192 stitches and thrown out of the club, swearing to get even.

Pusser moved to Chicago in August 1957 to take a job with the Union Bag Company. In 1958, Pusser began wrestling professionally. Before one match, he met Pauline Mullins, a twenty-four-year-old divorcee with two children. Pusser and Pauline married in 1959. The Pusser's newlywed period was rudely interrupted on January 4, 1960, when Pusser was arrested on a warrant from Corinth, Mississippi, and charged with the December 13, 1959, armed robbery and attempted murder of W. O. Hathcock. The arrest stemmed from the beating Pusser had received at the Plantation Club two years earlier. Hathcock alleged that Pusser had gone to the Plantation Club to get his money back and to deliver some payback for the beating he had received two years earlier. At the trial, Pusser claimed that he was in Illinois on the day of the assault. He was acquitted, in large measure because the jury placed little credence in the testimony of Pusser's accusers, which included Hathcock and some of Corinth's disreputable police officers.

Pusser resumed his wrestling career, traveling around the south. Most of his matches were in small west Tennessee towns, and he once won $50 at a county fair for wrestling a bear. Pusser's only natural child, Dwana Aitoya Pusser, was born during this stage of his life, on January 9, 1961.

In 1962, Carl Pusser retired as Adamsville police chief. He had enough influence to get his twenty-four-year-old son appointed as his successor. In September 1962, he was elected district constable, a part-time position that allowed him to remain chief.

In November 1962, Pusser, along with two federal agents, participated in the first of what would be many moonshine raids. Suspecting that McNairy County sheriff James Dickey was in cahoots with the moonshiners, Pusser did not notify him in advance of the raid. This public slap at Dickey further exacerbated the already existing rivalry between the two.

Pusser ran for sheriff of McNairy County in 1964 as a Republican. Pusser's pledge was, "If you elect me, I will clean up the corruption and violence that has made the state line notorious. I'll make McNairy County a decent place to live and raise a family." The movie *Walking Tall,* which would make Pusser famous several years later, was replete with inaccuracies, one of which was the circumstances behind Sheriff James Dickey's 1964 death. In the movie, the Sheriff, pursuing Pusser, runs off the road and is killed. Actually, Dickey did die in an automobile accident two weeks before the August 1964 election, but Pusser was not involved. The suspicious timing of Dickey's death cast a shadow over the election, evidenced by Pusser's narrow 300-vote victory margin over his dead opponent.

Pusser, the youngest sheriff in Tennessee history, was sworn in on September 1, 1964, at the age of twenty-six. Carl Pusser served as his son's only deputy, running the county jail. Not long after becoming Sheriff, Pusser suffered his first serious injury at the hands of a lawbreaker, being stabbed by a hitchhiker in November 1964. The assailant was never caught.

Pusser ferociously pursued moonshiners in McNairy County, conducting forty-two raids during his first year in office. Pusser exhibited compassion toward some of the bootleggers, giving them Christmas away from jail if they promised to return and give him no trouble later on, but his relationship with the local underworld became increasingly combative. He arrested Louise Hathcock several times. Hathcock repeatedly gave money to Pusser to leave her alone, starting with $500 monthly payments, and later increasing the amount to $1,000 per month, but Pusser would not cooperate.

On one occasion Pusser responded to the scene of a fire in which several people were killed. He caught a man and woman at the scene that had moonshine in the back of their truck. Pusser leaped onto the truck's hood as they attempted to flee; the couple drove off, stabbing Pusser and hitting him with a pipe wrench as they escaped. The two were never caught.

Pusser's feuds were not only with the local underworld. They extended to other law enforcement agencies. In 1965, Pusser began receiving complaints about Tennessee state troopers that would force accident victims to use one wrecker service. Pusser demanded that the troopers stop, and they retaliated by setting up roadblocks and arresting McNairy County citizens. During one court appearance Pusser and the trooper captain got into an argument, which led to Pusser grabbing the captain by the collar. As a result of the public feud between Pusser and the troopers, Pusser succeeded in having most of the troopers transferred.

On February 1, 1966, the long-standing feud between Pusser and Louise Hathcock came to a head. An Illinois couple checking out of Hathcock's hotel accused her of stealing $125 from them. They called Pusser, who showed up with a search warrant. While searching Hathcock's residence, Pusser found illegal whiskey. Hathcock shot at Pusser twice; he returned fire, shooting her twice and killing her. After Hathcock's death, local underworld figures placed a $10,000 bounty on Pusser.

Pusser had become enormously popular in McNairy County by 1966. By most accounts Pusser and his father tried to run the local jail humanely. He performed some charitable acts and on more than one occasion helped pay funeral expenses for the poor. His brand of mercy also had a violent edge as well; Pusser once broke up a domestic fight by beating the abusive husband with a hickory limb because he knew the man was abusing his family. He was reelected in 1966 by a three-to-one margin.

The flamboyance and violence that had marked his life and career continued into his second term. On January 2, 1967, Pusser stopped a speeding car. As he approached the car, he was shot twice, but survived. Two suspects were questioned but were never charged, and the case was never solved. Attention centered on Carl Douglas "Towhead" White, the brother of Louise Hathcock. White, a well-known criminal entrepreneur in northern Mississippi and western Tennessee, was imprisoned at Fort Leavenworth, Kansas, at the time Pusser was shot.

The tragedy that made Pusser famous occurred around 5:00 A.M. on August 12, 1967. Pusser received a call to go to the Mississippi state line to check out some sort of trouble. For reasons still unclear, Pusser took his wife along for the ride. He drove at a speed of around ninety miles per hour on State Highway 57. While driving on Highway 57, a drive-by shooter shot Pauline Pusser as she sat in the passenger seat of the car. When Pusser stopped the car, the shooter returned, this time shooting Pauline again and shooting Buford in the face. Calling for help was hampered by their rural location, by the darkness, and by Pusser's inability to call for help on his police radio because a 30–30 slug had blown off his chin. Pusser had been set up and ambushed. In all likelihood, Pauline Pusser was not a target, but was simply in the wrong place at the wrong time. Pusser was transported to a Memphis hospital, where he was guarded by Shelby County police officers. Contrary to *Walking Tall*'s portrayal, Pusser did not attend his wife's funeral; he was in the hospital fighting for his life.

Speculation about the shooting ran rampant. Attention turned to several suspects. One was Carmine Raymond Gagliardi. After Pusser recovered he tracked Gagliardi to Boston. Before Gagliardi could be arrested, he was killed and his body was dumped in the Boston harbor. Another suspect was Kirksey Nix, Jr., of Oklahoma. Nix was a leader of the Dixie Mafia, a shadowy confederation of criminal organizations that had long dominated vice crime throughout the South, especially along the Mississippi Gulf Coast. At the time of Pauline's murder, Nix was serving a life sentence for robbery and murder, but Pusser suspected Nix nonetheless. Attention also centered on Carl Douglas White and W. O. Hathcock, but they were never charged.

Pusser underwent sixteen operations on his face. Recovering from his physical wounds was only part of the battle. Wanting to appear less conspicuous, he stopped wearing sheriff's uniforms and began wearing tailored suits. He changed cars often, and alternated between periods of depression and obsessive fear. Pusser vowed to carry a gun for the rest of his life.

Pauline Pusser's murder made Buford one of the most famous law enforcement officers in the United States. The first to capitalize on the Pusser tragedy was Eddie Bond, an occasional country singer, disk jockey, and record company owner. Bond paid tribute to Sheriff Pusser with a song called "The Ballad of Buford Pusser" in 1968, which Bond cowrote with Jim Climer. The record enjoyed enormous popularity in western Tennessee and northern Mississippi. Carl Pusser sold copies of the record from the jail.

Pusser's notoriety, coupled with sympathy because of his wife's murder, led to his reelection in 1968 by a two-to-one margin. Pusser's efforts to rid the area of many of the dives and gambling houses also gained ground. Many were closed down or burned down. Carl White was beaten severely by Pusser once and left in the swamp, but he did not die at Pusser's hands. White was killed on April 2, 1969, while trying to rob a hotel. The effort to silence Pusser had backfired; he became more popular than ever, while many of his enemies either died or were put out of business.

Several events made 1969 another notable year in Pusser's life. The second and last person to die at Pusser's hands was Charles Hamilton, a fifty-year-old alcoholic and convicted killer who shot at Pusser when Pusser answered a call to his house in December 1969. Pusser was also in another auto accident that same year. This time he almost did not make it to the hospital because an ambulance overheated while en route. Also that year the Tennessee House of Representatives named Pusser honorary sergeant at arms; he was named national police officer of the month by a New York detective magazine.

Pusser's term was set to expire in 1970. He was barred by law from seeking another term as sheriff, but he was elected third district constable. Pusser had also established a friendship with a fellow Tennesseean and writer named W. R. Morris. Morris teamed with Bond in furthering the Pusser image, and penned a 1971 biography about Pusser titled *The Twelfth of August: The Story of Buford Pusser*.

Pusser accepted a movie deal from Bing Crosby Productions, serving as technical adviser. His first criticism of the movie was its script. Pusser complained that the violence was toned down too much, but he did not object to other inaccuracies, the most prominent of which wrongly portrayed Pusser wielding a huge stick to mete out street justice. McNairy county locals were miffed that *Walking Tall* was filmed in three neighboring counties, and some officials disliked glorifying Pusser's violent behavior.

While serving as constable, he encountered legal troubles of his own, again stemming from his propensity to violence. In 1972 he was charged with assault with a deadly weapon for beating a man he claims pointed a gun at him. The charges were dismissed when the accuser did not appear in court.

The local animosity toward Pusser grew strong. He was defeated in his bid for sheriff in 1972, and Pusser blamed his loss on the movie, which had flopped. McNairy County laughed at Pusser because of the inaccuracies in the movie, especially Baker's portrayal of Pusser carrying the huge stick, which became the movie's trademark. He never rammed his car into a saloon and he never assigned the local judge to the courthouse bathroom as was depicted in the movie.

Stung by *Walking Tall*'s failure, Bing Crosby Productions redid the movie's promotional trailer, and the impact was tremendous. *Walking Tall* became one of the top box office draws of 1972 and 1973. *Variety* called it the year's best sleeper.

Photoplay magazine named it motion picture of the year. The movie starred Joe Don Baker in the role of Buford Pusser. Baker and Pusser became good friends, and Baker vowed to make the people of McNairy County sorry for rejecting Pusser.

According to Pusser, *Walking Tall* was about 70 percent fiction, but the public did not care. Pusser's character was a larger-than-life hero. The movie contained graphic violence (for its time), which the public also enjoyed immensely. Pusser was portrayed as a bold, incorruptible one-man crime-fighting machine. He unhesitatingly used his huge stick to wallop bad guys. He fought judicial ineptitude and corruption, and he did his best to make the sheriff's office representative of the population by hiring an African-American deputy (another fiction).

Pusser became one of the most sought-after public figures in the nation. CBS produced a documentary about Pusser. Governor Winfield Dunn declared October 21, 1973, Buford Pusser day in Tennessee. Pusser received $1,000–$2,500 for personal appearances and lived the high life, rubbing shoulders with the elite of Nashville's country music establishment. He began a romantic relationship with Anne Galloway, a Miss Tennessee winner. In his public appearances, Pusser would say that *Walking Tall* signaled a trend toward public respect for law enforcement. It is doubtful that *Walking Tall* resulted in any conversions toward a law enforcement mindset. It merely reinforced existing beliefs about the proper role of law enforcement, plus it was replete with violence, always a drawing card for American movie buffs.

Pusser's notoriety began to experience a negative shift as time went on. His brashness and violent tendencies made him enemies, and some began to question whether Pusser was the upstanding individual portrayed in *Walking Tall*. In an interview with an Ohio newspaper, Pusser's stepdaughter said that Pusser was a man to fear, and she made the highly questionable accusation that Pusser was responsible for Pauline's death, an accusation made more out of bitterness than fact.

It was ironic that one of Pusser's claims to fame was his penchant for busting moonshiners because Pusser was a drinker himself. He found more time for bar hopping after the release of *Walking Tall*. Once in a local Moose Lodge, a man accused Pusser of accepting money while he was sheriff so the man and his wife could sell illegal alcohol. An argument ensued, and Pusser beat the man so severely that the man literally defecated in his pants.

Pusser's friendships with some of the people that had made him famous soured as well. He had a falling out with Republican Party officials after backing democrat Ray Blanton in the 1974 gubernatorial race. Pusser's friendship with Joe Don Baker went south as well. Pusser, a republican, had serious political disagreements with Baker, a democrat. Baker called Pusser a fascist pig that would do anything to support the existing political establishment. Pusser called Baker a "conceited bastard," and claimed that Baker owed his career to him.

Bing Crosby Productions wanted to film a sequel to *Walking Tall* but negotiations with Baker proved fruitless. Pusser did a screen test and was awarded the part of playing himself in the sequel. Filming was scheduled to start on September 20, 1974, in Jackson, Tennessee. But Pusser would not live to play himself in the movie, nor would he live to become commissioner of public safety, the promise made by Ray Blanton in exchange for his support in the governor's race. Pusser had a history of driving fast, having had several accidents in his lifetime, but his notoriety and position as a law enforcement officer had gotten him out of several traffic tickets. It would not save his life. On August 21, 1974, while traveling more than one hundred miles per hour, Pusser's car crashed, killing him at the scene. Pusser's blood alcohol content was .18, almost twice the legal limit.

Rumors about his death brought unscrupulous conspiracy theorists out of the woodwork, at least one of whom succeeded in conning the Pusser family out of a considerable sum of money. Two more *Walking Tall* movies were made, but neither enjoyed the critical or commercial success of the first *Walking Tall* movie. A CBS television movie was made featuring Brian Dennehy as Pusser. Pusser's daughter maintains an Internet web site devoted to Pusser, complete with saleable items that capitalize on Pusser's name. Pusser's former home is now a museum.

Whether or not Buford Pusser will be remembered in the distant future is unclear. He was not an intellectual. He did not contribute any philosophical or technological innovations to the field of law enforcement. Pusser was admired more by those who did not know him than by most of those who did. Like Wyatt Earp, Pusser's advantage over many of his adversaries was that he lived long enough to have himself portrayed in film and literature as a hero, in many ways different from the real-life police chief, sheriff, and constable known to residents of western Tennessee.

SOURCES AND SUGGESTED READINGS

Alan Axelrod and Charles Phillips, with Kurt Kemper, *Cops, Crooks and Criminologists* (New York: Facts on File, 1996).

W. R. Morris, *The Twelfth of August: The Story of Buford Pusser* (Reagan, TN: Cherokee Press, 1971).

W. R. Morris, *Buford: True Story of the "Walking Tall" Sheriff, Buford Pusser* (Shiloh, TN: Poplar Books, 1983).

DISCUSSION QUESTIONS

1. In what ways was Buford Pusser's fame reflective of the times in which he lived?
2. Would the fascination surrounding Buford Pusser be as great if he had not died at a young age? Why or why not?

CHAPTER 23

LEE BROWN
(1937–   )

In Lee Brown, one finds a blend of several pioneering traits and accomplishments. He is a pioneering minority, among the first African Americans to serve in big city police leadership roles. Brown has been a tireless and high-profile advocate of community policing, the hottest policing idea of the past twenty-five years. He has found himself in the middle of some of American law enforcement's most controversial and infamous cases. In addition to being a law enforcer, Brown is an academic, among the most highly educated members of the law enforcement profession at the time he began his career, and among the few individuals as dedicated to the academic profession as to law enforcement. Brown has also moved among the highest echelons of American politics, using his law enforcement background as a stepping-stone to higher office in a way done by few in the criminal justice or academic professions.

Lee Patrick Brown was born on October 4, 1937, in Wewoka, Oklahoma, into a poor farming family. Brown's family moved to California when he was five, where his father took a job as a grape picker and his mother worked as a cook. By the late 1950s, criminology was slowly emerging as an academic discipline, albeit on very few college campuses. One of the schools that offered criminology was California State University at Fresno, the school Brown attended. Brown graduated with a degree in criminology in 1961. Also, municipal police departments in a few locales were beginning to open their doors to racial minorities. One of those locales was San Jose, where Brown began working shortly after graduating from Fresno State.

Brown worked as a police officer in San Jose for eight years, both as a patrol officer and as an undercover vice and narcotics officer, which, according to Brown, was a much safer job then than it is now. While he worked as a police officer, Brown continued his educational pursuits, a rare endeavor for municipal police officers in the early 1960s. Few police officers had four-year degrees at the time, and obtaining a graduate degree was extremely unusual. Brown obtained a master's degree in sociology from San Jose State University in 1964 and a master's degree in criminology in 1968 from the University of California at Berkeley, the institution that had pioneered criminal justice study at the collegiate level several decades earlier. Brown capped his educational career in 1970 when he obtained a doctorate of criminology from the University of California at Berkeley.

Brown left California and municipal law enforcement for a professorial position at Portland State University. He established Portland State's Department of Administration of Justice. Brown continued a career in academe, moving to Washington, DC, in 1972 to assume the position of associate director of the Institute for Urban Affairs and Research at Howard University while also holding the rank of professor of public administration and director of criminal justice programs.

Brown returned to law enforcement in 1975, entering the realm of politics for the first time by serving as sheriff of Multnomah County (Portland), Oregon. A year later Brown was appointed director of justice services, charged with overseeing all criminal justice agencies in the county.

Brown's steady climb up the law enforcement and political ladder continued, with his next move being the one that would make him nationally known both inside and outside law enforcement circles. In 1978, Maynard Jackson, Atlanta's first African American mayor, appointed Brown to the position of public safety commissioner. Brown's hiring was popular with many who knew of his reputation, and the more educated, erudite members of Atlanta's black community. However, Atlanta's poorer blacks were disappointed with the hiring of Brown, whose perceived aloofness and polished manners stood in contrast to Brown's earthy, populist (and by many accounts corrupt) predecessor, Reginald Eaves.

Brown owes his fame to a series of horrible crimes perpetrated on Atlanta's youth in the late 1970s and early 1980s. Between 1979 and 1981, twenty-seven children and young men were murdered, apparently by the same person. Atlanta was in a state of panic. Since all of the victims were black, conspiracy theories abounded; were the murders a racist plot? Did the Atlanta Police Bureau act quickly enough in view of the fact that most of the victims were poor? How much did government authorities know that they were not sharing with the public? Any neighborhood stranger came under suspicion. Police officers were bombarded with calls from parents whenever a child disappeared for even the shortest length of time. Nightly newscasts both in Atlanta and around the country frequently began their programs with stories about the murders. The airwaves were flooded with public service announcements that featured local sports and entertainment celebrities and warning parents to know their children's whereabouts at all times. News outlets and tabloids from around the world descended on Atlanta in droves.

At the center of this firestorm was Lee Brown. He became a fixture on local and national television newscasts. As time went on and the murders remained unsolved, Brown and his department came under increasing criticism, not only for failing to solve the crimes using traditional investigative techniques, but for having a sloppy and disorganized investigation, and for making such embarrassing moves as hiring a feckless psychic to visit with the victims' families and visit the murder scenes, accompanied by Atlanta police officers.

A saturation of patrol resulted in the arrest of Wayne Williams, who was formally charged with two of the murders, but only after a few weeks of embarrassingly public surveillances of Williams's home. Williams was linked to twenty-five other murders and was convicted and sentenced to life in prison in 1982.

Brown gained considerable notoriety as a result of the murders and Williams's conviction. This recognition and Brown's history of not staying in one place too long led to his accepting the job of police chief in Houston in 1982.

Houston was beset by allegations of corruption, racism, and brutality at the time of Brown's appointment. Brown, the most well-known African American police official in America, was brought in to increase minority hiring and improve relations between the police and the minority community.

At the time, community policing ideals were seeping out of colleges and universities and into police departments. Brown, an academic in his own right, was determined to implement community policing in Houston. Brown's preference was for neighborhood policing, with officers ordered to become personally acquainted with citizens in their assigned area. Emphasis was placed on foot patrol, town meetings, crime prevention, and trying to assess specific neighborhood needs. Officers were not rewarded simply for the number of arrests made or the number of citations they issued; a decrease in crime was one of the sought-after goals of Brown's community policing model. Brown viewed violent crime as more than simply a criminal justice problem. He viewed it as a public health issue as well. With that in mind, Brown, in collaboration with the University of Texas Health Science Center, helped create the Center for the Study of Interpersonal Violence.

The defeat of Kathy Whitmire, the mayor that appointed Brown, and the election of David Dinkins to the mayor's position in New York City in late 1989 led to Brown's next position, chief of police in New York City, the most prestigious municipal law enforcement position in the United States. Dinkins admired Brown's work in Houston and wanted him to implement similar programs in New York City.

After a comprehensive review of the NYPD administrative structure, Brown proposed and received approval for a plan called Safe Streets, Safe City, which called for a sizeable increase in the number of uniformed police officers in New York. Despite the budget problems faced by the city, Mayor Dinkins approved Brown's proposal. Brown also launched Operation All Out, which, in accordance with the community policing ideal, required a greater emphasis on foot patrol, and required all officers, regardless of rank, to spend some time each week on the street. Town meetings were held with community leaders to assess crime-related needs. The number of minority and female officers also increased under Brown's administration.

Throughout the 1990s, New York City experienced a precipitous drop in crime, leading many to speak of the "New York miracle" achieved by the city's municipal leadership. While many attribute the "miracle" to the work of Mayor Rudolph Giuliani and William Bratton, one of Brown's successors as chief, one might credit Brown with at least initiating the miracle. During Brown's administration, crime dropped for the first time in thirty-six years.

On August 3, 1992, Brown resigned as chief of the NYPD to spend more time with his wife, Yvonne, who was in declining health. Brown returned to Houston, taking a professor's job at Texas Southern University. He would not stay long in that position either. In 1993, Brown was nominated by President Bill Clinton to head the Office of National Drug Control Policy, a cabinet-level post at the time.

After confirmation by the United States Senate, Brown assumed his duties as America's "drug czar" on June 21, 1993.

Offering up a fairly noncontroversial position at his confirmation hearings, Brown pledged to curb drug use by coming down hard on dealers and offering treatment for users, not "waging a war" against American citizens. Brown also claimed that American society had failed in its efforts to curb drug use by relying too much on the criminal justice system to deal with drug users. As with violent crime, Brown believes that drug use is not only a justice system problem.

Brown returned to Houston in 1997, this time to run for mayor. He was elected on December 6, 1997, and assumed office on January 2, 1998. Brown translated his community policing ideals into municipal government. Working off a principle he called neighborhood-oriented government, Brown has encouraged his staff to hold meetings with neighborhood and community leaders to assess neighborhood needs, just as he did when he served as police chief. Brown was reelected in 1999, and again in 2001 when he began his third and final term as mayor. Subsequent to the death of his first wife, Brown, the father of four children, married Frances Young, a Houston schoolteacher.

Brown's tenure as Houston's mayor ended in 2003. Brown already has amassed a lifetime of accomplishments. He was the first African American big city police chief, the first black police chief in Houston and New York City, the first African American drug czar, and Houston's first black mayor. Brown also represents the healthy marriage of academe and law enforcement, which should be of special interest to students of criminal justice.

SOURCES AND SUGGESTED READINGS

Alan Axelrod, Charles Phillips, with Kurt Kemper, *Cops, Crooks and Criminologists* (New York: Facts on File, 1996).

City of Houston, Mayor's Office, miscellaneous material.

City of Houston, Mayor's Office, Mayor Lee P. Brown Biography, www.ci.houston.tx.us, July 13, 2003.

Michael J. Stoil, "A View from President Clinton's Drug Czar: Dr. Lee Brown," *Behavioral Health Management,* 14: 6–7, 1992.

Alan M. Webber, "Crime and Management: An Interview with New York City Police Commissioner Lee P. Brown," *Harvard Business Review,* 3: 111, 1991.

Biography of Lee P. Brown, Director of ONDCP, http://clinton.nara.gov/White_House, July 13, 2003.

DISCUSSION QUESTIONS

1. What personal characteristics and historical events and forces have contributed to Lee Brown's success?

2. If Lee Brown had been born twenty years earlier, would he have become as prominent as he did? Why or why not?

CHAPTER 24

PENNY HARRINGTON
(1942–)

When Lola Baldwin worked as a police officer in Portland during the 1910s, she was perfectly content to focus on protecting women. She was a specialist; she had no desire to perform all of the duties of male officers. Likewise, the thought of actually serving as chief of the department probably did not enter her mind; such was the mindset of even the most maverick of female law enforcers during Baldwin's era. Between the 1920s and the 1980s, the role of women in the American workforce experienced a gradual but radical shift. Women entered the workforce in great numbers during World War II, taking jobs traditionally performed by men, many of whom were in the military. After the war, women, emboldened by "women's liberation," continued to make strides in the workforce.

To a greater degree than most other professions, men have dominated American policing. Among the few women who did enter the field, even fewer of them, especially those in large cities, could seriously entertain thoughts of being a chief. Penny Harrington was the first woman in the United States to attain the position of chief of a police department in a large city. Like Lola Baldwin, she made her name in Portland, Oregon. Although her tenure as chief was brief and stormy, Harrington paved the way for hiring other women police chiefs. Her tenure as chief notwithstanding, her career presents in microcosm the lot of women police officers since the 1960s.

Penny Ledyard was born in Lansing, Michigan, on March 2, 1942. She was the oldest of four children born to Edward and Mary Louise Ledyard. Penny grew up in a lower-middle-class household; her father was a superintendent of steel processing at a plant that manufactured wheels for automobiles. Mary Louise Ledyard worked as a secretary for a utility company in Lansing until she was fired when she became pregnant with Penny. One of the memories of Penny's childhood was that her parents assigned no gender roles in the family; there was no such thing as girls work or boys work.

Penny attributes her decision to enter police work to her meeting a Lansing (woman) police officer on a high school career day. After high school, she took a job as a legal secretary and enrolled at Michigan State University (MSU), one of the few universities in the country that offered a degree in police administration, a forerunner of its criminal justice program. During the early 1960s, most MSU men who were interested in criminal justice studied criminal investigation; their female colleagues studied juvenile justice and child psychology. In other words, men prepared for a career in police work and women prepared for a career working with juveniles.

Penny married a fellow police administration major while a junior at MSU. Soon after graduating from MSU, a former MSU professor offered her husband a job with the Multnomah County (Portland), Oregon, sheriff's department. So, Penny Orazetti, as she was now known, moved with her husband to Portland. Multnomah County prohibited hiring married couples, so while her husband worked for the sheriff's department, Penny worked as a legal secretary.

Penny sat for the Portland Police Bureau entrance exam in 1964 and passed with high marks. She was hired and went to work in a department that had 700 officers, including five African Americans and eighteen women. Penny was the first person ever hired by the Portland Police Bureau who had a four-year degree in police administration. Penny Orazetti's basic training experience illustrates what women police officers had to endure and how much has changed since the 1960s. The term *sexual harassment* was not in vogue in 1964 like it is today. Many of the men with whom she trained thought nothing of making sexual advances toward the female officers, even if both were married. Once during self-defense training, Penny had her sweatshirt pulled over her head by a male training partner, leaving her exposed with only a bra on, all to the whoops and laughter of the other trainees.

For the most part, though, the women in Penny's group were treated relatively well. One of the reasons that they received good treatment was that the male officers knew, or thought they knew, that the female officers would never be transferred from the Women's Protective Division. Therefore the women were not viewed as a threat to the men. Like other female officers, Penny wore a police uniform, but it consisted of white gloves, a hat, a tailored suit, silk blouse, and a pair of sling-back pumps. They were not allowed to carry firearms. The policewoman's primary function was to assist male officers and work with cases involving children, especially child abuse cases and runaways. Since Portland became a frequent destination for runaways in the 1960s, her plate was often very full.

Penny learned from an African American officer the importance of connecting with the community. Community engagement, said the officer, was the best way of preventing riots. In a time long before the term *community policing* came into everyday usage, Penny Orazetti understood well the importance of making sure that police officers tried to stay engaged with the community they served.

One of her first blatant encounters with discrimination in promotion came in 1968 when Penny tried to sit for the detective exam. She was denied admission to the exam because she lacked the necessary experience as a patrol*man*, experience she could not obtain because of her gender. Penny also complained because she and the other women in the bureau received less pay than male officers. She took the sergeant's exam but was passed over in favor of another woman who scored lower.

Although she inherited antilabor sentiments from her father, Penny Orazetti, frustrated by what she perceived as unfair treatment, joined the police officers' union. She became very active in the union, recruiting members and volunteering in her off hours. She lobbied for better pay and better work hours, and she advocated for the creation of a research and planning division within the bureau.

Her reputation spread, making her popular with many rank-and-file officers and very unpopular with management. When told by the bureau chief that she would leave the Women's Division only "over his dead body," Penny went to Mayor Terry Schrunk, who would not intervene. Penny angrily left his office but not before threatening to sue him. When she returned to her office, she found a message from the mayor stating the she had been transferred to the bureau's planning unit, effective January 29, 1970.

Not long after her transfer to the planning unit, her marriage, which had produced one son, fell apart, primarily because of her intimate relationship with her captain in the planning unit. In 1970, Penny became an officer in the International Association of Women Police. She also banded with other women in the Portland Bureau and filed a civil rights complaint over job requirements that discriminated against women, such as height requirements (which also affected Asians) and the title police*woman*. As a result all police officers in Portland were simply referred to as officers.

Every time Penny was interviewed for a promotion, she encountered questions that would not have been asked of men. One was whether she could juggle her family and childcare responsibilities and still devote enough time to her career. Penny had scored ahead of all others on the detective exam, but the bureau left five detective positions vacant rather than give one to her. Penny persevered, however, and was promoted to detective in February 1972, another in a long line of firsts for her. Although some of her male colleagues received her warmly, some did not. Penny received more help from secretaries than from other detectives. She received this anonymously authored note from a fellow detective:

> I don't know how a fat homley [sic] double chin hump back cow with two legs that resamble [sic] two fresh butchered hogs hanging sid [sic] by side and naked to within one inch of her crotch can expect to not be conspicuous. One look at a freak like you is enough shock to give a baboon the big jitters.

Over the next several years, Penny filed forty-two complaints against the Portland Police Bureau, constantly butting heads with officials within the bureau and in city hall. She was transferred to other divisions within the bureau several times. By 1974, the stress had become too much. Her situation was exacerbated by her newest job assignment, which required her to work on the bureau's new computer system in a slightly renovated bomb shelter, where she seldom saw the light of day. In November 1974, Penny suffered an acute anxiety attack and passed out. She became very depressed and suffered mood swings. In January 1975, a time when visiting a psychiatrist still carried a heavy stigma, especially for a police officer, Penny Orazetti started seeing one. Her immune system was depleted and she was advised to quit her job by her doctor. Instead, she took antidepressant medication and signed a suicide pact with her psychiatrist.

She returned to work in July 1975 as a uniformed patrol sergeant, becoming Portland's first female officer to supervise male officers. A uniform had to be specially designed for her. She was assigned to Portland's highest crime area, an opportunity she relished because it gave her a chance to do real police work. She liked her fellow officers and enjoyed working with the community and using innovative methods of dealing with crime problems, such as using administrative codes to close bars that sold to minors.

Penny's reputation grew in the Portland area, in part due to favorable media coverage, and she was promoted to lieutenant in 1977. On one occasion, she was reprimanded for insubordination after she struck her captain. She claimed the captain had grabbed her hand and placed it on his genitals.

In July 1980, Penny Orazetti became the youngest and the first female captain in the history of the Portland Police Bureau. One of her priorities was to increase the hiring of minority officers, a move that did not sit well with many of her colleagues. She emphasized the importance of understanding the different cultures in Portland. For example, many officers were perplexed at the lack of cooperation from recent Asian immigrants. Penny learned that the officers often made a fundamental mistake when dealing with them. When responding to a call, the officers would quickly ascertain that the adults on the scene did not understand or speak English very well. So the officers would speak to the children in the house, an insulting gesture to the adults. Penny suggested cultural diversity training to remedy such problems.

Penny married Gary Harrington, a fellow officer, in February 1982. Penny Harrington made history on January 24, 1985, when Mayor Bud Clark appointed her to head the Portland Police Bureau. Harrington became a national celebrity. She was profiled in magazines and on television shows; a Penny Harrington action figure was released.

Her tenure as chief would prove short-lived and tumultuous. She made several moves that upset rank-and-file officers and union representatives. She placed her sister Roberta in charge of internal affairs and personnel. She dismantled the narcotics unit and created a general vice unit. She reinstituted the juvenile division to attack truancy. She clashed with union leaders over budget cuts.

Harrington banned the use of the carotid hold after a Portland officer killed an African American security guard with the hold. The ban on the carotid hold was popular with the city's black leadership, but in response, some officers, who viewed Harrington as disloyal to her officers, started wearing t-shirts inscribed, "Don't choke 'em, smoke 'em." Some of the officers who wore the shirts were fired, which prompted lawsuits from the fired officers and a no confidence resolution from the union leadership.

Not all of her moves were unpopular. She was the first to ban smoking in police buildings, she implemented greater physical fitness regimens, and she increased diversity training for officers. Crime decreased in several categories.

However, Harrington never gained the confidence of union leadership, who blamed her for bad morale within the department, the drug trafficking problem in Portland, and for fostering an us-against-them mentality by favoring community leaders over police officers. The final blow involved her husband Gary. In March

1986, the Harringtons went to a party at a restaurant that had a reputation as a drug-dealing location. Gary saw a known drug dealer there and informed the manager that he should not let the drug dealer hang out at the restaurant. Unknown to Gary and Penny, police officers were conducting surveillance on the dealer.

This thwarted a planned drug bust of the restaurant, and police officers accused Gary Harrington of intentionally thwarting the investigation and the bust. Neither the district attorney nor the United States attorney found basis for criminal prosecution of either of the Harringtons, but the damage had been done. A mayoral commission recommended that Penny Harrington be replaced and that Gary Harrington receive a twenty-five-day suspension. The commission also cited problems with departmental morale and with her leadership as chief. Penny Harrington resigned as Portland's police chief on September 1, 1986, nineteen months after she assumed her duties.

Harrington left Portland. In 1988 she began working for the California State Bar Association, where she remained for seven years. Currently, Harrington works as a private consultant and public speaker. She remains active in women's police organizations such as the National Council for Women and Policing.

In an telephone interview, I asked Harrington if she would have done things differently if she had the chance to do it over again. She admitted that her problem was not being a good enough politician, not building adequate bases of support for her decisions, and in general not playing the political game well enough. She likes moves toward community policing, calling it "women's policing," but she also thinks the term is frequently misused. Like many other civil libertarians, Harrington worries that the events of September 11, 2001, are being used as the pretext for depriving citizens of privacy and due process rights. Although she acknowledges that women have made great strides in policing, she thinks that only when women achieve critical mass in a department, meaning at least 33 percent of a police force, will women truly impact policing. In 1999, she published her autobiography, titled *Triumph of Spirit*. Penny Harrington lives in Morro Bay, California.

SOURCES AND SUGGESTED READINGS

Penny Harrington, telephone interview, March 10, 2002.
Penny Harrington, *Triumph of Spirit: An Autobiography of Penny Harrington* (Chicago: Brittany Publications, 1999).

DISCUSSION QUESTIONS

1. How have conditions for women police officers changed since Penny Harrington started her law enforcement career?
2. In what ways does Penny Harrington's career demonstrate the importance of developing alliances with political leaders and leaders of the rank and file?

CHAPTER 25

GREG MacALEESE
(1947–   )

U nder ancient Chinese law, a person that provided an anonymous tip to the authorities about
a crime would be executed, even if the accusation turned out to be true. The fear was that an
anonymous accusation would make the accuser
unaccountable for his or her actions. Much has
changed since then; the American criminal jus-
tice system places heavy reliance on anonymous tips and on community involvement in solving crimes. One great influence in this area is Greg MacAleese, the
founder of Crime Stoppers. The power of Crime Stoppers worldwide is one of the
hallmarks of law enforcement since the 1980s.

Greg MacAleese was born on January 23, 1947, in Picton, Ontario. The son
of a Royal Canadian Air Force officer, MacAleese moved to Alberta as a youth. In
1961, when MacAleese was fourteen, his father moved the family to Albuquerque,
New Mexico. MacAleese attended the University of New Mexico on a baseball
scholarship, but an arm injury shortened his baseball career. MacAleese graduated
with a degree in journalism in 1969. He went to work for the *Albuquerque Tribune,*
where he had interned as a sports columnist. After one year as a full-time employee
with the *Tribune,* MacAleese went to work as the New Mexico state sports editor
for the Associated Press.

MacAleese, at the age of twenty-five, was voted Sportswriter of the Year for
New Mexico in 1972. Yet another medical problem would cut short his promising
career as a sports journalist. MacAleese developed an ulcer and nearly bled to
death. The ulcer was caused by the stress of his profession, the constant pressure to
meet deadlines, and the long and irregular hours that his job demanded.

Acting on the advice of his physician, MacAleese quit the journalism profession, and his doctor suggested he choose a profession that carried less stress and
emotional baggage and that might offer more regular working hours. Incredibly,
MacAleese chose law enforcement as the answer to his problems, not because of a
passion for public safety or crime detection, but because he thought that police
work would be a good vehicle for authoring books. MacAleese had not spent much
time on crime stories as a reporter, but, in 1972, he worked as press release coordinator for the successful United States Senate campaign of Pete Dominenci. While
working for the Dominenci campaign, MacAleese met law enforcement officers
from all over New Mexico and developed a strong interest in police work as a
result.

MacAleese began working with the Albuquerque Police Department in 1973,
walking a beat for the first six months and then being promoted to the department's
violent crimes section. MacAleese, like any other Albuquerque police officer, did

not get bored with police work. At the time Albuquerque had the highest per capita crime rate in the United States. MacAleese found his niche in policing, especially detective work, but one of his greatest frustrations as a detective was not being able to solve cases, especially when he suspected that someone in the community had useful information but would not or did not know how to supply law enforcement with the information. MacAleese tried for a long time to think of ways to get more public cooperation; he attributed lack of community involvement to apathy, fear of retaliation, and the police not being connected with community.

In 1976, a young man working in an Albuquerque gas station was robbed and shot to death. MacAleese thought the crime would be solvable if he only had some information that would point him in the direction of the killers. Based on the modus operandi of the killing, MacAleese suspected that the killers were responsible for a series of other armed robberies in the Albuquerque area. Falling back on his experience as a journalist and his contacts in the Albuquerque television market, namely Max Sklower, the general manager of KOAT-TV, MacAleese devised a plan to elicit tips about the murder. Based on the information available, MacAleese decided to reenact the crime with as much accuracy as possible, have KOAT film the reenactment, and then air it on the local news broadcast. A tip line was set up so that people with information could phone in. The gas station had offered a $1,000 reward for information leading to the killers' arrest and conviction.

MacAleese carefully arranged to reenact the crime with as much accuracy as possible. He knew the type of gun that had been used; he had a description of the car, and he had been told that the suspects were two young African American men. MacAleese arranged for the service station that had been the scene of the murder to be used to stage the reenactment. He visited the local job corps and recruited two of the participants to play the role of the killers. MacAleese hired a University of New Mexico drama student to play the role of the victim. He even visited car lots until he found a car exactly like the one seen leaving the scene; the car was a black and yellow Chevrolet Charger. Everything was set for a perfect reenactment save for one detail. The crime occurred at night, but the television station would not pay its film crew to work overtime so the reenactment had to be conducted during the day.

The day of the reenactment, everything went awry. The Chevrolet Charger had been sold the day before. The two youths from the job corps failed to show; in fact they were arrested later that day in a barroom disturbance. MacAleese was forced to use his own unmarked car, and he and his lieutenant played the role of the killers. As they acted out the shooting with the young drama student and fled, MacAleese did not realize that the shotgun casing they used to shoot blanks was so hot that it set the young student's clothes afire. The young man was left to desperately shed his clothes and extinguish the fire as MacAleese drove away, all to the delight of dozens of nearby schoolchildren that had gathered to watch the reenactment in full view of the cameras.

Distressed by the amateurishness of the video, MacAleese was sure that nothing would come of it. It aired on September 8, 1976, with MacAleese performing the voice-over. To his surprise and delight, not only was that crime solved, but so was another. The first call led to the solving of an eighteen-month-old unrelated gang-rape case; the second and third calls came from two people who remembered the car and hearing a noise, but they were too drunk to remember any more. Another caller knew the location of the car used in the robbery. MacAleese tracked the car and questioned the owner, who admitted to taking a share of the cut in exchange for the use of his car. He led MacAleese to the killers and the case was solved. At the time of my interview with MacAleese in late 2001, the two killers were still incarcerated.

The television station was delighted with the response they received to the reenactment. Other Albuquerque detectives wanted in on similar reenactments. Numerous reenactments were conducted with great success. Unfortunately, this bred laziness on the part of detectives, who would sometimes wait for the reenactment rather than doing the legwork necessary that could have solved the case up front.

Realizing that the program was growing quickly, MacAleese approached his chief with an eye toward getting a formal program established. MacAleese thought that the program was getting too large to be strictly a police-funded program and that more substantial public involvement was needed to sustain it. He also realized that since money was involved the possibility of malfeasance existed. MacAleese knew that outside oversight was needed to prevent such abuse. With that in mind, Crime Stoppers was formally established with a board of directors, procedures for operation, and fiscal accountability.

Early in the history of Crime Stoppers, MacAleese and another detective nearly found themselves in jail for trying to protect the identity of a Crime Stopper informant. A shooting had occurred in a high drug-activity area of Albuquerque. An informant, also a drug user, who feared retaliation, took MacAleese by the place where the shooters were located. MacAleese arrested the suspects and found other corroborating witnesses. Once the case got to court, defense attorneys, who knew the case had been solved through a Crime Stoppers tip, demanded that MacAleese release the name of the original informant. MacAleese knew that doing so would ruin the program. The judge agreed to take the contempt matter under advisement, and MacAleese spent several days not knowing whether he would go to jail for contempt and whether Crime Stoppers would survive. The local media were in a frenzy and were in favor of Crime Stoppers. The judge, perhaps thinking that the political fallout from ruining Crime Stoppers was greater than the legal issue involved, declined to hold the detectives in contempt.

As a result of his Crime Stoppers work, the Albuquerque Police Department nominated MacAleese for International Association of Chiefs of Police (IACP) officer of the year for 1977. The arrival of 12,000 police chiefs at the IACP meeting in Los Angeles was an enormous boon to Crime Stoppers. Crime Stoppers spread throughout the United States over the next several years. MacAleese eventually left the Albuquerque Police Department and maintained his affiliation with Crime Stoppers until 1983.

In 1984, MacAleese worked in Texas for the Criminal Justice Division of Governor Mark White's office, where he helped establish a Crime Stoppers unit. In

1986 he went to work for the greater Dallas Crime Commission as its executive director, a position he held for five years. In that role, MacAleese sought support for police work from local businesses. MacAleese was also involved in Crime Stoppers and other crime-centered television productions. He was involved in a three-hour television show that profiled narcotics trafficking and its associated violence, with special focus on the recent influx of Jamaican drug dealers in Dallas. The show consisted of two hours of documentary and one hour of town hall meetings. The documentary offered reasons for drug use, pictures of known drug dealers, a profile of the Dallas drug market, and a help line for informants or those wanting treatment. Hundreds of phone calls came in, from those asking for help and those wanting to finger drug dealers. MacAleese grew frustrated with the Dallas Police Department, which was beset with bad morale, community relations problems, and poor training budgets.

Crime Stoppers now includes more than 1,100 programs in more than eight countries. Crime Stoppers claims to have cleared more than 1 million cases, led to more than 400,000 arrests, doled out in excess of $60 million in rewards, and recovered at least $1.3 billion in property and more than $4 billion in narcotics. Perhaps even more significantly, Crime Stoppers reenactments spawned other crime-oriented reality shows, such as *Cops,* and, most significantly, *America's Most Wanted,* an idea that came to the show's creator while he was watching a Crime Stopper reenactment on a hotel room television. The question of whether such shows constitute quality television viewing is beyond the scope and range of this book. However, whether Crime Stoppers' legacy will be positive or negative has not been decided. Some criticize the cozy relationship that such organizations foster between the media and police departments, fearing that it may compromise the independence of both entities. MacAleese believes this is nonsense. Organizations such as Crime Stoppers and shows like *America's Most Wanted* bring the police and the community closer together. As a former police officer and former journalist, MacAleese provides an informed perspective on the proper role of both the police and the news media.

MacAleese returned to New Mexico in 1991; from 1991–1995 he served as executive director of Crime Stoppers. Feeling burned out, MacAleese decided to try his hand at business. MacAleese's first wife was former Albuquerque city councilwoman Jo Marrs, who passed away in 1991. He remarried and now resides in Colorado where he works as a private law enforcement and private security consultant.

SOURCES

Crime Stoppers web site, www.crimestoppers.com, November 2, 2001.
Greg MacAleese, telephone interview, January 18, 2002.
Greg MacAleese, "The Crime Stoppers Story," www.c-s-i.org, November 10, 2001.

DISCUSSION QUESTIONS

1. How has Greg MacAleese's background as a journalist contributed to his law enforcement accomplishments?

2. Along with *America's Most Wanted,* how has Greg MacAleese's career influenced other ventures between law enforcement and the entertainment media?

CHAPTER 26

CLARENCE DARROW
(1857–1938)

Clarence Darrow may have been the greatest courtroom lawyer of the twentieth century; he was certainly the greatest courtroom orator. To his admirers, his name has become synonymous with fighting for the right to think and speak freely, championing the rights of the underdog, and leading the charge against a cruel and capriciously applied death penalty—the quintessential American defense attorney or, as he has been called, the "attorney for the damned." To his detractors, he embodied several distasteful aspects of America's legal culture and liberal thinking. Darrow was derided as a godless, amoral atheist, a cynical defender of cruel, remorseless criminals, and an overtly political partisan, rather than an emotionally detached advocate for his clients. No matter what one would call him, no one ever accused Clarence Darrow of being dull.

Clarence Seward Darrow was born on April 15, 1857, in Kinsman, Ohio, the fifth of eight children born to Emily Darrow and her husband Amirus, a village undertaker and coffin maker. Perhaps in a foretelling of his opposition to the death penalty as an adult, young Clarence Darrow supposedly never visited his father's shop. The thought of seeing stacked coffins and corpses exacerbated his abiding fear of death.

Darrow attended law school at the University of Michigan and stayed for only one year before being admitted to the bar in Ohio in 1878. He served as an apprentice in Youngstown for one year. He married Jessie Ohl, a farmer's daughter, in 1880. The marriage produced one child, Paul, who was born in 1883, fifteen years before Clarence and Jessie divorced. Darrow remarried in 1903, this time to Ruby Hammerstrom, a woman fifteen years younger than he. Darrow began his law practice in Ohio, first in Andover, then in Ashtabula, where he was also elected in 1885 to the part-time position of city solicitor. His first case as a defense attorney involved a boy accused of stealing a $15 harness, a case that he took to the Ohio Supreme Court and for which he was paid $5. Darrow practiced law in his home state until he moved to Chicago in 1887.

Although Darrow represented a multitude of defendants accused of innumerable crimes, he gained fame by immersing himself in four social issues that made their way into an American courtroom. The mark of a truly celebrated criminal case is one that transcends legal circles and is well known to those outside the working world of criminal justice. Darrow was involved in several such cases, each involving four of the most controversial sociopolitical issues of his generation. The four issues were (1) organized labor, (2) freedom of speech vis-à-vis religious beliefs, (3) civil rights, and (4) the death penalty.

In 1894, Darrow became involved in the first case that would thrust him into the national spotlight when he represented Eugene Debs, president of the American Railway Union and one of the most controversial labor leaders of his generation. This was the defining moment in Darrow's career. He had been associated with railroad management since moving to Chicago, and he could have been a success in the traditional manner of corporate attorneys of his time, but Darrow admired the burgeoning labor movement in the railroad industry, so he quit the railroad to represent Debs. From that moment on, Darrow usually linked himself with defendants he perceived as "the underdogs."

Pullman Railroad employees had gone on strike in March 1894. The strike turned bloody, resulting in several deaths. The striking employees were ordered back to work, courtesy of a court injunction requested by Pullman management. When the workers refused, Debs was arrested and charged with criminal conspiracy and contempt of court for encouraging the workers to stay on strike. Darrow defended Debs passionately and eloquently, even telling jurors the case would "count much for liberty or against liberty," but that did not save Debs. He was convicted and sentenced to six months in jail, but the notoriety from the case made Darrow and Debs famous, solidifying Darrow's reputation as a great courtroom orator.

Darrow continued to represent the interests of organized labor for the next two decades, until a 1911 case caused an irreparable break between Darrow and organized labor. Brothers James and John McNamara, two labor activists, were accused of bombing the *Los Angeles Times* building on October 1, 1910, a blast that resulted in twenty-one deaths. Their arrest came several months later as a result of an investigation headed by William Burns. Delighted by another chance at the national spotlight, Darrow undertook the brothers' defense with his usual zeal. He accused Detective Burns of kidnapping the pair by illegally arresting them in Indiana. He argued that the McNamara brothers were the victims of a conspiracy against organized labor. With the help of other labor leaders, Darrow whipped the country into a frenzy. Newspapers around the country reported on the case, many siding with the defendants and Darrow. Darrow's defense and accusations of a conspiracy disintegrated when the brothers changed their plea to guilty in the middle of the trial. Darrow successfully argued for a life sentence instead of death, but his reputation with organized labor was ruined. To make matters worse, Darrow was indicted on charges of jury tampering, a charge of which he was eventually acquitted, though a great deal of evidence pointed to his guilt. It would take Darrow several years to repair the damage to his reputation, which he accomplished by publicly advocating the American war effort during World War I (1917–1918).

Darrow's most famous clash against the death penalty came with his defense of Nathan Leopold and Richard Loeb. Leopold and Loeb were teenaged friends (they were actually gay lovers, but the newspapers of the day only made subtle reference to that) who wanted to commit the perfect crime, purely for a thrill. They were wealthy, educated (Leopold had an intelligence quotient above the genius level), and attractive (Loeb, handsome and athletic, became a matinee idol, receiving numerous marriage offers from female admirers). Richard Loeb had devised what he thought to be the perfect crime, and he needed Leopold's assistance in pulling it off. In the summer of 1924, Leopold and Loeb abducted Loeb's fourteen-year-old cousin, Bobby Franks, as he was leaving school; they bludgeoned him to death, used acid to disfigure his sexually mutilated body before dumping it into a creek, and telephoned Franks's father demanding $10,000 ransom for his safe return.

Darrow, whose career tanked after the McNamara brothers' fiasco, found himself back in the national spotlight, this time to take on another nemesis of his, the death penalty. The killers were cruel, cynical, and remorseless. Unlike most other criminal defendants, they could not fall back on poverty or lack of education as an excuse for committing crime. Leopold and Loeb, it seemed, were poster children for the death penalty.

In a brilliant but unexpected move, Darrow had the two defendants plead guilty. He had no doubt of their guilt and he knew that they stood no chance of acquittal before a local jury. He also knew that if the decision to sentence the pair were left to a jury that death would almost certainly be the outcome. With a guilty plea, Darrow figured his chances of sparing the two men's lives would be better if the sentencing hearing were conducted in front of a judge. Plus, while preparing for the case, Darrow discovered that, in Illinois history, only two men of Leopold and Loeb's age had been executed, and they were offered a life sentence in exchange for a guilty plea. His strategy worked, in part because of his brilliant mercy plea, and also because the judge, John Caverly, also opposed the death penalty. Leopold and Loeb were sentenced to life in prison plus ninety-nine years.

Darrow's next high-profile case came in 1925, this time in Dayton, Tennessee. Several years prior, Tennessee had enacted a law banning the teaching of evolution in public schools. The law sat largely unnoticed and was not enforced. Government and business leaders in Dayton, eager for the money and attention that a celebrated trial would bring, secured the cooperation of a high school physics teacher named John Scopes to play the part of a defendant charged with violating the law. Contrary to the image depicted in *Inherit the Wind*, a fictional play based on the trial, Scopes was a willing participant in the proceedings. The then recently founded American Civil Liberties Union (ACLU) also relished the prospect of such a trial so it could advance its reputation and agenda. The ACLU enlisted Darrow to aid in Scopes's defense, and William Jennings Bryan, whose 1896 presidential bid Darrow had supported, was hired as a special prosecutor.

The stage was set (intentionally) for high drama, and the Scopes Trial lived up to its billing. It pitted Darrow, the greatest courtroom orator of the era, against Bryan, the most eloquent political orator of the era. The case consisted mostly of emotionally laced and theatrical speeches made by Bryan and Darrow. The highlight came when Darrow, stymied in his attempts to have academic experts testify on Scopes's behalf, questioned Bryan on the stand, and poked holes in Bryan's arguments supporting a literal interpretation of the Bible. Darrow humiliated Bryan, leading him to make such nonsensical statements as, "I do not think about things that I do not think about," to which Darrow retorted, "Do you think about things that you do think about?" Wanting to avert an impassioned closing argument by Bryan, Darrow had Scopes plead guilty; his sentence, a $100 fine. Scopes's conviction was subsequently overturned by the state Supreme Court, but on procedural grounds; Tennessee's law against teaching evolution was left intact. Although Darrow lost his battle in the legal arena, he won in the court of public opinion. The teaching of evolution flourished, while Bryan, suffering from bad health and despondent over his performance in the Scopes Trial, died shortly after the trial.

Darrow became a celebrity among civil rights advocates for his defense of Ossian Sweet, an African American doctor in Detroit. Sweet purchased a house in an all-white neighborhood, and in 1925, faced with protesters in front of his house, fired several gunshots from inside his house, killing one of the protesters. The first trial ended in a mistrial. Darrow defended Sweet during his second trial and won his acquittal, convincing an all-white jury that Sweet had acted in self-defense.

Another racially charged case, the last significant case of Darrow's career, took him to Hawaii. In 1932 he took on the defense of Navy Lieutenant Thomas Massie and three other men who were accused of killing a native Hawaiian. The deceased had with other men allegedly raped Lieutenant Massie's wife. Darrow managed to have the defendants exonerated, in exchange for Massie's wife agreeing to drop rape charges against the other Hawaiian defendants. In the eyes of some, Darrow had contributed to racial harmony in Hawaii, which was still an American territory at the time.

Darrow's notoriety and penchant for taking on left-wing causes did not escape the attention of the FBI, which conducted surveillance of suspected subversives during the 1930s. In May 1936, Darrow contributed an article to *Esquire* magazine called "Attorney for the Defense," in which he laid out some of his beliefs about the justice system and his courtroom tricks of the trade. An agent was assigned to read Darrow's article and relay his impressions about Darrow to FBI assistant director Clyde Tolson. During Darrow's lifetime, there were few if any highly paid jury consultants and researchers. Even the most prominent defense attorneys relied on their own beliefs, past experiences, and gut instincts in selecting a jury. Even though he was competent in the technical aspects of the law, Darrow's greatest talent (and he knew it) was his own persona and his ability to play on a juror's emotions. Said Darrow, "The more a lawyer knows of life, human nature, psychology, and the reactions of the human emotions, the better he is equipped to select the twelve good men, good and true." He thought it important that the attorney discover a potential juror's reading habits, type of friends, ethnicity, and religious beliefs, as Darrow was considered an almost fanatical atheist.

During the 1930s, prior to the age of political correctness, Darrow expressed his preferences and prejudices regarding certain ethnic groups and jury service in the *Esquire* article. Said Darrow, the "Irish are emotional, kindly and sympathetic, must have him . . . the German is not keen on individual rights, his ways are fixed by his race . . . the Scandinavians and Lutherans are quick to convict." Darrow avoided prohibitionists because they were "too solemn and holy." Darrow said that he avoided any "Presbyterian who rolls up his umbrella and calmly sits down." He reserved his greatest disdain for Baptists, his prejudice no doubt influenced by his experience ten years earlier in the Scopes Trial. Said Darrow, "The Baptists are more hopeless than the Presbyterians. They, too, are apt to think that the real home of all outsiders is Sheol and you do not want them on the jury, and the sooner they leave the better." Not surprisingly, Darrow expressed a preference for agnostics. He also liked having Jews on his juries.

Darrow's greatest preference was for a man that laughs; his greatest prejudice was against wealthy men. He also expressed relief that his career was coming to an end as more and more women were starting to serve as jurors, because, in his words, women jurors "took their roles too seriously." The *Esquire* article provided some insight into Darrow's worldview, which carried over into the types of cases he selected. One passage of the article, underlined by Tolson, best summarized Darrow's attitude toward the American justice system. It stated, "The litigants and their lawyers are supposed to want justice, but, in reality, there is no such thing as justice, either in or out of court. Most trials are contests between rich and poor."

The *Esquire* article was Darrow's last publication. In 1938 he began to grow weak from heart problems, which eventually rendered him an invalid. The last year of Darrow's life was spent in semi-seclusion. He died on March 13, 1938, at the age of eighty. Although the *Esquire* article was his last published writing, a hand-written piece discovered after his death was his last actual writing. It affirmed and summarized the worldview that drove his work. Darrow expressed admiration toward his father, a man who often found himself ostracized because of his unorthodox social and religious beliefs. Darrow's father passed on his unbending belief in the worth of the individual against a tyrannical majority. Darrow wrote: "The fact that most of the community were on the other side made him so much surer of his cause."

SOURCES AND SUGGESTED READINGS

Martin Calabro, *Great Courtroom Lawyers: Fighting the Cases That Made History* (New York: Facts on File, 1996).

Clarence Darrow, *The Story of My Life* (New York: Grosset and Dunlap, 1932).

Gilbert Geis and Leigh B. Bienen, *Crimes of the Century* (Boston: Northeastern University Press, 1998).

Darien A. McWhirter, *The Legal 100: A Ranking of the Individuals Who Have Most Influenced the Law* (Secaucus, NJ: Carol, 1998).

Irving Stone, *Clarence Darrow for the Defense* (Garden City, NY: Doubleday and Company, 1941).

Kevin Tierney, "Darrow, Clarence," www.anb.org, *American National Biography Online,* Freedom of Information Act web site, http://foia.fbi.gov, November 1, 2002.

DISCUSSION QUESTIONS

1. What has been Clarence Darrow's impact on American society?
2. Which of Clarence Darrow's cases was the most significant?

CHAPTER 27

■ ■ ■ ■ ■ ▬▬▬▬▬▬▬▬

ROGER NASH BALDWIN
(1884–1981)

Few organizations are as alternately admired and detested by the American public as the American Civil Liberties Union (ACLU). Whatever one's opinion of the ACLU, no one can deny that it has been a major force in the legal and social arenas of American life for more than eighty years. The life of its founder, Roger Baldwin, is a window into the ACLU's history and mission.

Roger Nash Baldwin was born on January 21, 1884, in Wellesley, Massachusetts, the oldest of six children. His parents, Lucy Nash Baldwin and Frank Fenno Baldwin, were native Bostonians, direct descendants of the seventeenth-century *Mayflower* expedition. Frank Baldwin was a successful leather merchant, and Roger enjoyed a childhood of wealth and privilege. The Baldwins were Unitarians, which excluded them from some prominent Boston religious circles. Roger Baldwin attended public schools in Wellesley. He performed well in art and music, which, coupled with his Unitarian beliefs and lack of athletic ability, set him apart from many of the popular students at school. The tendency toward nonconformity to those around him would be a trait of Baldwin's throughout his entire life.

Baldwin's childhood reflected the naive and hypocritical attitude of some wealthy, liberal New Englanders. The Baldwin family proclaimed the doctrine of equality for all races and ethnic groups, but they had little interaction with anyone other than white Protestants. Once, when an African American man visited Baldwin's elementary school (so the young Wellesley children could actually see and talk to a black man in person), Baldwin asked the man if he was "black all over."

Baldwin enrolled at Harvard in 1901. After graduating from Harvard (in only three years) with a degree in anthropology, he earned a master's degree in anthropology and philosophy from there as well. While at Harvard, Baldwin showed no signs of his proclivity to social activism and political radicalism that became his life and career.

Baldwin grew disenchanted with his family and with the conformist life of Boston. He wanted to get away from Boston, where he could be more than his "grandfather's grandson, his uncle's nephew, and his father's son." He moved to St. Louis and took a job as director of a settlement house called the Self Culture Hall; he also took a position as the first teacher and director of the now-famous sociology department at Washington University.

Baldwin no longer lived among Protestant bluebloods as he had in Boston. He lived in a poor neighborhood and interacted with minorities that he had shunned as a youth. Although he still possessed a courtly and patrician air and personality, his worldview became more liberal. Sheltered from the problems of the poor as a child, Baldwin was affected by firsthand looks at the poverty, racial segregation, and ethnic discrimination he witnessed in St. Louis. He grew increasingly intrigued with anarchism, socialism, and Communist thought. Baldwin became a local social activist, mostly lobbying against discrimination in housing laws.

Baldwin would often follow some of his troubled youthful acquaintances to court when they ran afoul of the law. A skillful and passionate advocate, the juvenile court judge thought Baldwin a natural for a juvenile probation officer's job. A year after arriving in St. Louis, Baldwin assumed the job of chief probation officer for St. Louis's fledgling juvenile court system, even though at twenty-four he was four months shy of the minimum age for probation officers as prescribed by Missouri law.

With juvenile courts still in their infancy, Baldwin was able to shape juvenile justice in St. Louis in his own image. Unlike most of his more bureaucratic colleagues, he realized the importance of working with the news media. He persuaded local media outlets to omit the names of juvenile arrestees from the paper. He successfully lobbied for a law disallowing children under fourteen from selling newspapers. With Colorado's Benjamin Lindsey, he helped organize a national probation association, which later became the National Council on Crime and Delinquency. He coauthored a training manual called *Juvenile Courts and Probation,* which was used by probation officers across the country.

While single and still in his twenties, Baldwin assumed legal guardianship of two eleven-year-old boys. He struck up a friendship with Emma Goldman, one of the most famous (or infamous) and articulate spokespersons for radicalism in the twentieth century. This friendship further steered Baldwin in the direction of radical political and social beliefs.

Baldwin left probation work in 1910, accepting a position with the St. Louis Civic League. His interest in social justice at all levels was increasing, and Baldwin thought he had a better chance of effecting social change in all areas of life with the league than as a probation officer. His interest in civil liberties became more pronounced as well. In 1915, Margaret Sanger, known for her controversial advocacy of birth control, was denied permission to use a St. Louis auditorium to deliver a speech. Baldwin took up Sanger's cause, and he succeeded. The situation repeated itself with the International Workers of the World (IWW), a radical labor organization.

In April 1917, with Europe in the throws of World War I and the United States on the brink of entering the war, Baldwin publicly proclaimed a commitment to pacifism and went to work with a pacifist organization called the American Union against Militarism (AUAM). The AUAM was founded by a group of social workers that included Jane Addams, a Chicago juvenile justice pioneer. Baldwin moved to New York City, the home base of the AUAM. America entered the war in 1917.

On October 1, 1917, a subgroup of the AUAM formed an organization to defend conscientious objectors to the war. The new organization, which Baldwin joined, called itself the Civil Liberty Defense League, and soon changed its name to the National Civil Liberties Bureau (NCLB). The NCLB vowed to make spirited efforts to not only defend conscientious objectors but to defend free speech, seeing it as "the living essence of democracy."

The NCLB evoked the ire of many government authorities, especially those promoting the war. Government authorities openly accused Baldwin of espionage. Their offices were raided and members were placed under frequent surveillance. The government tried to silence Baldwin another way. In October 1918, Baldwin, now age thirty-four, was ordered by the local draft board to take a physical. Baldwin refused, believing that violence was the wrong means to achieving a noble end, and he was arrested for violating the Selective Service Act.

Baldwin was sentenced to one year in the penitentiary. The move to silence Baldwin backfired. He became a hero to many, and his name became well known to supporters and opponents of the war alike. Baldwin became more famous while incarcerated than he could have hoped for while living on the outside. To Baldwin's surprise, the NCLB welcomed him back as their leader. After World War I ended, some thought that the NCLB and other civil liberties would have no mission. The NCLB found other interests to defend, namely the rights of laborers to organize and strike and the right of socialists and anarchists to speak out.

Baldwin was released on July 19, 1919. On August 8, 1919, he married Madeleine Doty, a thirty-nine-year-old journalist and lawyer that he had met in 1913. Doty was also a prison reform advocate; she once spent a week in the New York state penitentiary at Auburn under an assumed name so she could witness prison life firsthand. The two lived in Greenwich Village, always a haven for the political and social left of New York City.

On January 20, 1920, the NCLB changed its name to the American Civil Liberties Union (ACLU). Its stated purpose was that "all thought on matters of public concern should be freely expressed, without interference. Orderly social progress is promoted by unrestricted freedom of opinion." Baldwin assumed leadership of the ACLU.

In contrast to other civil libertarians, who preferred to work away from the public spotlight, Baldwin recognized the need for publicity and cultivating good relationships with the media and as many government officials as possible. This was not possible with the Bureau of Investigation, then under the direction of William Burns and later under the leadership of J. Edgar Hoover, both of whom loathed Baldwin. J. Edgar Hoover called him a "parlor pink," a derisive term for those thought to have Communist sympathies; William Burns accused him of being a "paid agent" of the Communist Party, a common labeled applied to those on the political left after the Russian Revolution.

In contrast to other political radicals, dissidents, and civil rights activists, Baldwin thought the best arena for promoting his agenda was in the courts, not in the streets. Much like it does today, the ACLU sought out court cases they thought were significant touchstones for civil liberties issues, often challenging local laws and ordinances they viewed as unconstitutional. However, Baldwin was no stranger to demonstrating the streets. He was arrested and charged with sedition for participating in prolabor rallies.

Under Baldwin's leadership, the ACLU involved itself in the most celebrated criminal cases of the day, but only peripherally. It supplied expert scientific witnesses and funded expenses for the defense of John Scopes, a schoolteacher tried for violating Tennessee's law against teaching evolution. (The witnesses were not allowed to testify.) The ACLU aided in the defense of the so-called Scottsboro Boys, nine African American men convicted of raping two white women in an Alabama railroad car. However, the ACLU's main priority were cases involving the First Amendment.

During the 1920s Baldwin, by then firmly in control of the ACLU, involved the union in international affairs. Creating a new socialist order around the world became the priority. Baldwin aligned the ACLU with proponents of Indian independence from Great Britain. Baldwin naively believed that the newly formed Soviet Union would be the vehicle for the new socialist order, even though he denounced Soviet repression of its citizenry, especially after visiting the Soviet Union. Political prisoners around the world became a priority for Baldwin, both in the Soviet Union and in other countries. He even left the ACLU for a brief time to head the International Committee for Political Prisoners.

During the 1930s, many Americans, thrown into economic and psychological desperation by the Great Depression, turned to socialism and communism as the answer to their frustration. The majority of Americans detested communism, which brought them into conflict with the ACLU. Likewise, right-wing radicalism, led by the Ku Klux Klan and the American Nazis, was on the rise during the 1930s. The ACLU, which despised the KKK and Nazisim, still thought it better to have their ideals discussed openly, in the hopes that the American public could see them for what they were. Despite their tepid endorsement of the rights of right wingers to express their views, and their disenchantment with Soviet communism, the ACLU, both under Baldwin and subsequent leadership, aligned itself with left-wing causes more than right-wing organizations and ideals.

During World War II, Baldwin did not concern himself with antiwar efforts as much as he did with protecting Americans prosecuted for espousing unpopular views. In fact, the ACLU, motivated in part because of its hatred of fascism and Nazism, supported American involvement in the war. Baldwin, who by now had lost sole control of the ACLU, criticized the union for not speaking out more forcefully against the internment of Japanese Americans on the West Coast. The ACLU did not oppose prosecution of those who aided the causes of the enemy governments of Germany, Italy, and Japan.

When the war ended in 1945, the ACLU turned its efforts to protecting free speech in the age of the civil rights movement, the Cold War, and anticommunism, even though the ACLU had officially taken an anti-Communist stance in 1940. The ACLU expended great efforts defending Americans accused of violating the 1940 Smith Act, which made it illegal to belong to organizations or distribute material that advocated the overthrow of the United States government.

By the late 1940s, Baldwin lost the energy and interest needed to administer the daily activities of the ACLU. Board leadership forced Baldwin out as leader. He resigned on January 1, 1950, but stayed on the board of directors until 1955. Baldwin opposed American involvement in the Vietnam War in the 1960s. He voiced concern over treatment and suppression of antiwar activists during the Vietnam conflict as well. He joined the ACLU in calling for President Richard Nixon's impeachment in 1974. Nixon resigned to avoid impeachment.

After his departure from the ACLU, Baldwin remained active in promoting civil liberties. He spent most of his time in New Jersey with his second wife, Evelyn Preston Baldwin. (Baldwin and his first wife had divorced in 1934.) Evelyn Baldwin died on June 11, 1962, while Roger was in Puerto Rico teaching a university course on civil rights. Baldwin was a frequent speaker in educational and political forums, both in the United States and abroad. Baldwin became less of a radical and more of a conventional liberal as he got older.

Baldwin died on August 26, 1981, in Ridgewood, New Jersey, at the age of ninety-seven. Baldwin believed that the criminal justice system could be used to protect democracy, but that it could also be the means of its destruction. He loved the United States and believed in democracy. He once said, "Democracy works. I have hope, but not optimism. But if you want to put a label on me, I'm an unhappy optimist."

SOURCES AND SUGGESTED READINGS

American National Biography Online, www.anb.org, March 20, 2003.

Robert C. Cotrell, *Roger Nash Baldwin and the American Civil Liberties Union* (New York: Columbia University Press, 2000).

Peggy Lamson, *Roger Baldwin, Founder of the American Civil Liberties Union: A Portrait* (Boston: Houghton Mifflin, 1976).

DISCUSSION QUESTIONS

1. Given Baldwin's privileged upbringing, is it surprising that he lived his adult life as a perpetual fan of people he viewed as underdogs?
2. Most Americans have strong feelings about the American Civil Liberties Union. Given that you probably have an opinion about the ACLU, what are your thoughts about Baldwin's place in history?

CHAPTER 28

■■■■■

EARL WARREN
(1891–1974)

Earl Warren served as chief justice of the United States from 1953–1969, one of the Supreme Court's most tumultuous periods. Warren has been credited, or blamed, with leading the so-called due process revolution, which significantly affected the way criminal justice officials in America, especially law enforcement officers, conduct their daily activities. John Jay and John Marshall had tremendous influences on the Supreme Court's establishment as an institution and a force in American government. However, in terms of the daily aspects of criminal justice administration, no chief justice has been as influential as Earl Warren.

Earl Warren was born on March 19, 1891, in Los Angeles, the son of lower-middle-class immigrant parents (a Norwegian father and Swedish mother). He had no middle name because his father claimed the family was too poor to give him one. Warren spent much of his childhood in Bakersfield, California. At the turn of the twentieth century, Bakersfield was a true frontier town, with all of the vices common to Wild West blue-collar areas. Bakersfield, like most other towns in California prior to World War II, systematically oppressed the ethnic minority group that bore the brunt of much West Coast prejudice at that time, the Chinese. Warren's father, Matt, struggled to make a living as a railroad car repairman. The plight of California's working class and the anti-Chinese discrimination witnessed by Warren in Bakersfield remained an important influence on Warren throughout his career.

Warren attended the University of California at Berkeley where he graduated from the Boalt Hall School of Law in 1914. After serving in the Army during World War I, Warren joined the Alameda County District Attorney's Office as an assistant. He worked as a prosecutor there for eighteen years, the last thirteen as district attorney.

Warren gained a reputation as a tough, effective prosecutor. During the 1930s, Warren, who would eventually be vilified by American law enforcement, was a frequent speaker and honored guest before Peace Officer Associations around the country. He befriended police chiefs throughout the country, including August Vollmer and O. W. Wilson. Warren's fame as a district attorney led to his election as California attorney general in 1938. In 1942, shortly after America's entry into World War II, he was elected governor. During his gubernatorial term, Warren signed legislation creating the California Department of Corrections, which centralized authority over all California prisons in one body.

As governor, Warren would make one of the most momentous decisions of his professional life and one that stains his name in the eyes of many Americans today. Warren, the great civil liberties hero of the 1950s and 1960s, oversaw the evacuation of Japanese citizens to internment camps during World War II. Late in life, Warren acknowledged in his memoirs that the treatment of Japanese Californians had been unjust.

This move by Warren, though reviled by many today, was a popular decision in 1940s California. Warren was elected to the governorship three times, though he did not finish his third term. Warren's enormous popularity in California spread to the rest of the country. In 1948, he was chosen as republican presidential candidate Thomas Dewey's running mate. Though Dewey and Warren lost the election to Harry Truman, Warren's name became better known than ever before.

In 1952, republican candidate Dwight Eisenhower was elected president. Warren had done much to send California votes Eisenhower's way; plus, he had done the party a favor by grudgingly turning down the vice-presidential nomination in deference to fellow Californian Richard Nixon. Eisenhower had promised Warren a position on the Supreme Court when one became available. Soon after Fred Vinson's unexpected death in September 1953, Warren assumed the duties of chief justice of the United States Supreme Court.

Warren assumed the helm of a deeply divided Court that faced several landmark cases. The first landmark case was *Brown v. Board of Education of Topeka, Kansas*. *Brown* paved the way for school desegregation, and it signaled the beginning of the end for the "separate but equal" doctrine on treatment of racial minorities that had been upheld in the 1896 case *Plessy v. Ferguson*. Perhaps what was most remarkable about *Brown* was that a Court that had been viciously fractured in recent years unanimously decided its outcome. Always regarded more for his political acumen than his giftedness as a legal scholar, Warren won high accolades for his ability to build a consensus on the Court, as evidenced by *Brown*.

In the ensuing years, the Warren Court led the due process revolution in America. The Warren Court effectively settled the "Incorporation Debate"—the argument over whether the rights contained in the United States Constitution applied to the individual states. In *Mapp v. Ohio,* the Court held that the exclusionary rule—the rule that illegally obtained evidence can not be admissible in a criminal trial—applied to the states, overturning common law enforcement practice as well as *Wolf v. Colorado* which had been decided only twelve years prior to *Mapp*.

Many decisions handed down by the Warren Court were extremely unpopular with the American public, particularly with police officers. Despite the *Terry v. Ohio* decision, which was a victory for police officers, Warren was accused of handcuffing police officers and court officials and unleashing a crime wave with the *Mapp v. Ohio, Miranda v. Arizona,* and *Gideon v. Wainwright* decisions. He was accused of interfering with the electoral process in *Baker v. Carr,* and of improper social engineering in *Griswold v. Connecticut* and *Brown*.

Prior to his appointment as Supreme Court chief justice, Warren had been a lifelong republican, albeit a moderate one compared to some of his contemporaries, such as Joseph McCarthy and Richard Nixon. He became very unpopular with his fellow Republicans, including President Eisenhower, who reportedly said that Warren's Supreme Court nomination "was the biggest damn fool thing I ever did." Eisenhower also stated that he would like to shoot the person who first recommended Warren as chief justice. Warren's former running mate, Thomas Dewey also became disenchanted with the chief justice, calling him a "judicial wrecker."

Warren will also be remembered for a role he reluctantly assumed at President Lyndon Johnson's request in the mid-1960s. After President John F. Kennedy's assassination in November 1963, Johnson asked Warren to head a commission to investigate the assassination. Warren and several other distinguished politicians and statesmen, including future President Gerald Ford, issued a report on the assassination, which has been the subject of intense scrutiny and criticism since its release in September 1964. Politicians, journalists, conspiracy buffs, and even Hollywood filmmakers, many of them defaming Warren's name in the process, have hotly debated the Warren Commission's findings.

Criminologist Samuel Walker stated that Earl Warren underwent a transformation from a tough law-and-order prosecutor, attorney general, and governor, to a champion of civil liberties as chief justice. Walker suggests that Warren's transformation was in keeping with changing times. According to this view, Earl Warren, along with Supreme Court colleagues William Brennan and Thurgood Marshall, symbolized and embodied the transformation of the American conscious in matters of criminal justice and believed in protecting the rights of the "little guy" from all powerful state and majority interests.

Warren biographer Ed Cray suggested that Warren did not really undergo a radical ideological transformation. Warren was always a strict disciple of law and order. He was also a strong proponent of the procedural due process rights that criminal justice officials should employ when enforcing the law. Warren practiced what he preached in this respect long before he became chief justice. An intruder murdered Warren's father in May 1938. The investigation led police to a San Quentin inmate serving time on other charges. When Bakersfield police officers suggested that a planted stool pigeon or eavesdropping device be used to catch the killer, Warren refused, stating he would not stoop to underhanded police methods, even to catch his father's murderer. His father's murder was never solved.

Warren died in 1974, five years after retiring from the Supreme Court. Regardless of whether one thinks he was a great civil libertarian and jurist, or the catalyst who provoked a "great American crime wave" of the 1960s, Earl Warren's place as one of the most important Chief Justices in history is solid, as is his place as one of the most important figures in the history of American criminal justice.

SOURCES AND SUGGESTED READINGS

Ed Cray, *Chief Justice* (New York: Simon & Schuster, 1997).
Rolando V. del Carmen and Jeffrey T. Walker, *Briefs of Leading Cases in Law Enforcement* (4th ed.). (Cincinnati: Anderson Publishing, 2000).

Jack H. Pollack, *Earl Warren: The Judge Who Changed America* (Englewood Cliffs, NJ: Prentice Hall, 1979).

Samuel Walker, *Popular Justice: A History of American Criminal Justice* (2nd ed.) (New York: Oxford University Press, 1997).

DISCUSSION QUESTIONS

1. Of all decisions handed down by the Warren Court, which one do you think is the most significant?
2. Throughout most of his career, Earl Warren was viewed as a friend to police officers, but by the time of his retirement, many police officers detested many of his decisions. What caused this—did Warren change or did the times change?

APPENDIX   Landmark Criminal Justice Cases Decided by the Warren Court

CASE CITATION HOLDING

Draper v. United States	358 U.S. 307 (1959) Information from an informant may be probable cause for an arrest if it is corroborated by a police officer.
Mapp v. Ohio	367 U.S. 643 (1961) Evidence obtained illegally is inadmissible; the "exclusionary rule" applies to the states.
Wong Sun v. United States	371 U.S. 471 (1963) Evidence derived from an illegal police act, or "fruit of the poisonous tree," is inadmissible.
Gideon v. Wainwright	372 U.S. 335 (1963) Anyone charged with a felony in state court is entitled to appointed legal counsel if they cannot afford an attorney.
Escobedo v. Illinois	378 U.S. 478 (1964) A person charged with a serious offense is entitled to counsel while in a police station.
Sheppard v. Maxwell	384 U.S. 333 (1966) Reversed the conviction of Dr. Sam Sheppard ("The Fugitive" murder case) because of the judge's failure to protect the integrity of the proceeding from the effects of pretrial publicity.
Miranda v. Arizona	384 U.S. 436 (1966) Information and confessions obtained from a suspect undergoing custodial interrogation is inadmissible unless the suspect understood that he/she had certain rights mentioned in the *Miranda* decision.
United States v. Wade	388 U.S. 218 (1967) A criminal suspect has the right to the presence of an attorney during a lineup.
Katz v. United States	389 U.S. 347 (1967) Electronic surveillance that is an invasion of privacy constitutes a search and is subject to the rules pertaining to illegal searches.
Duncan v. Louisiana	391 U.S. 145 (1968) A person is entitled to a jury trial if they are charged with a "serious" crime.
Terry v. Ohio	392 U.S. 1 (1968) Police officer "stop and frisk" is valid if it is based on reasonable suspicion.

CHAPTER 29

WILLIAM KUNSTLER
(1919–1995)

If anyone deserves the title of America's premier radical lawyer, it is William Kunstler. Kunstler biographer David Langum called him "the most hated lawyer in America." The desire to be loved and admired would cause most human beings to abhor such a label. Kunstler relished such titles. He reveled in taking on unpopular clients, or as he called them, "unacceptable outcasts," particularly those on the political left. Kunstler viewed his job not so much to defend his client, but to put the criminal justice system on trial instead.

Like anyone who assumes unpopular positions, lack of confidence was never a problem for Kunstler. Kunstler sought the spotlight throughout his career and usually found it. His appearance was as unforgettable as his personality. A large man with long unkempt hair, Kunstler seldom entered any room unnoticed. As a lawyer who traveled frequently, he saw little need to make good lasting impressions on court officials or criminal justice officials that were aligned against him.

William Moses Kunstler was born on July 7, 1919, in New York City, the oldest of three children born to Frances Mendelbaum Kunstler, a housewife, and Monroe Bradford Kunstler, a physician. William Kunstler grew up in a Jewish household near Central Park West. His identification with lawbreakers emanated from his own adolescent antics in New York. He belonged to a gang called the Red Devils, who specialized in petty theft and vandalism. Kunstler graduated at the top of his high school class in 1937 and entered Yale University. Even during his teenage years, Kunstler's activities provided some indication of his proclivity toward being a daredevil. In 1935, while visiting Europe, the sixteen-year-old Kunstler drove an ambulance in the Spanish Civil War but came home at his mother's request.

At Yale, Kunstler embarked on a medical degree, assuming that he would follow in his father's footsteps. He changed his major to French, graduating in 1941. Kunstler enlisted in the Navy in June 1941. He was rejected by the Navy and enlisted in the Army on September 5, 1941, three months before America's entry into World War II. While in the Army, Kunstler married Lotte Rosenberger, the daughter of family friends that had fled Germany in the 1930s amidst Nazi persecution of Jews. Kunstler spent most of the War in New Guinea, rose to the rank of major, and received the Bronze Star.

After the War, Kunstler enrolled in Yale Law School. While in law school, Kunstler put his literary talents to work, writing book reviews for the *Atlantic Monthly,* the *New York Times,* the *Chicago Tribune,* and other magazines and newspapers. After graduating from law school, Kunstler practiced family law in New York City with his brother Michael. He taught part-time at New York University Law School and developed an interest in civil liberties law.

In Kunstler's view, the job of the defense attorney was not only to vigorously defend his client but to place the criminal justice system and sometimes the entire United States government on trial. He knew he was unpopular with much of the public and that his efforts would cost him friends; sometimes even his family criticized him. None of this deterred Kuntsler; he believed that what he did was right and that his efforts represented an important step in bringing true justice to all Americans, and in healing divisions within American society, whether based on racial, religious, or political differences.

Kunstler's list of clients reads like a who's who of the political and social left in the United States. It includes (1) Lenny Bruce, a stand-up comic and political satirist who was convicted on obscenity charges during the 1960s; while Kunstler and other attorneys were appealing his convictions, Bruce died of a drug overdose; Bruce had provided drugs to Kunstler on at least once occasion; (2) Stokely Carmichael, a member of the radical Black Panthers who was indicted for sedition by the state of Georgia; Kunstler was successful in having the law invalidated; (3) Hubert Geroid "Rap" Brown, another African American 1960s radical that Kunstler called his best friend from the 1960s era; Brown was arrested and indicted for numerous crimes across the United States, some related to his advocacy of violence against "white oppression"; (4) Adam Clayton Powell, an African American congressman and minister from New York City's Harlem community; upon beginning his eleventh term, Powell was denied a seat in Congress by his colleagues, claiming that he was unfit to serve because of several fraudulent acts; Kunstler carried Powell's case to the United States Supreme Court, where he succeeded in having Powell reinstated to his congressional seat; (5) Kent State; on May 4, 1970, four Kent State University students were killed and nine were wounded when National Guardsmen opened fire against a group of students that had gathered to protest American involvement in the war in Vietnam; two of the dead were protesters and two were merely passing by; twenty-four students and one faculty member were indicted for inciting a riot; Kunstler and several other attorneys worked to get one defendant acquitted and got the remaining indictments dismissed; (6) Attica; on September 9, 1971, more than 1,200 inmates at the Attica Correctional Facility near Buffalo, New York, took over the prison, holding fellow inmates and staff members hostage and demanding better living conditions; the inmates requested that Kunstler and several others be called to mediate the dispute between the inmates and state authorities; while Kunstler and the other mediators were negotiating inmate demands with the state, New York Governor Nelson Rockefeller ordered the prison retaken by force; in a calamitous raid by state authorities, thirty-nine people, including inmates and hostages, were killed, and dozens more were injured; (7) Martin Luther King, Jr.; Kunstler filed several injunctions on the civil rights leader's behalf, and represented several of King's close associates; he had agreed to file a federal lawsuit, at King's request, on behalf of striking Memphis sanitation workers; King was assassinated in Memphis before he got a chance to review Kunstler's lawsuit; (8) Freedom Riders; in 1961, Kunstler went to Jackson, Mississippi, at the request of the American Civil Liberties Union to aid the Freedom Riders that had been jailed for violating laws against segregation; he represented Nathan Schwerner, the father of Michael Schwerner, one of three civil rights workers murdered in Philadelphia, Mississippi, in 1964.

Although it is difficult to pinpoint Kunstler's most significant case, three cases may embody the essence of his career: American Indian Movement (AIM) leaders, El Sayyid Nosair, and the case that Kunstler thought was his most significant, his personal Rubicon, the infamous trial of the Chicago Eight.

THE AMERICAN INDIAN MOVEMENT

The American Indian Movement (AIM) was founded in 1968. It was composed of Native Americans dissatisfied with the operation of the Bureau of Indian Affairs and the status of American Indians in general. Their early activities included occupying the abandoned federal prison complex on Alcatraz Island in California and a takeover of the Bureau of Indian Affairs building in Washington, DC.

Kunstler became involved with AIM in 1972, when he defended members of the Iroquios Confederacy in Philadelphia on charges of resisting arrest and inciting a riot. In 1972, members of AIM, seeking to wrest power from reservation leaders, and to commemorate the 1890 slaughter of 300 Minneconjou Lakota at the hands of American soldiers, began moving in large numbers to the federal reservation at Wounded Knee, South Dakota. AIM leaders took control of the reservation, refusing to let anyone, including federal authorities, on the reservation unless they were affiliated with AIM. Federal authorities sealed off Wounded Knee, refusing to allow the protesters to leave or to let others enter the reservation.

The federal government wanted to remove AIM from the reservation, but AIM issued several demands; Kunstler was one of those brought in to mediate the dispute. Actually, Kunstler was clearly on the side of AIM, and he sought to prolong the dispute in the hope that it would bring attention to the plight of Native Americans around the country. After seventy-one days, the Native Americans that had taken over Wounded Knee were allowed to leave, claiming that they had reached an accord with government negotiators. Kunstler claimed that the government reneged on every promise it made.

AIM leaders were indicted for several crimes, including illegally occupying Wounded Knee. Kunstler represented Russell Means, one of the leaders, in a 1974 trial in St. Paul, Minnesota, that lasted more than eight months. Kunstler and his cocounsels argued that their defendants were political prisoners. True to form, Kunstler made an impassioned plea before the judge and jury in his closing argument, replete with references to promises broken by the American government, to the plight of Native Americans in the United States, and to the alleged misdeeds of the FBI.

The defense strategy succeeded, but in an unusual way. One juror became ill during deliberations, and the prosecution refused to submit to an eleven-member jury verdict. Furious over the prosecution's unwillingness to compromise, the presiding judge dismissed the charges and scolded the FBI in the process. Kunstler was elated over his victory but was soon dismayed when he realized the Wounded Knee saga did not improve the lot of Native Americans. Kunstler, who had practically no knowledge of or exposure to Native Americans prior to Wounded Knee, continued to work with AIM leaders and for Native American causes throughout his life. Wounded Knee in many ways embodied Kunstler's legal career. Once he believed that his client's cause was just, especially when he thought the political establishment was persecuting the client, his zeal became unquenchable.

EL SAYYID NOSAIR

Kunstler knew that many Americans, including many government officials, political conservatives, and practically anyone in law enforcement, hated him. He relished his unpopularity, in large measure because he cared as little for his critics as they did for him. But most of the cases he undertook at least made him popular with his small circle of friends and his family members. In his defense of El Sayyid Nosair, Kunstler demonstrated that he would even forsake friendships and family relations for the sake of a client.

Meir Kahane was the founder of Israel's anti-Arab Kach political party and the Jewish Defense League, a militant Zionist organization. Many Jews in and out of Israel and practically all Arabs disliked Kahane. Most governments, even those friendly to Israel, distanced themselves from Kahane and his anti-Arab rhetoric.

In late 1990, Kahane was assassinated in New York City. Kahane's death was not universally mourned to say the least, even in Israel. However, many Jews were nevertheless appalled when Kunstler agreed to assist in the defense of El Sayyid Nosair, his accused killer. Members of the Jewish Defense Organization picketed his house and even his own family expressed their displeasure with his defense of Nosair.

Kunstler believed in the right for self-determination for Arabs just as strongly as he did for Native Americans, seeing some similarities in the status of the two ethnic groups. He viewed Kahane and his ilk as impediments to Middle East peace. Kunstler believed that peace between Jews and Arabs was possible, and that although Arabs were responsible for many atrocities against Jews, some Jews were equally capable of barbaric and murderous acts against Arabs.

Kunstler's initial inclination was to plead insanity, but he changed his mind when he saw a chance to have Nosair acquitted, believing that the prosecution had a weak case. Kunstler's strategy was partially successful. On December 21, 1991, a Manhattan jury found Nosair guilty of gun possession, assault, and coercion; but he was acquitted of murder. Kunstler and his fellow defense attorneys had successfully defended a client already found guilty in the court of public opinion.

THE CHICAGO EIGHT

The most turbulent year of the twentieth century, at least in the United States, may be 1968. Opposition to the Vietnam War, racial tensions, the assassinations of Martin Luther King, Jr., and Robert Kennedy, a generation gap between young and old, and other social and political issues reached a boiling point in 1968. The place for that boiling point to explode was at the Democratic National Convention in Chicago.

Riots and demonstrations had become routine fare on the evening news by 1968. Given the political and social climate, most Americans fully expected some sort of demonstration at the convention. Few, however, anticipated the ferocity of what would actually occur. Some of the protesters saw the Chicago convention as the birthplace of another American Revolution. Later many people faulted local authorities, specifically Chicago Mayor Richard Daley, for failing to anticipate and plan for the demonstrations.

During the month of August, approximately 10,000 young people descended on Chicago. The greatest object of the protesters' wrath did not even attend the convention. President Lyndon Johnson, the democratic incumbent that had presided over the escalation of the Vietnam War, had chosen not to seek another term and did not attend. The Democrats had assembled to nominate Johnson's vice president, Hubert Humphrey, and the protesters feared that Humphrey would continue the Johnson policy in Southeast Asia.

In retrospect, much was learned as a result of the carnage of Chicago. In recent years, local law enforcement officials have tried to work with protesters in advance of large-scale conventions, in hopes of avoiding what happened there. Mayor Daley viewed such willingness to accommodate as weakness. Daley abjectly refused to recognize the protesters' right to demonstrate and ordered his police to use every violent means necessary to subdue the protesters, hoping to show democratic leaders and the rest of the world who really held power in Chicago. Some of the most militant of the protesters were just as uncompromising and would not have agreed to cooperate with police officials anyway, actually hoping that the demonstration would turn violent.

Daley's tactics backfired, horribly. Police officers beat and clubbed demonstrators in a full-scale battle between Chicago police and thousands of American citizens. Newspaper and television cameras captured all of the carnage, and the riots disrupted proceedings in the hall, with Mayor Daley caught on camera screaming profanities at convention speakers who criticized the actions of police officers. Humphrey's nomination was overshadowed by the riots, and it fractured the party enough to hurt Humphrey in the November election, which he lost to Richard Nixon.

After the convention, United States Attorney General Ramsey Clark brought indictments against eight police officers for interfering with the protesters' civil rights. None were ever convicted. Eight of the protesters were indicted under what was commonly called the Rap Brown Statute, which prohibited conspiring to travel across state lines to incite a riot. The eight defendants represented a cross section of the 1960s counterculture. Although the defendants were all acquainted with one another, they were not a tight-knit group. The government, led in part by FBI director J. Edgar Hoover, viewed the eight as the quintessential group of hippies, college radicals, and militant black leaders that needed to be dealt with forcibly as a deterrent to others of the same political persuasion. The eight defendants and their affiliations were: Rennie Davis and Tom Hayden (Students for a Democratic Society), Dave Dellinger (National Mobilization Against the War), John Froines and Lee Weiner (teachers), Abbie Hoffman and Jerry Rubin (Youth International Party), and Bobby Seale (Black Panther Party). Seale represented himself at trial.

The trial, which in Kunstler's view was designed to put the 1960s itself on trial, was pure theater. The defendants exhibited no respect for the court or for the proceedings. They were disruptive, abusive toward the judge, and deliberately incorrigible. The trial lasted for two months. The defendants, along with Kunstler and his cocounsel Leonard Weinglass, reached unprecedented heights in audacious courtroom behavior. Bobby Seale's behavior so outraged the presiding judge that he was bound to a chair and gagged during the trial, a move that played right into the hands of the defense's efforts to portray the government as the oppressor and the defendants as the oppressed. Seale was bound and gagged for three days, until the presiding judge declared a mistrial in his case, making the Chicago Eight the Chicago Seven. On February 20, 1970, Davis, Hayden, Dellinger, Hoffman, and Rubin were found guilty. All seven defendants, plus Kunstler and Weinglass, had also been sentenced to prison for contempt. All convictions and most of the contempt citations were eventually overturned on appeal.

During the Chicago trial, the presiding judge told Kunstler that he was getting "awfully chummy" with his clients, due to his mirroring their abrasive behavior both in and out of the courtroom. The American Bar Association was also critical; so was conservative columnist William Buckley, who wrote that Kunstler should have been disbarred.

LEE HARVEY OSWALD AND JACK RUBY

The murder that occurred in Dallas, Texas, on November 22, 1963, ranks as the most infamous crime of the twentieth century. On that day, President John F. Kennedy was assassinated while riding in an open car in a parade. Texas governor John Connally, who sat in the front seat of the presidential limousine, was seriously wounded as well. Lee Harvey Oswald, a professed Marxist and the nephew of a well-known New Orleans mobster, was apprehended later that day and held as a suspect in the murder of President Kennedy, the shooting of Governor Connally, and the subsequent murder of a Dallas police officer.

On learning that Oswald had been detained for more than forty-eight hours without legal representation, the American Civil Liberties Union contacted Kunstler and asked if he would fly to Dallas to represent Oswald. Believing that the trial of an accused presidential assassin would bring him enormous publicity, Kunstler accepted the offer. Shortly before Kunstler was scheduled to fly to Dallas, Oswald was assassinated in front of a national television audience by Jack Ruby, a Dallas nightclub owner and small-time mobster.

Ruby was convicted and sentenced to death for Oswald's killing. While his conviction and sentence were being appealed, Kunstler joined the Ruby defense team. Kunstler believed that Ruby was mentally unstable. In 1966, Kunstler and his fellow lawyers convinced the Texas Court of Criminal Appeals that a statement made by Ruby after the shooting ("I'm glad I got the son of a bitch.") should have been excluded from admission based on *Miranda* grounds; the court also ruled that Ruby's trial should have taken place outside of Dallas County. Despite the fact that the murder of Oswald was captured live on national television, Ruby's conviction was overturned on October 5, 1966, and a new trial was ordered. Ruby died from cancer on January 3, 1967, before his second trial started, robbing Kunstler of his place in the limelight.

Kunstler died six years before the World Trade Center towers were destroyed by terrorist hijackers on September 11, 2001. So it is impossible to know whether he would have rushed to the defense of those associated with that unfathomable mass murder. He was alive and practicing law when the World Trade Center was bombed on February 26, 1993, killing six people and injuring more than 1,000 others. It would be difficult, even for the most fervent or naive advocate of civil liberties and due process, to embrace or grant credence to some of Kunstler's pleas on behalf of the 1993 World Trade Center bombers, like this one contained in his autobiography (Kunstler and Isenberg, 1996).

> I agree that bombing the World Trade Center was crazy, and I don't condone it. I can, however, understand why someone would want to bomb it for political reasons, for the building is a monument to American corporate structure and capitalism. I regret, as I suppose the bombers also regret, that people died in the process.

The last statement by Kunstler is at best naive, and at worst, despicable. Nonetheless, such was the essence of Kunstler. Kunstler wanted to defend the accused bombers but was denied permission by his peers with the Southern District of New York Criminal Justice Act Panel, who claimed Kunstler was not qualified to represent the defendants.

Kunstler's last controversial case was that of Colin Ferguson, who murdered six commuters and wounded nineteen others on the Long Island Railroad on December 7, 1993. Ferguson, who was by many accounts severely deranged, was allowed to represent himself at trial. Kunstler pursued Ferguson's case on appeal, angering many by raising the issue of black rage as a form of insanity in Ferguson's defense.

Kunstler's life away from the courtroom was not dull either. He displayed his theatrical ability on the big screen. In 1992, he portrayed a judge who imprisons the title character in Spike Lee's *Malcolm X*. He played opposite Val Kilmer as Jim

Morrison's lawyer in *The Doors*. Kunstler's first marriage ended in divorce in 1973. He attributed the marital breakup to his frequent travel and to his own marital infidelity. Kunstler rationalized his sexual misadventures by claiming that young, attractive women aggressively pursued him because of his celebrity status. One was Margaret Ratner, an attorney who had worked with Kunstler on several cases. Kunstler and Ratner were married on October 6, 1975. Kunstler fathered four daughters.

Kunstler's fantasy death scenario was slumping down on a courtroom lectern after delivering an impassioned summation in a criminal trial. Kunstler's fantasy did not come true. After experiencing declining health for several months, he suffered a heart attack and died on September 4, 1995. He was seventy-six years old.

SOURCES AND SUGGESTED READINGS

Marian Calabro, *Great Courtroom Lawyers: Fighting the Cases That Made History* (New York: Facts on File, 1996).

Paul Finkelman, "Kunstler, William Moses," *American National Biography Online,* February 2000, www.anb.org, August 19, 2002.

William Moses Kunstler and Shelia Isenberg, *My Life as a Radical Lawyer* (Secaucus, NJ: Carol, 1996).

Darien A. McWhirter, *The Legal 100: A Ranking of the Individuals Who Have Most Influenced the Law* (Secaucus, NJ: Carol, 1998).

DISCUSSION QUESTIONS

1. Despite his unpopularity, why does the American legal system need people like William Kunstler?
2. What will be William Kunstler's legacy in fifty years?

CHAPTER 30

F. LEE BAILEY
(1933–   )

If Clarence Darrow was the most famous defense attorney for the first half of the twentieth century, F. Lee Bailey deserves the title of most famous criminal defense attorney for the second half of the twentieth century. When Americans think of great defense attorneys, F. Lee Bailey inevitably comes to mind. At a minimum, Bailey has earned the title of America's premier celebrity criminal defense attorney since the 1960s. His client list includes names linked to several of the most celebrated criminal cases of the twentieth century.

Francis Lee Bailey was born on June 10, 1933, in Waltham, Massachusetts, one of three children. His father left the family when Bailey was ten, leaving Grace Mitchell Bailey, a nursery school owner, to raise him. He lived a life of relative privilege, attending prep school in New Hampshire and gaining admission to Harvard to study English. Bailey grew bored with college life and decided to enlist in the Navy in 1952. Wanting more exposure to flight, Bailey switched to the Marines. While stationed in North Carolina, Bailey became interested in the Marines' legal system, and served as chief legal officer at his base. After Bailey left the Marines, he wanted to embark on a civilian law career. He was admitted to the Boston University School of Law in 1957; his legal experience in the Marines exempted him from the normal requirement of at least three years undergraduate experience.

Bailey's greatest preparation for his legal career came from his experience in the Marines and later as a private detective. It was in the Marines and as a private detective that he learned the importance of painstaking investigation, research, and preparation before going to court. In a February 1967 interview, Bailey told a magazine reporter that any lawyer that does not investigate "should be yanked for malpractice." Bailey has always been critical of law schools, claiming they do a poor job of preparing students for legal careers, especially in the area of criminal law and courtroom tactics. For those who wonder how Bailey could make substantial amounts of money representing criminal defendants, Bailey replies that the key has been securing publication and film rights to the high-profile criminal defendants he has represented; plus, the reputation he would acquire from representing high-profile but poor clients would aid him in securing wealthy defendants.

While he was in law school, Bailey operated his own private detective firm. Most of his work was done for criminal attorneys and it afforded Bailey first-hand experience at criminal investigation work, something that few defense attorneys had. He worked more than 2,000 criminal cases before selling the firm to a former Massachusetts police officer, whom Bailey worked with for many years afterward.

He also attended the Keeler Polygraph Institute in Chicago, which would pay dividends early in his legal career.

Bailey's knack for getting high-profile cases came early in his legal career with the "torso" murder case. In 1960, the same year he was admitted to the Massachusetts bar, authorities discovered the torso of a woman allegedly killed by her husband. The defendant, an elderly man named George Edgerly, had been accused of killing and dismembering his wife and throwing her remains in the Merrimack River. Edgerly failed a lie detector test administered by police, and the prosecution used that failure against him in court, as polygraph evidence was admissible in Massachusetts courts at the time. Bailey was one of the few attorneys in Massachusetts that was knowledgeable about polygraphs. Only twenty-seven years old at the time, Bailey took control of the defense and won an acquittal, in large measure because of his ability to poke holes in the testimony of the prosecution's polygraph administrator. The case made Bailey a national celebrity.

Another high-profile criminal case from the 1960s involving Bailey was the Sam Sheppard murder case, which inspired the television series *The Fugitive*. In 1954, Sam Sheppard, an Ohio physician, was convicted of murdering his wife and blaming the murder on a "bushy-haired" intruder. Sheppard was convicted after a trial that became the media circus of the decade, mostly due to the conduct of the presiding judge. Bailey was hired to enter the Sheppard defense in 1961, while Sheppard was serving a life sentence. For the next five years, Bailey methodically filed appeals until he was able to secure Sheppard's release on bond, pending the final appeal of the case. In 1966, the case reached the United States Supreme Court. In a landmark decision, the Court, led by Chief Justice Earl Warren, ruled that Sheppard did not receive a fair trial due to pretrial publicity and that the judge had not protected Sheppard's right to a fair trial. Sheppard was subsequently retried and acquitted.

Bailey's reputation for brilliance was solidified with his defense of Albert DeSalvo, the man thought to be the infamous Boston Strangler. Between June 1962 and January 1964, thirteen women in the Boston area were murdered by strangulation. Their characteristics differed, but all of the women were single and all were murdered in their homes. The murders, labeled by the press as the Boston Strangler murders, became Western culture's biggest serial murder sensation since England's Jack the Ripper murders of the nineteenth century.

DeSalvo, who had been arrested and incarcerated off and on throughout his adult life on charges ranging from fondling young girls to burglary, was arrested on rape charges in November 1964. The court ordered DeSalvo transferred to a state mental hospital for psychiatric evaluation. While in the hospital, DeSalvo became acquainted with another patient named George Nassar, who was accused of murdering a gas station attendant. F. Lee Bailey was Nassar's lawyer. Bailey met DeSalvo through Nassar, after DeSalvo began bragging about committing the Boston Strangler murders. Bailey interviewed DeSalvo several times, sometimes in the presence of police detectives. He became convinced of DeSalvo's guilt, and his attention turned to sparing DeSalvo from conviction and execution, even though Massachusetts had not carried out an execution in more than fifteen years. DeSalvo knew he would spend the rest of his life in some sort of institution; he wanted to spend it in a hospital rather than a prison.

Bailey and the police officers knew that the state did not have enough admissible evidence to have DeSalvo convicted on murder charges, even though all were convinced of his guilt. Instead, officers sought to have DeSalvo prosecuted on burglary and sexual assault charges. Knowing that the court would impose the maximum on these charges because of DeSalvo's link to the strangler murders, Bailey sought to have DeSalvo acquitted on grounds of insanity. Nevertheless, DeSalvo was declared legally sane, convicted on the charges, and sentenced to ten years to life. Despite the seeming failure of the case, Bailey had at least succeeded in not having DeSalvo convicted of the strangler crimes, in spite of the fact that DeSalvo had repeatedly bragged about and confessed to the crimes. DeSalvo was murdered in prison in 1973.

In the early 1970s, Bailey became immersed in one of the most distressing episodes of a painful chapter in American history. On March 16, 1968, U.S. Army troops under the command of Captain Ernest Medina killed more than 500 Vietnamese civilians, many of who were women and children. Photographs of the My Lai massacre were disseminated throughout the world, much to the embarrassment and dismay of the American military establishment. Blame was placed on Captain Medina. As an expert in the Uniform Code of Justice and as an attorney accustomed to the spotlight, Bailey was uniquely qualified to defend Medina. He took on Medina's defense for which he was paid $79.

Bailey attempted to prove that Medina had not ordered the massacre, had no advance knowledge of it, and was not present at My Lai when it occurred. In fact, when Medina arrived at the scene, he ordered his men to cease-fire. As he had done in other cases, Bailey skillfully used polygraph testimony to substantiate Medina's claim. Bailey and military investigators were able to shift blame for the My Lai massacre to Lieutenant William Calley, one of Medina's platoon leaders, who was convicted of twenty-two of the My Lai murders. In representing Medina, Bailey took on a case in which the defendant had been judged guilty in the court of world opinion. Nevertheless, the military jury acquitted Medina after less than one hour of deliberations. After the trial, Medina went to work for Enstrom Helicopter Company, which was owned by Bailey.

One of Bailey's few unmitigated high-profile failures came with his defense of Patricia Hearst. Like many of Bailey's cases, the facts will forever be in dispute. At her trial, Bailey claimed that Hearst, a nineteen-year-old heiress to the Hearst publication empire, was kidnapped on February 4, 1974, by the Symbionese Liberation Army (SLA), a violent, left-wing political group. The kidnapping was as much politically as financially motivated, with the SLA proclaiming her a prisoner of war against America's capitalist structure. At her trial, Bailey claimed that the SLA brainwashed Hearst into adopting their radical political beliefs and that they coerced her into committing several crimes, most notably a bank robbery on April 15, 1974. Hearst was captured on film brandishing a firearm; she went from being perceived as the sympathetic victim of a kidnapping to assuming a place on the FBI's Ten Most Wanted list.

With some of Bailey's high-profile criminal cases, the defendants had little money to pay. With Hearst, money was no object. The Hearst money could not buy an acquittal. Judging by media coverage surrounding the trial, Bailey had presented the story of Hearst being kidnapped and brainwashed in a very credible manner (even though he faltered during closing arguments), so credible in fact that *Newsweek* magazine prepared a cover story announcing Hearst's acquittal. At the last minute, *Newsweek* had to change its cover story to "guilty" as the jury did not buy Bailey's defense. Hearst was convicted and sentenced to prison; President Jimmy Carter commuted her sentence in 1979.

After the Hearst fiasco, Bailey faded from the public eye. His celebrity status was reborn in 1994 when he was hired as part of the legal "dream team" that represented O. J. Simpson, the Hall of Fame football player and actor accused of murdering his wife, Nicole Brown Simpson, and Ronald Goldman, a Los Angeles restaurant employee, in June 1994. The basic facts of the Simpson/Goldman murder were well known to practically every American who owned a television set during the mid-1990s, including the infamous Bronco chase through Los Angeles on June 17 which was carried on live television, in which Simpson, driven by a friend, was chased down California freeways by police officers after realizing that he was the prime suspect in the murders. Bailey watched the chase on television from his Florida home, and he was subsequently added to the team at the behest of lead attorney Robert Shapiro, an old friend who had defended Bailey on a California drunk driving charge in 1982. The Simpson pretrial proceedings alone were the media event of the decade, as was the trial itself, and the announcement of Simpson's acquittal was one of the most widely watched broadcasts in television history, even though it was carried in the middle of the day rather than during prime time.

Simpson assembled a multimillion dollar team of attorneys, including Johnny Cochran, Jr., Barry Scheck, Carl Douglas, Robert Shapiro, and Bailey. Shapiro added Bailey to the team partly because of Bailey's reputation for defending men accused of killing their wives. Each of the dream team attorneys used the Simpson case to promote their careers, especially Johnny Cochran.

The Simpson team succeeded in taking the prosecution's case in myriad different directions, accusing virtually anyone that took the stand for the prosecution of everything from incompetence to conspiring to frame Simpson. Bailey's opportunity to bask in the glow of the television spotlight came with his cross-examination of Los Angeles police detective Mark Fuhrman. Bailey, playing the "race card" to the predominantly African American jury, played on Fuhrman's reputation as a racist by trying to convince the jury that Fuhrman had conspired to frame Simpson by planting evidence. Bailey questioned Fuhrman repeatedly on whether he had used the "n word" (a phrase introduced to the American vocabulary at that point) as a police officer. Fuhrman denied Bailey's accusations, making Bailey appear foolish, at first. Several weeks later, a quasi-dramatic performance featuring Fuhrman using the "n word" dozens of times and bragging of planting false evidence surfaced.

Fuhrman ultimately pled nolo contendere to perjury and Bailey was vindicated with his place as one of America's premier defense attorneys restored, even though he was upstaged at the Simpson trial by the more theatrical Johnny Cochran.

Since the Simpson acquittal, Bailey has not been involved in many high-profile cases, other than his own. In 1996 he was sentenced to six months in federal prison for contempt of court; he served forty-four days. In November 2001, Bailey was disbarred from practicing law in Florida for a minimum of five years because the Florida Supreme Court accused Bailey of committing "some of the most egregious rules violations possible" and lacking "respect for the justice system." Bailey's offense was mishandling almost $6 million in stock owned by a drug smuggler he represented. The violations also included giving false testimony, disregarding a judge's orders, using his client's assets for his own benefit, and compromising his client's best interests. The court stated that "Bailey's self-dealing and willingness to compromise client confidences are especially disturbing."

Bailey's personal life has been as colorful as his professional life. He has been married two times and is the father of three sons. He relishes being seen in flashy clothes and has never shrunk from publicity. Unlike Clarence Darrow, Bailey has never been a social crusader, although one of Bailey's quotes provides a glimpse of his view on the United States Congress. Bailey once said that the Bill of Rights would never get through the Congress today and that it would never even make it out of committee.

Bailey is also unlike Darrow in another way. Whereas Darrow was often long on style and emotional appeal, but often short on preparation and substance, Bailey is more plodding and is an articulate but less charismatic courtroom orator than Darrow or Johnny Cochran. He is relentless and merciless on his courtroom adversaries and was compared to a "determined badger" by one magazine writer. Bailey believes that criminal defendants are entitled to the best defense possible, and he believes that the government should be put to as much trouble as possible in their effort to deprive a person of their freedom or their life. In the minds of his detractors and his admirers, F. Lee Bailey will go down not only as the "lawyer to turn to when you kill your wife" as some have called him. He will also be remembered as one of the ablest criminal defense attorneys in American history.

SUGGESTED READINGS

F. Lee Bailey, *The Defense Never Rests* (New York: Stein and Day, 1971).

Marian Calabro, *Great Courtroom Lawyers: Fighting the Cases That Made History* (New York: Facts on File, 1996).

Les Whitten, *F. Lee Bailey* (New York: Avon, 1971).

DISCUSSION QUESTIONS

1. F. Lee Bailey has gained a reputation as the lawyer to hire when a man kills his wife. Is that label fair? Why or why not?
2. In what ways was F. Lee Bailey's path to prominence different from what one might expect?

CHAPTER 31

G. ROBERT BLAKEY
(1936–   )

On November 22, 1963, twenty-seven-year-old Robert Blakey traveled to work as usual in Washington, DC, to the U.S. Department of Justice. The young attorney spent the morning meeting with his boss, Attorney General Robert F. Kennedy, discussing plans for increasing organized crime prosecution efforts in Chicago. The meeting adjourned for lunch and was scheduled to resume that afternoon. The meeting never reconvened. During the lunch break, news reached Washington that John F. Kennedy, the thirty-fifth president of the United States and older brother of the attorney general, had been assassinated while riding in a motorcade in Dallas, Texas.

The assassination of President Kennedy was the most infamous crime the United States experienced during the twentieth century. Like December 7, 1941, and September 11, 2001, it was an unforgettable event in the lives of individual Americans. The Kennedy assassination had a profound personal and professional impact on Robert Blakey. It hurt him personally because he knew and liked President Kennedy and he had special admiration for Robert Kennedy. Also, it brought Blakey to the realization that fighting sophisticated criminal enterprises, like the one that Blakey maintains was responsible for Kennedy's murder, would not work with the business-as-usual approach employed by the criminal justice system. Once Kennedy had been murdered, it was too late for police officers to simply arrive at the crime scene and make an arrest; the damage to Kennedy and the nation had been done. Thus began Robert Blakey's successful endeavor at writing legislation that would serve as the most influential criminal law of the second half of the twentieth century, the Racketeer Influenced and Corrupt Organizations (RICO) Act. RICO, through its stiff criminal penalties and, most notably, its stinging civil asset forfeiture provisions, has devastated criminal enterprises ranging from multimillion-dollar Wall Street junk bond schemes to major mafia families to low-level drug dealers in small towns.

George Robert Blakey was born on January 7, 1936, in Burlington, North Carolina. He grew up in a Roman Catholic household that lived in predominantly Protestant central North Carolina. His father was a banker who died in an auto accident in 1945. The remainder of Blakey's childhood was spent in a single parent home. Blakey attended public schools in Burlington, and like many good students in central North Carolina, he planned to attend the University of North Carolina at Chapel Hill. A night of teen frivolity changed the direction of his entire life. One night when he was about seventeen, Blakey returned home from a night on the town with friends to find his mother and uncle waiting up for him in the family living room. Angry that he had stayed out too late, Blakey's mother told him that he needed a good priest. Much to his dismay, Blakey's mother informed him that he was going to attend the University of Notre Dame in South Bend, Indiana, where his brother was already attending, and which was several hundred miles away from his home state of North Carolina.

His mother's directive would serve Blakey well, both personally and professionally. Blakey enrolled at Notre Dame in 1953, intending to stay only for one year. While at Notre Dame Blakey met his future bride, Nancy, a New York native who was attending St. Mary's, the female counterpart to Notre Dame. He stayed at Notre Dame for his entire undergraduate career and graduated with a degree in philosophy in 1957.

An honors student, Blakey was admitted to the Law School at Notre Dame on a scholarship. Unlike many law school aspirants, Blakey did not attend law school with immediate hopes of earning fame and fortune as a corporate attorney or as a famous courtroom lawyer. What attracted Blakey to the study of law was the chance it provided him to analyze legal texts. He longed for the opportunity to integrate his fascination with philosophy and Roman Catholic religion with the study of jurisprudence. Blakey has said that during law school, he thought like a Roman Catholic on Sunday, Tuesday, Thursday, and Saturday, and he thought like a lawyer on Monday, Wednesday, and Friday. He enjoyed reading and analyzing the writings of St. Thomas Aquinas in its original Latin form. Blakey also enjoyed melding the writings of Aquinas with the philosophy of law to see how they conflicted and coincided.

Blakey's desire for knowledge rather than immense wealth would pay dividends in later years. After graduating second in his class from Notre Dame Law School in 1960, Blakey went job hunting. Although Blakey was fascinated with the purely philosophical aspects of the law, he did have one practical interest, and that was labor law, an irony given that he hailed from North Carolina, a historically labor-hostile state. He jokingly refers to himself as a "labor bomb thrower." If Blakey had a mission in life as a young man, it was to make the world a better place for working people. In his view, a good understanding of the law as it applied to labor issues was the avenue for doing that.

Blakey wanted to work with the National Labor Relations Board (NLRB), but an interview with the Department of Justice's (DOJ) honor program came along first. Although he would have preferred working with the NLRB, the DOJ position was offered on a take-it-or-leave-it basis. Blakey, married with a young child, felt he could not afford to take the risk, so he accepted a position with the Department of Justice, hoping to catch on with the DOJ's labor rights unit.

To Blakey's dismay, he was assigned to the DOJ criminal division. Blakey had never taken a course in criminal law or criminal procedure. At the time he assumed his position with the DOJ, Dwight Eisenhower was president of the United States. John F. Kennedy succeeded President Eisenhower in 1961. Kennedy nominated his thirty-five-year-old brother Robert to serve as attorney general.

Throughout the 1950s the Kennedy brothers had established reputations as two of America's leading soldiers against organized crime, especially in the area of labor racketeering. While in the United States Senate, John Kennedy served as a member of the Senate Select Committee on Improper Activities in the Labor or Management Field. Robert Kennedy served as the committee's chief counsel. The Kennedy brothers' well-publicized (and some say visceral) effort to rid the Teamsters Union of corrupt leaders like Dave Beck and Jimmy Hoffa, was one of the factors that catapulted John Kennedy into the White House.

Even though Blakey was a holdover from the Eisenhower administration, he and Robert Kennedy developed an excellent working relationship almost from the start. Both were young, idealistic prosecutors; both had Roman Catholic backgrounds; both embodied the somewhat paradoxical characteristic of being both a crime fighter and a political liberal.

Blakey seemed an odd figure to combat organized crime. Unlike many big-city attorneys and politicians from cities like New York and Chicago, the term *organized crime* did not resonate with the small town North Carolina native, nor did he identify with the ethnic dimensions so often associated with the study and prosecution of organized crime. In reference to his ethnicity, he was once asked, "what he was," to which he simply replied, "American," though he would later say he was Irish because of his mother's ancestry.

The Kennedy crusade against organized crime was viewed as paradoxical by some and downright hypocritical by others. Their father, Joseph Kennedy, Sr., had a long and fruitful association with organized crime. Some mobsters worked to get Kennedy elected to the presidency, feeling that they would have a pipeline to the White House and the Justice Department, in part because Chicago mob boss Sam Giancanna and John Kennedy shared a mistress.

Attorney General Kennedy's virtual declaration of war against organized crime enraged American mobsters, many of whom swore to get even and deal with John and Robert Kennedy as with any other mafia turncoat—by killing them. According to Robert Blakey, they did get even on November 22, 1963, when John Kennedy was assassinated in Dallas. After the assassination, Robert Kennedy's war on organized crime came to a halt.

Blakey came to Washington in 1960 brimming with idealism, which was only enhanced by his association with Robert Kennedy. Like many other Kennedy staffers, he left Washington dispirited. Blakey also left with the realization that certain forms of crime required an entirely different mindset than the traditional reactive law enforcement approach. There was no mechanism for going after group criminal activity, the sort that Blakey believed perpetrated Kennedy's murder. Most criminal laws were aimed at individuals, not powerful groups. With scant help from J. Edgar Hoover's FBI, America was ill-equipped to tackle organized crime.

A few months after Kennedy's death, Blakey returned to Notre Dame to teach in the law school. Blakey viewed (with extreme skepticism) the findings of the Warren Commission Report on the Kennedy assassination. Blakey had no doubt that Lee Harvey Oswald fired the shots that killed Kennedy, but he is firmly convinced that Oswald did not act alone, that there was a conspiracy to kill Kennedy, and that Oswald's nationally televised murder at the hand of Jack Ruby was the Rosetta stone of organized crime's involvement in Kennedy's murder. The reason, Jack Ruby, aka Jack Rubenstein, far from being a zealous patriot that loved his president, was a sleazy Dallas nightclub owner with organized crime ties dating back to his boyhood in Chicago, where he worked for Al Capone.

At Notre Dame, Blakey had a chance to reflect on his experiences with the Kennedy Justice Department. He had time to analyze the strengths and weaknesses of the prevailing attitudes and mindsets toward prosecuting powerful criminal groups. Blakey saw Robert Kennedy as being rich in people skills, political savvy, and organizational ability, but Kennedy's approach to tackling organized crime lacked procedure and substance.

While at Notre Dame, Blakey worked with Lyndon Johnson's administration, writing papers on organized crime for his commission that evaluated the state of criminal justice in the United States. Blakey stated that one challenge in the fight against organized crime was evidence gathering. Many criminal organizations were and are difficult to penetrate, and it is difficult to use traditional physical evidence in cases of group criminal behavior. Blakey outlined several keys to combating criminal behavior by groups, including using the grand jury as a strong investigative tool, making greater use of wiretaps and covert surveillance, enacting an immunity statute for those willing to come forth with information, creating a witness protection program for those who testified against organized crime figures, updating perjury statutes, and enacting more useful gambling statutes. Prohibiting membership in a criminal organization was also a key, and it served as the touchstone of the RICO law Blakey would write several years later.

The presidential election of 1968 brought on a shift in political affiliation for Blakey. He initially campaigned for his old friend Robert Kennedy, even chairing his campaign organization in Indiana. This stopped when Robert Kennedy was assassinated in June 1968 in Los Angeles. Although he was a lifelong democrat, he campaigned for republican Richard Nixon. His loyalty to Nixon produced one of the great "what ifs" of American history. Sometime during the course of the Nixon campaign, after it had become clear that Nixon would secure the republican nomination, Nixon campaign chair John Mitchell offered Blakey a position as special White House counsel. Blakey declined, but he recommended John Dean III, who he had met while working for the Senate. Dean accepted the job, and he would become the most instrumental White House figure in the Watergate scandal, which would lead to his own imprisonment, Nixon's resignation as president, and the permanent altering of American history. In email correspondence with the author, Blakey stated that he is not sure how history would have been different if he, rather than Dean, had accepted that job.

Although Blakey's career is marked by many accomplishments, three stand out: (1) his help with the wiretap provisions of the Crime Control Act of 1968, (2) his help with the Title IX (the RICO provision) of the Organized Crime Control Act of 1970, and (3) his work as chief counsel to the Select House Committee on Assassinations in the late 1970s. The Crime Control Act of 1968 included a provision written by Blakey authorizing the expanded use of wiretaps to infiltrate criminal organizations.

From 1969 to 1973, Blakey served as chief counsel for the Subcommittee on Criminal Laws and Procedures, chaired by Senator John McClellan, a long-time organized crime fighter. In 1970, Congress and the Nixon administration enacted the Omnibus Crime Control Act of 1970 and the Organized Crime Control Act of 1970. Title IX of the act is called RICO, or Racketeer Influenced and Corrupt Organizations Act. In order for an offense to qualify as a RICO violation, prosecutors must prove a pattern of racketeering-type crimes, that is, two of the crimes listed under RICO within a ten-year period. Federal RICO violations carry penalties of up to twenty years in prison and a $25,000 fine, plus the threat of forfeiting assets gained as a result of the crimes.

RICO prosecutions were rare during the early 1970s, primarily because prosecutors did not know how to use them. RICO prosecution accelerated in the 1980s and succeeded in making sizeable dents in many powerful criminal organizations, including the five major crime families in New York. RICO also helped launch the political career of Rudolph Giuliani, a federal prosecutor who gained fame for his organized and white-collar crime prosecution in the 1980s.

RICO offenses carry greatly enhanced prison terms, and they also carry the prospect of civil asset forfeiture. State RICO offenses, based largely on the original federal statute but in some cases written with Blakey's input, have been used to confiscate houses, boats, and cars from drug dealers. They have even been used to prosecute abortion protesters, an example of RICO's misuse, according to Blakey.

Blakey worked at Cornell University for the remainder of the 1970s, conducting research at Cornell's Institute on Organized Crime. In 1977, Blakey returned to investigating the event that had spurred the writing of RICO. He served as chief counsel for the Select House Committee on Investigations. The committee did not provide a final definitive answer as to who was involved in the Kennedy assassination—likewise for the 1968 assassination of Martin Luther King, Jr., which the committee also investigated—but Blakey's views on the assassination are found in his appearances on the A&E Network and in a 1981 book he co-authored with Richard Billings titled *The Plot to Kill the President: Organized Crime Assassinated J.F.K.* Among their propositions: (1) President Kennedy was fired at by two gunmen and was shot by Lee Harvey Oswald; (2) after his arrest, Oswald was stalked by Jack Ruby, with Ruby even being heard talking during a press conference in police headquarters; (3) Kennedy's murder was a revenge killing for his and Robert Kennedy's prosecution of mob bosses in Chicago and New Orleans.

Blakey returned to Notre Dame's law school in 1980, where he remains. He has served as a consultant to both the House and Senate Judiciary Committees as an expert on organized and white-collar crime. In 1991, he was listed by the *National Law Journal* as one of the one hundred most influential lawyers in America. Blakey, the accidental Notre Dame student who was forced to attend the school by his mother, is the father of eight children, all of whom are Notre Dame graduates.

SOURCES AND SUGGESTED READINGS

G. Robert Blakey, telephone interview, December 5, 2001.

G. Robert Blakey, resume, December 21, 2001.

G. Robert Blakey and Richard N. Billings, *The Plot to Kill the President: Organized Crime Assassinated J.F.K.* (New York: Times Books, 1981).

Margaret Cronin Fisk, "Profiles in Power: The Most Influential Lawyers in America," *The National Law Journal*, March 25, 1991.

Stephen Fox, *Blood and Power* (New York: William Morrow, 1989).

Joe Queenan, "G. Robert Blakey versus Michael Milken," *Forbes*, May 1, 1989.

Gregory J. Wallance, "Outgunning the Mob," *ABA Journal*, March 1994.

DISCUSSION QUESTIONS

1. None of the plans that Blakey had for himself as a young man worked out as he initially planned, yet he has been enormously successful. What lessons can a young college student learn from Blakey's life?
2. Given RICO's impact, what will be Blakey's legacy fifty years from now?

CHAPTER 32

THOMAS EDDY
(1758–1827)

Criminal justice historian Mitchell Roth stated that it is difficult to overestimate the importance of Thomas Eddy in the early history of the American penitentiary movement. Eddy is often compared to England's John Howard, the world's most renowned prison reformer of the eighteenth century. The founding of the American penitentiary is due as much if not more to the work of philanthropists like Thomas Eddy than to government officials. He was one of the primary movers in the establishment of the Auburn system, one of the dominant philosophies of the early American penitentiary.

Thomas Eddy was born in Philadelphia on September 5, 1758, the son of James and Mary Darragh Eddy, both Irish immigrants. In Ireland, James Eddy was a mercantile businessman; Mary Eddy stayed home to care for her family, which would include sixteen children, only two of which would live beyond a very young age. While living in Dublin, the Eddy's converted to Quakerism, a bold and unpopular move in eighteenth-century Roman Catholic Ireland. Hoping to find an environment more friendly to their newfound Quaker beliefs, the Eddy's immigrated to Philadelphia in 1753, five years before Thomas's birth and twenty-three years before America declared its independence from Great Britain. In Philadelphia, James Eddy worked in the ironmongery business until his death in 1766, when Thomas was eight. Mary Eddy carried on her late husband's hardware business until 1796.

The Eddy's relocated to Buckingham, Pennsylvania, where Thomas Eddy spent most of his childhood. His childhood education was poor, as qualified teachers were rare in his area. Political differences impacted local education in Eddy's community. Americans were divided over whether to seek independence from Great Britain. He lived in an area dominated by patriots seeking independence, but the Eddy's were loyalists. Most teachers in the area were loyalists as well, but the patriot influence negatively affected the education of most students in Eddy's community. As a result, Eddy was largely self-taught.

Like most poorly educated young men of his era, Eddy tried to learn a trade. In 1771, he began an apprenticeship to learn the tanning business. He worked as an apprentice for several years, until the outbreak of the Revolutionary War. Because of his loyalist sentiments, Eddy was forced to move to Virginia during the war. He returned to Philadelphia after the British evacuation.

During the American Revolution, Thomas Eddy spent most of his time working as a merchant in New York City, at the same time that Englishman John Howard was working to improve prison conditions in Europe. In April 1779, Eddy went into the shipping business with his brother Charles. His first brush with prison life, an event that influenced his subsequent prison reform work, came in 1780. While traveling by boat to visit his family, he was shot at and captured by the New Jersey militia. The militia suspected Eddy of spying and he was locked up in a filthy crowded dungeon in Middletown, New Jersey. Eddy later said that during his initial days in the dungeon, he did not think he would live another hour, so deplorable were the conditions. Eddy adapted well enough to survive ten days in the dungeon, when he was released in a prisoner exchange arrangement and allowed to return to New York.

Eddy married Hannah Hartshone on March 20, 1782. Like many loyalists, Eddy feared retribution at the hands of vengeful patriots after the British left America in 1783. Many loyalists, including Hannah Eddy's family, left America for Nova Scotia. Eddy remained in the United States at his mother's request, but he relocated to Fredericksburg, Virginia, in 1786 and remained until 1788, running his late brother's tobacco business.

Eddy moved to Philadelphia in 1788, then to New York City in 1790, where he became a successful insurance broker. In 1793, Eddy was elected director of the Mutual Insurance Company, and he assumed directorship of the Western Inland Lock Navigation Company. Eddy was also active in improving navigation along New York waterways. Once he started making substantial amounts of money, Eddy became active in philanthropic work and public service. Eddy had a number of natural gifts that served him well in his business and philanthropic career. He was an articulate, convincing, and animated public speaker. One observer reports being "struck with the simplicity of his manners, and the reasonableness and benevolence of his views." He was also personally impressive, a sharp dresser, standing five feet six inches (average height for an eighteenth-century American man), with a muscular build, a large head, and strong facial features. Eddy biographer Samuel Knapp wrote, "The elevation of his eyebrows gave the whole countenance an air of profound meditation."

One of Eddy's first philanthropic efforts was establishing a penitentiary in New York. To modern minds, building a prison may seem diametrically opposed to contemporary definitions of charity. However, between 1790 and the 1830s, many Americans saw penitentiaries as a humane alternative to corporal punishment and other forms of public humiliation. Correctional reformers like Eddy also saw the penitentiary as a chance for offenders to make penitence (hence the name penitentiary) for their past wrongdoings, learn a vocational trade, and get a least a minimal amount of academic education.

Eddy had heard about penitentiary experiments in Pennsylvania and wanted to put the idea to work in New York. In 1796, with the help of Philip Schuyler, Eddy wrote a bill proposing a penitentiary for New York. The bill passed, and Eddy was placed in charge of building the facility, which was to be located in Auburn, New York.

Eddy was a product of Enlightenment era thinking, an age in which reformers and thinkers attempted to improve the condition of mankind through the use of the scientific method and rational thinking. Enlightenment thinking was also present in the areas of law and penology. Eddy was influenced by the writings of the Italian penologist Cesare Beccaria, English penologist John Howard, France's Montesquieu, and Pennsylvania's William Penn. In 1801, Eddy published an account of the state prison of New York, in which he borrowed ideas from Enlightenment era philosophers.

Punishment was not on the minds of Eddy and most early penitentiary advocates. Instead, he wrote, "The end of human punishments is the prevention of crimes. In the endeavor to attain this end, three things are to be considered: the amendment of the offender; the deterring of others by his example; reparation to society and the party injured. Of these objects, the first, without doubt, is of the highest importance. Society cannot be better secured against crimes, than by eradicating the evil passions and corrupt habits which are the sources of guilt. Justice is not revenge."

No doubt recalling his own brief experience with incarceration in a filthy New Jersey dungeon, Eddy believed that prisons should be clean and prisoners well fed, not an easy proposition in a day when hot running water and indoor plumbing were inconceivable. In his 1801 report Eddy wrote, "By the great attention paid to cleanliness in every part of the prison, they have shown their opinion of its importance in aiding reformation. Its benign influence on the physical character, though well understood by many, is not duly estimated by the bulk of mankind. Though its effect on bodily health be more obvious, its less striking but equally certain effect on the mind has been no where more fully experienced than in this prison."

Eddy's plan called for educational opportunities and segregation according to seriousness of offense. Like all other advocates of the early penitentiary, Eddy believed that religious and moral instruction was fundamental to the penitentiary experience. Eddy expected the clergy to have the same philanthropic attitude as he had, "It is expected that the public preachers of the gospel in the city will cheerfully devote a small portion of their time to the service of these unhappy beings, who have so much need of their instruction, and of the counsel of the truly good and benevolent." Eddy believed that the commission of crime was rooted in moral factors and that removing a young person from the temptations afforded by urban life to a more docile rural setting would have a redemptive effect on the prisoner. Alcohol and gambling were the two primary culprits: "*Baiting* of animals with dogs, and every species of amusement which may tend to harden the heart, and render the manners of the people ferocious, ought to be prevented by a well regulated police."

Like many penal reformers throughout American history, Eddy realized early that the lofty goals of the penitentiary did not measure up to their outcome. Two years after the opening of New York's penitentiary, he noticed many errors while conducting his frequent visits. Logistical realities and human imperfections got in the way of attaining the penitentiary's aims. He noticed that keeping several prisoners in a cell thwarted the ideal of having inmates spend time alone, where they could make penitence for wrong deeds. Allowing inmates to share a cell would allow them to be "all joined by sympathetic villainy to keep each other in countenance." Allowing prison staff to administer corporal punishment backfired as well; it was used vindictively and had no positive effect.

Over the next two decades, Eddy continued to lobby for improvements in the New York prison system. Eddy lobbied for other facilities, one for offenders under the age of sixteen and separate facilities for men and women. He suggested having a prison that did not allow the use of tobacco (a move currently in vogue with prisons and jails of today) and that inmates be disallowed from having any books except the Bible. One problem with the idea of encouraging reading was that most prison inmates in the nineteenth century were illiterate, thus the hoped for reformative effects of the Bible would be lost.

On January 7, 1825, Eddy proposed four remedies for the problem of crime: (1) every poor family should be able to participate in Common Schools, since, in Eddy's view, crime was caused by pauperism and pauperism was caused by illiteracy; (2) establish a house of refuge for juvenile delinquents to keep them away from street life, which would address the inevitability that some juveniles would run away from home; (3) each county should have a prison for drunks, prostitutes, gamblers, petty thieves, and vagrants, and other prisoners serving sentences of three to thirty days; (4) have two state prisons for serious offenders. Remedies one, three, and four have come to fruition in the United States. All Americans have access to free public education; most counties have their own jails for housing those convicted of minor offenses; and most states have a few large facilities for incarcerating serious offenders.

One practice that Eddy denounced did not come to fruition during his lifetime. He did not like the idea of imprisonment for debt but did not live to see it abolished. Like many other Quakers, Eddy was active in advocating fair treatment of Native Americans, in particular the Mohigans, the Delaware, the Oneida, the Onondaga, and the Seneca, all of whom, in his view, had been mistreated by whites and deserved to learn the best practices and habits of whites while maintaining their own cultural identity. Eddy preserved a letter from an Indian chief, also a graduate of Dartmouth, who asked how whites could call Indian nations savage when some whites were imprisoned for debts while other whites lived in castles.

Eddy corresponded with penologists from around the world and visited prisons in other states. Eddy never concerned himself with improving justice in southern states. Like the French statesman Alexis de Tocqueville, whose writings on his visit to America have become pillars of American historical study, Eddy thought it pointless to talk about fair treatment of prisoners in states that allowed slavery. He admired the efforts of the English to deal with crime through the use of prisons. One reality that got in the way of prisons achieving their aims was crowding. Now viewed as the ultimate punishment within a prison, solitary confinement was originally viewed as the key to rehabilitation, but it became logistically impossible because of crowding. Eddy was disillusioned with the prisons he visited, as opposed to those about which he read. Of the New Jersey prison, Eddy stated that he was disappointed to find that the building plan was bad. There were fifty-nine convicts, fifty-seven men and two women, who appeared decent, orderly, and industrious; they were employed in the manufacture of nails, shoes, and cloth. He naively believed prison officials when they told him that inmate labor was sufficient in defraying prison expenses. He wrote, "Some of the prisons established in America have not answered the expectation of the advocates for the penitentiary system, most of whom were led to believe, that the avails of the labour of the convicts would be sufficient to defray all the expenses of their maintenance and care." Nevertheless, Eddy still believed that the prisons' positives outweighed their negatives.

Prisons were not Eddy's sole philanthropic endeavor. He was a founding member of the New York Bible Society. He was a passionate advocate of free public education. In another foray into a well-intended experiment gone awry, Eddy was instrumental in the establishment of New York's first mental hospital in 1820, which, in keeping with the vernacular of the day, was called a lunatic asylum. He was active in the New York Manumission Society, an organization dedicated to the abolition of slavery. Eddy and his wife had three children. Their son John, though rendered deaf at age twelve by scarlet fever, became a renowned botanist, poet, and painter. Around 1825, Thomas Eddy began to slow down, feeling the effects of advanced age and declining health. Eddy, who always penned his letters "thy assured friend," died on September 16, 1827, at the age of sixty-nine, the cause of death listed as "paralysis." He left behind his widow and two daughters.

Despite its shortcomings, Eddy always believed that the Auburn prison was the best in the world. In examining the life and work of Thomas Eddy, there is no doubt that he had the best of intentions in advocating the penitentiary as the primary mode of punishment for criminals. The question of whether the well-intentioned efforts of Eddy and other penitentiary advocates were ultimately successful has not been answered to this day. Few Americans have faith in the ability of prisons to reform offenders and all but a tiny minority believe that the prison experience actually does more harm than good. Even though 175 years have passed since his death, Thomas Eddy's place in criminal justice history has not been decided.

SOURCES AND SUGGESTED READINGS

Thomas Eddy, *An Account of the State Prison or Penitentiary House in the City of New York* (New York: Isaac Collins and Son, 1801).
Samuel L. Knapp, *The Life of Thomas Eddy* (New York: Conner and Cooke, 1834).

DISCUSSION QUESTIONS

1. Do you think that Eddy would have been as active in penal reform had he not been imprisoned during the American Revolution?
2. What will be the legacy of Eddy and other early penitentiary pioneers one hundred years from now?

CHAPTER 33

■ ■ ■ ■ ■ ▬▬▬▬▬▬▬▬▬▬▬▬▬▬▬▬

JOHN HAVILAND
(1792–1852)

The Commonwealth of Pennsylvania provided the blueprint for the American penitentiary concept. The concept of solitary
confinement and hard labor was the conceptual
brainchild of Pennsylvania penologists. One of
the first prisons in America was the Walnut
Street Jail in Philadelphia, which had been alternately used as a military prison,
temporary detention facility, and as a long-term facility throughout the eighteenth
and early nineteenth centuries. The Walnut Street Jail could not accommodate the
Pennsylvania concept. Advocates of the Pennsylvania system sought a facility that
would allow for solitary confinement for all its inmates. Although others devised
the concept of solitary confinement and hard labor that defined the Pennsylvania
System, it took the talent and efforts of English-born architect John Haviland to put
the Pennsylvania System into operation.

During the early years of the American penitentiary, two systems competed
for preeminence on the national and world stage of penology. New York's Auburn
System, or the congregate system, emphasized group work. The Pennsylvania system placed a premium on solitary confinement, thus providing the inmate an opportunity to make penitence, hence the word *penitentiary*. In theory, solitary
confinement would isolate the inmate from unhealthy or sinful influences that were
partially responsible for the inmate's incarceration. This idea presented a considerable challenge to any architect.

The concept of the Pennsylvania system originated in 1787 with a group of
reformers called the Philadelphia Society for Alleviating the Miseries of Public
Prisons; the name was later changed to the Pennsylvania Prison Society. There
were several driving forces behind the establishment of the penitentiary. One was
the thought that penitentiaries would serve as a humane alternative to corporal and
shaming punishments administered in public. Another was that offenders would
seek penitence if left alone to reflect on their actions.

John Haviland was born on December 12, 1792, near Taunton, England, the
son of Anne Cobley Haviland and James Haviland, a prominent Anglican minister.
Haviland, at fifteen, was assigned to work with James Elmes, a successful London-
based architect and writer. After acquiring the needed skills to set out on his own,
Haviland left England for St. Petersburg, Russia, around 1815.

Haviland stayed in Russia for only one year before immigrating to the United
States; however, he met several people in Russia that would significantly influence
his career and life. He met John Quincy Adams, the American minister (ambassador) to Russia, and a future United States president. Adams wrote papers of intro-

duction on Haviland's behalf to President James Monroe. Another Russian that had a strong influence on Haviland was Count Nikolai Semenovich Mordvinov, a naval minister and the husband of Haviland's aunt. Mordvinov was a good friend of Englishman John Howard, the world-renowned penal reformer that passed away in 1790 while touring Russian prisons. Haviland's interactions with his Russian uncle spurred his own interest in prison architecture. Haviland also met George von Sonntagg, an American-born admiral in the Russian navy. It was von Sonntagg that encouraged Haviland to immigrate to the United States, which he did in 1816, advising him that prospects for a successful architectural career were better in the United States than in Russia.

Haviland arrived in Philadelphia in September 1816, one of the few skilled architects in the young nation. Shortly after his arrival, he married Mary von Sonntag Wells, a widow with two children and the sister of George von Sonntagg. The couple would have two more children, one of which, Edward, would also become an architect. American architecture had been dormant for several years as a result of the War of 1812, and Haviland found Philadelphia ripe with opportunities. Not only was Haviland sought out for his penchant for creative designs in architecture, Americans were interested in Haviland's ideas on how to install central plumbing and heating systems.

One of Haviland's first jobs that received the attention of American government leaders and builders was a series of volumes he wrote called *The Builder's Assistant,* a pioneering work for American builders and carpenters who had little exposure to European architects trained in classic Greek and Roman orders of architecture. Haviland's first major project in Philadelphia was the design of the First Presbyterian Church, which was constructed in 1820.

The design that would garner worldwide fame for Haviland and that would also solidify his place in the history of American criminal justice was that of the Eastern State Penitentiary. The penitentiary, in which offenders were supposed to be isolated to reflect on their misdeeds and make penitence for them, was an emerging concept in American penology, but there was little idea of how to implement this concept. Pennsylvania, largely as a result of Quaker influence, was at the forefront of the penitentiary movement in the 1820s.

Haviland's design for Eastern was adopted, but he did not oversee actual construction of the facility. That job would fall to a rival architect named William Strickland. Soon after construction began, Strickland was fired and replaced by Haviland. Construction on the prison began in 1821, and was finished sometime between 1823 and 1825. The genius of Haviland's design made him and Eastern the object of attention from around the world.

At the time Eastern was constructed, it occupied eleven acres just outside Philadelphia. It opened its doors to prisoners on October 23, 1829, and, regarded by some as western civilization's first modern penitentiary (although, Western State Penitentiary, a less impressive structure had already been constructed near Pittsburgh), it immediately became an object of fascination. Two of the visitors to Eastern were Frenchmen Gustave de Beaumont and Alexis de Tocqueville, whose

1831 observations about America are classics in the study of American history and penology. They praised the prison, but Charles Dickens, the famed English novelist, did not, calling it in his 1842 visit, "cruel and wrong." On seeing Eastern, the first thing one noticed was the foreboding austerity and enormity of the prison. By design, Eastern, with its Gothic facade, resembles a combination giant fortress and castle, designed to intimidate its residents. Haviland designed the cells large enough to accommodate only one prisoner, as solitary confinement was the most essential aspect of the penitentiary idea. He also faced the challenge of making the cells large enough to allow inmates to work in them, thus each cell was used as a one-man workshop. The cells had high-walled exercise pens outside, so that prisoners could exercise outdoors and remain in solitude at the same time.

Security was also a concern with which Haviland had to contend. He adopted an idea from English philosopher and penologist Jeremy Bentham. Haviland's design was a radial plan in which a centrally located hub or station provided guards the ability to look down several corridors almost simultaneously. In order to fully implement the Pennsylvania concept of total isolation, inmates were disallowed from speaking with each other. The matter of enforcing this ideal was laid at Haviland's feet as well. To accomplish this aim, Haviland designed the prison's corridors and the pipes that ran along the corridors to be airy enough to detect the slightest sound, which would carry down the corridor to the guard station located in the middle of the building.

A challenge that faced all institutional facilities in the nineteenth century was sanitation, especially waste disposal. Flush toilets, septic tanks, and sophisticated municipal sewage systems were foreign to most Americans in the nineteenth century, and prisons and jails were always unspeakably filthy, smelly, and disease ridden. Through Haviland's design, Eastern State Penitentiary became the first large-scale building in the United States to have indoor flush toilets. Each cell had its own water tap and heating system, something found in only the most affluent American households at the time.

Other states and countries adopted the Pennsylvania concept, and with it, Haviland's design. Haviland's services were much in demand after the construction of Eastern. In 1830 the Pennsylvania legislature authorized the revamping of the Western State Penitentiary in Pittsburgh, with the conditions that it be designed to implement the Pennsylvania system of solitary confinement, and that John Haviland be hired as the architect. Haviland was paid $2,000 per year and, because he began to split his time between Pittsburgh and Philadelphia, was given $300 in traveling expenses.

On February 10, 1834, the Western State Penitentiary designed by Haviland opened with 108 cells to wide critical acclaim. The cells at Western according to one observer were "well ventilated, with sufficient light, and an admirable apparatus for observing cleanliness. The cells themselves are built of freestone, in a manner which reflects great credit on the skill and judgment of the architect and workmen."

In addition to the penitentiaries in Philadelphia and Pittsburgh, Haviland designed prisons in Rhode Island and New Jersey. The New Jersey prison followed an Egyptian design, as did a prison Haviland designed in New York, called the Halls of Justice, which was nicknamed "The Tombs." The Gothic style at Eastern was evident in his designs of the Pennsylvania Fire Insurance Company and the Pennsylvania Institution for the Deaf and Dumb. Haviland designed penitentiaries for Missouri and Arkansas; he designed county prisons in Harrisburg, Reading, and Lancaster counties in Pennsylvania. He also designed the Pennsylvania State Insane Asylum in Harrisburg.

Haviland's architectural skills did not save the Pennsylvania concept. The prison system in Pennsylvania fell victim to its popularity with the public and with judges by becoming overcrowded. Inmates had to double up in cells. Isolation, an extremely flawed idea to begin with, went away for practical reasons. The system of silence, also a flawed concept, gradually became impossible to enforce. The Pennsylvania system of isolation and silence was founded on Quaker religious ideals instead of any scientific hypothesis. Being quiet and sitting in contemplative meditation may have made for meaningful worship experiences, but as a way of institutional life, it was fundamentally flawed. The system was officially abandoned in 1913, though it had gradually broken down several decades prior.

Haviland's career as an architect thrived throughout the 1830s and 1840s, thanks to his work with Eastern and other Philadelphia landmarks, including several churches and theaters. He opened a drawing academy and taught at the Franklin Institute (later renamed the Atwater Kent Museum), a building he designed. In 1833 he revised a classic 1805 work titled *Young Carpenter's Assistant,* which was originally written by Owen Biddle. In 1836, Haviland cofounded the American Institution of Architects, a forerunner to the American Institute of Architects.

Haviland's most severe professional setback came about as a result of his work on Philadelphia's Labyrinth Garden in 1828. He invested his own money in its construction and operation, and the venture turned sour, compounding problems brought about by other ill-fated real estate speculations. At the time his debts were mounting, Haviland was under contract with the federal government to design the U.S. Naval Hospital in Norfolk, Virginia. To avoid bankruptcy, Haviland diverted government funds for the Norfolk project to cover his debts. His misdeeds were discovered, and although he was not criminally prosecuted as he might be today, the result was the termination of federal government contracts and a permanent stain on his reputation.

In 1958, the city of Philadelphia officially designated Eastern historic property. It was designated a historic landmark by the federal government in 1965. With the facility in general disrepair and becoming increasingly unsafe, Eastern State Penitentiary closed its doors in January 1970. Efforts to demolish the deteriorating facility were floated throughout the 1970s and 1980s, but a group of concerned architects, penologists, and other citizens lobbied Philadelphia mayor Wilson Goode to prevent commercial interests from taking over Eastern. Their efforts were successful, and Eastern opened for limited tours in 1988. Thanks to a grant from the Pew Charitable Trust, the facility was restored well enough to open its doors for tours in 1994. Today the prison and its museum attract more than 65,000 visitors each year. Its eerie atmosphere, even in the daytime, has made it one of Philadelphia's favorite party spots every Halloween, a tradition that started (illegally) during the 1970s while the facility was abandoned. Hard hats are required for anyone who enters the prison because of the danger of falling objects. One also notices that Eastern has two parts, one from the original construction, and another section constructed long after Haviland's death. One would presume that the newer portions would be in better condition. Such is not the case. The portions designed and built by John Haviland, although much older, are still in better condition than the newer portions of Eastern, due to the quality of Haviland's work and the slipshod efforts of those who came after him, an indication of how concern over quality of prison construction declined in the late nineteenth and twentieth centuries.

John Haviland died of a stroke on March 28, 1852, in his Philadelphia home at the age of fifty-nine. More than 150 years after Haviland's death, the place of the penitentiary in American history has still not been decided. Is the penitentiary good, bad, or a necessary evil? That is a question beyond the scope of this writing, but however one chooses to assess the place of the prison in American history, the name of John Haviland is inextricably linked to that history.

SOURCES AND SUGGESTED READINGS

Jeffrey A. Cohen, "John Haviland," *American National Biography Online,* www.anb.org, August 19, 2002.

LeRoy Beck DePut, *The Triumph of the "Pennsylvania System" at the State's Penitentiaries* (University Park, PA: Pennsylvania Historical Association, 1954).

Eastern State Penitentiary web site, www.easternstate.org, March 27, 2003.

Norman B. Johnston, "John Haviland," in Hermann Mannheim, ed., *Pioneers in Criminology* (Montclair, NJ: Patterson Smith, 1971).

Norman Bruce Johnston, Kenneth Finkel, and Jeffrey A. Cohen, *Eastern State Penitentiary: Crucible of Good Intentions* (Philadelphia: Philadelphia Museum of Art for the Eastern State Penitentiary Task Force of the Preservation Coalition of Greater Philadelphia, 1994).

Herman Mannheim, "John Haviland," *The Journal of Criminal Law, Criminology and Police Science* 45 (February): 5, 1955.

Obituary Notice of John Haviland, Esq., pamphlet (Philadelphia: Isaac Ashmead, 1852).

U.S. History.org, www.ushistory.org, February 24, 2002.

Wilson Biographies Online, http://jproxy.lib.ecu.edu, June 3, 2002.

DISCUSSION QUESTIONS

1. What would be the state of American penitentiaries were it nor for architects like John Haviland?
2. What does John Haviland's work say about the need for penologists to appreciate other academic disciplines, including architecture?

CHAPTER 34

JOHN AUGUSTUS
(1784–1859)

John Augustus did not invent probation. In fact, according to the modern definition of probation, John Augustus was not even a probation officer; he performed pretrial supervision, not probation supervision. Unlike most modern probation and pretrial supervision officers, he worked as a volunteer and never received compensation for his work. Despite the differences between Augustus's work and that of modern probation officers, he is rightly credited as the patriarch of modern American probation. Without John Augustus, someone else would have founded probation, probably the architects of the early juvenile justice system. Nevertheless, Augustus's contributions to the genesis of American probation are very significant, but he did not live to see how far his innovations would go, even in his hometown.

Some American courts had already begun using prison alternatives before John Augustus began his work. During the 1830s, Massachusetts judge Peter Oxenbridge Thacher, after finding a defendant guilty, suspended sentence and allowed her to be free on her own recognizance "for her appearance . . . whenever she should be called for, to go at large." During the 1830s, Massachusetts (illegally) used recognizance as a way of allowing first offenders to escape a criminal conviction.

One factor that separates John Augustus from many other community corrections pioneers is that he worked with adults. Most correctional innovators, including the founders of the penitentiary, the indeterminate sentence, and the juvenile justice system, directed their efforts toward young offenders, believing that adults over the ages of twenty-five to thirty were practically beyond help. Augustus did not subscribe to this idea.

Few if any historians have found serious blemishes on Augustus's character or his sincerity. Even criminal justice historian Samuel Walker, author of one of the most cynical works on criminal justice history ever published, said that Augustus had a "genuine sense of compassion for the downtrodden." The worst that can be said about Augustus is that he was puritanical, naive, and generous to a fault, and that his outspokenness alienated those around him. These same faults can be viewed as virtues. In any case, they defined Augustus's life and work.

John Augustus was born in 1784 in Woburn, Massachusetts. Little is known about his childhood or family background. Most of what is known about Augustus is contained in his own account of his work, called *A Report of the Labors of John Augustus,* which also contains some very sketchy biographical and supplementary material contributed by the American Probation and Parole Association. At age twenty-one Augustus moved to Lexington, Massachusetts, and became a shoemaker. The Jonathan Harrington house, now a Lexington landmark, was Augustus's base from 1811–1827. A successful businessman and landowner, Augustus always possessed a philanthropic mentality, evidenced by his donation of several acres of land to the local Lexington Academy in 1819.

Around 1813 he married a woman named Sally, who bore him one daughter named Harriet. Both Sally and Harriet died when Harriet was about a year old. Years later, Augustus married a woman named Harriet Stearns, who bore one daughter that died at about age ten; Harriet Augustus also gave birth to two sons.

Augustus moved to Boston in 1827 and continued his shoemaking business. He was successful enough to have several assistants work for him, which would eventually free enough time for him to engage in the philanthropy that would make him part of America's correctional history.

While operating his shoemaking business, Augustus was able to view Boston street life. He witnessed firsthand the activities and sorry states of many drunkards, prostitutes, and petty thieves. He observed the revolving door justice system in Boston, seeing the same people repeatedly arrested, disappearing for a while, and then reappearing on the streets, only to be arrested over and over for the same types of activities.

Augustus was an active member in several of the temperance societies in the Boston area during the nineteenth century. Antialcohol organizations were a powerful force in nineteenth century America. These organizations viewed alcohol as a social evil that destroyed lives, homes, careers, and the very moral and economic fiber of the entire country. Augustus wanted to rid Boston of the evil of alcohol, an ideal that seems naive by contemporary standards, but one that enjoyed considerable popularity among mainstream Protestant America in the nineteenth century. More importantly, Augustus decided to intervene in the lives of those who suffered the ill effects of alcohol, namely repeated arrests for petty crimes. Augustus made his first trip to a local Boston court in 1841. One day, Augustus saw a man being arraigned on a charge of drunkenness who did not have enough money to pay his fine. Augustus "requested that the man be allowed a short probation period and be placed in his care."

From that point on Augustus was a frequent presence in Boston's police and municipal courts. His primary targets at first were male drunkards, but he eventually offered his services to women as well. Augustus would look over the defendants as they were brought into courts and interview them to determine if they were receptive to his assistance.

In 1856, a Boston journalist named Ball Fenner, who had heard of Augustus, profiled him for a work called *Raising the Veil*. In *A Report on the Labors of John Augustus,* the American Probation and Parole Association quote Fenner extensively. Fenner provides one of the few external glimpses into Augustus's personality and home life. Fenner wrote that Augustus's home resembled a harem, except that the women were not attractive and they were not there to indulge his sexual desires. The women in his home were those he tried to assist. There is no indication that Augustus ever tried to take advantage of the women he helped. Likewise, he never exploited the men he helped for his business interests by requiring them to supply free labor.

By Fenner's account, Augustus would fit the modern profile of a type A personality. Fenner described him as a "fidgety old fellow." He lived in a constant state of excitement and agitation. One passage from *Raising the Veil* reads, "John can talk very rapidly. He will reel off more line from the end of his tongue in fifteen minutes than any ordinary man could accomplish in four times that space." Criminologist Sheldon Glueck called Augustus a "dynamic synthesis of Paul Revere, John Howard (an English penological pioneer), and Florence Nightingale."

Whether Augustus was aggressive about promoting his religious or political beliefs is not clear. Ball Fenner wrote that Augustus would not share his religious or political ideas with anyone unless asked. However, Augustus was fanatical about his work; he was also very brash. He never hesitated to vehemently disagree with judges, even in open court. One such encounter, recounted by Augustus in his memoir, provides an example of this brazenness:

> Mr. John Augustus, who was present, and standing near the prisoner, mildly observed, "she said, your Honor, that she had been in the House of Correction *once*."
>
> *Justice.* She did not say so,—I heard what the woman said, that *she never was in the House of Correction in her life.*
>
> *Police Officer.* That is true, your Honor, she said so.
>
> *John Augustus*—(warmly), But I said she did not say so! I heard the words she used, and I appeal to the spectators.
>
> Considerable excitement began to manifest itself among the few spectators of this highly dignified dispute, and several voices exclaimed, "She did not say so,—Augustus is right!" In fact there were not three persons present but heard Bridget distinctly admit that she had been in the House of Correction once.
>
> *Officer.* Silence in the court!
>
> *Justice*—(with temper), Mr. Augustus, hold your tongue, sir! Sit down, or I'll direct an officer to take you out of the room!
>
> *Augustus.* I *will* say what I heard.
>
> *Justice.* (Rising with a *show* of dignity), you can't say any thing! Take a seat, instantly sir! (The incorrigible philanthropist seated himself, and the justice readjusted his spectacle.) Sir, you intrude upon the patience of the court; you contradict me, and appeal to the spectators, as though I did not know what was said as well as they. (Augustus rising), keep your seat and be silent, or I'll have you taken out of the room. What right have you to interfere in a question of veracity between a highly respectable officer, so far as I know, and this woman?
>
> *Augustus.* But I wish to explain the—
>
> *Justice.* Not another word, sir!

Augustus was particular about who he assisted. He would target those who "were indicted for their first offence, and whose hearts were not wholly depraved, but gave promise of better things." Unlike today's community corrections and pretrial service officers, who use scientifically validated assessment instruments to gauge an offender's trustworthiness, Augustus had to rely on his own intuition, but he did try to use some sort of measuring stick of the offender's amenability to assistance based on his own experience. Augustus would determine depravity and promise by interviewing defendants as they arrived in court. He would take into account his estimation of a person's background and character, and what influences the person would likely be exposed to in the future. Although his methods were not scientific by modern standards, and Augustus admitted that he did not rigidly adhere to these criteria, his practice of targeting first offenders and those who seemed amenable to change set the standard by which probation operated for many decades and which still holds true to a great extent today. In fact, although Augustus was not scientific in his assessment of offenders fit for probation supervision, he probably exerted more effort in this area than most courts do today, as most offenders are placed on probation for the court's administrative convenience or as a result of plea negotiations or sentencing guidelines.

Augustus also set the standard for probation work by not defending his charges when they would not cooperate with his efforts at assistance. His offer of help was not unconditional. When bailing an offender, his announcement to the court would often follow this line: "I'll bail that young woman for thirty days, your honor. If I can't reform her, I'll bring her into court at the expiration of that time, to be disposed of as you will."

When Augustus was conducting his work in the 1840s and 1850s, there were no distinctions between adult and juvenile courts. Juvenile courts would not exist for another five or six decades. Juveniles went through the same judicial process as adults. Augustus often targeted teenagers for assistance. In his memoirs, Augustus recalled one rather touching account of his efforts to assist a group of teenaged boys. It demonstrates his utterly selfless dedication to his volunteer work. It also is one of the few occasions in which Augustus referred to his work as "probation" supervision:

> In 1847, I bailed nineteen boys, from seven to fifteen years of age, and in bailing them it was understood, and agreed by the court, that their cases should be continued from term to term for several months, as a season of probation; thus each month at the calling of the docket, I would appear in court, make my report, and thus the cases would pass on for five or six months. At the expiration of this term, twelve of the boys were brought into court at one time, and the scene formed a striking and highly pleasing contrast with their appearance when first arraigned. Seven of the number were too poor to pay a fine, although the court fixed the amount at ten cents each, and of course I paid it for them; the parents of the other boys were able to pay the cost . . . this class of boys could be saved from crime and punishment, by the plan which I had marked out, and this was admitted by the judges in both courts.

Naturally, Augustus had his detractors, most of whom were police officers. Some called him a "mock philanthropist." He was accused of encouraging criminal behavior through his "mollycoddling" of offenders. Once, when he became openly indignant because court officers had not saved a seat for him in court, he had a physical altercation with a constable that tried to remove him.

Some charged that Augustus sought to profit from his intervention, to which he replied that bailing prisoners "drains my pockets instead of enriching me," and that attempting to profit from bailing poor people out of jail was impossible, and that he had to work nights at his shoe shop to make up for time lost in court. Although many police officers and judges disliked Augustus, several of the local judges, most notably Peter Oxenbridge Thacher, and some in the local news media appreciated Augustus's work. Although Augustus always worked on a strictly volunteer basis, word of his efforts spread around Boston, and a few people contributed some money to help him out. He received no financial assistance from 1841–1842, during which he spent his own money. In 1843 he received $758 in contributions; he received $1,213 per year from 1844–1846. He received approximately $1,776 each year from 1847–1852, the year he penned his personal memoirs.

Augustus kept meticulous records of the number of people he bailed and assisted, including the amounts he paid for bail. From the time he started in 1841 until the time he was forced to stop in 1858, Augustus had supervised 1,152 men and 794 women. Augustus's generosity ruined his business. He received financial support from several well-known philanthropists, such as Horace Mann, Theodore Parker, and Wendell Phillips. But that did not rescue Augustus from financial peril. Augustus eventually went broke and gave up his shoemaking business before his death in 1859 at the age of seventy-five.

Augustus did not live to see probation become an integral part of the criminal justice system. That task would fall to his successors, most of whom supported Augustus during his lifetime. Augustus did not even live to see Massachusetts appoint America's first paid probation officer. Edward Savage, a Boston police captain, became the first paid probation officer in the United States in 1878, nineteen years after Augustus died. Although it is likely that someone else would have eventually started probation had Augustus not performed his work, it is no coincidence that the first paid probation officer worked in Boston and that other pioneering probation and pretrial service work originated in the Northeast, especially in Massachusetts.

Augustus's idealism is seldom found in American courthouses today, and his unswerving devotion to rehabilitation is not as common in probation supervision as it once was. Augustus would frown on the law enforcement focus that has overtaken probation in the twenty-first century, and, if he were alive today, he would care little for research reports suggesting that rehabilitation does not work. Augustus believed that human beings could be redeemed; he believed that substance abuse was the great evil of his time, and he believed that as a "probation officer," he was performing God's work by assisting petty criminals. Augustus did not care how many failures he experienced with his charges, as long as there was one success. His philosophy is best summed up in a scriptural adaptation he related to Ball Fenneer: "I don-no what proportion (of his clientele are reformed), but suppose one out of ten was reclaimed, would not that be well worth the time, labor and money that is expended on the whole? Do we not read that he who turns one sinner from the error of his ways, shall save a soul from death, and hide a multitude of sins?"

SOURCES AND SUGGESTED READINGS

The American Probation and Parole Association, *A Report of the Labors of John Augustus* (Lexington, KY: Author, 1984 [1852]).

Robert Panzarella, "Theory and Practice of Probation in the Report of John Augustus," *Federal Probation* 66 (3): 38–42, 2002.

Samuel Walker, *Popular Justice: A History of American Criminal Justice* (2nd ed.). New York: Oxford University Press, 1997).

DISCUSSION QUESTIONS

1. How is John Augustus's work similar to and different from that of modern probation officers?
2. Was John Augustus's religious devotion a positive or negative legacy for American community corrections?

CHAPTER 35

DOROTHEA DIX
(1802–1887)

One of the greatest challenges facing American society is proper treatment of its mentally ill. The American criminal justice system has found itself on the front lines of this challenge for more than two centuries. Courts and lawmakers wrestle with definitions of insanity and other mental health issues brought up by defense attorneys seeking to mitigate the crimes committed by their clients. Even more vexing is the problem of the chronically mentally ill who continually populate American jails and prisons, many of which are ill-equipped to treat the truly mentally ill. Although this problem remains, the state of America's mentally ill population would be much worse had it not been for Dorothea Dix, one of the most active and passionate social reformers of the nineteenth century.

Dorothea Lynde Dix was born on April 4, 1802, in Hampden, Maine, one of three children born to Joseph and Mary Bigelow Dix. As a descendant of Boston's elite social and economic class, Dorothea Dix, nicknamed "Dolly" by her parents, lived a life of privilege, attending the finest schools in New England. The Dix's climb up the Boston social ladder was halted when Dorothea Dix's paternal grandfather died in 1809. Joseph Dix, a minister and wealthy landowner thanks to his deceased father, moved the family to Barnard, Vermont, in 1812, just as war with the British erupted. In Vermont, Joseph Dix opened a business selling tracts and sermons written and delivered by John Wesley, the pioneer of the Methodist faith. To the consternation of her Methodist parents, Dorothea Dix found her religious home in the Unitarian faith.

Unhappy with her home situation, Dix ran away to her grandmother' house at age twelve, but returned shortly thereafter. She left for good in 1816 at the age of fourteen to live with Sarah Fiske, a wealthy relative in Worcester, Massachusetts. She eventually settled in Boston, taking custody of her nine-year-old brother Charles after their father's death in 1821. Dix biographer Thomas Brown indicates that her childhood and early adulthood were marked by a frustrating search for happiness and a sense of purpose. She opened a school, but was unpopular with her students, mostly because of her stern manner, which led to the closing of the school. She prized her sense of independence and, though she dated frequently, never married, which led to frequent bouts of loneliness and depression. Other health problems would dog Dix periodically throughout her young life, including a bout with tuberculosis in 1827 and a collapsed lung in 1836.

Dix found a niche in writing, publishing five children's textbooks and storybooks in the late 1820s. Thanks to the help of wealthy New England friends with whom she often resided, Dix traveled extensively, not only throughout New England, but also to other parts of the world.

Dix traveled to the Caribbean in 1830, spending most of her time that year in the Danish West Indies. It was there that she had her first encounter with slavery, an extinct institution in New England by that time. Throughout her life Dix possessed an attitude toward slavery that was inconsistent with her otherwise compassionate attitude toward the downtrodden. While slavery was tearing America apart in the first half of the nineteenth century, Dix could not understand the uproar over an institution whose cruelty seemed to escape her attention. She made scant mention of slavery in her writings from the West Indies, and in later years Dix would decry both militant proponents and opponents of slavery. During a visit to Raleigh, North Carolina, in 1848, Dix remarked, "The negros [sic] are gay, obliging, and anything but miserable," and "thoughtless and irresponsible." Her disregard for the evils of slavery would well serve her subsequent crusade for the mentally ill in a roundabout way. Had she been a staunch abolitionist, she would not have been able to gain access to southern mental hospitals and jails, let alone legislatures in southern states as the southern and northern states grew increasingly alienated from one another.

Dix's interest in education and spreading the Christian faith led to her helping prisoners and the mentally ill. The major turning point in Dix's life, which gave her the mission in life she had always sought, was in 1841. She visited the Middlesex (Massachusetts) County jail where she taught Bible study to the inmates and invited local ministers to preach sermons. She also generated enough local support to start a prison library and to start construction of a prison chapel.

Another seminal event in Dix's life was her reading of a pamphlet written by a Boston physician named Edward Jarvis. The pamphlet, titled *Insanity and Insane Asylums,* discussed an emerging strategy for the treatment of the mentally ill. The strategies for treating the mentally ill had long been characterized by primitive, aggressive measures such as bleeding, and it was assumed by many in the religious community that most mentally ill people were under the control of malevolent spirits. Jarvis advocated "moral treatment," which was characterized by attempts to instill a sense of self-control through gentle persuasion. Dix, with her strong religious values, saw memorization of Bible scripture as a key ingredient in this approach.

Dix began visiting prisons, jails, almshouses, and insane asylums throughout Massachusetts in 1842. She was often appalled at the conditions of the mentally ill prisoners in jails and prisons, but she would attribute their conditions more to pervasive and malign neglect than outright abuse. She would find this to be the case in most other facilities in other states as well. Adopting the moral treatment approach to treating the mentally ill, Dix used religious instruction and literature as her primary treatment tools.

Dix was not content to work for prison reform within the prisons. She wanted to effect change at a higher level. Dix analyzed Massachusetts's laws regarding the treatment of the insane and became determined to change those aspects that she viewed as unfair to the mentally ill. One law required that insane paupers not in hospitals be housed in county jails. Dix wrote *Memorial to the Legislature of Massachusetts,* which demonstrated her writing ability acquired from prior publication experience. Claiming to have relied solely on first hand observations, Dix, according to Thomas Brown, wrote, "I tell what I have seen!" She claims to have seen the mentally ill in "cages, closets, cellars, stalls, pens . . . chained, naked, beaten with rods, and lashed into obedience." Although *Memorial* was widely renowned by its readers, it did not persuade the Massachusetts legislature to enact any significant change.

Despite this setback, Dix knew she had found her calling. Dix traveled to other states seeking similar reforms. She traveled tirelessly, to Vermont, New Hampshire, Rhode Island, and into Canada, usually by stagecoach at night so she could visit facilities during the day. She experienced success in Rhode Island, persuading private donors to establish an insane asylum for the poor near Providence. In 1843, Dix went to New York, visiting sixty county jails in ten weeks, an incredibly arduous task even with modern transportation facilities. She presented a report to the New York legislature in 1843, evaluating each jail and almshouse she visited, noting that abuse and neglect were common. She reported seeing insane paupers confined to dark cellars, chained to beds, and scarred from beatings. Dix advocated a new facility for insane paupers, but only succeeded in having wings added to an existing mental health facility in Utica.

Dix kept up her hectic pace, visiting Pennsylvania, New Jersey, Ohio, Maryland, and Virginia. In contrast to her earlier efforts, Dix gradually ingratiated herself to the medical establishment in the states she visited. No longer a lone pioneer, Dix sought to enrich the moral approach to treating the mentally ill. She thought that mental illness was attributable to brain lesions or defects instead of spiritual flaws. In addition to writing, Dix found that she had a penchant for personal lobbying. Reluctant legislators would often come around to Dix's point of view after meeting with her in person. By 1845, Dix had traveled 10,000 miles over a three-year period, visited more than 300 almshouses, 300 county jails, eighteen state prisons, and numerous hospitals and insane asylums.

In 1845, Dix weighed in on one of the great penological debates of the nineteenth century. The debate was whether the congregate system in New York prisons was superior to the solitary system in Pennsylvania prisons, especially the Eastern State Penitentiary near Philadelphia. Dix decided that the Eastern system was better because perpetual isolation was more conducive to spiritual growth and rehabilitation than having prisoners work in groups. She also advocated corporal punishment for some unruly inmates, not unlike even the most fervent penal reformers of her day. According to criminal justice historian Samuel Walker, Dix stated that whipping might be the only way "by which an insurrectionary spirit can be conquered." She also advocated the "prudent and careful use" of shower baths. Dix taught Sunday school at Eastern and recruited well-known ministers to deliver sermons to the inmates, her reputation well-established enough to attract the best known clergy wherever she went. Her *Remarks on Prisons and Prison Discipline* made her one of the most admired women in American public life during the 1840s.

Dix began earnest reform efforts in southern states, something that many New England reformers would never have attempted, given that the aversion to slavery would have precluded serious efforts to work with southern politicians. She successfully advocated for the building of an insane asylum for poor prisoners in Kentucky. She experienced success in other southern states as well, ignoring the plight of slaves but tirelessly advocating for mentally ill prisoners.

Throughout the 1850s, the increasingly rancorous debates over slavery and secession bored and annoyed Dix, who could not understand why such a seemingly innocuous institution could threaten the very existence of the United States as a nation. Dix even supported the infamous *Dred Scott* decision of the United States Supreme Court, which essentially placed an official government imprimatur on the institution of slavery. She was a frequent visitor to the presidential mansion (the term *White House* was not yet in common usage) during the 1850–1853 administration of Millard Fillmore. Had Fillmore alone been the deciding voice, Dix would have been successful in having enormous federal funds set aside for institutions for mentally ill paupers, but Fillmore, one of the weakest presidents in American history, could not persuade Congress to accede to Dix's request. Fillmore's successor, a fellow New Englander named Franklin Pierce, an even more feckless president, was not enthusiastic about Dix or her efforts. Pierce's attention was focused on slavery, keeping America united, and avoiding war.

During the 1850s, Dix traveled to Europe and Russia to engage in similar reform efforts. In 1854 and 1855 she worked in England and Scotland, which ultimately resulted in Queen Victoria's appointment of a royal commission to investigate the plight of England's mentally ill. Parliament passed laws mandating better treatment for the mentally ill throughout Great Britain. Although her reform efforts in Europe resulted in some success, she was frustrated with the inertia of European governments and wrote that Americans should be grateful for what they had.

Another reason for Dix visiting Europe was Florence Nightingale. Nightingale, a British-born nurse, had made herself an internationally renowned figure for her efforts to aid wounded soldiers in the Crimean War, a military quagmire that pitted Russia against Great Britain, France, and Turkey. Dix viewed Nightingale, now acknowledged as the matriarch of modern nursing, as her role model. Dix did not meet Nightingale, but she did meet other European dignitaries, including Pope Pius IX.

Although Dix's indifference to slavery made her anathema to northern abolitionists, she was viewed positively in the South, where many saw her as a unifying and intersectional healing force. Despite such hopes, America erupted in civil war in 1861. The outbreak of war saddened Dix, but she viewed the war as a necessary evil to heal America of its divisions. Although her efforts to aid mentally ill prisoners slowed because of the war, Dix set out to become the Florence Nightingale of America. She treated war prisoners on both sides, seeing all of America's war casualties as victims of, as Thomas Brown states, the American penchant for giving in to uncontrolled passions. She thought that the Civil War was much ado about very little, and that she should act as a divinely inspired healer in the bloody rift between the two sides.

Dix met President Abraham Lincoln at the White House in April 1861. She petitioned President Lincoln and Secretary of War Simon Cameron to oversee administration of a group of military hospitals. Although military hospitals are commonplace today, they were not in 1861. Only Florence Nightingale had undertaken such an effort before. Dix had many obstacles to overcome, one of which was military doctors' opposition to having women serve as nurses in a military setting. Medical qualifications for nurses were minimal, so Dix, who had no formal medical training of her own, made moral and spiritual qualifications the most important factor in deciding who should serve.

Characteristically, Dix plunged into her new job with all of the energy she could muster. However, as the Civil War dragged on much longer and became much bloodier than the Union had predicted, it took its toll on Dix. She lost weight and suffered another bout of extreme depression. Her vision of the war acting as a form of spiritual cleansing faded. Dix's public reputation took a pounding as well, with many people, especially disgruntled job seekers, critical of her administration of the military nursing department.

Dix survived the Civil War, receiving two national flags for her efforts to aid Union soldiers. She resumed her advocacy on behalf of the mentally ill in prisons, jails, and hospitals in the United States and other countries, even convincing the Japanese chargé d'affaires, who was paying a visit to Washington, to have an insane asylum built in Kyoto. However, she did not pursue reform on behalf of the mentally ill with the same vigor as she had before the Civil War, partly because she was well into her sixties. She continued to visit hospitals, jails, and insane asylums, many of which were constructed as a result of her earlier efforts.

In October 1881, she visited the New Jersey State Lunatic Asylum in Trenton, the construction of which was one of the crowning achievements of her career as a reformer. While there she collapsed, complaining of chills and pain in her lungs. When it became evident that Dix was not able to take care of herself without constant care, arrangements were made for Dix to live in the asylum on a permanent basis, alongside the other residents for whom she had so tirelessly advocated years before. Although her medical attendants predicted that Dix would not live for long after her admission, her condition stabilized, and she was able to live a somewhat normal existence within the asylum, reading constantly and entertaining guests as best as her health would allow. Gradually, Dix's eyesight and hearing failed. She died on July 18, 1887, at the age of eighty-five.

The plight of the mentally ill is still a blight on the social conscious of the United States. Mental illness still carries a negative stigma that is a holdover from the days when practically nothing was known about such conditions. In the eyes of many criminal justice professionals, the idea of mental illness conjures images of slick defense attorneys inventing syndromes in order to have defendants escape responsibility for their misdeeds. Others view the mentally ill as a burden on courts and local jails. The plight of the mentally ill, especially those who are poor, is still a vexing problem for the criminal justice system. Dorothea Dix only made a dent in the problems facing America's mentally ill, but she did succeed in raising the consciousness of the nation. America and its criminal justice system still have much progress to make in this area, but much of the progress that has been made can be credited to Dorothea Dix.

SOURCES AND SUGGESTED READINGS

Thomas J. Brown, *Dorothea Dix: New England Reformer* (Cambridge, MA: Harvard University Press, 1998).
Samuel Walker, *Popular Justice: A History of American Criminal Justice,* 2nd ed. (New York: Oxford University Press, 1988).
Andrew G. Wood, "Dix, Dorothea Lynde," *American National Biography Online,* February 2000 www.anb.org/articles/15/15-00181.html, August 19, 2002.

DISCUSSION QUESTIONS

1. How far has the state of mentally ill prisoners come since Dix's lifetime? How far does it need to go?
2. What are your reactions to Dix's ambivalent attitude toward slavery in light of her compassionate attitude toward the mentally ill?

CHAPTER 36

■ ■ ■ ■ ■ ────────

RUTHERFORD B. HAYES (1822–1893)

Most Americans remember Rutherford B. Hayes as one of the rather anonymous gray-bearded presidents of the Gilded Age, his name sandwiched between Ulysses Grant and James Garfield as the nineteenth president of the United States. Hayes is remembered for the controversial election that placed him in the presidential mansion, an event that was revisited by the news media during the heavily disputed 2000 presidential election.

Hayes's place as a trivial footnote in presidential history is unfortunate, for his life was filled with adventure and was characterized by a strong devotion to improving life for many Americans and to improving the operation and humanitarian aspects of American prisons. Hayes enjoys the distinction of being the only American president to be strongly involved in prison reform. Much of his prison reform efforts came after his presidency, which was fortunate, because although Hayes is not remembered by twenty-first-century Americans as one of the country's greatest presidents, his high-profile status as an ex-president greatly served the cause of penal reform during the 1880s and 1890s, when his name was still a household word.

Rutherford Birchard Hayes was born on October 4, 1822, in Delaware, Ohio, the youngest of four children born to Sophia Birchard Hayes, and Rutherford Hayes, a storeowner who died three months before his youngest son was born. Later in life, Hayes's personal letters indicated that he had strong allegiance to Christian ideals, and he frequently attended church throughout his life, though he never joined one.

A strong advocate of public education during his political career, Hayes never attended public schools. He was educated at home by his mother and uncle until he entered Kenyon College in 1838. Hayes graduated at the top of his class in 1842 and entered Harvard Law School, from which he was graduated in 1845. Hayes practiced law in present-day Fremont, Ohio, until 1849 when he began practicing law in Cincinnati. While living in Cincinnati, he met Lucy Webb, whom he married on December 30, 1852. The Hayeses would produce eight children, three of which would die before the age of three.

Hayes's opposition to slavery, the most hotly debated issue in the country, was evidenced in his law practice. Cincinnati was a frequent destination of runaway slaves from neighboring Kentucky, and Hayes on more than one occasion defended runaway slaves. Hayes's success as an attorney and his Republican Party contacts paid off with his election to the office of solicitor, his first formal foray into politics.

Hayes did not complete his term as solicitor. The American Civil War began in 1861. Hayes joined the Ohio twenty-third volunteer company as a major. Hayes was offered the rank of colonel, but turned it down for the same reason he never joined a church; he felt unworthy. Hayes realized great glory as a combat soldier. He was wounded six times during the war and rose to the rank of major general. Fellow Ohioan and general (and future twenty-fifth president) William McKinley called Hayes the most beloved man in the regiment. His accomplishments as a soldier did not go unnoticed to the citizens of southern Ohio. Before the war's end, Hayes was elected to the United States House of Representatives, even though he never campaigned. In fact, Hayes did not assume his congressional seat until December 1865, eight months after he was supposed to, because he refused to abandon his military responsibilities.

Hayes's later prison reform efforts were rooted in his observations of Confederate and Union prisons during the Civil War. The most infamous prisons for captured soldiers were located in the South, but there were plenty of abusive situations in northern prisons as well. In an 1864 letter, Hayes wrote, "War is a cruel business and there is brutality in it on all sides, but it is very idle to get up anxiety on account of any supposed peculiar cruelty on the part of Rebels. Keepers of prisons in Cincinnati, as well as in Danville (Kentucky), are hard-hearted and cruel."

After serving a term in Congress, Hayes was elected governor of Ohio in 1867. He became active in prison reform both within and outside Ohio. One of the most significant events in American correctional history took place under Hayes's governorship. In October 1870, Cincinnati hosted the National Congress of Penitentiary and Reformatory Discipline. From what has since been dubbed the Cincinnati Congress came the ideas that guided American penology for the next several decades and which are still very much in evidence today. Hayes, as governor of the host state, played a great role in arranging the congress's location. He also presided over the congress. The star of the congress was Zebulon Brockway, who introduced the ideas of prison reform, industrial training in prisons, the indeterminate sentence, and separate detention facilities for juveniles. Although Brockway was the star, Governor Hayes was the facilitator. The congress was also the birthplace of the National Prison Association. Hayes was selected as the organization's first president. The National Prison Association, renamed the American Correctional Association (ACA) in 1954, is still the premier professional association for corrections in the United States.

As governor, Hayes also promoted the work of the Ohio Board of State Charities, which was occupied with prison reform issues. Soon after Hayes left office in 1871, the board was abolished, but it was reinstituted when Hayes was elected governor again in 1875.

Hayes received the republican nomination for the presidency in 1876. It was customary that nominees not attend their party's nominating convention, and it was also customary that presidential candidates not campaign in public, or at least not much. In his nomination acceptance letter, Hayes vowed to create a civil service system based on merit rather than political patronage, and he vowed to heal the venomous antagonism between the North and the South, both of which were still reeling from the effects of the Civil War that ended in 1865.

The election that pitted Hayes against his Democratic opponent, Samuel Tilden, ranks along with the 2000 election as one of the most bizarre and controversial presidential elections in American history. As election night ended, Tilden had a substantial lead in the popular vote and he seemed to be leading in the electoral vote as well. During the night and into the next day, Republican Party leaders figured that the election could be saved. The vote was believed to be close in South Carolina, Florida, Louisiana, and Oregon. A tilt in Hayes's direction from these four states would throw the electoral vote majority to Hayes. Telegrams were sent to republican leaders in the four contested states, with instructions to count the votes very carefully, and local republican vote counters had the authority to judge and disqualify so-called fraudulent ballots.

By the time vote counting was finished several days later, Hayes was judged to have won South Carolina by 600 votes and Florida by 94 votes. The vote counting in all of the states was rife with irregularity and accusations of fraud, especially in Louisiana. On December 6, 1876, the electors cast their ballots, but party officials in the contested states sent two sets of electors. Tilden, without the votes in the contested states, led Hayes 184–165 in the electoral vote count, with 20 votes still contested, and 185 being the winning number. Congress created an electoral commission composed of seven Democrats, seven Republicans, and one independent, a Supreme Court justice named David Davis. In the interim, Davis was elected to the United States Senate, and the task of deciding the election was given to Supreme Court Justice Joseph Bradley, a republican. This sealed Hayes's victory.

Naturally, a cloud of suspicion hung over Hayes, the Republican Party, and the election itself, but some southern power brokers acquiesced. The acquiescence was due to Hayes's promise to withdraw Union troops from southern states, ending the Reconstruction era so despised by southern whites, and bringing on the Jim Crow laws that cruelly oppressed southern blacks. A debate over the rightness or wrongness of this move, and its accompanying social ramifications, deserves much more attention than can be given here. However, it would produce in later years at least one unintended positive effect for Hayes's prison reform efforts in southern states.

It is unfortunate that Hayes's name is associated with his dubious presidential election. Hayes was by most accounts a decent and honest man. He was an effective president that did much to restore a sense of integrity to the office after the undistinguished and scandal-plagued terms of Andrew Johnson and Ulysses Grant. His integrity stood out during a period known for extremely unscrupulous politics. Hayes chose not to seek a second term as president, keeping the promise he made in 1876.

After leaving the presidency, Hayes and his wife returned to live in Spiegel Grove, Ohio, but he spent much of his time traveling. During his postpresidential period, Hayes became very active in several philanthropic activities and dove head-long into prison reform. In 1882, he was again elected to head the National Prison Association; each year for the rest of his life he would stand for reelection and each year he would win. He was active in fund-raising for Ohio State and Western Reserve (now Case Western Reserve) universities; he served as the first president of the Slater Fund, an organization dedicated to improving educational opportunities for African Americans, and he was very active in promoting prison reform.

Hayes used his fame as a former president to promote prison reform. One of the hallmarks of Hayes's penal philosophy was the idea that people could be rehabilitated. He thought it society's duty to facilitate rehabilitation and to forgive the offender who tried to better himself. He once wrote:

> I have often quoted, and shall continue to quote as long as I speak on prison reform, the significant words of Governor Horatio Seymour in his inaugural address as president of the National Prison Association: I never yet found a man so untamable that there was not something of good on which to build a hope. I never yet found a man so good that he need not fear a fall.

Hayes believed that industrial education was one key in preventing recidivism. Teach a young man a legitimate trade, he asserted, especially during the emerging Industrial Revolution age, and the young man was less likely to seek a life of crime. In an 1889 address delivered in Nashville, Hayes said that, "Education, as I undertake to emphasize, is the means by which any prison can best reform the convict."

Despite his advocacy for good prison programs and facilities, Hayes knew those factors were unimportant if they were poorly administered. One of Hayes's priorities throughout his political career was civil service reform, and he applied that priority to prison reform. Many government jobs throughout the nineteenth century operated under the spoils system. Under the spoils system, government jobs were handed out based on political patronage for the winning candidates instead of qualifications. This resulted in government (including prison management jobs) being doled out to unqualified, brutal, political hacks. In an 1891 address delivered in Pittsburgh, Hayes stated that "Merit, ability, experience, ought to be the controlling consideration in all appointments of prison officers. The spoils doctrine is nowhere more out of place than when it controls the appointment of prison officials." Hayes believed that a bad prison system managed by a good man is better than a good system managed by a bad man.

Although many Americans, especially African Americans in the South, were critical of Hayes's decision as president to withdraw Union forces from southern states, thus withdrawing federal protection from African Americans, his decision, though politically motivated, had an unintended positive effect on his prison reform efforts. In 1886, the National Prison Association held its annual meeting in Atlanta. Hayes's Georgia hosts warmly greeted him, because of his move to end the Reconstruction era that so many white southerners despised. They expressed gratitude for his ending Reconstruction, and as a result of their gratitude, were, according to Hayes, much more receptive to penal reform ideas from him than they would have been from most other northerners. Hayes denounced Georgia's convict lease system, under which prisoners were leased out to often unscrupulous businessmen and used as virtual slave labor. He called for segregated facilities for women and children. Although these practices did not end overnight, Hayes's message was heard and heeded.

Hayes never claimed to be an intellectual, but he possessed unerring self-confidence, a strong sense of integrity and forthrightness, and innate common sense. His common sense told him that his stature as a former president would open doors to promote prison reform that would be closed to others. Hayes would use any forum to promote prison reform, including political forums, saying that rehabilitation of offenders was in the best interests of society. Almost all prisoners will leave prison one day, thought Hayes, and it was in society's best interest to see that they left prison better prepared to rejoin society than they were when they came in. He advocated Walter Crofton's Irish ticket-of-leave system, under which an offender earned his way to an early release by working hard and exhibiting good behavior.

Hayes detested the emerging school of thought known alternately as criminal anthropology and positivism. This strain of thought, advocated by adherents to Darwinism such as Italy's Cesare Lombroso, suggested that tendencies toward criminal behavior were inherited or traceable to physical characteristics. Hayes believed that the right environment coupled with opportunities for self-improvement could make a positive difference in anyone's life.

Hayes carried his prison reform message to America's churches. He appealed to church parishioners as a fellow Christian on humanitarian grounds, no doubt remembering the plight of Civil War prisoners horribly mistreated in military prisons. He preached the gospel of forgiveness as well, maintaining that it was the duty of Christians to forgive wrongdoers. He recalled a situation he dealt with while serving as Ohio's governor. Once, when a young woman had been sentenced to death, a petition for clemency reached Hayes's desk. Intrigued by her story, Hayes, wearing a disguise, decided to visit the young woman in her cell, without revealing his identity. Moved by her penitent attitude, he commuted her sentence, saving her from execution. Hayes never regretted his action.

On January 8, 1893, Lucy Hayes passed away. Hayes's diary entry for that day included the following: "My feeling was one of longing to be quietly resting in a grave by her side." He died nine days later on January 17, at the age of seventy.

During his life and since his death, much has been written and said about Rutherford Hayes. But much of what has been said and written is related to his performance as president of the United States, as governor of Ohio, as a United States congressman, and as a Civil War hero. Much less has been written and said about his efforts as a penal reformer. In June 1893, at the National Prison Association's annual conference, Roeliff Brinkerhoff, another Civil War hero and penal reformer, paid tribute to Hayes.

To the world at large, General Hayes as a prison reformer is of little consequence. To us who believe that its solution is of more vital importance to the American people, and more essential to the perpetuity of the Republic, than the solution of the questions about which political parties are now contending, General Hayes as a philanthropist has rendered a service as worthy of remembrance as any deeds of his contemporaries in statesmanship or in arms.

In terms of what he once referred to as his favorite "hobby," Hayes's philosophy can be summarized by remarks from an address he gave to the Cincinnati Congress in 1870: "I must begin my address for the Prison Congress. How will this do for a first sentence? One of the tests of the civilization of people is the treatment of its criminals."

SOURCES AND SUGGESTED READINGS

Michael Beschloss, *American Heritage Illustrated History of the Presidents* (New York: Crown Publishers, 2000).

Ari Hoogenboom, *Rutherford B. Hayes: Warrior and President* (Lawrence, KS: University Press of Kansas, 1995).

Ohio Historical Society Internet web site, www.ohiohistory.org, April 21, 2003.

Charles Richard Williams, ed., *Diary and Letters of Rutherford B. Hayes, Volume IV* (Columbus, OH: Ohio State Archaeological and Historical Society, 1924).

DISCUSSION QUESTIONS

1. How did Hayes's war experience impact his attitude toward penal reform?
2. How did Hayes's status as a former president affect his penal reform efforts?

CHAPTER 37

ZEBULON BROCKWAY
(1827–1920)

Parole, a primary component of community corrections, has its genesis in the prison. Parole, which in recent years has come under fire more than any other component of the criminal justice system, was founded with high ideals and with a firm reliance on the indeterminate sentence, under which the amount of time inmates serve depends on their behavior while incarcerated. One of the most instrumental figures in implementing the indeterminate sentence was Zebulon Brockway, the "grand old man" of American wardens who served as superintendent of New York's Elmira Reformatory from 1876 to 1900.

Zebulon Reed Brockway was born on April 28, 1827, in Lyme, Connecticut, one of seven children born to Caroline and Zebulon Brockway, the latter a wealthy businessman, politician, state prison commissioner, and philanthropist. The younger Brockway spent his childhood in Connecticut, attending good schools and having a steady dose of Christian teaching. Why Brockway developed a keen interest in prison work is not revealed in his autobiography. With his family wealth he could have had a successful business career, but, perhaps guided by a sense of noblesse oblige, he chose prison work.

His first prison job was as a guard at the Connecticut state prison in Wethersfield. The Wethersfield facility had been strongly influenced by a family of prison wardens named the Pilsburys, who had turned the prison into a giant and profitable industrial facility. Although the Pilsburys no longer worked at Westerfield during Brockway's tenure as guard and later as a clerk, their influence remained. While at Westerfield, Brockway became enamored not only with management's ability to use prison labor for industrial purposes, he also became interested, as did most early prison pioneers, with the use of Bible study as a rehabilitative influence.

In 1851, Brockway accepted a position as deputy superintendent at the Albany (New York) County Penitentiary, in part because he wanted the opportunity to work directly under Amos Pilsbury, who he had come to admire through reputation. Brockway called his work at Albany "a period of severe but serviceable training." The county penitentiary, which had initially been little more than a county jail, became a profitable enterprise under their leadership.

Pilsbury recommended Brockway for the warden's position at Rhode Island Penitentiary. Instead, Brockway accepted a job as superintendent of the Municipal and County Almshouse at Albany in 1853. The Almshouse, which catered to the "diseased, defective, and dependent denizens who furnish the perennial supply of misdemeanant offenders who people the jails and short-term prisons," was located less than a mile from the Albany penitentiary. While there, Brockway oversaw construction and presided over America's first county hospital for the insane. Also in 1853, Brockway married Jane Woodhouse, who would give birth to two daughters.

In 1854, Brockway became superintendent of the Monroe County (Rochester), New York Penitentiary, where he remained until 1861. He maintained his allegiance to prison industry, stating, "Public expenditure for prisons should be limited to the cost of providing the plant." He established Bible study classes at Monroe County, in large measure due to a religious revival that swept Rochester, referred to as the "City of Revivals" at the time. Unlike most other wardens at the time, Brockway utilized academic education as a means of rehabilitation in addition to vocational and religious instruction. Although not a bleeding heart as later accusations indicated, Brockway was much more humane than many of his contemporaries.

Brockway's real passion was working with young offenders, who he believed were more amenable to rehabilitation than offenders over thirty. With that in mind, he accepted a position as director of the newly built Detroit House of Correction in 1861. Under a law just enacted by the Michigan legislature, felons between the ages of sixteen and twenty-one were no longer sent to the state prison at Jackson, but to Detroit instead. The House of Correction accepted its first inmates on August 1, 1861.

As he had before, Brockway made industrial output and vocational education one of the basic and successful ingredients of the Detroit House of Correction, quite a remarkable achievement given that most inmates served sentences of less than one hundred days, thus allowing for little training time. Brockway instituted regular school sessions, getting teachers, professors, and college students to teach classes, which usually met two nights per week. Lecture topics included the nobility of work, how to do business, ancient architecture, flowers, humorous poetry, chemical combinations of bread, money management, banking, and the emerging field of psychology. While at Detroit, Brockway's beliefs about the causes of crime crystallized. He began to discount the idea that free will was the sole determinant of criminal behavior. Nor did he buy into the long held idea that crime was equated with sin. Like many other penitentiary pioneers, he believed that factors in an offender's social environment were strong correlates of criminal behavior. In addition, Brockway joined a growing number of penologists in the United States and Europe who believed that physical and medical factors were correlated with criminal behavior. In his autobiography, he wrote that the dismissal of free will and sin "cleared the field of our endeavor and opened wide to science that which had been dominated by sentiment alone." Brockway did not abandon religious instruction of inmates, but he began to see that religious instruction alone would not rehabilitate inmates.

In 1869, Brockway wrote a bill for the Michigan legislature called the "three years law," which allowed prison administrators discretion in releasing inmates, and which allowed prison authorities to arrest recently released inmates for misdeeds and re-incarcerate them. Thus, the indeterminate sentence and parole supervision were born. The law applied only to women offenders in Wayne County (Detroit) and it soon became useless, dependent largely on judicial interpretations of how the statute was to be applied. Nevertheless, Brockway was encouraged by the results of the experiment and received public praise from many notable citizens, including Dwight L. Moody, the most renowned Christian evangelist of the nineteenth century.

The event that assured Brockway's place in American penological history was his presentation in 1870 of a paper titled "The Ideal of a True Prison System for a State" at the National Prison Congress in Cincinnati. The meeting gave birth to the National Prison Association, later renamed the American Correctional Association. Brockway's address set the stage for penology for the next several decades. The central thesis in Brockway's speech was:

> The prison system of a state should partake of the same spirit of the other parts. Legalized degradation of any criminal inflicts injury upon the whole social organism, while efforts for the highest and best welfare of any person promote the general good.

Brockway viewed the job of prisons to either cure the inmate of his wrongdoing ways or restrain him from harming society if he will not or cannot be cured. He called for graduated freedoms among inmates, culminating in a planned program of release into the community, with community supervision being conducted by local law enforcement. He also called for specialized institutions for young offenders, for elderly offenders, and for women. The crux of his plan was the indeterminate sentence and parole supervision, an idea that had already been implemented in Ireland and Australia by British authorities.

Despite his exalted status within the field of penology, Brockway's tenure at Detroit came to an end shortly after the Cincinnati Congress as a result of public accusations of serving unsuitable food and inflicting harsh discipline, the latter accusation being one that would recur many years later. Although he was exonerated of any wrongdoing, his reputation was tarnished. In December 1872 Brockway went to work for the Michigan (Railroad) Car Company in Detroit. He remained in this position until May 1876 when he was offered the chance to put his prison administration principles into operation at the New York State Reformatory at Elmira. The invitation to accept the position came from Louis Pilsbury, the son of Amos Pilsbury, whom Brockway had worked under in the 1850s. Although the Reformatory had a board of managers, which included Louis Pilsbury, Brockway had a free hand in running the facility. Brockway drafted an indeterminate sentence law in 1877, which was enacted by the New York legislature.

Brockway instituted a marks system, under which prisoners earned or lost marks depending on their behavior and progress toward rehabilitation as perceived by prison staff. The more marks prisoners earned, the more privileges they were given, and the sooner their release date. Brockway's marks program functioned as the first formal parole program in the United States. Volunteers in the community supervised those who were released on parole for six months.

Although he held firm to his religious beliefs, and he believed that reforming prisoners was the essence of the Christian ideal, Brockway had lost faith in evangelism as the primary tool of rehabilitation. Instead, he believed that education, vocational training, and coercion were the best instruments of rehabilitation. Elmira suffered a blow in 1888 when the New York legislature, under pressure from organized labor and business groups, banned inmate labor that competed with similar labor in the private sector. Although he initially fought to preserve such labor, Brockway was relieved when the ban came to pass, because he no longer had to worry about turning a profit with the reformatory, freeing him to concentrate on reforming the prisoners. He concentrated on instilling military-style discipline among the inmates by bringing in a former West Point instructor to train the inmates in drill and caring for their cells. The reformatory had a state-of-the-art gymnasium, both for recreation and for testing inmates' mental and physical agility. The gymnasium contained gymnastics and exercise equipment (basketball had not been invented). On the purpose of the gymnasium, Brockway wrote:

> The intention was to invigorate by means of physical culture the entire prison population and, particularly through specific scientific physical renovation, to improve defectives and dullards in their mental and moral habitudes.

According to Brockway, identifying and treating crime had become a scientific process. Brockway and his staff became immersed in the now largely discredited pseudoscience of phrenology. He advocated sterilization of inmates who came from criminal backgrounds or were judged as degenerates (sex offenders). Brockway also experimented with changing the caloric intake of inmates but the results of these experiments were inconclusive.

One of Brockway's greatest innovations was his system of classifying inmates. His system was based on intellectual capacity and physical abilities. Although his system seems rather crude by modern standards, it was innovative for its time. Inmates were placed in one of seven categories:

1. Five grade divisions based on the character as it is determined during the imprisonment;
2. Three school grades and twenty-eight school classes governed by the ascertained intellectual quality and proficiency alone;
3. Thirty-six trade divisions looking to industrial efficiency and economical engagement on or after the release;
4. Four battalions and sixteen military companies, which embraced all the able-bodied prisoners;
5. Five religious divisions according to the denominational affiliation;
6. Three general divisions and seventy-five subdivisions, interchangeable, of the manual training class;
7. Six designated groups of the very defective prisoners arranged on the basis of the physician's opinion of requirements.

Brockway became renowned the world over for his work at Elmira, most notably for his use of the indeterminate sentence and parole, but also for his bold experiments in prison management and rehabilitation. However, as was the case in Detroit, he encountered serious opposition close to home. Allegations of brutality surfaced again. Rather than deny the accusations, Brockway admitted that he and other prison officials utilized the "paddle" to administer corporal discipline to inmates who, Brockway thought, could be reached no other way. Corporal punishment, which the penitentiary was designed to stop, had fallen out of favor with most New York penal reformers. In addition, Elmira, like many prisons during the 1890s, was beset by crowding and fiscal problems. The problem at Elmira was aggravated by the massive immigration from Europe to New York shores during the 1880s and 1890s.

In 1900, New York Governor Theodore Roosevelt appointed a commission to study ways to improve New York prisons. According to the commission, one way was to surreptitiously ask Brockway to resign, which he did in July 1900, because of "disability due to old age." The Brockways stayed in Elmira with their widowed daughter. In 1905, he was elected mayor of Elmira on the short-lived fusion ticket. He served a two-year term and was defeated in his reelection bid.

Both before and after his term as Elmira mayor, Brockway spent much of his time delivering speeches and consulting on prison administration throughout the United States and Europe.

Jane Woodhouse Brockway died on February 8, 1911. Brockway's concluding words in his 1912 autobiography, titled *Fifty Years of Prison Service,* were: "At this writing, March 13, 1912, the eighty-fifth anniversary of the birth of my lifelong companion, I am indeed bereft and sorrowfully tarrying to meet my own last summons." Although he remained active, Zebulon Brockway lived his remaining years lonely and heartbroken. He died on October 21, 1920, in Elmira, New York, at the age of ninety-three.

SOURCES AND SUGGESTED READINGS

Zebulon Reed Brockway, *Fifty Years of Prison Service: An Autobiography* (New York: Charities Publication Committee, 1912).

Sandra Opdycke, "Brockway, Zebulon Reed," *American National Biography Online,* www.anb.org/articles, August 19, 2002.

Samuel Walker, *Popular Justice: A History of American Criminal Justice,* 2nd ed. (New York: Oxford University Press, 1997).

DISCUSSION QUESTIONS

1. After reading about Zebulon Brockway, how do you think idealism collides with reality in the area of penal reform?
2. What legacy did Zebulon Brockway leave for American parole?

CHAPTER 38

THOMAS OSBORNE
(1859–1926)

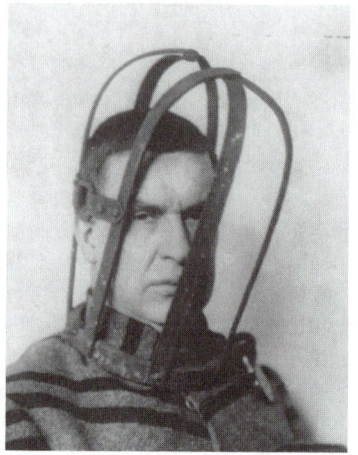

Those who try to improve the lot of people despised by most of society subject themselves to more criticism than do pioneers in most other fields. It takes a strong and unorthodox personality to withstand such negative scrutiny. Thomas Osborne was a correctional pioneer and had a very unorthodox personality. His personality would be his greatest asset as a penal reformer and it would also work to his detriment.

Thomas Mott Osborne was born on September 23, 1859, in Auburn, New York, the town whose name is attached to one of the major schools of correctional thought in the nineteenth century. Auburn was the home of New York's first penitentiary, built in large measure through the efforts of Thomas Eddy. Osborne was the third of four children born to Eliza Wright Osborne and David Munson Osborne. A sense of social conscience ran through Osborne's family. His great aunt was Lucretia Mott, one of the great philanthropists of American history. Another aunt was married to William Lloyd Garrison, one of the nineteenth century's most famous advocates of abolishing slavery.

David Osborne was a wealthy farm implement manufacturer. Osborne was a self-described "momma's boy" who enjoyed sewing and other traditionally feminine activities as a child. He attended public schools through grade school, even though his father could have afforded private schools. He did attend a private prep school and was admitted to Harvard in 1880. Like most young men at Harvard, Osborne assumed he was destined to enter business with his father after graduation. The idea of following in his father's footsteps did not appeal to Osborne, whose passions were football, dancing, the piano, and, above all, acting. Throughout his adult life he was active in the Unitarian Church and has been described by his biographers as spiritual but not an adherent to religious dogma. Osborne spent much of his time with other social liberals, like his uncle William Lloyd Garrison, who described Osborne as a natural leader, but somewhat cool and aloof. Osborne developed many other friendships while at Harvard, but he also made some important enemies that would later haunt him, including William Randolph Hearst, the future newspaper magnate that would persecute him in the press, and Theodore Roosevelt, the future New York governor and United States president.

After graduating from Harvard in 1884, Osborne returned to Auburn and reluctantly took over his father's business. In 1886 he married Agnes Devens, a young Bostonian. The marriage would produce four sons before Agnes's death in 1896. Osborne never married again, saying that to do so would be polygamous.

Soon after his father's death, Osborne gladly sold the business to International Harvester, which freed him to do the things he loved most, such as local theater and concert productions, local politics, and philanthropic endeavors.

Over the next three decades, Osborne dabbled in local politics and philanthropy. His first foray into public service came in 1885 when he was elected to the local board of education, a position he held until 1894. Though he came from a republican family, Osborne served as a delegate to the Democratic National Convention in 1892. He made an unsuccessful bid for lieutenant governor on the Citizen's Union Ticket in 1894. He was elected mayor of Auburn that same year.

Given Osborne's personality, it was strange that he enjoyed success as a politician. Politics is about slyness, conformity, and compromise, none of which was part of the Osborne personality. He was forthright and abrupt rather than sly, he seldom conformed to anyone's norms other than his own, and he tended to be very uncompromising when he believed he was right, a trait that made him many enemies. Even as a warden, he stubbornly opposed interference from his superiors who dared to question any decision he made. He detested the Tammany political machine that dominated New York City and the New York state legislature, and he did not get along with the most prominent New York politician of the era, Theodore Roosevelt. Roosevelt referred to Osborne as part of the "lunatic fringe" in New York politics, a phrase he made famous. Rudolph Chamberlain, author of Osborne's biography, wrote "Few men have ever been so unerring in their choice of the losing side." Osborne once wryly admitted that his great mistake in politics was failure.

Nevertheless he was reelected mayor of Auburn. He decided to discover firsthand some of the problems confronting Auburn residents on the streets but felt he could not do it adequately if citizens recognized him. So he embarked on what became his trademark, going about town incognito. He relied on his intuitive theatrical ability to alter his appearance and his personality, visiting Auburn streets and saloons in disguise and using the alias Harun-al-Rashid.

Not only was Osborne interested in improving living conditions for Auburn's citizens, he developed an interest in reform at the state penitentiary in Auburn. As a child he had visited the penitentiary but stayed away because the experience traumatized him, but he grew less scared and more interested in effecting positive change as he grew older. The turning point came in 1912 after he read Donald Lowrie's *My Life in Prison,* which crystallized all of his beliefs of prisons as a failure. Osborne once stated that trying to study criminals in prison was like studying "polar bears from one bear in a zoological garden." He saw courts and prisons not as assets but as impediments to reforming criminals. In a 1906 speech before the Congress of the National Prison Association at Albany, Osborne said that prisoners must have as much freedom as possible as only liberty can prepare a man for liberty.

The answer, said Osborne, was inmate self-governance, an idea he acquired from another penal reformer and prison warden named William George, who while serving as warden at a New York juvenile reformatory, created a system known as George's Junior Republic. It consisted of an inmate self-governance structure, a governance manual, and prison recreation programs. From the moment he began believing that inmate self-governance was the key to penal reform, Osborne never wavered; once he reached a conclusion or decision on any issue, no reasoning could move him.

Osborne once remarked that he had put himself "on trial in the court of conscience and a verdict has been rendered of 'guilty'—guilty of having lived for many years of my life indifferent to and ignorant of what was going on behind these walls." In September 1913 Osborne decided to put his words into action. Osborne went into the warden's office at Auburn prison at 10:00 A.M. He emerged as Thomas Brown, inmate #33,333x. Osborne, a former Auburn mayor and one of New York's leading citizens, had with the warden's permission assumed the identity of an inmate and was going to spend one week in prison at hard labor. Osborne contemplated going without the warden's knowledge, but fearing that the inmates would discover his identity and view him as a spy, he went in with the warden, staff, and inmates all aware of his true identity, even though he lived under an assumed name.

Osborne's sense of drama and theater served him well in his participant observer research endeavor. He completely immersed himself in the role of inmate Tom Brown. While he was working in the inmate factory, a tour group came through the prison, which included Osborne's nephew and some friends. Osborne's transformation into Tom Brown was so complete that he was not even recognized by his friends and his nephew. Osborne wrote in his diary, "Within Prison Walls," that he objected to having to sleep in his underwear without pajamas, to sleeping in a bed without linens, to throwing slop buckets with human waste into the river, and most of all to constantly being told what to do and where to go.

Osborne quickly adopted the inmate attitude toward the prison guards, all of who were aware of his true identity. Osborne thought some guards were brutal individuals, but that most were decent men working in a brutal system. In his diary he wrote that "in prison, as elsewhere, when men are dominated by fear, brutality is the inevitable result."

Osborne observed that men placed in solitary confinement entered sane but came out raving mad, so he faked a work stoppage to get himself placed in solitary. After spending three hours in solitary, a guard opened Osborne's cell door and told him he could leave. Osborne, by now even more immersed in his Tom Brown role, refused, out of pure hatred and resentment toward the man that opened the door. How dare he, thought Osborne, presume to deprive him of his freedom and restore it to him in just as authoritative a manner. He stayed an additional eleven hours. He emerged from solitary and later that week from prison, convinced that he had seen the light and that he would be God's instrument in making a difference in penal reform. Word of Osborne's experience spread to newspapers across the United

States, with some criticizing his efforts, some applauding; the *New York Times* called it "well intended yet ill advised."

In December 1913, with the warden's permission, Osborne started an inmate governance organization called the Tom Brown League. Forty-nine inmates served as the general committee, with "Tom Brown" elected as chair, even though he was no longer an inmate. The league drafted a set of bylaws and an organizational structure. The league would include forty-nine delegates elected every six months, with a nine-member executive board. A grievance committee, sworn in by the warden, vowed to promote fair dealing between inmates and guards.

The league changed its name to the Mutual Welfare League (MWL) and its membership stood at 1,350, each of whom wore a small green and white shield on his coat. All of their initial actions were radical and in many cases unprecedented in American prison history. Their first action was to ask for the right to hear music; they were successful in abolishing the rule of silence, which disallowed inmates from openly speaking with each other. They abolished "Blue Sunday," which required inmates to "rest" all day long in their cells, a maddening monotony that often led to fights on Mondays. The MWL established an inmate athletic program that allowed recreation facilities in the yard. Guards feared that the yard would be a location for settling scores; instead on the first day it was more akin to a family reunion as inmates finally openly communicated with each other after months and years of having to communicate in silence.

Although the MWL was a success in many respects, it suffered from some unsolvable problems. Contrary to the dictates of the league, inmates refused to report other inmate violations, still fearing the snitch label. Another problem was the manner in which violations were handled. Many guards still used physical punishment, much to the consternation of the league. Political infighting within the league became a problem as inmates jockeyed for power. The novelty of privileges wore off, and inmates began to take them for granted. Inmates whined more than before, which Osborne detested. The only thing he hated more than brutality was pampering.

Despite its shortcomings, word of the MWL spread around the country. On December 1, 1914, Osborne was appointed warden of New York's infamous Sing Sing prison in Ossining, with a mandate to establish an MWL there as well; Sing Sing inmates called their organization the Golden Rule of Brotherhood. The inmates requested weekend visitation, the right to purchase stamps and write to people not on a preapproved list, to have movies shown on Sunday, better facilities for the crippled and sick prisoners, and no more doubling of prisoners in small cells.

Accusations of scandal soon surfaced about Sing Sing. One was the allegation that regular inmates had been allowed access to talks with death row inmates about their cases. One instance especially irked the incumbent New York governor because he had been the prosecutor in that case. Osborne made no secret of the fact that he would stay up all night talking with death row inmates just prior to their execution, and he made no secret that watching an electrocution sickened him, although he was not categorically opposed to capital punishment.

The biggest blow to Osborne's administration came from the allegations made by an inmate named James Harvey, nicknamed "Jack the Dropper" because of his frequent participation in homosexual activity. Harvey claimed that he had "given himself" to twenty-one inmates for sex and that Osborne knew about it. Osborne did know about it, and he claimed that he punished the inmates involved, but his critics accused him of behaviors ranging from not punishing the misdeeds enough to actual participation in prison sex.

On December 28, 1915, Osborne was indicted by a Westchester County grand jury on charges of perjury, neglect of duty, and engaging in "various unlawful and unnatural acts with inmates of Sing Sing Prison, over whom he had supervision and control." The legal proceedings were widely reported in the press, with numerous character witnesses lining up behind Osborne, including some who he had known thirty years earlier at Harvard. Many former inmates and well-known penologists also lined up behind Osborne, as did many of the New York newspapers. Osborne was successful in painting prosecution witnesses as unreliable. Most of them were former prison inmates; some were former staff members. The charges were dismissed before the case came to trial.

Osborne returned to Sing Sing in July 1916 to a hero's welcome, but the damage to his reputation was irreparable, and he resigned in October of the same year. He continued his prison reform efforts, resuming his Tom Brown persona to investigate the naval prison at Portsmouth, New Hampshire, in January 1917. On August 1, 1917, he took over as warden at the prison, even though he had never been in the military, and he implemented an inmate self-governance structure there as well. One of the programs he established tied directly to his lifelong passion; he established an inmate drama club.

On March 17, 1920, he resigned from Portsmouth and returned to Auburn. He was sad to discover that conditions at Sing Sing had returned much to the way they were prior to his working there. The new warden had practically dismantled the MWL, making it a puppet organization for prison administrators. He toured the country, serving as consultant to state prison systems and giving speeches and consulting on prison matters throughout Europe. Speaking, not writing, was his forte, but some of his ideas were written down including his opinion of Sing Sing as an "ancient citadel of evil." Osborne stated, "we know nothing certain about any criminal except that he has done a particular act, and that he is a human being who cannot safely be left at large," but that society is in the dark about his moral guilt. He advocated two courts, one of condemnation, just to ascertain whether one committed a criminal act, and a second, called a court of release, that consisted of experts who should decide when to let a person out. Osborne did not believe that judges should be expected to decide both guilt and punishment in one proceeding.

The question of what rights prison inmates should have is still a thorny one for prison managers and all Americans. Although much of Osborne's dreams of prison reform went unfulfilled, many of his changes and reforms were not forgotten and some are still in evidence today. His approach to reform may seem naive to some today just as it did then, but Osborne felt the same dilemma that faces modern American society; he detested prisons but saw no acceptable alternative.

Osborne died on October 20, 1926, at the age of sixty-seven; he dropped dead on an Auburn street while walking home. Former Auburn inmates served as pallbearers at his funeral.

SOURCES AND SUGGESTED READINGS

Rudolph Wilson Chamberlain, *There Is No Truce: A Life of Thomas Mott Osborne, Prison Reformer* (London: Routledge, 1936).

John Jay Chapman, "Thomas Mott Osborne: Osborne's Place in Historic Criminology," *Harvard Graduates' Magazine,* Boston, 1927.

Frank Tannenbaum, *Osborne of Sing Sing* (Chapel Hill, NC: University of North Carolina Press, 1933).

DISCUSSION QUESTIONS

1. Should more correctional officials do as Thomas Osborne did, actually living in a prison for a short period of time to get a firsthand idea of what prison life is like?
2. What do you think of Osborne's ideas about inmate self-governance?

■ ■ ■ ■ ■

CHAPTER 39

MIRIAM
VAN WATERS
(1887–1974)

Of the pioneers discussed in this work, perhaps none had more obstacles to overcome
or faced greater controversy than those who
worked in prisons. No correctional pioneer encountered more controversy than Miriam Van
Waters, a turn-of-the-twentieth-century scholar who spent his life trying to improve the lot of female offenders in the community and behind prison walls by applying the principle of maternal justice. Her private life is shrouded in mystery and
intrigue as well, and it has made her the object of fascination to those who are interested in corrections and female sexuality.

Miriam Van Waters was born on October 4, 1887, in Greensburg, Pennsylvania, the daughter of George B. Van Waters, an Episcopalian minister, and Maud
Van Waters, who had six children, five of whom survived childhood. Miriam was
the second child, but her older sister died at age two, before Miriam was born. The
Van Waters family moved to Portland, Oregon, in 1891, where George Van Waters
served as rector of St. David's Episcopal Church for seventeen years. Miriam assumed many of the maternal duties over younger siblings, in part due to her
mother's physical and emotional problems, which often kept her away from home.

George Van Waters's embodied the social gospel movement of the early
twentieth century. The social gospel movement merged Christian ideals with a liberal social agenda in the belief that the two could rectify social inequalities. Between her father instilling in her a sense of social justice and her quasi-maternal
role in her family, Miriam's future as a matronly social reformer seemed preor-
dained from childhood.

Never one to accept the lowly position of so many women of her era, Van
Waters took the unusual step of earning a bachelor's and a master's degree in philosophy from the University of Oregon between 1905 and 1910. Unlike most
women of her era, she never married; she embarked on a career, thinking that wom-
anhood and public service were perfectly compatible, but she did not engage in behaviors that were thought to be radical at the time, such as smoking and wearing
makeup.

Van Waters enrolled at Clark University in Massachusetts in 1910, where she
earned her Ph.D. degree in anthropology in 1913. Although her degree was in anthropology, Van Waters was at heart a devoted social worker, but social work degrees were a rarity in the 1910s, though the field was growing rapidly at the time.
One of her greatest influences was Jane Addams, and Van Waters adhered to
Addams's belief that modern civilization lacked the appropriate channels for

youthful impulses. Based on her Boston and Portland experiences, Van Waters believed that recreation, education, and labor were proper treatments for criminal behavior, and that most criminal behavior was traceable to environmental factors, especially a dysfunctional home life, as opposed to the psychological and mental explanations that were in vogue at the time. While at Clark, she passed the Massachusetts bar exam, but never practiced law. Van Waters also studied medicine and interned at a mental hospital, but she was not a physician. Although she did not agree that biological or Freudian factors caused crime, she believed that the scientific method could be successfully applied to correctional intervention. She spent a year as a social worker in the Boston Children's Aid agency and worked as a probation officer in a juvenile court.

In 1914, Van Waters returned home to Portland and started work as superintendent at the Frazer Detention Home, a juvenile facility. She put her maternal justice ideas into practice there by eliminating corporal punishment, improving the diet for the juveniles, and improving sanitation and medical facilities. Far from being a strictly bureaucratic warden, she would take the children to her father's rectory for religious instruction; she would also take them on outdoor excursions to her family's summer camp. Van Waters worked herself into a state of exhaustion by 1915, though more than likely she had contracted tuberculosis. Like so many penal reformers, her efforts were short-lived. After she left, the home reverted to the jail facility it had been before.

Van Waters moved to Pasadena, California, to seek medical treatment. In 1917, she was well enough to take a civil service job at the Los Angeles County Juvenile Hall working with young delinquents. Los Angeles County was experiencing greater growth than any other county in the United States because of western migration, which brought increased delinquency. She worked as a juvenile court counselor until 1920 when she was appointed juvenile court referee, a quasi-judicial position. While in Los Angeles, Van Waters earned a national reputation for implementing her maternal justice ideals, seeing young delinquents as children that needed a mother figure. She gave keynote addresses before major gatherings of correctional and juvenile professionals; she taught part-time at UCLA. She served on the 1926 Harvard Crime Survey at the request of future Supreme Court Justice Felix Frankfurter. Van Waters headed the juvenile section of the Wickersham Commission, a first-of-its-kind task force established by President Herbert Hoover that studied criminal justice in the United States. Van Waters hired medical and psychiatric staff; she sought to improve morale among children by emphasizing the "redeeming power of recreation." Van Waters was praised by the *Los Angeles Times* and *Good Housekeeping* for her "unfailing courtesy, and chivalry." Although her administration was popular with the press and with most offenders, she was not popular with much of the staff, even surviving one poisoning attempt from a disgruntled staff member.

In her widely acclaimed 1925 book *Youth in Conflict,* Van Waters presented her views on the causes and remedies for juvenile delinquency, especially among females. She blamed social disorganization in large cities, popular entertainment that promoted sexual promiscuity in females, impoverished environments, and maintained that all children were innately good and that delinquents could trace most of their problems to bad parenting. Because of its sense of vision, its straightforwardness and its emphasis on compassion, *Youth in Conflict* became required reading in the United States and the United Kingdom for many who studied delinquency. Van Waters's *Parents on Probation,* published in 1928, was not as critically acclaimed as *Youth in Conflict* but it also sold well.

Van Waters never married nor did she bear any children, but in June 1929 she adopted a seven-year-old girl that she met in court; she changed the girl's name to Sara Ann Van Waters. It was also during the late 1920s that she met Geraldine Thompson, a native New Yorker fifteen years her senior. The two women became lifelong friends and pen pals. Their letters have become the object of fascination to gay studies students and Internet surfers today. Very few American women would publicly admit having a lesbian relationship during the 1920s, especially a woman like Van Waters who was in the public eye and worked with delinquent children. Whether the two actually had a sexual relationship is not known, but allegations of being a lesbian would haunt her in later years.

Van Waters was appointed superintendent of the Massachusetts Reformatory for Women in Framingham in March 1932. An outspoken critic of the fifty-five-year-old reformatory, Van Waters was determined to make social service, not punishment, the prime focus of the institution. She faced an uphill battle. The 1930s was the era of the Great Depression and few people cared about reforming female prisoners. Creating a homey environment was also of paramount importance to Van Waters, who stated that the goal of the "modern institution must be to have institutional life approximate outside normal life as nearly as it can."

Van Waters tried to run the reformatory like a school, even referring to the inmates as students. Good behavior led to increased privileges, including access to letters and better meals. The "school" had a library, an unusual feature for prisons of the 1930s. Van Waters actively solicited community involvement in the reformatory. She encouraged local women's groups to volunteer in the facility. In another groundbreaking move, Van Waters initiated an internship program for recent college graduates.

Despite the public shift toward social conservatism, Van Waters continued the Social Gospel tradition of blending Christian ideals with secular correctional intervention. She adhered to what she called the Social Gospel truth: Every child is a child of God and is capable of redemption. She championed "Christian penology," stating that she tried "to dwell within the Law of the Kingdom of God on earth—and laws of health, medicine, psychology and social work." She defied a purely clinical approach, choosing to blend spiritual and psychological approaches to rehabilitation. Van Waters, ever possessive of the scientific mindset, viewed her reformatory job as a research experience and as a model of progressive education. She believed that the students could learn from doing. She had them work eight-hour days making flags and clothing, staging plays and concerts, and organizing a

Glee Club. In a time long before the study of black history was in vogue, she encouraged the African American inmates to study black history, and she encouraged volunteer work from the National Association for the Advancement of Colored People, a radical idea for its time. Van Waters invited an editor from the *Atlantic Monthly* to teach a poetry class. She initiated a program for mothers and babies, allowing mothers frequent contact with their children, even those who bore their children out of wedlock. The reformatory had a nursery with lessons in health care and maternal education. She organized a weekly mothers club so inmates could gather and share concerns.

The prevailing thinking in most correctional circles is to discourage offenders from having contact with one another. Prison and parole authorities usually discourage inmates from having contact with each other once they leave the facility. Van Waters, however, encouraged some women to continue friendships after release, and she encouraged them to maintain contact with the reformatory as well. Van Waters established a transition program for those whose release dates were approaching and set up domestic cleaning jobs for them in the community. Some inmates even got jobs working at the prison after they were released.

Van Waters openly criticized prison sentences for women convicted of alcohol offenses and prostitution, calling such behaviors social rather than criminal problems. She expressed outrage at women being sent to prison for lewd conduct when their offense was publicly admitting to bearing a child out of wedlock and then actively pursuing their former lovers for child support.

Van Waters never embraced the role of a typical warden; she never approved the use of force as a punishment. She dreaded visits from the parole board, because they tended to pay more attention to past failures than recent inmate progress. She stuck unfailingly to her liberal convictions; her only compromise was that she appointed a few political cronies to appease some of her superiors.

Despite her lofty ideals and strong outward appearance, Van Waters was full of self-doubt as indicated in some of her diary entries. She was frustrated by not being able to create a kingdom of heaven on earth, and being unable to change lives or the social system that produced female criminals. Her attempts to make a kingdom on earth collided squarely with real-world opposition in 1948 in a very public and embarrassing way.

Deputy Commissioner Frank Dwyer charged that a former reformatory inmate had been beaten to death as a result of homosexual jealousies, when the death had initially been ruled a suicide. The incident opened up other charges, such as the misuse of inmate labor, employing former inmates to work in the facility, and the charge that Van Waters was condoning and perhaps participating in homosexual relations among inmates. William Randolph Hearst, the famous San Francisco newspaper magnate, joined the bandwagon, saying that Van Waters had been chased from California to Massachusetts for homosexual scandals.

The incident became a public battle to preserve Framingham, with many women's rights advocates lining up behind Van Waters and others lining up against her. America was swept up in anti-Communist hysteria, and anything that smacked of perversion also smacked of communism and things that were deemed to be un-American. Some also charged that Van Waters associated with Communists in Framingham.

Van Waters was fired from the reformatory on January 7, 1949. In firing her, Governor Paul Dever charged her, in addition to the charges just mentioned, with being too liberal with the inmates by allowing them to attend movies, eat in restaurants, and the like, but the greatest focus was on sex within the prison. Van Waters remained warden pending appeal. Between January 13 and March 11, 1949, the hearings became a cause celebre for "women's libbers" around the country. A woman known only to penologists and social workers suddenly became a household name because of the press coverage.

Van Waters won her appeal, but her life was never the same. One positive result from the hearings was the founding of the Friends of Framingham, a group of Van Waters supporters who successfully lobbied for legislation that legalized inmate apprenticeship. Still the accusations of rampant homosexual behavior persisted. A Smith College student entered the prison posing as an inmate for ten days, and she emerged with stories of vicious homosexual behavior among the women in addition to narcotics smuggling. Van Waters was further hurt by the death of her daughter in an auto crash in 1953. Van Waters began an intimate relationship with Helen Bryan, a former inmate in 1953, but Bryan left when the affair was made public and she was suspected of Communist sympathies.

Van Waters's behavior would seem abhorrent to many modern correctional authorities, as it did then, but Van Waters simply could not deal with the increasing bureaucratization of prison administration. She did not understand the need for keeping her personal and professional lives separate. She had always viewed the reformatory as a sort of home for women who had been rejected by mainstream society, and she was sincere in her attempts to nurture and rehabilitate them in a homelike atmosphere. By the 1950s she was dealing with a different class of inmate than the ones she worked with in the 1930s. Escapes became more frequent as did racial conflicts between inmates.

Miriam Van Waters retired from the Framingham Reformatory in October 1957. She lived with two former Framingham inmates for several years, and she continued to support inmates and their children. She collaborated with Burton Rowles in a sanitized, journalistic autobiography titled *The Lady at Box 99*. In 1972 Van Waters suffered a stroke that left her in poor health until her death on January 17, 1974, in Framingham at the age of eighty-six.

SOURCES AND SUGGESTED READINGS

Estelle B. Freedman, *Maternal Justice: Miriam Van Waters and the Female Reform Tradition* (Chicago: University of Chicago Press, 1998).

Burton J. Rowles, *The Lady at Box 99: The Story of Miriam Van Waters* (Greenwich, CT: Seabury Press, 1962).

DISCUSSION QUESTIONS

1. What would modern correctional officials think of Van Waters's conduct, especially her fraternizing with former inmates under her control?
2. Van Waters's sexuality was a beneath-the-surface issue throughout her career. Should the sexuality of a correctional official be a factor now as it was during Van Waters's lifetime?

CHAPTER 40

▪ ▪ ▪ ▪ ▪ ━━━━━━━━━━━━━━

JOSEPH RAGEN
(1897–1971)

The history of American prison reform is strewn with good intentions gone awry. Well intended reformers like Thomas Osborne and Miriam Van Waters have been frustrated in their attempts to make prisons democratic centers of humanity, both because of inmates that abused the privileges afforded them and because of outsiders distrustful of people that are overtly kind to convicted criminals. Many prison officials have gone in the opposite direction, preferring brutality to anything smacking of kindness and humaneness. Others have sought a balance, preferring a more impersonal, bureaucratic approach devoid of physical brutality but also devoid of any semblance of affection. This was the approach of Joseph Ragen, the warden of the Illinois Penitentiary at Stateville from 1936–1960, referred to by some as the world's toughest prison of its era.

Joseph Ragen was born on November 22, 1897, in Trenton, Illinois. He grew up in an area of southern Illinois referred to as "Little Egypt," a very poor area replete with dirt roads, miners, and farmers. Ragen's father, William, was the exception, spending most of his working life on the public payroll, just as his son would. William Ragen served as sheriff of Clinton County for three terms and as judge for one term.

Ragen, twenty years old when the United States entered World War I, served in the Navy during and just after the war. In 1922 he began working for his father as a deputy sheriff, a position he held until 1926, when he was elected sheriff of Clinton County. Shortly before he was elected sheriff, Ragen married Loretta Heyer, who would bear two children. Like many small town sheriffs of the 1930s, the Ragens lived in a small apartment on a floor above the county jail. Ragen served as sheriff until 1930. Ragen's biggest challenge, like many Prohibition-era law enforcers, was bootleggers. Most of the bootlegging Ragen faced originated in East St. Louis, Illinois, a haven for bootleggers. Ragen left law enforcement in 1930, preferring the office of Clinton County treasurer, also an elected position and one he held until 1933.

During his tenure as sheriff and treasurer, Ragen made political contacts in Illinois that would serve him well in years to come. He also learned the art and science of politics. In 1933 he received a gubernatorial appointment as warden of Menard Penitentiary in Chester, Illinois, a town sixty miles southwest of Clinton County. Despite being only thirty-six years old when he took over as warden, Ragen impressed his superiors, including the governor, who in 1935 appointed him

210

to the most lucrative but daunting task in Illinois corrections—running the Illinois State Penitentiary at Stateville.

On making his initial visit to Stateville, Ragen realized he had an extremely daunting task before him. One of his first observations was the smell. The odor of pet smells was noticeable, as was the smell of marijuana, which was not only smoked openly but was actually grown on prison grounds. An atmosphere of blanket permissiveness and a complete lack of discipline pervaded Stateville, both among the staff and inmate populations. Inmates were allowed to come and go at will, even in places where it was clear they did not belong. Many inmates spent most of their time sitting in the prison yard. Organized gambling operations operated openly. Liquor was sold openly. Prison gangs ran the institution. Shanties with posted signs reading, "officers not wanted" served as gang headquarters. Unauthorized conjugal visits took place with the consent of officers. Bribery was rampant, part of which Ragen attributed to the fact that guards only made $112 per month. Neither inmates nor guards were properly attired.

Upon arriving to work the first day, the thirty-year-old Ragen was told by his embittered predecessor, "Hello, warden. There's an execution tonight. It's your job now." Ragen's first task was to not only supervise an execution, something he detested because he did not believe in capital punishment, but to mobilize officers to control a near riot among those wanting to view the execution.

Ragen took immediate and strict control of Stateville, vowing to radically change the attitudes and behaviors of the staff and the inmates. Many of his measures are part and parcel of prison administration today, but were not very common in the 1930s. He announced a ten-point plan for running Stateville:

1. *Eliminate politics from the hiring of guards and prison personnel.* Although Ragen's ability to practice politics in his own right and for the good of the facility was one of his strengths, he knew that many corrupt and inefficient hires and promotions were based on political connections. Ragen had the strong backing of the governor in taking this first step. His strength was picking loyal middle managers. One former staff member stated, "There's not a lieutenant that don't think the Warden's God." Civil service reforms that were under way in state government helped as well.

2. *Build an efficient guard force through careful selection and set up training facilities for new guards.* "As of now, the first guard to appear on friendly terms with an inmate will be fired," was one of Ragen's first announcements as warden. Far from viewing this as brutal, Ragen saw this measure as a way of preventing favoritism and corruption among staff. Only selected guards were allowed to use force, and only in cases where an officer had been struck. Ragen forbad staff from associating with inmates, former inmates, or the families of inmates. One officer was reprimanded for letting a recently released inmate buy lunch for him. He issued a staff handbook that contained 89 general rules and 1,222 specific rules. He fired guards that were not physically fit. The off-duty lives of officers came under

Ragen's control as well. They were not allowed to loiter or gather in places of ill repute such as gambling houses.

3. *Keep the inmates working.* Ragen, who saw Stateville as a potentially self-supporting enterprise, allowed no idle gangs, where, he observed, trouble develops. Inmates were required to work either on farms, in coalmines, or in one of the industries in the prison. He believed that idle hands are the devil's playground and that many inmates had never learned good work habits.

4. *Closely regulate all prisoner movements.* Regimentation became the rule at Stateville. All inmate motions were subject to control. Ragen had to control 3,500 inmates in one-tenth of a square mile. He successfully lobbied for an increase in the number of staff. He reached his goal of having 300 officers and 100 clerks and foremen, a ratio of roughly twelve inmates per staff member.

5. *Enforce tight restrictions on the things an inmate may possess.* Ragen allowed no money in the prison yard at any time, for any reason. Liquor and gambling businesses were shut down. Guards tightened up on contraband enforcement.

6. *Give every prisoner equal treatment.* Stateville housed Illinois's most notorious criminals, some of whom had acquired hero status within the inmate population and in the free world. Guards and inmates alike had placed inmates in a hierarchy, something that Ragen officially forbade. Whether this was a good move is debatable. Even Ragen's protégé, future Texas prison boss George Beto, believed that prison bosses must recognize and choose inmate leadership so as not to allow inmates to pick leaders themselves.

Although inmate assaults declined under Ragen's administration, they did not disappear. In 1936, Richard Loeb, who with codefendant Nathan Leopold had committed the infamous "thrill kill" murder of Bobby Franks a few years earlier, was murdered by another inmate. The killer claimed that Loeb had made sexual advances toward him, and he was acquitted at trial. Ragen recognized and appreciated the work of Nathan Leopold, who collaborated with academicians to produce some of the leading works on criminal psychology during his stay at Stateville. Leopold described Ragen as strict but fair.

7. *Place first emphasis on security, secondary emphasis on rehabilitation.* Ragen believed that before the latter could be accomplished, the former must be present. A strong work ethic and educational opportunities were the prime ingredients in Ragen's rehabilitation scheme.

8. *Permit no prison bargaining groups or other intercessories.* Each prisoner was allowed to approach the warden directly with requests and complaints. At no time were inmates allowed any organizations of any kind. In a model diametrically opposed to that espoused by reformers like Thomas Osborne, Ragen abolished all inmate organizations unless he officially approved them. This made all inmates equal and placed total control in the hands of prison administration.

9. *Anticipate trouble and, when possible, deal with it beforehand.* If trouble occurs, deal with it with quick, direct measures and no show of weakness. At no time, even during a time of trouble, were inmates allowed a voice in the operation of the prison. Ragen was a tall, heavy, imposing man. His mere presence cowed some abrasive inmates and guards. He walked around the prison unaccompanied and without a weapon, seeing it as a show of strength and authority.

10. *Operate the prison with a maximum of cleanliness and neatness, both as a matter of health and as an essential part of security.* Pets were removed from the prison; inmates and staff alike were required to make cleanliness and neatness an absolute priority.

Ragen was widely hailed for his reforms at Stateville, but a new governor in 1940 caused Ragen to fear for his job. He resigned in March 1941, and, with the Department of Justice worried about sabotage and espionage as American involvement in World War II seemed inevitable, Ragen got a job setting up internment camps for illegal aliens. He also worked for a short time as superintendent of security at a car company.

Ragen was rehired at Stateville in October 1942; thanks to an escape by a well-known criminal named Roger Touhy, which cost the warden his job. When Ragen returned, Touhy told him, "Well, Warden, I got your job back for you." For the next twenty plus years, Ragen, who gradually assumed celebrity status within the field of penology, ran Stateville, making it a model prison for observers from around the world. Texas prison boss George Beto modeled his system after Ragen's. Celebrities, including actor Jimmy Stewart and boxer Rocky Marciano, visited Stateville, which expanded to include several prison units, 5,000 inmates, and almost 500 staff.

Stateville's prison industry included the largest farm in Illinois. Each year it produced 300,000 gallons in its cannery, 4 million pounds of soap, 1 million yards of fabric, plus mattresses and shoes. The prison had a bookbinding center, a stone quarry, a sheet metal factory, and a barber college. Ragen still ruled inmates and staff with an iron hand, exercising more authority over his nonunionized staff than most wardens would be able to do today.

Ragen was a sought-after speaker, sharing his views on prison administration and crime causation to audiences around the country. He had an overbearing presence as a speaker, stemming from his imposing physical stature, his direct gaze, and his deliberate methods of speaking. His views on the causes of crime reflected Midwestern conservative ideals. A religious man himself, Ragen advocated church attendance as a method of preventing crime. He saw the dissolution of the traditional family structure as an important factor in delinquency. He once said, "We must all help the children of today, who may be the criminals of tomorrow unless all members of society take an interest in them. Long experience has taught me that proper discipline in the home and in the school are important. A lack of discipline has permitted more than one boy to start on a career of crime." Compared to many other prison administrators in the United States who still ran brutal chain gangs, Ragen expressed relatively liberal ideas. He advocated the use of the indeterminate sentence, even for murderers. He spoke out against the death penalty, believing it did not deter crime. In short, Ragen stopped being a disciplinarian and became a penologist.

By the 1960s, the Ragen era in Illinois had faded. Inmates and staff alike gained more rights through unionization and litigation. Some labor and business interests complained that inmate labor constituted unfair competition. Although he was still well known in Illinois political circles, a new political era had dawned. Ragen was asked to resign in 1965 at age sixty-eight. He continued consulting and making occasional public speeches after his retirement. Joseph Ragen died on September 22, 1971, in Joliet, Illinois, at the age of seventy-four.

There was nothing fancy or stylish about Joseph Ragen. Throughout his life, Ragen was very down-to-earth, so down-to-earth that he did not fly on airplanes because he wanted to keep his feet on the ground, literally. He cared little for international travel, save Canada, because he thought America had everything that one needed. He was not flashy or flamboyant and did not try to win popularity contests, either with prison inmates or with the people that worked for him. Some called him the J. Edgar Hoover of prisons. Like Hoover, he inspired great loyalty from many of the people who worked for him, many of whom went on to assume positions of leadership in prisons around the country. Although no prison warden can or should aspire to be popular with inmates, Ragen, despite his no-nonsense bureaucratic style of prison administration, had his ardent admirers among that group as well. One inmate wrote a poem about Ragen that read:

> There's a Man in charge at Stateville
> Who has changed things all around
> From a madhouse to a prison
> Wherein Hope and Cheer abound.

SOURCES AND SUGGESTED READINGS

Donald Clemmer, *The Prison Community* (Boston: Christopher, 1940).

Gladys A. Erickson, *Warden Ragen of Joliet* (New York: Dutton, 1957).

James Jacobs, *Stateville: The Penitentiary in Mass Society* (Chicago: University of Chicago Press, 1977).

Nathan Kantrowitz, *Close Control: Managing a Maximum Security Prison* (Guilderland, NY: Harrow and Heston, 1996).

Joseph E. Ragen and C. Finston, *Inside the World's Toughest Prison* (Springfield, IL: Charles C. Thomas, 1962).

DISCUSSION QUESTIONS

1. Ragen was not a well-traveled man and was in many respects the prototypical dry bureaucrat. Was that a help or a detriment to his work as a prison official?
2. What do you think of Ragen's assessment of the American family and its impact on crime?

CHAPTER 41

CLINTON DUFFY
(1898–1982)

Few Americans have their destiny seemingly mapped out for them from birth, but there are exceptions. Clinton Duffy, who served as warden at California's San Quentin prison, was one of those exceptions. Although he took a few detours along the way, Duffy was destined for a career in prison work. The same can be said for many people who work in corrections, who may have gotten into such work due to the influence of a parent, but Duffy's commitment to kind treatment of inmates in a prison long associated with nothing but the darkest side of human nature makes him a notable figure in the history of American corrections.

Clinton Truman Duffy was born on August 4, 1898, in San Quentin, California, in the town's prison village. He was the son of William Duffy, a farmer turned prison guard who had a thirty-five-year career at San Quentin. Clinton Duffy grew up in the San Quentin prison village, or "prison town" as it was often called, living in a prison environment and associating mostly with the families of other prison employees. He attended San Quentin Grammar School, which was primarily populated by children of other prison employees. Rather than playing cops and robbers or cowboys and Indians, Duffy and his friends would play "guards and prisoners," with most of the children wanting to be the inmates because they knew and liked them.

One of the children with whom Duffy grew up was Gladys Carpenter, the daughter of a guard. The two childhood sweethearts were so immersed in prison culture that when they played make believe, they would climb the warden's terrace and pretend to be "Mr. and Mrs. Warden," a childhood dream understood only by those who grew up in a self-contained prison village like San Quentin. However, to Duffy, being a warden was a pipe dream; he thought he had as much chance of being warden as he did of "winning the Chinese lottery."

One of Duffy's vivid childhood memories was walking the streets of the San Quentin village and hearing prisoners cry in pain from hours spent in a straight jacket. Duffy had vivid memories of prisoners being punished for reading newspapers, being forced to wear straight jackets from their neck to their ankles, and being forced to swallow laxatives and wear a straight jacket for a week, which sometimes resulted in the inmate being permanently crippled.

Convinced that the son of a prison guard could not rise to prominence in San Quentin circles, Duffy enlisted in the Marines after graduating from high school and served during World War I. After the war ended in 1918, Duffy returned to the California Bay Area and took a job in Sausalito with the Northwestern Pacific Railroad. He married Gladys Carpenter, by then an elementary school teacher in San Quentin, on December 31, 1921. Their son, Jack, was born in November 1922.

Duffy continued working for the railroad and then for a construction company until 1929, when he visited San Quentin's prison to notarize a document. While there he was offered a job as secretary/assistant to the warden; Duffy began his duties on November 1, 1929. Duffy's career in prison work began not as a guard, as it had with his father and father-in-law, but as warden's assistant, a position he would keep for seven years.

During this time, Duffy's correctional philosophy took shape, but he could do little to put it into practice. The original prison at San Quentin was a floating hulk that settled at San Quentin Point during the San Francisco gold rush of the 1850s. It had been a political football for California politicians since its inception, and was often staffed by incompetent political hacks that knew or cared nothing for humane and secure administration of penal facilities, prisons being in their infancy in the nineteenth century. Corporal punishment and filthy living conditions were the hallmarks of San Quentin from its beginning to Duffy's arrival in 1929. One of the most unpleasant aspects of Duffy's position as assistant was attending executions, which he was forced to do because his warden boss refused to witness them alone. Although he grew up in San Quentin, there were certain of the prison's darker aspects with which Duffy was not familiar. In 1930, Duffy went to San Quentin's dungeon for the first time. What Duffy found shocked him, despite his lifetime of living practically within the confines of the prison. Inmates lived in deplorable conditions with no light or ventilation; officers would poor buckets of lye on inmates as punishment, and how long an inmate stayed in the dungeon was a matter of officer discretion.

One of Duffy's duties as assistant was notifying inmate families of bad news, such as an inmate death. Duffy developed strong sympathies for the wives and mothers of inmates, realizing that incarceration inflicted punishment on people besides the inmates themselves. In addition to developing an anti–corporal punishment stance, Duffy also developed an antipathy toward the death penalty, in large measure because of the prospect of wrongfully convicted inmates being executed. Once, on hearing that new evidence had been found that pointed to an inmate's innocence, the governor's office telephoned Duffy and instructed him to halt a scheduled execution. Frantically, Duffy phoned the execution chamber only to find out that the inmate had already been hung. After informing the governor's representative that the execution had already taken place, Duffy was told to forget about the phone call and that the governor's office would deny the call had ever been made should word leak out. On another occasion, an inmate hung himself in his cell shortly before Duffy found a letter on the warden's desk from an appellate court stating that his conviction had been reversed.

Scandals plagued San Quentin throughout the 1930s. In 1935, four inmates shot, beat, and robbed the warden at his official residence and escaped with his car. The local district attorney killed one escapee; two more were convicted and hung, and another was given a life sentence. That same year the Secret Service busted a major counterfeiting ring operated by San Quentin inmates. A new warden brought his assistant with him, which resulted in Duffy's reassignment to the position of historian to the Board of Prison Directors; he also served as a secretary to the Board of Prison Terms and Paroles. Although the warden was replaced, little changed. Inmate crime continued to flourish as did abusive behavior by staff, and the infamous dungeon was still in full operation.

As scandal, inmate unrest, and tales of brutality continued to filter from San Quentin to the governor's office in Sacramento, the governor, tired of dealing with San Quentin headaches, fired the prison board for which Duffy worked. However, a suggestion was floated that Duffy, since he had spent most of his life within San Quentin walls, serve as temporary warden at San Quentin. Even though appointing a career San Quentin employee and resident seemed to be the least likely way to change the mindset at San Quentin, Duffy was appointed for a thirty-day period starting July 13, 1940, while state officials took time to look for a permanent replacement.

Those who thought that Duffy would continue business as usual were surprised. Duffy was a quiet, nonthreatening, staid person without swagger or a macho facade. His meek demeanor belied a fierce sense of integrity and liberal idealism that was put into action at San Quentin. His first act was to abolish the dungeon. He fired six guards for brutality. He banned the use of whips, rubber hoses, and all forms of corporal punishment, which had long been a staple of San Quentin discipline and which was common in most American prisons at the time. Duffy abolished head shaving for inmates, a holdover from California's Spanish colonial period. He abolished the wearing of numbers on inmate's backs, thinking it was dehumanizing to refer to humans as numbers.

Duffy's changes were acclaimed by some, but not by all, especially those who were old enough to remember him as a child and viewed him as a young meddler. He galled and amazed veteran guards by walking through the recreation yard alone, something totally unheard of at San Quentin, especially in light of the near death of one of Duffy's predecessors only five years earlier. Duffy improved the quality of food provided to inmates, and he insisted that all inmate clothes be ironed. The actions of the young (age forty-two) Duffy impressed state government officials so much that he received a four-year appointment in September 1940. Duffy and his wife, Gladys, took up residence at the official warden's mansion; his childhood pipedream had come true.

Although he still opposed capital punishment on moral (not a deterrent, fell heavily on the poor) and legal (lengthy appeals, chance of error) grounds, Duffy took steps to at least make the death penalty more humane in its application. He authorized the expenditure of $15,000 to install a gas chamber and abandoned the gallows. Duffy detested presiding over executions, calling hangings in particular a "brutal spectacle." He allowed condemned inmates a few last minutes of exercise (one last breath of fresh air) and a chance to write a last letter. As warden, Duffy encountered some of the most infamous inmates in California penal history. One of these was Caryl Chessman, one of the twentieth century's first celebrity death row inmates who fought his case in the courts for twelve years, an extraordinarily long length of time for that period.

What Duffy was renowned for was not his opposition to capital punishment but his unswerving devotion to the idea of prisoner rehabilitation. Prior to Duffy's time, rehabilitation was primarily characterized by efforts to convert inmates to Christianity. While a professing Christian, who believed that inmates could benefit by exposure to religious teachings, Duffy was not a strong believer in the forced feeding of religious instruction. Instead, he relied mostly on secular attempts to rehabilitate inmates.

Giving the inmate a sense of self-worth through constructive activities and appropriate medical treatment were Duffy's primary means of assistance. His efforts were buttressed by the 1942 election of Earl Warren as governor. Warren, a former Alameda County district attorney, former state attorney general, and future chief justice of the United States, endorsed Duffy's attempts to rehabilitate inmates. Duffy ordered corrective surgery for inmates with obvious physical deformities whenever possible. He set up an inmate debating society; Caryl Chessman was one of its best debaters. Duffy allowed the establishment of an inmate newspaper, the *San Quentin News*. It was California's first prison newspaper that was sold to the public. For a $1 per year subscription fee the public could get a look at "Mr. Average Inmate," which was entirely appropriate according to Duffy since "Mr. Average Citizen" was footing the bill for prisons. The paper was free to inmates. Duffy contributed a column to the paper, usually to quiet untrue rumors that might be spreading through the prison. Duffy allowed inmates to have radio headsets. They could listen to radio programs from six to nine each evening, including some programs that originated within the prison. The San Quentin prison radio show, titled "San Quentin on the Air," debuted on KFRC in San Francisco on January 12, 1942. Within weeks it spread to more than 200 radio stations across the United States, thanks to the Mutual Broadcast Network. The program's primary feature was songs written and performed by San Quentin inmates.

A bedrock of Duffy's penal philosophy was instilling a good work ethic for the inmates. He believed that most inmates lacked good habits and thus found crime the easiest way to get what they wanted. One key to instilling good work habits was having an education. Duffy implemented literacy classes, thinking that an inmate's morale increased when he learned to read. Early in his administration, he recruited schoolteachers from the local high school. He established grammar school and high school diploma programs at San Quentin through San Rafael High School. Duffy established college preparatory programs through the University of California, which prepared many inmates to enter the university after their release.

Duffy worked for the increased use of parole, primarily because of the "guiding hand of the parole officer," which was so important to protecting public safety after the inmate's release. One of Duffy's most notable contributions came about as a result of an inmate survey he oversaw. He found that 65 percent of newly admitted San Quentin inmates claimed either that they were alcoholics or that alcohol played a part in the commission of their crime. Duffy conceded that alcohol does not make anyone do anything, but believed it took "off the breaks of what is within you." All prison employees, not just counselors and psychologists, received substance abuse training.

Duffy took the radical step of inviting representatives from Alcoholics Anonymous (AA) to visit San Quentin once each month, eventually establishing an AA chapter within the prison. Prison wardens across the country promptly criticized Duffy for doing something—bringing drunks in to talk with other drunks—that is now commonplace in American prisons. Duffy's AA experiment helped make his name known around the country, and he often spoke to AA groups outside the confines of San Quentin, where he would sometimes meet former inmates who thanked him for starting an AA chapter at San Quentin.

Duffy lobbied the California legislature for a bill that allowed inmates to make their own hobby goods and sell them to other inmates. The result was the San Quentin Hobby Association, which produced belts, wallets, picture frames, and other goods, the proceeds of which often went to inmate's families. Duffy's efforts attracted the attention of famous gossip columnist Walter Winchell, first lady Eleanor Roosevelt, and blonde bombshell actress Mae West, whose visit to San Quentin evoked considerable excitement among the inmates. Other celebrities, including actors William Powell, Glenn Ford, Edward G. Robinson, Caesar Romero, and baseball manager Leo Durocher also visited San Quentin. Duffy's reputation also garnered a visit from Harry Houdini, the twentieth century's greatest escape artist.

Duffy's reputation increased to the point where Doubleday and Company invited him to write his story for publication, which he did (with Dean Jennings) in *The San Quentin Story,* which was released in 1950. In 1954, he was contacted about an hour-long television pilot based on his life and career. As the idea developed, an additional eighteen minutes were added. The result was a motion picture titled *Duffy of San Quentin.* Actor Paul Kelly, who had served time at San Quentin for manslaughter in the 1920s, portrayed Duffy. A sequel, also starring Kelly, titled *The Steel Cage,* was released later. In 1959, Gladys Duffy wrote her account of life at San Quentin titled *The Warden's Wife.*

Duffy retired in 1952, after serving twelve years as warden at San Quentin. In subsequent public speeches and books, Duffy, as he always had, advocated that prison systems should be in the business of making better neighbors, always making people mindful of the prospect that anyone could have an ex-convict as their next door neighbor.

In his later years Duffy savored the tales of inmates he encountered. One inmate, a former prizefighter who fought under the name Kid McKoy, was serving time for the accidental killing of his girlfriend. According to California folklore, McKoy once got into a bar fight with a man who did not believe he was the real

Kid McKoy. After McKoy floored the man in the bar, the man admitted, in a line that was repeated in the local press, that his assailant was "the real McKoy," and the term *real McKoy* became a part of everyday language, thanks in part to McKoy's efforts at self-promotion.

Duffy filled his books and speeches with colorful stories that could be told by many people who work at large prisons like San Quentin. What set Duffy apart from the others is his allegiance to rehabilitation and his able administration as a warden of one of the country's most notorious prisons. His allegiance to the rehabilitative ideal may seem quaint or even contemptible by today's standards, but Duffy was way ahead of his time in many respects. For those who think that such a philosophy could not work, it should be noted that during Duffy's twelve-year tenure as warden, San Quentin did not experience a single major riot or disturbance. Duffy, who took the bold step of walking through the recreation yard alone when he first became warden and made a habit of dining with inmates at least three nights each week while he was warden, was not a naive do-gooder; he was a competent and no-nonsense prison manager. After working for penal reform and as an advocate for AA for many years, Duffy died in 1982 at the age of eighty-two.

SOURCES AND SUGGESTED READINGS

Clinton Duffy, "Prisons, Prisoners and Parole" (Los Angeles: Pacifica Tape Library, 1963).
Clinton Duffy and Dean Jennings, *The San Quentin Story* (Garden City, NY: Doubleday, 1950).
Gladys Carpenter Duffy, *Warden's Wife* (London: Gollancz, 1959).

DISCUSSION QUESTIONS

1. Could Clinton Duffy thrive as a warden in today's correctional environment? Why or why not?
2. If you had your choice, who would you hire as warden, Clinton Duffy, Joseph Ragen, or Thomas Osborne? Why?

CHAPTER 42

GEORGE BETO
(1916–1991)

"He was tough as nails, but he had a big ol' bleeding heart." This is a description of George Beto, a man as paradoxical as he was articulate and colorful. He enjoyed a good laugh but could just as easily cower a subordinate, an inmate, a college professor, or a student with one quick stare. He called himself a liberal, but was once referred to by a critic as "enlightened, but reactionary in some of his correctional practices." He proudly presided over the rise of a world-renowned prison system, only to watch it systematically dismantled by social change and judicial mandate.

Many of the attempts to shape and reform America's lawbreakers are rooted in religious ideals. Many of the pioneers in eighteenth- and nineteenth-century American penology were deeply religious people. The word *penitentiary* was coined in the hopes that inmates would seek penitence, or divine forgiveness, for their wrongdoings. This belief in the redemption of wayward humankind has dominated American corrections. One person whose life and career held true to this lofty ideal was George Beto, the "accidental penologist" who directed the Texas prison system from 1960–1972.

George John Beto, the son of Louis and Margaret Beto, was born in Hysham, Montana, on January 19, 1916. Soon after his birth, his family moved to Rockford, North Dakota, where they lived until George was three. Most of Beto's childhood was spent in Lena, Illinois, where his father served as a Lutheran pastor for thirty-one years. The frugality, compassion, and staid Midwestern morality that were a part of Beto's childhood in the household of a Lutheran minister would define his life and career.

Beto embarked on a career as a Lutheran minister while still a teenager. After attending high school in Milwaukee, Beto attended Valparaiso University, a Lutheran university in Indiana, where he received his bachelor's degree. After graduating from Valparaiso, Beto enrolled at Concordia Seminary in St. Louis. In 1939, shortly after graduating from Concordia Seminary, Beto took a job as instructor at Concordia Lutheran College in Austin, Texas, teaching history from 1939–1949. While there, Beto met Marilyn Knippa, whom he married in 1943 and with whom he would raise four children.

In 1944, Beto was ordained as a Lutheran minister at St. Paul's Lutheran Church in Austin. He worked part-time as St. Paul's assistant pastor. In 1949, at the age of thirty-three, Beto became president of Concordia Lutheran College, a post he held until 1959. While serving as president, Beto earned a master's degree in medieval history, and a Ph.D. degree in educational administration from the University of Texas at Austin.

Working and living in Austin, Texas's capital, was a fortunate coincidence for him, and a fortuitous circumstance in the history of the Texas penal system. In Austin, Beto became immersed in state politics and in the operations of the Texas penal system. In 1953, at the request of Texas governor Allen Shivers, Beto began work on the Texas prison board, where he met Texas prison director Oscar B. Ellis. Thus began Beto's career as a penologist—at age thirty-seven—and his career as an influential mover and shaker in Texas political circles. Beto's ability to influence politicians would serve him and the Texas prison system well for the rest of his life.

Shortly after his appointment to the Texas Prison Board in 1953, Beto attended a meeting of the American Correctional Association in Toronto. There he met Joseph Ragen, the warden at Illinois's Stateville Prison, who Beto called his correctional mentor. The two men established a friendship that would endure for many years. They shared similar values, a similar worldview, and a similar philosophy on how prisoners should be treated and how prisons should be administered. Although Beto had a very keen intellect and a knack for moving comfortably in political circles, he knew little about running prisons. Ragen, who was nationally renowned for running one of the country's toughest prisons, would be his greatest influence in prison philosophy.

Following Ragen's suggestion, the governor of Illinois appointed Beto to the Parole Board. While living in Illinois, Beto remained active in affairs of the Lutheran Church, serving as president of Concordia Theological Seminary in Springfield. During his term as president, he surveyed prisons in Germany (Beto spoke fluent German), France, England, Denmark, and Holland. While on his occasional travels to Chicago on church business, Beto would stop and spend the night with Ragen in Stateville. His Parole Board experiences, the interactions with Ragen, and the trips to Europe helped shape Beto's correctional philosophy. Strict rules, security, and a hands-on managerial approach were characteristic of this philosophy, paired with a strong belief in the redemptive power of education, a strong work ethic, and religious influence.

Beto's return to the Midwest would prove temporary and short-lived. Texas prison boss O. B. Ellis died in November 1961. Despite Beto's lack of experience at actual prison management, he was offered Ellis's job but initially turned it down out of loyalty to the Lutheran Church and Concordia Theological Seminary. Beto accepted when he was allowed to simultaneously serve as chief chaplain. He assumed the directorship of the Texas Department of Corrections (TDC) on March 1, 1962, vowing that he would not serve longer than ten years.

Beto set about shaping the Texas prison system in his own image and not by accident. One book that strongly influenced Beto's managerial style was Chester Barnard's 1938 work called *The Functions of the Executive*. Echoing Barnard, Beto once said, "Organizations are largely the shadows of their executives. It does not matter whether one is talking about Harvard U, the Chrysler Corp, or the TDC. The executive's skills and abilities, his sense of mission and dedication to duty, are decisive in determining how—and how well—an organization runs."

The force of Beto's personality was probably the most notable aspect of the TDC during the 1960s. Beto stood at about six feet three inches but somehow seemed even larger up close. Beto had sharp, piercing eyes, which it was once said, "could freeze a man with a stare." He had a knack of establishing great rapport with whomever he came into contact with, inmates and staff alike, and he had a great talent for remembering names. Beto acquired the nickname "Walking George" because of his penchant for showing up at TDC units unannounced and walking about prison yards and hallways to talk with whomever he met, both inmate and staff. It seemed impossible, thought some TDC staff, that Beto was only one man. In a state as large as Texas, with prison units scattered hundreds of miles apart, it seemed impossible for one man to make so many visits to so many prison units. The use of a private airplane for TDC use helped Beto implement his hands-on management philosophy.

Another book that significantly influenced Beto's management of prisons was *Inside the World's Toughest Prison* by Joseph Ragen, which was released in 1962 just as Beto was assuming control of the TDC. Ragen's influence was very evident in Beto-run prisons. Like Ragen, Beto was very security-conscious, but he strongly advocated correctional intervention, thinking that prison environments could be used as change agents for prison inmates. In contrast to some prison bosses that tried to run prisons as quasi-autonomous fiefdoms apart from the rest of the world, Beto was sensitive to the place of corrections in the criminal justice system, recognizing prisons as an integral part of the judicial system and state government. Through his experience interacting with state government leaders in Austin, Beto was able to bend the political environment to help him and the Texas prison system. He made it a point to maintain good relations with the incumbent governor, be it a democrat or a republican. He lobbied for legislation that allowed the prisons to make and sell many of the goods that were produced on prison farms and shops. Beto set out to run the Texas prison system as an efficient business, primarily in the area of agriculture but in other areas as well. In doing so, Beto was able to do what few prison bosses have done; he made his prison system an international showcase and a source of pride among state government leaders.

Beto's "Texas Control Model," as it came to be called, emphasized strict obedience to the rules, a healthy work ethic, and education. Under Beto, all prisons were maximum security and were run accordingly. Beto's prisons were organized along paramilitary lines. Inmates were required to walk between lines painted on floors rather than moving randomly down the center of a corridor. Inmates were required to shave and bathe regularly, and they had to wear white uniforms at all times. All illiterate inmates were required to go to school one day per week. All physically able inmates were required to work in the field for the first six months of their sentence. The Beto philosophy extended to personal relations with inmates.

He once stated, "You must keep some social distance between the inmate and the free law-abiding citizen. I never shake hands with an inmate." The basic idea driving his policies and practices was rehabilitation, which meant, "making people who were never responsible be responsible." Beto once said, "Some of these men don't even know how to buy a shirt, so we teach them."

In addition to prison farms that produced much of the food for TDC, TDC industries included a dental lab, a garment factory, a bus repair shop, a tire recapping plant, a coffee roasting plant, a wood shop, and a records conversion plant. Perhaps to a greater degree than any other prison system in the nation, Beto helped make the Texas system self-sufficient, due in part to Beto's skillful lobbying among Austin politicians. In 1963 he persuaded Governor John Connally to enact a state's use law that required state agencies to buy goods made by prisons. TDC's manufacturing output increased from $600,000 in 1964 to $6 million per year in 1972. Under Beto, the TDC had the first fully accredited prison education program in the United States; it also had a work release program. The TDC also offered junior college and vocational technology classes.

TDC became the focus of attention from distinguished penologists and the news media, not only from Texas media outlets but from national outlets including CBS television, which described Beto as being as comfortable with a prison manual as with a Bible, and as a man who could quote the classics in one breath and chew out subordinates in the next.

Beto's model was a mixture of carrots and sticks; punishment and rewards were swift and certain. Beto believed in being very liberal with the granting of good time, but he brokered no dissent or protests from inmates that were reluctant to follow the rules. Beto fell back on another of his favorite books, written by Martin Luther, titled *Secular Authority: To What Extent It Should Be Obeyed,* in which Luther wrote: "If wrong is to be suffered, it is better to suffer it from rulers than that the rulers suffer it from their subjects." Beto did not recognize the right of prisoners to rebel, he tolerated no complaints about quality of food, and he did not grant inmates any say in how prisons should be run.

Soon after succeeding Ellis, Beto was faced with a situation that tested his ideals. A group of inmates at Texas's Harlem farm refused to work. After talking seemed to do no good, Beto sent several wardens on horseback with a wet rope and put them to work, and soon the inmates were back to work. This prompted one inmate to remark, "Old Beto couldn't be beat, the preacher man with a baseball bat in one hand, a Bible in the other."

Despite his strict belief in an unbridgeable status gap between inmates and staff, Beto claimed that he was just as interested in staff abuses as he was inmate misconduct. During his frequent walks through Texas prisons, he would receive and act on letters from inmates that he met while walking. Abusive behavior on the part of staff was a detriment to the rehabilitative ideal, and it contributed to an overall breakdown of order, an absolute taboo in prison management. Beto believed in the idea that prison authorities should wield worldly power to protect and guide those who could not do it themselves. Beto told penologist John DiIulio, "In order to offer a range of educational and other programs, it is first necessary to establish and maintain safety and security. Work and recreational opportunities can be pursued meaningfully only in an orderly environment. 'Orderly' does not mean repressive. Quite to the contrary, it means simply that degree of formal control which inmates have a right to expect and society has a duty to provide."

Beto expected dedication from prison staff. Beto would often walk into a prison cafeteria, at any hour of the day or night, taste the food to see if it was satisfactory, and then leave. Although Beto's style of running Texas prisons would have its critics, especially after his departure, no one could accuse him of lack of dedication to the work ethic that he preached to staff and inmates. He worked constantly, only taking one brief vacation in ten years.

Another hallmark of Beto's prison was the building tender system, a system that he inherited from previous TDC administrations. The building tender system utilized tough veteran inmates, called *building tenders,* to maintain order and discipline in Texas prisons. Many staff and some outside observers advocated the building tender system, but others, including many inmates, detested it. Building tenders, or BT's, were often given a free hand in controlling their assigned area, and they sometimes employed brutal means of maintaining order and imposing discipline. The BT system would eventually become a lightning rod for criticism of the TDC, but Beto defended the system, claiming, "Either you pick your leaders or they do." Beto had no illusions about the depravity of some inmates. Regarding especially loathsome inmates, Beto was known to say that the man was so low he would "rape a snake through a brick wall."

Beto's Texas system became the object of admiration from correctional administrators the world over. Beto was sought out frequently—by other southern states to the federal government to the United Nations—for advice. Beto was a frequent speaker for both correctional and religious organizations. He chastised churches and America's religious community for not doing enough to help prison inmates or to prevent crime from occurring. Beto said that churches had failed with convicts, and that American churches had become middle-class social organizations that did not reach the type of people that wound up in prison. Beto claimed that Christians have historically ignored prisoners, criticizing the church as being a spectator rather than a participant in crime prevention. He advocated a return to the *koinonia* ideal, which refers to a vibrant first-century Christian church that depended on fellowship, not programs, buildings, rituals, or protocol.

Beto lamented the poor state of the American family, saying that the "family character-building role is gone." He said, "We live in the enlightened and, in a sense, highly regulated twentieth century. Nevertheless, our marriage laws are in many respects vestiges of the nation's first frontier. Common-law marriages and casual relationships which cannot and should not be dignified with the name 'marriage' are too frequent." He did not oppose welfare but saw it as a necessary evil because of men that would not support their children. Beto said, "Interviewing hundreds of convicts who were either parties to or products of these common-law marriages has persuaded me that while little can be done to prevent people from living like animals, the reasonable interests of society require that they be prevented from propagating their kind. Rigidly controlled sterilization may be a solution." He criticized the court system in urban areas for using rural prisons as dumping grounds for the mentally ill and retarded.

Beto, ever the devoted Lutheran, was an unapologetic believer in the power of spirituality and religion in the lives of inmates. During his directorship, he served as chief chaplain. He strongly encouraged worship, even offering incentives and rewards for inmates who attended worship activities, although his encouragement had limits, some of which were questionable and some of which did not stand up to legal scrutiny. At one point in the 1960s he directed officials to place all Muslims at one unit, ostensibly as a way of encouraging them to practice their religion together, but it also may have been a method used to exercise control over the Muslim inmates. A Buddhist inmate named Cruz filed suit against Beto and the TDC for denying him the opportunity to worship and proselytize. Beto's defense was that Cruz's advocacy of Buddhism would create disorder. Cruz won his legal battle against Beto. A federal court found Beto liable for unlawful intimidation and unlawful punishments, and awarded $10,000 to thirteen inmates, in part due to denial of legal access.

Beto retired from the TDC in 1972, leaving its directorship to his hand-picked successor, W. J. Estelle, and fulfilling his vow to leave the directorship after a ten-year stay. Beto took a position as professor at Sam Houston State University, with whom the TDC had enjoyed a long relationship for training and educating TDC staff. The university is located in Huntsville, a small east Texas town dominated by prison facilities. He traveled frequently, serving as federal monitor for Alabama prisons, and as an evaluator of prisons throughout the Middle East and East Asia. Beto remained a frequent presence at TDC facilities, especially those in the Huntsville area, and he watched with dismay as the system he had so proudly presided over seemed to disintegrate. Judicial mandates, brought about by several inmate lawsuits, and the social changes that were sweeping many American prisons brought about a TDC that differed radically from the system built and maintained by Beto. The Texas system was still the object of worldwide fascination, but the fascination with TDC industry and efficiency gave way to the fascination with inmate lawsuits and prison gangs, the new dominant force in TDC prisons, the BT system having been abolished by court order.

While at Sam Houston State, Beto taught corrections courses, mostly to graduate students. He served as dean of the College of Criminal Justice on two occasions. He established an endowed chair that bore his name. Beto, a strict but compassionate taskmaster with prison inmates and staff, carried his TDC philosophy into the classroom. He enjoyed informal lunches, banter, and debate with students, having a particular affinity for Asian students, but he brokered no foolishness. Unlike other professors, he did not allow food or drink in his class, and any tardy student would find himself on the receiving end of Beto's piercing glare and sharp wit.

In 1991, Beto retired from Sam Houston State and moved to Austin to serve as chief of chaplaincy services for the Texas Youth Commission. On November 9, 1991, Beto gave his last formal address, at Valparaiso University, his alma mater. Unfortunately, for all of his efforts, Beto was left with the same realization as many other correctional reformers throughout American history. In his speech, he stated, "As I reflect on forty years involvement in the criminal justice system in one capacity or another, I cannot escape the conclusion that the system is no better than it was almost one-half century ago." On December 4, 1991, Beto died suddenly of a heart attack while dressing for work. One Texas prison unit bears his name, as does the Criminal Justice Center at Sam Houston State University, a Texas Youth Commission halfway house, and the Academic Center at Concordia University in Austin.

SOURCES AND SUGGESTED READINGS

Dan Richard Beto and Melvin Brown, Jr., "An Accidental Penologist's Assessment of Correctional Leadership," furnished by the authors.

George J. Beto, "Prison Administration and the Eighth Amendment," speech delivered at Valparaiso University School of Law, November 9, 1991.

George J. Beto, "Probing Prison Problems," *Lutheran Witness,* March 1968.

Ben Crouch and James W. Marquart, *An Appeal to Justice*: *Litigated Reform of Texas Prisons* (Austin: University of Texas Press, 1989).

Paul M. Lucko, "Beto, George John," *The Handbook of Texas Online,* www.tsha.utexas.edu, April 15, 2002.

DISCUSSION QUESTIONS

1. What do you think of Beto's encouraging inmates to participate in religious activities?
2. How did Beto blend the worlds of academe and prison work? Why is that significant?

CHAPTER 43

■■■■■

JANE ADDAMS
(1860–1935)

Many of the subjects in this book possess (or possessed) a strong social conscience, one that enabled them to work toward detecting and reacting to crime in some extraordinary ways. It also takes a strong social conscience to work toward the prevention of crime, especially when it involves working hand in hand with the lowest echelon of society. Jane Addams possessed the rare gift of being as comfortable with Chicago's poorest turn-of-the-century immigrants as she was with the highest political and business leaders of her day in Europe and the United States. With these talents, this controversial author and social reformer made a name for herself that lives on to this day, and the phrase "Hull House" has been indelibly etched in the annals of literary and criminal justice history.

Laura Jane Addams was born on September 6, 1860, in Cedarville, Illinois. Jennie, as her family called her, was the eighth of nine children born to John Huy Addams and Sarah Weber Addams. John Addams was an active republican Quaker, who would be the greatest influence on Jane Addams's career and life. John Addams stressed the importance of helping those less fortunate than he, and he instilled a sense of social responsibility in his daughter. John Addams owned a grain mill, served as a bank president, owned interests in railroad and insurance companies, and was one of the founding members of the Republican Party. A vocal opponent of slavery, John Addams served in the Illinois state senate and was a close friend of Abraham Lincoln, another pioneering Illinois republican. Sarah Addams died in 1863, leaving Jane's rearing to her older siblings until her father remarried in 1868 to Anna Haldeman.

Jane Addams enrolled in the Rockford Female Seminary in 1877, one of the few institutions of higher learning for women in the United States. Addams served as class president for four years. In 1881 she was the school's first graduate and its first valedictorian. The same year she enrolled at Women's Medical College in Philadelphia. Her career there was cut short by health problems, but she recovered well enough to visit Europe from 1883 to 1885.

Throughout most of her life, Addams was a strong adherent to the Christian faith, her adult life spent in the Presbyterian Church following a Quaker childhood, but Addams criticized modern religion for being long on dogma and short on love and self-sacrifice. Frustrated by a desire to effect social change and the limitations placed on most women in her day, Addams expressed her frustrations and opinions through a medium that suited her well, writing. She began writing in earnest for college publications while at Rockford and continued writing from the time she was in her late thirties until her death.

A gifted writer, Addams was not content to live the life of someone who wrote about life and advocated social change. She was determined to bring about social change through her own efforts as well. While in Europe Addams visited Toynbee Hall in London, a settlement house for London's poor, especially its destitute women, both those who ran away from home and mothers with no other means of support.

As the Industrial Revolution and increased urbanization swept the United States, Addams was appalled at the living conditions of Chicago's poor. Like Dorothea Dix, Addams was frustrated, in part because of her own experience, at the paucity of opportunities for women in American society. Determined to do something about it and a firm believer in the idea of noblesse oblige, Addams established Hull House, a settlement house in Chicago set up along the lines of London's Toynbee Hall in 1889. The name came from the previous owner of the house, Charles Hull, who had the mansion built in the 1850s. Addams and Hull House became the topic of great interest and discussion throughout the United States. Poor immigrants, widows and single mothers, and other women who had no other place to turn came to Hull House and received nurturing, care, and a chance for self-improvement.

Addams's original intention was to make Hull House a place where women intellectuals could have esoteric discussions on literature and poetry with poor, uneducated women, but real-world problems altered, without derailing, that intention. Hull House offered practical services such as day-care services, basic literacy, medical care, and legal services. Nevertheless, Hull House was a center of cultural education and activity. Art exhibitions, small theater productions, music classes, and recitals were a part of life at Hull House. A coffeehouse and gymnasium were added in 1893. For several decades, thousands of men, women, and children participated in Hull House activities. Most of them were part of Chicago's lower class; many were poor immigrants who stood little chance of being exposed to anything but a life of abject poverty had it not been for Hull House.

Although she was aloof in personal interactions, one of the most remarkable aspects of Addams's personality was her ability to interact not only with street people and poor immigrants, but also with Chicago intelligentsia. This was one of the keys to the success of Hull House. Addams succeeded in bringing in some of Chicago's leading political theorists, musicians, artists, writers, and poets to Hull House to share their ideas with each other and Hull House residents.

Not content to let Hull House be her sole endeavor, and in sync with the Progressive Era thinking that characterized America during the 1890s, Addams plunged headlong into an effort to improve social and living conditions for Chicago's poor. One of her concerns was garbage collection, which was atrociously inadequate, and resulted in the breeding of all sorts of diseases in Chicago's slums. In Addams's view, the problem was the politicization of the city's sanitation department. She worked for civil service reform to reduce the role of politics in that department, the goal being to improve the overall quality of life for Chicago's poor. Addams was appointed garbage inspector for Chicago's nineteenth ward in 1895.

While Hull House was a remarkable achievement in many ways—one of which was that it was the forerunner of the modern halfway house, an integral tool used by the modern criminal justice system—Addams can lay claim to even greater achievement in the area of juvenile justice. A passion of Addams's was the state of Chicago's justice system, especially with respect to the city's youth. There was no separate court or correctional facility for children. Addams was one of the prime movers in the establishment of America's first juvenile court system in 1899 in Chicago.

Addams spread the word about Hull House through prestigious publications, including the *Atlantic Monthly, Christian Century,* and the *North American Review.* In 1902, she published her first book, *Democracy and Social Ethics.* In the book, Addams expressed her view that the human race should and was moving toward a higher social morality, and that members of a democracy are bound to move together. Addams wrote *Newer Ideals of Peace* in 1907, *The Spirit of Youth and the City Streets* in 1909, and her crowning literary achievement, *Twenty Years at Hull House,* in 1910.

Dedicated to her father's memory, *Twenty Years at Hull House* describes the formative influences in her life, her father and Abraham Lincoln, the latter she credits with giving America its title to democracy. Addams exhibited her emotional side in describing the heart-wrenching lives of many people who sought care at Hull House. Between 1910, when it was first published, and 1935, the year of Addams's death, *Twenty Years at Hull House* sold 80,000 copies. Called by at least one critic "an indispensable classic of American intellectual and social history," the book reflects Addams's gift for blending social thought and action. She viewed Hull House as true democracy in action, exemplifying the best undertakings in philanthropy and civic and educational action, and as an attempt to socialize democracy.

Between 1890 and 1910, Addams spent much of her life and directed most of her energy to improving life in Chicago, capped by serving on the city's school board from 1905 to 1909. After the release of *Twenty Years at Hull House,* Addams, now internationally famous, continued her work at Hull House but focused less energy there and more on other issues and causes. She worked for women's suffrage, convinced that voting women could undo many of the world's problems. Addams traveled to Budapest, Hungary, in 1913 and was the keynote speaker in a women's suffrage meeting. In 1912, she attacked prostitution, another social evil visited on women, in *A New Conscience and An Ancient Evil.*

As the 1910s wore on, Addams became involved in efforts to promote world peace, against a rising tide of warmongering that was sweeping through Europe and which culminated in the outbreak of World War I in 1914. Addams, who had met Leo Tolstoy (the author of *War and Peace*) during a visit to Russia in 1896, was impressed with his belief that war only begat misery. She campaigned for peace throughout the United States, but encountered opposition and downright hostility for her outspoken opposition to America's 1917 entry into World War I; her opponents included many former friends from America's progressive sector. Addams's pacifist attitude during World War I cost her dearly in terms of popularity, and it cost Addams her alliance with former President Roosevelt. Addams viewed war in general as a pathetic means of resolving human differences and as antithetical to the positive evolution of the human race.

After the war ended, Addams formed the Women's International League for Peace and Freedom, and supported the creation of the League of Nations. Although she was the most admired woman in America prior to World War I, second only to Thomas Edison among all Americans, her reputation never fully rebounded. In 1919, a year characterized by very strong antisocialist, antiradical, and antiforeign sentiment and actions, the New York state legislature blacklisted Addams in reaction to her defense of anarchists and radicals. Addams had never wavered in this area. As far back as 1901, she defended Abraham Isaak, an anarchist arrested for his alleged involvement in the assassination of President William McKinley. Hull House, which was populated by many Russian Jewish immigrants (an ethnic group often accused of having a disproportionate number of political radicals), had long been attacked as a hotbed of radical political and social thought, but the accusations became stronger and more intense during World War I. Addams was viewed by military hawks as a dangerous radical and as a traitor, a reputation enhanced by her support for socialist Eugene Debbs's unsuccessful presidential bid in 1920.

Nevertheless Addams continued to work, serving with future President Herbert Hoover in his famine relief efforts for Europe. Hoover was elected to the presidency in 1928, less than one year before the stock market crash of 1929, which signaled America's spiral into the Great Depression of the 1930s. President Hoover bore the brunt of American anger about the Depression. In 1932, Franklin Roosevelt, his democratic challenger, trounced Hoover. While Hoover was abandoned and vilified by millions who had supported him four years earlier, Addams did not abandon her old friend, publicly advocating Hoover's reelection.

Addams's energies in the 1920s were focused on promoting peace and attending and speaking at conferences dominated by women's groups aimed at avoiding future wars. As we've learned from history, such efforts were futile. After only a brief respite from war during the 1920s, World War II erupted in Europe and Asia in the 1930s. However, Addams succeeded in repairing the damage to her reputation that had occurred during World War I. Her determined peace efforts were rewarded in 1931 when she shared the Nobel Peace Prize with Columbia University's Nicholas Murray Butler for her European famine relief efforts.

Addams never married. Her close relationship with Mary Rozet Smith has given rise to speculation that Addams was gay. Although Addams and Smith were very close, spending summers together and alone at Smith's home in Maine, it is unlikely that their relationship was sexual. As with many single women of America's nineteenth and early twentieth centuries, the more likely scenario is that the two women were lovers, but in a nonsexual context; at that time sexual relations between women were seldom seriously contemplated in private, let alone acknowledged or discussed in public.

Addams was diagnosed with a tumor in 1931 and underwent surgery to have it removed. The initial diagnosis was promising, but the surgery ultimately was not successful. Yet Addams lived on for several years. She died of intestinal cancer on May 21, 1935, at the age of seventy-four.

Addams might scoff at being labeled a crime prevention pioneer; her thinking went beyond the mundane activities of administering a system of criminal justice, yet her efforts to improve the life of America's (and the world's) poor can be labeled just that. Hull House and other settlement houses of that era were the forerunners of the modern halfway house, or at least a distant vision of what such a facility could or should be. Her most important contribution to the administration of criminal justice may be her role in the creation of the Illinois juvenile justice system. While many who work in criminal justice can take issue with Addams's political philosophy, all will agree that Jane Addams is synonymous with many of the reforms and changes of America's Progressive era, including the founding of its juvenile justice system.

SOURCES AND SUGGESTED READINGS

Jane Addams, *Twenty Years at Hull House* (Urbana, IL: University of Illinois Press, 1990 [1910]).

Jean Bethke Elshtain, *Jane Addams and the Dream of American Democracy* (New York: Basic Books, 2002).

Victoria Bissell Brown, "Addams, Jane," *American National Biography Online,* February 2000, www.anb.org/articles, August 19, 2002.

DISCUSSION QUESTIONS

1. How has the juvenile justice system changed since Jane Addams's time? Would she approve of the contemporary juvenile justice system?
2. In what ways did Jane Addams embody the Progressive era?

CHAPTER 44

▪ ▪ ▪ ▪ ▪ ▬▬▬▬▬▬▬▬▬▬

BENJAMIN LINDSEY
(1869–1943)

America's first juvenile court was founded in 1899 in Cook County, Illinois, but Illinois was not the only state that experimented with juvenile courts at the turn of the twentieth century. While the idea of establishing separate courts for juveniles was gaining strides around the country during the Progressive Era (1890–1920), the efforts of several pioneers were very instrumental in shaping the modern juvenile justice system. One pioneer was Benjamin Lindsey, the eccentric judge that presided over the founding of the juvenile court in Denver, Colorado.

Benjamin Barr Lindsey was born in Jackson, Tennessee, on November 25, 1869. His father was Landy Tunstall Lindsey, a former Confederate captain; his mother was Letitia Barr Lindsey, the daughter of a Tennessee plantation owner. Ben Lindsey's childhood was unstable, mostly because of his father. Landy Lindsey was the likely source of his son's unconventional way of thinking. When Ben was five, Landy Lindsey had his entire family converted from the Episcopal faith to Roman Catholicism, a highly unusual move in predominantly Protestant Tennessee.

Landy Lindsey's next unusual action was moving his family to Denver, Colorado, in 1880, in part to escape the dominance of his father-in-law. Benjamin's stay in Denver was short-lived. He was sent to boarding school at Notre Dame, where he would remain for two years until his father lost his job with the railroad, forcing Benjamin to return to Tennessee to live with his maternal grandfather. He stayed in Tennessee for three years, attending college prep at Southwestern Baptist University, no doubt an influential factor in Lindsey's subsequent decision to abandon the Roman Catholic faith, while still retaining a strong Christian value system. Lindsey was a gifted public speaker, winning medals in prep school and college.

Lindsey returned to Denver in 1887 because of his father's deteriorating health and financial problems. His father committed suicide while Lindsey was still in his teens, leaving Ben, the oldest of four children, the head of his family. Throughout his short-lived college career, Lindsey had been fascinated with the study of law, and he did not let the absence of a college degree keep him from embarking on a legal career. Like many lawyers in his day, Lindsey prepared for the legal profession by getting a job in a law office as an office boy and studying the law while at work and during his spare time. While working in R. D. Thompson's law firm, Lindsey also helped make ends meet by delivering papers in the morning, working as a janitor in a Denver office building at night, and working in a real estate office.

Lindsey struggled both financially and emotionally as a young man. The burdens of heading his family, trying to advance his own life, and his despondency over his father's suicide at times were too much for him. He attempted suicide once by pointing a gun at his head and pulling the trigger; fortunately the gun jammed and Lindsey had a change of heart. Despite the burdens placed on him, Lindsey passed the Colorado bar exam in 1893. In 1894, Lindsey represented his first criminal defendants. He served as court-appointed council for two young boys accused of burglary. From then on, Lindsey carried a passion for helping children get a fair shake in court.

He started his own firm in 1896, in partnership with Fred Parks, a well-known democrat in Denver. Parks's political connections, coupled with Lindsey's personal success in his new profession and his own passion for Democratic Party principles, led to Lindsey's appointment as public guardian for Arapahoe County in 1899. His job involved making arrangements for the care of abandoned or delinquent children. It laid the foundation for his future work as a juvenile court judge. In 1901, Lindsey was appointed to a judge's position, becoming at age thirty-two the youngest judge in Colorado history.

A seminal event in the career of Judge Lindsey occurred during the winter of 1901. A teenaged boy was brought before him charged with stealing several lumps of coal. The boy offered no defense and had been caught in the act by a railroad detective. Lindsey promptly sentenced the boy to a reform school, which prompted a blood-curdling scream from the boy's mother, who was seated in the courtroom. Badly shaken, Lindsey had the boy's sentence suspended, even though doing so was not legal under Colorado law at the time. That night, Lindsey visited the boy's home, where he found the boy's father dying from lead poisoning. The family lived in cold, abject squalor. The boy had stolen coal to heat his family's home. Lindsey left, shamefully mindful of the way the justice system was perceived by the poor people of Denver. Shaken by this experience and mindful of his own childhood poverty, Lindsey resolved to make a difference in the lives of young people who came before his court.

Lindsey was as much a spokesperson for the newly emerging field of sociological jurisprudence as he was a judge. Unlike most judges of his day, he looked beyond the statute books in trying to reduce crime. He searched for crime's root causes, much as sociologists in his day were doing. Like most of the juvenile justice pioneers and sociologists at the turn of the twentieth century, Lindsey believed that juvenile crime was primarily the product of economic injustice, and that treatment, rather than punishment, was the proper remedy. Lindsey took pity on many of the young offenders that came before his court. In cases of theft, he would investigate the reason the young person chose to steal. If he found that severe poverty or a dysfunctional home life was tied to the theft, he would often go easy on the youngster, sentencing him or her to probation instead of incarceration.

One of the crowning achievements in Lindsey's career and an act that has cemented his place in history is his writing and promoting of legislation to establish a juvenile court in Denver. He requested that all defendants under age sixteen be sent to his court, where he would informally suspend their sentence and place them under supervision. He was elected to the post in 1900 and was continuously reelected until 1927, taking time along the way for an unsuccessful gubernatorial bid in 1906. In 1907, Colorado officially established a juvenile court. While serving as juvenile court judge, he married Henrietta Brevoort in 1913. The Lindseys had one adopted daughter.

Lindsey's colorful antics on the bench made good newspaper copy. Lindsey's tendency to view the world through a different lens than that used by most criminal justice officials also made for good reading. Once, an eighteen-year-old boy, who was a frequent "visitor" to the Denver police station, appeared in Lindsey's court. Lindsey thought the boy was amenable to rehabilitation. For years, Lindsey had utilized his own honor system. Under his honor system, those sentenced to confinement were allowed to leave the court free from constraint, commitment papers in hand, under the promise that they report to the jail at the appointed time. This was done for two reasons: one to aid in the rehabilitation of the young offender by building character and two, to fight the graft in local jails which stemmed from the fees that jailers would charge indigent inmates. This particular eighteen-year-old was ordered to jail but was allowed to leave on his own upon promise that he report to jail later that night.

Since the boy had been in jail thirteen times and had attempted to escape at least once, the jailer was surprised when the boy reported to jail as ordered. The next morning, a police captain told the judge that he would fail if he took any more chances with the boy. Lindsey asked why he would fail, and the captain replied that the boy had been in jail thirteen times. Lindsey asked the captain, "Well, didn't it ever occur to you that the jail had failed thirteen times?"

Not only did Lindsey practice innovative ideas for juvenile offenders, he passed on some of his ideas about juvenile crime to adult offenders. He pioneered legislation holding adults legally responsible for contributing to the delinquency of a minor. In 1903, Colorado enacted the Adult Delinquency Act, which put the idea into law. He tried to keep juvenile offenders from the glare of public scrutiny, a practice that continues to this day. It was one of many "Lindsey Bills" that the Colorado legislature would act on in the early part of the twentieth century.

Lindsey, who detested institutions because he thought they were breeding grounds for crime, only incarcerated offenders as a last resort. He refused to charge anyone under age sixteen with a crime, a radical step for the time. Unlike most judges who would (and still do) confine themselves to the courthouse, Lindsey acted as a strong advocate for cleaning up neighborhoods that he viewed as breeding grounds for crime.

Lindsey was a small man, only five feet tall and weighing one hundred pounds. He was shy and unassuming, with a meek, nonthreatening demeanor. However, his winning personality and easygoing facade belied a fierce sense of independence and nonconformity. Never one to easily take no for an answer, Lindsey, a pronounced nonconformist, often found himself on the receiving end of abuse from Denver's political power structure. In fact, one of Lindsey's weaknesses was his tendency to view those who disagreed with him as enemies. Political officials were especially angry at Lindsey's attempt to generate support for his ideas by taking them public when political officials refused to support them. *The Beast,* published by Lindsey in 1910, chronicled his fight against corruption in Denver's government.

During the 1910s, Lindsey, while continuing his work as a juvenile court judge, stepped outside of this role to advocate several controversial causes. He went to Europe in 1915 along with Henry Ford to denounce World War I, which America entered two years later. Far more controversial were his stances on social issues. He joined a small but increasing fringe group of writers and academics who spoke frankly about sex, in a manner unheard of by most Americans prior to the 1920s. He stated that sex was a natural part of life. Unlike most adults who decried the "decadence" of 1920s youth, he expressed optimism because of the exuberance and energy possessed by youth of the Jazz Age, which was replete with short-skirted, liberated, tobacco-smoking women and daring young men. During the 1920s he advocated birth control for young women (even for those who were not married) and sex education in public schools, both of which he thought would reduce illegitimate pregnancies and abortions; both ideas were outlined in his book *The Revolt of Modern Youth.*

Lindsey's most controversial action by far was his advocacy of trial marriages. Contrary to the perceptions of his critics, his book *The Companionate Marriage,* coauthored with Wainwright Evans, did not express hostility to permanent, monogamous marriages. In fact, the beliefs Lindsey espoused in *The Companionate Marriage,* which he tried to apply in his own court, were harbingers of things to come in the area of family law. He saw marriage and divorce laws as impediments to happiness. He advocated liberalizing divorce laws; he criticized alimony payments for women who were young and childless. He argued against the idea that divorce was contrary to Biblical precepts. He argued in favor of people being married just to have companionship and not necessarily for the sake of bearing children.

Lindsey served as juvenile court judge in Denver until 1927. It was during the 1927 election that his political enemies were finally able to harm him. Lindsey had clashed with the Ku Klux Klan, which enjoyed a national resurgence during the 1910s and the 1920s. The chief targets of KKK anger in Colorado were Jews and Catholics, as the African-American population in the state was very small. Lindsey, himself the partial product of Catholic upbringing, denounced the KKK, stating of dues-paying Klan members, "They had paid ten dollars each to hate somebody and they were determined to get their money's worth." Throughout the 1920s the Denver KKK targeted Lindsey for defeat. Lindsey won his 1924 reelection bid, but the election was challenged. Lindsey's opponent charged voter fraud. The case reached the Colorado Supreme Court in 1927, and the election was ruled invalid. In a move denounced by legal scholars around the country, Lindsey, the world's most famous juvenile court judge, was forced to resign on June 30, 1927. To make matters worse, Lindsey was accused of accepting payment for advice he

offered in a New York case, something prohibited for judges in Colorado. The scandals forced his resignation from the bench and resulted in his disbarment in 1929, after he had left Colorado.

Lindsey moved to Los Angeles in 1928 and was promptly admitted to the state bar, California authorities believing the charges against him in Colorado were baseless. In California, Lindsey carried out reform efforts similar to those he had instituted in Colorado. He established California's first juvenile court. In 1934, Lindsey was appointed labor compliance officer for the National Recovery Administration, one of the labor relief agencies created by President Franklin Roosevelt to provide employment during the Great Depression. He was elected superior court judge for Los Angeles County by an overwhelming margin in November of that same year. While serving as superior court judge, Lindsey lobbied for creation of a law called The Children's Court of Conciliation Law, which held that in any divorce case involving children, either spouse could petition the court to prevent a divorce before it was officially granted, which was believed to be the first law of its kind. While in Los Angeles, Lindsey continually lobbied for official appointment as juvenile court judge, not having a passion for other legal matters, but each year his request was denied.

While in Colorado and California, Lindsey garnered world fame (and considerable hostility) for his efforts. He served on numerous commissions, including the White House conference on child welfare. In addition to writing myriad pieces of legislation in California and Colorado, Lindsey authored several books, articles, and pamphlets. Most of them reflected his beliefs about the way juveniles should be treated by the justice system. He wrote two stage plays and one screenplay, also reflective of his views on juvenile justice and delinquency.

In 1931, Lindsey published his autobiography, *The Dangerous Life*. By 1935, the KKK's influence in Colorado politics had waned, and Lindsey's petition for reinstatement to the state bar reached the Colorado Supreme Court. The Colorado Supreme Court reversed his disbarment, holding that the procedure was filled with improprieties. Lindsey chose to remain in Los Angeles rather than return to Colorado. He died of heart failure on March 26, 1943, at the age of seventy-three. True to his maverick spirit, Lindsey had requested that he be cremated and that no conventional funeral service be held. At his memorial service, Lindsey's widow read a letter from President Franklin Roosevelt, which read, "The memory of Ben Lindsey is best honored in the name of youth."

SOURCES AND SUGGESTED READINGS

Ginette T. Aley, "Ben B. Lindsey," *American National Biography Online,* www.anb.org, March 21, 2003.

Charles Larsen, *The Good Fight* (Chicago: Quadrangle Books, 1972).

Benjamin B. Lindsey and Wainwright Evans, *The Revolt of Modern Youth* (Garden City, NY: Garden City Publishing, 1925).

Benjamin B. Lindsey, *The Companionate Marriage* (Manchester, NH: Ayer Publishing, 1972 [1927]).

Benjamin B. Lindsey, *The Dangerous Life* (New York: Horace Liveright, 1931).

National Cyclopaedia of American Biography, "A Biographical Sketch of Benjamin Barr Lindsey" (New York: J. T. White, 1943).

DISCUSSION QUESTIONS

1. What impact did Benjamin Lindsey's childhood and young adult life have on his career as a judge?
2. Which was more important, Lindsey's work as a judge or his influence with lawmakers?

EPILOGUE

This book has briefly chronicled the lives of forty-four people who impacted the United States' criminal justice system. Much more could be said about these forty-four people than has been said, and the list of people examined could and should be much longer. These forty-four people, like everyone who has ever worked in the criminal justice system, were, or are, human beings, no more and no less. They are neither angels nor demons. Too often when studying famous people, we tend to vilify or sanctify them, failing to realize that no human being is perfectly good or perfectly evil. Everyone who has ever worked or will work in the criminal justice system has and will make mistakes and commit acts that are wrong, and everyone has something positive to contribute. To hope that the readers of this book will avoid the mistakes made by these people is wishful thinking as is the hope that everyone that works in the system will exhibit the bravery possessed by many of the same people. Nevertheless, contemporary students and practitioners of criminal justice should continue to explore the simultaneously rich and shameful past of their chosen field. Exploring the lives of those who came before them is one way to do just that.